DATE DUE

~~OC 23 '08~~			
~~MY 11 '99~~			
~~RENEW~~ ~~MY 22 '99~~			
~~MY 4 '00~~			
~~DE 19 '00~~			
~~AR 10 '04~~ ~~AE 6 '07~~			
DE 9 '08			

DEMCO 38-296

ALSO BY DAVID K. SHIPLER

Russia:
Broken Idols, Solemn Dreams

Arab and Jew:
Wounded Spirits in a Promised Land

A Country
of Strangers

A Country of Strangers

Blacks and Whites in America

David K. Shipler

Alfred A. Knopf NEW YORK *1997*

THIS IS A BORZOI BOOK
PUBLISHED BY ALFRED A. KNOPF, INC.

Library of Congress Cataloging-in-Publication Data
Shipler, David K., [date]
A country of strangers : blacks and whites in America / David K.
Shipler. — 1st ed.
p.   cm.
Includes bibliographical references and index.
ISBN 0-394-58975-0 (alk. paper)
1. United States—Race relations. 2. Stereotype (Psychology)—
United States. 3. Race discrimination—United States.   I. Title.
E185.615.S48   1997
305.8'00973—dc21   97-2810
CIP

Manufactured in the United States of America

First Edition

*In memory
of my father and friend,
Guy Emery Shipler Jr.*

For now we see through a glass, darkly;
but then face to face: now I know in part;
but then shall I know even as also
I am known.

—I Corinthians 13:12

Contents

Preface

Discussions of race are imprisoned by words. The words whose meanings we think we know label and circumscribe peoples and ideas, honeycombing the untamed world with an illusion of clarity and order. As if that were not enough, meanings shift constantly.

"Tolerance" is an example. Long understood by its first definition in the dictionary (recognizing and respecting others), it is now tainted in many minds by its second and third definitions (leeway for variation from a standard and the capacity to endure hardship). Understandably, black Americans do not want to be "tolerated" as one tolerates deviance or pain. Anyone who advocates tolerance today risks being misunderstood as grudgingly accepting the unpleasant qualities of another group. "Integration" is the same. Once the nation's noblest goal, it is currently taken by some to imply assimilation and loss of identity. Words that seemed so dependable have become little mines planted along our way.

Since words are my only tools, I approach this endeavor in a spirit of careful humility, mindful of how difficult it is to capture the racial reality of America within the matrix of our vocabulary. I use "tolerance" rarely, but I do so in its most generous meaning. I devote the first chapter to exploring the dynamics surrounding "integration." I employ the latest versions of the self-labeling that has evolved, just in the course of my lifetime, from "colored people" to "Negroes" to "blacks" to "African-Americans" to "people of color," the last embracing all who are not "white." Since we seem to be stuck in what may be a period of transition, when "black" and "African-American" are still used interchangeably, I follow that style, mixing the two terms without endorsing any of the passion that often attaches to one or the other. Not many years from now, I imagine, this language will seem antiquated, perhaps even offensive, as the ear is trained to hear another lexicon.

Even the concept of "race" is suspect. It is too clear, too categorical to reflect the genetic whirlwind that has deposited humanity at the brink of a new millennium. Too much mixing has occurred to satisfy physical anthropologists that one or another person falls wholly within one or another racial box. Furthermore, those who call themselves "white" and those who call themselves "black" (or "African-American") imagine their differences not merely as biological but as ethnic and cultural. Many prefer "African-American" precisely because it has an ethnic and cultural connotation, not only one of skin color or race. People's images and prejudices, which may be triggered by the physical characteristics of the other's body, range far beyond the racial, or biological, and well into realms of ethnicity. I succumb to the necessity of using familiar words: "black," "white," "racial." But much, perhaps most, of what we call "racial conflict" between blacks and whites has all the hallmarks of ethnic conflict. It does not always rely on a belief in genetic inferiority; indeed, it has become fashionable for white bigots to postulate a black *cultural* inferiority. "Racial," then, is meant to include the swarm of ethnic tensions and interactions that infest the black-white relationship.

"White" is also an unsatisfactory term, for it encompasses a multitude of ethnic groupings and socioeconomic classes that relate to blacks in various ways. Most Americans of Hispanic origin are classified as white, but I use the term to mean whites of European descent, who still form the country's majority, hold the power, and set the tone of the black-white aversion.

This book focuses on blacks and whites and lets the country's other ethnic and racial divides fade into the background. Volumes could be done on the prejudice and hardship faced by Latinos, Asian-Americans, and American Indians and on discrimination among whites of various ethnicities; these have also been crucial in defining the American experience. But the fountainhead of injustice has been located between blacks and whites, and that legacy remains the country's most potent symbol of shame. Nothing tests the nation, or takes the measure of its decency, quite like the rift between black and white. No improvement would be felt as broadly as that between black and white; fundamental progress in that arena would reverberate throughout the other ethnic problems of the land.

I have not written a geographical study to compare South with North or East with West. Each region of the United States has its own history of racial strife that influences the present. But the South's past of slavery and de jure segregation does not exonerate the North, and the North's present of urban poverty and de facto segregation does not exonerate the South. I have sought and found common denominators at a level of attitude that transcend the boundaries of place. Everywhere I have looked, I have seen a country where blacks and whites are strangers to each other.

I have avoided the extremes in this book. I have not dwelled on the hate mongers, either white or black, who get so much attention in the press, but rather on the quieter middle ground where ordinary blacks and whites attempt to live their daily lives without a rancorous agenda. This is not to dismiss the poisonous influence of the noisy bigots who disguise themselves as politicians and professors, as ministers and talk-show hosts; their coded appeals to fear and their prejudices masquerading as scholarship or Gospel contaminate the atmosphere and impede true dialogue. But my preference is to listen to real people, not performers, who are rarely heard by the larger public and have something to teach us.

All the people in this book are real. There are no composite characters. Those few who did not feel comfortable with their real names in print have been given pseudonyms which are clearly labeled as such, either by quotation marks on the first reference or by explanation in the text. They, as well as those who are named, contributed immensely with their time and insights.

This book has been something of a family project. In our house there was no escape from the subject, since I was consumed with it for many years. My wife, Debby, offered perceptive judgments on racial interaction from the standpoint of mother, teacher, family therapist, and critical reader. Many of my observations originated with her. She added substantially to my understanding of what I was seeing and hearing, she made crucial suggestions on organizing the material, and she deftly took her pencil to the manuscript. Two of my children, Laura and Michael, came of age with this book; it has been shaped by their experiences, and their experiences have probably been shaped in part by my fascination with the problem. Laura was a constant source of ideas, anecdotes, and creative thinking about race; she read the entire manuscript and proved to be a tough and sensitive editor. Michael, who was twelve when I signed the contract and will be twenty when the book is published, acted as an extra pair of eyes and ears, providing a steady stream of vignettes and insights that enriched my understanding of racial encounters, especially among teenagers. He also made incisive comments on parts of the manuscript. My oldest, Jonathan, was well into adulthood and therefore less a captive of my obsession, but he was always a good listener to my endless tales of discovery.

Roger Wilkins helped orient me at the outset of my journey, tuning me in to the nuances of black-white miscommunication and giving me a sense of what I ought to look for on my search. At the end, he read the manuscript and offered good guidance. David Burnham assisted me on police matters, crime statistics, the case of Richard Arrington, and other aspects of the book, which he also read. My agent, Julie Fallowfield, supported me with encouragement (and chiding) through these long years, and my editor, Jonathan Segal, skillfully zeroed in on the weak spots and provoked improvements.

To a larger degree than I have been able to indicate in the text, I owe gratitude to many others for their assistance along the way, including Fox Butterfield, Mary Childers, James DeLaney, Ann Grimes, Ted Hitchcock, Ronald Joe, Robert Lerman, Evan Lieberman, Charles Miller, Charles Moskos, Jim Newton, Don Offerman, Clarence Page, Dorothy Redford, Sherlynn Reid, Ron Smothers, Lucia Stanton, Roberto Suro, and Amy Wallace. Maggie Nyabera checked Swahili translations, and a few friends and relatives let me freeload in an extra bedroom as I traveled the country: my cousin Betty Wojciechowski, Ed and Michelle Walsh, Nancy Uscher and Bill Barrett, and Tim Rattner.

I am grateful to William Diaz, at whose initiative the Ford Foundation provided me with a grant to study Teaneck, New Jersey, in the aftermath of the police shooting of a black youth. The Council on Foreign Relations and the Woodrow Wilson National Fellowship Foundation, which sent me to lecture in various parts of the country, made it financially possible for me to get to many places where I could also do research on race.

My thinking about race and group identity has been heavily influenced by the work of my father-in-law, the late Harold R. Isaacs, whose *Idols of the Tribe* gave me the idea to organize the middle section of this book around bundles of stereotypes. The title of Chapter 4, "Body," comes from that book, and the subtitle, "Dark Against the Sky," from Gwendolyn B. Bennett's poem "Heritage":

> *I want to see lithe Negro girls,*
> *Etched dark against the sky*
> *While sunset lingers.*

A few sections include passages from an op-ed piece I did for *The New York Times* on April 12, 1993; my review of *Kwanzaa and Me* in the *Times* of February 19, 1995; and my piece on affirmative action in the *Times*'s "Week in Review" of March 5, 1995.

It has often been said that every American is an expert on race. I have concluded the opposite: that no American is an expert on race. Each of us has our own experience, and sometimes it is intense enough to make us think that we know the subject thoroughly. When we recognize that we do not, we will have taken the first step toward learning.

D.K.S.

January 1997

A Country
of Strangers

Introduction

The Color Line

> Behold, human beings living in an underground den
> . . . here they have been from their childhood, and
> have their legs and necks chained so that they cannot
> move . . . and they see only their own shadows, or the
> shadows of one another, which the fire throws on the
> opposite wall of the cave. . . . To them, the truth
> would be literally nothing but the shadows of the
> images.
>
> *—Plato,*
> Republic, *Book VII*

A line runs through the heart of America. It divides Oak Park from Chicago's West Side along the stark frontier of Austin Boulevard, splitting the two sides of the street into two nations, separating the carefully integrated town from the black ghetto, the middle class from the poor, the swept sidewalks from the gutters glistening with broken glass, the neat boutiques and trim houses from the check-cashing joints and iron-grilled liquor stores.

The line follows stretches of the Santa Monica Freeway in Los Angeles and Rock Creek Park in Washington, D.C. It runs along the white picket fence that divides the manicured grounds from the empty field where the slaves' shacks once stood at Somerset Place plantation in North Carolina. It cuts across the high, curved dais of the Etowah County Commission in Alabama, where one black member sits with five whites. It encircles the "black tables" where African-Americans cluster together during meals at Princeton University, Lexington High School in Massachusetts, and a thousand corporate cafeterias across the country.

At eleven o'clock Sunday morning, which has been called the most segregated hour in America, the line neatly separates black churches from white churches. It intertwines itself through police departments and courtrooms and jury rooms, through textbooks and classrooms and dormitories, through ballot boxes and offices, through theaters and movie houses, through television and radio, through slang and music and humor, and even through families. The line passes gently between Tony and Gina Wyatt of Florida; he is black, she is white, and they both reach gracefully across the border. It tangles the identity of their teenage son, Justin, who looks white but feels black.

"The problem of the Twentieth Century is the problem of the color-line," W. E. B. Du Bois wrote in 1901; the prophetic words became the opening declaration of his lyrical work *The Souls of Black Folk*. In the succeeding decades, that line has been blurred and bent by the demise of legal segregation and the upward movement of many blacks through the strata of American opportunity. But it remains forbidding to black people left behind in poverty and to others, more successful, who may suddenly confront what Du Bois called a "vast veil"—the curtain of rejection drawn around those whose ancestors were brought in chains from Africa. Today, when sensibilities have been tuned and blatant bigotry has grown unfashionable in most quarters, racist thoughts are given subtler expression, making the veil permeable and often difficult to discern. Sometimes its presence is perceived only as a flicker across a face, as when a white patient looks up from her hospital bed to discover that an attending physician is an African-American.

And so, as the close of the century now approaches, I offer this journey along the color line. It is a boundary that delineates not only skin color and race but also class and culture. It traces the landscape where blacks and whites find mutual encounters, and it fragments into a multitude of fissures that divide blacks and whites not only from each other, but also among themselves.

Americans of my generation, who were youngsters when the civil rights movement began in the 1950s, grew up on awful, indelible images. I am haunted still by the cute little white girls who twisted their faces into screams of hatred as black children were escorted into schools. I saw for the first time that the face of pristine innocence could be merely a mask.

Here was the enemy. And the solution seemed obvious: Break down the barriers and let people mingle and know one another, and the importance of race would fade in favor of individual qualities. Blacks would be judged, as Martin Luther King Jr. was preaching, not by the color of their skin but by the content of their character. The perfect righteousness of that precept summoned the conscience of America, and I remember how King translated the argument into touching personal terms when I interviewed him once for the college radio station at Dartmouth. We sat backstage in an auditorium where he was to speak, and I can still hear the majestic timbre of his voice, the weary outrage as he told of his young daughter seeing an amusement park near Atlanta, called Funland or Playland, as I recall. Again and again she asked to go, and her father tried and tried to avoid confronting her with the angry truth. Finally, he had to explain that she could not go, because she was not white.

The simplicity of the injustice made it seem brittle and vulnerable to attack. And the next time I saw King, at the Lincoln Memorial in that summer's March on Washington in 1963, the clarity of his call for the liberty of his dream infused the multitudes of us, black and white, who were packed together across the Mall, with the conviction that history was being made at that moment, and that the country would never be the same.

That turned out to be true, but we did not get the revolution we anticipated. As the Jim Crow segregation laws were overturned, less tractable problems were revealed, and they frustrated King toward the end of his life as he tried to bring his campaign to cities in the North. There, villainy was less easily identified. Rooted in the prejudices, the poverty, the poor education, and the culture of hopelessness that divided blacks and whites, the racial predicament proved too deeply embedded in the society to be pried out by mere personal contact and legal equality. Perhaps it was naïve to think that all that would have to happen was for people to look into each other's eyes, to give blacks as many opportunities as whites, to open the doors. I put this to Reverend Bill Lawson, the black pastor of the Wheeler Avenue Baptist Church in Houston, who had been in the movement and had a long perspective.

"You're not naïve," he said generously. "You share what most of us share. This is a can-do country. It's a nation that came from nothing. We were people who were fleeing tyranny, and we established on a frontier this little set of colonies, and out of that we built a nation which ultimately became one of the most respected nations in the world. And we've been proud of this country, and we've made some assumptions about it, one of them being that there's a national conscience, and that if you appeal to that national conscience, you will do what is right. So, everybody from Dr. Martin Luther King down to the smallest of us who was out there marching someplace believed that the American dream was not only a reality but was a reality that was close to being fulfilled, and that all we needed to do was to let the American people know 'You're in error here. And here is the right way to go, so if the children of slaves and the children of slaveholders can join hands' . . ." And here his voice trailed off for a moment. "So it was not a matter of naïveté. I think that it really was a matter of optimism, of good American optimism, and I think we still have it to some extent. And frankly, I'm glad that we do."

Lawson was tall, slim, and distinguished-looking. A smattering of gray salted his short, kinky hair, and he dressed carefully: light brown jacket, dark slacks, cream-colored shirt, and rust-colored tie. Settled into a deep leather chair in his spacious office, he spoke precisely about the limitations of change induced by the civil rights movement: the public versus the private. "I think that there has been a redefinition of relationships over the last, say, forty years," he said. "There has been, on the one hand, a push toward eliminating the old segregation laws and, on the other hand, a resistance to changing community and neighborhood patterns. So there has been a tension between what we felt was right and what we felt was expedient. There has been the allowance of public contacts. Blacks can ride in the fronts of buses or eat at lunch counters. There has not been a significant change in intimate, personal attitudes. There is still some feeling that we don't want to live too close together, that we don't want to have too many close connections in places [where] we worship, or that we don't want to have too much family contact. We still have some problems with dating and marriage. So in the more public relationships, there has been at least a tolerance that says, let's each one have our own freedom. But anything that becomes more intimate or personal, we tend to have a little bit more resistance."

In Birmingham, Alabama, an old civil rights warrior, Reverend Abraham Lincoln Woods of the St. Joseph Baptist Church, saw the movement's accomplishments as more cosmetic than substantive. "Birmingham has gone through tremendous changes," he said, "and the fact that we have gone from a city where blacks were shut out of the process to having a black mayor and a predominantly black city council—we now have black policemen, in fact we have a black chief now—many things have changed of that kind. But I find that in spite of what seems to be a tolerance of the races and a working together, I find still, somewhat beneath the surface, sometimes not too deeply, those same old attitudes."

But it is behavior, not attitudes, that concerns David Swanston, a white advertising executive whose wife, Walterene, is black. He sat in his handsome town house in McLean, Virginia, one evening and took the measure of America in terms of his own interracial marriage. "It was against the law in a number of states twenty-five years ago," he observed. "It just seems to me that this world was institutionally significantly more racist, overtly racist, than today. Now, each individual black and white within the country may be about the same place they were twenty-five years ago, as regarding interracial marriages and other issues. But it seems to me that's very secondary to the fact that institutionally, we are much beyond that—and it's the institutions that hurt you, that can have the impact on your lives. And by and large, if the twenty people we see in the mall don't like it, and those twenty people wouldn't have liked it twenty-five years ago, I don't really care. The fact that our marriage is recognized by the Commonwealth of Virginia, that we're not criminals, those are the areas where it just seems to me incredible change has been made."

The disjunction between attitude and behavior was not that clear-cut for Steve Suitts, a white Alabaman in his forties, a tall man with sandy brown hair. As the executive director of an old-line civil rights organization, the Southern Regional Council in Atlanta, he had done more thinking than most whites about race. Yet before he answered a question, he considered it silently for a long time and then spoke slowly, reflectively, sometimes repeating the question or rephrasing it as he looked down at the floor or out the window of his nineteenth-story office on Peachtree Street. "When does making people feel better about each other translate into making life better for each other?" he asked himself. "I don't know. I think we've assumed . . . that if you could somehow get people to understand each other a little better, they would do better by each other."

In the South, he noted, bigotry often coexisted with friendship, challenging the assumption that association tempered prejudice. "During the latter days of legal segregation," Suitts explained, "you could always—even among the ardent, rabid segregationists—you could almost always find a caring relationship, not necessarily equal, but a genuinely caring relationship between that white and a black. . . . The paradox was that southern whites loved blacks as individuals and hated them as a group." Something beyond contact was needed. "It is a sense more of sharing than of understanding," Suitts said, "sharing not just their lives, but sharing things that matter, like sharing power, sharing responsibilities, being placed in a situation where your future, your success is directly related to how someone of another race also performs in the workplace." People whose interests overlap can find their commonalities, he thought. "Nevertheless, for those of us who grew up in a segregated society and who had been inculcated by segregation's ways, both blacks and whites, it is a constant vigil to try to—even when you have those sorts of sharing experiences—to not let old stereotypes seep into new relationships."

Unlike most other parts of the country, the South has confronted its racism and struggled through momentous change. Many blacks find white southerners more overt and easier to read than white northerners, who are often suspected of opaque duplicity. As a northerner, I find the South more complex: Liberal southern whites are the deepest and most interesting of any whites I have interviewed on race. But the transparency that blacks see in other southerners eludes me; many whites in the South sugarcoat their hostile views and exaggerate their region's tolerance in a kind of gauzy self-congratulation, which can be penetrated perceptively by blacks with a southern background. After roaming the country, I have a strong sense that "old stereotypes seep into new relationships" everywhere, not just below the Mason-Dixon Line. Geographical boundaries are intriguing but hardly decisive in describing patterns of attitude. So, in diagnosing the South, Steve Suitts spots the universal American cancer of embedded prejudices—sometimes latent, ever ready to work their will.

There is scarely a consequential interaction between a black and a white in the United States in which race is not a factor. Even as it goes unmentioned, as it normally does, race is rarely a neutral element in the equation. It may provoke aversion, fear, or just awkwardness, on the one hand, or, on the other, eager friendliness and unnatural dialogue. Even in easy contacts that are fleeting and impersonal—between a diner and a waiter, a customer and a salesperson, a passenger and a bus driver—race does not always drop to zero; it possesses weight and plays some role in the chemical reaction. "There's always something there," said a young white Princeton graduate working for the *National Journal,* a Washington magazine. "It can be mitigated or it can be worsened by a lot of other factors: social class, culture, the status hierarchy in the office." But it never quite goes away, as he realized when he observed how the mixture of race, class, and hierarchy led him to feel more comfortable with the white reporters than with the black secretaries and receptionists.

If race distorts individual relations, it also magnifies most major social and policy issues facing the American public. Poverty, crime, drugs, gangs, welfare, teenage pregnancy, chronic joblessness, homelessness, illiteracy, and the failure of inner-city public schools are usually viewed through the racial prism. They are seen as black problems or as problems created by blacks. The most popular solutions—cuts in welfare for teenage mothers and long sentences for repeat offenders—are codes for cracking down on blacks' misdeeds. Where race enters the realms of politics, health care, economic injustice, and occasionally foreign policy (as in Haiti and South Africa), the debates are charged with an additional layer of emotion. Despite the upheavals brought by the Supreme Court's 1954 ruling against segregated schools in *Brown v. Board of Education,* by the civil rights movement, and by the resulting 1964 Civil Rights Act and the 1965 Voting Rights Act, race is still central to the American psychological experience, as it has been for more than two hundred years.

Over their entire history on this continent, African-Americans have struggled as a people in every conceivable way, short of widespread armed insurrection, to share in the pursuit of happiness. By social reflex or by calculation, by happenstance or ideology, blacks have been servile and militant, passive and hardworking, dependent and self-sufficient. They have used the church, the mosque, the schoolhouse, the university, the military, and the corporation in an effort to advance. They have tried to go back to Africa, and they have tried to function within the political system of the United States. They have tried peaceful demonstrations and violent street riots. They have tried sweet reason and angry rhetoric, assimilation and separatism. They have appealed to the nation's conscience and to its fears. It would be wrong to say that none of this has worked: Individuals have succeeded. But neither deference nor defiance has been effective for black Americans as a whole. No degree of personal success quite erases the stigma of black skin, as many achieving blacks realize when they step outside their family, neighborhood, or professional environment into a setting where their rank and station and accomplishments are not known. "I didn't come from a deprived family," says Floyd Donald, who owns a small radio station in Gadsden, Alabama. "I grew up with books. I grew up with china. I grew up with silver. My background is impeccable, so far as my education and my parents' education and their positions in life and their abilities and so forth. So I had that advantage. However, out of my community, I was just another black. You see, it doesn't make much difference about the status that a black achieves. He is black in America."

In five years of crisscrossing the country to research this book, I was struck by the ease with which most blacks I interviewed were able to discuss race and the difficulty most whites had with the subject. I had anticipated a certain wariness among African-Americans, who might wonder why they should let a white man probe their inner feelings and painful memories. In reality, however, only one out of all the hundreds of people I met raised such a concern. She was Colette Walker, a junior at Drew

University who came from Roselle, New Jersey, and sat mostly in silence through a long evening I had with black students on campus. Finally, toward the end, she told me angrily that it was useless for me to do a book. "Racism is a big business now, so they're writing these books," she scoffed. "But nobody I know will buy it. First of all, they can feed a family of three on what it costs to buy a hardcover book these days. There are no bookstores in my neighborhood. And the people who are going to pick it up and read it—they know it or they don't know it." Anybody who wants to know should talk to her, she said; she could tell them better than any book could.

The next day, she happened to be in a class where I spoke, and she raised the issue again but in a way indicating that she had been pondering the phenomenon of a white writing about race and had grown more curious than challenging. Did I really think this book would change anybody's mind? she asked skeptically. Why was I doing it? I told her that it was my way of coming home. After many years abroad, after writing about the countries I had lived in—Vietnam, Russia, and Israel—I wanted to write again about the country I was living in: my own country. And in my own country, there was no more intractable, pervasive issue than race. I didn't know if this book would change minds or help people to think differently, but I knew that I had to do it for myself. To understand my own country, I had to attempt to unravel racial attitudes, to dig and question and try to comprehend. It was an act of discovery, and I needed to undertake it as a personal quest. She nodded, and I thought there was a little less anger in her gaze.

Otherwise, black Americans were enormously generous of spirit and time in reaching into their experiences to lay them out for me. Gradually, I came to understand what should have been obvious at the outset: that a black person cannot go very long without thinking about race; she has already asked herself every question that I could possibly pose.

By contrast, most whites rarely have to give race much thought. They do not begin childhood with advice from parents about how to cope with racial bias or how to discern the racial overtones in a comment or a manner. They do not have to search for themselves in history books or literature courses. In most parts of America, their color does not make them feel alone in a crowd; they are not looked to as representatives of their people. And they almost never have to wonder whether they are rejected—or accepted—because of their genuine level of ability or the color of their skin. As a result, few whites I interviewed had considered the questions I put to them. Many struggled to be introspective, but most found that I was taking them into uncharted territory, full of dangers that they quickly surrounded with layers of defensiveness.

Still, my white friends and acquaintances were always keen to hear what I was learning. The news that I was working on race was a real conversation starter, as my wife, Debby, noted after a party one evening. I would be questioned closely or told unsolicited stories in which whites were often the victims. Two white professors at a conference on international issues approached me separately to talk lightheartedly about playing basketball with blacks. One, as a boy in New York City, had gotten into a fracas as the only white on a black team and had been rescued by a huge black kid who had lifted the black antagonist off the ground and said, "Don't mess with my white hope." The memory still made him smile. The other professor had been playing a pickup game with a black who took long, inaccurate shots without ever passing to him, even when he was in good position. Finally, he and another white had decided to sit down on the court in protest. The black stopped, stunned. "We're staging a Montgomery sit-in," the white professor said. The black laughed, got the message, and started cooperating.

But other discussions were sometimes disheartening, for they revealed dimensions of attitude I had not seen before, even in people I had known for years in other contexts where we had talked about politics or Russia or the Middle East but not about race.

"Jim," a middle-aged professional who shared my interest in Russia, took a long detour during a phone call one day to make me understand how little initiative black children had. At a PTA meeting, it seemed, he and other parents had complained about poor teaching of grammar and writing at their children's elementary school. In the tradition of American voluntarism, they had been invited to do something about it, so three of them had agreed to teach a writing course several mornings a week for fifth- and sixth-graders.

Only one black pupil had signed up, Jim said, pausing to let the significance of that fact sink in. (He did not say how many white children had failed to enroll.) And when he had told the class that each child would need $21 for a grammar book not provided by the school, the black girl had informed him that under some scholarship arrangement with the school system, she was not required to pay any extra fees. Jim had then bought the book for her himself, but she had never returned to the class. He was bitter. He noted that two Chinese girls had come and worked hard; in ten years they would probably be at Harvard or Yale, he said, and the black girl would be yelling for affirmative action.

The coldness of this man's tale was startling. He gave no evidence of having asked himself whether other black students, hearing in advance of the fee, had been discouraged from attending, whether they had been gently steered away by teachers who believed they couldn't benefit, whether early academic defeat had already robbed them of the confidence they would need to push themselves and embrace such a course. Nor did he seem to realize that he might have inadvertently embarrassed the black girl who could not afford the book. I asked if he had spoken to her later or inquired as to why she hadn't returned. He said no. His conclusion needed no further research: The incident clearly reinforced all the stereotypes of blacks lacking drive, he declared. To bolster the indictment, he went on to describe two adults, one black and one white, he had recently met working in Ukraine. Their intellectual energies were so disparate that only one of them—guess who?—had bothered to learn the local language. So, carrying his baggage with him, Jim saw race alone as the governing variable in his two examples, and, armed with these two cases, he confirmed the very prejudices that had shaped his perceptions in the first place.

It was disturbing enough to see a mind that seemed intelligent in other areas trading in simplistic images of race. But equally troubling was how invisible his biases had been through the few years I had known him, how mistaken my sense of him had turned out to be. If he had learned from his teaching experience that images were valid, I learned that they were only shadows on the wall; my earlier picture of him proved as deceptive as his was of blacks. It was a lesson in the insidious camouflage of bigotry.

Many whites are confused over how they should be thinking about racial issues now. Some adopt an air of smooth indifference, an emotional distance. They often hesitate to say what's on their minds, lest they be accused of racism. Others work quietly, sometimes in frustration, to improve blacks' opportunities in their companies or universities or military units; indeed, I have discovered that more sincere effort goes on than ever gets reflected in press portrayals of America's racial problems. But nothing adds up to a neat sum anymore. How does a white person—even a liberal—sort out the anti-white prejudices, the black self-segregation, the manipulation of history, the endless message of white guilt, the visible achievements of prominent blacks coupled with the deepening poverty and violence of the inner cities? Across much of the spectrum of white America run common themes of distress and impatience with the subject of race, a national mood of puzzlement and annoyance.

This is salted with a dash of fear, an anxiety among some whites that the society is disintegrating into warring camps, that blacks may rise up against the system that has oppressed them, or that violent class struggle lies just over the horizon. The apocalyptic vision was held by David Berg, a white lawyer in Houston. "Every major city, including this one, is a racial powder keg, ready to go off," he said. Accommodation between the races was only a thin veneer, he thought. "I promise you, in twenty years, I'm telling you, this country is headed toward revolution if we don't do something about the inner city. If the poor people of this country, black and white and brown, ever realize that what unites them is greater than what divides them, we're in terrible trouble."

That kind of talk seems more prevalent among whites than among blacks, although my daughter, Laura, heard some of it from students at Spelman, the black women's college in Atlanta, where she spent a semester during the second trial of the white policemen in Los Angeles who beat Rodney King, the black motorist. If the cops were not convicted and imprisoned, a couple of black students predicted, rioters the second time would not confine themselves to black neighborhoods but would take guns into white areas. In a course on revolution in Cuba, Nicaragua, and elsewhere, some black students raised the possibility of revolution in the United States; the professor, also black, discounted it as impossible, given the alignments of power.

The question most often asked me by whites is whether racial matters are getting better or worse. It is an odd inquiry for people to make about their own country. I am used to being asked by Americans how things are going in Russia or in the Middle East, where I have lived and traveled and they perhaps have not. But to have so little feel for the situation right at home betrays the corrosive nature of our racial legacy: how it eats away at our equilibrium, our sense of direction, our navigational skills. We simply do not know where we are, and we are not even quite sure where we have been.

What's more, there is no neat answer to the question. Sometimes I ask in return, "What is your reference point? Slavery? Jim Crow? The height of the civil rights movement? The last five years? Are we measuring economic success or personal attitudes? Are we counting black college graduates or anti-black hate crimes? And what if we decide that pockets of hopefulness are tucked into the midst of despair? Shall we feel virtuous and relax?"

If any sum can be reckoned, it is one of acute contradiction. In the

1920s, the Ku Klux Klan had about two million members; by the mid-1990s, the estimated membership was down to between 2,500 and 3,000, out of 20,000 or 25,000 altogether in various hate groups, including skinheads and militias. Furthermore, prospects have improved for blacks with high skills or advanced degrees in the sciences, business, law, medicine, and other professions as more and more white-run institutions have grown eager to find talented African-American men and women to serve diverse constituencies, improve profits, and demonstrate a commitment to "equal opportunity." But other black people, dragged down by the whirlpool of poverty and drugs, have fewer and fewer exits. The United States has more black executives and more black prison inmates than a decade ago.

The answer may be that things are getting better and worse at the same time. Racially, America is torn by the crosscurrents of progress and decay. Practically every step forward is accompanied by a subtle erosion of the ground beneath.

Anyone who left the United States a couple of decades ago and returned today would be stunned by the visible prominence of so many African-Americans. Thirty-five years after Mal Goode became the first black network newscaster (on ABC in 1962), black achievers are all over television screens as correspondents, anchors, actors, comedians, talk-show hosts, and musicians. But every point of progress has a counterpoint: Blacks are also featured on the eleven o'clock news in handcuffs, in pools of blood, in mug shots, in police sketches of wanted men.

Fifty years after Jackie Robinson first took the field for the Brooklyn Dodgers, highly paid black athletes have the run of the baseball diamond, the football field, and the basketball court, where they project their appeal far across racial lines. But even in the positions they play and the commentary that sportscasters sometimes deliver, blacks are nagged by old expectations that they will be more physical than cerebral.

American letters today would be fundamentally poorer without black poets, novelists, and playwrights. Gwendolyn Brooks, who has written twenty books of poetry, became the first African-American to win the Pulitzer Prize, in 1950. Alice Walker then won the Pulitzer for *The Color Purple*. August Wilson, the playwright, won it twice, for *Fences* and *The Piano Lesson*. Toni Morrison received the Pulitzer for her novel *Beloved* and in 1993 was awarded the Nobel Prize for Literature. Walker, Morrison, and other black writers, including poet Maya Angelou, have spent long periods on *The New York Times*' best-seller list. Angelou was invited by President Bill Clinton to compose and recite a poem at his inauguration in 1993; the result, "On the Pulse of the Morning," called powerfully upon America to celebrate its diversity. The same year, Rita Dove, also a Pulitzer winner, became the first African-American selected by the librarian of Congress as Poet Laureate of the United States.

In some minds, however, such writers are not quite part of the mainstream: Their works are not on the shelves in the major department of "Literature" at Borders Books & Music, a large and excellently stocked store north of Bethesda, Maryland, but are kept in a separate, smaller section labeled "Black Literature." Numerous colleges also segregate black writers, including them not in regular courses on American literature but in "black literature" classes taken by relatively few white students.

In government, firsts have been scored so often that the news value has diminished even as traditional expectations have been foiled. Republicans have tried hard to find moderate or conservative blacks. Twenty-five ran for Congress in 1994, the largest number in history; two of them won seats. In the same year, the Republican governor of New Jersey, Christine Todd Whitman, chose a moderate—James H. Coleman Jr., the son of a sharecropper—as the first black nominee to the State Supreme Court. In 1991, Republican President George Bush, replacing Thurgood Marshall in the "black seat" on the United States Supreme Court, nominated Clarence Thomas in an intriguing concoction of racial and ideological politics. Bush's conservative predecessor, Ronald Reagan, appointed General Colin Powell as the first black national security adviser, and Bush then elevated him to be the first black chairman of the Joint Chiefs of Staff.

Other inroads have also been made. In 1983, John Charles Thomas, a partner in the Richmond law firm that helped defend the constitutionality of school segregation in *Brown v. Board of Education*, became Virginia's first black Supreme Court judge. In the same year, Guion S. Bluford Jr. became the first black astronaut to fly in space, and in 1992, after a total of four blacks had gone into orbit, Dr. Mae C. Jemison became the first African-American woman to do so. Dr. David Satcher became director of the Centers for Disease Control and Prevention. President Bill Clinton named four blacks to his first-term cabinet, the largest number in history. And his administration broke the white male club at the upper echelons of the FBI when a woman, a Hispanic man, and a black named Paul R. Philip were appointed assistant directors. Nonetheless, the FBI's ranks remained hostile to nonwhites, according to complaints filed by some black agents.

Very gradually, African-Americans have increased their representation in elective office. In 1992, the first election after the redistricting that followed the 1990 census, the number of blacks in Congress jumped from 26 to 39, and then to 41, the highest in history, after the 1994 election (and slid to 40 after 1996). Between 1970 and 1993, blacks holding elected positions at the federal, state, and local levels went from 1,469 to 8,015. The number of black state legislators rose from 307 in 1979 to 511 in 1993 (amounting to 8.2 percent of all state senators and 7.1 percent of assemblymen); members of city governing bodies went from 1,697 to 3,181 in the same period; school board members from 1,085 to 1,617; and mayors from 48 in 1970 to 338 in 1993. Despite the significant gains, however, blacks counted for only 1.6 percent of all elected officials in the country. And the Supreme Court had begun whittling away at the practice of drawing electoral districts to improve blacks' chances for representation.

The half-full, half-empty glass in elective politics exists also in academia. Even to recite the gains is to sound a note of regret at how belated the change has been. After 104 years, the *Harvard Law Review* elected its first black president in 1990. After 123 years, Smith College became the first prestigious college in the Northeast to appoint a black president, in 1994: Ruth Simmons, the daughter of a Texas sharecropper. As of 1990, there were only 133 black presidents among the 2,433 college and university presidents in the United States.

Many institutions of higher education are scrambling to attract the best and the brightest blacks as undergraduates, and the result has been a narrowing gap between the percentages of whites and blacks with college degrees. In 1940, four times the percentage of whites as of blacks had at least four years of college; by 1995, the multiple had dropped to 1.82 times—24 percent of whites against 13.2 percent of blacks. But 26 percent of all blacks still lacked a high school diploma, compared with 17 percent of whites.

Furthermore, few African-Americans go on to graduate work. While black people make up about 13 percent of the country's population, only 4.7 percent of the college professors are black. And the number of blacks earning Ph.D.'s has remained low—1,393 in 1994, just 4.4 percent of the total, and rarely in the sciences. In 1990, not a single black received a Ph.D. in applied mathematics, molecular biology, elementary particle physics, oceanography, philosophy, ecology, geology, or biophysics.

The economic portrait also contains a strange duality. From 1940 to 1990, as the nation's black population doubled, the number of blacks in white-collar jobs rose nearly ten times, from just under 200,000 (mostly teachers, clergymen, and small storekeepers) to nearly 2 million, and they spread into a wide variety of professions. But the burgeoning of the black middle class and the departure of upwardly mobile people from inner-city neighborhoods have also distilled the remaining ghetto populations into a concentration of poverty and social corrosion. Median family income in such neighborhoods has declined; unemployment has grown.

Some resolution of traditional wage inequities has taken place between blacks and whites, especially for women. Black women with high school diplomas earn nearly as much as white women ($926 per whites' $1,000), and those with four years of college virtually the same ($992 per $1,000). By contrast, black men with high school diplomas and college degrees earn only $723 and $767, respectively, for every $1,000 earned by white men.

Overall, the income distribution of black families has not changed much; if a graph is drawn showing the percentage of families along a scale above and below the median annual income for blacks, the result is anything but a bell curve. At the lower end of the earnings spectrum, on the left, the line looks like a mountain peak, representing a large number of impoverished households. Moving to the right, where earnings exceed the median, the line drops precipitously, indicating how few blacks have made their way above the working class. Moreover, the shape of the curve shows little shift between 1979 and 1995, despite a gradual reduction of the black-white gap. In 1995, according to the Bureau of the Census, 29.3 percent of black Americans lived below the poverty line, compared with 11.2 percent of whites; in 1979, the proportions were 31 percent and 9 percent, respectively.

The median income for black families, figured in constant dollars, rose slightly between 1970 and 1995, from $21,151 to $22,393, while white families' annual earnings moved from $34,481 to $35,766 in the same period. This basic stability in incomes masked a deteriorating situation that is especially acute for blacks: the widening disparity between the median incomes of married couples and female-headed households. In 1979, black families headed by women with no husband present earned only 40.8 percent of what black married couples made; by 1994, that percentage had dropped to 34.4 as the number of female-headed households mushroomed.

A significantly greater disparity between the races is revealed by the gap in family net worth—the savings and property that represent a cumulative history spanning generations. Overall, the most recent figures show the median net worth at $43,800 for white households and

$3,700 for black. Even blacks and whites with roughly the same income possess such different financial assets and real estate that placing them in the same class of material well-being, as the income statistics generally do, is misleading. The median net worth of those considered middle-class ($25,000 to $50,000 in annual income) is $44,069 for whites and only $15,250 for blacks. At all other levels, too, the asset gaps are much greater than the income gaps. Consequently, blacks who make it into the middle class often have no cushion; they rightly feel that they are barely hanging on to their newfound status, that a single reverse could drop them back into poverty.

These are some of the tangible facts that mark the contours of race in America, like rocky outcroppings in a turbulent sea. Among them run the deep, abiding currents of racial attitude, which draw on old perceptions and beliefs that submerge but never quite dissipate. In covert form, they can still prevent black youngsters from getting into honors classes, black managers from the circle of decision making, black politicians from commanding solid white support. Fears and assumptions, often far beneath the surface of propriety, tend to prevent honest discussion from taking place in classrooms, corporate conference rooms, and congressional committee rooms. When it comes to race, we do not know how to talk to one another. "We are a country of strangers, and we are having a great deal of difficulty with our differences," says actress Anna Deavere Smith, "because ultimately, we lack the ability to look at specific human beings."

This is not a book on statistics or issues of public policy. It is about people and the way they think, about blacks and whites and their images of one another, about what happens when their paths intersect. It is a journey along the crucial fault line of America.

It is a book about the present, not the past, but it begins by tracing roots and finding wellsprings. Part One, "Origins," opens with an exploration of the competing impulses of integration and separation, the reference points by which the races navigate as they venture out and withdraw, the biculturalism that many blacks perfect as they move back and forth between the white and the black worlds, and the homesickness some blacks display for the all-black comfort of separateness. Then comes a portrayal of interracial families and their multiracial children, who are expert guides through the clashes created by racial blending in a nation that craves simple dichotomy. The final chapter of the first part measures the burden of history, examining the differing ways in which whites and blacks now carry the weight of that troubled legacy.

Part Two, "Images," dissects blacks' and whites' stereotypes of each other, laying out the distinct components: the physical body we see, the mental qualities we imagine, the moral character we attribute to the other and ourselves, the violence we fear, the power we seek or are loath to relinquish.

Part Three, "Choices," recognizes that we have the power to shape our racial landscape—not to eliminate every tension, surely, but to reconstruct the texture of our relationships. Racial strife is not some storm sweeping inexorably across our land; it is of our making, and we can choose something else. This closing section examines nuances of racism and methods of coping. It assesses the complexity confronting blacks and whites alike as they struggle to define and recognize the racial motivations that may or may not be present in a thought, a word, a deed. It documents the silences that prevail, the listening that isn't done, the conversations that don't take place. It looks at the chemical reactions between victims, including blacks and Jews, blacks and Koreans. It explores the human dimensions of affirmative action, the intricate contacts and misunderstandings across racial lines among coworkers, neighbors, policemen, soldiers, and others who interact daily. It focuses on the expanding universe of attempted remedies, including diversity workshops and sensitivity training, especially in the military. The final chapter considers the invisible privileges of whiteness, the black-white chasms that result, and the contradictions of caring and neglect that mark America's approach to its racial dilemma.

A key test for any society is whether or not it is self-correcting. And to be self-correcting, it must first be open and truthful about itself. This work is dedicated to that purpose.

PART ONE

Origins

CHAPTER ONE

Integration

Together and Separate

You could be very, very close, but there was always,
like, a slip of paper between your hands, and you
couldn't put them together.

—*A white man*
from Cambridge, Massachusetts

Clustering

When the lunch period begins, the lines dissolve in an instant of fluidity. The hallway rings cheerfully with raucous teenage slang in many tongues. A swirl of faces cascades through the corridor in a blurry kaleidoscope of colors and casts, a flood of continuous movement.

Suddenly the moment of motion is over. The hall is almost empty, the cafeteria full, the blending now fragmented and hardened into separateness. At the first long table inside the door, all the students are black. At the second, all are Russian, speaking Russian. The third is the Cambodian table, and the language is Khmer. In the far corner is another group of black students, some sitting, some standing. A couple of white tables are at the side. Integration is scattered only tentatively around the room: A black girl sits with an Asian girl, a black boy sits with a group of whites.

Edward R. Murrow High School in Brooklyn has no single racial or ethnic majority, but rather an array of groups as extensive as at any school in the country. Its neighborhood, in the Midwood section not far from Coney Island, has New York's characteristic diversity: A kosher Chinese restaurant named Shalom Hunan stands a couple of blocks away on M Street. By all accounts, relationships among the students are fairly congenial, with markedly less friction than elsewhere. Yet the clustering is finely tuned, and the boundaries are clear enough that, one day, students in the Council of Unity, representing every ethnic organization at Murrow, wanted to draw me a map on the board to show where various kinds of people congregated before school, after school, and during free periods.

Andrea, who is half Dominican, drew four rectangles representing the four floors (although the school is H-shaped). Beginning on the first floor, she pointed to the area near room 140, where handicapped students gathered "because that's where the elevators are," she said. "Brown lockers is the Italian world. On the stairs, the Irish. Cafeteria, black people mostly, and Russians right here. And then you have people who don't speak English. Then a mixture, by the windows."

As she continued, she got a lot of help and argument from other students, who called out instructions on filling in the pieces of their ethnic geography.

"The Avenue L entrance, that's all African-American. By the music hall, rockers, a lot of rockers."

Then to the second floor: "Near room 240, WASP, prep, AP."

"That's white world," said Kim, an African-American girl in a yellow dress with black polka dots.

"All the theater people hang out together. They're not all white," countered another black girl.

"Two-forty is the assimilation place," Andrea explained. "In between 240 and 210—Asian," and she pointed to the middle of the hallway. The others weren't satisfied with the label "Asian," and under pressure Andrea changed it to "mixed."

"The second-floor bathroom is all black," said Kim. "I know 'cause that's where I am."

Then to the third floor: at the lower-left-hand corner, near room 340, Asians and some whites; near 310, mixed. "And again, by the bathroom, it's African-American," said Kim.

"I get so confused," Andrea complained. "I want to write down 'black,' but I don't want to offend anybody, so I write 'African-American,' and it takes so much more time."

When they got to the fourth floor, the students were shouting and arguing about someone's suggestion that African-Americans bunched themselves together in the middle with Hispanics around them.

"They're dark-skinned. They're Panamanian and Dominican. They're not African-American," one black girl insisted.

"They *are!*" shouted another. "I know them!"

Then the argument was cut short by the key question, posed by the adviser to the Council of Unity, a young white teacher named Joseph Zaza: "Do people of other races feel afraid to walk into those areas? Is there intimidation?"

They all said yes, but as the discussion progressed, it emerged that nothing was actually done to give them that uneasy sensation—no looks, no comments. It was just a feeling inside themselves, and "feel" was the operative word.

"I just don't feel comfortable, people looking at me."

"When you walk through a place, you feel out of place."

"It's just a feeling. Nobody says anything. Nobody looks in a certain way."

"Like a new kid on the block."

"It's your basic upbringing. You're going to feel intimidated by people you don't know."

Across the country, white people are indignant about black people segregating themselves. A white mother is angry that black parents have formed their own committee at her son's private school in Washington, D.C. A white corporation executive in New Jersey is bothered by blacks sitting together in the company cafeteria. White officers at the Air Force Academy are troubled and suspicious when black cadets prefer to eat or socialize with other blacks. White college students express sadness, outrage, resignation, or moral superiority over the clustering and exclusivity of many blacks on campus.

I watched the process one fall semester at Princeton's Forbes College, a large residence hall for freshmen and sophomores, where I lived for three days a week while teaching a course. In the first blush of newness in September, the freshmen mixed themselves up thoroughly in the large dining room, blacks and whites and Asians and Latinos and others taking their trays and settling all together at the large tables for animated introductions and conversation. This lasted a couple of weeks, and then, little by little, the students began to sort themselves out until one evening, when I arrived for dinner, the separation was complete: one table of Spanish-speaking Latinos, another of Asians, another of blacks, and the rest of whites. They had finally found their comfort zones.

Thus do young people practice for adulthood and set the stage for the clustering that Balkanizes America. In multiracial elementary schools, children innocently mix themselves into cornucopias of color. By junior high, however, they usually begin to spin off into groups of common ethnicity. In high school, friendship patterns tend to harden along racial boundaries. And then the university provides little sanctuary from the racial chemistries that dominate the outside world. Clustering among students is no anomaly; it is a metaphor for the nation at large.

Of all the racial and ethnic walls built in America, the black–white divide is particularly poignant. More than three decades after the civil rights movement's victories over forced segregation, few white people can understand why so many African-Americans appear to want voluntary segregation. The movement dreamed that the individual could transcend the group, that race could recede as personal merit prevailed. Now the impulse toward self-separation defeats the dream. Black clustering feeds into white aversion, and together they render the goal of the color-blind society as elusive as ever.

Many blacks are faintly amused by whites' anger. They delight in the novelty of a situation that whites, for once, cannot enter or control. "It says that we are going to live independent of you, and we really don't need you to get along here," said Jaslin Salmon, head of the NAACP in Oak Park, Illinois. Black students who don't care about mixing make you feel impotent and undesirable. "That's a sense of rejection," Salmon added, and then, lifting his voice in mock surprise, " 'You mean they don't want to be with us?' "

These reactions come from the " 'woo-shoo phenomenon'—who's wooing and who's shooing," according to Thomas Kochman, a white specialist who runs corporate seminars on black–white cultural differences. "As long as blacks and immigrants were petitioning to integrate, then whites were in the controlling position of how accepting they would be. So once blacks no longer choose to be whites," he said, whites get annoyed at losing their dominance over blacks' acculturation.

Salmon, Kochman, and others note that all kinds of people, including whites, coalesce into circles of affinity, as at Murrow High School, where the handicapped, the theater crowd, the advanced-placement students, and other clusters form around attributes or interests that are not racial. Among whites, subgroups are less obvious visually but no less exclusive. They include fraternities and sororities, for example, which are founded on the principles of compatibility and rejection. "Affinity houses" at many universities have been set up not only for African-Americans but for foreign students or French majors. At dinnertime on some campuses, there are tables where the college newspaper's staff, the swim team, or the glee club tend to congregate.

"All over this country, wherever you go, that's what you'll find, and that doesn't disturb me," said Salmon, a sociologist who hails from Jamaica. "I expect it to happen that way. Frankly, if I go someplace, and I happen to realize that there's a group of Jamaicans over there, guess what I'm going to do. I'm going to go and join them. If you're in Europe and there's a group of Americans, guess where you're going to go. So that's understandable." Yes, I've seen that in myself. When I lived in Vietnam, in Russia, in Israel, I had Vietnamese, Russian, and Israeli friends, to be sure. But when I really wanted to kick back and relax and be absolutely at ease, I gravitated to Americans, and not only to Americans but to American correspondents—in other words, to people like me.

Yet blacks are the ones largely blamed for the separatism along racial lines. Many whites seem captivated by an optical illusion: As they gaze out over a vast dining hall of all-white tables, their eyes are drawn to a black group sitting together. They see the blacks separating themselves; they rarely see that the whites have separated themselves as well. They sometimes remain stubbornly blind to this even when it is pointed out, as it was to a group of nine white freshmen at Lake Forest College, north of Chicago, who were taking a course on the history of the American suburbs. They argued that since whites were the majority, they could not be held responsible. It was up to the minority members to disperse themselves, they insisted, and they were offended that blacks rarely did so. When whites ask why no black comes to sit with them, however, blacks sometimes reply with a question of their own: Why don't any whites come sit with blacks?

"It wouldn't be something you would do," explained a young white woman who had just finished high school in San Antonio, Texas. "You aren't invited." Do you have to be invited to sit down with somebody in the lunchroom? "Well, no, but when you sit down with somebody at a table, you don't just sit down with people that you don't know. And if they don't invite you, you're not going to walk over."

The eight others shared her discomfort. Of all the racial issues that might have been upsetting to them, black separatism provoked the most distress, a powerful resentment over what the students had seen in their various high schools, which were scattered from Texas and Florida to Missouri, Illinois, and New Hampshire. It hurt them, angered them, practically drove them to distraction when black students seemed to adopt a posture of apartness and radiate vibrations of enmity. These were difficult to document but pervaded the atmosphere like smoke, which the white teenagers could see and smell but could not grab and show to an inquiring writer.

"It's like an attitude, I don't know," one woman said. "It's like they try to scare you. I don't know."

Can you be precise? What do they do to scare you?

"I don't know, I feel like they're looking at me like I think that I'm better than them, even though I don't. But they just perceive that we all think that, and so they try and, like, have this rule by fear, like the only way maybe to defend themselves is to scare you, I guess."

So it's the look? Body language? "Yeah, they would look at you: 'Why are you coming to sit with us?' Or sometimes they think that you're trying to be, like, diversified . . . so then they have the attitude 'Oh, you're just coming over here because you want to meet us because we're black.' "

Did that actually happen to you? "No." She giggled. You just imagine that it would? "Well, I mean, that's just why I don't go over. It happens in our cafeteria. I don't know if you've noticed, but for the most part they all sit in the corner. Even if I, like, start going toward the salad bar or something, I get looks."

I was at Lake Forest for a week, and I watched. There was a "black table" near the windows, straight across the cafeteria from the door, but I never noticed any "looks" at whites who approached the salad bar. How much was reality and how much, imagination?

Trying to get tangible illustrations from the white students was like trying to nail a custard pie to the wall. One assertion after another dissolved under questioning. A freshman from Manchester, New Hampshire, described in detail black kids standing menacingly in his school's courtyard, ready to tease any white who walked through their group. "You don't have any desire to get made fun of by going and sitting down at that table," he said. "When they stay together and do things like that and be unfriendly towards other people just because they're different, it's just reverse discrimination."

What things did they do, what did they say to tease you? He let the question roll away with a simple "I don't know" and quickly continued: "Also, they'd stare at people, and if you were to look at them, they'd be, like, 'What are you looking at?' Just to be able to start a fight or make a person feel uncomfortable." It was certainly conceivable, although he had no concrete examples to give. Above all, he trusted his feelings, and feelings—not observable incidents—dominated these accounts, as they often do also when blacks discuss racial tensions. For whites and blacks alike, this suggests that perception is as real as reality itself, that expectations are as powerful as experience.

Margie Stamper, a white senior at Berkeley who once ventured into a meeting of multiracial students, recognized that her acute discomfort was coming more from inside herself than from outside. About thirty-five people were sitting in a circle when she arrived, and she carefully took a chair outside the circle, behind someone who, she hoped, would make her invisible. "I'm obviously not multiracial," she said. "I felt I couldn't say anything, that everybody was wondering why I was there." Nobody took any action to make her feel unwanted, she acknowledged. No comments were made, no looks were thrown her way—nothing. Yet she felt so miserably out of place that just fifteen minutes into a discussion that followed a forty-five-minute lecture, she couldn't stand it any longer and left. She recounted the experience in a journal for a course called "Roots of Ethnic Conflict and Cooperation," and she received a rebuke from the teaching assistant, a woman who described herself as having African, Native American, and European ancestry. Never before, Stamper wrote, had she encountered a student organization in which she felt she did not belong. The teacher jotted down a reaction: "And you perpetuated that by leaving."

White students are not always fantasizing when they expect a negative reception, and while they might not be able to pinpoint just what blacks do to make them feel uncomfortable, a group of African-Americans at Lake Forest offered specifics. I put the question to them: Let's say you're in the cafeteria, you're sitting together, all black students at a table. How would you respond if a white came and sat down with you?

They snickered. "Do we know this person?" asked Michelle Pulce from Little Rock, Arkansas. Some whites might be welcomed if they have established themselves with black friends, but our hypothetical student didn't qualify. He was known only casually around campus.

"I'd probably kind of laugh to myself," Michelle declared, drawing her words out theatrically: " 'Well, OK, so I guess we're having company, or whatever.' " She got a burst of laughter. "I mean, this person doesn't normally sit with us."

"We'd question his place, his position," explained Shari Jones of Memphis. How would you question it? Give him dirty looks? "I don't know." She thought for a moment, then stared, wide-eyed, and said, "Wow!" in a tone of wonder. But she quickly corrected herself. "I wouldn't say, 'Wow,' but I'd just kind of look. I'd wonder why he wanted to join us."

So the white students were not far off in anticipating an uncomfortable greeting, which led all but one of them to place the blame for the tense distance entirely on the African-Americans.

"I think it's the blacks who put up the wall," said a white man from Naperville, Illinois, a suburb of Chicago. "They are segregated, they always stay together."

One woman sat quietly for a moment, isolated in a thought. Then she raised a lone appeal to broader responsibility. "From my experience," she said, "it's actually equal, and both groups contribute to this symbolic wall we're talking about."

The other whites did not buy her evenhandedness. They were angry, and they focused special resentment on blacks whose numbers reached some critical mass. Individually or just a few at a time, African-Americans did not disrupt the whites' sense of how things ought to be. But in large groups blacks appeared hostile, even fearsome, to their eyes.

"When there's a group of them, they act differently than they did when there was just two or three of them with other white kids," said a young white man whose school in Webster Groves, Missouri, was about 30 percent black. "Like they were superior. They acted like they controlled the area, the hall that they were walking in. They didn't move out of anybody's way. I felt that the white people gave them more respect than they gave us."

Both blacks and whites report symmetrical stories about "friends" from the other race snubbing them in public. A white may be congenial to a black in a safe setting, only to cut him when other whites are present; blacks sometimes do the same. "I would talk to black kids in class when they weren't around a lot of other black kids and have a perfectly good conversation," said one young man. "But if I were to see them with other black kids, they wouldn't even acknowledge that they knew me or anything. I'd say 'Hi' to this person and they wouldn't say 'Hi' back if they were with these other people. It doesn't make much sense to me."

Superficially, the whites were reacting to rudeness and arrogance; at a deeper level, to a violation of the customary codes of deference in which blacks are not supposed to have power over whites. When blacks carve out a small, temporary zone of power in a hallway or a doorway, they destroy traditional roles, disorienting some whites and making them indignant. Bullying by any group deserves an angry response, but blacks are not just any group. What they may see as pride and solidarity, whites are often quick to interpret as hostility. And where blacks mean their behavior to be antagonistic, as some surely do, they are granted less room before they trigger whites' resentment; in many settings, the threshold for them is rather low, and some of them enjoy crossing it.

Furthermore, most white Americans have been taught to see themselves as individuals, not as members of a privileged group, so they are shaken and angered when blacks deal with them as part of a group, not as individuals. To many whites, this seems a kind of ethical violation. To many blacks, it seems merely realistic. It marks a fundamental difference in perception about the way the world works, with blacks more inclined than whites to recognize the broad forces that determine a group's position in society.

When African-Americans sequester themselves, it is hard for whites to see past the sheen of bravado and solidarity into the sense of vulnerability that lurks beneath. Black pride is a yearning. Separatism runs along the edge of easy hurt. Mostly white settings are often felt as inhospitable, hence the search for the safe harbor of shared support. Brother. Sister. "It's a Black Thing. You Wouldn't Understand," the T-shirt says.

It makes white people mad. The message seems accusatory to some, nihilistic to others. Some take personal offense; others simply deride the illogic. "If you say whites never understand and then blame whites for never understanding," complains a white student, "it's a lose-lose situation."

For many whites, the T-shirt's slogan defines a place way out of bounds to them, a region so rich with mystery and suffering that no mere white majority mind can grasp the riddles there. Being black is elevated to the unattainable, deepened to the unfathomable, expanded to the incomprehensible. Black people are not supposed to be so complicated and interesting, so remote that they escape control, so possessive of something that whites cannot have.

All these white youngsters seemed in anguish about race, awkward about dealing with blacks, bitter about blacks' self-segregation, and helpless to overcome it. Much of what African-Americans intended as positive gestures of self-comfort and cohesion, the whites interpreted as assaults on community and mutual respect. And it was clear, through these white eyes, that many black youngsters did not know how, or did not care, to splice their sense of community into the larger whole.

If the chemistry of race is especially disappointing in schools and colleges, settings in which black and white students possess every possibility for finding common ground, it must be said that their elders have given them no better example. Even on professional athletic teams, where blacks and whites achieve harmonious solidarity, clustering takes place off the field. Richard L. Schaeffer, a former attorney for the National Football League Players Association, observed friendship patterns aligned by position—defensive linemen pal around with other defensive linemen—and by race as well. "There's still a tendency for blacks to hang with blacks and whites to hang with whites," he said. "White players' wives are friends with white players' wives. Some of that is probably racist at its bedrock."

A white AT&T executive recalled a noontime celebration in his office for Martin Luther King Jr.'s birthday. So many whites and blacks showed up that people had to stand. A black Baptist minister gave a fire-and-brimstone sermon on some tough racial issues, and a woman sang spirituals.

But then, after the ceremony, as people drifted down to the cafeteria for lunch, they split into separate racial groups, table by table. The white executive looked out at the scene and reflected sadly on how the spirit of King, which had so infused the gathering just moments before, had dissipated. He was bothered, and he thought about it for a long time until he came to see it as something more innocent, that "these people were having lunch with who they wanted to," as he later explained. "They didn't feel forced to do anything, they didn't feel bad because they weren't over at the other table. It was clear from where we had just been that there was welcomeness, and they were all talking about the same thing, talking about how good the program was. And a lot of us had never really been in something like that, and it was really good. I stopped being bothered by it." Then he hesitated and added, "Maybe not totally, or I wouldn't have said anything about it. I wonder about it more than being bothered by it."

Had he looked more closely, he might also have noticed that race coincided with a stratification in the corporate hierarchy: clerical workers, middle managers, executives. A young white woman, fresh out of Princeton, was struck by how the National Gallery in Washington, where she worked, was "segregated by floor," as she put it. "All the security guards are in the galleries, which are on the bottom floor, and the food service is like on the lower floor, and as you get on higher and higher floors, it becomes more white and more male. And then you get to the seventh floor, which is blocked from all the other floors, and that's the power floor where all the white males are and there's nobody else." She smiled thinly.

"Where I get on the Metro is sort of a splitting point," she continued. "My train I get on, it goes to Virginia, and it's primarily white people who take that train. And the other train, it must go to Southeast or Northwest, it's the Green Line, and there's not a single white person. It's like they put all the black people on the train and take them away, and they put all the white people on the train going the other direction and take them away."

One of her friends, also white, lamented his emergence from the rarefied atmosphere of the multiracial Princeton campus—even with its clustering and boundaries—into a largely white world where his encounters with blacks were fleeting and distant, an odd sensation in the mostly black city of Washington. "I had much more real contact with nonwhite people at Princeton than I do today," he complained. "Today my office is all white, and the people I spend time with socially are almost exclusively white, and the only blacks that I encounter on a daily basis are security guards and kitchen staff and people on the Metro. I really don't have very much contact. I find that troubling and strange, that Princeton is going to be the place where I had the most diverse perspective."

Such imposed separation forms the incubator of the separateness in which many African-Americans find comfort today. Sometimes for a single human being, the seminal event, the action that provokes the reaction, is so slender that it scarcely registers on others, as for W. E. B. Du Bois, who recalls in *The Souls of Black Folk* how it begins and how variously it can end. The feelings have hardly changed in nearly a century since these words were written:

> I remember well when the shadow swept across me. I was a little thing, away up in the hills of New England, where the dark Housatonic winds between Hoosac and Taghkanic to the sea. In a wee wooden schoolhouse, something put it into the boys' and girls' heads to buy gorgeous visiting-cards—ten cents a package— and exchange. The exchange was merry, till one girl, a tall newcomer, refused my card,—refused it peremptorily, with a glance. Then it dawned upon me with a certain suddenness that I was different from the others; or like, mayhap, in heart and life and longing, but shut out from their world by a vast veil. I had thereafter no desire to tear down that veil, to creep through; I held all beyond it in common contempt, and lived above it in a region of blue sky and great wandering shadows. That sky was bluest when I could beat my mates at examination-time, or beat them at a footrace, or even beat their stringy heads. Alas, with the years all this fine contempt began to fade; for the worlds I longed for, and all their dazzling opportunities, were theirs, not mine. But they should not keep these prizes, I said; some, all, I would wrest from them. Just how I would do it I could never decide: by reading law, by healing the sick, by telling the wonderful tales that swam in my head,—some way. With other black boys that strife was not so fiercely sunny: their youth shrunk into tasteless sycophancy, or into silent hatred of the pale world about them and mocking

distrust of everything white; or wasted itself in a bitter cry, Why did God make me an outcast and a stranger in mine own house? The shades of the prison-house closed round about us all: walls strait and stubborn to the whitest, but relentlessly narrow, tall, and unscalable to sons of night who must plod darkly on in resignation, or beat unavailing palms against the stone, or steadily, half hopelessly, watch the streak of blue above.

By the dictionary definition, integration is the blending of parts into a unified whole; this has never been accomplished in the United States. It is a promise unfulfilled, a dream unrealized. And so its luster is gone. For many blacks and whites alike, the failure has discredited the word itself and stolen its aura of hope and justice. At best, it seems an idea from a naïve time, a goal unattainable and perhaps undesirable if it means—as many blacks understand it to mean—assimilation.

True racial integration means more than the physical presence of blacks among whites. It means sharing power and shifting control; it means African-Americans who are in a position to make decisions and exercise authority, even over white people. Pockets of such integration have evolved here and there, but not with wide scope. In settings that look integrated, African-Americans often feel that they are invited but not fully accepted. And therefore, many blacks search for alternative paths to access and equality and belonging; frequently, the search turns inward, into the strengths and sustenance of black friendships, black institutions, and black culture.

Nowhere can the yearning be seen more vividly than on campus. Universities have become laboratories of frustration, alienation, and separation, all the more grievous because they constitute rare communities in which black and white students have egalitarian relations devoid of the hierarchies of the working world. Yet on the campuses of mostly white colleges, blacks often feel rootless and adrift unless they can find a circle of other blacks. Otto Green Jr., a big man wearing an Africa pendant on a black string, rolled with laughter as he described his family's hunt for black people when he arrived at the University of Nebraska in the very white town of Lincoln. "It was amazing," he said. "I'll never forget my first two days here. We literally tried to get lost in a city that we didn't even know our way around in, trying to find black people. And when we saw a black person, we slowed the car down: 'You see?' "

Black students "feel like they are in an alien environment," observed Nell Painter, an African-American history professor at Princeton, "in which they know the language that people are speaking, and they can speak it. But they're sort of aware of translating, so they have to rephrase their concerns or censor them. And they find that they must swallow objections—gut-level objections—to things that people say in seminars, knowing that what people say is not meant with any kind of ill intention." And so they gravitate to one another.

Whites occasionally learn what the alienation feels like, but it seems to generate more annoyance than empathy. Christina Fichera and Rebekah Pokart, white students at Drew University in New Jersey, took a nineteenth-century literature course from a black woman who virtually ignored the whites in her class, Christina thought, and who short-changed the study of such white authors as Henry David Thoreau, Ralph Waldo Emerson, Walt Whitman, and Edgar Allan Poe, in Rebekah's view. While blacks were effusively praised for mediocre comments in class, whites were rarely called on, Christina complained. "We were practically nonexistent, and we had to make an exceptional point to be noticed." She was convinced that if the situation had been reversed, black students "would have raised the roof." But she didn't feel free to complain directly to the professor, and when she and another student approached a white dean, they were brushed off. So she was limited to writing a scathing evaluation at the end of the course, when it could not affect her grade. "I was thinking, Let's not rock the boat," Christina remarked. "What if I am wrong and this professor feels that it's just necessary to pay more attention to blacks to kind of bring them out into the discussion?" Still, the experience made her feel small and insignificant. "You know when you have a garden, and you're tending your garden, and you have the roses growing and you have the daisies growing?" she said. "Well, we were the daisies and they were the roses, and she was like cultivating those roses to be the biggest and best roses."

Since Drew is overwhelmingly white, whites can escape from such situations. Blacks have more difficulty doing so. "White people have an option to feel uncomfortable or not. We don't have that option," observed an African-American sophomore, Al-Quiyamah Faiz. She could not easily avoid a class just because "you don't want to deal with the racism, you don't deal with the stereotypes, you don't want to deal with that attitude, that mentality you know is there, no matter how subtle or how apparent it is."

That's right, said a white student, Carla Guerriero. "I've never dropped a class because I felt uncomfortable in the class, but I know blacks who have dropped classes because they felt uncomfortable."

The issue is one of belonging, explained Steve Suitts, the white civil rights veteran in Atlanta. "White folks don't understand how important this notion of ownership is for black folks, and being able to be in a place where it appears that you're not there by the grace and goodwill of someone else. . . . People want to be at home. They want to be at home in where they are and what they do. They want to feel that this is the place that is theirs, these are the things that are theirs. There's a sense of ownership that goes to one's sense of identity. If white folks in general had experiences in their lives where they spent most of their time as a minority of the people around them, I think they would understand a little more sympathetically the urge that a lot of black folks have about going to the places where they can be at home."

Home. The Harlem Renaissance Center at Colgate University is home. Known as a "black dorm," it is open also to white students who want to learn something of the African-American experience. But for black students there, it provides an essential respite from a white world that is not always congenial, a retreat from the constant sensation of being onstage, on display, an object of curiosity.

Colgate's gray stone buildings stand on a hilltop in the small town of Hamilton, New York, surrounded by farmland. It seems a friendly place; students smile and greet a stranger trudging up a path on a windy February day. Underneath, however, blacks feel a racial tension that whites may not sense. In East Hall, seven African-American students have been selected by a black dean to sit around a wooden table and discuss their lives on campus.

The incidents they mention range from the blatant to the insidious: Some years ago, brothers of an all-white fraternity threw a "jungle party," painting their faces black and simulating African natives, and then expressed bewilderment when they were accused of racism. The Afrocentric historical views that many blacks bring to campus are rejected by professors, so students "lie" to get good grades. In a pickup basketball game, a black student hangs from the rim, and a white professor scolds, "This is not a game for monkeys." A black woman gets the highest score on a test in a religion class, and the professor asks her if she is surprised—meaning, in her view, that *he* is surprised that an African-American could do so well.

"There are little, subtle things that many Caucasians do on campus that they don't think is racist," says Lawrance Evans, a sinewy sophomore with a single gold ring in his left ear. "Like one Caucasian male told me one day, jokingly, not knowing it was a racist statement, that 'Don't you know honkies steal, too?' Now, when I say that Natasha is pretty, *too*, that infers that somebody else has been pretty before her. So he's saying Caucasians steal, too. So obviously there's somebody stealing before the Caucasians, meaning black people: You people steal, but we steal too."

And so the Harlem Renaissance Center, also known as HRC, becomes a safe place, like a good family, in which to take sustenance. "If the dorm wasn't on campus, I wouldn't be at Colgate," says Michelle Atkinson, a slender young woman with tiny braids hanging over her forehead. "I remember, like, freshman year, being in a white classroom, listening to the professor talking about Europe and looking at me to suggest that I haven't been to those places. The Harlem Renaissance Center—at least I had someplace to go home to after class."

"The center is like our embassy in a foreign country," declares Diantha Joiner, a senior, who longed for the refuge during five months as the only African-American in a group of white students studying in Wales. "It got to be so difficult because I was with these people almost twenty-four hours a day, and they did not respect me at all," she says, her voice trembling. They played drinking games with unflattering rhymes about blacks. They mimicked and mocked ghetto slang. The women, chatting among themselves, remarked on how uneasy they felt when black men spoke to them on the street. "From that experience I just really prefer not to be close to them or have conversation with them or anything."

"Most of us come from predominantly black neighborhoods," explains Sydney Morris, a freshman. "Now, [if] you're at home one day and the next day you're at Colgate and there's no dorm like that, I mean, what do you do? . . . You walk around campus and look for black people and collect them in one place once a week and go, 'Oh, boy, this is what I needed, my once-a-week whatever'?"

Natasha Redwood, also a freshman, is using the dorm to avoid some of the pain of high school in Englewood, New Jersey, where most of the students were black but she had many white friends. Because her mother works for an airline, she has traveled abroad, "and I was the quote 'accepted' black student because I was educated, I had traveled worldwide," she says. "I would not want to subject myself to that again, and if HRC were not here on campus, I don't think I would be here, I would not want to be here. Because I'm not going to be called the 'accepted' person. I haven't had that experience here because I haven't allowed it to happen. But in high school, it was a thing where my white friends were like, 'Well, only you and a couple of your friends can come, OK?' Because we were the ones who could be most like them. They couldn't accept my other friends because of whatever differences they might have with black people or whatever, and they didn't realize that that was a racist thing. But I just won't deal with that here."

Even if you were a black person who lived in a predominantly white neighborhood, "you had something, you had a support system, being your family," explains Trevor Woollery, a tall senior from New York. "You could go back home at night. Now, most blacks on this campus, they come here from, say, the Bronx, Brooklyn, New York City, or as whites term it, the inner city, OK? They leave home, and they come here, no parents. HRC represents that parent, that place where you can go for support."

African-Americans who seek separate refuge do so not only to escape racism but also to find a complex of comfort where their humor, music, and hairstyles will be accepted without friction.

Hair is a key reason that many black schoolgirls and college women want to retreat into familiar, all-black territory where they won't be interrogated. "How often do you wash it?" "How long does it take to braid?" "Why are you so afraid of being in the rain?" The incessant questions from whites who are usually just trying to show some friendly interest irritate African-Americans who grow weary of explaining themselves. One evening, a little girl, her head covered with lovely braids, was approached by two white women before a show for Black History Month at Bethesda–Chevy Chase High School in Maryland; they ooed and cooed and asked her how long it took to do them. She just winced.

Shari Jones, her hair straightened and combed back in a ponytail, tried to describe the subtle sense of sisterhood that she could not find with whites, even on so small a point as what happens when naturally kinky hair gets wet. "When I'm walking with my white friends and it's just sprinkling outside, I'll say, 'Look, I've got to get an umbrella because I will have a big 'fro with the water.' With the black girls, they understand, like, 'Hey, grab the hat!' "

Music also marks a racial divide, pitting rap against rock, hip-hop against heavy metal. The clash of tastes has caused tension between blacks and whites in college dorms and army barracks, albeit tempered now by the invention of the Walkman, which has allowed students and soldiers to isolate themselves in their own musical worlds.

At Chicago's Brother Rice High School, a Catholic institution with 12 percent black students and no black teachers, the 1991 senior prom broke into two parts over the issue. African-American seniors, excluded from the prom committee, had no say in how the music was to be chosen: Each senior would list three songs, and those mentioned most would be played. That would obliterate blacks' preferences and load the dance with "hard-rocking, bang-your-head-against-the-wall kind of stuff," as one boy put it. The curriculum and culture of the school were so heavily white that blacks looked to music as a vehicle of pride and identity. When it also became the focal point of frustration and rage, the black students held their own, separate prom. They invited whites to come too, but none did.

Music promotes racially separate parties on many campuses, where students say they can enter a dorm room, look at the tapes and CDs, and tell the race of the occupant. The assumptions also include some comical stereotyping. Laura, my daughter, once had a couple of black friends walk into her room at home, look over her tapes, and exclaim, "Where's the heavy metal?" They were truly confused that she didn't like what white teenagers were supposed to like.

La Tanya Wright, from Washington, D.C., picked music as one of the most alienating features of her life on the mostly white campus of Claremont–McKenna College in California, her first predominantly white setting. She felt so different that it took time before she ventured out and tried for acceptance. "I want to go home more and more now, just because I miss that black culture," she said when she was a junior. "I mean here, just in social life, there are so many things that are different, and I have no control over. I can't go up and say, 'Play these twenty songs at parties.' . . . There's maybe two parties a year that have the kind of music I like, like R and B. I like rap."

Although music marks the divide, it can also be a route across the line. Richard Orange, who is African-American, remembers growing up in a dialogue of music, at the confluence of cultures, and he recalls the precise beginning of his education. He smiles openly, showing a gap between his front teeth. A thick gold chain around his neck is visible through the open collar of his denim shirt.

His profession is teaching corporate executives and middle managers how to cope with and welcome and utilize diversity across the lines of both race and gender, and he tries to explain to whites the significance of music to blacks.

"I have this little shtick," he says. "I talk about how I remember coming home in elementary school and telling my mother, 'Gee, Mom, today we learned about classical music.'

"She said, 'You mean European classical music.'

"I say, 'What are you talking about?' She was a schoolteacher. I said, 'No, it's classical music.'

"She said, 'No.' So she sat down and played Rachmaninoff on the piano. She said, 'Now, that's great stuff.' She played Liszt. Then she played something from Erroll Garner, you know. She said, 'That's *your* classical music.' She would play Joan Sutherland and Maria Callas, and then she'd play Sarah Vaughan. And then she would play Mario Lanza, you know, and then she might play Billy Eckstine. And she said, 'Understand that in our frame of reference we have our own classical art, music, literature, and if you lose that you'll be lost forever and be significantly less strong in the world than you have to be.' So that's how she educated us. So I talk about that."

Humor is also a rationale of separation, for many blacks believe that their style of wit conveys an intimacy and rapport that whites simply cannot grasp. When a white person enters a circle of black friends who are joking with one another, the intrusion can be as inhibiting as if a foreigner with broken English sat down at the table. The outsider doesn't catch the references, people have to explain, and the banter bogs down. The conversation may be interesting, but it takes considerable psychic energy, especially from those who have grown up in virtually all-black neighborhoods and have never been close to whites.

Many blacks delight in thinking that they have a special warmth of humor that leaves whites out. A black consultant merrily recalled an IBM computer workshop for teachers and administrators where "all the blacks were sitting around the table, cracking on each other," when a white woman wandered over.

"Gee, you seem to be having a good time over here," she said.

"Yeah, and you're not!" a black woman replied.

The group of blacks erupted into laughter, and the white "went back to this boring table," the consultant said. He chuckled with satisfaction. "We have a joking relationship; we have fun with each other. We spend hours on hours just talking shit and busting on each other and having a good time. When I get bent out of shape, I can just go to my local joint, and even when I feel mad and angry I just sit there for about half an hour or so, and I'm out of it. People come up and say, 'Oh, look at you—blue, hoo, hoo.' "

At Iowa State, Bruce King first hung out with whites, then discovered that he could never be himself and so moved back toward blacks by joining the gospel choir. "I loved being at the choir rehearsals because we were laughing, people were joking. There's a common language, there's a common understanding," he said. "You didn't realize what being in the black community meant until you removed yourself from that community." Joking with whites was easily misunderstood, he felt. "White people always thought that I was angry or that I was just too cynical, and I hurt people's feelings all the time, and I was always apologizing and everything. . . . But in the choir rehearsals, people knew. . . . There's a great sense of support that people understand who you are. You're not constantly educating people that this is who I am."

"When I'm with black students, we talk about different things, we find different things funny, and we find different things just saddening," said Shari Jones, the Lake Forest student from Memphis. "Conversations with whites are more conservative, in that—it's so hard to explain . . . you talk about general things such as classes and teachers and groups. You never focus on one person or talk about anybody." Meaning gossip? "Yeah, gossip. That's the word." She gave a huge laugh. "You just don't do those things. You never get down into those real deep conversations, personal conversations. Whereas with blacks, it's different. Things are so funny, and we just basically have fun with each other." She gestured at a young man across the table. "I could just really insult him, and he would just laugh and everybody else laughs and nobody's really hurt by it. I guess the phrase would be, we crack on each other, and it's just different."

Cracking, capping, signifying, bagging, hiking, slipping, sounding, snapping, serving, ribbing, playing the dozens—whatever the expression, the masterful insult is a game among friends, usually a style of humor that works best in circles of intimacy where even the slur "nigger" can be turned into a term of camaraderie. "Your mother is so fat, she has her own area code." "Your breath smells so bad people on the phone hang up." "Your sister is so ugly, she went into a haunted house and came out with a job application." These are among more than 450 examples compiled in *Snaps*, a book by two black Dartmouth graduates and a white collaborator. The game is "about maintaining your cool," according to the foreword. "The point is not to appear emotionally vulnerable. Talking fast and talking smooth are all part of not letting them know you're scared."

Whites can fling affectionate insults at each other too, but without the sense of persecution that makes the zone of safety so precious and the joke so necessary to survival. Barbara Wyche, a black sociologist, got a lesson in just how necessary when she asked her mostly black class at Virginia State University where they would place humor in the hierarchy of human necessities: under primary needs (food, shelter), secondary needs (education, law), or integrative needs (art, music)? "Ninety percent of my students put a joke under 'primary needs,'" she recalled. "What I had tapped was the culture. And kids were telling me, 'If you're living with someone big, you have to tell a joke in order to survive.'" And she exploded in a great roar of delighted laughter.

Blacks find shared support in various ways. Sometimes, an unspoken tie binds African-Americans in the simplest encounters: a kind word and a little banter between a customer and a salesclerk, a gesture of generosity from a bus driver or a bureaucrat. Black students occasionally ask black teachers and professors to go a little easy, an assumption of favoritism that some teachers accommodate and others resent. Such overtures come to Mark Vance, who teaches African history at Oak Park and River Forest High School west of Chicago. "Some of the black kids say, 'Mr. Vance, we're from the same stock.' They quietly come and say, 'Mr. Vance, cut me some slack on this.'" One boy followed the plea by touching the dark skin on his forearm. "I said, 'Thank you for telling me that, but no. And even more so, I'm gonna be even harder on you.'"

At Lincoln University, the oldest historically black college in the country, a white professor asks to remain anonymous as he reports, "This place is very comfortable. They gain from being here. They're very uncomfortable around whites, and they're very uncomfortable around middle-class living, and so this is a nice stopping-off point for them. It's like a womb. Concessions are made to them. It does give them a confidence. Blacks at Penn State, I don't think they have the fortitude to go on. They've been wounded. Our students go on to graduate with enthusiasm."

But then he shows me two essays to mark the contrasting calibers of his students. One, entitled "Mother," is beautifully written by a young woman who hides her brilliance in class by keeping her hand down and staying quiet, for, she tells the professor, anyone who is always shooting her hand up and giving the right answers gets ridiculed by other students. Another paper is riddled with spelling and grammatical errors, but its subject touches a nerve of raw reality. It is called "Surviver," spelled just that way, and it contains the sentence: "If a black male gets to the end of the week, he's a surviver." The professor has peppered the essay with pencil marks; lines cut diagonally through words, through phrases, discounting but not correcting, rejecting but not reinforcing. The margins are left mostly devoid of suggestion or explanation. And at the bottom, the professor has written "D+" and his entire comment: "You should pay more attention to the details of writing."

Anyone who has taught writing knows how long it takes to do a thorough critique of a paper and how tedious it is to deal with one so mechanically disastrous. But the D+ and the cold comment are like two quick punches in the stomach, the blows of utter defeat. At least, I say, the kid is writing about something he knows, something important to him. Can't he be encouraged and helped? The professor looks at me blankly.

All this proves that damage can be done anywhere, even at the black university where Langston Hughes and Thurgood Marshall were nurtured as undergraduates. But it is a safe bet that if the mostly black colleges had more money for scholarships, more black students would choose them. The pull is very strong, sometimes just as a stopping point to make contact with black culture before moving on into the mostly white working world. As a freshman woman at Lincoln remarked in simple explanation of her choice, "I wanted to learn about me."

Many African-Americans thrive on the play between blackness and integration, taking what they need from each. This requires a fluidity of spirit, a rejection of rejection. Sherlynn Reid is such a person. She is black, she raised her three daughters in the integrated Illinois town of Oak Park, and she has worked for many years as a professional integrationist overseeing the town's community relations department. But when her daughters went to college, all three chose black schools—Howard, Spelman, and Alabama A&M. "They needed to have some sense of who they really were." Growing up during Oak Park's early days of integration, "they probably suffered a lot in this experiment," she said, "because they had to deal with teachers who had never had black students and who had all the stereotypes about they can't learn, they're lazy, their parents are uneducated, you know. And we had to do a lot of educating of the teachers." At a black college, you could "be in a class and know if you didn't get the grade, it was because you did not do the work. It didn't have anything to do with the color of your skin, even though the professor may be white or Asian or black or whatever."

After college, the three daughters—one now a social worker, one a bank auditor, one a fiscal clerk for a parks authority—all settled in integrated communities. "They're all single, but that's all right," their mother said. "I'm looking for three BMWs—three black men working. I don't know what they're looking for, but that's what I'm looking for."

Venturing into the white world and keeping solid contact with the

black world, achieving the balance of mobility and rootedness, is a difficult accomplishment for many African-Americans.

Sometimes they jealously guard the black environment from white
intrusion, as my daughter learned during a semester at Spelman College
in Atlanta. When six black freshmen discovered that Laura was about to
move into a room on their floor, they visited her new roommate, a black
exchange student from New York University, and said firmly that they
did not want a white on their hall. The roommate deflected their appeals, told Laura they were racists, and she moved in. At first, four of the
six gave her "sticky-sweet" greetings that were clearly insincere; then
they reached the point where they could have some light banter; and
finally—as the school year ended—they told Laura that they would truly
miss her. The other two never spoke to her, though. She had apparently
spoiled their hope for an all-black setting.

Of course, every argument has its counterpoint, every observation its
opposite. And on every campus, in every high school, black students can
be found who move easily back and forth across racial lines, undeterred
by cultural discomforts. Christopher Howard arrived at a certain equilibrium between identity and assimilation, excelling at the Air Force
Academy, winning a Rhodes Scholarship, and suffering the epithets from
fellow blacks in the process. He came from Plano, Texas, about twenty
miles north of Dallas, where he was one of just twenty-six blacks in a
large, vastly white high school; he was elected president of the senior
class and went by the motto "Act your age, not your color." This made
whites comfortable and enabled him to establish friendships across racial
lines. "Black males, and particularly young black males, think a lot of
times that they have to be militant," he observed. "They're upset and
mad about all this oppression that we've suffered these last two hundred
years, and they rebel against whites. . . . That's not right. You don't have
to do that to be black. Colin Powell, I think, is a great example of a
strong black man. I just don't think you can walk to class with your
dashiki on and black shades on and sit back there with a scowl on your
face and expect to be a good military officer. We have to kind of give up
a little bit of ourselves for the good of the organization. Black cadets who
can't give up that black militance, or whatever, are not going to do well
in the air force, period. I think the same thing [about] a white cadet who
is from the Deep South and has certain prejudices against blacks. You
can't take that into a professional environment.

"I've had blacks call me 'Oreo cookie'—you know, black on the outside, white on the inside," Howard continued. "So sometimes some of
the toughest things in black-white relationships are black-black relation-

ships. You have to be comfortable with who you are, because there's going to be insecure blacks that withdraw within their own clique. And what they want to do is call you a 'whitey' or call you an 'Uncle Tom' behind your back. It seems like a majority of them are from inner-city schools. Most of them grew up around blacks, so they're the flip side of my other friends from the Deep South who grew up around white kids."

Black college students are pulled in many directions. Their parents occasionally try to govern their affinities by remote control. "Some parents dropping their kids off at school say, 'I'd really like them to be more involved with black students. Could you keep an eye on them? Try to get them to do more with black students,' " said Bruce King, who was Lake Forest's director of minority affairs before he moved to a similar position at Carleton College. "Sometimes it floors me. And then we have black parents who call me and say, 'My son has worked very hard to achieve the things he's achieved. He's achieved them because he has worked hard, and I don't want him to be a minority there. So I prefer that you not include him in any activities of your office.' " King shook his head and declared, "It is the student's choice."

As King himself learned in college, blissful free choice is uncommon. More often, black students have to struggle against a gravitational force that pulls them closer to each other, a kind of moral code that dictates solidarity and cohesiveness, and punishes those who stray into white circles of friendship. Only if a campus has too few African-Americans to reach a critical mass of peer pressure, or if an individual black has gained special stature as a star athlete or student government leader, is he exempt from the expectation that he will hang out with other blacks. And this demand is made not by whites but by blacks themselves.

King began at Iowa State by hanging out with the whites on his floor, and he was quickly rejected by blacks. He went to beer parties, sat in the dining hall at his floor's table, not at the black table, and finally found that he missed the warmth and comfort of black company. Going back was difficult. "It's very chilly at the black table if you have chosen to sit with white people," he noted. "Once you've been outside of the community, it's very hard to get in. You go to events, and people are very suspicious of your motives. 'You weren't hanging out with us last year, you were trying to be white, we thought you were a Tom,' and you have to go through all that. It's almost like an initiation rite, that people can say anything they want, they can treat you any way they want, see if you're gonna stick with it."

To Mellody Hobson, the line between the races was always permeable, and she liked it that way. At St. Ignatius, a Catholic high school in Chicago, she stayed with her best friends from grade school, all but one of whom was white. She did not follow the usual pattern of eating lunch at a "black table." She lived in a mostly white neighborhood on Lake Shore Drive (her mother was a real estate developer) and then moved to River Forest, an upscale suburb west of the city. And she talked "white," as some blacks would say, without a trace of a "black" accent or dialect.

When she arrived at Princeton, Mellody quickly discovered the rough choice that black freshmen there confront. "I expected college to be very freethinking," she said. "I thought, 'There will be black people just like me when I get there.' " Instead, she saw most blacks clustering jealously together in tight cliques with a clear message: You're at a crossroads; if you select the white route outside, you cannot come back. "It really bothered me. I called it 'the tribe.' Do you join this tribe that needs each other, it seems, or are you willing to venture out? And I've never had a life around just black people. I didn't understand why it was necessary in my case. So I chose to be friends with whoever I liked." And since most of those were white, she was alienated from other African-Americans.

The separatist demand is often based on the painful belief that "everything out there is against us, so if you leave, you must be against us," as another black student put it.

"It was never directed at me in a confrontational way," Mellody said. "It was very subtle isolation. When you walked into the dining hall, all eyes were on you. It was a very uncomfortable feeling. And I was even more upset by the fact that I didn't see it on the white side. And so I went through this very hard time . . . I couldn't understand. I did talk to a lot of black people on campus about it. Their experience was very much like mine: You had to make this choice."

Mellody's choice meant profound rejection, for she was branded with the cunning epithet that Princeton's black students use against those who go to white parties, join the mostly white eating clubs, and seem to lack sufficient fervor about black pride. The word is "incognegro."

It is an efficient, penetrating curse: a black identity disguised by an old subservience. "Incognegro," or "incog" for short, has taken its place in the lexicon beside "Uncle Tom," "Oreo," "Afro-Saxon," and other such labels. It has caused many wounds over the years at Princeton.

"It was very upsetting," Mellody said. "I'd call home all the time and say, 'Mom, we did something wrong.' "

"She'd say, 'What are you talking about?' "

" 'Well, these people just don't like me.' "

While the core of black students was unwelcoming, she found most whites accepting, with a notable exception that stood out as one of the few blatant incidents of racism that she had experienced in her lifetime. It took place in the Tiger eating club. "I was standing at their tap and I was waiting to get a beer, and this guy would not give me one. I mean, absolutely. Everyone else but me. I mean, it was like fifteen minutes of me standing there. So I became very, very angry. I can't even believe I did this, but I just looked at him, and I go, 'If I were blond-haired and blue-eyed, I would have been the first one served.' And he just looked at me, and I looked at him, and I turned around, and I have a lot of friends in the club and this guy was standing there, and he said, 'What's wrong?' And my eyes just welled with tears. And I said, 'He would not serve me.' And he said, 'Mellody, that's just ridiculous.' And I said, 'He wouldn't. He just wouldn't.' I just kept saying it: 'I can't believe it.' And someone else came up to me, and he said, 'You know, there are assholes everywhere.' I just turned around and walked out. And I said, 'I'm going to my own club.' And then I found myself going home, I was so upset."

Her club was called Cottage, and she had argued with herself before joining. Along Prospect Street, the high-ceilinged mansions that housed Princeton's version of fraternities had a reputation as bastions of whiteness, and she was torn. "Prospect Street was considered very prejudiced," she said. "Black people did not take part in this. It was a different way of life. Prospect Street was not receptive to minorities. The drinking and everything else was not what minorities were used to. Do I join and look like I'm trying to fit into this WASPy society?" She chose to have what was called the full "Princeton experience" and found that Cottage had a better black representation than most—14 members out of 140.

"To say, 'I want to have the Princeton experience,' " Renea Henry countered, "is almost tantamount to saying, 'I don't want to have a minority experience at Princeton.' " She had come to Princeton from a background quite unlike Mellody's: a public school and a low-income family in New Orleans. Renea now headed the Organization of Black Unity on campus, a vantage point from which she saw a heavy white responsibility in the black-white dichotomy that had developed.

"To fit into what is a 'Princeton experience,' " she said, "you have to leave that racial baggage where you got it from, because the campus isn't comfortable with you bringing up the fact that you're black, that you think this country is racist or whatever, at the eating club. That makes everybody really uncomfortable, and that's not an acceptable thing to do." When white students would talk about how minority students "should mainstream," she translated it as "assimilate" and asked a pointed question: " 'Why is it that minority students have to give up those things which make them comfortable with their ethnicity so that you can feel comfortable with them? Why don't you assimilate yourself to their cultural quirks, if you want to call it that? Or better yet, why does anybody have to assimilate?' That's such an ugly word. Why can't we all come to a point where we respect each other's cultural differences and create spaces where everybody feels free to be who they are? There's this attitude on campus that if you have any kind of pro–black nationalist feeling, then you're militant. This guy asked me if I was a Muslim. No, I'm Catholic." It made her laugh. "I don't see why having an opinion that's pro-black makes me militant. It's really a fear of difference. This is why I call it a superficial diversity. You can be as diverse as you like if you fit into that mainstream model of diversity. You can be black, Asian, or Latino at Princeton, but you have to make a choice. You can have the 'Princeton experience,' or you can have the 'minority experience at Princeton.' "

She did not extend her ideal of respecting differences to those who chose not to have that "minority experience," however. "A black student who comes in and acts white, who socializes white, who thinks white, who has white viewpoints, et cetera, is called an 'incog,' " Renea declared. "And either you're 'down' or you're 'incog.' Either you're with black people or you're against them. Especially freshman year, there's a lot of pressure. If you do something that makes you deny part of who you are, that's where the problem comes in, and that's probably where I would call someone an 'incog'—not to the point of exclusion, but as a point of reference; I would say this person has a problem with their iden-tity." What would someone have to do to earn that label? "There are black students who avoid other black students. Espousing political views or theories that just aren't consistent with the reality of being a minority. It just boils down to that person's denying a part of them. That person's so uncomfortable with their ethnicity or whatever that they either aren't dealing with it [or] they've decided that it's not a factor. One of my favorites is: 'People aren't black or white; they're just shades of gray. Black and white, that doesn't matter; we're all just people.' It's a feel-good sort of phrase, but it's not true. And they use those little clichés and maxims to the point that they don't confront issues that are right in front of them. I think that would make someone an incog."

The racial consciousness that Renea Henry was looking for became a source of argument one day among black students at Colgate who bris-tled when one in the group, Ian Forde, questioned the wisdom of having a black dormitory. Forde was different. He lived currently in Yonkers, New York, but his parents were from Barbados and he had spent many years in England. This alone made him somewhat suspect, and his disagreement on such a basic article of faith brought him tangible contempt from the others.

"I've lived in a predominantly white neighborhood, I've lived in a predominantly black neighborhood," he told them. "I've learned to live among people of different kinds—"

Sydney Morris, a freshman wearing a black shirt with a map of Africa, interrupted and sneered, "You've learned to live among people of different kinds—people who look like me, people who don't look like me. . . ."

"It's a classic example of some birds being taught to be cats," said Lawrance Evans, the gangly young man from Rochester who liked to lob little parables and unflattering metaphors at his opponents. He smiled thinly and drew his words out slowly, letting each one hang in the air and make its point. "Therefore, those birds with catlike qualities can live among the cats better than us who have pure birdlike qualities."

"I went to a predominantly black grade school and junior high school," Morris said to Forde. "For high school, I went to a predominantly white school . . . in Williamstown, Mass. Now, you say you've seen all these different cultures, you've lived in a black neighborhood, you've lived in a white neighborhood. That's fine and dandy, but what did living in a white neighborhood do for you? I mean, you can understand them, so what? What do they do for you?"

Quickly, Forde tried to bolster his credentials as a victim. "I had the experience of walking down the street and being called 'nigger,' " he said. "That has happened to me. It has happened more than once."

"I'm not saying you have to hate white people, but they're not *you*," said Michelle Atkinson.

Forde came back, "It seems as though on this campus, there's this pressure that if you're black, you have to have a quote 'black consciousness.' "

"What's wrong with that?" Atkinson asked.

"What's wrong with having a black consciousness?" asked Morris.

"If you *are* black!" said Natasha Redwood, sarcasm thick in her voice. She had very light skin, green eyes, and wavy brown hair. Now everybody in the room was charged with anger.

"What it seems," Forde said, "is that I'm being preached to all the time, that I'm not allowed to have—"

"For instance," Morris interrupted again. "I live in HRC [the Harlem

Renaissance Center], but I don't hang around there all the time. I branch out. It's not like I stay with one center twenty-four hours a day. When I go to class, I'm around white people for all that time. I'm experiencing a white center. When I go back to my dorm, to where I lay my head at night, you know, I'm in a black-centered environment."

"That's the difference, you see," said Forde. "You have a complex toward the whites. I just have a center."

"No, no, no."

"That's the way I see it."

Evans aimed another metaphor like a well-guided missile. "If you ask me, it's the difference between a yo-yo and a broken yo-yo." Natasha giggled. "The yo-yo always comes back to the center. It always comes back to the center. Some yo-yos are broken and continue to dangle out here, out of their grip."

Whites in some settings have their own cliquish antagonisms, and they have even invented terminology that mirrors "incognegro." The word in some high schools is "wiggers," applied by whites against other whites who hang out with blacks. So naturally had this term entered the vocabulary at Bethesda–Chevy Chase High School in Maryland that some whites who used it nonchalantly did not even recognize its origin; they were taken aback when my son Michael pointed out that it was an insulting combination of "whites" and "niggers."

In Millard, Nebraska, a suburb of Omaha, Tamika Simmons discovered in the late 1980s that as an African-American, she represented quite a liability. Not only was she tacitly considered ineligible for coveted spots on the high school cheerleading squad and drill team, she said, "I had one [white] friend whose mother told her that she wouldn't ever make the drill team if she kept hanging out with me."

Bill Page, a white facilitator who advises corporations on racial problems, found himself the target of intense resentment from white managers at Du Pont who grew nervous and angry as he challenged their vice presidents. They expected and accepted pressure from his black colleague, Richard Orange. But a white man pushing them on racial issues seemed almost traitorous, and finally they asked for Page's resignation. Orange told them bluntly that if Page went, he would go as well; the Du Pont managers backed down, and both Page and Orange stayed on. But the whites' indignation stayed on as well, a standard occupational hazard in Page's professional life.

A double stigma attached itself to Richard Winchester, a white man with white hair, a ruddy face, and impeccable liberal credentials established in 1968 as a delegate for Eugene McCarthy to the Democratic Convention. As chairman of the history department at Lincoln University, he shuttled from one rebuff to another every time he traveled the three miles between the black campus and his home in the rural white town of Oxford, Pennsylvania. "There were times when my politics changed a hundred-eighty degrees when I traveled that road," he said. "I was seen as a honky here, and I was seen as a sellout to the white race by some people there. I was the same person, but in terms of those two environments I was pursuing a completely different life."

Today, two X's mark the separatism of pride. One is used by certain blacks, the other by certain whites. Both trace the echoes of slavery but with wrenching dissimilarity. One originated as a symbol of the lost heritage of the slaves, replacing the African names forgotten, the slave owners' names imposed. The other called the slave owners into battle to defend and to honor their misbegotten right of possession.

Born of the same history, then, the two X's now summon up reverberations of clashing memories. Even as the two peoples display the emblems as parallel statements, the meanings diverge. Each may contain an aura of militance, an exclusion of the other, but they are not at all the same. The symbol of the oppressed cannot do as much injury as the symbol of the oppressor.

The X that Malcolm Little substituted for the last name he inherited from some distant slave owner has become a brand on baseball caps and T-shirts. With the release of Spike Lee's film on Malcolm X in 1992, the appearance of the X rose to a crescendo, signifying a range of black attitudes from cultural affection to tough self-reliance, from the assertion of rights to the hint of violent self-defense that Malcolm seemed to suggest in his oft-quoted slogan, "By any means necessary." By 1996, however, several black college students in Mississippi were speaking of the X in the past tense, since it had lost popularity. They were also giving it a benign interpretation. "Malcolm X never killed anyone or enslaved anyone," a young man noted. "Most teenagers wore the X as a fashion statement, nothing more," a woman insisted. "It meant your history, pride," said another young man.

Still, seeing an African-American wearing the X, whites often see unapproachable hostility. Whether intended or not, the message is received that the bearer of the X is not amenable to comfortable contact across the line.

So it is with the other X, the star-studded St. Andrew's cross of the Confederate flag. For many whites who fly it, the flag means just what many blacks think it means: white racial pride, a gritty nostalgia for the antebellum South, fierce rejection of the liberal agenda of civil rights. In the North as well as the South, the flag can be seen on bumper stickers and pickup truck antennas, on shoulder patches and dormitory walls. But for poor whites in the South, its connotations carry far beyond race.

"That flag has one meaning for folks who understand the history of the Confederacy and its preservation: slavery. But it also has, in parts of the white community, a wholly different cultural meaning," explained Steve Suitts, the native Alabaman who now lives in Atlanta. "I think the rebel flag is probably the only cultural symbol that poor white southerners think they own. It's a bogus symbol. It's as bogus as a Confederate dollar is right now, but it is what poor white folks have, and it's about the only thing they have in their life that gives them a sense of 'This is who I am.' They don't own their house, they don't own their car, they don't own much land. I think it is a symbol that represents their sense of ownership of something. And they don't give a damn about what it may have meant to somebody else. They know what it means to them."

Does it mean racism? "No. It may include that, but it means more. You can't get into a discussion on the flag with white folks, blue-collar or poor white folks, without this part coming up. They'll then say to you, 'Well, look, ever since Lyndon Johnson, we've been giving black folks something. The government's been giving them this, been giving them that. And now what they want is our flag. And they're just not going to have it. If they think they can take over the government, that's all right, but this isn't theirs. It's ours. It means that white folks have value. It's a flag that we have maintained. It belongs to southerners. It was the property of southern whites. It was born in this region, like us; it stayed in this region.'

"It's the same phenomenon that David Duke was able to use in his campaigns in Louisiana, in which he said, 'I'm not anti-black, I'm just pro-white.' And that captures the sense of what people think about this flag: 'This flag isn't anti-black. This flag is just pro-white. And by God, we're gonna keep something in this world that's pro-white.' And that ends the conversation."

Variations on the Confederate flag still have official sanction in parts of the South, where they have been targets of turbulent efforts at reform. The X—the white stars on crossed bars of blue against a red field— enjoyed a renaissance as a defiant symbol during the civil rights movement of the 1950s and 1960s. In 1961 and 1962, respectively, Alabama and South Carolina adopted laws requiring that the Confederate battle flag fly atop their statehouses, beneath the American and state flags. Georgia and Mississippi incorporated the "stars and bars" of the battle flag into their state flags.

The NAACP launched an effort in 1987 to get the flags removed by all four states. In 1988, four black legislators in Alabama were arrested for removing the flag from the Capitol; they finally won their victory in 1993, when it was officially taken down. In Atlanta, the flag was removed from the Atlanta–Fulton County Stadium, where the Atlanta Braves played. But an uproar greeted Governor Zell Miller in 1992, when he began a campaign to replace the Confederate battle emblem. The flag remained. In South Carolina, Charles Condon, a Republican who was elected attorney general in 1994, reversed his predecessor's refusal to defend the state in a lawsuit brought by business, civic, and political leaders seeking to remove the flag because they saw it as a reminder of slavery and—not incidentally—an obstacle to tourism and economic growth. In 1996, Governor David Beasley proposed moving the flag from the Capitol to a nearby monument.

The Confederate flag embraces such an array of meanings that it is accepted even by an occasional black American. "I'm from Richmond, the Confederate capital, and I own a rebel flag, too," said a young black man, a recent Ivy League graduate. For blacks to fight against the flag is to say, "Oh, the Civil War never happened, or afterwards we got even," the man argued. "It's a part of my heritage. I had relatives that fought on both sides of the war, both blacks and whites. It's acknowledging that I have a very diverse but very interesting heritage," he said. "It's another way for me to get a link with my past."

That link was precisely what bothered another black man, a third-year cadet at the Air Force Academy, when a white southerner on his floor hung the flag on the wall of his room. The black cadet took a step that few Americans of any race seem capable of taking: He calmly explained the feelings that the flag evoked. "I told him that I didn't appreciate him hanging it up because to me it represents slavery and the hardships that we had to go through and my ancestors had to go through, things like that," the black man said. "After I talked to him for a while, he finally understood where I was coming from, and he took it down. And so I kind of respected him for that, for taking it down."

Venturing Out

The journey is hard. The path leads out of the all-black comfort of family, neighborhood, and culture into the alien landscape of mostly white America. There the rewards may be bounteous, but life can be lonely. Buffeted by strangeness, the traveler is scorched by curious stares, exhausted by questions, stung by the nettles of a thousand assumptions about his failings.

There is no real choice for most African-Americans but to pursue their potential in white-dominated territory. All-black settings offer certain opportunities, as many excellent teachers, physicians, and pastors can testify. But the full horizon opens up only under a white sky; such is the present structure of the United States of America. So, many black Americans choose, if they are able, to venture out to classrooms, factories, offices, and construction jobs where whites, mostly, hire and fire and make the rules and determine the styles of interaction.

In that world, a peculiar chemistry of culture envelops black people. Those who carry along elements of black pride may stimulate white aversion; those who try to leave "blackness" behind may lose their grounding in themselves. Few whites recognize this dilemma that nags at their black classmates and coworkers, few discern the hidden art of inner compromise that tears at black souls. If they did, perhaps they would be gentler.

Two black cadets found themselves at just this juncture. Having sent militant, allegedly anti-white messages through the Air Force Academy's computerized electronic mail system, they had been brought up on charges and were sitting in a small office to seek the advice of a black officer, Major Curtis Alatorre-Martin, a professor of English literature.

The phone rang. The major answered. On the line was a white major, in charge of the cadets' squadron, who went by the title AOC—-Air Officer, Commanding. He asked the major whether one of the cadets was in his class, and then a remarkable conversation followed. According to Major Alatorre-Martin's recollection, it went something like this:

WHITE MAJOR: What is the class?
BLACK MAJOR: Afro-American literature.
WHITE MAJOR: I want him out of the class. I don't want him going to that class.

BLACK MAJOR: What's the problem?

WHITE MAJOR: Well, one thing is that he doesn't have the time. He's having problems in other classes, and he doesn't have the time to be doing it. And the other thing is, I think that the ideas and the philosophies, and those types of things that you're talking about there, are detrimental to him.

BLACK MAJOR: Wait a minute. You want me to give him a direct verbal order that he cannot come to this class?

WHITE MAJOR: Yeah, I want him out of the class—now. By the way, are you black?

BLACK MAJOR: Yeah. That's irrelevant to anything. Yeah, I'm black, I'm an academy grad. What else would you like to know? I have a master's degree in English. I know what I'm doing here.

The black major was infuriated. "My bell started going off," he told me. Not only had the cadet earned a B so far, but he had experienced a "social and spiritual uplifting since he got in the class," Alatorre-Martin argued.

"As one of the other cadets was telling me, this is the only class in which they can explore. They can look at Malcolm X. They can look at Martin Luther King. And they can say, 'Well, maybe Malcolm was as important as Martin. Maybe the [potential] violence was as important as the nonviolence. And let's explore that, as opposed to the system that says Martin is the hero and Malcolm is the villain.' My particular system says you need both of them to get the political machine to move."

This seemed a fair analysis of the American reality, and the Air Force Academy tolerated it in the classroom. But when it got into e-mail and black cadets added the inflated rhetoric of militant Islam, white officers grew nervous.

Indeed, the class I witnessed went quickly beyond literature and into life, into a lesson on how to cope with integration. Most of the cadets were black, but there were a few whites; they sat at desks in curved semi-circles along four tiers of the classroom. The atmosphere was relaxed, and Major Alatorre-Martin encouraged a black church style: call and response, call and response. In essence, he transported a pocket of black culture into the white academy.

He began by leading an animated discussion of how black writers from Richard Wright to Toni Morrison and Alice Walker portrayed the white male and female, the black female and male. Then the class talked in detail about everyday stereotyping, about black-white interactions. He gave counsel about dealing with white people. "If you think of them as immoral, you're going to lose your support," he said. "I think most white folks out there don't give a damn about black folks. They don't think about black folks, except for the black drug addicts and criminals. So if you think of them as immoral, you lose them." Whites weren't "evil or racist," he said, merely "ignorant."

A white cadet added a bit of homespun wisdom. "It's taken for granted that you're gonna have to work with whites," he advised. And whites will just dismiss anyone who accuses them of personal responsibility for racism. "I'm gonna say, 'That is a bunch of B.S. What have I done to you?' But [if] you say, 'We have a *system* that puts us down,' I can understand that."

Toward the end of the class, the white student echoed the standard platitude of the air force: that the only color you should see is the blue of the uniform.

"Yeah," the major replied, "*you* can do that. But a black doesn't have that luxury."

A tall black man in the back row spoke up with a non sequitur: "The white man did an ingenious job of destroying a race on the face of this earth."

Quick as a flash, a white man in front of him came back, "Well, at least we did something right!"

At the beginning of the semester, they couldn't have joked that way, the major said later. The white probably wouldn't have made the crack, and if he had, blacks would have jumped on him and tagged him as a racist for the rest of the term. But now, after getting to feel comfortable with one another in this freewheeling course, everyone—blacks and whites alike—greeted his remark with a roar of laughter, and he got a high five over his shoulder from the black cadet in back.

This all seemed pretty therapeutic in a society that rarely has an honest discussion about race. Some of the hard truths being told would make many whites uncomfortable. But the military has been one of the most enlightened institutions on racial issues since the mid-1970s, and when the major resisted removing the cadet from his class, the academy backed him up. The registrar told him that the white AOC had no authority to order such a step, so Major Alatorre-Martin filed a complaint that brought the AOC some counseling.

"What the cadet told me was, during his whole year he's been getting harassed by this particular AOC," Alatorre-Martin said. "I cannot imagine being a cadet in that AOC's squadron." Given the context, he could even understand the cadets' anti-white computer messages. But the academy demanded that they apologize for their writings or face expulsion. What to do?

Alatorre-Martin spoke to the cadets from his own experience. He had devised a careful balancing act to get along in the air force without losing integrity. "I can't appear to be too radical; I can't appear to be an Uncle Tom," he explained. "So there's this line that I have to walk. If I can approach that, I can survive. I can live in this world, in this white military world."

Somewhat sadly, therefore, he advised the cadets in his office to apologize. When you're pro-black, he observed, the white establishment considers you separatist. "You can do it, but you'll be walking a tightrope the entire time," he told them. "One of the ways to make the American system work is to get inside it."

The cadets involved were clearly having trouble seeing themselves as being inside the American system. "The American army is an army of slaves," one of them, Kwame Abdullah, had typed on his computer. "The Elder al-Shabbazz's army is just the opposite." (The reference was to the Arab name taken by Malcolm X, which he spelled "Shabazz.")

Abdullah assumed the role of instructor for other black cadets, gave himself the computer name "Brother N.D. Know" (Never Denying Knowledge), and also signed his messages "the Minister of Education." Another cadet used the initials "H.N.I.C." (Head Nubian in Charge). They distributed messages to a wide list of blacks through Falconnet, the academy's e-mail system, and called their network of electronic pen pals "Nubian Edutainment Television." According to copies Abdullah gave me, their discussions ranged across a host of topics, from Martin Luther King Jr. to the 1991 war against Iraq, in a way that alarmed the white upperclassmen who happened to see some of the messages when they were randomly printed out.

"I view the military and Bush as the Pharaoh of the 90's," Abdullah wrote as he sat at his desk in room 2D60 of Sijan Hall, tapping on his Unisys computer. "I am in the armed forces at this present time because of the same reason that most Black people submit to this slavery. It is for an opportunity to progress. . . . I have no nation. I have been robbed of my nation, robbed of my language, robbed of my name, robbed of my heritage. My nation is the skin that I am in. Yes, I will die for it. . . . I have no career in the service. Or, to put it in more understandable terms, I have no desire to be a house nigga for the rest of my life. . . . An all Black squadron is fine. However, an all Black nation should be our goal."

Abdullah later conceded that his "methods of communicating" might have been construed as racially offensive, but he saw no reason to abandon his views. "I was accused of being a racist," he said. "At one point, they even asked me, 'Are you anti-white?' I said, 'No, I'm not anti-white. I'm pro-black.' " When he wrote that the military was a form of slavery, "they took it out of context," he argued. "In today's American society, the military seems to be the only way out for most young black men and black women. They're forced into it because of their economic standpoint, therefore making it some kind of forced labor. I use harsh words. However, the main point is right."

The military, which has made racial harmony a top priority, has little patience with divisive behavior, whether by whites or by blacks. The youngsters who come into the clear mountain air of Colorado Springs, bringing their baggage from white towns and black streets, from poverty-ridden ghettos and racially charged suburban high schools, run into a set of homogenizing standards. And when Abdullah and the other two black cadets hit that new atmosphere, neither they nor the academy's mostly white power structure handled the consequences very well. Neither seemed able to tell the difference between black pride and anti-white antagonism, between mutual support and separatism. Neither side had an ear good enough to tune in on the other.

The confrontation began as an innocent effort among black teenagers to bolster one another in a mostly white military world that they found difficult. Kwame Abdullah still went by the name Lorne B. Moore when he graduated from Little Rock High School in Arkansas and entered the Air Force Academy's preparatory school, which provides a year of remedial help before certain students start at the academy itself. By chance or by design, a group of blacks happened to be housed together in part of a dormitory. They formed friendships and quickly fell into the usual pattern of gathering at the same tables for meals. But they added elements that made them look exclusive: prayer and organized discussion.

"Some of the whites began to refer to the blacks in B Squadron as the 'ABC,' which meant 'All Black Conference,' " Abdullah recalled. "And since we all were roommates living in a 'segregated' part of the squadron, they referred to that part of the squadron as the 'ghetto.' This was the beginning of a lot of our problems. We never exactly reserved any tables for ourselves. However, there was a table that we always sat at, and the majority of the whites refused to sit there. A handful of them sat with us on occasion. We all welcomed them without hesitation. But one day we were accused of discriminating against the white cadet candidates by refusing to allow them the opportunity to sit with us. We quickly protested the accusation. However, we were not heard. We were told that from that point on, no more than two of us should sit at the same table."

"We feel that we have been charged with simply spending too much time together," Abdullah wrote in an explanation at the time. "We are only practicing the concept of friendship. Obviously, the friendship which we have acquired has in one way or another offended, and frightened, some, if not all, of the Caucasian population here."

Their white superiors were alarmed not only by the racial clustering but also by the artifacts of black pride. Any scent of African identity or black nationalism provoked a stern response against the symbol, the expression, the T-shirt, the poster, the book. For a while, Abdullah's roommate, Taurus James, got away with having a poster headlined "Africa" on his wall. Beneath a map of the continent was the word "Motherland." Eventually, though, James said, "my sergeant told me to take it down because of the perception. I took it down and put it in a corner. He came in several times and told us to take down all the African stuff and books Kwame had about Malcolm X, so it couldn't be seen. He said it was perception."

Indeed, black-white perceptions at the preparatory school were severe enough to produce tensions that occasionally broke out in fistfights. And one morning, black students woke up to find a Confederate flag pasted to each of their doors and a Confederate flag on the flagpole, the halyards taped so tightly that it flew for hours before anybody took it down. Worse, the officers who had reacted so sharply to the X of Malcolm seemed considerably less aroused by the X of stars and bars that formed the centerpiece of the "rebel flag." A sergeant ordered everyone into the auditorium and told them that such incidents were not allowed and that they were not to discuss this one, a tactic guaranteed to keep the wound festering. There was no investigation, no punishment. "We couldn't understand why nothing was done," said James. "It was just swept under the rug."

Some of the black students approached a black major with their anger, Abdullah recalled. "He told us, 'I grew up in the military. When something like this happens, you just have to salute smartly and carry on.' Salute smartly and carry on? They're doing something wrong." Blacks nicknamed him "Major Sellout."

The prep school experience persuaded Abdullah that he needed a new formula, and he told himself: "I'm going to try to do my best to survive and be successful in the air force without having to suppress my pride and heritage." So in the summer between prep school and the Air Force Academy, he abandoned his given name and joined a community known as the Nubian Nation, an alternative to the Nation of Islam. He swept into the academy radiating his fresh identity but quickly saw that his version of self-respect wouldn't work. "The only way that you can survive in the military," he finally concluded, "is if you subordinate yourself, you don't show your black pride. People at the academy get in trouble for wearing T-shirts saying 'Africa' or 'Proud to Be Black.' Black women had T-shirts made—'Proud to Be a Black Woman'—and they got in trouble."

As a Muslim, Abdullah came under special scrutiny during the war against Iraq. He was questioned repeatedly by officers and upperclassmen about his attitudes on the fighting, and his noncommittal answers deepened their suspicion. He and other blacks were subjected to room searches by superiors looking for copies of the Nation of Islam's newsletter, *The Final Call*, and they were harassed over posters of Malcolm X and Louis Farrakhan. Abdullah also led an unwelcome movement criticizing a fact book, entitled *Contrails*, which contained "knowledge" about the air force that first-year cadets had to memorize. The "knowledge" omitted substantial black contributions, he argued, such as those of the Tuskegee Airmen, a corps of black pilots and crewmen created in 1941 and based at Tuskegee, Alabama. In his e-mail messages, Abdullah told black prep school students that they should learn black "knowledge" and that he and others would be testing them when they arrived at the academy. A black-dominated student organization, the Way of Life Committee, also engendered apprehension among whites. "They think we're plotting," said one black cadet, shaking his head.

Other blacks saw the Air Force Academy draw from a broad arsenal of punishments against those who displayed black pride. One young man explained that there were "certain regulations," not invoked for most cadets but used against particular blacks. "You get a certain amount of demerits if you have your hands in your pockets, certain demerits leaving trash in your trash can," he said. The consequences included "confinements" and "tours." Under confinement, a cadet had to remain in his room, silent and with his door open, except to go to class and the bathroom. A tour was a march in dress uniform with a rifle on the shoulder. Abdullah said that he had received six months of confinement and one hundred tours.

After the e-mail messages were found, three cadets were initially ordered expelled. Abdullah left the academy. Taurus James and the third cadet appealed, gave conciliatory explanations, and won the right to stay. For James, who lived in the slums of Southeast Washington, D.C., where "you could be hit by a bullet at any time," the military was an escape route that he would not lightly cut off. "Going to the academy was an open door, an opportunity to get out," he said. Ultimately, however, he faced intense scrutiny, was brought up on various other charges (including assault for pushing his girlfriend, who later became his fiancée), and was judged unfit to be an officer. He left the academy in bitterness just before graduation and finished at the University of Colorado. The third cadet graduated and was commissioned second lieutenant.

For January, it was unusually warm in Massachusetts, and the drizzling rain made the day gloomy and raw. The white teenagers walking to Lexington High School trudged through the dismal dawn not far from the town common where minutemen had confronted British troops the morning of April 19, 1775. The black youngsters piled off two yellow buses, onto the campus of brick buildings, and into the stresses of another culture. Like the Air Force Academy, this was integration at its most carefully managed, yet it too revealed deep fissures along the color line.

Lexington is one of thirty-two predominantly white suburban towns that have voluntarily accepted black pupils from poor Boston neighborhoods. The undertaking, born in 1966 out of the turbulence of Boston's busing controversy, is a gesture of civic conscience known by the acronym Metco, for Metropolitan Council for Educational Opportunity. It provides the communities with additional state funds as compensation, but the true benefit lies in the intangible—an enriched experience for both whites and blacks who would otherwise have no such contact. And by one measurement, the results have been impressive: 78 to 80 percent of Metco's graduating seniors go straight to college.

The program also creates a laboratory of tensions at the junction of race, class, and culture. Most towns take only small numbers of black children lest they inundate the schools and (it is implied) drag down the academic level. Therefore, just 3,300 participate, and a long waiting list forms in the city. Parents have been known to carry their newborns into the Metco office to have them registered.

Most black children in the United States have never attended mostly white schools, and most white children have never been in classes with significant numbers of blacks. This has been the case across the entire sweep of American history, both before and since the 1954 Supreme Court decision in *Brown v. Board of Education*. The laws mandating segregation have been struck down, but segregation remains, sustained by economic disparities and the resulting residential patterns, white indifference and aversion, the undercurrent of black resistance that has grown in recent years. A truly integrated school has been the rare exception. No constitutional rulings, no intricate court orders, no fine platitudes of conscience and vision have been powerful enough to turn back the tides of separation that still engulf the races.

In assessing schools, statisticians use two definitions of segregation. One labels a school "segregated" when it has more than 50 percent "minorities" among its students. The other reserves the "segregated" classifications for a student body that is more than 90 percent black, Hispanic, or Asian. Schools in the first category—with a majority of "minorities"—have hardly diminished. Throughout the country— including the South, where court-ordered desegregation plans were focused—growing percentages of African-Americans are now attending schools in which most students are black, Hispanic, or Asian: The percentage dropped from 77.6 in 1968 to 63.6 in 1972, held steady during the 1980s, and then by 1995 rose to 67.

Schools in the second group—at least 90 percent minority—were more successfully attacked by desegregation efforts. The proportion of black children attending such schools nationwide declined from 64.3 percent in 1968 to 33.2 percent by 1980 and then by 1992 rose to 34 percent, where it has remained since. In Illinois, Michigan, New York, and New Jersey, the most segregated states in the country, a majority of black youngsters go to schools with fewer than 10 percent whites.

The separation is even more severe than the data suggest, for many junior high and high schools that are considered integrated—with 10 to 35 percent minority students—are internally segregated along academic and extracurricular lines. Basketball, football, and track teams provide racial intersections where solid friendships are often formed. But few blacks work on the school newspaper or hang out with the theater crowd. Few whites join the Student Coalition Against Racism. Most troubling, academic tracks are defined starkly by race. Walk through Lexington High School in Massachusetts, Bethesda–Chevy Chase High School in Maryland, Oak Park and River Forest High School in Illinois, Teaneck High School in New Jersey, and you can almost always tell just by glancing into a classroom whether it is an honors course or not. If there are no blacks or only a couple, chances are it's honors or advanced placement. Blacks who might be qualified are screened out by a host of factors. Some get peer pressure not to "act white" by emphasizing their studies; some are stereotyped by teachers as incapable; some feel awkward in mostly white classes; some have parents who do not push them or do not know how to be advocates with a school administration that they find intimidating.

"It's one of the tragedies of my oldest son," said Marge Zuba, a white guidance counselor at Oak Park. "He says, 'I went into honors courses having loads of black friends; I left having very, very few.' And as a parent, I'm furious about it. And had I realized the extent to which that had an impact on my son's life, I would have pulled him from the honors courses."

My son Michael dropped down from an all-white honors American history class to a regular course to get a better teacher and in the bargain realized that he had gained the opportunity to study his country's history with black students, a valuable experience that he would have lost at the honors level. But most whites are not exactly clamoring to overturn internal segregation. Many white parents are frankly comforted by the whiteness of their children's honors classes, which probably defuses some opposition to integration in good suburban schools.

Putting it another way, the honors courses are a filter, letting in blacks who have acquired speech patterns, body movements, and visible attitudes that send nonthreatening messages announcing their acclimation to "white" culture. Laura, my daughter, doing a high school paper on race at Bethesda–Chevy Chase High School, discovered that she was most comfortable interviewing blacks who were in honors—blacks who seemed most like herself. Those prepared to move into white culture were more accessible to her, she thought, but they didn't feel they could open doors for her to other blacks who didn't mix with whites. Those others, Laura hesitated to interview—and felt annoyed at her own inhibition. "They would hang out at a particular corner," she recalled. "They were intimidating to me. I wanted to talk to them, but I never had the guts. I felt surrounded and alone when I walked through there—a lot of body language that was sending some signals of a tough exterior." She had hit some of the walls within the walls.

Integration itself is far from an absolute concept; it has the elasticity of a fantasy as seen through one or another misshapen lens. What whites may regard as a fair representation of blacks in a given setting, the blacks themselves may see as tokenism; where whites may perceive an overwhelming presence of African-Americans, the blacks may feel scattered and lonely. A black *New York Times* editor, sitting at the Metropolitan Desk, was once startled when a white colleague looked across the block-long newsroom and remarked approvingly on how many black reporters there were now. "I looked out and saw three," the black editor said, laughing. "He must have seen thirty. Cognitive dissonance."

Housing researchers have discerned a "tipping point" of about 8 percent at which the rising proportion of blacks in a neighborhood will frighten whites into wholesale selling. Real estate agents in Oak Park, Illinois, were so convinced that the schools were being overrun by blacks in the 1970s that town officials had to take the agents on a school visit to prove that only about 5 percent of the students at the time were black. In most settings, a threshold exists at which the number of blacks begins to look dominant to white eyes. And polling shows that whites' racial intolerance is expressed more and more overtly as larger proportions of blacks are introduced into the hypothesis. For example, whites who are asked if they would oppose sending their children to school with blacks change their responses depending on whether black children would account for just a few, half, or more than half of the student body. The percentages of whites in opposition, by the date of the poll, are as follows:

Where Blacks Would Constitute . . .

	A few	*Half*	*More than half*
1963	23%	47%	70%
1969	11	34	62
1975	6	29	59
1978	4	22	57
1983	3	23	62
1988	3	20	47
1994	4	7	39

The level that makes blacks comfortable is probably about the point at which whites get nervous. Therefore, when a mostly white suburban school system offers to take some inner-city black children, it tends to keep the numbers small.

The towns that accept blacks from Boston through the Metco program insist that the youngsters begin in the early elementary grades, not in high school, so that they can be acculturated both socially and academically. "The feeling in Lexington," explained Cheryl Prescott, Metco's coordinator there, "was that the earlier you can place the children, the better the chance they would have of being bicultural, so to speak, being able to operate in their world and this world. People really do see it as two different worlds, mine and yours. And 'mine and yours' may smack of black and white. It certainly has a lot to do with urban and suburban, which are totally different ways of living. It has to do with street savvy or street naïveté. It has to do with whether or not you know how to take the T!" She burst out laughing at her own reference to the subway system, such a normal part of life for the city kids, so alien to many suburban teenagers with cars to drive. "You will hear people refer to 'our world' and 'their world.' Right there, there is separation."

The sense of separation is felt by black youngsters in many ways—in the difficulty of penetrating white cliques, in the racial stereotyping that goes in both directions, in the assumption that they are to blame when something is stolen from a locker, in the differences of income, in academics, in the cultural clashes that involve clothes and music and styles of interaction.

Sometimes a crude incident will strike like a bolt. "When they did a play at one of our elementary schools in Brookline and a black boy tried out," recalled Jean McGuire, the voluble director of Metco, "the principal said: 'You can't be that. You're black.' It was a Shakespearean play. He couldn't be in it because he was black. And he was furious. We had to go out there—the stupid fights. Oh, you fritter away your energies with this stuff. He's retired. Thank God they put him out to pasture. But that's who's running the country: these old white men who grew up on *Amos 'n' Andy*—yassah, boss man. Shit. You know, tap dancing, singing, playing football, running a race on the track; that's for blacks."

Mostly, the hardships are subtler. Metco students are sometimes caricatured with false compliments by teachers with good intentions. "During gym class, the gym teacher noticed that I was very quick," Yolanda Scott remembered. "He made a statement: 'A lot of you Metco kids are really good runners, good sprinters. You should really go out for the teams.' And to me that was kind of insulting. Basically he was saying, 'Black people are so athletic.' "

Sadada Jackson had a teacher who called her by the wrong name, mixing her up with another black girl: a case of the old they-all-look-alike syndrome, Sadada thought. "Then there are those who are just like, 'Oh, I understand where you come from,' and, you know, who pity you," she said acidly. "You just don't want that pity. But at the same time, you don't want people stomping all over you because you're black. You want to just be equal, like everybody else. You know, you take off my skin, you're gonna see the same thing."

Sadada chewed reflectively on her green gum and blew a bubble. She had found the conundrum of integration: opportunity and pain, exhilaration and exhaustion. One could argue that much worth doing in life is a bit scary, that every bold endeavor generates a little fear, and that comfort is a sign of complacency—in which case the black experience with integration surely has value. Venturing out is unpleasant but necessary, as Sadada recognized as she pondered her contradictory reactions to the task of going to school in a white suburb. "I think the situation more or less prepares me for future encounters with people of the other race," she said. It's not easy training. "There's no curriculum that says, 'Here, this is how you do it.' This is an everyday thing, and I think you learn a lot from your experiences." But she found it tiring. "As I got older, I started to kind of get this racial shield about me," she said. "I build this shield where there are days when I feel that I just don't want to interact with these white people, I'm just fed up."

One skill that integration imparts to African-American youngsters is acute sensitivity. These teenagers were keenly attuned to the vibrations from their teachers—the racial slights, the earnest caring, the indifference, the concern.

"There's this one teacher," said a junior named Latasha. "He's a math teacher, no names. I guess he thinks of our kids' attitudes as bad, but I guess he doesn't understand because, I mean, they don't mean harm. Most of the students have never gotten higher than a C or a B minus. They could be doing so well, but he's a very mean teacher to all the students, and especially to the Metco students. He thinks of our students as disrespectful or very bad students or mouthing off. But that's how they express themselves; they're not meaning any harm. That teacher really puts stress on the kids.

"But we have some excellent teachers here that will stay after just for you, to give you extra help," she added. "These are the teachers who really care about you. I appreciate teachers staying after school to help me when I need help."

Yolanda agreed and liked being challenged. She was now a senior, thin and wiry, with an articulate intensity. "When I went to school in Boston, I was always one of the highest students in the class, so I never really had to push myself that much. Yet when I got here to Lexington, despite what grade you get, the teacher's constantly pushing you, constantly asking you to give more." She adjusted her glasses. "But there are those teachers also who have these—I don't know—these stereotypes of what a Metco student can achieve. . . . They just assume that if they give you a passing grade, that you will accept that. There are a lot of Metco students who do not accept a passing grade. They want to go beyond that."

It takes a strong hand at the top to create an atmosphere free of biased behavior. And the principal, David Wilson, portrayed himself as eager to do just that. "I'm very frank with them," he declared. "I had a biology teacher, and I said, 'Look, it's clear to me that we've had, over the last four or five years, six or seven issues and they're all with black students. The kids perceive you as being racist, and here are the issues.' I don't see how one couldn't see it. Kids felt that if they had a test returned to them and they went up to ask for an interpretation, he was more patient with white kids than he was with them." Sometimes he would raise a white student's grade, but not a black's, Wilson said. A black youngster would enter the classroom late, and the teacher would say sternly, "I want to see you after class." A white would be tardy, and "sometimes he would just let it slip by and the kid would come in and sit down, and no issue was made of it. The kids quite clearly see that kind of thing very quickly. And as I said to him, I said, 'This kid has five other classes, they're not complaining about their teachers being biased, so the impression is more important than whatever perception you have. The impression is there.' And he said, 'I'm really not intending to—' So I say to him, 'Consciously or unconsciously, it's there. I don't want to see it again.' . . . The last three or four years I haven't had any complaints, and he does have black kids in class."

As in black-white encounters nationally, the divide of economic difference drives an additional wedge into the fissure of race. Although a few blacks in the high school live in Lexington, most African-American students come from working-class or poor families in Boston; most of the whites are Lexington residents who have known nothing but upper-middle-class privilege. Some whites believe this takes a toll on the black youngsters' self-esteem.

"I think it's difficult for the kids," said Wilson. He was the model of a principal: gray hair, gray mustache, blue short-sleeved shirt, dark blue tie with tennis players on it, smooth and expressionless oval face—a bland, friendly, low-key man. "Let me give an example. One night a young man was stranded here, and I could have taken him down and dropped him at Alewife [the subway station], but it was late at night, so I said, 'I'll drive you home.' " Wilson could see that the boy was torn, eager to have his principal meet his mother, embarrassed by the route to his apartment. He lived in the projects, and "as we walked up the stairs with the garbage on the floor and urine all over the place, I could see him change," Wilson said. "He just closed in. We got to the door, knocked on the door, his mom came to the door, opened the door, ushered us into just a lovely apartment." The boy relaxed. "I think for kids whose friends are being shot at, whose uncle may be involved in drugs, who fear for their own lives and security in the area they are in, to come here and expect them to be open and resilient, you're almost asking an impossible task of a kid, to be a superhuman kid who can overcome. The values have to be in place, and there has to be support in the home in order for that to happen. If it isn't, the kid's gonna have an awfully hard time."

To ease the hardship, each black child from Boston is assigned a host family in Lexington as a home base for after-school visits and overnight stays. Some youngsters form strong, lasting attachments with their white hosts, who often come out to plays or games to lend support as substitute parents. But in the intimacy of white homes, the blacks are also assaulted by confusing contrasts, which illuminate questions about family life, morality, struggle, and social justice.

Curiously, the contact sometimes leads both blacks and whites to romanticize each other's worlds, as if everything that one lacks the other enjoys in abundance. As a white teacher and a black student looked into each other's cultures, for example, they saw the defects of their own filled in the other's.

Peggy Dyro, who taught English and history, was an acute, pleasant woman with pale blue eyes. She loved having blacks from Boston in her classes, and she detected strengths and connections that were absent for the Lexington whites. "Kids who live in the inner city much more readily know what community means than kids who live in suburban ghettos," she said bluntly. "People [in Lexington] are very busy with career making, and many of them don't see their children for any length of time to truly know them. And the irony is, of course, they're out earning and getting, partly for their own self-aggrandizement, but also to give to their children. But there isn't the richness of culture that I see a lot of black kids coming from in the city. They [whites] don't have such touch with their families—you know, grandparents, that sort of stuff. There isn't that much conversance with what struggle really is: reaching down there and finding—when you've got nothing left—new resources. There isn't a whole lot of that. By the same token, because there is this created thing called poverty, and this created culture called inner-city life, it lives on the underbelly of capitalism. It wants real fancy sneakers and real fancy leather goods and real shiny gold."

To Sadada's eye, however, the white families of Lexington, especially the mothers, lived rather enviable lives. "They have time for work and also have time to come home and cook their husbands and their families dinner," she noted. "The black woman—I look at my mother, and she's just a paycheck away from poor. . . . And I see her struggling. She'll come home, she won't have dinner ready. . . . She'll have to rest 'cause you can tell she's so tired from whatever she was doing . . . and never is there time for her and my stepfather to get together and maybe enjoy their own company. The white women always have time. Dinner's always ready when you come home. There are snacks always here. . . . Maybe Sunday night we'll go out and see the opera . . . whereas the black family, we're struggling for the next day, like there's no tomorrow."

Being in Lexington made Sadada more eager than bitter. "It makes me reach higher than my mother," she said. "My mother was born in the projects. And my mother said to her mother one day, she said, 'I'm gonna live in a big white house on the corner on top of a hill.' Well, she didn't get on top of the hill, but she did get a nice white house on the corner. And that was her dream. And I know that my dream will be bigger than that, and I want to pursue that. So that makes me want to reach more for my dream, whereas I think if I was white, I'd take for granted what I have." A chorus of agreement rose from other black youngsters in the classroom, who insisted that they now treasured their few possessions. "Exactly," Sadada replied. "You appreciate much more."

"My mother, she always wanted a Mercedes," added Syretta Bollin. "I'm gonna get to that point. I'm gonna be that successful—another successful black woman in this world. And every time I come up here and I see these kids driving around with their nice cars—" An uproar of groans interrupted her. "It gets me."

"It makes me want more," said another girl.

"I feel mad," Syretta continued, "because my mother, our family, she's been working for twenty years now, over twenty years, and we still haven't got it yet. We've been struggling so hard, and we still have not got it yet, a nice car, that Mercedes that she wants. And I just get angry sometimes."

As Yolanda moved back and forth between the two worlds, she developed a formula for success in mostly white Lexington: Imagine that you belong. As she told entering freshmen: Act like a Lexington High School student, not a Metco student. "What you have to do is to achieve academically," she said. "That's the first thing I stress: schoolwork. They have to have their mind set on doing well in those classes, because if they don't, nothing else will work. If you can't do well in class, then you don't feel good about what's going on around you. And then I try to tell them that, if you have a talent, whether or not you can act, sing, play basketball, play the trumpet, you know, do something like that. Get involved in those organizations that you think you would enjoy. And don't let yourself, just because you're a Metco student, limit what you're doing.

"Freshman year, I went out and I ran for student government, 'cause I like to be in the middle of things, and I ran for president of my class, and I made it. There were many times, eight, nine, ten o'clock at night, I was catching the T home. Don't let anyone tell you just because you're black you cannot do it and you cannot achieve it. A lot of kids get hung up with that. They think, Oh, I'm black and I'm out here and the school is predominantly white and no one's gonna let me do anything, and I'm not gonna be able to achieve. And I always try to tell kids that if you believe you can achieve, you honestly to God for goodness know in your heart that you can achieve anything you set down to do, then do it and don't let anyone else tell you otherwise. Because once you do, once you start doubting yourself, you leave an opportunity for other people to come in and try to shoot you down. And what you want to be is like the moon. You want to be there so people can constantly see you, they can constantly know you are there, that your presence is felt, and that your presence has an impact on what's going on in their lives as well as yours."

Teachers love that kind of attitude, of course, and several white teachers saw the presence of black students as deepening class discussion. Some Metco students had academic and behavioral problems. But Peggy Dyro learned that if she tuned in culturally, she could see the strengths that coexisted alongside the weaknesses. Youngsters in standard courses were "almost all print-deficient," she said. "They don't read as well, they don't write as well. They speak beautifully. They have real facility with oral communication—rich, colorful, expressive, wonderful. They can tell beautiful stories, they read character to a T, they're people readers from miles away. They're right on the money. And I notice this all the time."

Black Biculturalism

Every morning, Consuella Lewis consciously transformed herself as she drove to her job as director of the Office of Black Studies at Claremont-McKenna College. About a block away from the lush southern California campus of low buildings and graceful palms, she reached down to her radio, lowered the volume, and changed the music from throbbing rap to soothing classical. Along with the clothes she was wearing and the vocabulary and accent she would use at work, Lewis was deliberately crossing into the white world. And she had no apologies, even for the change of radio stations. "You're riding around, you may see someone, it's a small community, so you do the switching thing," she explained. "You don't really feel like you're selling out. You know what your core values are. And I don't feel like I'm acquiescing, because I actually like both types of music. But it's better to do that a block away." She laughed and added, "I'm serious."

From early childhood, many African-Americans learn to move easily across the boundary between black and white. As a little girl, Walterene Swanston saw the line vividly every time she took the train from her home in San Francisco to her relatives' in Baton Rouge, Louisiana. Blacks and whites could mingle together until the train reached Clovis, New Mexico, heading into the segregated South. There, a curtain would be hung across each car, separating blacks from whites. "They'd put the curtains up, and that was the wall and that was the signal," she recalled. "So going back and forth, I got used to living in those cultures from the time I was four years old. And so I knew how to go back and forth."

The curtain still hangs, invisibly now. To pass through it effectively, to succeed in predominantly white schools or workplaces, African-Americans find they must master the nuances of the white world. Biculturalism is their route across the frontier of separation. They substitute dialects, they adjust body movements, sometimes they change the clothes they wear and the music they listen to.

I saw the dramatic shift when I sat in on Major Curtis Alatorre-Martin's African-American literature class at the Air Force Academy. Most of the students were black, and they took easily to the call-and-response style that he allowed. Nobody raised a hand; people just spoke out when they wished. At the end, he invited students to stay and tell me about their experiences at the academy. Fifteen black cadets did so, remaining in their seats as I took a position at the front of the room.

Suddenly, with a white man standing before them, their style became "white." Mouths closed and hands went up. Nobody spoke until I pointed or nodded or gave recognition. As if they had flipped a switch, they turned off their "black" culture and turned on their "white" mannerisms. And they were flawless at the metamorphosis.

African-Americans fall along a broad spectrum of cultures, and of ability and willingness to adapt to whatever they may define as "white" forms. At one end is the black person who has grown up among whites, who speaks with a nondescript "white" accent, who is more comfortable among middle-class whites than among lower-class blacks. At the other end, perhaps from the impoverished inner city, is the person who speaks, dresses, moves, and identifies in a "black" culture that is not easily abandoned. The style of this "homeboy" or "homey" is sometimes emulated by middle-class blacks trying to embrace their blackness.

In the center of the spectrum, millions of black Americans travel between cultures every day, struggling to maintain their identity while fitting into what they believe is "white." What is white is hardly monolithic, of course. Numerous white subcultures organize themselves around class, region, religion, and ethnicity; Italian-Americans, Jews, and WASP Episcopalians are not culturally alike. But they do meet on some common ground, which Thomas Kochman, the specialist in black-white cultural dissonance, calls "Anglo culture," a corporate (largely white male) set of values and behavioral patterns that has established the tone in much of the working world. As it has spread into the society at large, this cultural lingua franca has faced growing challenge by those who resent its domination. But it remains the route by which cultural minorities still move into successful lives.

Blacks' cultures possess their own complexities. "There are so many different kinds of being black," noted Eamon Buehning, a multiracial Los Angeles woman. "There's southern, rural black, which was the larger definition of black through, let's say, the thirties through the late fifties, early sixties. I mean, that's what people were seeing as black: greens and black-eyed peas and all that stuff. That's what black people did. Then you had in the sixties the emergence of the urban black, which had some of the southern cultural things. But then you had this new spin on black English, which is basically southern English, which is a southern style of English that a quote unquote 'lower class' of people spoke. Now a lot of middle-class blacks have a real struggle. If they use standard English, if they listen to fusion jazz instead of rap, they're not black anymore, they're not black *enough* anymore. So I think, in part, the definition of being black is changing again. And that's why a lot of people are feeling a lot of pressure and people are confused and there's a lot of anger going on within the black community."

All the American subcultures, whether black or Chicano or Chinese, are also American, a point too often forgotten in the whirlwind of debate over multiculturalism and "political correctness." They are parts of the whole, and the whole would be diminished without them. They do not escape the influence of the American common ground, just as the common ground is not insulated from them. In this symbiosis, aided by boundaries that are permeable and blurred, citizens may move to and fro across lines, engaging in the great American compromise. That means checking at the gateway to the common ground their particular subculture's attributes of language, dress, manner, and perhaps values. These can be picked up on the way out—every evening or every holiday or just when the older generation is gathering. In a perfect society, each American would be permitted to keep this cultural baggage with him as he enters the common ground; he would be allowed to advance and excel without relinquishing his cultural attributes. But it is not a perfect world: America's common ground remains rather unwelcoming to other, non-Anglo cultural styles.

The mechanism of adaptation, used by millions of immigrants who embraced their American identity above all, was once called the "melting pot." Today, those who acknowledge the multiculturalism of American society prefer competing metaphors such as "tossed salad" or "beef stew," in which each ingredient flavors the others but retains its own identity. For many black Americans, though, the way into acceptance feels more like a sieve; only the traits most amenable to "mainstream" white culture are allowed to pass, while others are filtered out. That is why "integration" is often denounced now as a code word for "assimilation." Gerald W. Barrax begins his poem "Black Narcissus" with the sardonic lines:

> *You want to integrate me into your anonymity*
> *because it is my right*
> *you think*
> *to be like you.*
>
> *I want your right to be like yourself.*

At Lexington High School, Peggy Dyro saw black students losing something in this process, as if their traditions had been sterilized and filtered by the white suburban standards. "The language has been extremely honed," she said. "The sort of extravagance and richness and volatility of human interaction gets called inappropriate. So what they've been schooled to value is quite antithetical to what they live."

Everyday misunderstandings arise along the line where the cultures meet. Qasim Abdul-Tawwab, director of student services for Metco, remembered a black first-grader who was considered disruptive and uncontrollable. "His teacher, who of course was white, was saying with some emotion how she would have to shout at him to get him to do what he was supposed to do," he recalled. "She had to shout repeatedly. And she was really emotional as she said this. Something clicked. I said, 'The tone of voice you're using now, is that shouting?' She said, 'Yes, yes.' I said, 'Well, you have to understand, if you were working in a Boston public school, you would be regarded as almost whispering.' And I asked the mother, 'Would your voice level be higher than hers?' And she laughed, and she said, 'Of course.' I said, 'I think it is quite possible that he is not perceiving you as raising your voice when you're talking at that level.' "

In schools across the country, white and black teachers alike observe how black students raise the volume in the hallways, how they shout and laugh and carry on with such thunderous merriment that some teachers, especially whites, react harshly. The loudness may be more urban than racial, but African-Americans tend to claim it happily as their own. "That is a cultural thing," said Veronica Valentine, a black Metco coordinator who as a child was bused to the suburb of Braintree. "I get annoyed sometimes when I hear the kids very loud in the hallway, because they come to me and they're really upset when stereotypes of them are negative but don't realize how they reinforce the stereotype: walking down the hall, talking loud, laughing loud." When she tries to quiet them down, they ask her why they can't just be themselves. "And I say, 'You can be yourselves, just on a lower decibel level, please.' "

On the streets as well, a black policewoman in Baltimore has had to calm white officers because they misread the cultural cues, just as white teachers often do in school hallways. "Black people talk loud," she said bluntly. "A lot of Hispanic people talk loud, they talk with their hands. If you go on a call, you know, when you get there, especially in a black neighborhood or a black family, it's not uncommon for everybody to be talking loud. But see, working with some of the guys here, when they go in, especially the white officers, and these people are talking loud and their hands are going in all different directions, they go—" She lowered her voice in mock seriousness: "—'OK, this is really a big disturbance here, you know, I really have something.' And sometimes they tend to aggravate the situation themselves."

It is impossible to overstate the amount of conflict around such behavior in schools. When Valentine tries to explain it to white teachers as a cultural issue, some agree to laugh off the noise and horseplay. But others sternly reject the excuse. Black youngsters often think that if they accede to teachers' demands, they will be accused of abandoning their blackness and "acting white."

The difficult task for African-American teenagers, said Yolanda Scott, the Lexington senior from Boston, was "to find out what the administration expects of you and try to conform to those requirements as much as possible, but not really give up who you are. Because if you conform too much you're only a clone." Finding the balance is hard. "Some people say, 'I'm African-American and I don't need to understand the Caucasian culture,' when that's not at all true. You have to understand it in order to be able to get along and even to achieve what you're going to have to later on in life. . . . If you are biculturally intelligent, you know what your culture has and what your culture has done for you, what other people's culture is and what it is like; it lets you be able to play the cards in your favor [so] that you feel more comfortable with what you're doing."

Cheryl Prescott, the Metco coordinator at Lexington, had a simple formula for her students. She observed that white teachers were less tolerant of disruptive behavior by the Boston children (read "black") than by the Lexington children (read "white"). Her advice: "Stop doing that behavior. There are some things that are OK for me to do. There are some things that are OK for some people to do but not me. That's the way life is." Many blacks call this assimilation, not integration.

Moving between cultures often means shifting between styles of language and clothes. "Our language is so much different than the white American language," said Latasha, who was bused from Boston out to mostly white Lexington. "When I come out here, I usually talk like I'm educated," she said. "But at home—I mean, *ain't*'s a big word in my house. And we usually tend to switch our letters around at the end of words." Indeed, the habit of some blacks to reverse letters—saying "aks" instead of "ask," for example—is occasionally used as a cunning technique by Rush Limbaugh, the conservative talk-show host, to ridicule a black viewpoint in quick, stiletto fashion. It is a code that sends the same message as if he crudely mimicked a black accent.

White teachers sometimes get flak from African-American students for making them speak "white English," a demand interpreted as dishonoring "black English" and the culture it represents. One September, a popular black English teacher was transferred out of Wakefield High School in Arlington, Virginia, and Michelle Walsh, who is white, was assigned to take the class. Most of the students were black; they had signed up expecting to get the black teacher, and they groaned with disappointment as Michelle walked in. A thick tension hung over the classroom during the initial days, until a student finally demanded to know why they had to learn all those words. Michelle answered: because they were essential to speaking and writing good English. Well, the student said, if we have to learn your words, then you should have to learn our words.

What are some of your words? Michelle asked. And the youngsters called them out one by one, bits of slang that Michelle had never heard. She wrote them on the board, and then the kids challenged her: If you learn our words and take a test on them in a couple of days, then we'll learn your words. They wouldn't give her the definitions, but she got them from some other blacks, passed the test, and won her students' respect by respecting them.

Linguists tend to see black dialect not as a mishmash of bad grammar to be corrected but as a distinct linguistic structure. It is "systematic, regular, and complex insofar as it involves a vocabulary or lexicon, a phonology or sound system, and a grammar," John Rickford of Stanford University told the *Washington Post*. Consequently, the Linguistic Society of America has endorsed its use as a tool for teaching standard English to children who know no other way of speaking. Experiments in that approach have been tried in Los Angeles, Dallas, San Diego, and other cities where black youngsters fall far behind in reading and writing. But a furor erupted in 1996 when the school board in Oakland, California, voted to recognize black English, also called "Ebonics" (from the words "ebony" and "phonics"), as a "genetically based" language to be used in classrooms as a bridge to standard English. This brought contemptuous outcries from whites and many black leaders and educators who thought the school system planned to teach black English as such. They feared that students would be deprived of the language skills they needed to advance in American society. After a few weeks, Oakland's school board revised the resolution with "minor clarifications" that deleted the assertion about Ebonics as genetically based but retained the goal of "respecting and embracing the legitimacy and richness" of black English.

Some white teachers, fatigued and worried about accusations of racism, give up and let black students speak dialect. Many black teachers seem less accommodating. Haki Madhubuti, an African-American poet, tells his mostly black classes at Chicago State University, "The language that you speak, which is African-American English, which is black English, is not only correct, it is good and it's the best and it's legitimate. Why? Because you're able to communicate with those people that you love—your mother, your father, your aunt, your grandmother, and so forth. However, here at Chicago State, you just have to learn another language. You've got to become bilingual, which means that you learn the language of the academy. It also means that once you graduate from the academy, you'll probably have to learn another language. You'll have to learn the language of business, you'll have to learn the language of commerce."

The issue was put in similar terms by Alatorre-Martin at the Air Force Academy. "When I'm dealing with you, I have to watch which portions of black vernacular come into play," he told me. A little slang is considered "hip and cool," he said. "But I can't do much of that, because my value in the economic community will go down. On the other hand, when I go back home, one of the first things I had happen to me as a cadet was, when I went back and talked to my quote 'homeboys,' my homies back on the block, I talked about ten minutes and everybody shut up. They said, 'You're talking white. You better than we are now?' And so it was a matter of cultural survival for me to get back into black English so I could go home and feel at home, and then come back to this place and feel at home. It hurts."

James Dixon, a young black minister in Houston, remembered his schoolmates chiding anyone who took on mannerisms that seemed white. "If you didn't say 'ain't,' if you said 'aren't' or 'not,' you were said to have been trying to act white," he recalled. "Most of your academicians were white, most of your A students were white, and so blacks would decide not to do anything that made them appear to be copycats, even if it meant not making straight A's. If you dressed extra nice, drove a new car, and handled the English language properly, you were just, you know, you were white. Period. And so blacks would do things like purposely abuse the English language—purposely. You have a lot of that today. Purposely. Just to say, 'I am not being molded. I'm here, but I'm still my own person.' "

Language contributes to white antagonism as well. To the white freshmen at Lake Forest, thinking back to their various high schools, the ethic of black dialect harbored anti-white attitudes and eroded any spirit of commonality. "I've heard black people say they don't want to talk white," a young woman noted. "They talk in slang or whatever, and you can't understand them. Because the white people have discriminated against them for so long, they're trying to get back at us or make us feel the same way that they've felt for so many years. But I don't really think that's helping anything." She felt it as "reverse discrimination" and concluded, "They're doing everything just to be the opposite of white people. I don't consider speaking good English a white thing. I think it's something that everyone should do." Another student believed that when blacks spoke their slang they were "isolating themselves."

To many blacks, though, language is a bond, not a barrier, because many of them can move back and forth between accents, idioms, rhythms. "It is a dual consciousness," explained a black student at Princeton. "Catch me with my frat brothers, it's 'Yo, what's up, man?' You know. You get incomplete statements, all sorts of grammatic slaughter. But we're communicating messages, and occasionally we can get into a conversation and nobody understands what we are talking about. So it's like a foreign language. With the music and the subtle nuances, you do have to know how to play the game."

Clothing is also a powerful symbol of culture. "We tend to dress differently, with the big sneakers and the jeans and the black hoods over our heads, the hats and the jackets," said Latasha, the Boston student at Lexington High. Whites in Lexington often mistake team jackets for gang jackets. "I can be walking down the street in Lexington, and I've had a cop come over and ask me where I was going. And I wasn't doing anything, and it was just because of the way I was dressed on that particular day. I had a large red goose jacket on, and I had on a pair of high-top red Adidas, and I had a Walkman on with the really big earphones, and you know, they saw that and they were wondering what was going on, because police have been trying to crack down on drug distribution. So he must have assumed, having seen me walk off the school campus without a book bag, that I was doing something that I wasn't supposed to be doing. Then when I took off my hood and showed him who I was and showed him my school ID, he let me go about my way.

"There are two fashion worlds that go on in Lexington," she continued. "One, there's the Boston scene. A lot of kids usually dress to the fashion of the city. Most kids either have on the Adidas or they have on the Patrick Ewing sneakers or they have on different kind of Nikes. That's the Boston kids, whereas the Lexington kids, they maybe wear, they have on the Reebok pumps or Asics Gels or maybe New Balance. Usually the Boston kids dress the way they feel comfortable in being seen when they get off the bus. You know, you get off the bus at two-thirty, three o'clock in the afternoon, you're in the middle of your neighborhood, and so they feel comfortable wearing the clothes that most of their friends in Boston are wearing. Whereas Lexington kids, they usually go along with the flow of the style. Whatever's new in Burlington Mall, that's what they'll wear."

At 3:05 p.m. on this drizzly January day, two bright yellow school buses loaded with black students pulled out of the Lexington High

School parking lot, turned onto Waltham Street, picked up Route 2, and headed east. One of the buses threaded its way through several suburban towns and finally into Boston, where it stopped on Massachusetts Avenue to discharge four or five youngsters by Symphony Hall; they went into the T station for the ride home. Two more got out on Washington Street and walked away toward bleak apartment buildings. The bus wound through Roxbury's forlorn, dilapidated streets, where the children, appropriately dressed, stepped back into their other world.

Many African-Americans experience no contentment as they leave their blackness at the doorstep. A history teacher in a midwestern high school gave his explanation with a grimace: "When we enter the building, we try not to act black." It was not a proud duty.

A black minister once used an anguished metaphor: "What I have to do to make whites feel comfortable is a form of strip mining. And what do you think that does to me?"

It can be brutally wearing for a person to strip away her natural culture and put herself on display in a largely white institution. After hearing me describe this process in a speech to Haverford College students, a young black woman stood and reinforced what I had said. She began to talk about the trial of always being something not quite what you really are, and then her composure dissolved and she began to weep. She tried to talk through her tears and finally sat down, and we all—all of us white people in the room—made comforting and compassionate noises. But I doubt that we brought any comfort, for the hardship is not necessarily a product of malice.

"Some blacks call it 'fronting,' " said Thomas Kochman. In such settings, blacks make more sacrifices than whites, he believes. As they enter the workplace, both blacks and whites may lose their individuality. But in the process, whites gain their identity—that is, their professional identity. By contrast, he said, "when black men lose their individuality, they lose their identity" and are more likely to see a loss than a gain as they adjust to the workplace in a masking process that conceals who they really are. (White women, it should be noted, must also leave a great deal behind to move into the maleness of the working world.)

Even as a consultant who followed a somewhat independent orbit in the companies where he worked, Richard Orange made an effort to assimilate, and his discomfort led him to come out arguing that companies should lighten up and embrace diverse cultural styles along with diverse racial composition. "I tried," he said. "I don't know how long it was, maybe a year, eighteen months, I tried, and I was miserable. I remember speaking, trying to talk differently. Trying to not even let anyone think or see that I had any anger, any intensity, 'cause I think I'm one of these passionate folks when I talk. I was trying to contain my energy, and I would purposely try to speak softer. I would even dress differently: much more Brooks Brothers, Ivy League. . . . I said, this is awful. I hate this." Then he stopped trying to be somebody he wasn't. "I just started trusting myself more," he said, and he began observing other African-Americans in the corporate world with sorrow. "It's as if someone drills a hole in their brains and extracts their spirit. They don't have permission to be free."

Many African-Americans describe "black culture" with definitions of contrast: black is better than white in one or another dimension, such as the inventiveness of humor, the closeness of family, the honesty of friendship, the spontaneity of feeling, the dignity of struggle, the sexuality of love, the rootedness in reality and the suffering of the street.

The differences come in explicit and subtle forms. Daphne LeCesne, an African-American psychologist at the high school in Oak Park, lived in a black area of Chicago called South Shore, and she used culture to explain issues of time, status, and organization that affect how she thought black children learned. Her comparisons were heavily value-laden. "African-American learners," she insisted, "respond to a warm, interactive style, sensitivity to relational issues, and interact with you—accept interaction from you—on the basis of your personal attributes. The reason is, in a slave culture . . . you acquire strength and power by being verbally adroit, like an old-time minister, like the orator, by just being able to pull people into your power. Whereas there's tons of research that suggests that a European style is more dependent upon positional authority: your status, your role, the job you've been given. By virtue of the fact that you are dean, you're a notch higher than the teacher, and by virtue of the fact that you're an administrator, you're a notch higher than the dean, and if you're really in trouble, oh, boy, you could be sent out to the dean and you could be sent out to the principal, and that means something. Even the fact that you are sent up the scale is kind of intimidating. It's more European to be very time-conscious and role-conscious.

"Suburban birthday parties are a wonderful example," she said, and she laughed all the way through the telling. "A great suburban birthday party for white folks—I discovered with the first party I went to—starts promptly at two, just like it says on the invitation. And if you run late, people will call you and say, 'You comin'?' 'Of course we're comin'.' 'Well, we're waiting.' 'You're waiting? You're holding the party and waiting? OK, we'll be there.' You go, it starts promptly, there are no parents in sight. Everyone drops off their kids, they leave. When you stay, they look at you like, 'You have an anxiety problem or something? You know, you can go shop.' 'Well, I don't leave my kids and go shop.' 'Well, OK, fine.' 'You need any help?' They look affronted: 'You think I'm not organized here?' And at four, these people come back, and they take their kids. And of course, since you came late and your kids aren't used to this, they're, like, 'Can we stay and play?' 'No, I don't think so. I'm not too sure here, either, but I don't think so.'

"A great African-American party or Hispanic party doesn't start on time. If you come on time you expect to cook, OK? And you're needed to help cook because it is an extended family event. You better have food enough for the adults, and you better have adult-quality food. It's terrible—you got hot dogs here. Where's the chicken? Don't expect it to start on time, and don't expect it to end abruptly."

Body language also sends out cultural vibrations. Whites who ran a conflict resolution program for black schools in Baltimore had to negotiate their way through a tangle of concerns about whether adult instructors could touch the children. "When we started sending in black males to the elementary schools," the white program director explained, "the kids went after them like popcorn—grab them around their legs, sit on their laps, hug them. And if this had been a white private school, I'd have been worried about hearing something from the parents or the teachers about this."

The blacks thought that touching was fine; the whites worried about charges of sexual abuse. The white director proposed that only women touch; the white women, insisting on egalitarianism, said that they wouldn't touch if black males couldn't. The blacks argued that in their community, black males and females could certainly touch with impunity and that the white leadership should accept those mores. In the end, a "protocol" was hammered out, in which black and white women were allowed to touch but black and white men were to be essentially passive. "We let the children approach, but they wouldn't touch back," the director said of the men. "So if a child's hugging, that's fine, but they wouldn't do anything. And if they touched, it would be primarily in the shoulder area. It was very interesting how the two groups saw the issue from a different perspective."

Richard Orange tries to get whites to accept black styles by showing them tapes of Johnny Carson and Arsenio Hall, made shortly before both went off the air. Orange emphasizes what he calls "my vitality and energy as an African-American man: I'm not Lawrence Welk, I'm Stevie Wonder. I'm not Johnny Carson, I'm Arsenio Hall. Carson doesn't move around a lot. Carson always has a desk between him and his guest. Carson doesn't talk a lot to his audience. Arsenio interacts with his audience. Everyone defers to Johnny Carson. They bow, they salute. Arsenio interacts. You see Arsenio's audience, Arsenio touches them. Then I use that as a way to talk about what's different between us." Another difference, perhaps inadvertent, lay in how Orange used Carson's last name and Hall's first, contrasting distance with kinship, calling up the familiarity of black brotherhood.

Eamon Buehning of Los Angeles has her own perspective as a multiracial woman with a foot in each culture. Her father is white; her mother is a mixture of African-American, American Indian, and white. "Except for some church experiences, I don't know black people who shake hands unless they're in a white environment," she said. "Handshaking just isn't part of the cultural expression." (Except for the shake followed by the power grip, made popular by the Black Panthers, or the intricate, coded handshakes that some black Vietnam veterans still use.) "Eye contact is real different," Buehning continued. "European-American eye contact tends to be more often, more intense, where my experience in African-American communities is, you don't necessarily look in someone's eyes a lot unless there are some specific agendas, unless there's a specific relationship. You just don't do it. It's offensive. It's like getting up into somebody's face. It's as though you were standing nose to nose with them and want to start something. I had a real hard time in college learning to look my professors in the eye, having that kind of interaction that made them feel comfortable. A lot of times it will be a power thing, just like, 'Look at me when I'm talking to you.' That's exerting power. So if you walk into a grocery store and the clerk isn't looking at you, then they're not acknowledging your power."

She has worked consciously to adapt to white styles. "That's what I think anybody who's not of the culture that's in power has to do," she said. "It's why black middle-class people who learn the skills to work in white corporate America get accused of denying their blackness. They've just learned what it takes to get along in the power structure, which happens to be acculturated white. It's not that they're less black; it's just that they learn to use the system to get what they want."

James Dixon saw the bicultural route as fraught with problems. "It's difficult now for blacks to leave, to grow up in an all-black environment, go to the corporate setting, become successful, and then come back to the black community and receive an open welcome," he said, "because typically, he has to make so many cultural compromises to survive in that white setting that he's not accepted when he comes back. He's seen as a traitor, 'cause here's this guy stuck in the middle. He's too black to be white, but he's too white to be black."

La Tanya Wright endured the accusation from her teenage cousins. "When they hear me on the telephone talking to a credit company: 'La Tanya, you sound white,'" she said. When she's stubborn in her convictions, "They say, 'You just think you're better than we are because you go to that white school.'" When she asks the older cousin if he's thinking of going to college, "He'll say, 'With all them white folks?'"

"Acting white" can be effective as a put-down if you take the charge seriously, but some blacks just laugh. Russell Ballew, a young black man from Atlanta, shook his head and chuckled as he told this story: "There's a beautiful car, a Volvo 760 GLE, on the street once, and one of my friends, a black guy, and I were walking, and I said, 'That's a beautiful car.' And he said, 'You don't want no whitey car. You don't want no honky car.' He'll never go and pick up a consumer magazine guide and read it and say, 'Well, the Volvo 760 GLE's the best car for the buck that you can buy' and say, 'I'm gonna do that,' because he's been limited. There are some magazines that a black man wouldn't pick up, just because it's a whitey magazine."

Between black and black, much of the friction runs along class lines. A couple of African-American Dartmouth students, Zola Mashariki and James Riddick, from the Brooklyn neighborhoods of Fort Greene and Bedford-Stuyvesant, respectively, watched with annoyance as ghetto styles became the fad among blacks from Darien, Connecticut, and posh prep schools. "I think there's a general sentiment that in order to be quote unquote 'black' you have to have an inner-city mentality, and you have to dress a certain way, talk a certain way, think a certain way, eat a certain way," Riddick said. "It's really bothersome, especially for me, because I'm from the inner city and personally I don't have all of the traits that others associate with being an inner-city black male, for instance. I just get really mad because certain people adopt these attitudes, and they don't see the everyday things, they don't see what you go through in your life back home."

"It's definitely a glorification of the inner city—these kinds of clothes, saying things this way, having a certain accent," Mashariki said with contempt. "People love it, and they kind of adopt it. And to me that's bothersome, because everything I've done, all of the lessons that I've learned and the things that I've adopted from the inner city have basically been about survival. These people come up here, they come from Deerfield and Choate Rosemary, and they'll buy, like, clothes and talk a certain way and curse and adopt slang. But they don't go home with me. And they don't deal with what I have to deal with when I go home. And I'm like, it's not fun to have to run from the police. It's not fun to not be able to catch a cab at night because I'm with my brother or my boyfriend. It's not fun to not be able to go to certain parts of Brooklyn. And these people, they don't understand that. They just glorify and adopt what they think is cool. If that's not your experience, you should be happy and run."

As black Americans embrace black culture in its various configurations, they revise the concept of racial justice. Instead of accepting the notion that race should disappear from consciousness so that color blindness might prevail, they welcome racial difference as a reality and argue for its celebration. Instead of regarding race as a superficial deception that masks the true person beneath, they see it as a deep vessel of culture and history that must be recognized, not ignored, if the whole individual is to be known and accepted.

Although some blacks may want the awareness of race to recede, many are infuriated by whites who declare themselves oblivious to color by stating, "I don't even notice that you're black; I just see you as a person." Woven into that self-conscious blindness is the unwitting assumption that black is not beautiful, that seeing a person as black is automatically demeaning, and that the best compliment is to eliminate his race as a characteristic. "That would really tick me off," said a dark-skinned Baltimore policewoman. "I would say, 'Well, how is it that I would see what color you are, and not only what color you are, but the colors you're wearing? And as dark as I am, how are you going to tell me you don't even notice my color? You know that's a lie.' There's nothing wrong with acknowledging the fact that I'm black, you know, or I'm brown. If you asked a little child maybe two or three years old what color I was, they would tell you, 'Brown.' If you don't even notice that I'm black, what else are you gonna notice about me? Because this is something that's almost jumping right in your face. Are you telling me that what pertains to me is irrelevant? It is really an insult."

Too often, blacks who form friendships with whites are tormented by the well-meaning, insulting compliment: "I like you; I don't think of you as black." This attempt to confer honorary whiteness on a favored African-American hardly ever goes down well. When Mica Scott, a student at Louisiana State University in Shreveport, told a close white friend that she would not talk to a group of white racists on campus, the friend was baffled and asked why. "How can you expect me to speak with these people," Scott asked, "knowing how they feel about my race?"

"But, Mica, you're not black; you're cool," the white friend replied.

"Well, because I'm cool, ergo, I'm not black?"

"Well, you don't act like them."

"Who is *them*?"

"Them" may mean blacks who radiate black pride, who adopt ghetto slang and clothes and swagger, who trigger tough and thieving images. Some whites call such people "niggers" and differentiate between "niggers" and other blacks who act more "white" and are therefore acceptable. "There are two kinds of blacks—regular blacks and niggers," a white eighth-grader in Maryland told my son Michael. "Regular black people accept what they are, and niggers think they're gods of the world." The boy then went on to mimic black dialect derisively. Even some middle-class African-Americans, talking among themselves, make similar distinctions with identical terminology, but they bristle if whites do it.

Russell Ballew, the young black man from Atlanta, spent part of his childhood in a small Wisconsin town that was virtually all white. "The students there, they set me apart," he recalled, "because they would make remarks about the students in the city. They used the pejorative term for blacks," which Ballew carefully avoided repeating. " 'Those—' " And he paused, to let the imagination fill in the blank. " 'They did this, and they're that, they're scummy, they're stupid,' and the typical jokes about fried chicken and so forth. But they always said, 'Russell, we're not talking about you.' It made me feel bad, because I knew that I was black. These were my friends, or supposed to be my friends, or I wanted them to be my friends.

"The effect it had on me at that time was to make me reject everything black. I did not want to be identified as a black person. I tried to avoid things associated with black people, while at the same time, wherever I was, I was highly conscious, supersensitive to the number of blacks in the room, their status, their importance. It got to the point where, on TV shows, I would look for blacks and see what they were doing."

A corrosive tension developed between being black and not wanting to be seen as black, between wishing to be accepted and wishing to melt into acceptability. "I was very conscious of my place in any situation," Ballew said. "I wasn't ever assertive. I wouldn't ask girls out for dates. When we played a game, I'd try to show that I was good enough to be picked, but I wouldn't try to be the best."

The proper response to such debilitating bigotry, many African-Americans believe, is pride in blackness. And racial pride precludes any discussion about transcending race. Whites may talk among themselves about the ideal of race fading as a human category, but that conversation rarely goes well between whites and blacks these days. I tried once at Claremont-McKenna College with a group of black students and faculty shortly after I had seen *The Glass Menagerie* with an all-black cast led by Ruby Dee at the Arena Stage in Washington, D.C. The students and faculty had not seen the production, so I could only describe my re-actions and then hear their reactions to mine.

Tennessee Williams wrote of a South—or, in this case, of a family in the border state of Missouri—infected with pathologies not necessarily rooted in racial attitudes. Doing the production with black actors turned into an intriguing experiment. My first feeling was: This works, absolutely. This is a black family, and all of the problems and the strengths and the sicknesses that Williams wrote into his white characters have transferred from white culture to black culture. I heard only one false note, in the fantasy about old boyfriends and the line that one had gone to Wall Street and made a million bucks. Ouch, I thought—not for a black man in those years. But by the time I got past the first act, I stopped thinking about race; it just disappeared, at least for me. As the play's power swept up the audience, the black cast was able to accomplish the task of true literature, making it both particular and universal, the story of these precise people and of a larger humanity.

My African-American acquaintances weren't buying this at all. The theory of race disappearing did not appeal to them one bit. "There's not a time when I don't want to stop thinking about race," said Consuella Lewis, the woman who switched from rap to classical music on the way to work, "because if I have transcended the issues of ethnicity, that means that I have sort of devalued part of who I am and part of my culture."

I tried again. Perhaps I was having the peculiar experience of a mixed white American who is part Polish, part Scottish, part German, English, French, Irish. For people like me, the ideal may be to look past all the ethnic, religious, national attributes into the person. And when I was sitting in that theater, and after the play was over, I thought how interesting this mental process had been, because the characters onstage had finally ceased being people with certain ethnic backgrounds. They had become people with intensely personal problems that did not really depend at all on the racial or ethnic culture from which they had come.

"That's unrealistic," Lewis replied. And then she gave me a little lecture on how right it was to bring along the baggage from my various cultural backgrounds, all of which, as I seemed unable to explain, have long since merged and faded into distant generations. A student then told me how the black cast had transmitted a subliminal message, that "way back in here, they're black." And that was good, she said, because commercials usually feature whites, "and it's important that we get some black Colgate commercials and some black *Glass Menageries* in our unconscious." In other words, they were very eager for me not to forget that the cast was black.

This polite little exchange touched the nerve of a larger set of issues: blacks' suspicion that integration means assimilation, the debate over how much blacks should adapt, and the contradictory advice that diversity trainers and other mentors give to black students and employees about how to get along in the white world. "There's a whole school of black consultants around this diversity piece who work very differently than I do, so it makes the job that much more difficult," said Richard Orange. "They tell people, 'Well, you need to dress for success, learn how to play squash, learn how to play golf.' And I'm telling people, 'Be more empowered. Focus on your own excellence. Go for it. And don't go for it alone. Go for it with some other people. Develop some alliances within your own, and develop some alliances with people who are different from you. And go for it. Crack the code. But be yourself.' "

Some whites are attracted to black styles—first in music, where so much American rock and jazz and blues have such strong black roots; then in clothes; and sometimes in language. Often the affinity is happenstance, not explicitly racial. A white Dartmouth student who attended an inner-city high school attributed her friendships with blacks to city life rather than race. "I'm feeling more comfortable with black people and white people who went to inner-city schools, who come from cities," she said, "because there's a culture, there's a way that you speak, there's a way that you act."

Sometimes the attraction is pragmatic, as in politics. Kathy Whitmire, the former mayor of Houston, who is white, had straightforward advice for anyone wanting to build political support among black voters. "I think you have to spend time in the black community to become comfortable with the culture and the people, and I particularly recommend the black churches," she said. "Through my many years in politics, I learned to move comfortably between white culture and black culture. When black people are together in a majority black environment, it's sort of like being at a family reunion—the way the language is used, the things that are said, you learn to understand the phrases and the slang. 'That's really a *bad* hairstyle you're wearing' means it's really great." She avoided using black slang herself, however. "I think some people do, but I think that it's probably not appropriate for me to try to pretend that I'm black, because anybody can see I'm not. But you become comfortable with the language and with soul food and the historical experience that people have."

Whites can easily let black dialect creep into their speech, and it is not always appreciated, a fact that forced intricate thoughts for Sandra Owen. She was a white assistant director of Boys Harbor, a building brimming with after-school programs for youngsters in Harlem. One afternoon, she encountered four eleven-year-old boys peering through the door to the swimming pool. They weren't sure where they should be, and as she helped them find their way, she slipped into a slight southern black accent laced with "Sugar" and "Honey" and oozing with warmth. Later, when I pointed it out to her, she said she had not even noticed and felt ambivalent about it.

"I talk to kids folksier sometimes, so as to not put them off," she said. When she first began work there, she "almost fell into a totally different speech pattern, which was more or less an acceptance kind of thing: 'Please accept me,' " she explained. "I'm not going to talk the Queen's English and try to separate myself." On the other hand, she recognized the risk of being patronizing, saw value in being herself, then vacillated and came down on every side of the question. "This is me. I speak like this. This is what I am. I find that I still do that somewhat with kids so that I'm not threatening to them, especially if they don't know me, because they had too much of that white teacher schoolmarm mentality. They see people like that, and I guess that's my way. That may not be right, even so, to do that. And I wasn't even conscious of it, as a matter of fact. But I know I do it."

Whites can be brutal with other whites who adopt black styles. In 1993, six white teenagers quit a virtually all-white school in Morocco, Indiana, after being harassed for braiding their hair and wearing "hip-hop" clothing. "This is a white community," a sixteen-year-old named

Brandon Belt was quoted as saying. "If they don't want to be white, they should leave." One girl found a death threat on her locker.

Similar intolerance exists among blacks. In a New York public school, a white girl dressed in African garb for a play was peppered with a barrage of ridicule from two black boys in the hallway. "Oh, look at her! She's trying to be a sister!" the boys shouted. They followed her and a friend down the corridor, tormenting her with nasty remarks. "It's for a play," she finally shot back, "and besides, what does that matter? Maybe I'm interested in your culture. Maybe I'm interested in your roots."

African-Americans do on occasion confer the informal status of "honorary black" on whites who blend in well. When Jessica Prentice took a year away from Brown University to spend as the only white at Tougaloo College in Mississippi, several friends there gave her the black name "Shanikwa" as a way of defusing her whiteness. "A lot of people," she said, "just decided I wasn't white. I mean, that was how they dealt with it. Either they kind of mistrusted me, or they would say, 'Well, she's not white anymore.' I'm an honorary black, kind of thing, exactly the same way white people have always dealt with blacks in terms of, you know, 'You're not really black, you're one of us now.' "

When Jessica slipped into black dialect, black friends would make fun of her, but not contemptuously. Every once in a while, though, when she jokingly referred to chronic lateness by adopting their practice of saying "c.p. time," meaning "colored people's time," she found that "someone would give me a look, like I wasn't allowed to say that, even though they said it all the time." Despite the acceptance she achieved, she respected boundaries. She never joined her black friends in calling each other "nigger," although she got delighted laughter by once referring angrily to her white boyfriend as "that honky." Nor did she have license to participate in nasty conversations about appearance. "They would be really critical of somebody's hair being kinky, or somebody's skin color," Jessica said. "I just didn't engage in that sort of criticism. And they wouldn't have appreciated it if I had."

"Brendan," a young white man, had practically no white friends during his high school years in Cambridge, Massachusetts. A distance runner who identified being fast with being black, he spent most of his time with blacks, made his friends on the mostly black track team, and put himself into social limbo: rejected by whites and never truly accepted by blacks.

"It was comical to them when you tried to be black," he said. Black youngsters got mad "when they saw white kids start wearing goose-down jackets and wearing their hats backwards, wearing medallions, really, really getting their hair nappy," he recalled. "There was a kid on our team who was a hurdler who was white, and he tried in every single way to be black, 'cause he said to be black means that you're faster, black means you're a better athlete, you can attract more women. And they just cracked on this kid all the time. You know, Eric was a dork. He would dress like them. The hairstyle was that way. He would try to have like a high-top fade or dreadlocks or anything. The big thing in Boston, Cambridge, was in winter you'd have these coats with fur on them here, and then you'd have a fur cap like Russians. And he would get all this stuff. He would spend all his money buying shoes. There was a definite homeboy look he was aiming for. And the harder he tried, the farther he was.

"We used to play this game, it was called 'Suicide,' where you'd have a tennis ball and you'd throw it off the wall. If you tried to catch it and you missed, you had to run to the wall before they hit you with the ball. So whenever he would play, he would be the one who would be hit the most." Brendan started laughing. "Even if he didn't miss the ball, they'd throw it at him and run to the wall and tag him. He was such an ass, let's just beat on him a little bit so he can get the idea." It was almost as if he were trying to steal their culture.

Brendan avoided such blunders, although he did listen to rap and hip-hop, and he found when he went home from college that he slipped into a little black slang. "At home, when someone's sacking someone it doesn't mean they're going to bed," he explained. "It means that they're, like, following them around and trying to impress them. So, if you're always sacking a girl you're trying to impress her." At college, he had to watch his vocabulary carefully. " 'He's the man.' That means, 'You're big stuff, you're hot.' 'She's the girl.' Same way: It's actually a compliment, but here it's taken as offensive, almost." These days, white females in college are *women*.

As loyal as he felt to his black friends, a slight distance remained. "You could be very, very close, but there was always, like, a slip of paper between your hands, and you couldn't put them together. It seems like that's how it is. I don't know if that's how it always will be, but that's how it is now."

Some whites find black culture more vibrant than their own. They are drawn by a sense of ease, a warmth, a laughter that is so deep and liquid that it boils up and overflows and envelops. Some are mesmerized by the rhythm of the black preacher, by the poetry of song. For Bill

Page, it was the music of colors in an African marketplace that sealed his fascination.

He was in his fifties, a lean, ruddy man with thick, iron-gray hair, a craggy face, and piercing eyes. He grew up in a trailer park south of Miami—he called his family "trailer trash"—and his great-grandfather had been in the Ku Klux Klan in New England, where the targets had been mostly Jews and Catholics. Then he worked with Richard Orange, trying to help corporations embrace racial diversity. And Richard Orange worked with Page, introducing him to black culture.

"I remember I visited him one weekend," said Page, "and we got up on Saturday morning, and he said, 'How would you like to take a walk through Harlem with me?' . . . We were out there the whole day, went to the theater, went to museums, walked up this street, down that street, and I was totally immersed in this black place, walking with this black man. Initially, I was enormously frightened. I didn't know what the hell would happen. I had all the stereotypes about Harlem."

He came away with a multitude of impressions, mostly "an enormous appreciation for their gifts and contributions," he said. He remembered a jazz concert "in which the crowd was ninety-nine percent black, and listening and standing, standing among three, four, five thousand black people and listening to the music." Then he began to read black writers, and he saw similarities between the music and the literature. He marveled at the virtuosity of the jazz musicians' improvisation; he was entranced by writers who could soften and blur "the wall between what we call real and fantasy," he said, a boundary he found much harder in the white world. He began to see "an enormous contribution in areas where I had felt deprived as a white person," he realized. "You see, I began to experience my own cultural deprivation. That does not mean that I'm talking about European culture, or American, as being bad. There are areas that we didn't grow, that we're afraid of. For example, we're afraid of the conscious-unconscious. We don't play well with that. Hell, one of them just has to do with the use of color. . . . My color spectrum was this wide [he held his hands a few inches apart] in terms of my dress. And now suddenly it was opened up. And if you go to my house, my closets are full of these shirts."

He visited a marketplace in Gambia with a group and a guide, separated himself, and meandered alone among the startling array of colorful fabrics. "I went in really deep, and pretty soon I was so caught up in the fabric and the colors and the movement of people around me and the voices that I forgot all about who I was. And pretty soon I was handling the fabric, I was sitting with these old men who had sewing machines, and through an interpreter I was explaining to them how I'd like to make something out of this fabric. And all of a sudden out of nowhere the guide came, and he was pissed at me, 'cause I think he felt I was in danger. But for that thirty-five or forty or fifty minutes or whatever it was, I just lost who I was, you know. . . . I felt whole parts of myself that I never knew were there, and I could never have experienced those in New Hampshire or Massachusetts. So I began to recognize that there was a kind of deprivation . . . in the sense that parts of me didn't grow because of the culture I grew up in." In recent years, in his spare time, Bill Page has become a painter.

White America misses a great deal by failing to welcome the positive features of black culture. But many white Americans are made nervous by its artifacts, are repelled by the anti-white hostility they read into it, and feel threatened not only by the swagger of the "homies" but also by displays of African fashion. In a Virginia town in 1995, a teacher was denounced for wearing an African robe and headpiece to school every day; she compromised by dropping the headpiece but seemed baffled by the reaction. One white girl remarked on a television newscast that the style of dress was "racist." In a suburb of Washington, D.C., a hotel tried to dismiss a black worker for wearing her hair in tiny, African-style braids; she got the decision reversed through publicity and the threat of legal action.

Many other whites across the country experience similar discomfort with blacks in African dress, and this affects the way they interact. "I'm more formal with the people who are in this garb," said a recent Princeton graduate working in Washington. "I feel there's going to be more of a cultural gap between us in communicating."

Such aversion made Carla Guerriero impatient. As an Italian-American who grew up in a mostly black neighborhood of Orange, New Jersey, she saw a double standard. Whites don't look with contempt on white ethnic enclaves, she noted. "You don't say, 'Why are all the Italian-Americans living there? Are they separating themselves? Are they trying to be segregationists?' But when a black person rejects the melting pot as a model and says, 'I want to have my own cultural thing, just like Italian-Americans have theirs and Polish-Americans have theirs,' white people get very threatened and scared. . . . I would be disappointed in my African-American friends if they were not as proud of their culture as I am of mine. And I think that white people, we get very tense when

African-Americans assert themselves. I think we get tense because we're conditioned to believe that a black person should be forgiving, that a black person should always be smiling. These are stereotypes that we grew up with. A black person should always be passive."

Five white students at Drew University, who met twice with me to search through their attitudes toward blacks, uncovered in themselves a significant aversion to African-Americans' emphasizing identity and culture. All said that they had had some black friends in high school, and all said that they were intimidated by blacks who embraced inner-city styles or African cultural roots. "What put me off were the girls, and the guys, who sort of had their own subculture—the big gold earrings, the street language that I just don't understand," said Rebekah Pokart, a public school graduate from Manhattan's Upper East Side. "Like, it's sort of a whole subculture that I really feel excluded from, and I wouldn't want to be friends with somebody who wanted to exclude me because of my race."

"Yeah, I agree with that," said Christina Fichera, from Stanfordville, New York. She was wearing round glasses; her hair was tucked up into a blue baseball cap. "I notice that I won't try to reach out to someone who looks like that, because why bother? Because they don't want to be friends with me."

"Maybe I want my friends to be whiter, but I don't think so," Pokart added. "I think I just want to be able to connect with them on common ground, and I don't have a common ground with somebody who wants to exclude other people and who wants to make me feel uncomfortable for who I am. . . . I think they feel that they need to exclude other people because for so long they've been excluded themselves."

In their experience, anyone who stressed black cultural identity seemed to have a chip on his shoulder. "When the subculture's really strong in people," said Fichera, "you're trying to talk to them, and you're trying to understand or let them know that you understand about the past history and everything, and they'll turn to you: 'You can never understand. You're not black. You don't know what it's like.' So right there, you're always excluded. . . . And it really takes away from what you're trying to do, even if it's just to reach out to one person or to twenty. It makes it much harder."

Pokart felt more antagonism from blacks who radiated ghetto chic than those displaying African garb. "I don't want to say the rap culture, but that's what it seems like—the girls with the big gold earrings and the gold jewelry and the pants down around their knees." She and Fichera snickered. "They always seem to be very hostile. In class they didn't want to talk to you." Pokart once tried to join several black girls who were complaining among themselves about a math teacher. When she told them she agreed, they pretended not to hear, as if to say, "That white girl's trying to talk to us!" "I got a lot of that in high school—not from the people who were reclaiming their heritage," Pokart said. Students stressing their African roots "I can be friends with," she noted. "That's accessible."

Stephen Burka, who comes from Milford, Connecticut, found it possible—but difficult and rare—to reach past the African styles. "Where you see a group of black students dressed in African wear and they're all black, you can't get over that," he said. Only if you try to make some contact by asking something like "What did you think of the Yankees last night?" could you break the barrier, he said. "Once you make that connection, then you can start. Very few times can you make that connection."

All of this was summed up candidly by Chris Johnson, a sturdy athletic type with a crew cut who had come to Drew from the southern New Jersey town of Millville, where he said the Klan had held a rally a couple of years earlier. "It seems to me that for white people to become friends with blacks, it seems like those black people are generally somewhat white, so to speak. Or they might come from a middle-class background, they're generally better educated, they share a lot of common interests, they speak the language the way middle-class people will instead of an inner-city way. I think that's the best way to put it. I'm not trying to put anyone down; I'm just saying that's generally the way it is."

Homesickness

Before Hopewell, Virginia, got its floating bordello, which made it the wildest place north of Hell, it was so boring that you wished for a fire. That's how Barbara Wyche remembers her hometown. Then came school desegregation, splitting her childhood along a great divide: on one side, the protective cocoon of blackness, where children were taught deference to adults and were gently steered away from racial frictions; on the other, a colder world where teachers didn't seem to care.

"The white folks lived right across the street," she recalled, "except you didn't have too much to do with them. There was a road called Arlington Road, and I lived here at a fork called Freeman Street, and it was like a field. And you'd see white folks' homes right through the woods, but it wasn't real dense woods. And then further down in this bend there was a white family, a Russian family named the Durskies, and they owned a lot of the houses. We rented from the Durskies. And we knew the Durskies and played with them till a certain age. Then, you know, parents pull you away from playing with folks because they know the social system is beginning to affect children's play, so they pull you away to protect you from being ultimately rejected or being told your status. You were almost always protected from situations where you would have bad things happen to you or where you would have to deal with the negative aspects of being black.

"White folk lived over here, and you could see their houses, and they weren't that much different from black folks' houses, and you could see their cars, and they didn't have much more than black folks. And certain black folks had more than they had. . . . I don't think they served black folks at George's Drugstore. You didn't really know, because you would go downtown, and you went in certain places and you never went in other places. . . . You weren't allowed to be adventuresome and go out. It was like a code you had to follow like a child."

Wyche, who is now a sociologist, attended segregated schools until the tenth grade, and the black classes, the black teachers, the black institutions that enveloped her remain fixed in her fondest memories. When the order came to desegregate, one black school refused to merge unless it could carry along all the clubs and awards that constituted its structure of community. "You know, all those years of treasures," she said, "club memberships, offices, yearbooks." For a while, both schools' clubs and yearbooks were maintained, until finally the blacks' trophies and such were put away somewhere and lost. "Stuff is still in people's basements, because nobody knows where it disappeared to."

It is sad and strange to hear the nostalgia for segregated schools from Wyche and others who went through the upheaval that then seemed so hopeful and just. Whites generally thought that integration would be purely good for blacks without recognizing the hardships blacks would face or the benefits of situations they had left behind. "I had teachers who were very, very good about making sure you had your basics," Wyche said of her black schools. "They were very much dedicated to you having your skills, and they put in extra time. You showed you had ability, they would push you and give you a second book—not only give it to you, make you go through it. Give you your third book and make you go through it.

"I went to the predominantly white school when I was in the tenth grade. It was, hmmm, you know, having to walk through the white community and them siccin' their dogs on you, that was a part of it. They did that. My mother paid for us a cab so we wouldn't have to walk." Academically, the integrated school seemed to be a step down. She saw better math skills, for example, among the blacks who came from all-black schools—"the segregated schools, where people cared," she said. "Since white schools didn't hire blacks with Ph.D.'s, a lot of them were teaching in predominantly black schools.

"I hardly found a person who cared about me the whole time I went through predominantly white schools: the time, the extra energy. I often say, my education stopped when I left. Not that I didn't learn what I could learn. But in terms of people giving me that extra attention that can make the difference between in-depth and really sharp discipline, I didn't get it. And I know I didn't get it. So I rode all the way on what I had been taught in the segregated system."

If anyone should have been invested in integrated education, it would have been Larry Walker, the black vice principal of Oak Park and River Forest High School near Chicago. It is an excellent school in a town that makes racial integration an official policy. The money for the school system is there. Walker, in a striped shirt, blue tie, and gray slacks, leaned back in his black leather chair, arms folded, and looked across his glass-topped desk. And yet he spoke with longing and wonder about the segregated schools he had attended in Meridian, Mississippi.

"I think it was bad, I really do," he said of integration. "It may have been necessary, but I think for the average African-American it was probably one of the worst things that ever happened in this country. That's looking back on it." Then he caught himself. "I shouldn't say the worst thing that ever happened. I think that it had to happen, I really do. I think the only way, especially in the South, there was going to be any assurance of some kind of equality, whatever that is, was that people had to be in the same school."

But nothing could replace the nurturing by the black school or the sense of identity it provided, he felt. "I remember so well having a course called 'Negro history,' ninth grade," Walker said. "And I learned about Sojourner Truth, you name it—all the black pioneers and everything. And I graduated from high school in 1956, so I'm talking about 1952. Yes, it was segregated. Yes, the books were probably five years old, but they were wonderful books—Carter G. Woodson and that kind of thing. When I came here [to Chicago], one of the things they were fighting for at Proviso East was an African-American history course or black history. I couldn't believe that things were worse here educationally than they were in the South. Curriculum, in terms of what I needed to know to establish my identity, was there. There were no foreign languages in the school. So that was bad. There were no counselors in the school. That was bad. The books we got came from the white schools; when they were done, they passed them over to us. You could see in the back of the book the names; they didn't even pull the labels off. So you knew you were using outdated texts. But boy, there were some great teachers there. There were some teachers who could just take anything and make it come alive for me. Yeah, there were some discipline problems, but there were times when you just didn't want to turn your head from what was going on—in literature, some of the other kinds of things. Maybe it wasn't Shakespeare, but you were interested in what was going on.

"Integration took all that away because, number one, who were the teachers who were let go? Black teachers, African-American teachers. Principals were let go. So what you found yourself in was a school that was supposedly integrated, that had none of the things that you were really interested in. . . . There were a lot of good teachers lost and a lot of good administrators lost, and those who didn't lose their jobs I'm sure were made to feel inferior."

It would be hard to find an African-American who would trade the choice and opportunity that have opened up since the 1960s for the days of Jim Crow, of course. But many are infected with a growing sense of what has been lost. The warm memories overwhelm them with a home-sickness for the loving community that once thrived within the walls of segregation.

The pull has brought some blacks back to the South, a curious reverse migration in search of the certainty, safety, and community that have been smothered by the urban anonymity of the North. Janet Bowser returned to the rural country of eastern North Carolina, near Columbia, where she was born and reared and schooled in segregated classrooms. Working now at a Head Start center, she has an aura of soft-ness in her large and dreamy eyes, her quiet voice, her shoulder-length hair, which she wears in a gentle wave.

"This might not set so well with some people, but I don't think inte-gration was necessarily the best thing for everybody," she declared. "In this part of the country, anyway, the [black] kids are still sitting in the back row. And when there were black teachers teaching black kids, they knew your mother, they knew your father, and you had to be account-able to that teacher. She was more than a teacher. The principal was like our grandfather, an authoritative figure. When you walked down that hall, you better not do anything. . . . You knew that you had to carry yourself in a certain way. . . . You had to have respect. . . . We didn't have the best materials, but we had the best nurturing. The teachers knew what we had to face and knew that we had to try extra hard, and they tried harder to make us to strive. Now it's, like, 'Take it or leave it, here's the agenda, here's the curriculum; you take it or leave it.' And for the black child, if they leave it, there isn't anybody there to push them."

Bowser had gone to college in Raleigh, had moved to Harlem, had worked for the post office, and then had come back to North Carolina in 1988 when her son, Zachary, was ten years old, going on eleven. "I saw a change in him," she said. "He had started to act different. In fact, he had started having two lifestyles. He was a boy who was raised in church." She sighed. "And I started getting calls from school saying that he was in trouble, he had gotten into a fight. They would say he was rude, and this wasn't the boy that I knew. And I felt like he didn't have that southern culture in him, and I wanted him to have that. I didn't want him to be raised up in New York City, all his life never knew the quietness and the mannerisms of the South. And so I brought him back home."

Zachary detested the virulent bigotry among whites in North Carolina, such as the shop teacher who told the boy that AIDS came from Africans who had sex with green monkeys. But he had benefited from immersion in his enormous family of fifty cousins and several uncles, his mother believed. "When I was growing up, I felt so secure," she said. "Just walking around, it's like nothing can happen to you because there's always somebody there who's gonna look out for you." In New York, she had missed the sense of relaxation that she has recaptured in North Carolina; she had missed the dark back roads with no streetlights so you could see the stars. Home in the South, she said, you "could be charming without somebody trying to take advantage of you because they think you're weak or nice. I could be myself; I could be humble. It's an attribute here, where in the city it's like a target for hustlers."

Even the most severe apartheid held fond memories for John Charles Thomas, the first black justice on the Virginia Supreme Court. "I lived in a housing project in Norfolk called Liberty Park, but I never lived without hope," he recalled. "I don't remember anybody living in there in the fifties and sixties who didn't think that they were going to get out of there and buy a house one day and get out of there and go to school one day. And that was in the time of the most vicious segregation in terms of housing. In the projects you would have teachers . . . and postmen and folks like that, and we never felt we were going to be there the rest of our lives. But now there are people who expect to be there the rest of their lives, and that makes for a whole other world. You've got all these opportunities out here, but you've got a different sense of expectations in the people themselves. And it makes things worse, I think."

Dismantling the barriers of discrimination drained away people with the most potential, he said. "They moved 'cause they had the money to move, and the neighborhood was left with leadership that was not as profound as that leadership had been. And then at some point all the real leadership was just about gone, and there were no instant models . . . where people could say, 'Now, you can be like Dr. Blah de Blah, and you can have a car like that, and you can speak that way, and so forth.' Those models are not there."

Even if every solution creates at least one new problem, Vivian Gussin Paley seems determined to keep solving. A white kindergarten teacher at the University of Chicago Laboratory Schools, she has written a couple of slim and powerful books—*White Teacher* and *Kwanzaa and Me*—that struggle candidly and gently with the hardships that black children may face in her integrated classroom.

In *Kwanzaa and Me*, her gradual realization that such difficulties accompany integration is brought home to her by a former pupil, a black college student named Sonya, who appears at her doorway after school one day. They wrap each other in a warm hug, then sit at a low table. Many years before, Paley greeted the racial mixture in Sonya's class with excitement, but now she needs reassurance that it was, and is, a good place for black children. One black teacher has written an article advising black parents not to send their small children to this school, where only 15 percent of the pupils are black and 80 percent of the teachers are white, Paley tells Sonya. Another teacher has argued that black boys "survive more intact if they spend their early years with black children and teachers" and enter a predominantly white school only after sixth grade. A black sociology professor refuses to send his daughter to a white school because he won't have her feeling dumb and ugly.

Paley is waiting, but she does not get the reaction she wants from her former pupil. Sonya stares at crayon marks on the table, then shifts in her chair, glances at her watch, and seems oddly unmoved. Finally, she says that she, too, has been made to feel dumb and ugly "plenty of times." Paley takes her hand; Sonya is suddenly on the brink of tears. "I was walking on eggs the whole time. Hell, I still am. All these places I've been sent to are racist. They can't help it. My mom hates when I talk this way to a white person."

Thus begins Paley's 1995 reexamination of the integrated classroom, which she first explored sixteen years earlier in *White Teacher*. Then she discovered her own discomfort with race and described how the subject had brought her to a state of paralysis and silence. Now, by the end of *Kwanzaa and Me*, she has developed sensitive storytelling techniques for children, open consultations with black teachers and parents, and a deepening conviction that teachers—better called "integrators," she believes—can identify "the minorities built into any group, those who act, feel, look, think, or learn differently. Then each child's special attributes could be included in the common culture."

Her long journey illuminates the capacity for introspective whites to overcome the hang-ups, the assumptions, the prejudices, the unconscious slights, the awkward sense of helplessness that often afflict them in racially mixed settings. Behind the frozen inability to discuss race honestly, Paley recognizes, stereotypes are free to gambol destructively. "Each year I greet thirty new children with a clear picture in mind of who shall be called 'bright' and who shall be called 'well-behaved,' " she writes in *White Teacher*. "Ask me where these 'facts' come from and I will probably refer to my professional background. Yet I doubt that the image I carry of the intelligent, capable child has changed much since my own elementary school days. It has been intellectualized and rationalized, but I suspect it is much the same, and that image was never black. The few adult blacks I knew were uneducated laborers and I never played with a black child."

Consequently, she confronts a telling truth about her white liberalism: If the capable child is never imagined as black, then racial tolerance means ignoring race. "In the beginning it was more comfortable to pretend the black child was white," she observes. "Having perceived this, I then saw it was my inclination to avoid talking about other differences as well. Stuttering, obesity, shyness, divorced parents—the list was long." Once, when Paul (white) told Alma (black) that she looked like chocolate pudding, a few children laughed. "I became rigid and pretended not to hear," Paley confesses. "Alma was looking at Paul with interest. She did not seem to feel insulted. Is it an insult or not? I couldn't decide. Do I react? To what? She does look the color of chocolate pudding. But he shouldn't say that! You never say anything like that to colored people. . . . If I say anything to draw attention to her blackness she'll never talk to me." At a faculty meeting, teachers agreed that color must be disregarded. "We must bend over backward to see no color, hear no color, speak no color," she writes. "I did not argue against this position because I could not justify another."

It made for a kind of invisibility, as Vivian Paley gradually came to understand by reflecting on her own memories of being Jewish in a mostly Gentile classroom. The teachers never acknowledged the children's Jewishness. "They insisted we were all just children, which meant we were all Gentile children since that was the only kind of child they thought about or talked about." This threw her into a quandary. "The more my parents provided me with roots in my own culture, the more I felt my differences from the culture of the school. Failing to be recognized as a Jew, and knowing I was not a Gentile, I did not know what I was at school."

Then a black mother told her that black children knew they were black and that parents wanted the fact recognized as a positive difference. Finally, when a black pupil, Michelle, pointed to a picture of a blond girl and said, "I wish I looked like her," Paley's best instincts led her in the most supportive direction. "Michelle, I know how you feel," she said. "When I was little I also would have liked to look like this little girl. She doesn't look like anyone in my family, so I couldn't have looked like her. Sometimes, I wish I had smooth brown skin like yours. Then I could always be dark and pretty." It is so rare for white people to tell black people that their dark skin is pretty.

"Michelle looked down at her skin," Paley writes. "So did everyone else. I don't know what she was thinking. But I knew the feelings I had expressed were true, though I did not know it until I spoke."

Having found her voice, Paley now encourages people to take an unusual step: to talk to one another about race. She does so herself. She invites black parents into class and listens to children propose new chapters in the parables that she invents to represent the emotions and the differences that flourish in her classroom. When three black girls play with a white doll and ignore a black doll, Paley creates an African princess, Annabella, as a character in a continuing story about a runaway slave named Kwanzaa. She names the black doll Annabella, and the children begin to play with her and, in their sketches, draw brown faces.

Paley shows the children some empty pages for the next chapter and asks them what they think might happen. Kesha, who is black, worries about a small witch named Beatrix, who does not get along well with the others. If there are other witches in the forest, she says, "let them have their own school. That way Beatrix will get used to school. After that, she can go to Schoolmistress's school." But Martha thinks that Beatrix will get used to the witches' school and will want to stay there. "Then let her go to one school in the morning and one in the afternoon," Kesha offers. "And when she's older let her decide which one she likes better."

• • •

Black supporters of integration tend to couch their arguments in purely pragmatic terms these days. "My mother's not a real big fan of white people," remarked Laura Washington, editor and publisher of the *Chicago Reporter*, an investigative monthly. "But she said to me: 'You've got to live with them. If you're going to be professional and go out into the world, you're going to have to work with them every day. They're probably going to be your bosses. You need to learn how to understand how they think and how they live and the cultural differences, and you better learn it as early as you can. So go to an integrated high school.' " So she went to an integrated Catholic school in Chicago.

Her long, thin braids ran along the top of her head and hung down her back, over her shoulders. She talked fast, in a husky voice. "I think going to an integrated high school and then going to Northwestern, which is overwhelmingly white, upper-middle-class, I found that I was able to adjust much better to that experience than my peers," she continued. "My black peers who started school with me ended up dropping out or ended up transferring, because they couldn't deal with the culture shock of going into that kind of society. And so I'm a big fan of integration just in terms of educating young people, especially black people, in terms of making the adjustments." For blacks, then, the alternative to integration is marginalization. "And I think for whites it's important too," she said. "In Chicago, whites are going to face the same situation. Even if they're living in a lily-white suburb, they're going to come downtown and work with black people in the office."

As Laura Washington also pointed out, however, integration is not a panacea for racial friction. "Sometimes an integrated workplace can be a laboratory where racism can fester and grow and at least be maintained," she said, "because people come in with these prejudices."

The romantic notion that negative stereotypes will disappear simply by people getting to know one another has been proved false by experience. Proximity alone does not mean affinity. Before going to Colgate, for example, Sydney Morris regarded white people as models. "I had always thought they were the standard," he said, "and the goal was always to be equal to white people. I believed that white people didn't drink," he remarked, looking sheepish at his own innocence. "When I came to Colgate and there were white people throwing up in my suite in the bathroom, I just realized that they are not the standard."

The same principle works in reverse. In the words of Ruby Hurley, the NAACP's southern regional director during the civil rights movement, "These white folks are gonna learn that we ain't no worse, and then they're gonna learn that we ain't no better, than them."

The antecedents to integration remain fixed in memory, and memory is a fickle thing. Inside its labyrinth, nostalgia coexists with suffering. Around each turning, one or another recollection rises from the landscape of segregation into wishfulness or bitterness. And so it must be remembered that despite the yearning of many blacks for the comfort of pure blackness, and despite the delight of many whites in the ease of pure whiteness, many also recognize the scars of separation. Race has a way of branding a moment so vividly that a rebuff, a joke, a single bigoted word can persist with acute clarity across a chasm of decades. In the midst of homesickness, it is a duty to keep alive those searing moments:

• Master Sergeant Dorothy Maney of the army is lecturing in an austere classroom at Patrick Air Force Base in Florida, training men and women from the armed services in the techniques of monitoring racial problems in their units. She is describing how institutional racism can be supported even by people who are not racists. And to illustrate, she takes her class back some forty years or more to a moment that is engraved in her memory as a little black girl under Jim Crow laws.

She and her family, who live in Los Angeles, have crossed into segregated territory to visit relatives in Texas. At a bus station, she goes innocently to a snack bar to ask for a milk shake. The young white woman behind the counter says, "We don't serve colored people."

Little Dorothy doesn't understand, and so she hopefully repeats her request for a milk shake.

Again the saleswoman says, "We don't serve colored people."

At last the awful meaning penetrates, and Dorothy begins to cry. And when she looks up, she sees tears in the white woman's eyes as well.

• David Berg is eight years old, a white boy living in Little Rock in 1950. The Harlem Globetrotters are in town, and his mother is going to see their fancy displays of acrobatic ball handling. David doesn't want to be left alone, and he's throwing a fit, whining and crying and carrying on.

"You're not going to be left alone. Pearl's here," his mother says.

Finally, David yells, "Why do you want to go see a bunch of niggers?"

What happens next is still etched into Berg's sense of justice. "My mother hit me so hard that I went flying across the room," he says, a nostalgic look in his eye. "That's one of those beneficent acts of child brutality that had its powerful impact. She hit me really hard. And I'm glad it happened."

Berg sits in his Houston law office, tapping on his computer to check his e-mail. He has represented a black mayoral candidate and ragtag protest groups that have been denied parade permits. He has sued a Klan member for calling him a Communist and has thus become a target of Klan harassment. "They left human excrement at my door."

In civics class at the age of twelve or thirteen, before *Brown v. Board of Education*, "I had a teacher named Mrs. Cook," he remembers. "I will never forget her. She, right now as we are sitting here, is roasting in Hell, I promise you. And I hope it is a long, hot period for her. Mrs. Cook stood me up the second semester and said, 'I want you all to know that I tried to get him out of my class. I tried to get David Berg out of my class, because all David Berg cares about is niggers getting their way.' "

• Mary Wills plays first clarinet as one of the few black children in her high school band and orchestra in Lexington, Kentucky. She is a sophomore, and it is 1963, the early days of integrated schools.

Every year, the band is bused to the Laurel Mountain Festival in Pikeville, where it marches in a parade and competes for awards, and every year on the way back the director treats his musicians to lunch at a Red Lion restaurant.

The two buses pull into the restaurant's parking lot. The kids pile out, are made to line up outside, are clowning around as the director goes in to tell the folks at the Red Lion that they've arrived.

"The next thing you know, we're all getting back on the bus," says Wills. "So the kids who had been in the band for a couple of years and knew they did this every year were saying, 'Well, what's the problem? Why are we getting back on the bus? Isn't this arranged? Aren't we gonna stay?' "

The director takes them to another place down the road, saying only that he's starting a new tradition. He tries to avoid talking about what has just occurred. It's not until a day or two later, after some of the parents call to inquire, that a white kid comes up to Wills and says, "We didn't get to do that because of you." Another child overhears the remark and goes to the director, and only then does he sit down and have a discussion with the band.

He explains that the Red Lion refused to serve the black children and the assistant bandleader, who is also black. The director says that he told the restaurant it would lose a good deal of money. The manager proposed that the blacks eat in the bus. Angrily, the director said no: The band was a team, and he would not play the manager's game.

Why he failed to explain this earlier he does not say, but Wills thinks he did not want to ignite the smoldering resentment that some white children and their parents felt about black youngsters' being in the band at all.

• Herbert Sklenar, a slim white man with horn-rimmed glasses, is trying to recruit more blacks into the upper ranks of his company, Vulcan Materials, which is based in Birmingham, Alabama, and operates 120 quarries. In his office lounge, adorned with Japanese prints, he sits at a round glass table and remembers with brittle clarity an incident long past.

He and the others on the University of Omaha's basketball team are in Detroit playing Wayne State, and after the game, back at the hotel, four or five of them grab a cab to go to a steak house. A black player named Bob Rose is among them.

The cab driver is acting a little funny, and Bob says, "I shouldn't be going. I don't think I should be going."

"Why?" asks Sklenar.

"This," Bob answers, and points to the skin on the back of his hand.

They pull up to the restaurant, and Bob hangs back a little. "As soon as we walk in," Sklenar recalls, "it's about ten-fifteen or something, things are still open, a lot of vacant tables, but the maître d', he rushes up, he tells us: no more service that night." They argue, but to no avail. And when they finally give up and leave, "Our cab driver's still waiting for us, 'cause he knew what was going to happen. Then he says, 'I'm taking a chance even riding you guys.' This was Detroit, Michigan, in 1950.

"I remember Bob, he felt badly. The cab took us back to the hotel, and Bob wanted to go to his room. The rest of us still wanted to go to a hotel place or right across the street, but he didn't want to go."

• For much of her life, Barbara Green has been able to "pass" as an African-American. Her skin has an olive cast, and her black hair, salted with gray, is short and kinky. To the best of her knowledge, she has no black ancestors. Her mother's father was an Orthodox rabbi from a little shtetl in what was sometimes Poland, sometimes Lithuania, and sometimes Russia, depending on where the border ended up after the last war. He got off the boat in Baltimore in 1894. Her father's family, also Jewish, came from a small town in Romania; her grandfather arrived in the United States, by way of Argentina, around the turn of the century.

But Barbara's appearance fools a good many blacks. During high school in Kansas City, Missouri, in the early 1950s, a black friend used to take her to dimly lit jazz clubs frequented only by African-Americans, and she thoroughly enjoyed the ease of switching identities. "It was just always assumed that I was black, and I rather liked that," she remembers now, "because I was doing it on purpose, because I was determining whether I was a white person or a black person. It was a game."

In later years, too, she has been mistaken for black, and it still pleases her to be able to shift. At the University of Michigan, trying on costumes for a chorus part in a play, she remembers having a choice of pink or blue. The black student beside her advised, "Let's get the blue; we always look better in blue." Barbara laughs. "That was her signal to me, I figured." In the 1990s, in Washington, D.C., where she is an attorney, she gets a dose of familiarity from a black woman in an aerobics class. "She always calls me 'girl,' " Barbara reports. "She says, 'Now, listen, girl, you come back here again.' And I figure anybody who calls a middle-aged white woman 'girl' must think she's a black woman. It's just too intimate a term."

But there came a blistering moment when acceptance by blacks turned to rejection by whites. Driving with her white boyfriend, George, to Ann Arbor, Michigan, the summer of 1952, she discovered the acid, angry taste of an identity imposed, not chosen. It was a hot day, and in midmorning, passing through Fort Wayne, Indiana, they decided to stop to satisfy their thirst and hunger. The restaurant was small and empty. Two waitresses stood behind the counter, but neither came to the table where Barbara and George had taken seats. They waited and waited, and finally George got up, went to the counter, and asked for menus and water. The waitresses said no. He asked why. One replied, "We don't serve Negroes here."

"But we're not Negroes," George said.

"You're not, but your lady friend is."

Barbara still looks astonished as she tells the story. "We were just totally nonplussed," she says. "That was quite a different experience from playing at being black."

• For forty years, a white man has been held in the grip of another's brief statement of tolerance. In 1955, Emmett Till, a black boy, had just been murdered in the Mississippi Delta for whistling at a white woman.

"I remember very clearly the day that I first heard the name of Emmett Till," Lewis Nordan, a white writer who grew up in a neighboring town, tells National Public Radio. "I was in a football locker room. We were getting dressed out, and the body had just been found. There were terrible jokes being made, and thank God I was not telling the jokes, but sitting there in that locker room listening to this, probably smiling, I don't know, and some old boy, he said words I had never imagined a white boy saying before; he said, 'It's not right to talk this way. He was just a kid who was killed, just like us. It don't matter what color he was.' And that moment I measure as the moment that changed my life.

"I had never questioned the WHITE and COLORED signs on the water fountains, or the separate restrooms or the separate schools. They were just a part of the water that this fish swam in.

"Nobody that day, or even in the months that followed, became suddenly civil rights workers or went out and joined the NAACP or whatever. But when this jury of white men let off the murderers, even though they actually even admitted the murder to *Look* magazine at one point, the black community boycotted the country stores that were owned by the murderers, and the white community also boycotted them. And ostracized them. And each one of them, and much of the family, finally moved away and were really not allowed back into the little town of Money, Mississippi, where this actually happened."

The crime has been written about by blacks—James Baldwin, Toni Morrison, Bebe Moore Campbell. But only decades later has Lewis Nordan been able to do so, in a novel. "I knew the murderers," he explains, " 'cause I went to school with some of the people in the family. My father was best friends with the brother of the murderer. But I didn't know that a little white boy growing up in the South—who was in some ways maybe even implicated in the guilt just by my whiteness—had the right to write such a story. And so I repressed it, I kept it in my heart and in my memory for all these thirty-eight years since the event, but I was obsessed with it."

• Perry Wooten is remembering the moment, back in 1978, when he violated the doctrine of black absence in a certain East Texas bar.

Wooten is short and muscular, with a firm handshake and an unwavering gaze. His biceps bulge under the short sleeves of his blue uniform shirt, which has a silver badge pinned over the left breast pocket. His gun belt is lying on the brown vinyl couch in the office of the Afro-American Sheriff's Deputies League in Harris County, Texas, where he is now on a campaign against racism in the sheriff's department. He had none of this impressive labeling and equipment in 1978, when he was working with juvenile delinquents for the probation department.

He, another black, and three whites had visited a wilderness camp for juveniles, were heading back to Houston, and decided to stop for a beer in Goat Hill, Texas. "It was the first time I'd ever been affected with racism," he said. "As soon as I walked in, you could feel the height of awareness, everyone looking around. You just sensed that you were in the wrong place. But you know, you try to think, 'Well, maybe I'm just paranoid.' "

The bartender served beer to the whites, but when the whites passed beers to the two blacks, the bartender said, "Hey, you can drink it, but they can't drink in here. We don't serve them boys in here."

"Hold it, wait a minute," one of the whites snapped. "They're my friends, and if they can't drink in here, bullshit."

Wooten looked around. "I saw the guys on the side over here with the pool sticks in their hands, the bartender reaching down—I saw his shoulder drop. I said, 'Hey, wait, I don't want a beer. I changed my mind. Just stop drinking. Let's get the hell out of here.' I started bagging out, and these good ol' boys were just raised up, and I could see the anger and the hatred in their eyes, and it stuck with my mind for a long time. I'm paying for a beer, [but] I can't even open a can. I'm not even asking for a glass, but he's going to deny me the right, because I'm black, to drink a beer. To me that was really traumatic." He was twenty-four years old.

• When Steve Suitts is still a small boy in rural north Alabama, many years before he joins with other whites who are working in civil rights, he sees a bus with a handful of black children, probably on their way home from the black school where they are sent each day. Very few blacks live in his county, and it is his first recollection of seeing anybody nonwhite. He asks his father, "Who dat?"

"Oh, those are the nigger kids."

He doesn't know what that means, exactly, although the word is used enough in his family that he senses its reference to people he and his folks have nothing to do with. Later, in the 1960s, when Governor George Wallace is railing against busing to achieve racial integration, Suitts thinks back to that vivid point of reference. "Of course," as he recalls now, "long ago in segregation those kids were being bused a long ways every day for racial segregation."

He is in second grade. His class is on a visit to Shiloh, the Civil War battlefield. His mother has given him a dollar, and in the gift shop, for reasons he cannot explain, he buys a blue cap rather than a gray one. He wears the cap for a long time, and the other kids, who have bought gray, call him a "damned Yankee," which is not a compliment in Winston County, Alabama.

He is in high school, in the mid-sixties. He is quite taken with how interesting it is to put words together, and he makes a speech to the full school about the Klan. "I talked about the hooded hoods who did not know that Halloween came only once a year and who were fools behind a mask of hatred and things of that sort," he says.

"I remember that two of my teachers asked me to come see them afterwards, and we chatted about something, I don't even remember. But it got late after school, we must have been an hour or so. And then one of them said, 'Well, since I've got to go home, I'll just take you home.' It took me a long time to figure out why all that happened. I clearly didn't have a sense of what was the danger of what was being said, and people protected me."

• It is wartime. Samuel Adams is not yet U.S. ambassador to Niger; he is a hungry college student in desperate need of money, and so his professor arranges a job for him at an aircraft plant in Nashville. The young black man presents himself as a precision lathe operator, a skill sorely needed in military industry during World War II.

"We can't use you until we build another toilet," the boss says. "Not a toilet for colored to use, but a toilet for colored to clean up."

Adams jots down notes on the conversation and mails them to the War Manpower Commission, which sends back word that he should report for work at the Norfolk Navy Yard. He travels by train, using up almost all his money, and has to sleep all night in the Portsmouth, Virginia, railroad station. In the morning, "I go bouncing out to the Norfolk Navy Yard," he recalls. "I had no idea what a navy yard was about, but the thing I never will forget was there was a sound system that was blaring out 'Onward, Christian Soldiers' when I got to the gate. And I said, maybe I can be a soldier for God. I'm not kidding.

"I walked through the navy yard to Shop 38, and I was fascinated by the torpedo boats and the aircraft carriers and the flags flying and all things like that. And I get to Shop 38, and there's a man who's standing at the door. And he asked what I wanted, and I just gave him my papers. I never will forget him. He was very caustic. He said the fewest words I ever heard anybody say, but the substance of it was 'Look, I'm the head man here. . . . I hope you're not an educated fool. I hope you know that anytime you refer to a white man here, you've got to refer to him as "Mister," and . . . that a colored boy has got to crawl before he walks.' " He sends Adams to the drydock to the leading man in the crew of the machine shop, a huge man who "just seemed so intimidating."

Local 440 of the AFL-CIO has no intention of letting blacks into the machine shop, so Adams is not allowed to do any real work. He gets paid overtime whenever the crew is paid overtime, but he is not to use a tool, not so much as to hit with a hammer. He may carry a toolbox for someone else, that's all. After many protests, he is shifted to a job, of sorts: He goes from ship to ship to take orders for hamburgers, Cokes, cigarettes and bring them back from the canteen.

One morning about two o'clock, he is stopped by MPs in a Jeep. What is he doing, a lone black man, walking through a base in the middle of the night? Well, he's back from delivering two Coca-Colas, he tells them. You've got to be crazy, they say. No, he insists, and pulls out his little black book where he writes his orders. They see the names of ships with coded notes beside them, and they rush him to naval intelligence for lengthy interrogation.

The incident provokes a spasm of common sense, and Adams is assigned to work as a machinist. He is given his own toolbox and jobs he can do by himself, so he won't have to work with whites. But after a few "accidents"—a forty-pound maul dropped on him and acid poured onto his back—he is teamed up with a young white man. They get along fine.

Adams then discovers in himself something so unsettling that he finally quits his job.

"One day we were putting on a deck winch," he says, "and this deck winch involved hammering some studs through the base of the winch into the deck, and you used a maul to drive the studs through. I took my turn, and we were just about through. We were all excited about how good we'd done the job. And it was my turn to hit the last thing, and the maul head slid off the handle and hit the fellow on his hand. He just shrieked with pain. But the thing that was disturbing to me—he had to go to the hospital, and he didn't say it was my fault, because it was the fault of the maul. But anyhow, I had a very disturbing feeling, because I didn't feel sorry for the man.

"Until that experience, I had never known white people as human beings. All my life, it never occurred to me that they had problems, that they cried or anything. There was never the natural relationship between us. It was always somebody I was afraid of. In this navy yard experience, although I could not sit down and talk with them, at least I listened to them talk about their children, talk about their families, tell jokes among themselves. I saw them as human beings. I saw some of them who were hurt when their children did something. But I was surprised at myself that I could have been related to causing harm to somebody so severely and then not feel sorry about it. And so I told myself that it had got to the point that, even though I was making more money than I had made in my life, I just couldn't stay in a situation like that. So I left."

CHAPTER TWO

Mixing

The Stranger Within

I have a center everywhere and a circumference nowhere.

—*G. Reginald Daniel,*
whose ancestors lived in Africa,
Europe, India, and North America

Taboos

Richard Orange, the black diversity trainer, gazed out at his integrated audience of about fifty corporate managers and made a request of the blacks among them: "How many African-Americans in this room know that you have white blood in your family? Please stand."

Papers rustled, chairs scraped, and ten of the sixteen black people in the room rose to their feet. The whites gasped in a shiver of amazement and stared at the spectrum of those standing: very light, medium brown, deep dark. "And this is white blood that you *know* about," Orange added, suggesting the secrets that lay beyond. Then he smiled at his success in dramatizing the revelation.

It is always this way, he says. In every group of African-Americans, only a few are left seated. "Blacks and whites have a relationship," Orange explains. "The reason I look different from that Ghanaian cab driver is that somewhere back there, something went on. It's like a dysfunctional family, and we won't talk about it. Black slave women were raped by the tens of thousands by white men, and white wives had to watch that. All the black Americans who have green eyes and light skin and straight hair were the result of that. And this country has never talked about that: a dysfunctional family that won't talk about the core of its dysfunction."

Race is a continuum, says Fatimah Jackson, a physical anthropologist at the University of Maryland. "The notion of pure races is absurd. The Europeans are not pure. The Africans are not pure. Nobody is pure.

That's one of the great blessings on this planet. We don't want to be pure. The pot has been on the stove boiling for a long time."

Race is fluid. Therefore, it can be viewed with clarity through those who embody its mixtures. People who interact intimately across the racial lines within family and within self are among the best guides into America's region of racial disharmony.

One of them is G. Reginald Daniel, who teaches sociology at the University of California at Santa Barbara. He has made racial mixing a subject of study because of his own example: American society labels him black, yet he is a blend of white, East Indian, and American Indian as well as black. He sees a future even more complicated than the present. Intermarriage today is "creating a whole new miscegenation, and it's not clear where it's going to lead, but it's not going to be the same as it was in the past," he predicts. "These kids are growing up and are going to do all kinds of weird stuff. They might marry other mixed people. They might marry people with Japanese and Mexican along with the mixture, or they might marry whites or blacks, who knows?"

This ambiguous reality has far outrun popular perception. Obsessed with racial categories, American society finds comfort in the neat matrix of black and white. Blurred lines, breached walls, swirls of coexisting identities cannot satisfy the passion for orderly definition imposed on our racial landscape. We do not use the word "mulatto." We do not allow mixed-race people to check more than one box on forms. We do not want to be confused by complexity.

Most black Americans, as well as whites, have bought into the black-white dichotomy, which dates to the "one-drop rule" of slavery, which assigned a black identity to anyone with just a strand of known black ancestry, a single drop of "Negro blood." Even those who know that whites were tangled somewhere in their roots still answer "black" when asked their race, and many do so with pride. Society allows them no alternative unless their appearance permits them to pretend to be wholly white. In this regard, the United States remains firmly locked in the eighteenth century.

Many blacks consider white ancestry an embarrassment; admirers of Malcolm X, for example, do not advertise his white grandfather on his mother's side or his nearly white grandmother on his father's. Other blacks, however, display the white relatives with a trace of wry amusement, as a little joke on America. That is more easily managed where the mixture comes from love rather than rape. "I can remember the picture of the first white man in our family hanging on the wall," said Tony Wyatt of Gadsden, Alabama. "Matter of fact," Wyatt added with an impish grin, "he's buried in the family graveyard." The ancestor was called "that white man," and Wyatt couldn't remember his name, only that he had come to Alabama from England and had been an outcast because of his ties with blacks.

"I have white relatives," Jean McGuire announced cheerfully as she sat in her Boston office. "My son-in-law is white, my brother-in-law is white, and my grandmother is white. Some of my cousins by marriage are white. In black families, we've got loads of relatives who pass, and we laugh about it." Then she paused before delivering the punch line: "And a lot of white folks, in their roots, are black."

Here is where the tables get turned. It's one thing for blacks to have some white in them, but many whites shudder at the thought that their bloodline may have been infiltrated by even a touch of black ancestry. When an African-American professor at Drew University spoke in class on the subject, she drew sharp reactions from her white students. One of them, Christina Fichera, was still spitting mad a year later. "She was saying that the masters raped the slave women and we probably have black in us anyway and don't know it," Fichera declared furiously. "I mean, a person's history is kind of personal and kind of important, and you don't throw that type of thing in there. And it could be true, but you'll never really know. And to uproot somebody's foundation like that is—it's uncomfortable."

On every social distance scale that sociologists use to measure the aversion of one race to another, the relationship that triggers the strongest ethnocentrism is marriage. Asked about their attitudes toward having blacks on their jobs, in their neighborhoods, and at their children's schools, white Americans express a tolerance that has grown significantly since the early 1960s; a majority at least *say* that they have no objections to blacks in such settings. Yet resistance to intermarriage remains strong; about two-thirds declare that they would disapprove of a close relative's marrying a black. This opposition has lingered at a personal level even as it has dissipated in the legal arena. Since shortly after the Supreme Court overturned anti-miscegenation laws in its 1967 ruling on *Loving v. Virginia*, the percentage of whites supporting laws against racial intermarriage has dropped from 53 to 16 percent.

The revulsion at intermarriage extends to lesser implications of sexual involvement, especially where the male is black and the female is white. In that realm, fantasies flourish. The image of black sexual aggression remains powerful in the minds of many white men, who still feel a

rising fear and fury over the specter of white women sexually involved
with blacks. For more than twenty years, a New Jersey high school has
managed to arrange a black teacher's schedule so that he has never taken
a white female out for driver's education, although a white man does so
frequently. At a Goodyear tire factory in Gadsden, Alabama, white males
vigilantly guard the purity of the race against even the most innocent
friendship. Suspicions in the plant were aroused when a black worker
named Robert Avery fell into frequent chats with a white woman. Their
main subject: soccer. The woman's son was on a team that played against
one that Avery coached. White men took her aside, Avery said, and "told
her she didn't have to be talking to me, and they better not catch her
talking to me anymore." She wasn't concerned, but Avery was. "My
behavior toward her changed, because I didn't want to jeopardize her."

This particular prejudice can boil up from unexpected depths. A
white executive who had a good record in combating discrimination in
his company, and in pursuing an aggressive program to hire and promote blacks, was suddenly confronted with an unpleasant glimpse inside
his own attitudes. When his daughter brought a black boyfriend home
from college, the executive surprised himself with a surge of worry. And
in that chafing distress, he saw ugliness buried in his feelings. He had not
known it was there, and the discovery brought him guilt and sorrow.

Another father, who was black, had to advise and comfort his son,
who was sixteen, after a white girl's parents forbade her to go with him
to their high school prom in Michigan. Curtis Alatorre-Martin floun-
dered somewhat as he spoke to his wounded child. "The only thing I
could say is: 'It's not the first time, and it won't be the last. This is the
America you live in today. This is the reality of the situation. And realize
that it's not about you. It's about their attitude, it's about white
people.' " The father fumbled for words, even in the telling. "It's almost
like saying, 'Don't take it personally.' Except how do you not?"

Away from parents, on college campuses where students make their
own decisions, interracial dating can still be surrounded by whirlpools of
myths and suspicions and pressures. Although the taboo is no longer
absolute and mixed couples are no longer a novelty, relations across the
color line tend to conjure up sexual fantasies. Several white men at St.
Olaf College in Minnesota confided to a black woman that they found
black females exotic. Black men and women at Morehouse and Spelman
Colleges told my daughter that they imagined white women as sexually
accommodating. At Claremont-McKenna College in California, a black
woman reported, "I've heard black males say things like, 'White females

are easier to get in bed.' . . . I've heard things from white females that black men are better in bed."

At the University of Nebraska, a black student named Otto Green Jr. saw many reasons why black athletes, for example, seemed to date white women. "It's accessible to you now, it's curiosity, it is a rebellion," he said. " 'I'm gonna get even.' A lot of brothers say that: 'I'm gonna get even for what I couldn't have.' It's very negative to both parties." He himself dealt with the hang-ups. "I got here, never in my life dreaming that I would have anything to do with a white woman," he said. "And it was a shocking experience for me when I finally did. And I realized, I said, 'Well, Jan, the only thing that makes us different is here.' " And he pointed to the skin on his arm. "So how do you make this something that's simple? It'll take a lifetime. And how do you make it right or wrong? It's not wrong that a black man is with a white woman or that a black woman is with a white man. What I see as wrong is if the reason you do it is not a love thing. If you don't love this person, I don't care who you are. Don't be with me because I'm black, OK?"

Not all objection to interracial dating comes from whites. In the spirit of black pride, black solidarity, black cultural cohesion, some blacks also resist and resent. Black women may speak bitterly of white women snatching the few desirable black men on campus. Black men may preach against interracial dating as disloyal and self-hating. The rhetoric hints at larger emotions involving rejection and vulnerability. Some black Americans opposed Clarence Thomas for the Supreme Court simply because his wife was white, which told them all they thought they needed to know about his alleged discomfort with his blackness.

When a parent reads that discomfort into a child's behavior, it can be alarming, and it worried a black mother in Teaneck, New Jersey. "My daughter was dating interracially for a good couple of years; she found it very difficult," the mother said. "I found her sacrificing her identity and assimilating into white. She doesn't look white in any way. It's just habits and things that she was doing. I just said, 'I don't know if you're always going to be happy doing this, so don't start talking about marriage and things like that if he's not comfortable. You're already pretending you're something you're not. That's not normal.' " And how was she pretending? "Speech, actions, dressing, all white friends," her mother complained.

The girl's father, a black teacher at Teaneck High School, made no secret of his opposition to interracial dating, even among his students.

He called one white girl's black boyfriend "a sellout" in front of a whole class, the girl said. He did the same to another young man who had befriended, but not dated, another white girl, Carrie Orapello. The teacher "made a comment to him," Carrie said, "something along the lines of being a sellout, and he deserved better than dating a white girl."

"First of all, we're not dating," the boy replied, "and second, I don't think that's any of your business."

When a white principal named Hulond Humphries did much the same thing in Wedowee, Alabama, he caused an uproar that caught the attention of the national press and the U.S. Department of Justice. In February 1994, he announced to an assembly of juniors and seniors that he would cancel their prom if any interracial couples attended. This brought an argument from a mixed-race student, Revonda Bowen; according to her account, he responded by denouncing her parents for making a "mistake" in having her. Humphries denied saying any such thing, reversed himself on the prom the next day, was suspended for two weeks, and was then reinstated by the local school board. Black parents, as well as some whites, were infuriated. The Justice Department weighed in and negotiated an agreement that removed Humphries to an administrative position and barred him from school grounds during school hours. That summer, arson destroyed most of the school; a twenty-five-year-old black man was arrested, tried, and found not guilty.

For Humphries, race was a rigid, brittle thing. Not so for mixed-race youngsters at Teaneck High. For them, the racial categories slide in fluid crosscurrents that melt and mix and merge platitude and prejudice. In the cafeteria one day, a teenage girl made a simple observation. "My father's black and my mother's white," she explained. "Every person I've ever gone out with has been an interracial relationship."

Marriage

Through an occasional crack in the pavement, a courageous flower struggles into the light. Tough and gentle, it blooms against every dictate of man and of the nature he has fashioned. The surrounding concrete is strewn with petals.

In blindness or certainty, in defiance or tranquillity, more and more couples now wed each year across the black-white color line. In so doing, they assert the power of personal affection over societal convention. Sometimes they must suffer strains within their families; more often, it seems today, they force their families to adjust and thereby form a circle of acceptance. In public, they weather the stares and learn to laugh at the assumptions; they carefully choose where to live and vacation, carving out secure niches in the hard landscape of America.

Since 1970, the number of black-white married couples has more than quadrupled, from 65,000 to 296,000 in 1994. This has hardly made the phenomenon widespread; it remains a tiny fraction of the whole, accounting for just over one-half of 1 percent of all marriages, up from one-eighth of 1 percent a quarter of a century ago. Yet even in its minuscule proportions, interracial marriage represents a soaring triumph of the individual over the group, of union over divergence, of common humanity over the boundaries and taboos that have stood at the heart of American racism.

Men and women who have married across racial lines do not generally describe their act in such heroic terms. They see simpler outlines: They meet, fall in love, get married with their eyes open, help their children navigate the troubled waters of identity, and find congenial surroundings to sustain their happiness. Many of them are annoyed by portrayals that emphasize the hardships of interracial marriage; a front-page *New York Times* report on the subject brought letters of protest, one from a white woman married to a black, who wrote, "We could not relate to anything in this unrelentingly negative article."

Race does not disappear from such households, however. Indeed, those marriages that work best seem to be those in which each partner sees the other as a human being first and then as a white human being or a black human being with all of the cultural and historical ingredients that come with membership in that larger tribe. Those who try to park race at the curb usually find that society has cunning ways of pushing it inside the door; in the end, biracial children will bring it home and put it into the middle of the dinner table. Therefore, the most successful interracial marriages are microcosms of the broader nation's most promising styles of racial interaction: unashamed discussion among people whose affection embraces the wholeness of the person, with every characteristic. And one characteristic is the person's race.

Many of those who marry are already comfortable in each other's cultures. The blacks have usually attained an easy biculturalism; some have been raised in white environments and don't yearn for all-black surroundings. The whites have often spent enough time with blacks to feel relaxed and attuned to racial concerns—although once married, the whites get a crash course in American racism. "I've learned so much about it," said Nancy Brown, whose black husband, Roosevelt, is a financial and tax adviser in Los Angeles. He opened a world as he talked to her and their children about his youth in segregated Texas and re-counted stories of his grandfather's generation in subservience. "I would never know this stuff or have a good sense of it if I wasn't married to him," she observed. And then she caught a glimpse firsthand.

She was pregnant. Roosevelt was behind the wheel as they drove through Victorville, California, on the way to Las Vegas. "We passed a car," she recalled, "and then that car got in front of us. The guy, he was driving by himself, and he turned around, he had his hand like this as if he had a gun, and he went like that"—she made her fingers into the shape of a pistol—"and then he swerved into us. And it was very scary." He did not manage to run them off the road, but a thousand fears flew through her mind: "Was this guy connected to the Ku Klux Klan? Was he gonna call his friends? Was something gonna happen?"

The incident ended there, and luckily it was rare enough to stick in her mind as an aberration, but one that always lurks at the horizon of possibility. She is a sandy blonde, and invariably, she and her children, she and her husband, are flooded with a spectrum of stares, from hostile to curious. "If I don't get it, it's almost unusual; I expect it," she said. "I feel sometimes like I'm a person of color. I have that strong a sense of what it's like because of being married to him. I think that I can put myself in somebody else's shoes who is a person of color and have just such a tremendous sense of empathy and understanding, as if I was." She took a breath and shaded her meaning a bit. "I know that I'm not, and I don't walk around thinking that I am."

For Doug and Nancy Deuchler, the outside world has not been deliberately hostile but rather "unintentionally rude," in his words. He is a burly white man with glasses and a full black beard; she is dark and trim, with a red bandanna over her straight hair. They live in a cozy, cluttered house in Oak Park, from which he ventures out each morning to teach English and she to manage a bookstore. In public places, they and their three children are repeatedly slapped with the assumption that they cannot possibly be connected to one another. "In stores, they always want to wait on you separately," Doug said, "and we always have to announce in restaurants 'We're all together,' because they want to give you separate checks. They can't imagine that you'd be together."

Then they told a story that had them both in stitches. In New Orleans a few summers ago, they went on a steamboat ride. A photogra-pher, perched on the end of the gangplank, snapped away at couples as they boarded. At the end of the cruise, the pictures would be pinned up for sale. "We were with another couple, and they were like in front of us in the line," Nancy explained. "They went up and they got their picture taken, and you could see this little twenty-year-old photographer was down there kind of confused, and we couldn't figure out if she got the picture or if she didn't." When they looked for themselves on display as they left, what they saw cracked them up. Nancy had been paired in the photographer's lens with a black man behind her who had come aboard by himself. Doug was nowhere to be seen.

"I was not in a picture," he said. " 'cause she couldn't figure out who to match me with. So we didn't have a picture of us." They laughed merrily, sardonically, at the skewed frames that box in the people of America.

The stares that interracial couples receive are often curious and benign, but sometimes they bore dangerously into a nerve. In 1989, in Waco, Georgia, Tony Wyatt, a black master sergeant in the air force, and his white wife, Gina, stopped for gas on a little back road. Tony got out. Full service only. "The guy's staring," Tony said. "The guy's out pumping the gas in the car, and he look over in the car and he see her, and I see this funny look on his face. He fill up the car and he didn't say anything. I gave him the money and he gave me the change, and I got in the car and left, and about a block away, there's this four-wheel-drive pickup truck with a huge rebel flag flying out the back, and guys in the back with the hoods on."

"Just the hood, not the full robe," Gina added.

"And I'm like, 'Get down, get down in the seat.' "

"And I said, 'Hit the floor.' " Gina was talking to their children.

"And they were everywhere. Everywhere," Tony remembered with a chill.

"I was scared to death. Tony got right behind them. I said, 'Tony, stay back and don't get up so close to 'em. They can see down in our car and can see us.' So he kind of backed away from them. They went on through, and we finally got on the highway." The children, ages eleven, eight, and six, wondered why they were being pushed down out of sight. The oldest, a boy, understood first. "They've got masks on," he said. Then: "Oh." The meaning clicked in. It is a hard education to see your parents gripped by fear.

In a restaurant in Rome, Georgia, in 1979 or 1980, members of a white family had just received their meals and were deep in animated conversation when Tony, Gina, Tony's sister, and her husband walked in and sat at the next table. Suddenly, the white father stopped eating and stared. Tony was in no mood to be conciliatory. "I literally take my chair, and I turn it around facing him," Tony said. "I look at him, and I just sit there. I was getting ready to go to his table and sit down next to his wife." But then the man commanded his family to get up and go, and they all obediently stood and walked out, leaving their meals unfinished.

"When we first got married," said Gina, "I was sort of scared a lot, but I've gotten over that. Now it doesn't bother me. . . . If you don't like it, that's too bad. As long as you don't come in my face and say something to me, you can look all you want, and you can give me your little dirty looks, I'll just look back at you and smile. Because I've grown up and gotten over that."

Still, the sense of being in the black camp can be disorienting for a white parent, as Walt Harrington suddenly discovered while sitting in a dentist's chair. In walked a visiting dentist who had no idea that Harrington, a white writer for the *Washington Post*, was married to an African-American. The dentist carelessly told a racist joke with a typical punch line about a black man's stupidity. "How many racist jokes have I heard in my life?" Harrington asks at the outset of his book *Crossings: A White Man's Journey into Black America*. "But today, for the first time—who knows exactly why?—I am struck with a deep, sharp pain. . . . This idiot's talking about my children!"

White parents of biracial children often endure "a tremendous amount of grief and pain and guilt" when they see their youngsters facing racism, according to Daphne LeCesne, the black school psychologist in the integrated town of Oak Park, Illinois. "I get a lot of stress from white mothers who never had an inkling of what African-Americans experience," she said. "You cannot shield them. It is out there. It's bigger than all of us. It's a new experience: Your own child encounters something you never grew up with.

"Your problem is the problem of black folks," she continued. "You may be somewhat separate. You may be white with a black child. You may have assimilated and moved well beyond the black community. But the problem you have is the problem of all black folks, so you might as well just come on home, get involved, get political, network with all the people who have the same problem." In her view, that meant joining African-American organizations and making African-American friends.

Most painful is the bigotry that a mixed couple may confront as it boils up from their own roots, their own parents. It can cut them off in poisonous isolation from broader family, it can force their children to leave a mother or father at home when they visit grandparents, or it can gradually ease and mellow and finally resolve itself into acceptance, perhaps even affection.

"I agonized very intensely before I ever told them about the relationship," said Nancy Brown. "I anticipated giving my father another heart attack and being disowned." She remembered acutely that back in junior high, she had been ordered to stop dating a black and threatened with boarding school if she disobeyed. Even as a young teenager in an innocent romance, she was assaulted by the customary scenario: She would expose herself to the society's scorn, a marriage would not survive, she would be "saddled with black babies." And so, in this more serious phase of life, when she went home to Teaneck, New Jersey, to reveal her relationship with Roosevelt, she circled her parents like a puppy, according to her mother's recollection. Inside, though, Nancy felt "like a champagne bottle about to pop."

She did not get the severe reaction she expected. Her parents were hardly overjoyed; they tried to dissuade her with the usual arguments. Her father labeled her relationship "the alliance," she said, "the alliance between you and this black person." But in the end, "they took the attitude that 'We can't stop you; you're an adult; you make your bed, you lie in it.' " She and Roosevelt moved in together in 1975, got married in 1977, and worked hard on her parents. "Out of my need to continue having their love," Nancy explained, "I didn't turn away and become angry and say, 'If you don't like this, blankety-blank you, forget it. I'm not going to talk to you anymore if that's how you're going to be.' I didn't do that, and I kept working at getting them to give themselves a chance to get to know him beyond his color." And they did, seeing his values as close to their own. Roosevelt and her father "ended up finding out that they had so much in common in terms of business interests," she said, "and my father taught him how to play golf—and now Roosevelt is an avid golf player." Her father, who died in 1985, ended up being the best white friend her husband had ever had.

Roosevelt's family was "warm and welcoming," Nancy recalled. But not all black families are. An Israeli woman who married a black physicist in northern California was reviled by his parents: His mother told her that half-breeds were not welcome in the black community. So she never felt free to accompany her husband and their small son when they went to visit. Ultimately the couple was divorced.

Maye Morrison did not even tell her father that her fiancé, John, was white. Her father found out "when they came to New York for the wedding!" she exclaimed, exploding into delighted laughter with her husband. "And his comment was, 'I'm sorry he's not black.' And that was the end of that."

In succeeding years, they wove a bond of cordiality; on visits to her parents in Danville, Virginia, her father extended himself charmingly to make John feel comfortable. "We were in the supermarket one day, the two of us and my father-in-law," said John, chuckling. "There was this white couple—what I would call a redneck couple—they're shopping and they kept staring. My father-in-law—there's a certain kind of graciousness about the South that sort of tries to clean up situations—he was like, 'Well, you know, John, they don't usually see people with beards here.' " John and Faye guffawed.

It can get less humorous. "I was disowned," Andreen Butler said flatly. She had a modest, appealing calm about her. Her complexion, the color of cream, was set off by a blue scarf, a gray dress, and brown hair worn short. She had a very pleasant smile even as she spoke of her estrangement from her parents when she married the first of her three black husbands. "I got written out of people's wills," she explained. "When they died, I'd get a copy. They went through the horrendous task of making sure that I knew it and was privy to it." Not that such contortions were necessary, since her parents had made their views quite clear. She could not go home. She was completely cut off. "The only time my children were allowed to go home was when my mother died and they had a ceremony. My father had been dead for some time, and my aunt said she was going to have us to the house."

In the vacuum created by her own family's hostility, she and her children were nurtured by her black in-laws, especially her first mother-in-law. "We're very close," Andreen remarked. "I literally feel that she's my mother, and when I have problems I go to her. And she's a true friend to my [current] husband. We're very similar."

After a frigid beginning, even a warming trend leaves a lingering chill, the ghost of a memory. In all the years after 1972, when Bob Sherrell married Kathleen, who is white, he never felt at ease with her family. Their initial objections were so bitter that long after they seemed to have adjusted to him, he found himself in constant anxiety, eager to be accepted, determined to differentiate himself from "those people that they have such a fear of," as he put it. "So much of me was invested in being careful and carrying the weight of black people on my back, in my relationship with the family. So much of it was making sure that I was not who they feared their daughter was going to be with. So in a lot of ways, I was being very careful, and I was taking care not to feed into the myth."

"I can always tell when he's talking to my mother on the phone," Kathleen said through a smile. "By the way he answers the phone, within thirty seconds I know it's my mother." How? "I don't know. Careful, maybe. Being careful."

• • •

Sometimes, at some level deeply buried, racial anxieties are carried into the marriage. Some blacks wonder silently how they are seen by their white spouses. Some white spouses, if they are honest with themselves, have to fight against ingrained prejudices. They have to scream inside their heads for the well-taught images to go away. And this is not an easy subject to discuss with a stranger.

"I think that I'm aware of the biases that I grew up with," said Nancy Brown. Going into New York City with her parents, she was fascinated by the array of people, and when her parents made disparaging remarks about the hair, the dress, the walk, the accent of this black or that Puerto Rican, "intuitively I knew it was wrong," she said. "It just didn't feel good."

Were there biases about blacks that she had to work through in her marriage? "I don't think there were major ones I had to work through, no. Not like some other folks, perhaps. Not to say that I'm without them, but if you ask me about major ones versus minor kinds of feelings or ideas—" She paused. What did she mean by minor? "Like—" She stopped again, gave a big sigh, and waited for a long time before resuming. "OK, the stereotype that maybe blacks don't take as much initiative or are as assertive as whites to get ahead for themselves, or to do this or do that. To a degree I've had that notion. But I know that that notion has been kind of passed down to me. . . . So I would consider that a minor one versus something more major that blacks are inherently different or somehow inferior to everybody else." Were there other minor biases? "Uhh. Hmmm. I'll think on it. I can't really come up with another one. Again, what I'm aware of is that these things were laid into me. It's very uncomfortable, very uncomfortable to even think or talk about it. The notion that blacks are—not only blacks but other people of color—maybe they don't keep themselves real clean. These are all things that are put into us by horrible images: bigger lips or wider noses or unkempt hair, always being the criminal, the dope person, or the poor person."

Even after twenty years of marriage, Bob Sherrell had to check with his wife about how she felt about black people, about him. "It's taken me a long time to be comfortable with being black," he confessed. "Probably my own discomfort with being black is why I married Kathleen, you know. . . . Certainly a large measure of my own identity is based on my bicultural capabilities, to live on both sides of the line, so to speak." And in that mixture of identities and discomforts there lurked a low expectation of how whites, including his wife, would regard him. "It's only been, I think, within the last eight or nine years, maybe even less than that, that I've begun to trust Kathleen," he said. "I'll give an example. Four years ago, when I was elected [to Oak Park's town council], I got a bunch of really negative hate stuff in the mail, very negative. And one of them was this list of 'fifty reasons to hate niggers,' or something like that. . . . The thing that bothers me is, I needed to find out from Kathleen if she felt that way. I said, 'After all these years of marriage, I still have to confirm whether you feel this way about black people.' "

She sat listening to him. She was a psychologist with short, graying hair; he, a retired phone company executive, a bald man with a salt-and-pepper mustache. They lived in a rather posh area of Oak Park where the houses were large and stately; their pleasant sitting area, in a corner adjacent to the kitchen and the living room, had big windows covered with venetian blinds. As he tried to sketch his present he was pulled by his past, and the line between them blurred until even he was not sure how thoroughly he had turned a corner and walked away from earlier obsessions.

"Somehow, underneath, I'm still afraid that Kathleen—why should Kathleen be any different than any other white person in America?" Bob continued. "What is her difference, then? What is her uniqueness that says race in our situation doesn't matter? And while we've made commitments and we are here and we have kids and we love each other and all those things, still nagging for me has been the preeminent issue in America, which is, Once you cut past all the stuff, race is still the factor. What's still nagging for me is, Is it really? Is it really the factor in our relationship? It's taken me, I would say, fifteen years, probably . . . to accept our relationship simply as man and woman."

How did Kathleen react to what he had said? Bob watched her as she sat in silence for a long while, gathering her thoughts. "I don't know." She took a breath. "I think it got played out in so many indirect kinds of ways, you know. We used to have horrendous fights about inconsequential things that were probably really about that. We had a very stormy first fifteen years—very stormy. We had a very stormy marriage."

As the only white in a household with a black spouse and biracial children, Kathleen endured the sensation of apartness that many white spouses experience. "I feel alienated from this family at times. I'm the one who doesn't belong, because I'm uptight and rigid," she declared, rehearsing characteristics that many blacks attribute to whites generally. She saw the black-white gulf in her family opening up "around music, around dialect," especially when her husband and children were locked in conversation. "They can go back and forth talking black, and then I just kind of back out and watch. And I'm kind of like an apprecia-tive audience at that moment, but I can't get into it, you know. And I envy that. I'm an outsider almost, at that moment, in my family." And then her daughter would fling the ultimate put-down: "Well, you don't understand, Mom, 'cause you're white."

For both Bob and Kathleen, the racial tensions were acted out as dis-agreements over child raising, differences commonly reported by mixed couples as clashes between black and white cultures. The black parents are often seen by themselves (and their white partners) as demanding (harsh), strict (restrictive), and loving (punishing) in a firm (unfair) manner. The blacks may view their passion for discipline as arising from anxiety over the child who must study harder, do better, and be exem-plary enough to ward off society's discriminatory impulses, a set of risks that the whites in the marriage do not fully comprehend. In turn, the white parents are often seen by themselves (and their black partners) as flexible (indulgent) in a way that supports (spoils) the child and encour-ages creativity (selfishness).

"It gets played out in terms of her being more liberal and my being conservative about the consequences of my worst fears about what can happen to my kids," Bob said. "That's the reality of racism from where I sit. Therefore, my kids have got to walk a tight line—now."

"It's culture," Kathleen insisted. "I don't believe in screaming at kids. I grew up in a very repressed household where we didn't express anger, we didn't express any feelings, really, and I think Bob grew up in a household where everybody screamed at everybody all the time. And so neither family really communicated. My family didn't communicate because we'd never talk about anything that was emotional, and his family screamed at each other all the time, but they never really commu-nicated with each other. So I would be very nervous about his screaming, that was one of the things. I didn't like him screaming at the kids."

"See, even the word 'screaming,' " Bob said. "To me, 'screaming' is not screaming. To me, when I talk loud and forcefully, that's loud and forcefully."

The trouble with this discussion lies in the inability to draw clear dis-tinctions between race and culture, and between culture and individual family styles. The associations flow too easily, perhaps; two sets of par-ents exhibit contrasting methods of parenting to their children. Their children then marry and disagree. Their parenting philosophies are attributed to culture, and culture is attributed to race. And in that way, race in a racist society can amplify marital discord the way political disharmony in an authoritarian country can exaggerate the most mundane family conflicts.

That is not to say that no cultural differences exist between black and white Americans. But a note of caution is in order: There are many black cultures, many white cultures. Many blacks do not spank their children, and many whites do. And not every disagreement over child rearing in multiracial families comes from racial-cultural roots.

Still, those are the sources that black and white spouses tend to see. "I think it's a more traditional attitude of parenting," Hank De Zutter said of the style of his black wife, from whom he was just separating. She would say, " 'Your job is to raise a kid who is independent of you. Your job isn't just to be nice and understanding and nurturing and all that,' " he noted. "She overdoes it her way, and I overdo it my way. We have big rifts where I don't think she's being nice enough and she thinks I'm being a sucker, letting the kids get away with murder."

On the other hand, some parents use their differences to play good cop, bad cop. Andreen Butler was raised with a lot of verbal discussion, while her husband, Jewel, who is black, grew up without elaborate conversation, just the message "Do it because I say so." "Well, I guess my husband does that a little bit too," she observed. "We put the two families together. He plays the heavy purposely, and I play the social liberal type. We play off one another fairly well."

Not all African-Americans defend strict discipline. Salim Muwakkil, a Chicago journalist who left the Nation of Islam after a stint as managing editor of its newspaper, *Muhammad Speaks*, has grave misgivings about the way many black children have been raised. "White children generally are allowed to operate as if this is their world, the world is their playground, they have no limits, no parameters—which may be a stereotype in itself," he said. "Our child-rearing style is 'No! Stop! No! No!' Very authoritarian. It punishes curiosity. . . . Sparing the rod and spoiling the child is a cardinal tenet; most black families believe in corporal punishment. . . . One of the reasons we do it is that curiosity was punished by lynching in many cases in the South, so mothers impressed their children, especially their male children, with the need to be reticent and not to be as curious and ready to venture out as white children are. . . . I think it does have that effect, to make black children less curious, less willing to explore the world, because there is a voice telling them, 'No! Stop! Stop!' "

Rosanne Katon-Walden has deliberately and categorically forsaken one particular aspect of child rearing that she attributes to her African-American heritage. An actress and screenwriter in Los Angeles, she has made her view clear to her white husband, Richard, on the matter of corporal punishment. "One of my sisters and I made a conscious effort that we would not spank," she declared. "We want to break with what we believe is a negative culture of the African-American community. And I think a part of it was out of necessity. . . . In the African-American community, you really needed to have your kids listen. What if they drank out of the white water fountain? Or if they whistled at a white woman? That was like a real threat. . . . We're still spanking and being authoritarian parents when the threat is not out there; it's not necessary anymore. It affects everything. My daughter goes to public school here. The kids who are acting out at public school are kids who can't act out at home, 'cause they'll get beaten. So they have to act out someplace, and it's safer to act out at school than it is to act out at home.

"Richard was never spanked. I was spanked. . . . I laid the law down to him. I said, 'This is an area we will split on.' I said, 'If you lose it and spank our daughter, you have to apologize for losing your temper and spanking her.' And the one time I spanked her, I apologized to her."

Rosanne Katon-Walden's daughter, Jamaica Kate, is her petal on the pavement. By embracing race, she transcends it. By recognizing herself, she accepts who she is. "I've never told her she was biracial," Rosanne said. "She figured that out. She doesn't understand why in the world one would choose one or the other. She's a lot less racist in ways that I will never be. It's really a gift. She'll look at a pregnant woman and say, 'Gee, I wonder what the baby's gonna look like.' She doesn't assume that the baby's necessarily going to look like the mother. It's never an assumption that she makes. Or sometimes I'll see someone and in describing them I'll say, 'Oh, I think she's biracial.' And my daughter will say, 'Well, how do you know? Do you know her mother and her father? You can't tell by how people look!' And it's true."

Offspring

At age seven, "Carolyn" began collecting mermaids, "because they're part one thing and part another, like me," she told her mother. By age eleven, she had collected so many stuffed pandas that her mother had trouble counting them.

"There are twenty-five," said her mother, looking around her room one day.

"No. Twenty-six," Carolyn answered.

"No. Twenty-five," her mother insisted.

"You don't get it. There's me, too. I make twenty-six."

At age thirteen, Carolyn chose black. She was biracial, had been adopted as a baby by a white couple, and had skin light enough to allow her to pass for white. But her friends were black, and that remained her preference as she went through high school, picked a man to live with, and had children. And even then her father was brought up short by her mother's comment that she had decided to be black. "I never thought of [Carolyn] as black," he said with surprise. "I've thought of her as white with black genes. All the talk we've done about this, and this is the first time it's occurred to me. I've never thought of her as black. Do you think of her as black?"

"I do now," her mother replied, "unless she chooses otherwise."

Choice in such matters is an elusive concept, which the multiracial children of America tend to learn too early in their budding lives. If an American is part French, part German, and part Polish, she may select one, two, or all three strands to call her own. If he is half Jewish and half Catholic and wishes to be known as one or the other, a simple statement will suffice. But anyone who is blended from black and white is subject to a perverse interaction between freedom and necessity—the freedom to embrace blackness, whiteness, or both and the necessity of surviving in a society that wants to rob you of the choice.

Increasingly, the children of mixed marriages insist that they possess the right to identify themselves as they wish. And many argue that they are, and can be, "biracial." A Bill of Rights for Persons of Racially Mixed Ancestry, distributed by a Los Angeles support group—Multiracial Americans of Southern California—begins, "We have the right to change our identities from how our parents identify us," and ends, "We have the right not to engage in racially limited partnerships and friendships."

If this is the ideal, society has some catching up to do. A coffee-colored girl, a junior at Teaneck High School, explained, "I am black, but I'm not exactly black. I'm half black and half white. But I'm black. I'm a hundred percent African-American, I'm a hundred percent Caucasian. That's just it, you know?"

This brought laughter and shouts of "Two hundred percent!" from some of the other kids who had gathered in the cafeteria for a discussion of race. "I mean, half of me can't leave," she continued. "Like, my white half can't go outside this room and stand over there, so I'm not fifty percent. I'm all white and all black. But in this society I have been forced to choose. And I can't base this on my personal feelings. I have to choose to be black, because if I don't, I won't be able to survive in this society. . . . If I go around thinking, 'Well, wait: I'm interracial, I'm interracial, I'm interracial,' but everybody else is seeing me as black, I won't be able to handle that." And when did she begin to realize this? "Oh, like, last year. Last year is the first time I realized that I was black. I didn't realize I was black before last year."

It seems as if Reggie Daniel has all of America coursing through his veins, that his tangled, mingled, blended genealogy is the genealogy of the nation itself.

"My mother and my father were the offspring of people who were themselves the offspring of several kinds of interethnic unions," he said. "Several were marriages, some were informal liaisons. My grandfather's father was half African and half Irish. My grandfather's mother was East Indian, from Bombay. This is on my maternal side, my mother's father. My mother's mother was half Jewish, half African-American. . . . My father's mother was half French and half African-American, and his father was part Native American and part African-American. But they all identify as black, and that was what they raised me to be."

The fact that black was only part of him, however, has produced life-long tension. In his earliest years in Kentucky, his color boundaries were permeable. "I knew that I lived in a world where a lot of different colors floated in and out, but I have to think that as a child I really didn't dichotomize things. I didn't see things as black and white. In the very fluid world that I lived in, I had white playmates. . . . The people who lived next door were white, and then some African-Americans lived down there, and it got a little more mixed here." His grandfather, one of the doctors in a small country town, treated people of every color, saying that the oath that he had taken was the Hippocratic, not the hypocritical.

Daniel's suspension in the limbo of innocence lasted until his play-mates were old enough to think about color. His light complexion earned him ridicule—from blacks. "I've been treated better by the white community than by the black community," he lamented. "European-American kids when I grew up were not cruel to me like black kids were. But I also knew I was a little nigger. I was never ambiguous about that. I knew there was a limit." Still, the disdain from whites was more diffuse; from blacks, it carried a rasping immediacy. "In terms of day-to-day tor-ment, [black kids] would call me names. Sometimes it was 'high yellow.' And because I was also reared to be a gentleman as well, I would get names like 'sissy' and 'mama's boy.' So that, along with the light face, didn't help."

Sometime between the first and fifth grades, Daniel was told about his multiracial ancestry. That planted a seed of desire deep within him. "The first time I remember talking about it was when I went to my first integrated school," he recalled. "I was in this class that was predominantly white, and the teacher was white, and I was one of the teacher's pets, kind of, and I was sitting at her table. And I remember out of a clear blue sky telling her, 'You know, my great-grandfather was Irish.' And she kind of looked at me . . . and she said, 'Oh, well, that's where you get these names: Reginald. Daniel.' But I was thinking to myself, No, that's not why I told you. The reason I'm telling you is I want you to know I have at least partial rights to sit here at this table, 'cause I'm part white, and you can't prevent me from being here." Daniel put on an ironic smile. "She didn't get it: I'm not telling you because of the names. I'm telling you because I want you to know: I have a right to be here. I'm part white!"

He surprised himself by his sudden declaration, and by his silent thoughts. They hinted at a mystery of attitudes. Even in the retelling, the episode made him whistle in amazement and then ponder "what kind of deep stuff is going on down in my subconscious that I don't even understand, that I had submerged, that bubbled up," as he phrased it. "And from that moment on, I had this great desire not to be rejected by European-Americans, because there were African-Americans who were very vicious and cruel to me, based just on the way I looked or the way I behaved. I just didn't behave like most of the black kids that I grew up around." And as he wrestled with the tentacles of his divergent backgrounds, he drew a ringing conclusion: "I just felt that I didn't belong anywhere, and yet I belonged everywhere."

Belonging everywhere, and nowhere, caused him a problem and put him on a search. "I could not get in my head how in the hell I could have East Indian and African and Native American and several European backgrounds and be Negro," he remarked. "How can you take one part of my whole background, the African part, and then get rid of all the rest? That's irrational. That doesn't make any sense. I just said, 'This is irrational.' "

His evolving picture of himself did not coincide with the lines and shapes and colors that the surrounding society drew of him. "All the way through adolescence, there was this great struggle to affirm being a multiracial person," he said plaintively. "I didn't have a label for it, but I was saying: I'm all of these things—why can't I just be all of them? Why is everybody having such a hard time with this? I'm not having a hard time with it, except what people make me have a hard time with."

The clash reached a crescendo at Indiana University. "It was then the turbulent sixties, when black was beautiful," Daniel said, "and all of a sudden I was on the front line saying, 'I'm mixed, but I'm your brother.'

" 'No, you can't be mixed and be our brother; you gotta be black.'

"And I'm saying, 'But I'm black and white.'

"And they said, 'No, you're not. You're black.'

"And I'm saying, 'No, but that's who I am.' "

And this dogmatism among blacks was given license by certain faculty members, especially a white anthropology professor whom Daniel despises to this day for practically turning over his class to black militants. "They were very uncomfortable, here in the midst of the black consciousness movement, with this little high-yellow boy coming around talking about he's mixed, when it's really not cool."

Reggie Daniel finally found the label he was looking for. "I read an article on race relations in Brazil. It was in *Ebony* magazine, and it was talking about the mixing going on down there," he said, "and I flipped when I saw the word 'mulatto,' and I almost had a cow. I said, 'I knew it. I knew there was a word for what I was. It's right here on the page!' I was so excited. Oh, my God! I have a name! I'm a mulatto! That's great! And also, I began to think, I'm going to Brazil. I'm getting the hell out of the U.S. I'm going to Brazil, 'cause there I get to be who I am." And so he took the academic route to Brazil, studying Portuguese, earning his Ph.D. in Latin American literature, living in Brazil for a year and discovering its own brands of racism. But Brazilians' prejudices did not detract from the novel experience of fitting into a comfortable category. "It's not a matter of wanting to be white; it's not a matter of denying being black," he said. "Not everybody does it the way the U.S. does. This is the only country in the world that uses the rule of hypodescent, which is called the 'one-drop rule.' . . . When I was in Brazil, people looked at me, and they knew exactly what I was. . . . I got a chance to be free of some of that legacy of five hundred years of hypodescent and got a chance to just reaffirm who I was in a way that was very healthy. But eventually I had to come back to the fact that you live in the U.S."

Daniel believed that it was not enough to be unique. He thought he needed to belong to something larger than himself. Specifically, he imagined that his real problem lay in the simple fact "that there weren't enough mixed people around," he explained. "I longed for them. I wanted this homeland, a multiracial Zionism, you know. I wanted to be somewhere and have a place where I could be who I am. And I could never find them. I remember in college, I would run up and see these students on campus who kind of looked like me, and I'd pretend that we were brothers and sisters, you know? They were black. End of discussion."

So he joined MASC, Multiracial Americans of Southern California. Initially, it was a joyous sensation, "of feeling like I was home for the first time. I felt a sense of family," he recalled. "It was just matter-of-fact. 'Oh, yeah, I'm multiracial' or 'I'm mixed' or 'I'm biracial' or whatever. I wanted it to be so matter-of-fact, and it was never that way, and all of a sudden I'm sitting in a room where there's twenty or thirty people, and it was like this feeling: Welcome home. And I mean, African-Americans always wanted that from me, calling me 'brother' and wanting me home, and it was never like home. . . . For the first time, I landed in a place called home."

And then gradually he began hearing pronouns that he didn't like: we and they, us and them, "our people." He laughed as he remembered his new understanding of himself. "I realized that after finding my own group, I'm not comfortable with having to be part of a group." He came to see where he was truly located. "My whole identity is premised on the notion that wherever you draw the boundaries, wherever you draw the circle, I'm going to be on the outside of that circle," he explained.

Nevertheless, he is connected. "I feel so excited that I have a known part of me that's Irish. Saint Patrick's Day has never been the same for me anymore," he said. "I feel a connection with Hinduism or with India. When I saw the movie that took place in Calcutta, *City of Joy*, I said, 'My great-grandmother could have come from a place like that. I may have family at this very moment in India. I may have relatives right now in Africa somewhere who don't even know I exist.' " He lowered his voice to a whisper: "They're there. They're alive. If I could track them down, I could go say hello. I could say, 'I'm one of your descendants in the New World.' . . . Just that feeling that I have relatives on the planet, all over the world, is just the most empowering thing for me, to know I belong everywhere. I have a center everywhere and a circumference nowhere."

Eamon Buehning looks white but feels black. Her skin is quite pale in the winter, even in southern California. Her nose is slender, her lips are thin, and her straight brown hair falls unpretentiously to her shoulders. The day we sat talking in a Los Angeles restaurant, she wore gold hoop earrings and a blue leather jacket. She was thirty-four, just old enough to have a sad wisdom about her.

"My father is European-American. My mother is African-American, European-American, and Native American." With that crisp statement, she fixed the starting point of her complicated definition. "Eamon" is a Gaelic name. Her mother, from Mississippi, let everyone (including Eamon's father) think that she was white until she divorced him in the late sixties. And then she allowed her blackness to emerge. "It depends on what day you catch her as to what she is," Eamon said. "Some days she's white; some days she's black; some days she's Native American; some days she's just a human being. Her identity switches a lot. . . . It sort of depends on how you catch her. So that has affected my identity."

Race trickled into the crevices of her family's conflicts like water into stone, widening fissures. "My mother thinks that I'm physically unattractive," Eamon explained, " 'cause I look like my father, you see: bad thing." She laughed tensely through her teeth. "I was always brought up as the smart kid. My sister was the pretty kid; I was the smart kid. And when the kids would tease me and tell me how ugly I was as a child, my mother wouldn't say, 'No, you're not ugly.' She would say, 'It doesn't matter what they think.' So some of my friends tell me that I send out vibes that turn people off because of my self-image of not thinking that I'm attractive. So that may be an issue apart from race or inclusive of race. It's hard to tell whether she thought I was unattractive 'cause I didn't look black enough or because I looked like my father, a particular person who she didn't care for."

One day, walking upstairs, her mother flung a remark at Eamon and gave a clue about how far race had permeated the family's frictions. Eamon and a friend were behind her when the friend observed, "You don't really look like your mother very much."

"No, I actually take after my father," Eamon replied.

Her mother turned and pierced her daughter with a glance. "Yeah, the white side of the family," she said sharply.

"Ohhhh, I guess she's black today," Eamon told her friend. Then she rebuked her mother. "Wait a minute, Mom. You guys have been divorced for, what is it, ten or fifteen years now, and you're still so bitter? Oh, isn't that lovely." And another fifteen years after that, across the restaurant table, Eamon managed a tinny laugh. "It was a real powerful thing to throw down the stairs."

Divorced parents often use their children against each other, and many families contain destructive relationships. But race magnifies, and when it is introduced into unhappy interactions, it throws the problems up on a big screen. Personal issues take on the added dimension of social conflict.

That was the case with a high school girl in Oak Park. Over the years, her father, who was black, had beaten her mother, who was white, to the point where the daughter had made the leap from detesting her father to detesting all black people. "She hates all blacks—I mean hates," said her guidance counselor, Marge Zuba. "She wants to kill her father and has planned it out to the point where I called the mother and said, 'Come in here.'" Her loathing was so vitriolic, Zuba said, that when she was assigned to a black teacher, "I had to pull her out of the class." And yet, Zuba observed wistfully, "she is one of the most beautiful young women I have ever met in my life and has loads of gifts."

A more intimate question is how that girl and other biracial Americans address themselves, how they see their lines of heritage, whether they weave their disparate racial threads into a whole. One may reject her blackness; another, her whiteness. A third, such as Eamon Buehning, may reach for a larger integrity by embracing all of her dimensions of identity even as she listens most sympathetically to the invisible inner voice of her blackness.

Eamon first sensed a kinship with her African-American roots when, as a child, she found herself inexplicably excited by a black family's arrival in her white neighborhood. "Oh, this is a good thing," she thought, without knowing quite why it was. Later, living her adolescence in mixed neighborhoods "where people start demanding that you fit into certain boxes" as a way of establishing their own identity as well as yours, "I began to notice things," she said. "I noticed that most of my friends tended to be black. I didn't know why, but that's where culturally I tended to fit in well. . . . I began to notice that I was listening to different music than everybody else. . . . Michael Jackson and the Jackson Five. You know, hmmm. The magazines I looked at were different. . . . Blacks started confronting me, like, 'Why do you listen to that?' Or 'Why are you wearing that?' Or 'Why are you dressing like that?' Or 'Why do you speak like that?' . . . There would be a lot of hostility: 'Why are you trying to pretend to be this?'"

In high school one day, after she finished singing a song in drama class, a white boy "just, like, stood up and said, 'Admit you're black! Admit you're black!' And he and I had never had this discussion or anything. He didn't know what my self-identity was, but he had decided from what he had seen culturally that I was black. He, too, wanted clear distinction." The recollection made her smile fondly, for she enjoyed the black part of her and liked the way it seeped up from the depths.

Most whites didn't see it, though. They derived a false sense of comfort from her appearance, enough to allow insensitivities and slurs. A white boss who loved *The Cosby Show* "became very irate when the youngest daughter named her twins Winnie and Nelson [after the Mandelas] because then the show became too black," Eamon said, offended. "That had just crossed the line for her." Other whites "crack jokes that they think all white people will, if not agree with, at least tolerate," she complained. "That's one of the hardest things about being as fair as I am and being connected to an African-American reality," she continued. "Whites are unguarded around me more than they would be around someone that they physically identify as black. So that can be very hurtful. I know a lot of people that are mixed, who have had a lot of negative experiences with the black community, and I have too. But because I am on the lighter end of the spectrum and whites assume that I'm white initially, I get a lot more of the negative from the white side."

The fact that she felt black prevented her from feeling white enough to relax around whites. "Now, if I go into a room that's all white, then I feel uncomfortable, because I know I have certain preconceived ideas about the way I'm going to be treated and what people are going to assume," she said. "I will have on thicker armor and have my listening devices up a little extra higher."

She might have defused the issue by defining herself, but that would have been exhausting. "In high school, if people asked me what I was, if I was in a good mood, I would say: My father's this and this and this, and my mother's this and this, and people deny it on both sides, and my grandmother says my great-grandmother's crazy about what she says she is, and there's all this denying, and so this is what we think we are—this kind of thing. I'd get into a long discussion, and it got very tiring. And so when I went to college, I figured I'm going to be in a new environment: If people ask me if I'm black, I'm just going to say yes. I'm not going to go into why I look the way I do, you know. But if that's what they identify me as, fine, whatever."

Now she tries to embrace all her parts. In the eyes of other Americans, however, her multiple identity seems a volatile mixture, unstable in the extreme, wanting always to be resolved on one side or the other of the color line. "Even with roommates," Eamon said in exasperation, "we'll have this discussion and talk about my background. I'll lay it all out: This is who I am. But they'll conveniently forget, because they don't connect it with their part of reality. They'll see me and don't identify me as what they consider black, 'cause maybe their definitions are limited to inner-city 'hood people who wear certain things and talk in black English all the time. I do speak black English, but generally with blacks and with blacks I know well. I always speak standard English in most cases. So whites tend to conveniently forget that I'm black. So people have said things, so I'll remind them. 'Oh, yeah' "—she snapped her fingers—" 'I forgot. Oh, yeah, you view things a little differently.' "

That could be painful, "because you thought they understood," she remarked. She had recently been bruised by a multiracial woman who, after twenty years of friendship, finally realized and said to Eamon, "You're not trying to be black; you're just who you are." "It hurt," Eamon said. "There had always been something in the back of her mind. 'Oh, she's just pretending to be black.' " So many years and so much friendship had been spent on the friend's acknowledgment and recognition that when it came, it came with an acrid taste. "She had always been loving and open, and we'd talked about all kinds of things," Eamon said sadly. "But that was like, Now, wait a minute; I thought this was settled."

It never seems quite settled in the outside world, as a tall gentleman from Ohio named Ted has been reminded since he was a small boy in the early 1940s. His parents were black, his grandparents were black, and his wife and children are black. He has always considered himself black, but nobody who encounters him sees anything African-American. All the cues are white: the pale shade of his skin, the craggy face, the accent and cadence of his speech, the way his body moves. Somewhere back down the family tree, sealed off from current knowledge, mixtures were surely made. But never was he told about them, so he can only guess—and he doesn't waste time on that. He simply defines himself as African-American. This takes him on a path different from the one followed by an aunt of his, who passed for white and bore children who were kept unaware of their black ancestry. He has done her the courtesy of avoiding them and pledges never to be as gauche as to announce, "By the way, I am your cousin and I am black." He seeks a peace between his outer appearance and his inner being, saying, "Other people may pass me, but I cannot pass myself."

Although his mother constantly corrected his speech to give him an exit from black dialect, she also enveloped him in an African-American ambiance. "This would be what you would stereotype as a typical black family with all the cultural norms and variables," he explained. "I can remember my mother always listening to the blues. I can remember the parties where the dialect would go on, and I'd be a part of that."

At age nine or ten, the first conscious memory dawned that he might not be *seen* as part of that. One day, his father, who worked for the post office, met him on a downtown corner in Cleveland, took his hand, and boarded a streetcar with him. It was a frequent excursion, but this time Ted noticed the stares and asked his father about them. "Well, they might be confused by the colors they're seeing," he remembers his father explaining. "See, if you notice, my skin is light brown skin, and they don't often see [such] people together, and especially holding hands. So they're probably curious as to who we are."

What he felt inside about his essence became disconnected from what others saw, and the two spheres chafed against each other. Riding the streetcar to school with "visibly black" friends from his block, he learned that certain intimacies were denied to him. "You remember that nigger down the street?" a friend asked one day.

"What nigger are you talking about?" Ted inquired.

"Shhh. Wait a minute, Ted. You can't say 'nigger' 'cause those white folks don't know you."

Ted filled with hurt and anger. "You're saying I have to act differently than you because of my color," he shot back, "and I resent that."

He is often disconcerted by the illusion of whiteness that papers over his essential blackness. "If I'm in a setting somewhere," he said, "and all of a sudden a person who is black is walking toward me—it could be a complete stranger—I have a tendency to look over at that person and sort of give a nonverbal, I-know-you're-there kind of thing. But I won't get the same response from the black. It's like I'm invisible, and the person walks by." Yet in a virtually all-black situation, a lone white may catch Ted's eye in recognition as if to say, "God, I'm glad he's here. I'm not the only one."

Ted's only solution is to explain who he is, to disclose his racial identity. Once, at a party where he was known by a few and had been introduced to the rest, some black males came in, saw him, and pulled him into the kitchen.

"Why don't you go to your own party? I suggest that you leave."

"Why?"

"You know why."

"Wait a minute. I'm black just like you are."

That took them by surprise, and it required more conversation before they were convinced. But they were in the end. "It might be that they have relatives or know friends," Ted said, faintly amused. "There are a lot of 'us' running around."

Consequently, until he has a chance to explain himself, Ted is usually forced into a certain detachment. "I always feel like I'm sitting in an audience watching the play," he remarked. "And you don't take on any substance to me until I can get into dialogue with you. Then you begin to take on some shape or form. It's like moving to a new city for the first time: You don't have a sense of being a part of that community until you're there for a while."

Disclosure has created new problems. "I began to realize that [white] people really didn't believe me when I told them I was black," Ted said, "but yet there was a change in the way they responded and interacted with me. A lot of them thought I was eccentric, that mentally there was something wrong."

However, the alternative of saying nothing about his blackness forced Ted, like Eamon Buehning, to hear bigoted remarks from whites who assumed that he was also white. The incidents stand like frozen monuments to his silence. A favorite teacher of his, years after he had been in her class at Lafayette Elementary School, "remembered me after we started talking," he said. "She asked me what I was doing, where was I living. I said, 'I still live in the area.' And she said, 'Aren't there a lot of niggers going there?' "

Inadvertently, he has benefited from whites' obsessions with color. When he was about to lease space to open a beverage store, his prospective (white) landlord considerately warned him about the risks posed by the "colored people" moving into the neighborhood. Ted did not reveal that he was one of those "colored people." Then, with the lease signed, the landlord invited him and his wife for dinner. She was obviously black, and when she arrived at the owner's house, "you could see a little change of expression on their faces," Ted remembered, "but still we were treated courteously, and we had what you call a friendly relationship."

On a more uncomfortable occasion, volunteering as a deputy sheriff, he merely listened as a senior officer told the men who were about to go out on patrol, "When you see niggers in the area, make certain that you stop them and check them out."

"I didn't say anything as he was talking," Ted confessed. Suddenly a white deputy stood up and objected, protesting that he did not appreciate the use of such an offensive word. "But I didn't say anything," Ted repeated. "I didn't come out with any support or do anything. And don't ask me why I didn't. . . . What struck me was that that was so unusual for that to happen, for someone of the same color to do that."

The event underscored a cardinal principle in which Ted now believes: When a white makes a racist remark, a reprimand from another white has more impact than a protest by a black. After all, a black who complains is merely being predictable; a white is being provocative. So now, when Ted makes his grievance known, he does not identify himself as African-American. "I want [you] to assume that I'm a member of your group and I'm challenging you."

Within the emotions of a multiracial person, black identity can churn and flow, attracting or repelling, embracing or rejecting, often pitting the inner sense against the outer image. Just as blackness draws Eamon and Ted, who appear wholly white, it pushes away Angela Alvarez and Dena Bonner, both of whom appear black.

Alvarez is Cuban, Mexican, African-American, and Irish. Her dark skin, flat nose, and full lips lead most strangers to see her as simply black—a decided disadvantage in Los Angeles, particularly among the Central American immigrants with whom she often interacts. "When they come here to L.A.," she asserts, "they're forced to live in really bad neighborhoods with black people who are really, really rough. They get this image that black people are really animalistic and really violent and all these other stereotypes. There's this fear that is instilled in them about black people from day one." She reaps the hostile harvest of those images. So does her son, who is called "nigger" by classmates.

Alvarez has never thought of herself as black. Culturally and linguistically, she calls herself "Latina," a beneficial identity that she hastens to advertise. "Especially on this side of town, [in] most eating places or markets or whatever," she says, "the overwhelming population of employees is Spanish-speaking. And whether I go in alone and sit down, or whether I go in with my kids, they'll immediately start struggling with English to communicate with me. And when I start speaking to them in Spanish, oh, all kinds of doors open up, and they start bringing me stuff and talking to me and asking me all kinds of questions, just being really, really friendly." Her Spanish decodes her identity.

Dena Bonner has no African-American strain to deny, as far as she knows. She is quite dark, like molasses. Her hair is long, black, and straight, accentuating her slimness and framing her large and liquid eyes. Cherokee, Creek, Sioux, and French ancestors populated her mother's side. She is unsure about her divorced father's ethnicity; his grandmother, she was told, may have been part white, part American Indian. She adamantly differentiates herself from the African-American label that others often apply to her.

"It's offensive to me," she says. "It's not exactly been a benefit to go around and label something that particular color and think that you're going to make it. Since when was that ever a benefit? I don't remember anyone ever throwing money down at your feet."

Bonner gets the full range of anti-black treatment in Los Angeles, where she lives. She gets followed by storekeepers who think she's going to shoplift. She gets catcalls from construction workers. She gets treated disparagingly in banks. This could be a diffuse reaction to her dark skin, which might trigger negative thoughts of: Mexican, Indian, alien. But she is unwavering in her belief that she is being mistaken for an African-American. "In a dating situation, or even in mixed company—men and women at a party—the general assumption is that I would want to sit next to someone that's black," she complains. And then she goes on to paint an unflattering portrait of black people, with whom she feels no kinship.

For example, she detests black dialect. Black and white men she has dated "can't understand why I sound the way that I do, and I said, 'Excuse me, my parents spent too much money on my education to come out sounding as though I lived on the streets. That's not gonna happen. . . . When I was growing up, I was not allowed to use 'bad English/black English/street English.' I had to speak a certain way when I was at home, and most definitely when I was in school, 'cause I went to parochial school. I had to speak in a way that is along the same level as educators'.

"Another way that I think that I'm different is my hair," she continued. "I keep my hair up, I'm sorry. I don't have this thing about walking out in the street looking like some strange person that never put a comb to her head. . . . I'm not going to walk around with these braids. I'm not going to walk around with beads in my head. I'm not going to walk around and put orange tint in my hair, which a lot of these young women are doing."

She also accepts the stereotype that blacks lack initiative, and she resents being associated with such a characteristic. "The average person out there on the street who considers himself black, they don't want an education," she declares. "They don't want to go any higher, because there's a pervasive feeling: Why should I try and work my butt off and have someone else able to come in above me, and they don't even know anything? So there is never really this push for more education, for more knowledge."

She has some sweeping condemnations of black men, too. "Maybe nobody would appreciate letting this part of the little dirty laundry out, but there's this whole fantasy thing from the black male perspective, where when they look at a woman, it's a conquest. It's something that they can take home and put up on a wall and say, She's mine. I own her. . . . And you just don't get that from other races."

She quotes the advice of her great-grandmother, who died at age 104: "It's not good to point someone out and say you don't like them because of their color. Don't go out in the street and jump up and down and say: 'I'm not going to get anywhere in life because people are just going to look at me and think I'm black.' You're not. Don't ever think that. Don't let someone tell you that, because you're half of what I am. You're part of what your mother is, your father is."

Mothers and fathers often struggle to help their multiracial children navigate the difficulties of identity, reaching out but not always knowing quite what to do. Self-definitions are so fluid that different ones churn up to the surface at different times, throwing parents off balance. Sometimes, one parent or another feels rejected as the child chooses the other's race.

When Karen got to Princeton, her sense of where she belonged began to shift decisively toward the black, and her mother expressed concern. Light-skinned with green eyes and straightened brown hair cut to just above the shoulder, Karen could have left the African-American label behind, if she wished. Since her mother was white and her father black, she had divided herself between those worlds, hanging out with black friends in high school and, after school, sailing with white youngsters on Lake Michigan. Black friends had needled her with good-natured teasing about the racial division within. "My black friends used to call me 'fifty-fifty,' " she said with a smile. They changed the percentage as they saw more "black" behavior. "Sixty-forty!" she quoted them as yelling as they cheered her on. "Oh, man, that was good—ninety-ten!"

Early on, the racial component entered her relationship with her parents. "Since I had a white mother, she didn't know how to take care of black hair," Karen said. "When I was little, my father used to take care of it. And then my mother cut it all off, because it was easier to take care of. . . . I was trying to learn how to do it myself, and all the other black girls had very nice pretty hair but their moms took care of it. I used to cry because it wasn't straight and I couldn't make it do anything."

At Princeton, Karen drifted into circles of black students more exclusively than she had in high school. Her mother's anxiety came through in Karen's recollections of their conversations.

"Well, don't you think you should have some white friends?" her mother would say.

"Well, like, well, yeah, but it didn't happen that way," Karen would answer. "It's not like I went looking for the black people. It just kind of materialized that way. And then all the organizations I got in were the organizations they were in, so I started getting more involved in the black community."

"By the time you get home, you're going to be so black I won't recognize you."

"Wait a minute, aren't you the one who told me to join organizations? It's just not the organizations that you want me in. That's the problem."

"This is isolating yourself," said her mother. "You're not broadening your horizons. You're limiting yourself by doing that kind of thing."

"I can see how looking from the outside in, it looks that way. But I think you have to make the distinction between being isolated and just kind of participating in your culture and maintaining an identity."

Her father, on the other hand, thought that moving resolutely into blackness was perfectly all right.

John and Maye Morrison took opposite roles when their daughter, Judy, defined herself as black. John, white, expressed satisfaction. Although they had not pushed it on her, he said, "I'm pleased that it came out that way. I think that has many fewer potential conflicts and problems." It made no sense to him when some interracial couples, including friends of theirs in New York, talked about their children being tan. "That's very unrealistic," he said. "You're looking at a social definition of race, not a genetic definition of race. It's unrealistic and probably ultimately not very healthy for the kids. . . . That's not the way society and people are going to define them."

"I had some concern about it," countered Maye, who was black, "because I said to her that she was denying her white heritage. She says, 'I'm not.' "

To listen to black and white parents talk about their biracial children is to eavesdrop on America's racial agony. Many admit that they had no idea what their sons and daughters were experiencing until late in high school or college, when the youngsters could finally talk about their trials. Unless the parents are also biracial, they have trouble knowing how to help. One couple watched in some pain as their two children strove to sort out their identities. The older, a girl, looked more obviously black and wanted in high school to be white; the younger, a boy, was often mistaken for white but tried his blackness on for size. "She wanted more to identify with the white community, and he's trying more to become part of the black community," explained their mother, who is white.

For both parents, the girl's reach for whiteness caused concern. "That's my greatest disappointment with my own parenting of my daughter," said her father, who is black. "My greatest disappointment is that [she] went the way where she chose mostly white kids to be her friends. And I think in some ways it was easier for her to do that than to do what I've done, and that is to live on both sides of the line." By that he meant moving culturally back and forth between black and white, something his daughter could do well.

"She can move back and forth between dialects," said her mother. "I envy that ability to be that creative. And I feel like if she would marry someone white she would lose that piece of herself that is so free and creative and 'street,' I guess. She can move between talking like she's in the street to talking like she's in the opera. She has that ability. But then she's got to be accepted at the same time. And her need to be accepted is [so strong] that she will forfeit that part of herself in order to be acceptable, which I think is very sad if she will lose that piece of herself, which is really the more free, kind of creative part of herself. Her creative side is more black than white. That's what I think."

A more sanguine view of biracialism was offered by Rosanne Katon-Walden, based on watching her daughter, Jamaica Kate. Granted, the girl has not yet reached adolescence, when the pressures to be black usually mount sharply. And granted, "the African-American community forces you to choose black," Rosanne said. "It is such a frightening concept to be at peace with more than one culture." She added, "I tell my daughter, 'Look, if someone really wants you to be black, be black for them.'. . . Sometimes when people ask if you're black and they want you to say that you're black, it's because they want you to say that you're part of them. You know, it's like a political statement. It's not rational."

But she sees change coming, thanks to the biracial children who now say the word "biracial" out loud, not just in a whisper, as it was spoken not long ago. "They're definitely going to be different," Rosanne declared. "They see culture as fluid, and they see culture as a series of tools that get them through the day, and they see themselves as having twice as many tools as anybody else!" She was shouting in laughter. "I wonder, how does that work? And I feel I'll never know. I don't know, it'll be like explaining to Stone Age man about the computer, about television or airplanes, you know? Here I am, making an ax out of a rock!"

Boxes

When Eamon Buehning applied for a job at Twentieth Century Fox in Hollywood, she was handed the usual form with the usual boxes for ethnic coding. So she checked the three boxes that represented her racial and ethnic makeup: "Black," "White," and "Native American." She got a call from a black woman in Personnel.

"She had an attitude, an attitude," Eamon remembered. "How dare I? How dare I not pick one? She had never met me, so she didn't know what I looked like, and she basically couldn't even deal with me. She pawned me off to her supervisor within a few sentences."

The supervisor, who was white, had interviewed Eamon and had assumed that she was simply white. "She was very confused," Eamon laughed. "I was using the very politically correct: I am European-American, African-American, and Native American. Well, she didn't know what European-American was. She goes, 'Well, I don't know what category we can put that in.' Well, I'm in trouble now. She doesn't even know that she's European-American. African-American she understood." As Eamon recalled, the rest of the conversation went like this:

"Well, you have to choose," the supervisor said.

"I have chosen," Eamon insisted. "You don't like my choice."

"Well, we really want people to self-identify."

"Well, I do self-identify. I'm doing that."

"Well, we need just one category. We will have to choose if you don't choose."

"Well, you do what you have to do."

Four days later, Eamon said, "I noticed that in the computer I was labeled as black."

Increasingly, multiracial Americans are demanding that the standard form be revised so that they are not forced to identify only one part of themselves. Since the categories used by the Census Bureau serve as models for many other institutions, it is the bureau that has been targeted by multiracial organizations in a campaign to get a "biracial" or "multiracial" box put on the questionnaire for the next census.

In a society impressed by the power of statistics and obsessed by the significance of race, it might seem logical to count the number of multiracial people. But while the Census Bureau knows how many interracial marriages take place, it has no idea how many offspring have been produced by those marriages, and so far it has refused to allow such children to define themselves in the census count as biracial or multiracial.

In 1920, it dropped the "mulatto" category. In 1994, it began inviting public comment on whether to reintroduce a mixed-race designation and was lobbied fiercely in both directions. Black organizations were afraid that if a "biracial" box were included, it would exacerbate the undercounting of blacks, diluting their perceived power in politics and the marketplace. Since the society sees the vast majority of black-white people as simply "black," the argument holds, they should be tallied as such; otherwise, the figures will distort a social reality. In 1997, the Clinton administration proposed that the 2000 census allow people to check as many boxes as they wish.

Past census forms have frustrated many who are multiracial. In 1990, they were given the following list, from which they had to choose only one: White, Black or Negro, Indian (Amer.), with name of the tribe to be written in, Eskimo, Aleut, Chinese, Filipino, Hawaiian, Korean, Vietnamese, Japanese, Asian Indian, Samoan, Guamanian, and Other Asian or Pacific Islander (to be written in). A final blank, for "Other race," permitted only one race to be entered, not several. A separate question asked about "Spanish/Hispanic origin."

Indeed, the Census Bureau's code lists required someone identifying himself as "black and white," in that order, to be coded as "black or Negro" and someone using the reversed order, "white and black" to be coded as "white." The bureau's report on procedures explained:

> During direct interviews conducted by enumerators, if a person could not provide a single response to the race question, he or she was asked to select, based on self-identification, the group which best described his or her racial identity. If a person could not provide a single race response, the race of the mother was used. If a single race response could not be provided for the person's mother, the first race reported by the person was used. In all cases where occupied housing units, households, or families, are classified by race, the race of the householder was used.

Many children of mixed marriages give in to convention and simply put a check in the "Black" box. "That's what I do," said Karen, the Princeton student. "Until they change the system to my benefit, I'm going to make the system benefit me and I'll write down 'Black.' "

Reggie Daniel does the same, but for a slightly different reason. "I don't have another alternative that I feel good about," he said. "I would love to be able to check 'Multiracial' and check whatever other boxes apply." Why not check "White"? "Because I don't feel that. To me, that is not accurate. . . . I don't represent the white community in terms of ethnicity. If anything, my experience is that of an outsider socially, and the people who need the number are people who are considered to be outsiders." He concluded, "The white community does not need my number."

Many of those who straddle the color line and blend the races have come to see themselves and their children not as a problem but as a source of health in a diseased environment. They find that affirming one's multi-racialism can have a healing effect, both on the individual and on his immediate surroundings. Doug Deuchler, who is white and whose wife is black, sees the disappearance from film of "the tragic mulatto, people with no race . . . always suicidal and sad" as a good sign. "The biracial child really draws his identity from both, and they feel more secure with both black and white because they've known a black parent and a white parent. They've known both black people and white people, and there isn't the fear. It's a hybrid identity, I guess, but people don't view it quite so tragically as it used to be."

In some measure, that is the result of careful efforts by organizations such as Multiracial Americans of Southern California, which runs support groups and provides schools with learning materials on multi-racialism. "We have all these wonderful books on multiracial kids," said Rosanne Katon-Walden. "So on the first day of school, when all the kids are bringing apples to the teacher, my daughter's bringing a packet of books that will go into the library, this is the classroom library. Teachers are thrilled to get it. Now, if we had gone to the board and said, 'We'd like this in the curriculum,' forget it. My daughter has never been questioned about being biracial, because everyone knows in the classroom what it is. They absolutely accept it."

This has given both Rosanne and her child some sense of influence. "I cannot eliminate race as a problem for my daughter, but I can show her that if you're part of the solution, you don't feel the sting of it," she said. "A lot of the pain that I felt from racism was the feeling that I just couldn't do anything. We're told that culture is stagnant, that it stands still. What I've learned is that culture is fluid, it's what I make it."

CHAPTER THREE

Memory

The Echoes of History

If you deprive a man of who he is, you can make him anything that you want him to be. But if you teach him his heritage and his culture, he will aspire to be greater than those before him.

—*Major H. L. Barner,*
a descendant of slaves

Beauty for Ashes

It is a September Saturday on the plantation. People are gathering for a day of reunion, and yellow ribbons are tied around the thick trunks of the cypresses planted two centuries ago by their enslaved ancestors. Families stroll in clusters toward the mansion, up the walkway of red bricks laid by those who went before, along the dirt carriage path that borders the narrow canal. The earth smells of ripeness and age.

The canal is soothing, and it strikes a chill. The placid water moves lazily in the late summer shade and harbors suffering in its murkiness. A double image shimmers beneath the towering trees. One is for those who do not consider the history; beauty shrouds the shame. The other is for those who recognize that they have come upon the site of a great crime and can feel a shiver of remembrance.

To drain a North Carolina swamp so that timber could be cut and rice could be grown, the canal was dug by slaves through two stifling summers and two raw winters in the 1780s; it ran twenty feet wide and six miles from Lake Phelps to the Scuppernong River, among tangled roots and swarms of blackflies and mosquitoes. Imagine the whistle of the whip, the ebony bodies glistening with sweat, the groan and cadence of the melancholy work songs. African-Americans too exhausted to return to their shacks at the end of the day were left behind, to be found dead at dawn. The canal they created is a lovely river of sorrow; it marks the divide in America between those who see the beauty and those who feel the chill.

The gathering today is of those who try to do both, who have traced their family lines back, back into slavery in this very place, on this particular ground, and who now stand on the same soil, pained and proud, reconciling themselves with history. Across the plantation drift the notes of a spiritual sung by two male voices, then the beat of four African drummers, then the sad and sour blues of a harmonica, like fragments of reminiscence.

The land is flat and the soil is rich, and the fields are deep in cotton and tobacco. Most of the back roads are paved now, slender traces of blacktop through the tranquil North Carolina countryside. With the arrival of air-conditioning and television, folks don't sit out on their porches much anymore to watch the gentle summer evenings settle over the woods and farms; many of the houses are bunched in suburban enclaves, where lawns are carefully mowed and azaleas lovingly fertilized so that they bloom in pastel reds and pinks in the springtime.

Near the little town of Creswell, the main road to the coast passes a small supermarket, a tiny restaurant, a Mobil station, and an historic marker that was finally erected a few years ago to acknowledge that human beings other than white planters had lived here and helped build the nation:

Somerset Place
Antebellum plantation of Josiah Collins III,
who grew rice and corn. Home in 1860
to 328 slaves. Located six miles south.

If you're white, you probably don't stop to think that the road you're driving may have first been cut by slaves, that the field you're passing may have first been cleared by slaves. Americans, especially white Americans, have short memories. We are impatient with the past, always hurrying into the future, moving on, getting beyond, not dwelling, leaving behind. "That's history," we say dismissively. Whatever reverence our European ancestors had for the power of history has been lost in the frontier culture of this continent; whatever deference later immigrants felt for the age-old rhythms of their homelands in Asia, the Middle East, Latin America, and elsewhere has not been transplanted well into the soil of the United States.

Although some whites appreciate the durability of the past in shaping the present, the sense of continuity held by other cultures has not found its way into the American mainstream. History here begins the day you are born: To most of white America, slavery is an evil long gone, the segregation of Jim Crow is deeply buried, and the civil rights movement has wiped the slate clean. Our ethic is practical, and problems are for solving; we do not easily admit to those that we cannot fix. Wrongs have been righted, the residue of guilt has been erased—this is the current creed of many whites, especially those too young to have seen those pictures of white girls' faces twisted in hatred as they screamed at little black children who were integrating their schools.

Some blacks acquire this habit of historical amnesia, but black America generally lives with a different memory, one that feels the reverberations of slavery, yearns for roots, searches for pride, and reaches back to grasp at ancient uncertainties. Present events occur in context, not in isolation, so they are interpreted according to what has gone before. Hence, in the eyes of many blacks, elements of the complex relationships of slavery are constantly being reenacted—between bosses and workers, between blacks and whites sexually, between African-Americans of lighter and darker skin, among blacks who suppress dissent within their ranks. Slavery is a permanent metaphor.

Rosanne Katon-Walden, for example, a passionate advocate of interracial adoption, engages in frequent combat with black social workers who oppose placing black children with white parents. When she wants to explain why her fellow blacks are uncomfortable having this dispute in public, she reaches for old patterns: "You don't rat to the massah about what's going on in the slave quarters," she says.

A black policewoman in Baltimore, noting that white women are almost never assigned with black men in patrol cars, sees a policy with distant origins. "It's a thing that goes all the way back to slavery," she says. "The white slave owners didn't want their wives to associate too much with the black slaves, and sometimes the wives were attracted to them, you know, white females were attracted to black males."

Reverend Abraham Lincoln Woods, the veteran black civil rights leader in Birmingham, Alabama, reacts swiftly to a question about the popular belief among many blacks that the drug trade is a white conspiracy to commit genocide. "Hogwash. Hogwash. Hogwash," he declares. "Nobody's making blacks use it and push it. So that theory is hogwash. It's like going back to slavery. What did the slaver do to enslave blacks? He took a shipment of arms, went to the African coast, and traded the arms to the African chiefs and other African leaders in charge, and they got the black slaves. History repeats itself. We're reenslaving ourselves. The slaver could not have so easily carried out the enslavement of blacks on the continent of Africa without the cooperation of those black chiefs."

A week before Christmas 1995, some African-American employees of the Library of Congress stepped off a sixth-floor elevator into the face of what they saw as a metaphorical statement of their own status at the institution: a large photograph of a white overseer on horseback looking down on black cotton pickers. "It reminded me of the white overseers here at the Library of Congress looking down over us to make sure we're in the fields doing our work," one employee remarked to a *Washington Post* reporter. The photograph was part of a traveling exhibition on slavery entitled "Back of the Big House: The Cultural Landscape of the Plantation," collected from interviews with former slaves in the 1930s and pictures from the library's archives. For twenty years, black and female staff members had been embroiled in a discrimination suit, which the library had just partially settled for $8 million. And somehow, in that context, the graphic reminder of slavery became a symbol of blacks' difficult history at the library, which some had sardonically nicknamed "the Big House."

The episode illustrated the unstable balance between respect for the power of the past and obsession with its injustice. Facing history can be liberating or imprisoning. It can unite or divide. At the Library of Congress, the angry protests brought quick capitulation, and the administration dismantled the display within hours.

It was then snatched up by a black-run institution, the flagship of the District of Columbia's library system, the Martin Luther King Jr. Memorial Library, where it opened to the public three weeks later. At a lecture there, the curator, John Michael Vlach, explained the exhibition as a view from the slaves' perspective, looking in from the fields and focusing on the shacks, the skills, the religion, the culture, the resistance, and the nobility of the slaves. And outside the context of the racial disputes at the Library of Congress, the exhibit lost its highly charged symbolism. From the audience, one African-American after another stood to thank Vlach for his caring and contribution.

Understandably, some of the finest literature by African-Americans is haunted by the ghosts of slavery. Toni Morrison's *Beloved* and August Wilson's *The Piano Lesson* lay bare the wrenching struggles that blacks have with themselves over how to coexist with that past—whether to bury it, fear it, despise it, deny it, revise it, memorialize it, or somehow to absorb and face it and take nourishment from the sorrow and the survival. And in all this the barriers of time become permeable, as in *Beloved* and Alice Walker's *The Temple of My Familiar*, where the shifting moments of history blur into mystical continuity. August Wilson's piano, purchased by a slave owner in exchange for the heroine's father and grandmother, stands at the pivot point of family, memory, history, and revenge. It is an unplayed instrument, a commodity, a shrine, an artifact of inner suffering.

Blacks and whites who manage to engage each other successfully across the racial line often do so by achieving concord in the historical dimension: Whites who are accepted by blacks are frequently those for whom black history has resonance. Blacks who are accepted by whites may tend toward the ahistorical, observing events in a vacuum and activating less white guilt as they put aside the prism of slavery and segregation.

More often, however, the black regard and the white disdain for history foster a collision of memories. Bearing the burden of history in its own manner, each group hears different echoes, tells a different story, creates a complete universe of perception that separates and disconnects. We need to listen to each other's echoes.

Somerset is in a mood of warm celebration, not mourning. Quite a crowd has now assembled, mostly of blacks, who are hugging relatives on the lawn near the old mansion, filling the grounds with laughter and joyous greetings.

On a makeshift stage, with the lake in the background, one of the musicians gets up from his African drums and approaches the microphone. "We're gathered here in recognition of our ancestors," he declares. "We're here on hallowed ground, where our ancestors lived in the physical world at one time. But they're still here spiritually. We're going to call our ancestors to come and be with us this morning." A hush moves across the crowd. "We'll follow the African tradition of pouring libation."

He instructs all those gathered to close their eyes and breathe deeply. Silence has settled over the plantation. "We ask that our ancestors, those who were left on the African continent, who go back to time immemorial, we ask that you come to be with us." He pours a little water from a green goblet onto the ground. "Ancestors, those who died in the middle passage, whose bones are buried beneath the Atlantic Ocean, all the way to the shores of North America, South America, the Caribbean islands, we ask you to come and be with us." The goblet is tipped again. "Ancestors, those who were in bondage in North America, South America, and the Caribbean islands, and those, in particular, here at Sunset

Plantation"—there are a few titters as he misstates the name—"we ask that you come and be with us." Another splash of water into the soil.

A children's choir of about twenty-five blacks and a dozen whites sings "Jacob's Ladder" and other songs, clapping and rocking back and forth in the black church style that the white youngsters have mastered well. Displays and activities are being set up. African incense sticks, perfumes, jewelry, masks, and wood carvings are being sold, along with ceramic figurines of blacks in work clothes. A white woman named Sylvia demonstrates the weaving of small kitchen baskets, showing three black girls how to do it; she arranges reeds in a cross, wraps another reed around, and hands it to one of the girls to complete.

A black woman, Mrs. Sykes, wearing a colorful dress and shawl and a baseball cap on backward, shows people how to tie sedge brooms; a young black man in crisp overalls and a white T-shirt splits oak into thin strips and makes baskets; a circle of people walks round and round a wood fire, making candles by dipping wicks again and again into a black pot of melted wax; an old white man is doing wood carvings; an African man is selling drawings and banana-leaf pictures of scenes in Zambia and Zimbabwe. Between the mansion and the lake, a big mural is under way on a six-by-ten-foot piece of cardboard. Under the title "This Is Harlem," a pencil outline of buildings has been sketched, and it is being colored by black and white children (and some adults) using water paints in big jars.

Malachi Brickhouse, four generations from slavery on this plantation, wears a baseball cap declaring "Jesus Is My Lord" and a yellow T-shirt with black letters that announce:

FEELING GOOD ABOUT LIFE!
Somerset Place
Coming Home
A Celebration of Family and Life

"I enjoy coming here," he says. "I get to see a lot of people that I haven't seen in a long time." Does it make him think painful thoughts about slavery? "That part don't bother me. I know where I came from and the way things was. You see, you don't go back in the past, you look forward."

Perhaps, but this day is sliding back and forth between the past and the future. Dorothy Spruill Redford is dressed as a slave might have been, in a skirt and blouse the color of burlap, her hair in a head wrap the color of field cotton. Radiating earnest energy and unyielding purpose, she strides to the microphone to give words of welcome. "As you're moving today," she says, "you're going to find that a lot of elders are here, so we want you to have an opportunity to interact and talk and learn from them. That's the most important aspect of a gathering. It's so that we can provide continuity from one generation to another. I've often said there is only one thing in life worthy of envy, and that's wisdom. And you only get wisdom through living. So today, more than anything else, I'd like you to interact with those who've lived long enough to be wise."

In 1986, out of her personal quest, Dorothy Redford first created this gathering at Somerset Place, where descendants of slaves and slave owners have come together every two or three years since. Embracing the past has meant a complicated journey for her.

Born a few miles from Somerset in 1943, she first encountered the enslavement of her ancestors by averting her eyes. "My parents were not much for history, for talking about the old days. But they did reminisce now and then," she wrote in her 1988 book, *Somerset Homecoming*. "Slavery was never mentioned around our house. The first time I heard the word, I thought some shame was attached to you if you even uttered it. I told myself it was just another thing about this place that had nothing to do with me. It was some kind of distant stain, something deep in the soul of the South. . . . When they talked about slavery in school, I was puzzled to think that an entire people could allow themselves to be enslaved—as puzzled as I was to see my parents allow little white children to call them by their first names."

This vague belief that the victims were somehow responsible for their own suffering has haunted other black families as well. Just as some Jewish survivors of the Holocaust have not talked of their trials to their children, some black grandparents have never spoken of their parents' or grandparents' lives as slaves. If black families are to travel back through generations, they must rely on the threads of oral history, which have frequently been cut.

Some African-Americans who begin the search find it so painful that they break it off, as did Mel Henderson, a former high school principal in New Jersey, after tracing his lineage to Henderson, North Carolina. His name, presumably acquired from his ancestors' owner, brings him mail from companies that want to sell him the Henderson family crest, the Henderson family history, the Henderson family tree. "My father is from North Carolina," he said. "You know what that means. He certainly didn't come over on the *Mayflower*." Once, trying to draw his family tree, he sat down with his father and uncle but stopped. "I got no further back than my great-great-grandfather," he said. "My great-great-grandfather was a slave. But it was so traumatizing, I have not worked on that since."

Some of those who now found themselves at the Somerset reunion had to reach beyond the silence of their elders to get here. "They died with their secrets," one woman lamented. "They kept them. And they must have been horrendous secrets. They would never come back and visit."

Their ties to Somerset were uncovered largely by Dorothy Redford, who was inspired by the 1977 television version of Alex Haley's *Roots* to seek out her own ancestry, hoping to follow Haley's path all the way back to Africa. It made no difference to her or to many other African-Americans that Haley had fudged the truth when he supposedly found his kin in Africa and through them traced his bloodline to the slave Kunta Kinte in the Gambian village of Juffure. For blacks who had felt historically adrift, *Roots* provided a reconnection that repaired the link so abruptly sundered by the slave trade. The tie was theoretical, in a sense; probably no black American can truly know from which African tribe or nation or culture she originates.

Such was Dorothy Redford's fortune. In her six years of searching, she determined the slave vessel on which her ancestors had probably arrived but not the African port from which it had sailed, and so hit a wall in her quest for her roots in Africa. "It was impossible to trace," she said. "I couldn't find a connection. And I don't even have that desire now. I'm OK being an African-American, being an American of African descent. Once I found Somerset I really didn't have that desire, because there was so much history here, so many contributions here that had not been acknowledged. I don't even care from where in Africa they came."

She began the way many blacks begin, with hazy recollections from her mother and by making notes of stories and ancestors' last names—Littlejohn, Honeyblue, Cabarrus, Baum, Hortin—then combing through census lists back to 1870, the earliest in which blacks were recorded as individuals instead of being lumped together under whites' property as "12 slaves," "135 slaves," "328 slaves." During breaks from scanning the microfilmed tables in the library, Redford browsed through whites' books of genealogy, noticing how detailed and authoritative they seemed compared with the fragmented information she had about her family. Assuming that slaves had taken their owners' names, she searched in the white archives for last names of her own forebears and found a

William Alexander Littlejohn, who had come from Scotland about 1760. The 1790 census showed him owning sixty-two slaves. Looking through deeds and bills of sale, she finally found a sale of thirty-two slaves by Littlejohn to Josiah Collins, who owned a plantation that he named Somerset after his home county in England. The slaves were listed, and some first names echoed those her mother had recalled. "It had to be," Redford wrote. "The woman named Elsy was my great-great-great-grandmother, my ancestral mother. I carried her blood."

Redford's eyes shone when she talked about what the discovery did to her perception of her own enslaved forebears. "You can't think of them in a non-noble way once they've been given life," she said. "We hadn't put names to people we called 'slaves,' so it was difficult for them to be thought of as heroic. Or people who had been given names in our lives, like my great-grandfather, I had never identified as a slave. You know, he was just Grandpa Alfred."

After threading her way through the census lists and bills of sale, after looking up diaries and catching glimpses of her family through the records and catalogued recollections of white people, Redford was ready for her first visit to Somerset—but not quite ready for the anger and sadness of seeing the white custodians' indifference to her past. The plantation, with its mansion of columns and balconies, had been preserved as a state historic site. Nearly all the visitors were white; she looked in vain for some suggestion of the vibrant presence of African-Americans on the estate and found only a token remembrance of her ancestors—a rotting sign in an empty field: SITE OF SLAVE QUARTERS.

"I don't know why I expected anything more," she wrote bitterly. "I had been to colonial Williamsburg, to Jefferson's Monticello. Tourists at those places weren't shown any slave quarters. There were no monuments to the black hands that had built the white homes that the white tourists strolled through. But I was no tourist here. This was my home, my family's home. . . . My people were born and were wed here. And when they died, they were buried here, somewhere."

In 1984, Redford was asked by the white manager of Somerset to set up a display of her genealogical study—"something on the slave experience," as he put it—for a Founders' Day fair. She made charts and maps and family trees and drove with her mother to the plantation. There, all the other displays were manned by whites and set up across the shady lawn, but Redford and her mother were put in the stuffy kitchen, a separate building where slaves had done the cooking—and where one had been raped by a Union soldier at the end of the war. "We sat inside that stifling room, my seventy-seven-year-old mother and I, watching white people come and go past the door, white people who weren't even interested in the displays their own kind had set up, much less a black woman's charts about her slave ancestors," she wrote. "Some glanced in, then kept moving. Some probably thought we worked there. Hired help."

She left, burning with humiliation. She contacted other families whose names she had turned up among the slaves, pressed the state bureaucracy for a homecoming, and won the attention of the press. Some blacks who had lived their whole lives in the immediate area expressed indifference, perhaps in shame and fear at a reminder of slavery. But when the first gathering was held, Alex Haley joined several thousand descendants of Somerset slaves congregated on the lawns of the old mansion. Some whites were there, too; one of them, aged seventy-eight, was Josiah Collins VI, a descendant of the owner.

And then, in irony's final conquest, Dorothy Spruill Redford was appointed manager of the Somerset Place plantation.

There is something delicious about seeing the bright blues and reds and oranges of men's African dashikis against the bland, buttermilk-colored mansion. There is some satisfying justice in feeling the beat of African drums thundering across this ground. Here, at the genesis of America's racial divide, blacks are recapturing a bit of what was stolen from them.

"When I got here," says Nettie Moore Dyer, "just walking on the grounds, there was such a different feeling. It was like a connection. It was like I almost felt like I was walking on sacred grounds." She speaks with a slight New York accent, testimony to her living for thirty-three years in Harlem, Brooklyn, and Long Island before returning in 1990 to her place of childhood, her place of comfort, in Columbia, North Carolina. With Dorothy Redford's help, she discovered that her great-great-grandfather Jack Sawyer had been a slave at Somerset.

"The first time I got here, I felt that there was something here that was part of me, even though the person that was giving the tour at the time wasn't very helpful," Dyer says. "She wasn't even a nice person. It was a young white girl, and it seemed as if she just didn't even want to be bothered—'cause my family came with me. We were all black, and we wanted a tour of the house and grounds. She seemed as if she didn't even want to be bothered giving us a tour. But inside of me, it didn't take away anything. I still had that connected feeling. I knew that I would be coming back at another time, and I would be made to feel welcome, and that did happen." Eventually, Nettie Moore Dyer began to conduct tours herself.

A brisk breeze comes off the lake and eases the midday heat. People are sitting around on folding chairs, eating traditional foods: fried chicken, black-eyed peas, mashed potatoes, and okra. They are talking about gathering strength from this reunion, seeing their ancestors as the true role models, as heroes who had the vigor, the dignity, the ingenuity to survive slavery. "You do have a feeling of, maybe not pain, but you feel this sadness to think what our forefathers went through," an old woman observes. "And sometimes we think that we have overcome, but then another thought comes—we haven't overcome. We have made progress, but we still haven't reached our goal. There's a long way to go."

Clara Small, a young history professor from Maryland, is in a reflective mood about this place of her ancestors, judging it a kind of neutral ground where people are searching for understanding. She smiles slightly. It is an interesting concept: neutral ground. Once, she notes, it was anything but neutral. Now it is acknowledged as a place that the whites owned but the blacks built. A curious equilibrium has been achieved, and with it a sense of calm that suspends Somerset in a temper of contentment. The moment is strange and intricate, tenuous and clean, for embracing the reality of the past creates an island of unreal harmony in the present. Surrounded by turbulence, isolated from the larger, contentious society, Somerset's tranquillity today is a lesson in the therapy of honest history.

"There's a lot of peacefulness here," says H. L. Barner, an army major who is researching his family background, "and it's kind of ironic that you would find that kind of peace in a place where there was so much tragedy. And I think God intervened in a lot of things, you know. He put that peacefulness here so that we can tolerate the presence of this place and also so that we as a people can come here. Though we have our differences, we can come here and share and reflect back and understand one another better."

Oscar Bennett thinks about slavery a lot, and so he enjoys this gathering at Somerset. He is seventy-nine, a retired barber and elevator operator at Rockefeller Center in New York. "My grandmother, she used to tell me about the slaves," he says. "Some of them worked hard. Some of them had house jobs, some of them had field jobs. Most of my ancestors, Bennett, they was carpenters. They did carpentry work. Well, [young people] should know their roots, they should know where they come from. Everybody understands that. Everybody knows we came over here on a ship. Everybody knows that. So it's nothing to be ashamed of. How can we forget those times?"

Over the loudspeakers, the extended clans are being called to assemble in the dappled shade by the canal for family photographs. Bennett. Littlejohn. Brickhouse. Collins. The names from history ring out across the lawns, and groups of people get up and begin to move, old folks walking stiffly, children skipping among them, until a white photographer from the North Carolina Department of Cultural Resources poses them with the mansion in the background, makes them laugh, clicks off a few frames, and lets them go. They linger awhile beneath the gnarled old cypresses and sycamores, talking with one another.

A spirit of remarkable charity pervades this place today. Oscar Bennett captures it directly. "I don't hold no madness against nobody, cause you didn't do nothing to me," he says. "Those people who done that is dead and gone. I don't hold you responsible for something somebody else did. That's the way I feel about it. I think we all should live together and be as one."

Such generosity seems to be one result of facing the past, as if knowing exactly who you are enables you to look clearly at others across racial lines, even across lines that run within yourself. Dorothy Redford's father's father was white, a source of distress and resentment that have dissipated only since the first gathering and the writing of her book. She says that she has now come to terms with "the fact that I had to acknowledge that there was both black blood and white blood."

For H. L. Barner, personal history is power. "If you deprive a man of who he is, you can make him anything that you want him to be. But if you teach him his heritage and his culture, he will aspire to be greater than all those before him," he says. He is now thirty-eight years old, and since childhood he has yearned to find his family's roots in slavery. "I'd just like to know where did they live, where did the slaves come from. When you're doing research, a lot of time you hit walls, you go to a dead end and you think there's nothing else that you can do. So you come to a place like this and you see people that successfully achieved what you're trying to do. It inspires you to continue. And that's why I'm here, for inspiration."

Barner pauses and looks over the throng of blacks, and a few whites, scattered across the lawn. Some of the whites are just local folks, but several are descendants of the Collins family of plantation owners. "Whites are the victims of racism, and blacks are the survivors," Barner declares. "Places like this and Black History Month and things like that, it liberates whites." The lies that have been told to whites have imprisoned them, he says. "If the whites can liberate themselves through our knowledge and information, then we can come together and develop a oneness as a human race and as a people. Until that, we will always have the problem that we have."

Then he adds, "Think of all the relationships that whites have deprived themselves of. . . ." His voice trails off.

There seem to be no grudges at Somerset, at least none that anyone admits to. Descendants of slaves mingle with descendants of slave owners; they stand together for pictures, they laugh together.

"I find that I cannot hold no grudges," says Terry Lee, a thin black man from Philadelphia who is wearing a white T-shirt, black shorts, and a Chicago Bulls hat. "I look at it as, the whites had to do what they did, the blacks had to do what they did, and now it seems like everybody's doing it together. That's how I look at it. I really do."

Even the myth used for generations by whites to put a pleasant face on slavery has been absorbed by some of the blacks here today. "One thing, he was good to his slaves," Oscar Bennett says of Josiah Collins, the slave owner. "He was definitely good to his slaves. He liked music, he liked entertainment. And if you had any kind of talent, he would bring it out. My grandmother told me."

Under a sycamore tree at the end of the yard, John Graham, a white man in a baseball cap and sunglasses, is helping out by selling sodas from great coolers of melting ice. He is a descendant of the slave-owning Collins family.

Some months before the gathering, John Graham greeted me in his small office at Duke University, where he worked as director of strategic planning. Piles of papers were stacked neatly on the floor in a kind of horizontal filing system. He was tall and had an aquiline nose. His sandy hair was thinning on top, and his blue eyes were touched with a bit of pain as he talked about guilt. He wore a dark green sweater and no tie, and his voice was soft.

Graham had a Ph.D. in international economics and economic development, which made him one of the most highly educated of the Collins family. Interestingly, many of the slave descendants seemed to have done at least as well as the Collinses, even better in some cases. Dorothy Redford found that the slaves at Somerset had spawned, after several generations, an orthopedic surgeon and a couple of other physicians; a chemist; an aircraft-maintenance engineer; a microbiologist at Walter

Reed Army Medical Center; a running back for the New York Giants; a supervisor in the District of Columbia's government; more than one professor; and the Democratic leader of the Maryland State Senate, Clarence W. Blount.

Graham was one of the achievers on the white side, but his consciousness of his family's involvement with slavery came to him only slowly, out of a blur of names and stories that contained no shame until he gradually awakened to the history's personal terms. He was related not only to Josiah Collins but also to Paul Cameron, who owned Stagville and Farintosh, two large plantations near Durham.

Graham's journey reflected the contemplative dimension of white America's encounter with race, the introspection that brings ambivalence and longing. He grew up during the fifties and sixties in Edenton, across Albemarle Sound from Somerset, although he never visited the plantation until his late twenties. His family talked about slavery "some, but not much," he remembered. "I didn't have a sense that the slave stuff was a secret, but it may have been. We didn't talk about it, that's true, so who knows? . . . There was a very strong oral tradition in the family, so I had an opportunity to know anecdotes about people. I knew a lot of anecdotes about Josiah Collins. And I had a sense of knowing a lot of these people personally from the stories."

When Graham was a boy, the county was just over half black, as he recalled, "and I grew up with quite a number of black friends—like a black guy taught me how to ride a bicycle, for example, and I used to go fishing all the time with a couple of black guys. From the time that I was like six years old, we would go out fishing and trapping and stuff like that on the water. And then we went to school, and it was segregated through part of school, and I lost touch. I didn't lose touch altogether, but we didn't do things as spontaneously as we had when I was younger."

Bigotry and racism were intertwined with what he called "friendships," a term that blacks probably used more judiciously, for the patterns of power often felt to them like echoes of the past. "A hell of a lot of people grow up with close black relationships," Graham said. "They have household servants, like we had a cook and a yardman, and we got to be very good friends. I mean, they were part of the family and still are. They're retired now, but we still see them regularly at Christmas or whenever I go home. . . . There's always the distinction that they're black. That's there somewhere, but there's a great affection." He acknowledged it as a "complex relationship."

Graham was in high school during integration, and he enjoyed hanging out with the first two blacks who arrived—his way of showing that at least some white would invite them into friendship. "They were the subject of a lot of abuse," he recalled, "and I always felt both angry and ashamed for the abuse, I think. But, on the other hand, I never took up for them." When whites called them racist names, he felt tempted to speak out and then a plunging guilt for not doing so.

Later, when he worked in Washington, D.C., he thought he learned a piece of what they had endured, because blacks made him the target of their bigotry. He'd play basketball at a local playground, often as the only white, and the blacks on his own team would throw the ball at his head as he was breaking or refuse to pass it to him when he was wide open for a layup.

While driving to the beach one day, Graham followed an impulse of curiosity and stopped at Somerset. It was his first visit, and the unseen culture of slavery did not register on him. Instead, as he strolled along the canal and walked through the mansion, his thoughts were flooded by the admiring stories his relatives had told about Collins. "He made a lot of very difficult and risky decisions all along the way," Graham said, "so I had some sense of him being a risk taker and a very hard worker, and someone who was very strict, in a lot of ways, with his kids." He meant constructively strict, for his image of Collins was quite positive. "I also had a sense of him as being a thoughtful person, and my disposition was to think of him in general as someone who had been humane."

As Graham walked about, he found himself musing on how family responsibilities might have been shared between husband and wife, what their parties had been like—the Collinses had been famous for inviting guests for weeklong festivities—and whether, when the visitors departed, Somerset had been a lonely place.

He considered the slaves only as a diffuse mass with the arduous task of creating the plantation. "I thought about them more as an overall group of people," he admitted, "but not as individuals, the way that I thought about the Collinses." He did not picture the slaves who were forced into the dangerous, debilitating work of digging the canal, and so he saw only the beauty of the accomplishment with only an "appreciation for how hard it must have been to do it," he recalled, "and the organizational skills that would have been required, and all the many logistical decisions that were necessary to pull it all off." He felt no chill.

He began to see the slaves more clearly only a decade later, after a relative suggested that he join the board of a foundation that Dorothy Redford was creating to raise funds to reconstruct the chapel, the infirmary, and some of the shacks used by slaves. This exposed him to the power of heritage, he said, and to "the fact that African-Americans have been robbed of theirs." It was a painful and illuminating discovery, troubling and uplifting. "I think all whites and blacks who are seeking resolution are continually looking to see the humanity of each other," he observed; this means that each must recognize that the other can suffer, and each must be able to say, "I'm available or I'm capable or predisposed to have compassion and pride and all the other things, the responses that I have to people I love." Seeing the slaves at Somerset as individuals, not merely as a collective, was part of "trying to cultivate that understanding," Graham said. "So I think it's very enriching. And of course, just as it is in many other explorations, it is disturbing, unsettling."

In 1990, Graham went to his first homecoming. "I loved it. I thought it was great. Since I was on the board, I knew a number of people already, and they introduced me to their families who had come. And then I just strolled around. There were big circles of families . . . and I'd just sit down with folks and visit. I was just interested to see where people had gone and what they were up to now and what their experience was like coming back to this. I thoroughly enjoyed it. . . . I didn't get any resentment at all. And I was introduced as a descendant of Josiah, and people were really very easily engaged. This was one of those occasions where I felt there really was an opportunity for a dialogue and a relationship. And it's curious, it's kind of ironic. One might expect some resentment or something."

In examining his slave-owning roots, Graham wrestled with the allocation of responsibility, something that few whites do. "I feel some sense of guilt about it," he conceded. "And I also sort of have an intellectual rationale that I'm a different generation, and as a result I'm not immediately responsible." Then he made an important statement of honest self-appraisal: "I suspect that had I lived in those times and been in their position I would have been a slave owner too. And I probably would have had my concerns about it, but there was the conventional wisdom and the power of the economics, and I'm sure that would have all been very influential for me. I've wondered about their humanity and how they treated the slaves, and that's always been a question I've had, and in the end I've gotten stories that suggest that they were humane, for the most part."

This image of benign relations is part of Collins family lore, reinforced by "the one story that we heard," says Cathy Collins Gowing, granddaughter of Josiah Collins V. In February 1843, two sons of Josiah

Collins III and two slave boys drowned in the canal, an incident passed down the generations as evidence of interactions remarkably kind. "The story that I heard over and over again was that the white kids and the black kids played together. That's why they were in the canal together," she says. "That's it. That was the only thing that I heard at all, was that one story."

On the shady lawn, Cathy Collins Gowing is standing in a bright, flowered dress, her dark hair straight and long and framing a beatific smile as she gazes around her. She and the several other Collins descendants—including her little girl, Amber, who is clinging to her skirts—are incidental to this day, and that seems right to her. "I think it's great," she says softly. "Oh, this is theirs. This is their place." She laughs. "It's wonderful. It means redemption. It means hope." She has come all the way from Oregon to be here.

Only in a vague, undefined way was the history of Somerset transmitted to her by her relatives, and the gauzy images were so abstract that they never encouraged her to think about her ancestors as the owners of slaves. "I knew it was here," she says, "but I didn't know any of the background. I knew that eventually it traced back to Somerset, England, but that's about all I knew." Here, too, a certain silence had descended over the generations.

"I was an anti-war activist by the time I was fourteen," she explains, "and became a revolutionary by the time I was seventeen. I organized May Day marches and lived in Paris working with the North Vietnamese. I was very concerned about racism and very angry." She laughs again. "Lots of marches, and lots of getting beat over the head with sticks and Mace and all of that. I gave my father Bobby Seale's book when I was seventeen—*Seize the Time*—and he read it." Her father would "always raise us saying, 'Never lose the common touch.' He was a humble man. So he challenged us to have open hearts. And I challenged him, too."

She and her husband, religious people, have schooled their children at home, and it was during the exploration of history that she unexpectedly came upon her own story. "I was teaching my children, so we had gone to Washington, D.C., and we had gone to be with Amish people through the Mennonite Church, and then we came back through Jamestown, Williamsburg. And to finish up a science project on flight, we had been to the Smithsonian, so we wanted to finish up with Kitty Hawk, and we thought we would just pass through. And when I came here and we met Dorothy, forget Kitty Hawk. We never even went. We just stayed here. I had never read her book at all or even heard about it, and so I stayed up three days and nights reading that, and I could not believe what an excellent job she did. It was painful, but it was good. And so it helped me face stuff that I had no idea about. I cried, and I prayed, and I cried. I thought it was wonderful. I thought, This is great, this is stark and real and concrete. I'm really grateful to Dorothy."

Had she known of her connection to Somerset? "Sure, but I had no idea about black history here. I had no idea what was going on. I knew that we had lots of relatives way back, but we didn't know about the slave culture. We didn't have any idea about that." She looks out over the grounds. "This is just excellent. I care about it being redeemed."

She pauses for a moment, listening to a spiritual being played over the loudspeakers, then hums along for a while before speaking again, her voice so low that it is nearly lost in the strains of the music. "I went home and I thought, What's the verse for this? And it's Isaiah," and then she paraphrases Isaiah 61:3: "To appoint unto them that mourn in Zion, to give unto them beauty for ashes, the oil of joy for mourning, the garment of praise for the spirit of heaviness; that they might be called trees of righteousness, the planting of the Lord, that he might be glorified."

Over the music, family names are still being called for photographs. How does she feel the descendants of slaves are seeing her? "Well, I would understand it if they despised me. That's all right. But most people haven't. So, if I expect that, then everything else is a bonus." And what is she feeling, what is she thinking? "I pray for forgiveness for all that's gone on here. You know, there's deep roots of wrong that my family has carried out that needs to be redeemed, that needs to be healed. I think that this is an excellent place for that to happen."

The day is coming to an end at Somerset Place. By six o'clock, most people have departed, blacks with blacks and whites with whites, into separateness once again, abandoning the plantation to the lengthening shadows cast by the towering cypresses and sycamores. The sun sinks toward the lake, and the breeze off the water seems a little cooler.

The block-printing stand has been folded up. The basket maker has pulled his van onto the walkway and is loading his wood and tools. Members of a dance troupe, some carrying sedge brooms that they've made, have gathered to board their bus.

Clusters of conversation are thinning out. The remaining descendants of slaves drift gently away, down the brick paths that slaves built, slowly saying farewells with handshakes and hugs and bursts of hearty laughter. Some pull the yellow ribbons, the symbols of homecoming, from around the tree trunks to take as pieces of memory.

In the deepening shade beneath the old, thick trees where families sat and talked, empty chairs are left in ragged circles on the lawn. Beauty for ashes.

The Fatal Stain of Slavery

No comparable regard for the truth uplifts the manicured tourist attraction of Magnolia Plantation on the Ashley River about ten miles from Charleston, South Carolina. Listed in the National Register of Historic Places and blessed with lush gardens, the plantation charges a hefty fee and then subjects the visitor to patronizing disdain on the subject of slavery.

On a tour of the small, elegant house, built just after the Civil War to replace the one burned by General Sherman, a matronly white guide pointed out every piece of antique furniture and glass and detailed the ten generations of the Drayton family, which still owns the place. But not once in the course of the twenty-five-minute tour did she utter the words "slaves" or "slavery." Afterward, when I asked how many slaves there had been, she said, "Three hundred." Four families still live here, she explained brightly, and other maintenance workers reside in old slave cabins. "Did you see the slave cabin near the parking lot?" she asked. "It's really neat."

The cabin had rustic charm. Reconstructed with broad, green-painted boards as siding, its two rooms of unfinished wood contained rough furniture, bowls carved from gourds, wooden utensils, and a life-size model of an old slave looking contented. A plaque outside provided a sly commentary that minimized the suffering and placed a touch of responsibility on the victims. "Before we reflect too sadly on the conditions afforded by such a homestead," it said, "we should remember that what we consider as hardships today were accepted without discontent by our forebearers [*sic*]. In actuality, this cabin offered its inhabitants more room and far greater comfort than did most of the one room, dirt floored pioneer cabins typifying those of the frontiers at that time, and like today, the accommodations of each house varied greatly with the industry of the occupant." The sign went on to assert the slaves' "indifference to mosquitoes," an enviable trait, apparently, since the guide in the house had just described how the Drayton family always fled to the North Carolina mountains from May to October to escape the heat and malaria.

· · ·

Here and there, in pockets of honesty, slaves have been stripped of their invisibility. Occasionally, they are depicted as more than mere victims, and their contributions are measured as greater than the physical and uncreative. A slide show at Charleston's visitors' center renders black Americans as integral to the development of the city's culture and architecture. Basket weaving, brought from Africa, was introduced into American practices and carried on. Enslaved artisans—carpenters, blacksmiths—were rented out to work on the beautiful houses that remain the heart of the town's charm. Thus, tourists are told, the slaves were as important as the architects.

At Mount Vernon, George Washington's estate, slavery was largely absent until recently. On a crisp autumn day in October 1994, many years after the silence should have been filled, tourists filing through the mansion received no hint that African-Americans had been enslaved at this place. The lapse could not have been the quirk of any individual, because a touring group was not assigned to a single guide. Instead, a different white woman was stationed at each major room and hallway giving a brief description as people walked slowly through. Never once was the word "slaves" spoken in the house. Only in the separate building that served as the kitchen did a guide finally add "slaves" to the end of her last sentence, like a passing afterthought. She said, "The kitchen was normally staffed by four people—two cooks and two helpers, who were slaves." That concluded the tour, and the visitors then emerged into the cool sunlight.

It was no wonder that blacks were not prevalent among the visitors. How different a presentation it would have been if done from the slaves' viewpoint. The kitchen must have been steaming hot in the humid summers. Slaves would have sweated over the fires, and when there were large parties, they would have lugged huge pots of food to be served while catching a bite to eat themselves between courses, perhaps even smuggling some out to the field hands, who were fed less well.

The antiseptic approach to life in Washington's day continued at the various outbuildings. To avoid mentioning slaves, signs of explanation were written in the passive voice. In the washhouse, "clothing for both family and guests was washed. . . ." In the smokehouse, ". . . 132 hogs were slaughtered. . . . Meats smoked here were eaten by the Washingtons and their guests." Never did the slaves wash the clothing; never did the slaves slaughter the hogs and smoke the meat.

The only hints of shifting sensibilities came in reconstructed slave quarters and in the pleasant woods, not far from the tomb of George and Martha Washington. Two monuments, placed more than half a century apart, testified to the evolving terminology by which white Americans identified the black slaves. The first, a stone tablet laid on brickwork in 1929, was inscribed, "In memory of the many faithful colored servants of the Washington family buried at Mount Vernon from 1760–1860. Their unidentified graves surround this spot."

The second, a stone cylinder with the top sliced off at a sharp angle, read, "In memory of the Afro-Americans who served as slaves at Mount Vernon." It was dedicated on September 21, 1983, by the Mount Vernon Ladies' Association, which purchased the estate in 1858.

By 1997, however, accounts of slavery had been grafted onto the serene nobility of Washington's home. A walk through the mansion still yielded no utterance of the words "slaves" or "slavery," even by the African-American man who had joined the crew of guides the previous year. But some of the outbuildings' signs had been changed. In the wash-house, "Two slave women worked up to six days a week washing table linens and clothing. . . ." In the coach house, "Several slaves took care of the Mount Vernon vehicles. . . ." And in the spinning room, "Wool from Mount Vernon's sheep was spun by slave women on the larger wheels." Moreover, beginning in 1995, a candid tour of slave life was conducted two to four times daily, often by Gladys Quander Tancil, a descendant of slaves from a nearby farm. She didn't sugarcoat anything. The overseer was stingy with food, she said. The reconstructed slave quarters was much better than the original, which had a dirt floor and nothing but old rags for slave children to sleep on. As she spoke, she searched the faces of the tourists, tailoring her account to their reactions, not wanting to offend. The belated attention to slavery has drawn more blacks to Mount Vernon, but some whites express resentment. One told her, "We came to hear about George Washington, not you."

Until the mid-1980s, the guides at Thomas Jefferson's estate, Monti-cello, referred demurely to his slaves as "Mr. Jefferson's servants." Until 1993, there were no tours of the area where the slaves' dwellings and workshops had been located, although the garden was favored with seven or eight tours daily. African-Americans made up the vast majority of the inhabitants of Monticello, but their history was relegated to its cus-tomary invisibility.

Only after white historians and descendants of Jefferson's slaves began to press for a fuller, more honest portrait of Jefferson's life did Monticello gradually permit inroads to be made by the facts of slavery. In 1992, John Charles Thomas, who had served six years as the first black judge of the Virginia Supreme Court, was invited onto the board of the Thomas Jefferson Memorial Foundation, which oversees Monticello. A committee of African-American historians and other prominent blacks was established to provide expertise in developing presentations on the slave community there. For schools, Monticello's education department printed a poster headlined "Who Lived at Monticello?" It depicted, with little white and black figures, the population in the late 1790s: Jefferson and eight family members; fourteen white "free craftsmen and laborers"; and, dominating the poster, 118 "enslaved African-Americans," all of whom were named and arranged in family groups.

Steps were taken on the ground as well. Mulberry Row—the area of workshops and slave cabins that had been allowed to disintegrate and disappear—was allocated guides six times a day, and a detailed brochure was printed enabling visitors to show themselves around. An archaeological dig in the early eighties had turned up a wealth of information about life among the slaves, according to Lucia Stanton, Monticello's senior research historian: bones that indicated diet, a jew's-harp and part of a violin, pierced coins that were relics of African culture, and locks that had apparently been hidden away by slaves to leave corncribs open and make their contents available to all.

There were no blacks willing to stay in the full-time corps of guides until the mid-1990s, Stanton said; because blacks had been ignored in the portrayals, because "it was on their backs that all this was created and shown to the world," she noted, African-Americans in neighboring Charlottesville were averse to working at Monticello. But the whites who gave tours were finally instructed to talk openly about slaves. And by 1996, four African-Americans worked as guides—one in the house and three on Mulberry Row.

On a raw February day, an all-white group of visitors was met at the door of Jefferson's house by Bess Kane, a short, brisk, middle-aged white woman with glasses. She described Jefferson as a "slave owner all his life," a "paradox" that she would discuss further inside. Jefferson had planned the brick structure ingeniously, crowned it with a dome, and chosen its site at the top of a small mountain (*monticello* in Italian), where he enjoyed a 360-degree view of the surrounding countryside. Kane led the group through the tall glass doors containing many original panes that created a mosaic of wavy, misshapen forms. She pointed to a clock, designed by Jefferson to be propelled by the weight of cannonballs, which marked the days of the week as they descended. And interspersed among her routine physical descriptions of what the tourists saw around them were her comments on what they did not see—Jefferson's ambivalence about slavery, which he called an abomination and tried to abolish in Virginia; his ultimate surrender on the issue, saying he would leave it to the next generation; his likening slavery to having a wolf by the ears, a wolf you cannot subdue and cannot release. She observed that Jefferson was in debt and that he freed only two slaves during his lifetime and five in his will. To this, an elderly white man in the group said, "Well, he would have gone broke," as if that made slavery acceptable or at least understandable. Kane referred to Jefferson's "slave butler" and his "slave artisans" and occasionally to his "servants," noting once that that's what the family called them: servants. Indeed, she spent more time on slavery than on freedom, more attention to Jefferson's holding slaves than to the concepts of democracy and individual liberty that had led him to write the Declaration of Independence.

One thing she did not mention, however, was the belief that Jefferson had fathered five children by a slave, Sally Hemings, with whom he may have had a love affair for decades after his wife died. Only when I raised the question did Kane answer it, and at some length, giving a fair account of the unresolved dispute by reporting that the tale had been started by James Thomson Callender (described by historians as a scurrilous scandalmonger who delighted in libeling presidents) and that most Jefferson scholars—relying on the family's skepticism and Jefferson's denial in private correspondence—had their doubts. She skipped over the finding that Jefferson had been with Hemings nine months before every one of the children in question was born, beginning in Paris, where he took her, at age fourteen or fifteen, to serve his daughters when he went as minister to France.

Callender first published his account of the Jefferson-Hemings liaison in the *Richmond Recorder* of September 1, 1802, writing derisively, "It is well known that the man, whom it delighteth the people to honor, keeps and for many years has kept, as his concubine, one of his slaves." In 1873, at the age of sixty-eight, Hemings's third son, Madison Hemings, published detailed reminiscences claiming Jefferson as his father. He said that Sally Hemings was the daughter of Jefferson's father-in-law, John Wayles, and a mulatto slave, Betty Hemings, who was descended from a whaling ship captain named Hemings. The modern historian who assigns the story the most credibility is Fawn M. Brodie in *Thomas Jefferson: An Intimate History*. According to family lore, Sally Hemings's first child by Jefferson was Thomas Woodson, and it is this line that has retained its identity most clearly. The descendants of three of the other four have passed into the white world, according to the late Minnie

Woodson, the family historian, but the Woodsons have constructed an extensive organization in the last twenty years and hold a biennial reunion. In 1992, they were invited to Monticello, where they noticed that Thomas was not listed in the Hemings family tree; no documentation existed of his presence at the plantation. But at their insistence, Monticello agreed to add his name with an asterisk indicating strong family and oral tradition as the basis. Monticello has been studiously agnostic.

The pattern of slave masters consorting with and forcing themselves on slave women was widespread enough to convince many black Americans that the Jefferson-Hemings liaison did take place. "You really have somewhat equal testimony on both sides," said Lucia Stanton. Testimony may create argument and illuminate reality, but it does not drive perception on such a matter. Perception is a function of symbolism—in this case, the ultimate symbolism of racial domination and mixture in America. Most whites may not have heard of the assertions about Jefferson and Hemings; for most blacks who have, they are not assertions—they are fact.

One of Thomas Jefferson's putative descendants was a small boy in Petersburg, Virginia, in the days of segregation just after World War II. His mother, getting him ready to go shopping downtown, had him go to the bathroom and drink as much water as he wanted, so that she could shelter him from the humiliation of separate facilities in the stores. But downtown, he saw the signs over the drinking fountains—WHITE and COLORED—and he wondered what colored water looked like. So he snuck over and turned the fountain on to see. He didn't drink any, just watched it arch up and splash and swirl down the drain. It looked the same. Puzzling.

His name was Robert H. Cooley III. He began "to learn the facts of life," as he explained, delivering newspapers and talking with a white kid on an adjoining route as they rolled up their papers and put them into their canvas shoulder bags. They compared notes on school; the white boy took courses in chemistry, biology, and other subjects that Robert didn't have in his school, and the white's English book was more advanced. Robert asked his father about it, and his father explained, and Robert was laden with a feeling of disappointment and helplessness.

One day, it was threatening to rain. Robert did not have his bike, so he boarded a bus and sat right behind the driver.

"You get to the back of the bus, boy!"

"I'm just going to go about three stops, and then I'll be off in a minute," Robert told the driver.

"Boy, if you don't get in the back of that bus, I'm going to call the police."

"Oh, it's not necessary to do that. I'll just walk." And Robert got off and walked on down the street. Confused, he told the story at home, and his father was livid. But what could he do? It was not yet 1955, and Rosa Parks had not yet made her rebellious decision, out of weariness and stubbornness, to stay right in her seat and thereby spark the bus boycott in Montgomery, Alabama, that began to roll back segregation.

Robert was twelve or thirteen, visiting his grandparents' home in Pittsburgh, when his grandfather and two uncles sat him down and said, "Son, it's time you knew about the family secret."

"OK."

"You're related—we're all related—to Thomas Jefferson."

The boy said, "Wow!" or something close to it and felt a rush of amazement and pride. They explained that Jefferson's slave mistress, Sally Hemings, had given birth to a child named Thomas, who was banished from Monticello at an early age to the farm of a white named John Woodson, acquired the Woodson name as his own, and ultimately moved to Ohio. "And then some of his children came to Pittsburgh, and here we are," Robert's grandfather said.

The news bathed Robert in "a sort of warm series of chills," as he remembered years later. But then they dissipated, because life didn't change for him; his Jefferson ancestry had no relationship to his real world, and when he told black friends, they just let it go—no congratulations, no dialogue, no snotty dismissals, just benign neglect of a wondrous fact. Perhaps it even created something of an internal problem for him, for looking back, he recalled, "sometimes I would think, 'Gee whiz, here I am the grandson of the president of the United States, the author of the Declaration of Independence, and I still can't do the things I'd like to do.' There was a time when I wanted to be white, because white folks, they didn't have barriers that I had, and I could see that they were able to progress faster and with much less difficulty than I." But he did not tell white kids about his Jefferson connection. "You keep that to yourself," he said. "Nobody would believe you, for one thing. You simply didn't discuss your heritage in terms of your white ancestry. I mean, you just didn't do it."

Years later, his son, also Robert, came home from Clover Hill High School complaining about a racist teacher who hated Jews and blacks and anybody else who wasn't white Anglo-Saxon Protestant. "He's real poison," Cooley said. "The guy is a killer up there." In desperation one day, Robert told him, "I'm related to Thomas Jefferson."

"Yeah, sure. Prove it."

So he came home. "Where's that book?" he asked his father. "Where's that book we got?" It is a sourcebook, a genealogical study, containing documents and letters recording the stories passed through the generations and assembled during years of painstaking research by the late Minnie Woodson, the family historian.

"What are you going to do with it?" Cooley asked his son.

"The teacher told me to prove it."

"The heck with that guy. You don't need to honor that. You know who you are."

In 1964, Cooley was an army officer in his early twenties, and the army sent him to take courses at the law school on the campus of the University of Virginia. Again and again, when he went to the law library and sat at a table, all the other students got up and walked away. The first time, he thought that they had to go to class. The second time, he realized what was happening, and he pondered the irony: this university had been founded by his ancestral grandfather, Thomas Jefferson, and he could not even be welcomed as a student here. Eventually, however, all three of his children were.

On April 13, 1993, the 250th anniversary of Thomas Jefferson's birth, Cooley was invited to represent the Woodson family at a gala dinner put on by Monticello. The few blacks there, who included Virginia Governor L. Douglas Wilder, Judge John Charles Thomas, and Julian Bond, were scattered among the tables. Mikhail Gorbachev, who cited Jefferson as an inspiration, was an honored guest. "Now, at my table, I suspect there was a woman who was a Jefferson, but she never said much to me, and I never said much to her," Cooley recalled, a smile playing on his lips. "This lady and her husband both looked as if they had been eating lemons, so I didn't have anything to say to them."

As the dinner ended, Cooley was approached by a white gentleman with a mission. He introduced himself as "a Jefferson descendant" and said that, as a professional historian, he completely rejected the account of the Jefferson-Hemings liaison described in Fawn M. Brodie's book.

"I can understand that," Cooley replied politely.

The gentleman added that Jefferson descendants had periodic meetings. "I couldn't imagine what the reaction would be if you showed up at one of those," he said.

"I couldn't do it," Cooley reassured him.

"Well, I'm from New England, and my ancestors were abolitionists."

"Well, thank God for them," Cooley answered dryly.

"But my Virginia cousins are not quite as understanding or as liberal, and I can't quite imagine how they would react."

"Well, I can understand that, too," Cooley said. "But let me tell you something about the situation: We've known who we were for the last two hundred years."

John Woodson's eyes are such a pale gray that they look almost blue. In his seventies, he describes himself as "bricklayer, schoolteacher, army engineer, oceanographer, architect, builder." He is a direct descendant of Thomas Woodson, but it was his late wife, Minnie, who launched the investigation of the family when she retired as a reading specialist in 1972. She contacted eight hundred people in three hundred families and by 1978 had pulled together enough information to organize the first Woodson reunion, which has taken place every two years since then.

They sat together in their small house in Washington, D.C., detailing the genealogy of the Woodsons, she correcting his slight misstatements and filling in his memory lapses, pulling out letters from relatives across the country recounting their recollections of the oral history that has been handed down across the generations. What is remarkable—or would be remarkable if the lineage from Jefferson had no basis—is that identical stories are told by widely separated people who had no previous contact with one another.

The family lore stands unquestioned. "When I was growing up," John Woodson said, "my grandmother was still alive. Now, my grandmother was the one who married Granville Woodson, and she told me, oh, I guess about 1926, '27, or '28, somewhere in that period of time, that Thomas Woodson was the son of Jefferson. I would have been nine or ten. All my brothers had heard this story before."

Minnie Woodson, a slight woman with a precise mind, read out of a thick, black loose-leaf binder from scattered letters she had received:

FROM PENNSYLVANIA: "My father, Howard Dillworth Powell Woodson, told me when I was ten to twelve years of age, in 1919 to 1921, his great-grandfather Thomas Woodson that, No. 1, he was said to be the son of Thomas Jefferson. . . ."

FROM OHIO: "Throughout the years, this has just been accepted fact. My grandfather, being a minister, was not one to fabricate such a story. The way I heard it, and as it has been passed down through the family, was that Grandfather's grandfather Thomas was the son of Thomas Jefferson and that Jefferson had sent him to Ohio and bought him a farm so that he would not have to be brought up in slavery. My grandfather and father told me that there was once a letter whereby Thomas Jefferson had written Thomas Woodson to ask him how he was doing in Ohio. . . ."

FROM TEXAS: "All of my life I've heard that my mother's family is descended from Thomas Jefferson. This information came from Aunt Minerva, my mother, and her brothers and sisters, and my maternal grandmother, who was given this information by my grandfather. . . . My sister and I were told that our great-great-grandfather was Thomas Woodson, and he was the son of Thomas Jefferson and his 'second wife.' We were told that the relationship between Thomas Jefferson and Sally was a wholesome one, and not a vulgar relationship of which we should be ashamed. We were told that foolish laws and regulations, stupid community mores, and the Jefferson family status would not permit Thomas Jefferson to marry Sally. He considered her as his wife. We were told that the family did not brag about our being descendants of Thomas Jefferson but that we must study hard, work hard, to establish our own identity and reputation as black people and carry on the rich tradition and heritage of our great-great-grandfather, Thomas Woodson."

When Robert Cooley sits down to discuss all this, he begins and ends the conversation with the biblical analogy that he can't help working over and over in his mind: "In my family especially, when you talk about the black Jeffersons and the white Jeffersons," he says at the outset, "we all attribute our parentage to Thomas Jefferson, which is similar to what Abraham did to the Arabs and the Jews." It is the Old Testament parable of embrace and rejection, of the center and the margins, of blood supposedly pure and tainted, and of the power of those bloodlines through generations. Abraham's illicit son Ishmael, born of the slave girl Hagar and banished into the desert, is taken by Arabs as their connection to the Patriarch; Abraham's son Isaac, born of his wife, Sarah, is taken by Jews as their forefather. As Cooley recognizes, one cannot talk about the parallel legends of the children of Jefferson, or about blacks and whites in America, without searching for the larger scale offered by biblical grandeur. As we finish and say our farewells, Cooley returns to Genesis in a parting remark: "I have thought so much about the parallel between Abraham and Ishmael, and Abraham and Isaac."

If there is any patriarch of the American idea, it is Thomas Jefferson. His declarations on individual liberty, which still serve as a moral and political compass, showed the brilliance of a transcendent mind. But he also embodied the most powerful contradiction of the American legacy. Not only did he own slaves (he inherited 20 from his father and 135 from his father-in-law), he also put into writing his belief in the racial inferiority of black people, demonstrating how even a great thinker can be a captive of the racism of his time. Just as his views on democracy have endured, so have his images of blacks, which came out of the context of his era and are echoed today in the stereotypes by which African-Americans continue to be afflicted.

That one man could simultaneously possess such vision and such blindness is intriguing; that his crosscurrents of attitude should persist in the culture at large, as they have, tells a troubling story about American society. Ennobled by democratic ideals and corroded by racism, Jefferson's legacy is also America's. "We routinely return to Jefferson and his era in order to discover the glory of America," wrote Charles A. Miller, a Jefferson scholar at Lake Forest College in Illinois. "We should also be willing to return in order to find early evidence of our distress." He added, "I believe that Jefferson was firmly—centrally and emblematically—in the stream of American anguish over slavery and race, and he knew it. I also believe that the present, in altered form, is like Jefferson."

In principle if not in practice, Jefferson showed no ambivalence about slavery. It undermined the morals and the liberties of the nation; it stood against divine righteousness and the inevitable turn of history. "I tremble for my country when I reflect that God is just; that justice cannot sleep for ever," he wrote in 1785 in his only book, *Notes on the State of Virginia*. Responding to an 1825 letter from his granddaughter Ellen Randolph Coolidge, who wrote from New England her impressions that in the South "The canker of slavery . . . diseases the whole body," Jefferson declared in agreement, "One fatal stain deforms what nature had bestowed on us of her fairest gifts." Years before, he had included a resounding denunciation of slavery in his draft of the Declaration of Independence:

> He [King George III] has waged cruel war against human nature itself, violating it's most sacred rights of life & liberty in the

persons of a distant people who never offended him, captivating &
carrying them into slavery in another hemisphere, or to incur
miserable death in their transportation thither. This piratical
warfare, the opprobrium of *infidel* powers, is the warfare of the
CHRISTIAN king of Great Britain. Determined to keep open a
market where MEN should be bought and sold, he has prostituted
his negative for suppressing every legislative attempt to prohibit
or to restrain this execrable commerce.

Regrettably, the Continental Congress deleted the passage from
the final version. Obviously pained by its removal, Jefferson included
it nonetheless, with an appropriate notation, in copies sent to those
with whom he corresponded. Had the denunciation of slavery been
retained, no doubt could have been raised that Jefferson intended blacks
to be encompassed by the Declaration's affirmation that all men are
created equal.

Jefferson was as complex as the society to which he gave direction.
He abhorred slavery but never abolished it, not as governor, not as president, not as plantation owner. The slaves he inherited came with thousands of acres of land that embedded him in the slavery-dependent
economy of eighteenth-century Virginia. And although he was no
businessman—his plantations were poorly run, and he died in debt—he
could not see a path for himself or his country out of the evil that had
been created. "He may have known a truth greater than he was," said
John Charles Thomas.

Jefferson regarded himself as benevolent, as indeed he was by the
standards of the day. He usually spared the whip. Although he did not
engage in commerce in slaves, he was so devoted to keeping families
together that he sometimes bought or sold a slave rather than allow a
couple to be separated. Still, he displayed a lack of foresight in writing
his will, which granted freedom to only five slaves. As a result, families
were split up as slaves were sold to pay Jefferson's debts. Joe Fossett, a
blacksmith, was freed by the will, but his wife and children were not, and
they were divided among at least four buyers. Fossett spent the next
decade scraping together enough money to reunite his wife and five of
their children by buying them himself. Such was Jefferson's contradictory legacy.

Most searing are Thomas Jefferson's observations on the supposed
inferiority of blacks. Writing in *Notes on the State of Virginia*, he endorses
virtually every stereotype—positive and negative—that today character-

izes the system of prejudices about black people physically, mentally, sexually, emotionally.

Observing blacks' "unfortunate difference of color," Jefferson constructs a hierarchy of physical beauty, with whites at the top, apes at the bottom, and blacks in between:

> The first difference which strikes us is that of color. . . . And is this difference of no importance? Is it not the foundation of a greater or less share of beauty in the two races? Are not the fine mixture of red and white, the expressions of every passion by greater or less suffusions of color in the one, preferable to that eternal monotony, which reigns in the countenances, that immovable veil of black which covers the emotions of the other race? Add to these, flowing hair, a more elegant symmetry of form, their own judgment in favor of the whites, declared by their preference of them, as uniformly as is the preference of the Oranootan for the black woman over those of his own species.

Jefferson engages in pseudoscience. "They secrete less by the kidneys," he writes, "and more by the glands of the skin, which gives them a very strong and disagreeable odor. This greater degree of transpiration, renders them more tolerant of heat, and less so of cold than the whites." He goes on to suggest a "difference of structure in the pulminary apparatus" as an explanation. "They seem to require less sleep," he continues. "A black after hard labor through the day, will be induced by the slightest amusements to sit up till midnight, or later, though knowing he must be out with the first dawn of the morning."

He ascribes to blacks markedly less ability than whites to anticipate consequences. "They are at least as brave, and more adventuresome," he writes. "But this may perhaps proceed from a want of forethought, which prevents their seeing a danger till it be present. When present, they do not go through it with more coolness or steadiness than the whites."

In his favorite example, recorded from conversation with a British diplomat in 1807, Jefferson described slaves carelessly misplacing their blankets as summer approached, in apparent thoughtlessness about the future turn of seasons. But another interpretation seems more plausible. In 1806, Jefferson had noted that for five years, an overseer at Monticello had "failed to distribute a single blanket," Lucia Stanton found. Knowing this, the slaves may have pretended to lose blankets that they were actually squirreling away, accumulating them in "the very opposite of what the master saw—an effort to prepare for an unpredictable future," she concluded.

An image of primitiveness runs through much of what Jefferson has to say about the sexuality, emotional capacity, and creative powers of black people. He writes:

> They are more ardent after their female; but love seems with them to be more an eager desire, than a tender delicate mixture of sentiment and sensation. Their griefs are transient. Those numberless afflictions, which render it doubtful whether heaven has given life to us in mercy or in wrath, are less felt, and sooner forgotten with them. In general, their existence appears to participate more of sensation than reflection. To this must be ascribed their disposition to sleep when abstracted from their diversions, and unemployed in labor. An animal whose body is at rest, and who does not reflect, must be disposed to sleep of course. Comparing them by their faculties of memory, reason, and imagination, it appears to me that in memory they are equal to the whites; in reason much inferior, as I think one could scarcely be found capable of tracing and comprehending the investigations of Euclid; and that in imagination they are dull, tasteless, and anomalous.

Jefferson struggles with the question of whether these imagined traits are innate to blacks or imposed by their servitude, a forerunner of today's muted and self-conscious debate over the role of racial genetics versus discrimination and poverty in shaping people's lives. Jefferson excuses black people's supposed "disposition to theft," attributing it to "their situation, and not to any depravity of the moral sense." He adds, "We find among them numerous instances of the most rigid integrity, of benevolence, gratitude, and unshaken fidelity." But in other matters, he oscillates between the two poles—the inherited and the acquired—as decisive for black people, asserting at one moment that "their inferiority is not the effect merely of their condition of life," then modifying his words to say that he puts forth this view "with great diffidence" and "as a suspicion only." In the sphere of intelligence and creativity, however, he tilts decidedly toward inborn characteristics as the explanation for what he observes:

> It will be right to make great allowances for the difference of condition, of education, of conversation, of the sphere in which they

move . . . yet many have been so situated, that they might have availed themselves of the conversation of their masters; many have been brought up to the handicraft arts, and from that circumstance have always been associated with the whites. Some have been liberally educated, and all have lived in countries where the arts and sciences are cultivated to a considerable degree, and all have had before their eyes samples of the best works from abroad. . . . But never yet could I find that a black had uttered a thought above the level of plain narration; never saw even an elementary trait of painting or sculpture. In music they are more generally gifted than the whites with accurate ears for tune and time, and they have been found capable of imagining a small catch. Whether they will be equal to the composition of a more extensive run of melody, or of complicated harmony, is yet to be proved. Misery is often the parent of the most affecting touches in poetry. Among the blacks is misery enough, God knows, but no poetry. Love is the peculiar oestrum of the poet. Their love is ardent, but it kindles the senses only, not the imagination. . . . The improvement of the blacks in body and mind, in the first instance of their mixture with the whites, has been observed by every one, and proves that their inferiority is not the effect merely of their condition of life. We know that among the Romans, about the Augustan age especially, the condition of their slaves was much more deplorable than that of the blacks on the continent of America. . . . [Nevertheless] their slaves were often their rarest artists. They excelled too in science, insomuch as to be usually employed as tutors to their master's children. . . . But they were of the race of whites. It is not their condition then, but nature, which has produced the distinction.

Such ugly suspicions, also tempered with diffidence, lurk deeply within mainstream white America today. They nag quietly at the platitudes and the fine principles and the professions of tolerance. As Jefferson demonstrated, they exist alongside an understanding of their damage to society.

Given his suffocating appraisals of black people's qualities, Jefferson could not imagine the integration of the races. He opposed racial mixing and intermarriage (which makes the Sally Hemings story all the more intriguing), and while he favored the abolition of slavery, he could not envision former slaves living freely among whites. In a 1789 letter, he wrote, "To give liberty to, or rather, to abandon persons whose habits have been formed in slavery is like abandoning children." He proposed that the United States establish a colony for blacks on the coast of Africa, provide patronage until they became self-sufficient, and replace them with voluntary white laborers from abroad.

"Why not retain and incorporate the blacks into the State?" he asks in *Notes on the State of Virginia*. He then gives his ominous answer: "Deep-rooted prejudices entertained by the whites; ten thousand recollections by the blacks, of the injuries they have sustained; new provocations; the real distinctions which nature has made; and many other circumstances, will divide us into parties, and produce convulsions, which will probably never end but in the extermination of the one or the other race."

These are the two histories of Jefferson, the two histories of America. If we face Jefferson, we face ourselves.

But one would never know from U.S. history courses, required in virtually every high school, that the most visionary thinker at the outset of the American experiment also created a seminal catalogue of stereotypes that are echoed in most of today's images and fears. The widely used and respected high school textbook *A History of the United States* by Pulitzer Prize–winning historian Daniel J. Boorstin and Brooks Mather Kelley, for example, discusses Jefferson's slave owning briefly but makes no mention of his images of blacks.

I have read Jefferson's words to many audiences, without identifying their author, and have then asked how many know whose words they are. Not many hands have gone up. At the World Affairs Council in Philadelphia, in a group of 200 highly educated, well-traveled people, only 3 could say. At a fund-raiser for the Nevada State Library in Carson City, the figure was just 6 of 150. Only 3 knew in a training course of about 25 journalists who cover racial and ethnic issues across the country. And only 3 of 65 members of the Executive Committee of the Anti-Defamation League of B'nai B'rith knew that the passages were Jefferson's. At Milton Academy, an elite private school outside Boston, a cluster of hands went up from the faculty, but only 5 or 6 among the 600 students. Invariably, when the question is asked and the name "Thomas Jefferson" is finally pronounced, a gasp sweeps over the mostly white groups. Blacks seem less amazed; many already understand how extensively the American myth is pockmarked by one ellipsis after another, and some have been told about Jefferson by their black high school history teachers.

Some Jefferson defenders label the condemnation of his racist writings as "presentism," meaning an unjust imposition of present-day standards on a distant and very different past. The argument has some merit. But even during his lifetime, Jefferson was called to account for his views. On March 12, 1791, the *Georgetown Weekly Ledger*, reporting on the team that was doing the original survey of Washington, D.C., noted that one of its members, a free black man named Benjamin Banneker, was "an Ethiopian whose abilities as surveyor and astronomer already prove that Mr. Jefferson's concluding that that race of men were void of mental endowment was without foundation." Banneker wrote to Jefferson in the same year:

> Suffer me to recall to your mind that time, in which the arms of the British crown were exerted, with every powerful effort, in order to reduce you to a state of servitude; look back, I entreat you. . . . You were then impressed with proper ideas of the great violation of liberty, and the free possession of those blessings, to which you were entitled by nature; but, sir, how pitiable is it to reflect, that although you were so fully convinced of the benevolence of the Father of Mankind, and of his equal and impartial distribution of these rights and privileges which he hath conferred upon them, that you should at the same time counteract his mercies, in detaining by fraud and violence, so numerous a part of my brethren under groaning captivity and cruel oppression, that you should at the same time be found guilty of that most criminal act, which you professedly detested in others.

An op-ed piece of mine for *The New York Times*, quoting extensively from *Notes on the State of Virginia*, generated a letter and a phone call that resolved any temptation to think of Jefferson's prejudices as extinct. A man in Brooklyn, giving his name and address, wrote by hand in bold letters, with appropriate underlining:

4-12-93

DEAR MR. SHIPLER —

REGARDING YOUR ARTICLE IN TODAY'S NEW YORK TIMES, <u>YOU KNOW THE TRUTH</u>! IT'S THERE, IN YOUR HEART. IT LIES DEEP, DEEP DOWN WHERE YOU'VE BURIED IT, HOPING TO HIDE IT FOREVER FROM THE WORLD AND YOUR OWN SELF. WHO DO YOU THINK YOU'RE KIDDING? <u>YOU KNOW THE TRUTH ABOUT THE</u>

BLACKS! LOOK DEEP INTO YOUR OWN HEART, MR. SHIPLER, IF
YOU DARE, IF YOU CAN SUMMON UP THE COURAGE. YOU KNOW!!

Another New Yorker called and began by asking, "Did you ever consider the possibility that Jefferson was correct?"

He was a Harvard man, he said, both undergraduate and graduate.
He had been a volunteer in Harlem from 1969 to 1970, trying to teach
reading to black youngsters ages ten to twelve. As a result, he agreed
with Jefferson's assertion that blacks were "much inferior" to whites in
reasoning ability and that "one could scarcely be found capable of
tracing and comprehending the investigations of Euclid," as Jefferson
had put it.

The children "didn't know the alphabet," the caller said; he displayed
little insight into whose fault that might have been. "I have never seen
any evidence of affinity for mathematics by blacks," he declared. As for
Jefferson's assessment of blacks' musical skills and lack of poetry, he continued, "There may be some black poets out there, but in music they
certainly appear to be very gifted and generously rewarded for being
gifted. There are so many black musicians and entertainers, certainly far
out of proportion to black physicists. I don't think that observation of
Jefferson is different than what we'd make today, or racist, or unfair. All
you've got to do is turn on the television."

Genetics explained practically everything for this man, providing an
easy analysis of the world order. "Everywhere you go, blacks are always
forming an underclass," he said. "Europe, North Africa. They're the
underclass, and there's always some historical reason that everybody
believes in. My interpretation is that Africans are different genetically, as
are many different races, as are Asians, and as Jews seem to be. . . . From
what I understand, there are very few African written languages, and that
a lot of these things that we take for granted, like writing, mathematics,
geometry, papermaking, the wheel, metallurgy, astronomy, navigation,
shipbuilding, these things didn't spring up on African soil. The Middle
East maybe, North Africa perhaps. What does that tell us? An accident?
Mistake? I mean, I just think that there's this reluctance to understand
the difference between African peoples and European peoples and Asian
peoples and Hebraic peoples. These are very great differences, and why
[should] a person be accused of being a racist for drawing these simple
conclusions?"

· · ·

When Michele March read my op-ed piece on Jefferson's racist writings, she was outraged and delighted, stricken that Jefferson had expressed such bigotry and deeply pleased that I had put it into the sunlight again for all to see. As an African-American member of the Bergen County Human Relations Commission, March was a highly visible activist in Teaneck, New Jersey, and she decided to help organize a movement to rename Thomas Jefferson Middle School after Harriet Tubman or Frederick Douglass or Sojourner Truth.

"We felt that if you honor a slave master, how can you not honor an American slave?" she said. The rhetorical question seemed simple to her, but not to others. In fewer than five days, she and her group gathered six hundred signatures on a petition, but they made a tactical error right on the fault line of the black-white divide over history. Even those whites who supported naming schools for African-Americans could not bring themselves to sign a document that would shatter the icon of Jefferson. March and her organizers failed to comprehend the great weight of that symbol. "Jefferson doesn't mean the same thing to black people as he does to white people, and I didn't know that," she admitted. "We didn't know this was going to start such hoopla."

A "renaming committee" of town residents was formed by the board of education to consider alternatives to some of the white males whose names now graced all the schools. It drew up lists of black slaves, civil rights leaders, contemporary black achievers. It considered naming schools after Jews and American Indians and women. But in the end, its black members and its white members could not agree. The seven blacks all voted to recommend changes in the names of at least some, if not all, of the schools; they were joined by only one white. A list of possible names, forwarded to the board of education, was ignored, and the schools' names remained unchanged.

I had not intended for Jefferson to be deleted from anybody's consciousness, of course, but rather for all of Jefferson to be absorbed—not to minimize his contributions to liberty but to inscribe the man's acute contradictions on our monuments of memory. That way, we could recognize where we really came from and deal with the competing impulses in American society. Again, if we face Jefferson, we face ourselves.

Many blacks, as well as whites, hesitate along the way toward honesty in looking at slavery. After decades of ignoring the fact that slaves made up at least half of colonial Williamsburg's population, after pressure from

historians, after due soul-searching by the proprietors of the reconstructed village, the tourist attraction gradually introduced black actors
in the 1970s to portray slaves and in the autumn of 1994 held a mock
slave auction. But it hardly won accolades from civil rights groups, which
were poised to denounce the performance even before it began. Protes-
tors broke into "We Shall Overcome." Demonstrators from the NAACP
and the Southern Christian Leadership Conference held signs and condemned the reenactment in advance as a degradation, a trivialization of
the African-American experience.

Then four black staff members from Williamsburg's African-
American Research Department played the parts of slaves, weeping as
their loved ones were dispatched by an auctioneer who pronounced the
word "sold" in cold finality. Afterward, one of the "slaves" answered
questions, describing how runaways were punished, how children were
forced to work in the fields. Despite the protests, some blacks in the
crowd thought it was important to emphasize the crimes and to
remember the triumphs of survival. When it was over, Robert Watson
Jr., who portrayed a slave named Billy, had a last comment: "Living history is hard on a lot of people."

Hard but necessary, Gerald Talbot says. On his wall in Portland,
Maine, he has a ten-foot wrought-iron chain and neck shackle from a
slave ship, marked with the year 1670. He bought it at an auction in
Kennebunkport, one of dozens of artifacts of a dishonorable past that he
has hunted down and usually paid for dearly. Scanning newspaper advertisements in the late 1980s, he spotted a list of items being sold from
abandoned safe-deposit boxes; included was the 1925 charter of a Ku
Klux Klan chapter in Androscoggin County, and he wanted it badly.

A small crowd had gathered, and the auctioneer asked for a bid of
$100. He was met by silence. He called for $50. Silence. Down to $25,
and Talbot made a bid. Someone behind him countered with a higher
offer, and the race was on, pushing the price back up to $100 and then
beyond, ending with Talbot's successful bid of $145 for the Ku Klux
Klan's charter. "It has about twelve names," he said. "It's a very beautifully done document, a large document, and I had it framed."

Talbot collects such memorabilia because he is a black man in one of
the whitest states in the union, where schoolchildren get little exposure
to black history. And so he takes the tangible evidence to schools—a pair
of hand shackles, a leg iron, the chain from the slave ship. "I lay it out on
the table," he said, "and they come around, and they can touch it, and
they can feel it, and they can see it. I've been all over the state. I take the

position that this is a part of our history, and it is a part of our history that we have to know. A lot of it is graphic, a lot of it is derogatory and painful, but that is our history, and our grandparents lived through this and put up with it and got me to where I am today."

He is now in his sixties. His ancestors on his father's side were slaves in Massachusetts; his mother's came from Canada. Some ended up free in the early 1700s, owning a brickyard in what was then Harlem, Maine, and is now the town of China, a change of names he could not explain. Other name changes, however, were instigated by Talbot himself after a startling discovery in a library. Thumbing through a book of maps, he found seven places in Maine with the word "nigger" in their names: Nigger Ridge, Nigger Lake, Nigger Creek, and so on. He began a campaign to get the offensive word deleted, got endless runarounds from state authorities, and finally won a seat in the legislature; from that position, he managed to get a bill passed eliminating the epithet in all seven cases. Some local people resisted, arguing that the place had always been called that; the state had to threaten to sue before folks up in Presque Isle would abandon the name Nigger Lake. It was 1974.

Racial history in America is so heavily laden with shame and yearning that whites and blacks often behave clumsily with each other about the past, even when no malice seems present. They grope for a handhold on the story, reaching to control the interpretation and thereby tame the grief and outrage of what has gone before. Such a drama was played out when private developers, first in Boston, then in Tampa, Florida, tried to design a pirate theme park around the replica of a ship, the *Whydah*, which had carried slaves on its maiden voyage before being commandeered by a multiracial crew of pirates under Samuel Bellamy, alias Black Sam. The *Whydah* had sunk off Massachusetts in 1717 and was discovered in 1984 by a salvage company, which recovered the bell, cannons, and other metallic objects, though nothing relating to the slave trade.

The idea of reconstructing such a vessel as a pirate ship, while virtually ignoring its role as a slaver, touched off opposition in Boston. So the developers tried Tampa, which had been celebrating piracy with an extravagant annual festival. Tampa's white-dominated business and political structure, thinking of tourism, not sensibilities, embraced the theme park, in which actors were to play pirates. Only as visitors were leaving would there have been a static representation of the *Whydah*'s involvement in the slave trade—"an afterthought," said Claudine K. Brown, deputy assistant provost for arts and humanities at the Smithsonian.

She and other African-American historians were brought in to comment on the proposal after it provoked a confusion of protests and disagreements among black people in Tampa. The panel of historians urged in 1993 that it be "revised, rethought, and renamed." The developers then agreed to portray more fully the ship's role in transporting slaves and to give African-American specialists responsibility for shaping the interpretation. In the end, however, major elements of Tampa's black community remained opposed, and the entire project was scrapped.

"The public felt distrustful," Brown said. "They felt that the middle passage shouldn't be treated in a theme park environment. They felt it should be treated with reverence and respect. People take the issue very seriously, and anytime anybody approaches it as entertainment, it's anathema, and you lose support."

Another historian, Molefi Kete Asante of Temple University, thought the project "might be useful in explaining and interpreting some portion of African-American history." But because it was "controlled by white people," he said, it generated anger that could not be overcome by belatedly inviting blacks' involvement. Furthermore, the portrayal of the multiracial crew of pirates as "just a happy group of people raiding ships" with no racial tension among them had drawn ridicule from some Tampa blacks, Asante reported. The idea that there could be "some kind of special relationship" between blacks and whites during that period of slavery was something "most people didn't believe happened," he observed.

A different analysis was offered by the project's administrative director, Jack Batman of Silver Screen Partners in New York, who concluded that the black community simply did not want the story told. "It had no slaves on it when it was taken by the pirates," he explained. "But twenty-five of the *Whydah* pirates were black freemen. The black community doesn't want that. If you're going to tell a story about free black men, they don't necessarily want the free black men to be pirates. . . . I was not quite aware that the black community doesn't want to remember the story. It seems to me that that is the case."

Perhaps. But for many African-Americans, the past is too freshly felt in the present to be entrusted to white hands. History isn't just a great yarn that you get to hear by paying admission. It is the stuff of honor, the raw material of respect. Many black people, still struggling to be accorded these qualities, take their past with a delicate, angry ambivalence, with an anxious reverence that is ever alert to profane variations. When the Walt Disney Company planned an historical theme park near the Civil War battlefield of Manassas, Virginia, for example, part of the opposition—from white and black historians alike—focused on a concern that slavery and other elements of the American past would be cheapened for the sake of entertainment. Disney ultimately withdrew.

Even whites who try sincerely are often tripped up by an absence of sound instincts. In the little town of Atglen, Pennsylvania, a white teacher named Mary Horning decided in 1993 to mark Martin Luther King Jr.'s birthday by demonstrating to her first-graders "how unfair it is to judge people by the color of their skin," in her words. So she picked the only two black pupils in her class, had them climb up on a table at the front of the room, and proceeded to act out a mock slave auction. The teacher told little Ashley Dixon that she would have been worth about $10 as a housecleaner, the child said. When the youngsters described the incident to a group of parents, teachers, and administrators, outrage boiled up among both blacks and whites. Horning apologized, the Justice Department's Community Relations Service mediated the dispute, an investigation by the Pennsylvania Human Relations Commission found no acts of racism, and the Octarara Area School District instituted an affirmative-action hiring program and a multicultural history curriculum, according to its superintendent, Tim Daniels.

"We diversified our hiring," he said. "We've adopted an exemplary diversity curriculum that features various nationalities—Japan, France, various African countries—in different grade clusters, so every kid coming through will have the total spectrum." And Mary Horning continued to teach.

A diminished sense of history diminishes the sense of responsibility for racial ills. If Americans do not tune in to the reverberations of the past, a gulf is opened between the present and its origins. To Steve Suitts, that gap has recently developed, at least in the South. "There clearly is no way in which the newer generations, the younger generations at this point, can understand how their relations and how the relations of others are profoundly shaped by what has been the nation's and their communities' past," he says with a gentle drawl. "And that is new. You did understand, you always understood. It was the most facile explanation for why segregation could exist: because it's always been. . . . And that whole appreciation for how what *is* is built upon what *was* has been obliterated by the new references by which people come to shape their own race relations."

If a young white person can choose friends without regard to race,

Suitts explains, and can choose to admire black entertainers and put posters of black athletes up in his room, he somehow transcends the past. "That pretty well means that I have no personal responsibility for the fact that 60 percent of the black kids in this country, or in my state, are poor," Suitts says. "That's their problem, not my problem. That seems to me the ultimate result of this lack of personal responsibility. And whether you liked it or not, when I was growing up and became at least old enough to analyze it, you understood that if you weren't responsible for something, your papa was, or your grandpapa. The obvious nature of segregation required compliance; it required complicity. It required everybody to say, 'We ain't gonna do anything about it.' It was in the laws, and we knew we could change them if we wanted to. So there was always this sense that there was a personal responsibility there. And I think that sense of personal responsibility has quickly disappeared."

The Myths of America

In the Soviet Union under communism, history was such a powerful commodity that the government and the Communist Party sought to possess it absolutely, altering its presentation as each former leader fell into disrepute. This led to a sardonic little riddle that the Russians used to tell:

> QUESTION: What is the definition of a Soviet historian?
> ANSWER: A person who can predict the past.

Although history in the United States is not government-controlled, an open society generates versions of the past the same way an organism develops defenses to cope with climate and disease. History has power, and rival interpreters in this country strive to possess it. As growing numbers of ethnic and racial groups accentuate their particular identities apart from the American whole, a struggle over history has erupted on talk shows and campuses, in museums and newsrooms, and inside people's basic assumptions about how the world looks.

Put simply, the question is how white the portrayal of the American past should be. From that beginning comes the question of how white the portrayal of the global past should be. The debate, played out along the black-white racial line, is more than an intellectual game. It is a drive for self-knowledge and esteem. It is a contest for control. It is, sadly, another method of defining one's own group by denigrating another.

And for many African-Americans, it has created a subculture of historical views entirely separate from the white-dominated versions. Armed with a set of alternative concepts about the past, many blacks describe a cynical, bifurcated mind-set: They have to get along in the white, "Eurocentric" world while subscribing privately to an "Afrocentric" perspective.

The technique was outlined by Lawrance Evans, the Colgate sophomore. "We are willing to say that Columbus discovered America. We are willing to say that the Greeks fathered philosophy. We are willing to perpetuate any white lies that we read in books because we want to succeed. [A] dean told us, 'You take two sets of notes—one for whatever insanity they're teaching you and one to keep your own sanity.' " As a student at Monroe High School in Rochester, New York, Evans recalled, "when I sat in the social studies class and they told me Columbus discovered America, 'OK, I'll write it down on your test, I'll get an A on your test, I'll bust your test out, but in reality I realize that you're just feeding me another white lie.' "

At the University of Nebraska, Walter Gholson, who had gone back to college in his forties and was about to get his degree, had avoided the required course in Western civilization as long as he could but now was excusing himself from a roundtable discussion to go take an exam. He had a salt-and-pepper beard and steel-rimmed glasses, and on his lapel he wore a red, black, and green pin in the shape of Africa.

"Western Civilization, a piece of cake," he said as he got up. I wished him good luck. "You got to lie," he shot back. "You can't tell the truth." And then he was out the door. He reminded me of the freethinking Soviet students I had known, who had learned one set of facts around the kitchen table but knew what they were required to say in school.

When Gholson returned after forty-five minutes, however, and I asked him and other black students in the room for some examples of lies they had had to write on exams, they couldn't think of a single one. What emerged instead from the core of their frustration were the silences in the telling of history.

"I just took this exam, OK," said Gholson, "and the only references to anything relevant to me were references to apartheid, and the answers were simple. I would have hoped that on one of the essay exams there was something that I could have elaborated on, based on imperialism, based on colonialism, based on the destruction of traditional African society. But there was nothing on there."

That was also Tamika Simmons's complaint about Western Civilization. "It's a course about white people, from the very beginning to the very end," she said, "and they leave us out entirely." Similarly, in a course on the history of the mass media, "we spent one class period talking about the contributions of black Americans. One class period!"

To Gholson, the omissions served a purpose. "You want to build a positive perspective with white students about their culture, so consequently, you really can't clutter up their minds with all this extra information that's not relevant to them," he said. "But what it does is a disservice to white students and fosters their belief that black people are inferior."

The uses of history are legion, to both honorable and nefarious ends. They serve to elevate or to derogate, to move a people to the center or to the margins of achievement, to paint broad groups with qualities of enterprise or failure. Like religion, history appears immutable but is quite malleable and can surround a wicked idea with an aura of legitimacy. So the silences that the Nebraska students felt have had their function.

"There are many, many ways to destroy people," said Charles Hines, a black major general in the army. "You can destroy them in Tiananmen Square with tanks. You can destroy them with shotguns in Soweto. You can destroy them in the ovens of Auschwitz and Belsen. You can destroy them by simply removing them from the literature." He said this very quietly, almost gently.

For most of the century, and perhaps for most of the country today, blacks have been left at the periphery of the American story. The impression they make in textbooks, required high school courses, films, museums, and the like is most vivid in slavery and then in the civil rights movement, and they are therefore remembered not as writers or inventors or cavalry riders who helped to win the West; they are remembered mainly as victims, first brutalized, then ennobled by their suffering and their struggle. Many black youngsters take from the images of slavery only a sense of incapacity.

"You're taught in school that blacks were inferior, they were slaves," said a black woman at Lincoln University, "and you get all these negative things coming out toward you. And you being black, you wouldn't have any high aspirations. So you'll become a thief."

In Brooklyn, a black high school girl also absorbed a subliminal message from her mainstream history courses; even if it wasn't intended, it was perceived. "They would never talk about Africa," she said. "They would always talk about the accomplishments blacks made in America—

like they civilized us. . . . It seems like the only time we did something was when we came here, and we had nothing in Africa. The only time we had something was when we got to America. They civilized us and they made us what we were, which was not true at all."

Kwanza Jones, a black student at Princeton, had the same complaint and made a plea. "Can't we be included in the history books just a little bit more than just as slaves or than just during the civil rights movement?" she asked.

That slave-and-civil-rights portrayal makes a severe impact. It pricks the consciences of whites, tells a tale of redemption, and relegates African-Americans to a role comfortably apart. As long as they are victims, blacks do not threaten to acquire any of the whites' credit for building America. That has been the white story.

The emerging black story is quite different. It seeks to put African-Americans into the mainstream of the country's intellectual, scientific, and practical creativity and sometimes to assert that whites stole from blacks' achievements. In its most Afrocentric forms, it searches for a reconnection with Africa and pictures ancient Egypt as a black African wellspring of Western civilization. The black story has begun to have an effect on the white story, which now fills some of the silences, especially in American history.

The invisibility of blacks in the American mainstream is being corrected in fits and starts, in pockets of public discussion and display. Often the vehicle is Black History Month, which evolved in the sixties from Negro History Week, founded in February 1926 by the African-American historian Carter G. Woodson to embrace the birthdays of Abraham Lincoln and Frederick Douglass. "Do not let the role which you have played be obscured," Woodson advised, "while others write themselves into the foreground of our story."

Woodson spent a career digging out facts about African-American accomplishments and uncovered some misdeeds by blacks, as well as whites. Among his documents, which were placed on display in February 1992 by the Library of Congress, was an 1809 bill of sale for a slave named John for $231—from Thomas Jefferson to James Madison. Census and tax receipts from Woodson's collection also showed that considerable numbers of free blacks owned slaves in 1830. Husbands sometimes owned wives to control them, and he documented one man's sale of his wife because she was difficult to live with. He made a $50 profit.

Woodson's papers threw a spotlight on little-known black entrepreneurs, such as Warren C. Coleman, who had been born a slave and eventually employed some three hundred blacks and a few whites in a large cotton mill he founded in 1896 in Concord, North Carolina. The exhibit offered information on the 24th and 25th Colored Infantry, which helped rescue the Rough Riders at San Juan Hill on July 2, 1898. It included correspondence about Lieutenant Henry Ossian Flipper, the first black graduate of West Point, in 1877, who commanded white troops and was unjustly dismissed from the army in 1882, and about another black soldier, Christian A. Fleetwood, who had won the Medal of Honor during the Civil War and then submitted an eloquent letter of resignation when neither he nor any member of his exceptional unit was made an officer.

One telling item in the collection was a form distributed by the U.S. Patent Office in 1913, asking for information about black patent holders for an exhibition on the fiftieth anniversary of the Emancipation Proclamation. E. J. Nolan, a Chattanooga attorney, had written on the form, "I never knew a Negro to even suggest a new idea, much less to patent one. And I have dealt with them all my life." Then he added a P.S.: "I have asked other lawyers around here for data of Negro inventions, and they take it as a joke."

Nolan was quite wrong, but in 1913 most other whites probably shared his ignorance, and perhaps do even today. Only in the last decade or so have black inventors and patent holders been celebrated, their accomplishments publicized. They have become the backbone of a broad revisionist effort to look again at the history of blacks in the United States, to take them beyond their traditional roles as slaves, civil rights leaders, athletes, and entertainers and place them squarely in the mainstream of science and technology.

These efforts have filtered into many quarters. When my son Michael wanted to do a Black History Month project on Jackie Robinson, his white sixth-grade teacher didn't want him stuck in such familiar territory. She thought he should learn about somebody other than an athlete, so she told him he could write about Robinson only if he also wrote about a black inventor, for example. Michael chose Garrett A. Morgan, the son of a slave, who invented a gas mask, which he patented in 1914 as a "breathing machine." He also invented a forerunner of the traffic light: an electric signal that raised and lowered STOP and GO signs and, unlike its predecessors, had a half-mast position that later became the yellow light. He sold his 1923 patent to General Electric for $40,000.

Michael could also have chosen Norbert Rillieux, a biracial resident of New Orleans who developed an improved evaporator for sugar refining, or Granville T. Woods, who invented a steam boiler furnace, a telephone transmitter, a telegraphic relay, and an electromagnetic brake for railroad cars in the late 1800s. Or he could have picked Lewis H. Latimer, who bought secondhand drafting tools, drew telephone parts for Alexander Graham Bell's patent applications, won a patent in 1881 for a process to carbonize lightbulb filaments, and went to work in 1883 as chief draftsman and patent expert for Thomas A. Edison.

The U.S. Postal Service has helped call attention to accomplished, little-known black people by featuring them on postage stamps. In 1994, a stamp was issued to fill a gap in one of America's most cherished pieces of history; it honored Bill Pickett, a black cowboy and rodeo star who lived from 1870 to 1932 and originated bulldogging, the art of twisting a steer to the ground.

Otherwise, try to find black cowboys in a shoot-'em-up account of the Old West or a traditional John Wayne–type western. According to William Loren Katz, the author of numerous books on the West, "a fifth of the United States Cavalry who rode to the rescue were the Buffalo Soldiers, the 9th and 10th Cavalry regiments, United States Colored Troops. Almost a third of the cowhands who drove cattle up the Chisholm Trail after the Civil War were African-Americans; 30 all-black towns sprouted in Oklahoma alone between 1890 and 1910, and from the first days of slavery thousands of African-Americans joined Indian nations." Katz noted that the 1951 film *Tomahawk* had cast a white actor, Jack Oakie, as the black pathfinder Jim Beckworth, who discovered Beckworth Pass through the Sierra Nevada in 1850 and became a Crow Indian leader. "*Tomahawk* audiences learned Beckworth was a prominent frontiersman, but not that he was a black man," Katz complained.

A corrective step was taken in 1992, when the army erected a monument at Fort Leavenworth, Kansas, to the two black cavalry and two black infantry regiments that had patrolled and fought for vast reaches of the West. In 1993, Mario Van Peebles introduced a racially mixed cast for his western *Posse.*

Other fragments of recognition are now scattered across the American landscape. *Glory*, a film about a black unit in the Civil War, won two Oscars, and a memorial to blacks who fought in the Civil War was commissioned in Washington, D.C. The National Civil Rights Museum has opened in Memphis and the Negro Leagues Baseball Museum in Kansas City; Ken Burns included extensive discussion of the Negro Leagues in his major 1994 PBS series, *Baseball.*

In February 1990, at the Syracuse airport, a little glass case was set up for a small exhibition on black pilots. A picture of a biplane—with insets

of the pilot, J. Herman Banning, and the mechanic, Thomas C. Allen—
was labeled FIRST TRANS-CONTINENTAL FLIGHT, meaning the first by a
black aviator. It took nearly three weeks from Los Angeles to New York,
from September 19 to October 9, 1932.

In Louisville, the Derby Museum put together an exhibit on black
jockeys, who had brought equestrian skills from West Africa and heavily
influenced horse racing on the North American continent. Slaves had
won their freedom in races here, the exhibit explained, and black jockeys
had dominated the first eleven years of the Kentucky Derby. They had
been edged out in the early 1900s, when pari-mutuel betting had begun
to make the race lucrative. No African-American has ridden in the
Derby since 1921.

Most readers of this book will not have known that black Americans
were colleagues of Bell and Edison, invented ingenious machines and
laborsaving devices, fought at San Juan Hill, helped tame the western
wilderness, starred in rodeos, made an early flight from coast to coast,
and helped shape American horse racing. And that lack of knowledge
simply proves the point: In the white memory, which has been the dominant memory, blacks are usually absent. They just do not figure in the
American story, except as slaves, as reminders of our guilt. And nobody
likes to be reminded of guilt.

At 8:27 a.m., in room 356 of Oak Park and River Forest High School,
just west of Chicago, an electronic tone over the loudspeakers signaled
the beginning of first period. Michael Averbach wrote on the board:

1. Du Bois background
2. His strategy
3. Positive and negative parts
4. Du Bois vs. Washington

He was a tall, fairly young white man with a pleasant manner and a
nice touch for bringing the class into a discussion. The walls of the room
were plastered with *Newsweek* covers, and the desks were arranged in a
U shape. Averbach paced around from the blackboard to the other end
of the room, sometimes leaning against the back wall, sometimes sitting
down at an empty desk among the students, always speaking in the historical present tense to embrace his class in the moment. "He's as educated as anyone in the whole country in the late nineteenth century,"
Averbach declared. "Du Bois is sort of a dandy. It's an old word. He's

sort of spiffy. He walks with a cane. Du Bois has almost an aristocratic air about him."

Averbach was setting the stage for a lesson on an important piece of intellectual history—the debate between W. E. B. Du Bois and Booker T. Washington about whether black people should press for full rights and integration into society, as Du Bois argued, or stress the self-help approach of agricultural and industrial education, as Washington urged.

But this was not American History, a course required of all students. This was African-American History, an elective, and in this mostly white school, all but five of the twenty-four in Averbach's class were black. Since no whites at all had enrolled in the initial offering several years before, the current number gratified him. "It's come to be a nicely mixed group," he said. "Now we're getting a nice, truly integrated bunch." But with 1,818 white students at the school, five per semester didn't add up to much white contact with black history. By and large, they wouldn't be getting it in their regular history classes; the notion of integrating black history into the main American history courses had never been discussed by the History Department. "It's very decentralized here," Averbach explained. "You're really treated very professionally. We can assume you can do the job: Just step in the classroom and do it. So every history class is taught differently." And most of the teachers, who did not have Averbach's graduate school background of black history as a minor field, did not include much of the subject in their required courses.

As a separate class, African-American history "is legitimate by itself," Averbach said. "But there should be even more inclusion in the central course, because it's an essential part of the story. It's not peripheral. It's an essential part of the story. You can't understand American history without understanding this stuff."

The situation is repeated across the country. At Bethesda–Chevy Chase High School in Maryland, all but four of the students in my son Michael's Black Experience class were black, and the American history courses gave short shrift to the black story. At universities where African-American studies courses or departments have been established, they have been flooded by blacks, but only a trickle of white students have signed up. This means that because of the virtual segregation of black history into its own niche in the curriculum, blacks and whites are learning different stories, even within the same institution. Despite considerable attention to "multicultural" curricula, the seepage of the black story into the main American history courses has been minimal, and so most whites still go through school without much sense that a black intellectual life has existed. They get virtually no academic exposure to the range and depth of black experience in America.

On the black side of the segregated curriculum, courses and writings in African-American and African history vary in quality. Averbach's seemed to exemplify the finest. Others, less carefully grounded in rigorous scholarship, have set historical knowledge adrift on a wild sea of uncertainties where facts (or what used to be considered facts) are tossed about in a storm of exaggeration and then submerged by new truths or new myths, depending on the viewpoint.

Take Benjamin Banneker, the self-taught mathematician and astronomer who participated in the original survey of Washington, D.C. As recounted in the *Dictionary of American Negro Biography*, a standard reference work edited by two Howard University professors, Banneker was tapped by the surveyor, Major Andrew Ellicott, to fill in as an assistant in the observatory tent, making astronomical observations and monitoring the clock, until Ellicott's brothers could arrive from a job in New York. Banneker worked from February to April 1791, then returned to his home in Baltimore County and began publishing an almanac, which first appeared in December 1791. He also built a striking clock whose gears he carved from wood.

The Banneker story, impressive as it was, got embellished in 1987, when the public school system in Portland, Oregon, published *African-American Baseline Essays*, a thick stack of loose-leaf background papers for teachers, commissioned to encourage black history instruction. They have been used in Detroit, Atlanta, Fort Lauderdale, Newark, and scattered schools elsewhere, although they have been attacked for gross inaccuracy in an entire literature of detailed criticism by respected historians.

In the science section of the *Essays*, Banneker goes from assistant in the observatory tent to surveyor. "Secretary of State and slave owner Thomas Jefferson appointed Banneker to survey the site for the capital, Washington, D.C., shortly after reading a copy of his almanac," says the paper. Banneker's wooden clock becomes "America's first clock" (although the Smithsonian's National Museum of American History traces American clock making back to Benjamin Cheney of East Hartford, Connecticut, in 1745, when Banneker was fourteen years old). A slightly grander story is told in the mathematics section of the *Essays*: "George Washington heard of Banneker's skills and called him to Washington to be one of a team of three to draw up plans for the nation's new capital."

In February 1992, Banneker was elevated again by the Potomac Electric Power Company's monthly newsletter, *Lines,* sent to its 700,000 customers in the Washington, D.C., area with their bills. Banneker "was on the survey team that laid out Pierre L'Enfant's plans for Washington, D.C.," says a front-page article marking Black History Month. "When Major L'Enfant left the project and returned to Paris, taking the plans with him, Banneker reproduced them from memory, making possible the completed survey of what would become the nation's capital." Susan Moyer, senior writer for the newsletter, had gotten the information from a book whose title she couldn't recall, she said, and she had found the same story in student workbooks. It is widely believed by African-Americans.

She quickly learned of her error. "I got several letters, one from the head of architecture at Howard University," she said. Chastened, Moyer found a definitive biography, and she ran an apology two months later with the more modest version contained in the *Dictionary of American Negro Biography.* "I was a researcher; I knew better," she said contritely. "I did not go back to original sources."

She had looked up Banneker in a couple of encyclopedias and couldn't find the account, which might have set off an alarm bell—but not necessarily, for in the case of blacks, absence does not prove a negative; they have been omitted from much standard historical material. And this is precisely the problem: The practice of omission, and the undocumented nature of so much black-white interaction, renders truth elusive and gives license to the makers of myths.

The vacuum allows room for variations that reinforce the image of whites as cruel and exploitative. Such a case involves Lewis Latimer. The embellished story was told one morning by an African-American girl at Edward R. Murrow High School in Brooklyn, while a group of other black students filled in details and nodded affirmatively. In her version, Thomas Edison was an opportunistic white man who exploited Latimer, stole his ideas, and claimed them as his own. "Other people helped Edison," she said. "The person who made the part—some part, I don't remember—the wick?"

"That's in a candle," said another youngster, and a chorus of voices shouted, "The filament!"

"Edison was sued," the girl continued. "You never learn about that. The only reason I know about that is because I was listening to a radio show."

Historians can show through documentation that in 1879 Edison developed various carbonized filaments of thread and cardboard, and that Latimer received a patent for his process of carbonizing filaments in

1881, two years before he went to work for Edison. Later, Latimer also wrote a classic guide for lighting engineers, *Incandescent Electric Lighting: A Practical Description of the Edison System.* But no documents can capture the full give-and-take in Edison's laboratory, the unrecorded conversations and exchange of ideas that must have filled the days. There is no way to prove absolutely that Edison never expropriated anything of Latimer's. So if you want to believe, you can believe.

Beliefs are windows into people's deepest pain. If many African-Americans are ready to turn white society's reverence for Edison into yet another tale of the white man cheating the black, it is a statement of agony and rage. If most whites would be surprised to learn that a brilliant black man even served on Edison's team, it is a confession of myopia and ignorance. Silence, answered by fabrication, conveys a kind of suffering on both sides, the kind that comes from missing the full richness of truth.

Blacks' exaggerations are as pernicious as whites' silences, for when the myth about the black historical figure is not reported by the white texts, racism and theft are charged. Two black students at Lexington High School in Massachusetts demonstrated the point.

"A lot of the things that are said to be invented by the white man at the time were actually done by black men," insisted Sadada Jackson, a gum-chewing sophomore. "And I think that if they started exploring black history, they'd have to write the whole history book over again, and I think that's more or less the fear."

"The reason why we didn't, as a black race, put out those inventions was that we were slaves," said another student, Charles, as he ate pretzels from a plastic bag. "We never had the chance to put out an idea. And if you had an idea, it was taken. You never had the money, I guess, to produce the product. That's why a lot of the times the ideas were taken by people who had the money."

A story widely accepted among blacks about Dr. Charles R. Drew illustrates how powerful the appeal of a racial legend can be. Drew was a surgeon and a leading developer of blood banks. His research (among others') was instrumental in determining how to retain and distribute plasma for use in transfusions, and he organized the first mechanism to collect and store large quantities of plasma, both liquid and dry. In 1941, he became head of the Red Cross blood bank in New York City at a time when blacks were excluded from donating blood, an irony that he protested.

Drew died in an automobile accident near Burlington, North Carolina, on April 1, 1950, and the story of his death has been spun into mythology. The standard version, taught in classrooms throughout the country and repeated in Portland's *Baseline Essays*, has Drew being denied crucial transfusions. "Tragically, he encountered white racism at its ugliest—*not one* of several nearby white hospitals would provide the blood transfusions he so desperately needed," the text declares, "and on the way to a hospital that treated Black people, he died. It is so ironic that the very process he developed, which had been saving thousands of human lives—was made unavailable to save his life."

This compelling parable of race in America strikes mesmerizing chords of outrage. It is the perfect piece of poetic history, injustice distilled to its purest form. That it seems completely plausible to many whites and blacks alike testifies to our common legacy of shame.

It is a terrible fantasy, however. The *Dictionary of American Negro Biography* dismisses the tale with one sentence: "Conflicting versions to the contrary, Drew received prompt medical attention." Drew's daughter, Charlene Drew Jarvis, a member of the Washington, D.C., City Council, has tried to demolish the myth since she discovered that many African-Americans were citing it as justification for refusing to donate organs, bone marrow, or blood. The most detailed refutation comes from his most recent biographer, Spencie Love, a graduate student in history at Duke who decided to use her skills as a former investigative reporter to do her doctoral dissertation on the case.

"Many people in the county believed the legend," she said. "Black people started telling me things in their own lives that were similar. What I began to realize was that this legend was an archetypal story about segregation, about segregated medical care. And what allegedly happened to Drew had happened in multiple ways to people over a long period of time. This whole business of being refused treatment outside the hospital had happened to a lot of people. It was pretty routine."

In fact, Love found that it had occurred in the same area to a young black World War II veteran named Maltheus Reeves Avery on December 1, 1950, eight months to the day after Drew died. Critically injured in an automobile accident, Avery was sent to Duke University Hospital, which refused him treatment because its beds for blacks were full. Although he had a grave head injury, he was shuttled to a small black hospital and died minutes after arriving. The incident caused enough of a stir to get local newspaper coverage, with the result that many people remembered the young veteran's story and the name of Charles Drew, and put the two together.

The events of Drew's death were quite different, Love learned. She examined hospital records and interviewed the two white doctors who had cared for him, the black orderly who had been present, the hospital administrator, Drew's widow, and some of his children.

Drew was an energetic man who pushed himself hard; he had spent a day in surgery and had given an evening lecture in Washington before setting out with others after midnight to drive to a conference in Tuskegee, Alabama. "They were driving all night because of segregation," Love said. "There were very few places to stay, and you didn't even want to try to stay in certain places. He was driving and dozed off. So you could say he died because of segregation."

When an ambulance rushed him to Alamance General Hospital in Burlington forty minutes after the accident, two young doctors— brothers named Charles and Harold Kernodle—immediately recognized his name and worked intensively to save him, according to all the evidence that Love could assemble. Both blacks and whites were routinely treated in the emergency room, although the hospital, which was mostly white, separated patients once they were admitted. Blacks were relegated to a couple of basement rooms with five beds. "They even had a black nurse, so that segregation wouldn't be violated," Love said. But Drew never made it that far. In the emergency room, he was given plasma and other fluids as doctors worked on him, but there was no time to match blood types for a transfusion of whole blood. Within about an hour and a half, he died of what the death certificate listed as brain injuries, internal hemorrhaging, and multiple injuries to the extremities.

His widow, many black doctors, and other blacks who knew Drew have struggled for decades against the assertion that he was denied proper care, Love said. "They found it very disturbing. To them, it was an affront." As a result of Love's findings, the *Baseline Essays* have been revised and, if republished, will correct the history, according to Carolyn Leonard of the Portland School District.

Love sees the legend's origins in the deep roots of African-American folk tales, many of which reinforce the notion that a black man can bleed to death in white hands. These stories, vividly recorded by Gladys-Marie Fry in her 1975 book *Night Riders in Black Folk History*, grew out of deliberate campaigns of psychological control by slave owners, whose overseers donned white sheets at night and rode noisily as "ghosts" through plantations to frighten slaves into staying inside. Then, too, the Medical College of South Carolina and other institutions advertised for slave bodies, either cadavers or "sick negroes considered incurable," for dissection and experimentation. The twin background of real abuse and fears of the supernatural combined to produce widely told tales about "night doctors" who wore rubber shoes and silently prowled neighborhoods, especially near hospitals, grabbed blacks, put them into carts with rubber wheels drawn by rubber-shod horses, took them to hospitals, and drained all their blood to be used in making medicines. It was a variation on the old anti-Semitic slander about Jews draining the blood of Christian babies to make Passover matzoh.

Whites have also had their own fantasies around the symbol of blood as a racial symbol, including the notion that one drop of "Negro blood" renders a person Negro. In southern white medical literature, Love noted, treatises were written on the dangers of blacks' blood. "The black blood distributed to the brain chains the mind to ignorance, superstition and barbarism," wrote one antebellum physician.

"Folklore works the way dreams do," Love said. "You kind of take pieces of something and weave it together in a way that makes sense to you."

The Lure of Africa

The old house on Longfellow Street in Washington, D.C., had been turned into a movie set, and its owners were away on a free weekend in a hotel. Roughly carved wooden statues and other pieces of African art had been carried into the comfortably worn rooms and placed conspicuously within camera range. Bathed in bright light, the dining-room table was covered with an African weaving of blues, yellows, and rusty reds. The lens was trained on two light-skinned African-American girls, Suzanne, twelve, and Loren, seven, who sat contentedly making necklaces from an abundant assortment of beautiful beads that were oval and round and heavy and fine and reflected a spectrum of earth tones.

The crew, picking their way over cables and props, were about to shoot a scene illustrating Creativity, the Sixth Principle of Kwanzaa, and the young actresses were warming up. "We want to see the same kind of smiles that made you famous yesterday," a white man said gently from behind the camera. "If you think it looks pretty, you say so. Now, Loren, remember that smile?" Her face lit up. "That's the one. On my signal, you're gonna put that on your sister."

He was Robert Gardner, a talented documentary filmmaker who had won Emmys and an Oscar nomination; now he had been hired by National Geographic Television to do a twenty-minute instructional

film for schoolchildren about the latest in the American panoply of
rituals: the pseudo-African celebration, Kwanzaa,* which lasts for the
week between Christmas and the New Year. Most of the actors
didn't observe the holiday. The adults playing parents and grandparents
made the confession a little sheepishly; of the children, only Loren, the
littlest, announced, "I celebrate Christmas and Kwanzaa." Joseph, a
twelve-year-old, admitted that he had known nothing about it before
acting in the film; conveniently, he played a boy who knew nothing
about it.

Still, Kwanzaa seems to be catching on among African-Americans
who yearn for a cultural observance that is distinctly theirs. Invented in
1966 by a California activist, Maulana Karenga, the celebration honors
African roots and promotes communal values so wanting in American
life. Karenga calls the holiday a "cultural synthesis" drawn from harvest
festivals throughout Africa and embellished with intricate symbolism
designed to address needs felt by many blacks in America. The seven
days are organized around seven principles, named with Swahili words,
whose broadest theme is a collectivist ethic stressing the oneness of
the African-American people and the virtue of mutual cooperation.
The First Principle is Umoja (Unity), followed by Kujichagulia (Self-
Determination), Ujima (Collective Work and Responsibility), Ujamaa
(Cooperative Economics), Nia (Purpose), Kuumba (Creativity), and
Imani (Faith).

The themes end up sounding like a blend of Boy Scouts and Sunday
school, with a touch of Marxism added by Karenga's advocacy of "shared
social wealth." He endorses "the fundamental communal concept that
social wealth belongs to the masses of people who created it and that no
one should have such an unequal amount of wealth that it gives him/her
the capacity to impose unequal, exploitative, or oppressive relations on
others." This he couples with an appeal to economic self-help and solidarity among blacks in their commercial dealings; they should buy from
black businesses, for example. In addition, Karenga's ritual contains
unacknowledged borrowings from Judaism. Along with gifts for children, a centerpiece of the holiday's paraphernalia is a candelabrum that
holds seven candles, one of which is lit for each day. The obvious resem-
blance to Hanukkah makes Karenga recoil; he admits that an African
candleholder may be difficult to find, and then he cautions against sub-
stituting a menorah, which "represents a culturally incompatible and

---

Kwanza means "first" in the Swahili phrase *matunda ya kwanza*, or "first fruits";
the final *a* was added to make seven letters, one for each day of the celebration.

aesthetically dissonant intrusion in the context of an African motif." All the while, he employs terms familiar to Jews, such as "diaspora" and the "ingathering of the people."

Gardner, who read extensively on Kwanzaa and then wrote the script himself, did not exactly play up the Marxist angle when he made his film for the blue-blooded National Geographic Society, but he was faithful to the holiday's principles. He created a happy little story prettied up by a sentimental Hallmark scene, as he called it. On the coffee table, adorned with weavings of kente cloth, the candelabrum held one black candle in the center (for black unity) flanked by three red candles (for struggle) and three green (for the future). Behind the glow of the flames were a bowl of nuts, ears of corn, yams, apples, pears, grapes, avocados, onions, grapefruit, a coconut, and a goblet (the unity cup for a libation to the ancestors). The flickering light softened the faces of the "family" sitting together on the couch. The rhetorical edge of Karenga's message was softened as well.

It's a safe bet that most African-Americans who observe Kwanzaa focus not on hard ideology but rather on the anodyne values and the sense of belonging that the celebration conveys. Many also think it's a purely African holiday, which generates a false feeling of participation in a deeper tradition.

This leads some white people to sneer at Kwanzaa as a synthetic celebration of a fictitious custom. The indignation boils up almost venomously, with a snort of contempt for what they consider the phony, feel-good Africanness that attracts many blacks. Diane Ravitch, a professor at New York University who served as an assistant secretary of education in the Bush administration, ended a conversation on the errors of Afrocentric history by urging me to write about Kwanzaa as a fraud created by an unsavory character. She seemed truly outraged by the whole observance. (Karenga was imprisoned in the early 1970s for ordering a woman beaten, and his Los Angeles organization, US, waged shoot-outs with the Black Panthers in Los Angeles. Gardner decided not to interview him for the National Geographic film.)

As the film demonstrated, however, white institutions and white professionals can easily embrace the holiday and even promote it. White-owned newspapers and television stations now do seasonal stories on Kwanzaa, alongside those about Christmas and Hanukkah. Broadcasters show Kwanzaa graphics during station breaks. Museums include the ceremonies in their programs. And as the celebration gradually gains ground, it also teaches family values that even Republicans would welcome.

"The first value is Umoja, which is unity—basically, the unity of family," explained Haki Madhubuti, the poet and book publisher. He is a slender African-American with a short beard, a mustache, and a fleeting, shallow smile. "The family remains the basis and center of African life," he said, and it can be used as a counterweight to the destructive phenomenon of the single-parent household in black America. "So we're bringing that back here to our teaching: that the family's the basis."

Madhubuti works out of his African-American Book Center in a run-down shopping district along South Cottage Grove Street on Chicago's South Side. The bookstore sells editions from his publishing house, Third World Press, as well as mainstream civil rights books, children's books featuring black heroes, and birthday and Christmas cards in which black people can find themselves portrayed. His office, upstairs in a loft, overlooks the classroom of an "African-centered" school run by him and his wife. There, children are encouraged to see teachers as extended family members and call them "Mama Dorothy," "Papa Thomas," as would be done, he argues, in an ideal African village.

For Madhubuti and many others, Africa becomes a universal antidote for what ails black America. In this Africa, however, there are no separate tribes, no warring ethnicities; in this generalized and romanticized Africa, the enormous diversity of the continent's peoples collapses into a misty glow of simple harmony and sensible priorities. Africa's "social collectivism" makes "moral or material misery unknown to the present day," writes Cheikh Anta Diop, a Senegalese physicist revered by black Americans who look to the virtues of Africa. "There are people living in poverty, but no one feels alone and no one is in distress," he says. The culture contains "an ideal of peace, of justice, of goodness and an optimism which eliminates all notion of guilt or original sin in religious and metaphysical institutions."

In contrast, Diop describes the "Northern Cradle," comprising Greece and Rome, as a place of "xenophobia" and "individualism, moral and material solitude, a disgust for existence, all the subject-matter of modern literature . . . an ideal of war, violence, crime and conquests, inherited from nomadic life, with as a consequence, a feeling of guilt and of original sin, which causes pessimistic religious or metaphysical systems to be built."

Therefore, the imagined cohesion and pride and self-reliance of African communities are posed as the opposites of family disintegration and drug wars and dysfunctional schools. If African-American children suffer from low self-esteem, if growing numbers of African-American children are born out of wedlock, then the steps to repair the problem are dubbed "African." "What we're trying to do is always inspire," Madhubuti explained, to make the child "more self-assured." In African-based education, "children represent the major reward of life," he said. "When I had my children, my whole life changed, because it wasn't mine anymore. . . . It meant that my wife and I had to be together for at least a minimum of twenty-five years. So if you know that you're going to have to be together for twenty-five years, then you try to make it work. It's as simple as that."

Madhubuti had learned the value of black pride by suffering its absence during his childhood. At thirteen, many years before he was moved to change his name from Don L. Lee, his mother sent him to the library for a copy of Richard Wright's *Black Boy*. He was gripped by embarrassment.

"I did not want to go," he remembered, "because I didn't want to go anyplace and ask for anything black. That's how ashamed I was at being who I was."

But his mother was firm, and he went to the library, found the book on the shelf, covered it up so nobody could see the title with the terrible word "Black," went into a corner, and began to read. At that moment, he found the power of literature. "That's when I discovered that my life had been totally false in terms of what I had been taught. I read half the book in the library. I took it home, but I didn't give it to her until I had finished reading."

The seed having been planted, it was nourished by the army. At seventeen, as Lee stepped off the bus for basic training, he was carrying *Here I Stand* by Paul Robeson, the great black actor and singer who had despaired of America and dramatically moved to Moscow. Lee was the only black man and the lone recruit in a bunch of white draftees.

"The drill sergeant saw Paul Robeson's face on the book, and he snatched the book from me, and he said, 'What's your Negro mind doing reading this black Communist?' So 'black' and 'Communist'— that's a double negative right there.

"He told all of us, he said, 'OK, all you ladies, get up against the bus.' He called us 'ladies,' you know. And he held the book over his head and tore the pages out and gave them to each recruit and said, 'Use this as toilet paper.'

"What I learned as a result of that was the importance of ideas. Ideas." They were powerful enough to make a drill sergeant tear up a book. "Yeah, it was akin to book burning."

Years later, Madhubuti found his response—in his publishing house, his teaching, his school, his African name. Most children who attend Madhubuti's school have been given African names as a way of reaching out to bonds and traditions beyond themselves. He and his wife have bestowed African names on their three children. "My children are Bomani, Akili, Laini," he said. "Laini, first name. The middle name is Nzinga, named after Queen Anne Nzinga. Bomani Garvey, named after Marcus Garvey. Akili Malcolm, named after Malcolm X. So they have names that represent something, to give them something to shoot for, something to believe in."

Today, a search for Africa at home has replaced the impulse to find a home in Africa; no massive "back to Africa" movement has generated the appeal of Marcus Garvey's failed attempt in the 1920s. In the current quest, the name becomes an emblem of connection. "All of us have African names," Kwanza Jones, the Princeton student, said of herself and her siblings. "I like that. It's nice. I have one brother, his name is Mahiri; his name means 'skillful, clever, and quick.' And I have a younger sister, her name is Meta; her name means 'falcon black beauty.' And my older sister's name is Kito, and that means 'precious jewel.' "

Some Africans find that the blacks who favor African styles know little more than caricatures of Africa. That was the impression of Levi Nwachuku, a Nigerian professor of African history at Lincoln University in Pennsylvania, where almost all the students were blacks from the United States and the Caribbean. Most could not name a single country on a blank map of Africa, he said sadly.

"It's unfortunate that most of them take what I may call a therapeutic approach to the study," he observed, "to elevate those things that they feel will give them joy." His students, prone to generalization, were "not very much concerned with the facts of the history," he said. "I complain about the concept of calling everybody from the continent African: 'Why don't you say a Nigerian, a Liberian, an Egyptian, just as in Europe you say a Frenchman, an Austrian?' They got angry about it. And that's understandable, because if they should stress or emphasize the localities or the countries, then where do they fit in the framework of things? They got angry. So I said, 'Look, you may be angry, but you have to be realistic here.' "

Nwachuku was a short, sturdily built, friendly man who was passionate about his scholarship. "You have to see history intellectually," he said, "rather than to see it as a curative thing, to make you feel good." Therefore, he did not mind angering his students with difficult facts.

Swahili, for example, struck him as an odd choice as the language adopted by African-centered blacks in America. "It doesn't make any sense to me," he declared. The enslaved ancestors of most black Americans came from western Africa, where Swahili is not spoken. "Swahili is not even African as such. It's a synthesis of African and Arabic. It's widely spoken in East Africa, so it is assumed to be *the* language. Other local languages are there, but this is the one that got elevated by the Arab masters who came there. So it is not a purely African language. It's not. If you talk about authentic African languages, you talk about Hausa in West Africa, the Yoruba, Wolof. Most of them are authentic African languages that have no mixture from outside influences."

When another Lincoln professor, Islanda Goode, arrived from the Soviet Union in 1991 and encountered the emphasis on African heritage, she was bewildered and annoyed. In her Russian language class, she reacted sharply one day to a young black woman who insisted, "I'm not African-American. I'm African."

Goode replied with a remark that had more cruel precision than intended; inadvertently, she touched a core of truth and loss. And her words were poignant because of who she was. Goode looked white, so she might have been dismissed as racially insensitive. She seemed Russian, so she might have been seen as unschooled in the American nuances of racial discourse. But she was the niece of Paul Robeson. Her mother was Russian, and her father, a "mulatto," as she described him, was the brother of Robeson's wife. Goode had spent a career teaching Russian to foreigners (including African students) at Patrice Lumumba University in Moscow until she learned that, by virtue of her father's nationality, she held American citizenship. Her insider's genes and outsider's perspective allowed her some unpretentious common sense about race; she had the insight to see through posturing and the immunity to speak candidly.

Goode cut her student down: "You don't even know where in Africa you're from. But you *are* from America. Why deny that?"

Haki Madhubuti, who had naïvely carried Robeson's book into basic training, had not met Goode but had an answer nonetheless, both to her and to Nwachuku. "I cannot trace my lineage to any place in Africa," he conceded. "That's why we acknowledge 'African-American.' We are American-based Africans. What that means is that we have the best of both worlds, so I can claim anything in Africa I want. I don't care what ethnic group it is, I can claim it. I don't have to get into the clannishness or tribalism that is wreaking havoc on Africa now. Uganda, Tanzania,

Zaire, or Nigeria, Senegal, it doesn't matter. We find something good that's going to help us develop, then we're going to claim it."

History and honor depend heavily on each other, as historian Carter G. Woodson saw with clarity when he wrote in 1933, "The educated Negroes have the attitude of contempt toward their own people because . . . Negroes are taught to admire the Hebrew, the Greek, the Latin, and the Teuton and to despise the African." He thus put his finger on a pulse of resentment, which has now turned into a movement. By the final decade of this century, large numbers of African-Americans recognized that the veneration of Europe as the font of enlightened civilization had a fatal defect: So brightly did the light shine on the gods and philosophers, the architects and warriors of classical Greece and Rome; on the artists and musicians of the Renaissance, the kings and the democrats of England, that it blinded most of the American consciousness to the non-Western world. Ancient greatnesses in what are now China, India, Japan, Latin America, the Arab nations, and Africa were left in the shadows.

Among many African-Americans and some whites, such learning has now been given the contemptuous label "Eurocentrism" and belittled as the study of "dead white males." This brings the rejoinder that those dead white males happened to think and write and build and create and lead across new frontiers of human endeavor, whether on the Acropolis, the ceiling of the Sistine Chapel, or the stage at the Globe Theatre, and that Europe had profound influence on the political and economic structure of the United States. And so a struggle that runs along political, gender, and racial lines now rages. In its noblest form, it becomes a battle for inclusion that may, it is hoped, reshape historical knowledge to embrace entire peoples whose cultures and contributions have been deemed unworthy of central consideration in the human story. In its most parochial and racially divisive, it is a contest to replace the supposed preeminence of whites with that of "people of color."

To African-Americans, the stakes are nothing less than their historical dignity. For generations, Africa was portrayed as the "Dark Continent," mysterious and primitive, devoid of significance in the evolution of civilization. "Spear chucker" is still hurled by American whites as a racist epithet against blacks, and Hollywood's images of simianlike cannibals remain imprinted in many minds long after they have been rendered unfit for films. It would be folly to think that stereotypes of Africa have no impact on stereotypes of African-Americans or on the way many blacks feel about themselves.

Until recently, little effort has been made to find countervailing images. How many readers of *The Three Musketeers* and *The Count of Monte Cristo* know that their nineteenth-century French author, Alexandre Dumas, was half black? His mother, of African descent, was from Santo Domingo. How many Russian literature classes emphasize the partial African ancestry of Russia's great poet and writer Aleksandr Pushkin? His great-grandfather on his mother's side was an African, Abram Hannibal, presented as a gift by the sultan of Turkey to Peter the Great, who adopted him as his godson. Pushkin began a fictionalized tale of this man and the consternation surrounding his liaisons with white women; the unfinished piece is entitled "Peter the Great's Negro."

"We got a lack of information from the school system," said Lauren Nile, an African-American attorney who does diversity training in corporations and government agencies. "To graduate from high school, I had to take Western history. To graduate from college, I had to take European history. And there I was, almost a senior in college, and I thought to myself, Have Africans contributed nothing to humanity? Have we been on the fringes of humanity? Have we done nothing in science, in math, in geometry, in architecture? If this is so, I want to know. But if it isn't, I want to know that too. So I took an African history course, and of course the stuff I learned just blew me out of the water, in terms of what came out of that continent. But I had to take an African history course to learn that."

People who search for their history are actually searching for themselves. The assault organized by African-American scholars and activists against the derogation of Africa, therefore, is a way of reassembling identity. Their fight has been launched not only for image but for reconnection, not only to correct the record but to repair the broken ties, to graft the severed roots, and to honor whatever fragments of their ancestors' cultures can be pieced together. By extolling Africa, blacks in America are trying to work their way into the story from which they have been excluded, to find pride. The result, under the unfortunate title of "Afrocentrism," is a hodgepodge of respectable teaching on African history, authentic and synthetic cultural practices, and legitimate and inflated claims of Africa's contributions to human advancement. "That's one of my problems with Afrocentricity," said Levi Nwachuku. "It's nostalgic. It's past-looking. It's not forward-oriented. It should be a basis for building the future."

The Afrocentric argument is exemplified by the *Baseline Essays*, composed for Portland's school district, which begin with the fact that fossils of the oldest humans (from 4.4 million years ago) have been found in

Ethiopia and extrapolate from that discovery into an assertion that virtually all of civilization's accomplishments have their foundations in Africa.
The *Essays* contain chapters that trace music, art, science, and mathematics to African sources, intertwining demonstrable influences with
fanciful claims to make a thicket too intricate to be untangled by any but
a team of scholars.

Afrocentrism has spun off into its own orbit where it contends that
the pharaohs were black, that Moses was black, that Jesus was black, that
the discoverers of astronomy, the developers of mathematics, the first
philosophers, and the inventors of many modern devices were black.
These claims have unleashed a backlash of defensive outrage among
some whites, who accuse the movement of manufacturing a synthetic
history to satisfy a psychological and cultural need. But the emotional
investment in Afrocentrism is considerable. When I asked Nell Painter,
the black history professor at Princeton, whether she thought the reform
of history had led to fabrication, she gave a tart retort. "As someone who
went to school in the fifties, don't talk to me about fabrication," she
declared. "What we had to put up with! I think you deserve a black
everything for at least a decade."

With that attitude, the field is open to a rich folklore, which is nourished not only by Afrocentric essays and textbooks but by radio talk-
show hosts and callers, by acerbic rap music, by conversation around the
dinner table, even by Budweiser Beer posters. In a hallway of Baltimore's
mostly black Chinquapin Middle School, slick drawings of "Great Kings
of Africa" are adorned in the lower-right-hand corners with Budweiser
labels and the caption "This chapter of history presented by the King of
Beers."

Intellectually, this atmosphere allows no distinction between wishful
thinking and historical fact. A remark, an assertion, a fragment of rumor
passes the feel-good test and thereby enters the lore. In Brooklyn, a
black high school student says casually that African philosophers predated the Greeks by centuries; he has heard it somewhere but can't name
any of the philosophers. Like a fragile religious faith, his conviction
trembles under questioning; his eyes dart, he looks unsettled.

Usually, though, the belief is dignified by an aura of certainty. Many
black (and some white) youngsters do not suspect—they know
absolutely—that Napoleon's soldiers shot off the Great Sphinx's nose
because it was broad and flat. They know that ancient Africans journeyed
to America and were here when Columbus arrived. They have been told,
and therefore are certain, that Cleopatra was black. They are sure,

because their teachers have read in the *Baseline Essays*, that ancient Egyptians invented batteries, flew in gliders, and shaped Greek philosophy. Some of this is captured in the rough poetry of rap.

> *Let's take a trip way back in the days,*
> *to the first civilization on earth,*
> *the Egyptians, giving birth,*
> *to science, mathematics and music,*
> *religion, the list goes on—you choose it.*
> . . .
> *So people that believe in Greek philosophy,*
> *know your facts: Egypt was the monopoly.*
> *Greeks had learned from Egyptian masters,*
> *You might say prove it, well here's the answers.*
> . . .
> *Any philosopher at that time was a criminal.*
> *He'd be killed, very simple.*
> *This indicates that Greece had no respect*
> *for science or intellect.*

Ironically, the Afrocentrists have adopted the Eurocentrists' fixation with ancient Egypt and made it the centerpiece of the campaign to promote Africa. This puts them on shakier ground than if they were to emphasize the indisputably black African kingdoms and cultures, which are largely unknown and unappreciated in the West. Since the ancestors of most African-Americans came from West Africa, a good three thousand miles from the area of ancient Egypt, even those Egyptologists who are the most open-minded in considering Egypt an African culture (some traditional scholars adamantly refuse to do so) are puzzled by the Afrocentrists' emphasis.

"One of the things that really strikes me as strange is this concentration by these Afrocentric people on Egypt," said Gay Robins, professor of ancient Egyptian and Near Eastern art at Emory University in Atlanta. "It seems to neglect the rest of Africa. It's taking Western values: All that's worthwhile in Africa is Egypt . . . instead of standing up and saying, no, Africa has a long history, and there are many, many different cultures and civilizations that have risen and fallen during that time that are worth studying."

But Egypt is a special sore point for the Afrocentrists, who believe that European scholars stole a great African civilization from blacks and turned it into something fictitiously white and non-African. Thus, in putting together the *Baseline Essays*, a decision was made that "if you can commandeer Egypt," then you can "combat the notion that African people had never done anything," according to Carolyn Leonard, the Portland School District's coordinator of multicultural/multiethnic education. "We are simply mirroring the kind of respect that universities and funding people have had for Egypt," she said. "The Egyptians were able to preserve things and have people in awe. The mystique generated the interest and generated a field of study."

Even the European infatuation with ancient Egypt never burnished Africa's image, however. When Egyptians were seen as African, they were regarded as incapable of any metaphysical thought that could have influenced classical Greece. When seen as creative, they were divorced from Africa. In modern times, Egypt has rarely been viewed as part of Africa, despite its location on the continent. Egypt is somehow suspended in its own sphere, remarkable and unique in its religion, art, and monuments but not a product of black Africa. Egyptologists at American universities are usually located in the Department of Asian and Middle Eastern Studies, the Oriental Institute, and the like, not under any section with "African" in its name. Indeed, the extensive volume *Art in the Western World*, by David M. Robb and J. J. Garrison, first published in 1935 and revised into the 1950s, begins with Egyptian architecture, sculpture, and painting, then moves into Greece, Rome, the Middle Ages in Europe, the Renaissance, and beyond. Egypt is placed in the "Western world," and nothing else of Africa is mentioned.

Asa Hilliard, a Georgia State University education professor who edited the *Baseline Essays*, calls this "decontextualized information." The problem in education "is not so much the presence or absence of fragments," he said, but that "you don't have the whole story." If you did, it could be fit together into a comprehensive understanding. This is the heart of the Afrocentrists' complaint and the thrust of their solution, which makes three key arguments: first, that the Greeks were heavily influenced by the Egyptians in their religion, philosophy, language, architecture, art, and science; second, that the ancient Egyptians were black; and third, that the great Egyptian civilization grew out of black African cultures that had gone before. Thus, the roots of "Western civilization" ultimately lie in Africa.

The first point is perhaps the least disputed. To acknowledge Egypt's impact on the Greeks is to return to an earlier view of history, before eighteenth- and nineteenth-century European scholars set out to divorce ancient Greece from its African and Phoenician influences, according to Martin Bernal in his controversial series of volumes, *Black Athena*. Bernal has been criticized by classicists for exaggerating the linguistic similarities between Ancient Egyptian and Greek, for postulating an Egyptian colonization of Greece, and for misinterpreting archaeological evidence. But his work has helped focus new attention on Egypt's influence.

He writes that "the dismissal of the Egyptians and the explosion of Northern European racism in the 19th century" occurred simultaneously and were connected. "For 18th- and 19th-century Romantics and racists, it was simply intolerable for Greece, which was seen not merely as the epitome of Europe but also as its pure childhood, to have been the result of the mixture of native Europeans and colonizing Africans and Semites." Therefore, Bernal says, an "Aryan Model" was developed to portray Greece as essentially European, a view that is under revision by scholars today but remains alive in the popular mind. Paradoxically, it relied on a derogation of Egypt as African; if Egypt were African, the logic held, then it must have been too primitive to have contributed to Greek philosophy.

"The first law for the historian is that he shall never dare utter an untruth," said Cicero. "The second is that he shall suppress nothing that is true. Moreover, there shall be no suspicion of partiality in his writing, or of malice."

If historians had been consistent about meeting this standard, Cicero's injunction would have been unnecessary. But the "suspicion of partiality," which may be more or less pronounced in various versions of the past, is especially apparent in the Afrocentric writings on ancient Egypt. No uncertainties seem to exist for the Afrocentrists, no unanswered questions, no doubts, no caveats or qualifiers or hedged bets. Everything is crystal-clear, as illustrated by the second point in the Afrocentrists' argument: the race of the ancient Egyptians.

The Portland School District's essay on art is an example. It makes a flat declaration: "Egypt was a black nation. The first 1,000 years of Dynastic Egypt during the first six Dynasties was a period of undisturbed Black rule, and was the period when most of the pyramids (and the Sphinx) were built."

With no room for ambiguity, the spirit of inquiry is snuffed out. Laura, my daughter, encountered among black women at Spelman College the complete conviction that Egyptians were black. When she said that she had been to Egypt and offered the contradictory evidence of her own eyes, they reacted blankly; some insisted that they had seen pictures, but they weren't inclined to explore her experience to question what they had been taught. I ran into the same imperviousness at Lincoln University, where I spent a week lecturing. In a sociology class, a young man in the front row raised the issue of the black Egyptians (although we had been talking about something entirely different). When I suggested that the question of whether or not the Egyptians were black could be a whole subject for discussion, he shot back, "It can't be a subject for discussion. I mean, right there is part of the perpetration, if we sit here and deny that Egyptians are black and say, 'Well it's a different discussion,' when it's the truth."

A more intellectually open approach was proposed by Diane Ravitch, an archcritic of Afrocentrism. "It is important to teach students about conflicting interpretations and about debates among experts," she wrote. "Students should learn, for example, that scholars disagree about whether Egypt was a black African civilization or a multiracial civilization. . . . Let students investigate the question; such an inquiry would send many children to books about ancient Egypt as well as to museums with Egyptian collections."

Nonetheless, the adamant insistence on Egypt as a black African civilization has opened a debate where almost none took place before. It has stimulated many white Egyptologists to consider the issue and to state clearly in lectures and writings and museum displays that Egypt was, indeed, in Africa. "It's made me think," said Gay Robins of Emory. "Now, when I give a general lecture on Egypt, I start off by pointing out that Egypt is in Africa." To do so before, she said, "never occurred to me."

Dorothea Arnold, curator of Egyptian art at the Metropolitan Museum of Art in New York, counts this as a healthy discussion and "one of the great experiences" of coming to the United States from her native Germany, where the controversy doesn't exist. The museum gets pressure, she said, sometimes reasonable pressure. "Then there are, of course, people who come and ask too much. They want to redo the whole thing and say everywhere, 'This is African.' And then you have to calm them down. But on the other hand, I always learn, even from the mad, overdone, emotional people. I find it very enlightening."

In response, in the early 1990s, she decided to have hung at the entrance to the Metropolitan's Egypt galleries a huge map of Africa, boldly outlining ancient Egypt and Nubia in the northeast corner of the continent. "It is true, and I think every Egyptologist would admit this today, that in the nineteenth century the image of ancient Egypt was too Eurocentric," Arnold said. "After all, Egypt is in Africa, and this is one fact that I always make when I talk about Egypt. This is one fact that has really changed in Egyptology in the last decade or two. Now comes the question, How far do you go? They were Africans, of course. But were they blacks in the sense that the term 'black' is used in the United States? And that is where I think much of the problem comes from."

As she guided me past the displays of sculpture and paintings and pottery, of sphinxes and jewelry and huge hunks of carved stone that speak of brilliant artistry across four thousand years and more, Arnold worked her way expertly through a labyrinth of faces, skin colors, and questions about race. "What is black?" she asked. "If you look at it properly, it doesn't exist. It is a range. There is a whole range of brown- and black-colored people, which in the beginning may have been a north-south range."

The problem was put succinctly by Lanny Bell, an Egyptologist at the University of Chicago. "Asking the question 'What color were the ancient Egyptians?' is like asking the question 'What color are the Americans?' Egyptians were on a crossroads. They had people coming down the Nile to them, across the Sinai Peninsula, from the Sahara. My feeling is that the racial mixture you get in Egypt today would have been about the same: The further north you go, the more Libyan they are; the further south, the more African."

One might think that with all the writings, skeletal remains, mummies, sculpture, and painting that have survived from ancient Egypt, a reliable record would be available of the racial makeup of the people. But Arnold and others who have spent their careers studying the artifacts caution that conclusions are not that easy to draw.

As writings demonstrate, the Egyptians were clearly aware of human diversity. They probably had a multiracial society, to use today's terms, but without evident tension around the matter of skin color, some Egyptologists believe. The concept of race, which is a modern invention, was alien to the Egyptians, according to scholars who resist its application to that ancient culture. Yet the Egyptians recognized and sometimes celebrated difference, as in the Great Hymn to the sun god, Aten, which was engraved on a tomb about 1330 B.C. Arnold read this verse to me:

> *You made the earth as you wished to alone,*
> *All peoples, herds, and flocks,*
> *All on one earth, that walk on legs,*
> *Or on high, that fly on wings,*

The lands of Khor and Kush,*
And the land of Egypt.
You set every man in his place,
You supply their needs,
Every one has his food, his lifetime, his country,
Their tongues differ in speech,
Their characters likewise,
Their skins are distinct,
For you distinguish the people.

Mummies show a variety of traits, according to Frank J. Yurco, an Egyptologist at the Field Museum of Natural History in Chicago. "Ramesses II, who reigned from 1279 to 1212 B.C.E., . . . is a typical northern Egyptian," Yurco writes. "He had fine, wavy hair, a prominent hooked nose, and moderately thin lips. This mummy may be contrasted with the mummy of Seqenen-Re Tao, who died on the battlefield about 1580 B.C. He was from Thebes, much farther south. He had tightly curled, woolly hair, a slight build and strongly Nubian features."

A more scientific approach to determining the physical characteristics of the Egyptians has been used by Dr. Shomarka O. Y. Keita, an African-American physician and biological anthropologist who has taken detailed measurements of the skulls of ancient and modern peoples in the region. He has compared contemporary Somalis, ancient Kushites (in Nubia), modern Greeks, and Bronze Age Italians with Egyptians in various periods, from the Predynastic eras before 3100 B.C., when the kingdoms of Upper and Lower Egypt were united, to the Late Dynasties from 525 to 330 B.C.

"The assumption is, when you measure crania you can recover genetic information," Keita explained. "But it does break down. It's not perfect." He pulled out tables crammed with numbers, the basis for the Ph.D. thesis he was writing for Oxford University.

Using thirteen cranial measurements, he found much closer similarities among ancient Egyptians and other Africans—most notably the dark-skinned Kushites—than among Egyptians and southern Europeans. "The people of ancient Egypt were more like people from further south in Africa than like people across the Mediterranean," he concluded. "The Egyptians can be seen, must be seen, as authentic biohistorical Africans, with the understanding that there is no one characteristic of Africans. There are Africans with thin noses and thin lips, flat

---

*Khor was in Palestine and part of Syria. Kush was in Nubia.

noses and thick lips." He rejected the concept of race and preferred "breeding populations, mating systems," as he called them. "Race is a metaphor for kinship, and kinship has to do with prestige." And that is what Afrocentrism is all about.

Whatever categories are used in trying to define ancient Egyptians, their painting and sculpture cannot be taken too literally, Egyptologists believe. "Egyptian art is not photography," in Arnold's words. "It is art. It is an attempt to say something." And what it says is that Egyptians thought of themselves as Egyptians, that they had an "Egyptian type" in mind as they created the images out of certain ideals. She pointed to a wooden statue of a woman from Nubia, which was painted white, and noted the broad shoulders, the round head, the deep-set eyes. Race, she said, is a modern concept that we are now trying to impose retroactively on the ancient Egyptians, and it doesn't fit.

In the art, however, facial features are not altogether stylized, and they show a variety of physical appearances. Arnold showed me the sculpture of a man with an aquiline nose and thin lips, and the head of another whose lips are full, whose nose is flat. We walked into a gallery dominated by the ten-foot-high statue of Mentuhotep, a Nubian pharaoh of four thousand years ago. His commanding countenance says "African" in his lips and nose, a physiognomy that would surely be labeled "Negroid" by the categories of today, although Egyptologists shun such compartmentalization. Furthermore, Arnold said, "he would never have called himself a Nubian. He was an Upper Egyptian."

Similarly, the stone face of Senwosret III has heavy eyelids, ample lips. "I think if you were to put that into a living face, wouldn't you put that into Africa?" Arnold asked. "You would."

Skin color and physiognomy do not always relate to each other, as anyone who has seen Nubians or Ethiopians knows; for the most part, they have dark skin but thin lips and narrow noses. The physiognomy in sculpture suggests that Egyptian kings took black Nubians into their harems, according to Gay Robins at Emory. But in Egyptian painting, skin colors are no reliable guide to race, she said: Sometimes they can be considered realistic, often not.

"I think it would be very like today: that you would have a spectrum of color, very pale in the north to dark in the south," Robins explained. "But the real problem is that we don't see this in the art." The art establishes archetypes whose skin colors are "entirely symbolic," representing status and gender, she noted. "The male Egyptian should have a reddish brown skin and the female Egyptian should have a paler, yellowish brown skin," signifying the man's work outdoors and the elite woman's province of the house and the temple. "A man with a pale wife is saying, 'Look, I can afford a wife who doesn't have to work in the field,'" Robins said. "And in the art, this becomes just a gender distinction, so that when you see ideal scenes of peasants working in the fields, even when there are women out in the fields, they tend to be pale-skinned.

"The other problem," Robins continued, "is that early on, the Egyptians divided the world up into the Egyptians, their southern enemies, their northern enemies, and they set up images. All the time what you're seeing is images of subject peoples to the south coming and bringing their tribute to Egypt. And also you see the king trampling his enemies, and there'll be a southern prisoner who will be clearly black with the typical features and a northern prisoner who will be pale-skinned and represent the Syrians or something like that. And so you get these stereotypes."

Therefore, she concluded, even if an ancient Egyptian were black, that image would probably not appear in his tomb, because "you don't want to make yourself look like the typical enemy." The standard image of an Egyptian would be used instead. "So I think what's going on in real life would be very different from what's happening in the art," she said. "The only thing that you have to ask yourself is: If the Egyptians were really what we think of as black Africans, why was that image not chosen for the typical Egyptian in the first place? And that's why I have problems with people saying the Egyptians were black."

Furthermore, black skin in a painting can mean something else. "Black is the color of the fertile soil of Egypt," Robins explained, "and so it's a color of resurrection. And so Osiris, the god of the dead, is often shown with black skin. And so here's this king, but he's in the typical form of Osiris. He's wrapped in mummy bandages and he has his arms crossed. Osiris is also shown green, because green, of course, is the color of new vegetation and again can represent regeneration and rebirth. So I think the skin color really is symbolic."

For some time, an African-American teacher conducted a searching correspondence with Dorothea Arnold. In one letter, the teacher wrote "a terribly important sentence," Arnold recalled. "She said, 'I went through your galleries with my daughter, and I saw myself in all these things.' And I thought, Gee, isn't this lovely? As a museum curator, it's really not up to me to tell anybody who comes here and sees himself in these pieces, to tell [them] they mustn't. This is so important, that somebody comes to a collection and sees him or herself. Who am I to tell her, 'You're wrong'? I take this very seriously. Isn't it wonderful? I said, 'Of course, you cannot now deny me to go along and say, "I see myself in those pieces." In this sort of emotional experience in this museum, we both have the right.' "

Beyond the question of race lies the question of culture and of what impact on ancient Egypt the indisputably black African ancient cultures may have had. This is the third point in the Afrocentric argument, which sees Egypt as principally an African civilization.

The authority much respected by Afrocentrists is the late Cheikh Anta Diop, who insisted that beneath a superficial impression of heterogeneity, all of Africa, including Egypt, was encompassed by cultural integrity. His 1959 book, *The Cultural Unity of Black Africa*, contends in a dense and rambling argument that ancient Egypt shared the rest of Africa's societal characteristics, particularly freedom for women, as contrasted with the restrictions placed on them in Asia. As an example he offers Isis, the chaste and faithful Egyptian goddess of fertility. "All the historians and ethnologists who have compared the African and Asian societies have been led to consider Western Asia as the land of lechery, in contrast to the healthiness of African customs," he writes. This is a remarkable assertion, given the brutality of certain rituals, such as clitoridectomy, that are inflicted upon women in twenty-eight African countries.

In the Portland School District's *Baseline Essays*, John Henrik Clarke, a retired professor of African history at Hunter College, deplores what he calls the European colonization not only of territory but of information. Egypt was born not of immaculate conception, Clarke says, but of earlier cultures in the interior of Africa. He writes of "the Nile River as a great cultural highway bringing people and creative talent out of inner Africa. Migrations constantly renewed the energy and genius of ancient Egypt until it became the greatest nation the world has ever known. . . . The ancient Egyptians were distinctly African people." He traces their prehistoric ancestors to Uganda and Punt (now Somalia).

But Clarke commits some errors. As a key piece of evidence, he cites the Edfu Text in the Temple of Horus, according to which "civilization was brought from the South by a band of invaders under the leadership of King Horus." But he fails to mention that Horus of Edfu was the most popular of a series of falcon gods, sometimes rendered as a hawk-headed man, and that Egyptian writings are rich in contradictory myths about Horus originating in either the south or the north. The question of where legend ends and reality beings is surely worth raising, but Clarke ignores all ambiguity.

He also quotes an assertion that the ancient civilization of Meroe, which was located in Nubia (south of Egypt in what is now northern Sudan), predated the Egyptian dynasties and developed the pyramid before the Egyptians did so. But his essay confuses the chronology, for carbon-14 dating has determined that the major Egyptian pyramids were built between 2700 and 1600 B.C. and Meroe's were not constructed until after 600 B.C.

Clarke points to a 1960s excavation at Qustul, a Nubian kingdom that allegedly predated the ancient Egyptian dynasties by several generations. But according to a specialist in ancient Nubia and Egypt, Donald O'Connor of the University of Pennsylvania, "the preponderance of evidence" suggests that the stone vases and other Egyptian-style artwork found in a cemetery there were imports made by Egyptians, not by the Nubians of the south.

These specific inaccuracies notwithstanding, however, the question of Egypt's debt to other African cultures is far from closed. Some scholars who have spent their adult lives in deep study of Egypt see shared traits among the Egyptians and the indisputably black civilizations to the south.

"It's quite clear that Egyptian civilization was rooted in Africa," Gay Robins declared. "The Predynastic cultures in Egypt clearly are connected all down the Nile Valley, so it doesn't stop at the border of Egypt. What's happening in Nubia is the same sort of culture that's happening in Egypt. . . . I think divine kingship itself is African." The Mesopotamian civilizations to the east, which had contact with Egypt, did not have divine kings until later. "The rulers of the city-states of Mesopotamia were human stewards for the gods who owned the cities," she said. "But in Egypt, the king was divine right from the beginning." Since the concept of divine kingship exists in modern Africa, she said, "I suspect that this was something that is typically African." But it must remain a suspicion only, as Robins concedes, until ancient civilizations in the interior of Africa are excavated and explored.

It has been Egypt, not the black African civilizations to the south, that has been the focus of European and American archaeologists. For many reasons—racial attitudes, accessibility, an infatuation with large monuments, and the search for treasure—the financing and the fascination have been fixed on Egypt, leaving other cultures largely unknown. One is the great Kerma civilization, located in a fertile plain of the Nile in what is now Sudan; it arose about the time of Egypt's Old Kingdom, which is dated from 2686 B.C., and lasted more than a thousand years, until the Egyptians destroyed it. Kerma's pottery is considered some of the finest ever found anywhere.

Excavations in Nubia have come in waves, first in the middle of the nineteenth century, then in two efforts to save and move artifacts when the first and second Aswan dams were built, in the early 1900s and the 1960s. That second campaign piqued scholars' interest in ancient Nubia, which continues today.

Still, the question of impact remains open. Despite the extensive interaction between ancient Egypt and Nubia, "it is very hard to identify anything in Egyptian culture that you would say is specifically Nubian," said Donald O'Connor. "That's not something peculiar about Nubia. It is very hard in Egyptian culture to identify anything from another culture. You do not see anything of significance from the Near East. You do not see anything of significance from the Aegean either. Egypt is extremely resistant to integrating cultural influences from anywhere. This was a very self-contained culture and very self-contained social system."

Although Afrocentrists want to make inroads into mainstream curricula, their cavalier approach to the facts is a major obstacle to their being taken seriously. Portland's *Baseline Essays* has spawned a small industry of detailed critiques by respected historians who have exposed erroneous dates, spurious claims, outdated research, and shoddy and selective sourcing. The criticisms have been solicited and distributed by Erich Martel, a history teacher at Woodrow Wilson High School in Washington, D.C.

"If they are to gain acceptance, revisionist interpretations of history must be based upon impeccable and thorough research," Martel writes. "The historiography of American history is replete with examples of inaccuracies and outright myths that were shattered by scholarly revisionist research. Such outstanding scholars as W. E. B. Du Bois, Carter G. Woodson, John Hope Franklin, C. Vann Woodward, and Kenneth Stampp were among the many who played crucial roles in opening up textbooks and curricula to the African-American experience. Because of solid grounding, their research withstood criticism and could not be ignored."

Another problem is that none of the Afrocentrists who write about Egypt are formally trained scholars of Egypt, which makes them vulnerable to attack by Egyptologists. A canvass of Egyptologists turned up a consensus that not a single African-American scholar was studying ancient Egyptian civilization. Dorothea Arnold and some others see this as regrettable, but it may not change easily, because budding black scholars can be discouraged early on. At a leading Ivy League university, one venerated professor who asked not to be identified told me, "I see African-Americans who want to take Egyptian or do a senior paper on Egypt. I no longer fall for that one." He paused as if this needed no further explanation. But I asked him what he meant. "I think an African-American who wants to do a senior paper on Egypt is just going to end up spouting the Afrocentrist themes," he said. Don't any black students take his courses? Some, he acknowledged. Are they all Afrocentrists? Well, he said, they don't argue with him because they know where he stands. He did not seem to consider the possibility that some black students may want to explore the issues honestly, that being black doesn't automatically make you a doctrinaire Afrocentrist.

The professor's attitude illustrated the difficulty of creating dialogue between Afrocentrists and Egyptologists, which means between blacks and whites. Many Afrocentrists undermine their case by playing loose with the facts and are then attacked by other African-Americans who want serious scholarship, as well as by whites. Many whites hear only the radical Afrocentrists and are deaf to the quieter tones of reasonable revision that run beneath the furor. Increasingly, as the Afrocentric claims filter into schools, music, and conversation, blacks and whites exist in two entirely separate worlds, each shaped by a landscape of assumptions about what happened in the past.

Whites react variously. Some are intimidated by Afrocentrism, others are infuriated by it, and few seem able to respond with a genuine intellectual curiosity that says, "Hey, I never thought about that before, and maybe I should reexamine my assumptions." That is a commentary on the anxieties that surround much black-white debate.

Stephen Burka found himself in the camp of the intimidated. He thought he could joke around with an African-American friend, a fellow student at Drew, who "started naming off how everything originated from Africa, just to get us going, and how Plato and Socrates took all their learning from Africa." Burka ribbed him, "Ohhh, yeah, sure. They didn't know about Africa."

This brought a flash of anger from the black student, who snapped, "Well, that's your limited point of view."

Burka had thought they were engaging in friendly repartee. "And I said, 'Hold on a second, I'm just kidding you. I'd have to do more research for myself to really do an argument on this.' " As a white, he had transgressed a tense threshold. "You're crossing something that he automatically now stands for—the black culture, which is fine, which is great," Burka said. "Well, I thought that Plato didn't have anything to do with Africa."

Whites in the infuriated camp tend to sneer at any Afrocentric "facts" that violate what they think they know. Their beliefs seem to be arranged in concentric circles, with those most susceptible to revision at the outer rims. At those margins, many whites are willing to correct for the exclusion of blacks from contributions to American progress by adding a few African-Americans to the pantheon of inventors and technicians, provided the stories don't impugn white icons such as Edison. But the beliefs at the inner rings are firmer, less malleable. The center of this array is built on a core of perceptions absorbed from childhood as fundamental and unquestionable. Egypt's whiteness has been at that core, making it a difficult conviction for the Afrocentrists to shake.

The infuriated whites often attack the intimidated camp. Diane Ravitch, whose specialty in the history of education leads her to watch the evolution of textbooks, expresses contempt not only for Afrocentrists who fabricate but for whites who tremble in the face of the fabrications. In return, she is portrayed as a racist by Molefi Kete Asante, the Temple University professor, who is considered the dean of the Afrocentrist movement. He denounces Ravitch's positions as akin to the "Freedmen's Bureau's establishment of black schools in the South during the 1860s . . . to control the content of education so that the recently freed Africans would not become self-assured." Asante uses power terms such as "white supremacy," "white hegemony," and "racial dominance" to indicate that this is a political struggle, not merely a question of historical accuracy.

Blacks are also divided among themselves. Some who would like a real debate worry that the exaggerations and misstatements by Afrocentrists give whites the license to dismiss the entire realm of black history. Others, such as Henry Louis Gates Jr. at Harvard, disagree with the focus of some of their colleagues. "You would think that the most urgent issue in Afro-American studies departments today would be the causes of poverty and how they can be remedied," he said. "But this is not the most urgent issue. The most urgent issue is whether Cleopatra was black. This is classic escapism and romanticism."

Rarely can there be a conversation as accommodating as the one between Dorothea Arnold and the black teacher who saw herself in the ancient Egyptian faces. As I was leaving the museum, Arnold had a parting remark on the healthy questioning that has been stimulated by the Afrocentrists. "I think for history it is very good that this happened," she said. "Even if today we are not able to talk too much to each other, our children will."

Nowhere does the intersection of symbol, faith, and history become more poignant than in the Afrocentrists' argument that Jesus was black. "In the church, you don't hear teachings about the prominence of blacks in scriptures," said Reverend James Dixon of Houston, a suave young black minister who speaks with charismatic passion. He preaches to his congregation that the Garden of Eden was on the African continent and has said in several schools he has visited that "you can't get to the Garden of Eden without getting to Africa." The reaction has been fierce. "White faculty members just can't take that," he noted. "That's blasphemy to them, because Africa is perceived as such a bad place. It's considered the Black Continent."

Furthermore, Dixon continued, "no one talks about the fact that the New Testament says that Jesus was exiled to Egypt, to hide him there among his own while he was a child, because the king wanted to kill him. No one addresses that." Whites seem to fear that something will be lost "if we really tell the truth about the prominence and significance of blacks in history and in Scripture," he remarked.

Given his view that Egyptians were black, was he saying that Jesus was a black African? "I'm saying that he was very dark." And Dixon laughed.

Across town, on the wall of his spacious office at the Wheeler Avenue Baptist Church, Reverend Bill Lawson had a drawing of a black Jesus with a crown of thorns and a full black beard. Lawson, more solidly part of the black establishment than Dixon, sat in his deep leather chair and gestured to the dark face, compassionate and suffering. "I like that picture," he said. "I would make no claim in the world that Jesus looked like that." He pointed to another drawing. "Here's a picture that our deacons gave to us, and it pictures Jesus and his disciples at the Last Supper, and they're all black. But it is based on the old Leonardo da Vinci painting, and that did not accurately describe what happened in that room, anyway."

He continued, "I love our people, and I believe in the fundamental dignity of our people, but I would really like to think that God made of our entire universe one extended family, which has infinite variety. And the reason that I like the picture of Jesus is that it says to a child, 'You need to identify with a Jesus who looks like your daddy or like your uncle, and that's OK.' You can say to the Chinese child, 'If you need to see a Jesus with an Asiatic [face] who speaks Chinese, that's OK.' You need to say to a Scandinavian child, 'If you like your Jesus to have blue eyes, that's OK.' The important thing is that God told us not to make any images of anything anyway, so fortunately we don't have any pictures of Jesus. And that means we don't know what he looked like. And that was sort of providential. It means we are able to identify him with us, and yet at the same time, we can't claim him as just ours.'

It is just this kind of embrace of all peoples, this inclusive spirit, that many critics of Afrocentrism fear is being lost from the American ethic. It is one thing to correct errors and fill in the blanks of history; it is another to do so with new fabrications. "This nonsense now can be very dangerous and very divisive," warned Saul Bruckner, principal of Edward R. Murrow High School in Brooklyn. "Public educational institutions shouldn't do things to destroy the common basis that we have. We have to recognize that the only way we're going to survive is on the basis of being united."

Diane Ravitch worries that the country's basic cohesion could be ruptured if the "particularist" school replaces the traditional "pluralist" approach. As a political theory, particularism allows each group the right to promote its own interest without regard to the interests of larger groups. Pluralism envisions each group's development of its own culture and interests within a larger framework of a common society. Some of the new materials emphasizing "multiculturalism," she believes, "have a political slant" and "are very downbeat," as she puts it. "Nothing good happened unless it was done by blacks and women. That's not going to make people feel that this is a country worth improving. You've got to love something before you can want to make it better." The conviction that "your ancestor oppressed my ancestor," she said, "encourages a sense of rage and victimization. . . . Instead of promoting reconciliation and a sense of shared community, particularism rekindles ancient hatreds in the present; its precepts set group against group. Instead of learning from history about the dangers of prejudging individuals by their color or religion, students learn that it is appropriate to think of others primarily in terms of their group identity."

But the same accusation could be made against the parochial versions of history long accepted in mainstream schooling, where young people have been taught for generations to think of others as members of groups to be envied, pitied, despised, ignored, or otherwise caricatured. Across the color line, these images and silences have worked their way into the disharmony of America. Whites who discover the problem only when black people seek to tell their story do their country little service. Somewhere in American life, there must be room for the multiple truths of a complex past, for the blend of many honest melodies.

PART TWO

Images

CHAPTER FOUR

Body

Dark Against the Sky

black (blăk) *adj.* -er, -est. 1. Being of the color black.
2. Without light: *a black, moonless night.* 3. Often
Black. a. Of or belonging to a racial group having brown to black skin, esp. one of African origin.
b. African-American. 4. Soiled, as from soot; dirty.
5. Evil; wicked: *black deeds.* 6. Depressing; gloomy.
7. Angry; sullen.

white (hwīt) *adj.* whit·er, whit·est 1. Being of the color
white. 2. Light-colored; pale. 3. Also White. Of or
belonging to a racial group having light skin col-
oration. 4. Not written on; blank. 5. Unsullied; pure.
6. Snowy: *a white Christmas.* 7. Incandescent.

—The American Heritage Dictionary, *1994*

Color

Rosanne Katon-Walden had a turned-up nose, and her skin was the
smooth, rich color of milk chocolate. She lived in Los Angeles now,
where she worked as an actress and screenwriter, but she spoke with just
the slightest trace of a New York accent from her childhood in Queens.

At first she told her story with composure and a flick of sarcastic
humor. Then, as she traveled deeper into memory, she was overtaken by
somberness, and suddenly by a breaking voice and a welling up of tears,
and she was putting her fingers to her eyes and saying, "Oh, God. I
haven't thought about this for so long."

She did not get much of an elementary education. Every morning,
when she and the other children arrived at her virtually all-black school
in Queens, her white teacher would turn on the television set at the front
of the room. "We would watch baseball. We would bet on the baseball.
Of course we loved it."

So as school integration began, her parents made sure she got into a better junior high school. A year before her class was to take a full complement of black children, she recalled, "I integrated Archie Bunker's neighborhood, Astoria—Woodside Junior High. I was the only black person in the seventh grade in Astoria.

"I had a couple of really uncomfortable moments. I remember one girl calling me a 'Negro slave,' which was supposed to be some sort of slur, and the whole class getting really quiet, 'cause they knew that she had overstepped the bounds. We were all doing this little kind of dance. The teacher just kind of excused herself, she was so aghast. She had no words for it.

"I had one really—" And here her voice cracked as she pushed on through gentle tears. "I had one really good friend, whose name was Terry, who got me through it. She was a little Jewish girl whose mother was crazy, so I guess she felt kind of ostracized, and she kind of understood everything. . . . Her mother was always going in for electric shock. And so I would kind of hold Terry's hand as she would tell me what was happening with that.

"But her mother was an artist." Rosanne shifted to an excited whisper. "I thought, an artist! That's just so amazing. I couldn't imagine someone who could actually do that. Her mother had taken a photo of me playing the violin, and Terry said her mother was doing her next piece, and it was going to be me. I couldn't imagine. Someone was going to paint me.

"My father was always very nervous about me staying in Astoria. So I was never allowed to go to Terry's house much. But I decided that I was going to sneak over to Terry's house. I wanted to see this painting, and Terry hadn't seen it. So she brought me over to her house and snuck into where her mother was painting."

Rosanne was crying delicately as she talked, and she spoke the next sentence quietly and quickly, as if to scurry past the pain: "Her mother had painted me white."

She hurried on. "And I remember, Terry and I were just looking, and we were speechless. And I think I remember mumbling something like, 'Well, she got the color of my dress right.'

"And, you know, on a certain level we both understood. It had to do with, back then, getting it sold. Gee, I haven't thought about this stuff for so long. Jesus, and I don't remember crying through any of this stuff. Maybe I can cry now because I know that it was happening, but back then you just went through it."

And then she took a breath and cleared her gaze. "But my daughter's not going to go through that. It's just not going to happen to her. It's a different world."

Color is the first contact between blacks and whites. It comes as the initial introduction, before a handshake or a word, before a name, an accent, an idea, a place in the hierarchy of class, or a glimpse of personality. It is the announcement, the label, the badge, the indelible symbol that triggers white assumptions about a black individual's intelligence, morality, reliability, and skill. From across a room or across a street, from a magazine page or a television screen, it is this most superficial attribute that suggests the most profound qualities.

After color comes shape. The eye reads the shading of the skin, then takes in the broad or narrow nose, the thick or slender lips, the hooded or delicate eyelids. For a white gazing upon a black, the facial features meet or defy instinctive standards of beauty. Together, the physiognomy and color define a distance, a perception of difference that increases as the features become less "white," more "Negroid." They stimulate silent, subterranean judgments.

Hair contributes to the impression by being kinky or straight, braided or "relaxed." Clothes can make statements about culture and politics and profession. Messages are sent by the way the body moves— in sedate, businesslike modesty or in an exhibitionist "pimp walk," as the novelist Tom Wolfe slyly called it when he wrote disparagingly of ghetto blacks in *The Bonfire of the Vanities*. All these physical, visual cues are collected by the eye into an appraisal before a single thought has been expressed.

Thus, even before he opens his mouth, a black person has been assigned an aura of proximity or remoteness. The darker his skin, the flatter his nose, the fuller his lips, the kinkier his hair, the more African or homeboy look to his clothing, the more flagrant his gait, the more unlike the white he will seem and the farther he will stand from the white person's zone of comfort. His image will then be either reinforced or revised by what he says. If his name is Salim or Kwame or Imamu, it is one thing; if he is called John or Paul or Bill, it is another. If he speaks "black dialect," dropped out of high school, doesn't have a job, or can't discuss subjects familiar to the white, the remoteness may be reinforced. If his accent, education, and work closely match those of the white person—whether lower-, middle-, or upper-class—the initial stereotypes may be tempered and the sense of distance generated by physical appearance reduced. In an office in Harrisburg, Pennsylvania, one white woman overheard another say to someone on the phone, "You don't sound black, so come in for an interview."

Of all these characteristics, the body is the least susceptible to change. Hair and clothing can be worn differently, of course. But the skin and the flesh and the bones are the essence, and they do not lend themselves easily to alteration. Minorities have long experience in trying to revise their features to conform to the majority's notions of attractiveness. In South Vietnam, women with mixed-race offspring by white American servicemen sometimes rubbed black shoe polish into their children's brown hair to make them look more Vietnamese. And in the United States, plastic surgeons have been kept busy by "fixing" the noses of Jews and removing the "slant" from the eyes of Asians. For American blacks, a substantial industry of skin lighteners and other cosmetics has developed around "white" standards of beauty. Some black men grow mustaches to diminish the prominence of their lips; some black women use lipstick to the same end and laugh at white women who apply gobs of lipstick as if they yearned for thicker lips.

In the end, however, there is no more potent attribute than the color of the skin. And there is no more powerful color than black.

From the opening lines of Genesis, blackness has been woven into consciousness not as a mere color, but as a concept. Primordial darkness predated light and life, when "the earth was without form, and void; and darkness was upon the face of the deep." Creating light, God saw "that it was good, and God divided the light from the darkness." Throughout the Old and New Testaments, the dichotomy of light and darkness is linked to the contradictions of good and evil, truth and ignorance, glory and sin. "He has fenced up my way that I cannot pass, and he hath set darkness in my paths [19:8]," wails Job as he clings to piety in his storm of suffering. "When I looked for good, then evil came unto me; and when I waited for light, there came darkness. [30:26] . . . My skin is black upon me, and my bones are burned with heat [30:30]."

The symbols and metaphors that derogate blackness and elevate whiteness are indelibly etched into the great works we read, the words we speak, the images that move us. And they are not confined to Western civilization, as Harold R. Isaacs observes in *Idols of the Tribe*. They are found in the Philippines as "an almost obsessive preoccupation with color"; in India, where "in classical Hindu texts, there is an association of colors with the main caste groups—white with the Brahmans at the top, black with the Sudras at the bottom"; and in Chinese and Japanese classical traditions, where "the celebration of whiteness as a criterion of feminine beauty is a familiar theme." They infiltrate slang in many cultures. In Sweden, when youths want to harass immigrants from Latin America, the Middle East, or Africa, they shout, "Blackhead! Blackhead!," a derisive epithet for foreigners. In *The New World of Negro Americans*, Isaacs writes:

> The concepts and usages of black evil and white goodness, of beautiful fairness and ugly blackness, are deeply imbedded in the Bible, are folded into the language of Milton and Shakespeare, indeed are laced into almost every entwining strand of the art and literature in which our history is clothed. They can be traced down the columns of any dictionary from white hope to whitewash, from the black arts to the Black Mass, from black-browed and blackhearted to blacklist and blackmail. "I am black *but* comely," sang the Shulamite maiden to the daughters of Jerusalem, and on that *but* hangs a whole great skein of our culture.

From our own era came Jefferson's rhetorical question on whether the subtleties of color and mood shown by a white complexion were not "preferable to that eternal monotony, which reigns in the countenances, that immovable veil of black which covers the emotions of the other race." Aversion to blackness has been the stuff of eloquence and poetry.

Even some black writers and orators who are sensitive to the connotations find it difficult to avoid the conventional symbolism of "black" and "darkness," and of "white," "light," and "bright." Louis Farrakhan, the fiery apostle of black separatism who heads the Nation of Islam, could not resist the imagery in his address to the hundreds of thousands of black men who were spread before him from the Capitol to the Washington Monument at the Million Man March on October 16, 1995. Deflecting accusations of racism and anti-Semitism, he declared, "Whether you like it or not, God brought the idea [for the march] through me, and he didn't bring it through me because my heart was dark with hatred and anti-Semitism. He didn't bring it through me because my heart was dark and I'm filled with hatred for white people and for the human family of the planet. If my heart were that dark, how is the message so bright, the message so clear, the response so magnificent?"

But browsing through an anthology by African-American poets also yields a set of vivid opposites in which blackness is admired and polished like precious stones mined from a wilderness: "Flowers of darkness . . . a bouquet of blackness" (Frank Marshall Davis); "Black Narcissus" (Gerald W. Barrax); "Black angels" (Imamu Amiri Baraka); "Black is a soul. . . . Cocoa filled breasts nippled with molasses" (Joseph White); "Caressed by ebony maidens" (Bob Kaufman); "Golden-black children of the sun" (Henry Dumas); "Cold black wavelets of hair" (Al Young); "Night has secreted us" (Richard W. Thomas); "The black soul cracks the universe" (Sterling Plumpp); "Ginger head mama, all sweet and brown" (Doughtry Long); "Black sapphires" (David Henderson); "The neatdark rows of pine trees" (Pearl Cleage Lomax); "Come O Ebony-hued Eurydice" (Alvin Saxon); "Black is best" (Larry Thompson); "I'm a black ocean, leaping and wide" (Maya Angelou).

Here and there, whiteness is reversed and made into a negative: "The fair are fair and deathly white" (Imamu Amiri Baraka); "It is still snowing . . . in screaming white clots" (Ishmael Reed); "The bodies of pale men . . . white lice" (Ebon). Some blacks like to make fun of blondes by calling them "vanilla ice cream cones."

These are deliberate anomalies, statements of defiance. They parallel the conscious campaign, which blossomed in the late 1960s, to take possession of the stigma "black" and turn it into a label of pride and power. More recently, a school of Afrocentrists has tried to redefine blackness through pseudoscience by imagining that the very agent that gives skin its darkness—the pigment melanin—is a source of intelligence, humaneness, creativity, and even extrasensory perception. In this view, humankind is neatly divided into the "sun people" of Africa and the "ice people" of Europe, according to Leonard Jeffries Jr., the professor of African-American studies at City College in New York who gained infamy for his stereotyped condemnations of whites, especially Jews and Italians. "Ice and sun are very real and very scientific," Jeffries declared. "We are sun people, people of color, because of the sun, the melanin factor. Europeans have lack of melanin and have lost a great deal of it, because much of the European development has been in the caves of Europe where you do not need melanin." Those with more melanin relate more warmly to others, the melanists contend, while the "ice people" are object-oriented.

The racist biology of the melaninists generates contempt among whites and many blacks as well. But the other efforts—literary, political, and cultural—have produced a crosscurrent of attitudes about the connotations of blackness. Here and there, some whites now acknowledge and try to purge their deeply rooted impulses that link blackness with negatives. The culture has not been cleansed of the ancient associations, however. They thrive in many forms.

They come to the surface when Jim Biedron teaches his Russian history course at Bethesda–Chevy Chase High School in Maryland. He draws a pyramid on the board to portray Russia before Peter the Great, noting that the structure of the Russian Orthodox Church reflected the society, with two classes—the white clergy and the black clergy. Which were on the bottom? he asks his students. "It is interesting that almost invariably they place black at the bottom and white at the top," he says, although in fact it was the other way around: The black clergy—those entitled to wear black vestments—were "the nonmarrying upper group that controlled the monasteries and the wealth of the church," he explains, while the "white clergy were marrying parish priests who were very similar to the common peasant." The occasional student who answers correctly has usually done some reading or guesses a trick, he says. The vast majority have absorbed by osmosis the potent assumptions about where black and white belong.

And no wonder. The symbols pervade the books youngsters read and the films they see. In *The Wizard of Oz*, Glinda the Good Witch is unabashedly dressed in white and the Wicked Witch of the West in black. In *Star Wars*, the ultimate villain, Darth Vader, is cloaked and hooded entirely in black.

The distaste many people have for dark skin, broad noses, and thick lips works its way into odd corners of behavior. When Fran Lebowitz wrote African-American characters into her children's book, *Mr. Chas and Lisa Sue Meet the Pandas*, white artists seemed uncomfortable doing illustrations. "The biggest problem was getting white people to draw children who looked black," she told National Public Radio in an interview. "They drew white children who were sort of cream-colored or beige."

There is less ambivalence when the character is not likable and blackness can be deepened to convey a sinister sense of wrongdoing. That was apparently *Time* magazine's purpose when it darkened the mug shot of O. J. Simpson and put it onto the cover in June 1994; the former football star had been arrested and charged with murdering his white wife and her white friend. Americans could see the effect vividly, because *Newsweek* ran the same cover photograph, undoctored. There stood the two magazines, side by side in the racks of newsstands, one showing Simpson as a man with amber skin, the other, with a face so dark his unshaven cheeks and chin matched the blackness of his jacket. Strangely, *Time* also printed the original mug shot on an inside page, so readers saw the infernal magic that had been worked by artists. A line from Toni Morrison's *Beloved* came to mind: "Whitepeople believed that whatever the manners, under every dark skin was a jungle. Swift unnavigable waters, swinging screaming baboons, sleeping snakes, red gums ready for their sweetwhite blood."

When the old notions surrounding blackness are combined with America's racial history, they produce a chemistry of emotions that many whites fail to recognize even in themselves. "Being black is a twenty-four-hour lifetime job," declares Jean McGuire, the director of the Metco school program in Boston. "If most white people woke up tomorrow morning with black skin, they would be crazy by twelve o'clock. They're not prepared in their life to deal with what they've been taught. White people teach their children that they are superior."

For any white who claims to have no negative reaction to dark skin, Andrew Hacker, a political science professor at Queens College, suggests an exercise. He presents white students with a parable: At midnight tonight, they are to become black. "And this will mean not simply a darker skin, but the bodily and facial features associated with African ancestry. However, inside you will be the person you always were. Your knowledge and ideas will remain intact. But outwardly you will not be recognizable." Each of them will live fifty more years as blacks. What compensation would they demand for such a change? "Most seemed to feel that it would not be out of place to ask for $50 million, or $1 million for each coming black year," Hacker writes. "And this calculation conveys, as well as anything, the value that white people place on their own skins."

The literature of fantasy contains magical and frightening transformations between white and black. Hugh Lofting, an English-born writer, gave generations of children an inventive character named Dr. Dolittle, an animal doctor who visits Africa with his friends—a parrot, a monkey, an owl, a dog, a duck, and a pig. In the early version of one story, they are captured by an African king with a hideous son, Prince Bumpo, who tells of having kissed Sleeping Beauty awake, only to have her shout, "Oh, he's black!" and run away. The prince yearns to be white. So, in exchange for their freedom, Dr. Dolittle makes a paste to whiten Bumpo's face—but it will work only temporarily, until they make their escape. The duck says, "Serve him right if he does turn black again. I hope it is a dark black."

Finian's Rainbow, the popular Broadway musical that is still a mainstay of community theaters, contains a little morality play that attacks prejudice but reinforces the curse of black skin. Senator Billboard Rawkins, a bigot, makes Sharon McLonergan so angry that she wishes he were black. It would be an idle wish except that when she makes it, she is unknowingly standing over a buried pot of gold that makes wishes come true. Rawkins turns black, a leprechaun gets the bigotry out of his soul, and the sheriff threatens to burn Sharon as a witch if she doesn't convert Rawkins back to white. She has no idea how to do it, but the leprechaun does. Rawkins is restored. Happy ending.

A curious sentence was uttered on September 7, 1989, by the anchorman of the eleven o'clock newscast on WRC-TV in Washington, D.C. Reporting on the search for a suspected rapist, the announcer declared, "Police say he is black with a dark brown complexion."

The confusion of symbol and color creates an easy paradigm, hardening the categories of blackness and whiteness. What if the newscaster had described the suspect merely as having a dark brown complexion? With the word "black," a host of images rushes into the mind; without it, the assumptions lose their clarity and certainty. After all, the designations "black" and "white" are metaphors. They are absolutes, opposite poles in an elemental divide. Physicists define "black" as the absence of light, the result when all light waves are absorbed, and "white" as the reflection of all wavelengths in the visible spectrum. One is truly the antithesis of the other. And that symbolism of contradictory extremes drives the language. It is not the eye alone but the associations triggered by color that have determined the labels by which Americans identify themselves and one another.

If language were designed to describe African-Americans and European-Americans accurately, it would embrace their true colors along a range of browns, tans, yellows, and pinks. As it is, the only people who seem capable of recognizing what their eyes see are small children, before they are taught how to look through an adult American prism. An Egyptian boy, entering kindergarten in Washington, D.C., came home during the first few weeks talking about other children as "brown." Soon he learned the American lexicon and switched to "black."

In Pennsylvania, an African-American youngster of six said to his mother, "A boy at school called me black. I'm not black, am I?"

"Yes, you are," his mother replied. "Your father and I are, too."

"No, I'm not. I'm not black. I don't want to be black."

"Well, but you want to be our son, don't you? If you weren't black, you wouldn't be our son."

Gently, she talked him toward acceptance, until he finally said, "Yes, I want to be black. I want to be your son."

On the day after the 1955 Montgomery bus boycott, Reggie Daniel got to his school in Louisville, Kentucky, a little late. As he was walking in, the class was singing the last line of "America the Beautiful," and the teacher began to talk about how glad she was that "we colored people had started standing up for our rights," as he recalled. "I had the concept of color, and that was peach and pink and brown, but this notion of colored people and whites—what's a white? I raised my hand to get a clarification: 'What are colored people?' There was dead silence. And the teacher: 'What's your problem?' She said, 'You and everybody in the school [are colored].' 'What color?' 'Colored people.' I thought I would give it another try, and that, of course, was my big mistake, 'cause I asked, 'What color? What do they look like?' 'Of course, brown.' 'Oh, OK, well then, I guess I'm not colored.' " His heritage was African, Irish, East Indian, American Indian, French, and Jewish, and his skin was a light tan; the only way he could match it was to mix brown and white paints. "I was never in the crayon box," he said. "My skin tone was never anywhere to be found. Crayola came out with these very fascinating rainbow colors that year. They had beige and tan, and they had this weird thing called 'flesh.' " That didn't correspond to his skin either. "I was never there. But I had an awareness of mixing the paints—so I had an awareness of being a mixture without knowing what that meant."

The visceral reaction to the idea of blackness has not been extinguished, despite all the efforts to surround the term with an aura of dignity. Some whites worry that calling a person "black" will be insulting, and some blacks find it so. A group of white students at Dartmouth confessed that they tended to avoid "black" in favor of "African-American," which they found politically safer. "That was my biggest fear, that someone would think that I was referring to them in a derogatory way," said a white football player from Alabama.

The aversion was reinforced by an eighteen-year-old from Newark, New Jersey, who had come to resent being labeled "black." "I not only think that the word 'black' when it's used toward people is negative," she said, "I think that 'African-American' is the correct term—not just politically but on a cultural level. We descend from Africa; we don't descend from black. Black is a color. You don't descend from white. Africans don't consider themselves black. You call them 'black,' that is an insult. They are Africans. We should adopt that belief too. Don't call me black. I can show you the darkest person of African descent, and they are not black." She pointed to a chair. "This is black. They are brown. Don't call me black. Call me African-American."

Even those whose racial prejudice is keenly honed can fool themselves by relying on color to put people into neat boxes. One proof lies in an old photograph that is kept by a black family in Gadsden, Alabama—a prized shot that causes a lot of laughter. According to Tony Wyatt, the picture shows his grandmother being kissed by Governor George Wallace in the days of segregation. "He thought she was white," Wyatt said with a big smile. "She has blue eyes. She has long, beautiful hair. She's lighter than you. Wallace was coming through campaigning, and she'd been hired to serve hors d'oeuvres, typical subservient role. And he sees her. And for a campaign picture, he says, 'Oh, let me!' and he puts his arms around her and he gives her a kiss on the cheek."

In a less amusing fashion, whites' obsession with color confronted Derek Greene, a nineteen-year-old African-American from Wilmington, North Carolina. He had a pink birthmark on his face. A splotch covered his right eyelid and extended onto his forehead above his right eye; his right eyelashes were blond. When he worked Sundays as a sacker in a supermarket in Shreveport, Louisiana, where he was going to college, he got so many tasteless questions about his birthmark from whites in the checkout line that he avoided spending any more hours at work than he absolutely had to. "One day, a lady just boldly came out and said that I wanted to be white but turned out black," he remembered painfully. "I didn't want to lose my job, so I just took it."

Because of the long-standing segregationist formula that a person was considered Negro with just "one drop" of "Negro blood," white Americans are not usually conscious of differentiating among African-Americans of various colors. A person is either "black" or not, and the relative lightness or darkness of her skin is irrelevant to the classification. At a deeper level of less explicit awareness, however, various shades of the skin do appear to have varying impacts on the attitudes of many whites. This can be brought home dramatically.

When a white couple in San Francisco decided that they wanted to adopt a black child, the county official in charge, who was white, sat them down and began showing them one baby picture after another. "He started off with jet, inky black," the father recalled, "and he said, 'That black?' " Then he produced another photograph, of a slightly lighter child, and so on, until he got to a very light, biracial girl, whom they chose for adoption. "It was a very interesting process, and it was very humiliating, actually," said the father. "He'd been through this before, and he knew. He did a very good job not only of pinpointing our sensitivity but also doing it in a way that was not hostile, not threatening."

But it did pinpoint that sensitivity to the shade of the skin, that galvanizing unsteadiness that whites often have around the very, very dark. In her Catholic school in Chicago, editor Laura Washington believed the white nuns "for the most part seemed to be very intimidated by the black students and very uncomfortable around them, and feeling a need to try to identify a black child in the classroom that they felt most comfortable with—and usually that child was very light-skinned, had straight hair, appeared more white and usually would come from a middle-class background."

Indeed, when white people want to be demonstrably tolerant, they often aim their welcomes at lighter-skinned blacks, who can seem less different. "They're expanding their own group while seeming to be egalitarian," Reggie Daniel observed. " 'Well, we have some. I mean, you're equal. You're just like me. I don't see any difference. This is a meritocracy.' " In fact, he argued, the result remains a hierarchy of skin color. "In the integration of the public schools in Louisville, what they did was to choose the lightest-skinned teachers to put into the white schools. My mother was one, and Mrs. Alexander—you couldn't tell her from a white person. They also would send another person who was just a little browner. . . . They were not threatening. They wouldn't have sent anybody in there with an Afro or braids or a dashiki."

One of the few studies of whites' attitudes on shades of color found that different skin tones elicited significantly different reactions in certain circumstances. The research was done in 1991 and 1992 by Nayda Terkildsen, then of the State University of New York in Stony Brook. She used a random sample of 348 whites from the jury pool of Jefferson County, Kentucky, giving each person a packet of information on one fictitious gubernatorial candidate supposedly running in a nearby state— a white male, a light-skinned black male, or a dark-skinned black male. The three "candidates" were created by using a photograph of a light-skinned African-American man and altering it to make him look either white or dark-skinned. The biographies and positions on issues were made identical so that the only variable would be skin color. Through a series of questions, the white voters were analyzed as to their level of racial prejudice and their tendency to be "self-monitoring"—that is, the degree to which they were "aware of the negative social consequences of expressing their prejudice," as Terkildsen wrote.

Overall, the white candidate received more positive responses than either of the blacks, confirming race as a significant factor in whites' political choices. Among racially intolerant voters, both the light-skinned and dark-skinned blacks got low marks; indeed, as prejudice increased, the rating of the light-skinned black fell more precipitously than that of the dark-skinned candidate.

However, when the prejudiced voters were divided into two sub-groups—those who were self-monitoring and those who were not—they displayed major differences in attitude toward the light- and dark-skinned blacks. Those who were not self-monitoring—who did not recognize or care about the results of appearing intolerant—were much more negative about the dark-skinned black than about the light-skinned black. In other words, they felt no compunction about expressing their distaste for dark skin. The self-monitoring, prejudiced whites were the reverse: They rated the dark-skinned black much higher than the light-skinned, suggesting that they were compensating for their intolerance by engaging in "the censorship of their judgments about the dark-skinned black candidate," Terkildsen said.

Several other researchers, black and white, have compiled evidence that skin tone influences professional success. The three authors of *The Color Complex*, Kathy Russell and Ronald Hall, who are black, and Midge Wilson, who is white, examined a list of blacks who have scored firsts—the first black chairman of the Joint Chiefs of Staff (General Colin L. Powell), the first black female cabinet member (Patricia R. Harris), the first black mayor of this or that city. "Look closely at the faces of these 'first' Black leaders," they write, "and notice what they have in common: they all have light skin. . . . For light-skinned Blacks, it simply remains easier to get ahead. Take a close look at Black urban professionals, or 'buppies,' with their corporate salaries, middle-class values, and predominantly light-brown to medium-brown skin color. They benefit not only from their social contacts with other light-skinned Blacks but also from looks that, in a predominantly White society, are more mainstream." The authors cite several sociological and anthropological studies that have uncovered strong correlations between lighter skin and higher earnings, between thinner noses and lips and higher socio-economic status. "Drive past any inner-city housing project, and you cannot help but notice that the majority of residents are dark-skinned," they write. "Even more disturbing, look behind the walls of the nation's prisons; they are filled with a disproportionate number of dark-skinned inmates. (A telling saying in the Black community is 'The lighter the skin, the lighter the sentence.')"

These patterns are not rigid, and the exceptions are numerous enough to leave room for debate about the weight of skin color in the equation of failure. Supreme Court Justice Clarence Thomas is an example of a very dark African-American who has been elevated to the pinnacle of power. "He throws the whole thing out of kilter," said Reggie Daniel, "except that his mind is as white as the driven snow. It's like, 'Clarence, you wanted to make sure there is no question about your credibility, didn't you?' " Born of a poor and broken family, Thomas earned the embrace of white conservative Republicans by adopting extreme right-wing views and by confirming their soothing myth that with hard work, anyone of any race or creed can rise. Toni Morrison notes how crucial it was for this dark-skinned man's white supporters to render him harmless from the outset: At the news conference introducing the nominee, Senator John Danforth, Thomas's foremost champion, put the judge's laughter high on his list of attributes. "It's the loudest laugh I have ever heard," she quotes Danforth as saying. "It comes from deep inside, and it shakes his body . . . the object of his laughter is most often himself." To Morrison, the fixation on Thomas's laugh—unthinkable for introducing, say, Robert Bork, William Gates, or even Thurgood Marshall—represents the white requirement for racial accommodation and obedience, made all the more essential by Thomas's darkness.

Skin color and facial features are so intertwined with concepts of physical beauty that they pervade casting decisions in the entertainment and advertising industries, thereby both reflecting and reinforcing the dominant "white" ideas about what is attractive. A study of magazines and mail-order catalogues by the New York City Consumer Affairs Department found that on the rare occasions when African-American models were used in upscale advertising, most of the females had light skin and "white" hairstyles. The ads "in effect say that only white is sexy and beautiful," the report concluded. "The seductive ingenues in 'Guess' clothing ads are white, the woman with the 'come hither' look in the Cointreau ad is white, ads for the Estée Lauder perfume called 'Beautiful' show a white woman with a white veil." In catalogues, the study found, "African-Americans are usually very light-skinned, and, with few exceptions, have straightened, i.e. 'relaxed,' hair. This sends a disturbing message: light skin tones are desirable, dark skin is not; straight hair is desirable, natural hair is not." Only 25 blacks appeared among 2,198 whites in Victoria's Secret catalogues, for example, and most had lighter skin tones. "By using very light-skinned minority models, cataloguers can say that they are racially diverse, without having to deal with the difficult and uncomfortable issues that blackness may present to some whites," the report declared. "The use of light-skinned models is intentionally ambiguous."

A 1996 Talbots catalogue, however, suggested that the taboo may start to break down. Among the 159 pages, a dark-skinned black model with close-cropped, kinky hair appeared fourteen times—not an overwhelming presence, but a beginning.

Some blacks who have studied American film and television believe that studios and networks also prefer lighter-skinned black women with slender noses and thin lips, because black women seem more desirable to Hollywood when they occupy an ethereal region of racial drift. Black men, on the other hand, must be darker. "No mulattoes," said Albert Johnson, an African-American film critic and professor at Berkeley. "Make sure that you know that they're black. It has been sad, through the decades, where great male black actors couldn't be cast because they were light-skinned and they had straight hair. Harry Belafonte could have become a great star, but the studios were afraid of having a mulatto black man, especially in the South."

While women must "meet the dominant standard in terms of beauty," said Reggie Daniel, "men are not judged that way—well, not consistently. The stallion image, the black stud, can be someone who's got the body of a Hercules, but whose face may not at all meet European standards, because it's strictly an erotic image. You find a lot of that. There's Wesley Snipes in *Jungle Fever*, the guy who played Shaft in the sixties, and James Brown. The simian image. The stud who's gonna maul the world is an acceptable image for men of African descent, because, as a sexual image, it's an image that people are accustomed to seeing."

For black men to be chosen for less brutal roles, however, they must usually combine reasonably dark skin with "white" physiognomy. Thus, Sidney Poitier "looks like a dusky Apollo," Daniel observed. Denzel Washington lacks a strongly African face, but he's "all chocolate," said Daniel. "So they're going to choose men whose skin is brown but with European features." The notable exception to these patterns is singer Michael Jackson, who has become lighter in skin and more European in features over the years, presumably through plastic surgery and other medical treatment. Adding an effeminate manner, he presents himself as the ultimate in ambiguity: neither black nor white, neither male nor female.

There are corners of the entertainment world where such hang-ups do not exist. The Arena Stage in Washington, D.C., frequently does color-blind casting, where blacks and whites play roles regardless of race. In Shakespeare's *Twelfth Night*, the two romances—between Orsino and Viola and between Olivia and Sebastian (Viola's twin)—turned out to be interracial because of the actors who were cast. In the Gershwin musical *Of Thee I Sing*, the part of Diana Devereaux, who wins the Miss White House contest and is supposed to marry the president, was played by Terry Burrell, who was black. Absolutely no racial implications existed; the audience was asked, in effect, not to see color at all. So it was also with Arena's production of *Our Town*, two of whose leads in that very white setting were black, and *The Visit*, by Swiss playwright Friedrich Dürrenmatt, who surely had not imagined a racially diverse population of characters walking through his fictitious Central European village early in the century.

Color-blind casting invites a suspension of disbelief. For a wondrous moment, human beings are illuminated by their humanity, not by their race; whatever nobility and weakness they display, whatever vision or cowardice they possess comes individually, not from some group identity. This brand of theater is of the real world and apart from it, created by reality and beyond its reach. The outside grit of life is filtered, purified, and distilled into the essential ingredients of human justice and tragedy.

The stage is unique. Where color-conscious casting exists elsewhere, some may be deliberate and some instinctive. When Robert Gardner, who is white, set out to do his short film on Kwanzaa for National Geographic Television, he chose the black actors he considered the best. As it happened, all were rather light-skinned (all three children in the film were biracial), and when the whites at the Geographic noticed, they were displeased. Some darker-skinned blacks were required, they told him, and so he had to withdraw the leading role from the actress he had hired, hold new auditions, and pick another woman with darker skin.

This shows that whites will often push for darkness when the character is supposed to be emphatically black. That happened when the television situation comedy *True Colors* was being cast. It featured an interracial couple, and Michael J. Weithorn, the white writer of the series, wanted a black man who looked unequivocally black. "It was very important to me that we not cast a light-skinned black as the father," Weithorn explained, "because it would look as if—and in fact would be—an attempt to back away from the premise a little bit." One excellent actor read for the part, but he was quite light-skinned and somewhat effete, Weithorn said. "He's very good, very funny, but it just was not right. It would seem to be minimizing the thing we were trying to do."

Otherwise, and in other shows, he insisted, color has not entered his calculations. "Quite honestly, I've never heard it come up," he said. "I've never felt any pressure from networks to cast lighter-skinned people. I'll tell you what is interesting, though. I honestly think, in my experience, blacks today focus on it much more than whites do. In the black culture there's much more emphasis on it. There was a fascinating thing. A girl came in to read for a part, a teenage girl, and sometimes they'll have their picture and résumé, and it's not just one picture but a composite, showing two or three different looks. And this girl had two pictures, one of her as a street girl, and one was as a nice, sweet middle-class girl. The nice, sweet middle-class girl picture was lit in a way that made her significantly lighter-skinned than the street picture. I bet anything that that was intentional, on the theory that she thought that she'd be able to get those parts more easily if she seemed light-skinned in the picture, and conversely, the street parts more easily if she seemed dark-skinned."

The actress may have been playing to her perception of white biases. But the argument that blacks care more than whites about color was reinforced by the reaction to a casting decision by ABC when Sidney Poitier was picked to play Supreme Court Justice Thurgood Marshall. Poitier was much darker than Marshall, leading Richard G. Carter, a columnist who described himself as a light-skinned black, to chide the film and television industry for ignoring color. "Mr. Poitier's acting ability notwithstanding," he wrote, "such lack of color-conscious casting is an insult to African-Americans. But it's par for the course in TV and movies." He accused white producers of insensitivity to the shades of color that black people cared about so strongly, and he cited case after case in which studios had made no attempt to match skin tones: Cicely Tyson, who is dark, played the lighter Coretta Scott King in a film that "also featured Howard Rollins Jr., who is dark, as the much lighter Rev. Andrew Young. Then there was brown-skinned James Earl Jones as the very dark heavyweight champion of yore, Jack Johnson, and short, dark Percy Rodrigues as the tall, light 300-pound former Mayor of Atlanta, Maynard Jackson." Carter concluded, "With black people, skin color counts. Even if Hollywood can't see it."

Caste

With black people, skin color counts. And so, like an insidious virus, the
bigotry long nurtured by white culture infects black values. It mutates
into a malignant strain of color coding, which influences marriage, child
rearing, friendship, churchgoing, career, music, and literature. Among
all the prejudices surrounding race in America, it is this obsession with
the shade of the skin that has been absorbed most thoroughly by the victims themselves—not all of them, to be sure, but enough to create powerful patterns of attitude and discrimination.

To express the various levels of contempt for various degrees of
color, a vocabulary of self-hatred has been generated among African-
Americans. It includes "rusty," "blueblack," "high yellow," and a nasty
little chant that darker children sometimes aim at lighter playmates:

> *Light, bright, almost white!*
> *Light, bright, almost white!*

"Maybe this is just me," said "Martha," a young woman at Louisiana
State University in Shreveport, "but have you ever noticed that there's,
like, a prejudiced line drawn between blacks of different colors?" Her
skin was a smooth coffee brown, and her question got a chorus of agreement from five other African-Americans around the table, young people
from Maryland, Texas, Louisiana, and North Carolina.

"Oh, yes!"

"I know!"

"That's something I feel—everybody does." Indeed, just as whites
often begin a description of another white by citing hair color, blacks
often begin by noting skin color: She's a bright-skinned girl, or she's a
dark-skinned girl or a brown-skinned girl. And these are not benign
categories.

Martha admitted that she was biased, and the confession came almost
gleefully. "I really know that I am," she said, "because the other day I was
walking down the street . . . and there was this rusty black man—" She
broke into laughter. Could she define rusty black? "Just like incredibly
dark, just like black beyond the part of all black." Others chimed in,
saying, "Blueblack," and they giggled naughtily.

"Like the eyes and his teeth were the only things that shined,"
Martha continued merrily. "He probably glowed in the dark. I don't

know, it was nasty. And like a greasy Jheri curl hanging all the way down his back. He said, 'Hey, baby.' And I was like, 'Ooooh.'" A lighter-skinned man walking with him she had found attractive, she said; the other students nodded with understanding. "And they were both black, and the ex-ter-eeeem-ly black guy was probably a perfectly nice person, and I didn't care and I felt bad 'cause I realized that that was probably a downfall on my part, because I should be able to accept them all. But the truth is that I was just like, 'Ewwww.'"

Now the conversation was ignited, and the banter quickly revealed crosscurrents of anti-dark and pro-dark feelings, anti-light and pro-light behavior. Tricia, who was quite light and wore her hair in waves to her shoulders, told of walking into a black club with friends darker than she. "Oooh! Oooh! She just thinks she's Miss It!" came the comments from the crowd.

"I'm just walkin' in just normally," she said. "I wasn't shakin', anything like that. I just walked in."

"She thinks she's Miss It! Look at her, all her light self! She's so yellow, she needs to get out of here! Oh, but she needs to get out of here!" The last line Tricia delivered in a high-pitched screech, but with a smile.

"I've encountered that up here," said a third woman, Adriane. "A young man up here told me, 'I prefer darker women because lighter women have an attitude.' I was very insulted."

"I got that," said Martha. "I got that quite a bit."

"This was from a black man," Adriane added. "He said he wouldn't date anybody who was lighter than him."

"I think that rusty black people deserve rusty black people," Martha sneered, laughing acidly.

"No, he's a pretty brown," Adriane countered.

Martha giggled. "I'm sorry."

"He's a pretty brown, he's a pretty brown."

And then the women started talking about somebody from Sudan. "And his skin was blueblack," one said. "He was beeeyoooootiful."

"I saw a man like that once," said Martha. "I went to school with him. His name was Darnell, and he had very white, very sculptured features, but he was black. He was beautiful, though."

All the hang-ups, piled on top of one another, make a jumble of contradictions. Dark is beautiful, mysterious, authentic. Dark is unruly, aggressive, lower-class. Light is beautiful, intelligent, ambitious. Light is ugly, uppity, effete. It depends on where the hue of your own skin places you in the hierarchy of color castes. The preoccupation is reflected in African-American literature, from the coarse poetry of rap to the lyrical prose of the novel.

Along the spectrum between virility and homosexuality, light skin is sometimes associated disparagingly with being gay, as one rap song suggests by contrasting a "straight" with a "light-skin fluffy." Conversely, it has been a mark of authority, as Charles W. Chesnutt writes in *The House Behind the Cedars*, his 1900 novel of a young "bright-skinned" woman who is induced to pass as white, only to be found out and plunged back into blackness. Chesnutt, who was very light himself, constructs his story as a tragic account of blacks' obsession with color. In one scene, the heroine applies for a teaching job, and a light brown schoolmaster, expecting "to see a pretty yellow girl," is struck by her radiance. He says, "A lady er her color kin keep a lot er little niggers straighter'n a darker lady could."

In another passage, Chesnutt sketches a precise portrait of the prejudice: "There were dark mulattoes and bright mulattoes. Mis' Molly's guests were mostly of the bright class, most of them more than half white, and few of them less. In Mis' Molly's small circle, straight hair was the only palliative of a dark complexion."

Much of black literature is populated by characters who care very much about color. The subject runs through friendly insults during a card game in Zora Neale Hurston's *Their Eyes Were Watching God*, which has become a classic since its publication in 1937. "Don't over-sport yourself, Ed. . . . You gittin' too yaller," one man says. "Move, over from me, Gabe!" says another. "You too black. You draw heat!" Later, Hurston writes:

> Mrs. Turner's shape and features were entirely approved by Mrs. Turner. Her nose was slightly pointed and she was proud. Her thin lips were an ever delight to her eyes. Even her buttocks in bas-relief were a source of pride. To her way of thinking all these things set her aside from Negroes. That was why she sought out Janie to friend with. Janie's coffee-and-cream complexion and her luxurious hair made Mrs. Turner forgive her for wearing overalls like the other women who worked in the fields. She didn't forgive her for marrying a man as dark as Tea Cake, but she felt that she could remedy that. . . . "Ah jus' couldn't see mahself married to no black man. It's too many black folks already. We oughta lighten up de race."

Alice Walker makes biting commentary as her characters in *The Color Purple* and *The Temple of My Familiar* struggle with the quality of skin and hair: "Harpo little yellowish girlfriend sulk, hanging over the bar. . . . The last thing niggers want to think about they God is that his hair kinky. . . . They are so black, Celie, they shine . . . try to imagine a city full of these shining, blueblack people wearing brilliant blue robes. . . . I felt like I was seeing black for the first time." "But soon another house was sold to lightbright blacks, and another. They didn't like us either—we were dark compared to them. . . . All the cadavers they'd worked on were from a certain range of shades between dark brown and black, and this had radicalized him. . . . He started to think there were no poor, really destitute, lightskin black people, and this made him very sad."

All these intricate evaluations are answered by Langston Hughes with a poem, "Harlem Sweeties," that rejoices in the delectable variety of colors among the women in his neighborhood of Sugar Hill.

> *. . . Brown sugar lassie,*
> *Caramel treat,*
> *Honey-gold baby*
> *Sweet enough to eat.*
> *Peach-skin girlie,*
> *Coffee and cream,*
> *Chocolate darling*
> *Out of a dream. . . .*
>
> *Caramel, brown sugar,*
> *A chocolate treat.*
> *Molasses taffy,*
> *Coffee and cream,*
> *Licorice, clove, cinnamon*
> *To a honey-brown dream.*
> *Cinnamon, honey brown dream.*
> *Ginger, wine gold*
> *Persimmon, blackberry,*
> *All through the spectrum*
> *Harlem girls vary—*
> *So if you want to know beauty's*
> *Rainbow-sweet thrill*
> *Stroll down luscious,*
> *Delicious, fine Sugar Hill.*

• • •

As a child, Linda was not happy with the color of her eyes, the set of her hair, or the tone of her skin. Alone with her private distress, she said her most frequent prayer: "God, please let me wake up with brown eyes and kinky hair and dark skin." Her eyes are green. Her hair is straight and dark brown, held now in a black band. Her light skin is set off by gold hoop earrings, plus a diamond button in each ear. She does not have full lips or a wide nose and could be mistaken for Hispanic or Arab until she begins to talk with a black accent.

She is sitting on the old couch in her cluttered town house, located between Baltimore and Washington. The living room is crammed with photographs and Thai rubbings. A wire coat hanger lies on the floor. A parakeet chirps loudly in a cage. Her young son comes in, shakes hands politely, then goes out to play; his father takes him some evenings and weekends.

Linda has worked on and off as a secretary, a teacher's aide, and a process server. Money is a chronic problem, but nothing compared to the problem of fitting her body together with her identity. Only now, in her late thirties, is she coming to terms with who she is.

Many African-American families value light skin, but not hers. She was made the target of mocking remarks. "She thinks she's white," relatives would say scornfully. One afternoon, when Linda came home from being tutored for dyslexia, her mother made a comment to her grandmother that burned like a slap across the face: "Listen to her, trying to talk like a white child."

Linda yearned for hair that needed pressing and straightening like her sister's; she watched enviously as her sister got all the attention with hot grease and a hot comb. "I put, like, over a hundred dollars in my hair trying to wear an Afro," she confesses. "The stuff was so tangled I had to cut it off."

Her skin color was never a neutral element in her friendships. A lot of white children "felt comfortable taking me to their parents' house," she said, " 'cause I didn't really look black. I had girlfriends that wanted to be my friends because of the way I looked, and I had girls who didn't like me because of the way I looked." Some children said, "I don't want to play with her, she looks like a white girl." Others automatically labeled her a snob, saying, "The bitch thinks she's cute."

"And that used to hurt," Linda recalls. "It made me very insecure as a child, 'cause I didn't look like other people. I thought I was an ugly child, and I was not; I was a cute little girl. I was convinced that I could be black one day. I used any kind of thing you could send off for in the back of magazines to make you dark, and lay in the sun for hours."

Her light complexion gained her one advantage, which she remembers with delighted amusement. "There was this swimming pool that was white-only in my neighborhood," she says, "and my godmother was a practical nurse and a midwife, and she worked for a family in the neighborhood, a white family. And they used to laugh because they used to send me to the swimming pool, where blacks weren't allowed." She took a breath. "I felt more racism from blacks than from whites."

Dimly at first, then with growing urgency, Linda's consciousness of her difference emerged and evolved into a mystery. She had no explanation for it. Her mother was darker than she. Her father, "Allen," who lived with the family until she was about five, looked nothing like her. He was short; she was large for her age. "He's about five feet, eight inches, as black as black can be, beady hair, and just not me," she says. "You don't get green eyes without blue being somewhere. There was no blue nowhere along the line. Just from reading, educationwise and learning about genetics and so forth in school, things just started adding up. When I started questioning everything, I guess I was about twelve." But her mother gave her no help. "She refused to talk to me," Linda said bitterly. "I asked her, 'Who is my real father?' And she says, 'You know who your father is, and I refuse to talk to you.' My mother was a very strict woman. What Mother says, Mother says, and you don't ask Mother no questions."

The questions continued to gnaw quietly, however. Bits and pieces of doubt were strewn around her family, and she began to pick them up and try to assemble them. She kept hearing that her mother had once lived in New York. Her godmother knew something but wouldn't reveal all of it. Peppered by endless questions, the godmother said, "No, [Al] was not your father. But it's not my place and I swore to your mother I would never do this."

Energized by hearing what she had already come to suspect, Linda was determined to find her real father. At nineteen, she took advantage of a moment, mixed her uncle some strong Scotches one evening, and got him to betray the family secret: Her father was a white man named James Smith, nicknamed "Smitty," a postal worker in New York City. He and her mother had been in love, the uncle said, but both were married, and the racial barrier could not be overcome. Her father had once come to Maryland looking for her mother, Linda was told. "She denied that she was pregnant. That was it."

Linda traveled to New York, to the central post office, looking for a

"James Smith," nicknamed "Smitty," who had worked there two decades
before. She had no middle initial, no Social Security number, no right
even to look through post office records. "I gave them a song and dance
that I was investigating the death of someone who had left an inheritance. They went looking through the files, gave me a stack of James
Smiths with the post office." And then, faced with the pile of personnel
forms, she did something she cannot quite explain. "The only thing I
could do was take a glance at them and walk out and cry," she remembers now. "I chose to stop looking. I became frightened. I had this basic
information, and I think I could have pushed it more, through the files. I
could have gotten more information from my uncle, been able to nail
down the route that he worked on, been able to go question the neighbors." And perhaps, just perhaps, she will do so. But not quite yet.

Fights among African-Americans in schools erupt over skin color. Children who are trained to be peer mediators in Baltimore middle schools
can cite case after case of disputes that arise because one child insults
another over color. Tony Wyatt remembers his light skin drawing hostility in his school in Alabama. "My brothers and sisters and I got teased
all the time about the cast of my skin, from blacks calling us 'high
yellow,' 'Light, bright, almost white.' And when we got good grades . . .
other blacks used to say, 'That's because of that white blood in you. You
fit right in.' "

For a person who wants to work in an African-American milieu, a
lack of identifiable blackness can do professional damage. Black identity
forms a major component of Eamon Buehning's self-definition, but her
multiracial ancestry has left her very light, and for that reason alone, she
believed, she received a dubious reception when she applied to teach a
class in an after-school program in the East Elmhurst neighborhood of
New York City. Part of her job was to put on a black history performance with the children, but the black administrators were "kind of
uncomfortable," as one put it to her, saying, "We don't know if this girl
can cut it." In other words, as Buehning explained, "I am not a visual
enough symbol." So, on the train to her crucial interview, she did an outline of the black history she would include in the program. She handed it
to the director and waited. The director looked it over and finally said in
a tone of resignation, "OK, I guess you know what you're talking about."
She got the job.

Since light skin has long been associated with privilege, much antagonism toward light African-Americans seems a displaced anger; whites may be inaccessible as targets, but light-skinned blacks are available. "The racism among blacks, I find, extends from slavery," says Linda Ross. "During slavery, I would work in the house, and that would be the good job, and the dark-skinned woman would have worked in the fields. This is where a lot of this light- and dark-skinned racism originated from. It's pretty sick that it still appears this way."

Anti-dark prejudices among African-Americans are at least as powerful as anti-light and were institutionalized into a virtual caste system in some parts of the country. According to *The Color Complex*, some black churches in the early 1900s painted their doors light brown, and "anyone whose skin was darker than the door was politely invited to seek religious services elsewhere." In Virginia, Pennsylvania, and Louisiana churches, "a fine-toothed comb was hung on a rope near the front entrance. If one's hair was too nappy and snagged in the comb, entry was denied."

Louisiana's particular history of color-consciousness among blacks has generated considerable comment and satire. In 1990, Black Entertainment Television ran an episode of the sitcom *Frank's Place* in which a professor-turned-restaurateur is invited by a friend to apply for membership in the Capital C club, an exclusive organization for light-skinned blacks. Ignorant of the club's color rules, Frank goes for an interview, where a snobby man questions him and looks him over. When he returns to his restaurant, a black waitress asks what in the world he was doing at the Capital C. He's baffled by the question. She pulls out a paper bag, holds it next to her arm, and asks which is lighter, the bag or her arm. The bag, he says. She holds it next to his arm: Which is lighter? Again, the bag. Well, she explains, you have to be at least as light as the bag to get into the Capital C—C for "Creole," a designation favored by light-skinned Louisiana blacks who resent the term "black." It turns out that Frank's friend wants him to break the color barrier at the club. Frank declines. "For years," he says, "I was the only black in this class, the only black on that team. I'm not about to become the only black in a black club—that's going a little too far."

James Miller, an expert on Louisiana history, notes that "Creole," a derogatory term in South America referring to someone born in the New World, became a term of status in Louisiana. In South America, a Creole couldn't be a governor or a viceroy; in Louisiana, a Creole was descended from the original French settlers, who predated the White Anglo-Saxon Protestant population that arrived after the Louisiana Purchase. Those of mixed black and European heritage whose ancestors lived there before 1803 define themselves as "Creoles of color," and many of them dislike blacks who have come from Alabama and elsewhere.

In 1967, when Miller was the only white teaching in a black slum school in New Orleans, he used to take seniors on Saturday tours around the city. Nobody had much money, so everyone would buy a bus transfer, tear the date off, and ride any day, all day, for a dime. The outings became so popular that after a while the group grew to about fifty, so Miller asked a black counselor in the school for some help. "I don't do anything with niggers," the counselor replied.

"But they're black like yourself," Miller said.

"I am a Creole of color. These are niggers."

Anti-dark prejudices kept Barbara Wyche from becoming a majorette in her black Virginia high school before desegregation. "Our majorettes used to only be light," she recalled. "By the time I grew up, I knew that if you were the light-skinned girl, pretty, with long hair, that you got certain things because of that. [Second] in the rank was the light-skinned girl with short hair, and a little below her was the dark-skinned girl with long hair. And if you were that little girl with short kinky hair and ugly on top of it, honey, you would have trouble. A lot of black folks do not even like for me to say that."

More than twenty years later, Angela Collins found the same dynamic among blacks when she attended integrated schools in a Chicago suburb. "I had a complex about being dark," she said, her voice too quiet, too calm for so much hurt. "The girls that were lighter-skinned, you know, they got more boyfriends. Or the girls that were on cheerleading, they were prettier because they were lighter and they had longer hair. . . . My little brother's going through that now. He can't get as many girls as a lighter-skinned guy. I don't know where it comes from, but it's just generation after generation. He's seventeen now."

Only when Collins went to Northern Illinois University did she begin to value herself as a dark-skinned woman. Black students made up 5 to 10 percent of the population, a group small enough to be cohesive and large enough to constitute a supportive subculture. On campus, a black newspaper published poems about skin color, letting her know that she was not alone, that others had suffered the same wounds.

When she auditioned for the campus television station, the white professor in charge rejected her as inarticulate, unable to pronounce some words. Anyone listening to Angela Collins for half a minute would know this to be nonsense; she speaks with complete clarity, finds precise vocabulary, and has just a hint of a black accent. It is impossible for her to escape the conclusion that she was rejected because she was very dark. Her verdict on the professor was simple: "I'll never forget him," she said.

Still, college allowed her to grow until she could find comfort in her blackness. "Now I can say that I'm a beautiful black, dark woman and I don't need to attract anyone, and I'm very happy," she said. "It just has to do with maturity—and being around people like yourself, too."

Skin color is such sensitive territory that an outsider enters at her own risk. Darini Nicholas, a Sri Lankan woman at Lake Forest College, learned this with acute consequences. "In Sri Lanka, as in most countries, unfortunately, the fairer your skin is, the better [off] you are," she explained. "That's something I hated when I first came over here. I realized what was going on, that it's not endemic just to one country." And because she disliked the color-consciousness, she was amazed at what came out of her mouth as she talked to her black roommate. "I said something, 'I guess I'm one of the fair ones in my country; I guess that's good,' or something to that effect. And she stood there and I saw her, and I realized what I had said, and I felt that I had just stabbed her. . . . I was so upset with myself . . . and I walked out of the room, and I grabbed my bag and I just left for class. I didn't talk to her for the rest of the day. And I saw her a couple of times, and she didn't look at me, and I knew: This is it."

The roommate told other blacks, and at dinner, as Nicholas approached their table, one made a crack about how lucky she must be to have fair skin. "Then I said that I wanted to talk to her—the friend, my immediate roommate," Nicholas said. "We were able to talk about it, and we got it straight, and I told her where it was coming from, and I told her it's something I hate, and I didn't expect to say that, and I told her I'd try to change it—that was subconscious and it was something that I still carried around, that I will change." But one of the other black women who heard about her remark "stopped talking to me," Nicholas said, "and we didn't click anymore."

Laced into the status of color are the hierarchies of hair and physiognomy. Whatever resembles the European model is valued by whites, even by many blacks. "Good hair" means straight or wavy, not kinky and African-looking. Attractive faces mean narrow noses, thin lips. Together, the three traits—skin color, hair, and facial features—combine to create an impression, a subconscious definition. If even one characteristic violates the model, it can be decisive, as Natasha Redwood of Colgate discovered when she tried out for the cheerleading squad. She had light skin, green eyes, and wavy brown hair. But her full lips and broad nose defeated her, she believed, along with the loose-limbed movements that she favored. Those who were chosen, including women of color, had finer hair, more European features. "I know I performed well, 'cause I love cheerleading," she said sadly.

A black professor in California, who looked more African than his mother, grew up surrounded by disorienting comments. He resembled his father, whom he rarely saw, and was raised by more European-looking relatives. "I was an outsider even in my own family," he said. "Somehow I was a colored boy in a white family. . . . As a child, when someone says you have bad hair, immediately it becomes confusing. 'Well, what's wrong with my hair?' And then you begin to realize that bad hair is not-straight hair. Straight hair is good hair." His relatives would tell him to pull on his nose so it would be pretty. "Well, is there something wrong with it?" he asked himself. "I thought I just needed it to breathe." Later in life, he realized that the remarks, made without ill intent, had undermined his sense of self, leading him to think, "I'm in this light family now, and there's something wrong with my nose, and my hair is bad."

Blacks and whites often gaze across the racial line with amusement at the other side's preoccupation with appearance. Half a dozen blacks, sitting around at Louisiana State University in Shreveport, laughed with delight at one woman's account of her white friends' elaborate use of makeup. "She's like, 'I got up so early this morning 'cause I really wanted to make a good impression on this guy that's in my class.' She got up at five-thirty in the morning to get dressed! I'm up, like, fifteen minutes before I have to go. I mean, her makeup was perfectly applied. And then another white female I ran into . . . she had on black eye makeup; she looked like she had been hit. This was serious nighttime makeup . . . in the middle of the day. I'm like, 'You look like a ho.' "

Even for the women in this group who were mocking whites about their makeup, however, their own hair was an obsession. "My hair's relaxed; hers is not," one explained. "It's like the natural curl. You can get it out through a process called a relaxer, which straightens the curl out. It's much like a perm, where you take straight hair and make it curly. . . . It's like pressing combs used to do, but it's a chemical process. You get it done about once every six weeks."

"And the hairdo is a big, big thing," said another. "It's a matter of acceptance, or not being accepted. When I was about seventeen, I cut all my hair off and I went natural, and the reaction—I even had an older woman tell me, 'Aren't you ashamed to have your hair like that?' I did it because I didn't really want to comb my hair. I was being lazy. . . . My older sister had natural hair, and she could do so much stuff with it, and I thought it was so beautiful, so I got the perm cut off my hair." She was peppered with criticism from black and white alike. "I hear, 'Why do you do that to yourself?' " she said. "You get it from all sides. And if I didn't have my family backing me up and if I weren't a stronger person, I wouldn't be able to handle it." Her sister, wearing a natural in Minnesota, "had a [white] woman say to her on an elevator one day, something to the effect of 'We ought to take you back to Africa and put you in a tree.' "

When black women want to deride a white woman, they sometimes do unflattering imitations of her tossing her long, straight hair. And white women are often amazed at the energy devoted to hair by so many blacks. Jessica Prentice, the only white student at Tougaloo College in Mississippi, found herself immersed in conversation about hair. "For the most part everybody was permed and the guys had fades," she said. "Fades, you know, where they shave here, and it pretty much fades into your hair, and then a flattop. It's a huge vocabulary. The things I learned, all the things I didn't know about hair. . . . I was living in a women's dorm, so they would be giving each other perms every night, and rinses, and all this different stuff. I never knew how black women did their hair. I'd never noticed it before, and all of a sudden it was around me all the time."

"Lady Jones was mixed," Toni Morrison writes in *Beloved*. "Gray eyes and yellow woolly hair, every strand of which she hated—though whether it was the color or the texture even she didn't know."

Body Language

Besides the visual impressions that are made by the color of skin, the style of hair, and the shape of facial features, blacks and whites are also driven by a network of myths and fantasies about other aspects of each other's bodies: hygiene, odor, sex, and movement—as in dance and athletics. These are not new images; they are merely new variations on old themes of stereotyping that have existed since Africans were first brought to the continent in the seventeenth century. It is enough to recall Jefferson's unsavory remark ("They secrete less by the kidneys and more by the glands of the skin, which gives them a very strong and disagreeable odor") to illustrate the antecedents of white society's attitudes about black bodies. This was the heart of much of the South's

segregationist impulse to enforce separate lavatories and drinking fountains, separate eating establishments, and whites-only beaches and swimming pools—all the while allowing blacks to prepare and serve food and
take intimate care of white children.

Today, with de jure segregation gone, the notion of blacks as unclean
is less explicit, more thoroughly diffused into other caricatures and aversions. But it can still be potent when it occasionally comes to the surface.
"It's kind of bad to say," a twenty-one-year-old white man remarked
during a focus group on race, "but, I mean, they do have an odor that's
different from the white people unless they cover it up with a deodorant
or cologne or something of that nature." Whites still flee neighborhoods
into which African-Americans move—or harass black newcomers until
they leave—not only because of the specter of violence but in the conviction that blacks will run down property values by throwing trash into the
streets and letting their houses go to ruin. And many restaurants still
keep blacks out of sight in the kitchen or in subservient roles as busboys,
while reserving waiters' jobs, with their lucrative tips, for whites. Somewhere, embedded in the tangle of other prejudices, lurks the resilient
suspicion that "black" is equivalent to "dirty."

Many blacks retaliate by aiming the same stereotype at whites,
turning the arsenal of bigotry on their persecutors. "I'm embarrassed to
say this, I just remembered it," said La Tanya Wright, laughing, as
she sat with friends in California. She was young and black, originally
from Washington, D.C. "We used to say things like 'If it rains and a
white person doesn't have an umbrella and her hair gets wet, it will
stink.' " A surge of laughter came from the other blacks. "I'm serious.
People believe that. It's like, don't get around a white person when it
rains, 'cause their hair stinks. And some of my friends still believe this
stuff, too, and they're in college."

Judging by which African-Americans across the country are familiar
with this calumny (many are not), it may be most prevalent in the District of Columbia. "I was told by blacks from D.C. that when they were
kids they were told, 'Never go near a white person in the rain, because
when their hair gets wet it stinks,' " said a black college student in
Louisiana.

"It does! It does!" said a woman who grew up just outside Washington.

"I've heard it does, I'm sorry," said a man who was raised in a military
family, on bases in Texas and Germany. "I'm sorry, it does." Of the
other half-dozen black students in the room, nearly all had heard this
and believed it.

The symmetrical images include a picture of whites as generally unclean. "I remember in high school, we always said the white girls were dirtier than we were and didn't practice good hygiene," recalled Laura Washington, the black editor in Chicago. And Bruce King remembered incidents from seventh grade that seemed to confirm the prejudice he had been taught.

His predominantly black school on Chicago's South Side linked up with a white school in a nearby neighborhood "and had these afternoon sessions in which the two schools would come together and talk about art and stuff like that," he said. "We would eat lunch together, and the white people would sit on the floor and have their lunch, and black people—we would be looking for chairs and tables because we just didn't sit on the floors. And I remember even then people talking about 'Oh, they're so nasty. That's why they're so nasty, because they sit and eat on the floor.' " What was meant by "nasty"? "Dirty," he said. "These were all the stories you would hear as a child: White people were nasty, they don't wash their hair. You can tell when they don't wash their hair. Some of them don't believe in deodorant. So you hear all these stories. And of course it proves it when you're sitting there—and they sit on the floor?" His voice rose in mock amazement.

"My grandmother always used to use the phrase 'dirty, barefooted, white children,' " recalled Carlton Chamblin, a black college student in Birmingham, Alabama. "When we were walking through town to the grocery store, there used to always be these white kids out playing stick-ball, and they wouldn't have any shoes on, and these white kids used to come to school and take their shoes off." He laughed. "My mother and grandmother would say, 'Well, white people don't use washcloths. They don't really clean themselves very well when they bathe.' "

During her year as the only white student at Tougaloo, Jessica Prentice found many blacks believing "that we were dirty," she said. By contrast, "they took, like, two, three showers a day—very cleanliness-conscious." And they devoted hours to their appearance. "As soon as I got there," she recalled, "I realized I had to iron every day, which I had never done. I mean, everything: jeans, T-shirts, everything had to be starched and ironed, and if you didn't, you were just—they'd tell you to go back to your room and change. . . . They would tell me I didn't have enough makeup, or the right kind, or my earrings were too small—all these kinds of things, so it was just constant. And I spent my first couple of months shopping and outfitting myself, because I could see immediately that that was one way to be kind of accepted, because people talk about clothes all the time. . . . They complained bitterly about the white students who had come down before [in an exchange program from Brown] with stringy hair and not wearing bras, and hippie clothes. . . . They thought it was dirty and ugly and filthy. And I think they had worked so hard in their families to kind of distance themselves from a certain lower-class appearance—and you know, people who had very little else had tons of nice shoes and a nice car. There's a sort of security in possessions."

Shari Jones and her white roommate at Lake Forest had fumbled around and struggled to find a decent relationship. And they had succeeded until one evening when they were watching the news and the carefully woven fabric of trust unraveled. Shari was an African-American from Memphis who carried a sense of cultural pride and an impatience with whites' irritating questions. Her roommate's main contacts with black people had been a Jamaican maid and *The Cosby Show*. The first semester was rough. Shari arrived at the mostly white campus feeling inferior, militant, and deprived. "I couldn't relate," she said. "I hadn't grown up in a private school in the really posh section of Manhattan or anything."

Her roommate challenged Shari's hairstyle, the music she favored ("This has to be the most stupid music in the world!"), and the clothes she wore ("That's loud. That's gaudy. Why don't you be more conservative?"). Shari was so distraught that she thought about transferring to a black school. Instead, she and her roommate decided to reach for a measure of understanding. Shari tempered her militance; her roommate tried "to get to know me and my culture," Shari said, by peppering her with questions that Shari began to recognize as expressions of genuine interest. "Like, 'When do you wash your hair?' 'Can I hear this blues tape?' 'Can I hear this rap tape?' And she asked questions about how I grew up in black [neighborhoods]. Essentially just questions, and I had to put down my anger and all that stuff and be her friend, and just drop all the egos and just relate."

Then came the Los Angeles riots. "We were sitting all cozy on the couch looking at the news, and we saw this black guy jumping on this car, and he was short and he had like a bald cut, kind of. And she was like, 'Look at that gorilla.' And I was like, 'Hold on. Hold on. No way. He is not a gorilla. He might be an idiot, and that's the way he's displaying his frustration and his anger . . . about the state of blacks in the inner city, and all that kind of stuff. He might be an idiot in the way he's doing it in trying to slaughter people, but he is not a gorilla. A black man is not a gorilla. He is not an animal.' "

A white might call another white a gorilla, but when the epithet is flung across the racial line, it picks up an ugly connotation. The roommate was clearly embarrassed at what had inadvertently come out of her mouth, perhaps from some depth of elemental prejudice that sees blacks as subhuman, primitive, animallike. The gorilla, the monkey, the ape add up to a long-standing caricature, and nothing hurts or infuriates more deeply. It is a whiplash with as much sting as the word "nigger," and the roommate did not know how to apologize or correct or erase or withdraw her instant of bigotry.

"Oh, oh, oh, my God!" she blurted. Then she said, "Well, I think I'll go read now."

"And I was like, 'No, come back and talk about this,'" Shari said. "'Don't call him an ape.'" Shari was surprised. She had not expected this; they had already achieved friendship. So they worked again, from the ground up, and finally made repairs. And yet Shari wonders. "I still question," she said quietly. "I call her a friend because I've done things for her and she's done things for me. But I don't know. It's still, like, an issue of doubt."

Trying to read white behavior is one burden of being black. "It takes too much energy," Shari confessed, "and you shouldn't have to take all that energy. You shouldn't have to. But that's the way the story goes."

In the autumn of 1993, AT&T published a cartoon in its house magazine, *Focus*, to illustrate the company's involvement in global communications. The artist, hired by the outside contractor who put out the journal, drew a collection of caricatures, all talking on the phone. Northern Europe was represented by a woman wearing a black dress, black boots, and a kerchief around her head. France was a mustachioed man in a beret. South America was a woman with wide hips, a ponytail, and a cockroach at her feet. Asia was a barefoot coolie wearing a conical hat. All these were bad enough. Africa was worse, symbolized not by a person but by a monkey.

From coast to coast, outraged employees and clients burned up AT&T's fax machines. Protests poured in from black leaders, religious leaders, political leaders. Reporters were calling. Stories appeared, and AT&T started losing business. "We lost all kinds of money," one black executive said. "People called in, changed their phone service. We had business customers who called and let us know that they were not making a decision to go with AT&T."

Top officials apologized, said they would not use the illustrator again, and fired the contractor (which in turn fired its art director), according to Burke Stinson, a company spokesman. But two long weeks passed before anything was done about the three AT&T employees who had produced the magazine. "If anyone had seen this and kind of shrugged their shoulders, they would have been fired," Stinson asserted. That was not the case, he explained. One of the three was African-American, and none had paid attention to the drawing as they processed it for publication. So they were merely transferred, and the magazine was shut down. The delay and the leniency gave the impression that senior managers didn't see the problem or thought it would just go away, the black executive said, as if their "lenses were not correctly aligned."

Some whites consciously use the ape as a vehicle of racist attack. In 1996, several employees of the Giant supermarket chain in Maryland did so by putting up pictures of monkeys on a bulletin board and labeling them with the names of black coworkers. More often, however, whites who consider themselves free of racial prejudice display blindness to the power and pain of the animal image, the monkey simile. That failing brought trouble to Dr. Frederick K. Goodwin, the Bush administration's top mental health official, who caused insult and unleashed an uproar with off-the-cuff remarks on February 11, 1992. Speaking to a meeting of the Advisory Council of the National Institute of Mental Health about an initiative aimed at identifying violence-prone individuals early in life, he digressed for a moment to mention a study of primates that a friend had just completed.

"If you look, for example, at male monkeys, especially in the wild, roughly half of them survive to adulthood," he said. "The other half die by violence. That is the natural way of it for males, to knock each other off and, in fact, there are some interesting evolutionary implications of that because the same hyperaggressive monkeys who kill each other are also hypersexual, so they copulate more and therefore they reproduce more to offset the fact that half of them are dying."

So far, so good. Learning about humans by studying monkeys has been long-standing scholarly practice. But Goodwin then swerved into racial territory—unwittingly, by his own account. "Now," he went on, "one could say that if some of the loss of social structure in this society, and particularly within the high-impact inner-city areas, has removed some of the civilizing evolutionary things that we have built up and that maybe it isn't just the careless use of the word when people call certain areas of certain cities 'jungles,' that we may have gone back to what might be more natural, without all of the social controls that we have imposed upon ourselves as a civilization over thousands of years in our own evolution."

After the meeting, Goodwin began to hear complaints, so he asked for reactions; two black colleagues had not been bothered by the speech (until they read the text and were upset), and some whites had been offended, he said. Indeed, as the reverberations increased and the story found its way into the press, his lecture was distilled by news reports, and the broader public was invited to be offended. WAMU, a public-radio station in Washington, D.C., reported simply that Goodwin had "compared inner-city youth to male monkeys in the jungle."

More than four years later, the details of the incident seemed freshly painful to Goodwin. He recounted them in a mixture of professed innocence, admitted guilt, and emphatic outrage that provided a glimpse of the difficulties whites have interacting with the country's racial legacy.

He had given the talk without sufficient preparation, he said, after a night without any sleep because his wife's mother had just had a stroke. That was his first mistake, he realized. In addition, he had not had race in mind when he spoke. "I was not even aware that 'monkey' is a derogatory term that racists have used against blacks," he insisted. "It wasn't something I ever heard; people in my circles never talked that way." Then he qualified his ignorance just a bit: "Maybe if I'd had a multiple-choice quiz I would have checked it off—yeah, it can be used that way."

But he was not referring to race as he spoke of the study or used the word "jungle," he maintained. "In my growing up, we had a movie called *Blackboard Jungle*, about an inner-city school, and everybody in it was white," he recalled. "A couple of days before, I'd heard Spike Lee talking about the 'jungle,'" he added. "It's OK for blacks to say, but not for whites to say." Maybe he should have cited Spike Lee, he lamented. He confessed to having been "insensitive" and "really dumb" and declared, "I hurt some people I respect, even some of my own black employees."

To bolster his credentials as a nonracist, Goodwin recited his record of bringing blacks into his agency at senior levels and pointed to his own research. "I knew that race and violence were not coordinated," he said. "Factors unrelated to race, like broken families, the absence of a father," were key elements in youthful violence. "Black people in the middle class are no more likely to be violent than white people in the middle class. I had been preaching the other way. I had pointed out that blacks in the middle class were *less* likely to use drugs than whites in the middle class."

Once vulnerable on the racial issue, however, he became the target of animal rights advocates, who had long protested his kind of research using monkeys; now they exploited his remark as the chink in his armor, he noted. So did criminologists who had fundamental disagreements with him about how to deal with youthful offenders. Furthermore, Goodwin felt deserted by colleagues. "There were a lot of people who knew better who could have come to my defense and didn't. They wouldn't get near it," Goodwin complained. "Race is like a third rail."

Ten days after his talk, he apologized publicly, and a week later he resigned as director of the Federal Alcohol, Drug Abuse, and Mental Health Administration. But it was hardly a career buster. He took the job he had wanted, which had been planned for him anyway—director of the National Institute of Mental Health—and later became director of a research center at George Washington University.

How the racial stereotypes sleep at the depths, to be aroused in a careless moment, nobody can be quite certain. Some scientists reflected soberly on the injustice of the accusation against the doctor; they noted how illuminating the research into primate behavior could be in gaining knowledge about humans. They might also have observed how illuminating the reaction to the remarks had been in providing insight into humans who live in a racially charged society. Where race in America is concerned, nothing happens in an historical vacuum; everything occurs within deep tradition and vivid memory.

When Frederick Goodwin mentioned that some male monkeys were "hypersexual," he flushed out another demon from the underbrush of caricatures. This is one that stalks many multiethnic societies, where one group sees another as prone to rape and sexual assault. In the United States today, explicit portrayals of African-Americans as primitive, bestial, well endowed, and sexually aggressive are the business of extreme racist organizations. But Ku Klux Klan and other white supremacist literature draws from a deep well of imagery that feeds broader American beliefs. Again, Jefferson illustrates the stereotype in his assertion that "they are more ardent after their female; but love seems with them to be more an eager desire, than a tender delicate mixture of sentiment and sensation."

Comics and horror movies have long been filled with dark monsters kidnapping white women, a metaphor played out to its ultimate in *King Kong*, about a giant gorilla who takes the fair beauty for his own. Even without being overtly racist, this theme taps amorphous fears that hover in the same region as racial fantasies: dark and light, primitive and vulnerable, the black seen as apelike—all with an overtone of sexuality. *King Kong* need not conjure up racial thoughts among its viewers to have the diffuse effect of reinforcing them; American racism pictures black people as similar to gorillas, as violent, as oversexed, as threatening to white females. That is enough to cause reverberations.

"Rapist" is a word that springs to the surface frequently among whites who are asked what comes to mind when they think of blacks. A focus group of white students at Drew University agreed that black men were seen as sexually aggressive and—by women—as especially frightening on that account. As soon as one student mentioned the word "rapist," heads nodded around the table.

"They always teach you that the rapist is a stranger," said Christina Fichera, "but most rapes are people you know. So, I mean, even though it's not right, I think it's the kind of thing our parents said to scare us and keep us in at night: 'The black man, the bogeyman, is gonna get you.' The bogeyman was always black. We had a lot of employees who were black, so my parents said, 'If you go out there, you pretty much bring it on yourself, so go ahead.' So of course I was scared to death. I think that's frightening for children."

But some whites in the Drew group struggled against the common view. "Not for me," said Stephen Burka of Milford, Connecticut. "Rapists are not based on race."

"I think whites are just as sexually aggressive, probably," declared Juliette Gaffney of Gaithersburg, Maryland. "It's definitely there, but if it were just a big white guy across the street, I'd probably be just as scared."

In a school near Cocoa Beach, Florida, Justin Wyatt joined the debate team. He looked white, although he was actually the child of a mixed marriage: His mother was white; his father, African-American with light skin. The boy considered himself black but did not advertise it. The debating coach, a white teacher, thought she had an all-white team.

One day, the teacher asked the students to choose a subject for debate, and they chose abortion. As the argument proceeded and various points were made, a girl who opposed abortion remarked that one circumstance, and only one, would justify ending a pregnancy: if a white woman were raped by a black man. "And all of them said: 'Yes, abortion is the answer,'" Justin's father, Tony, reported. "If a black man raped a white woman, abortion, absolutely—even the ones that had been saying abortion was totally wrong. And when my son asked, 'If a white man raped you and you became pregnant, what would you do?' 'Oh, we'd have the child.'" Justin simply listened in pain and did not reveal then that he was part African-American.

There is a flip side to this coin: In African-American lore, it is the white man who is sexually violent. It was the white man, the slave owner and the overseer, who raped slave women—black women who then bore their children into bondage. It was the white man, the drunk and the bully, who took black women at will, at gunpoint. Besides love, rape was the origin of the varying shades of skin tone that now mark the African-American population.

Against that backround, Tawana Brawley's story seemed credible. She was a black teenager. She disappeared after getting off a bus on the evening of November 24, 1987, in the Dutchess County town of Wappinger Falls, New York. Some ninety hours later, she was found in what seemed a daze, her body smeared with feces and labeled with slurs: "Nigger. KKK." She said that she had been kidnapped by two white men, taken to a wooded area, and raped repeatedly by a group of whites. She identified two of her assailants as an assistant prosecutor and a policeman.

Her cause of outrage was immediately taken up by a few of the black activists who are drawn to every flame of racial tension: Alton H. Maddox Jr. and C. Vernon Mason, who served as her attorneys, and Reverend Al Sharpton. For nearly a year, they waged a campaign of indignation and attack against the police, the prosecutors, the entire legal system of the state of New York. On their advice, which held that no white-dominated system could fairly deal with such a case, Brawley refused to testify before a grand jury convened to investigate.

Nevertheless, the grand jury spent seven months sifting through a wealth of testimony and intricate forensic evidence to issue a meticulous 176-page finding that no abduction and no rape had taken place. Brawley had smeared herself with dog feces, the grand jury concluded, and had written the slurs herself with a moist, charred rag; bits of the charred material were found under her fingernails and in a pair of gloves in her family's former, vacant apartment, where the grand jury came to believe she had spent most of the time. Laboratory tests traced the feces to a dog in a neighboring apartment.

Why had she done this? She had been staying out late at night, and the day she disappeared she had cut school. Perhaps she feared punishment from her mother's male companion, prosecutors speculated. Her choice of whites as her fictitious assailants—white law enforcement officers at that—suggested how she must have instinctively felt she could appeal to the adults in her life. Indeed, until the grand jury's investigation, she had been widely believed; knowing what we think we know about one another across racial lines, her ugly story was shocking but entirely plausible to both blacks and whites. In some minds, it still is: Even if it did not actually happen to Tawana Brawley, something similar has probably happened to someone, or would probably happen. So goes the reasoning that is drawn out of the fearsome mixture of race and sex.

African-Americans have deftly managed to take some of the stereotypes from white America and turn them into badges of superiority; these have mainly to do with physical prowess, widely seen as the antithesis of mental ability. In the racist caricatures, blacks aren't so smart, but they're strong; blacks aren't so clever, but they sure have rhythm. The patronizing compliment is a sly way to excuse and convey the condemnation. After generations in this undertow of bigotry, blacks have developed adroit techniques of survival. They now convert the white view that they "have rhythm" into a perverse pride that they can dance well and whites cannot. They translate the white image of black bodies as primitive and athletic into a conviction that in some sports, they can laughingly dismiss whites as inept. Twists on this stereotype interlace Ron Shelton's film *White Men Can't Jump*, in which Woody Harrelson plays a basketball player who uses his whiteness to hustle blacks on the courts. They assume he's a chump who can't play, so they bet against him and lose. There is only one thing Harrelson cannot do: jump high enough to dunk a ball. In the end, at the climax of a tournament, he manages that as well.

At Tougaloo, Jessica Prentice ran into "stereotypes like we can't dance, we don't have any kind of rhythm," she said. At Lincoln University, when I asked two sociology classes—entirely black except for one white man—to write down their images of whites, both groups listed "Can't dance," and one added, "No rhythm."

Bruce King, the black college administrator, chuckled all the way through his reminiscence about a football game that his virtually all-black high school in Chicago had played against a white school. "Our pom-pom squad went out, and they were just dancers, and they would dance to rhythm and blues," he said. "And then their pom-pom squad came out and, I think, danced to some Billy Joel record, and we thought that was just hilarious. There was just a lot of shaking and there seemed to be no rhythm to them."

When I asked Salim Muwakkil, the African-American journalist in Chicago, about blacks' stereotypes of whites, he listed "arrogant, imperialistic" and then thought for a long time. Finally, he said, "Angry at—angry at black success." Another pause. "Uuuummmm, scared, scared of blacks." Then, finally, "Can't dance." And he laughed. "Can't jump.

Let's see, uhhhh, in the service it was interesting 'cause the best dancer in our whole concern was an Italian guy from Brooklyn. He really messed up stereotypes."

When Laura, my daughter, spent a semester at Spelman, the black women's college in Atlanta, she was told after switching rooms that one of her former roommates, a freshman named "Sally," did not like white people. After that, Sally's comments snapped into focus for Laura. When music had been playing in the room and Laura had been fooling around by dancing, Sally had made fun of her, rolling her eyes. Another roommate had said lightly, "She'll learn to dance before she leaves." Sally had indicated that she thought it unlikely.

Laura handled the stereotyping with self-deprecating humor. She was the only white in a Martin Luther King Jr. Birthday show put on by students from Spelman and the neighboring men's college, Morehouse. The blacks welcomed her warmly, shouting cheerfully about having an "authentic white" to cast in white parts. In one scene dealing with the infamous concept of "separate but equal," a group of whites was supposed to dance, followed by a group of blacks. Playing the whites, Laura and black students wearing white masks were choreographed to do jerky, awkward movements; then the blacks came in to dance identical steps gracefully. Afterward, at the cast party, "the way it often does at parties, it turned into a circle and people were dancing," Laura said. The group called on its members one by one to get into the center and do some dancing. When they yelled, "Go, Laura! Go, Laura!" she stepped into the middle and did the goofy, mocking movements from the show, with arms flailing stiffly like a scarecrow's. She was flooded with an uproar of wonderful laughter. "Everybody thought that was so hilarious," she said. "They were very warm and good-natured."

Otto Green Jr. is black, and he is hefty. From around his neck, a big pendant of Africa hung on black string and swayed to and fro across the bold blue and black checks of his sweater. On the campus of the University of Nebraska at Lincoln, white students seemed to decide instantly that he was a football player on an athletic scholarship. "You can imagine my experience," he said, patting his ample chest. " 'What position do you play?' Not 'What is your name?,' 'Where are you from?,' or 'What is your major?' None of these questions. 'What position do you play?' And right away I know, Hmmm, this is going to be difficult." He was not an athlete.

Being a black athlete at Nebraska may imply less brainpower to many whites, but it's also a star role, according to Green and other blacks. "We're not supposed to be here," Tamika Simmons said bluntly. "That's the general impression: You're not supposed to be here if you're not playing basketball, if you're not playing football. . . . They don't expect you to sound intelligent; they expect you to like rap music, they expect you to dance and smile and fool with your hands, and you get so tired of that."

But black athletes bask in a glory that carries privileges and access that other blacks cannot touch. "They love it here," she said. "Nebraska doesn't have a professional team of any kind. We don't have any professional franchises. So the Cornhuskers are it. And they go around to different places in the state, and people ask them for their autographs. I mean, these are kids who are, like, nobody. And suddenly they're stars." They also get constant invitations from fraternities and sororities, Simmons said, "that would never invite me to a party."

There is something safe about blacks in sports, something non-threatening. It seems convenient to put a black into that box, even in the workplace. A human resources manager who monitors discrimination in a major corporation observed the pattern: Just as black females will be asked to help arrange a dance but not a marketing presentation, so black male employees will be invited onto an office softball team but not onto a task force. While white managers can imagine a black organizing an office athletic event, they cannot envision him running a department or dealing with a crucial customer.

As whites act on such images, they rarely seem aware that they are stereotyping. But some have learned sensitivity. And a few have learned so much that they tiptoe carefully through the most innocent conversation. An air force psychologist, Lieutenant Colonel Philip A. Irish III, was so keenly attuned to how blacks might interpret a comment that he once found himself unable to have a natural discussion. "I had a close friend who's black," Irish explained, "and we were sitting in a bar drinking together, and Magic Johnson came up on the tube, and I wanted to start talking about basketball, and I wanted to say, 'How do you think the Lakers are gonna do?' And then I sat there and went, Well, is it OK for me to say anything about basketball to him? I mean, I like basketball, but if I say, 'What do you think about the Lakers?' he may not know anything about basketball. Does that mean that I'm presuming that he knows something about basketball? And I'm sitting there in a strange moral dilemma, over nothing. And it caused me to catch my sentence."

Although blacks and whites can find common ground in sports, Irish had a point, since many black men complain of whites who don't seem to feel comfortable talking with them about anything else. If you were white, Irish argued, being sensitive to how blacks perceived your remarks was essential. However, he added, "sensitivity also causes one to become uncertain. If you begin questioning and doubting what you say and how you say it, then you start hesitating and make mistakes and withdrawing."

Athletics become a promise and a prison, a zone of racial equality and a canvas of racial caricature. The court, the diamond, the gridiron, the boundaries of the contest circumscribe an artificial place suspended from life's routine unfairness. At first glance, blacks as athletes seem to be awarded an honorary exemption from racially inferior status, as if they existed quite outside the culture of bias. A partitioning takes place: The game is divorced from society. The field is level. The rules create their own, color-blind universe. If you shoot from beyond the circle, it's three points. If you hit the ball over the fence, it's a home run. Success and failure result directly from performance, not from color, physiognomy, dialect, or connections. You do not catch a pass because of who you know or miss a basket because your skin is dark. "It is the only place in life where it doesn't matter anymore who your daddy was or how much money you have or whether you're white or black," said Richard L. Schaeffer, former attorney for the National Football League Players Association. "It is literally the even playing field we're always metaphorically searching for in this world."

Once blacks were admitted into integrated athletics, certain white attitudes had to be revised. Jackie Robinson "was the first opportunity for white America to see that a black man was equal to his counterparts in anything," Schaeffer noted. "So America was never the same after Jackie Robinson." Intricate bonds were formed across racial lines among players and fans. And the rising myth of blacks as "natural athletes" eased the integration of schools, some southerners believe. In pragmatic terms, whites discovered the usefulness of enlarging the reservoir of athletic talent to include blacks. "The first thing that caught the attention of the whites in the South, in my view, was that they started realizing that they could win football games with black athletes," said Ted Kennedy, the white chairman of B, E & K Construction Company in Birmingham, Alabama. "I really believe, when I think back, that that's what turned them around."

Nevertheless, much of white America cleverly defends its conviction that blacks are inferior. If they prove equal on the playing field, all whites have to do is to think, Well, that's physical. But things that take brains are something else again. So people compartmentalize their stereotyping, which allows for caricatures to be shattered by experience without throwing out the whole thesis.

So agile is prejudice that no matter what blacks may accomplish in one area, they cannot seem to overcome their negative images in another. Blacks can succeed brilliantly in professional sports and still be seen as inherently lazy, incompetent, and criminal. Positives are restricted by a policy of containment. Negatives, on the other hand, spread easily. Let one black man rape or murder, and his entire race is stained with the crime. Let failure or corruption occur in one sphere of life, and all others are tainted.

Consequently, a single black athlete can be adored by white fans who still detest his race, just as a white can consider a black friend an exception to the rule about most black people. Magic Johnson's devastating disclosure that he was leaving basketball because he had contracted the HIV virus brought sadness not only to liberals, but also to many whites with anti-black prejudices.

In some respects, the physical achievements by blacks in professional sports have been used to reinforce the impression of blacks as unintelligent. This was one connotation of a comment in the late eighties by Jimmy "the Greek" Snyder, a betting handicapper for CBS Sports, who said on *Nightline*, "The black is a better athlete to begin with because he has been bred to be that way" since the days of slavery. This came shortly after Al Campanis, then the general manager of the Los Angeles Dodgers, answered a question about why so few blacks were in executive positions in baseball.

"I don't believe it's prejudice," he said. "I truly believe they may not have some of the necessities to be, let's say, a field manager or perhaps a general manager." Campanis was helped to retire, but he had only said publicly what many in professional sports believed privately: that blacks could make their bodies perform but not their minds, that they had "the necessities" for the physical but not the mental. The statistics demonstrated how effective this prejudice had been in preventing blacks from moving up through the ranks of management. As of 1995, 80 percent of the players in the twenty-nine teams of the National Basketball Association were black, but only six coaches, eight general mangers or directors of player personnel, and not a single team doctor were black. In the National Football League, 67 percent of the players were black, but only three of the thirty head coaches, four of the general managers, and none of the team doctors. Blacks and Latinos made up 37 percent of the players' rosters in the twenty-eight major-league baseball teams, but only three blacks and one Latino were managers, one black was a general manager, and one was a team doctor. "Where the rules are public and clear, black people do very well," said Frank Watkins of Jesse Jackson's Rainbow Coalition. "Everyone can see who can shoot, who can run, who can hit. Now, who becomes general manager? What are the criteria? That's much more subjective."

It is the supposed contradiction between the physical and the mental that gives a racial charge to discussions about athletic abilities. This dichotomy is the reason that any comment on blacks' alleged superiority in certain muscle skills is thought to carry an automatic inference of inferiority in mental abilities. So when Dale Lick, the white president of Florida State University, said, "A black athlete can actually outjump a white athlete on the average, so they're better at the game [of basketball]. . . . The same is true for football. The muscle structure of the black athlete typically is more suited for certain positions in football and basketball," his words were taken as racist. Mike Royko, a *Chicago Tribune* columnist, pointed out that many black athletes make the same claims about their athletic talents.

The tendency to see the body and the mind as opposite poles has also shaped coaches' and sportswriters' perceptions, determining where blacks and whites play and how they are described. Studies from the 1970s, summarized in a 1980 report by the National Football League Players Association, found blacks markedly underrepresented in the "central" positions in both baseball and football: pitcher, catcher, quarterback, center, guard, and linebacker. These are considered the thinking positions, the report found, and those players "tend to have the greatest opportunity to have a controlling influence on the outcome." They require "frequent social interactions calling for interpersonal acceptability," and their roles call for leadership and decision making. Therefore, professional athletes drawn from such positions are most likely to be tapped later for managerial jobs, the study said. And if you've been a coach, you've got a better shot at getting hired as a broadcast commentator. The phenomenon is called "stacking." In baseball, it has extended even to base coaching, sportswriter John Feinstein has noted. Blacks have been kept at first, and hardly any have been considered sharp enough to coach third, where crucial decisions must be made on whether or not to send a runner home.

Black athletes are usually sorted out when they get to college, Schaeffer explained, especially if they've gone to a mostly black high school. "There are a lot of black college defensive backs who were quarterbacks in high school. Now, they'll make an argument that we're a passing offense and they played a running offense, you know, they did this and we do that. But in my mind, there is still definitely a resistance. I don't think most people in their minds are overt about it. I think it's a subtle, perhaps even subconscious, kind of bigotry."

"One of the most fateful lines that a black quarterback, let's say a high schooler, can hear is 'Can you run backwards?'" said Mike Hiestand, who covers sports for *USA Today*. "In other words, he'll become a defensive player."

Studies have found that college football coaches use the same descriptions of blacks and whites as they do for the qualities needed in peripheral and central positions. "The 'Black Positions'—running back, defensive back and wide receiver—were rated by the coaches as demanding physical speed, physical quickness, and high achievement motivation," said the report for the NFL Players Association. "Not surprisingly, these were also the same attributes which the coaches considered to be dominant among black athletes. In contrast, the 'White Positions'—center, guard, and quarterback—were rated by the coaches as requiring reliability, quick mental comprehension, and thinking ability. These were the same characteristics which the coaches perceived to be dominant among white players. Similar findings have been reported . . . from research on scouts and coaches in professional football: Black athletes were overrepresented at less-central playing positions which were thought to require strength, quickness, emotion, instinct, and speed; and were underrepresented at central positions believed to require intellect, leadership, poise under pressure, finesse, technique, and control." A poll by *USA Today* found the same views among fans, both black and white, most of whom ascribed the qualities of leadership, hard work, and intelligence to white athletes but speed and athletic ability to blacks.

The images carry over into what is said about black and white athletes by people in management, sportswriters, and broadcasters who spread the stereotypes into the public at large. The caricatures do not leap out at you, even when you're listening for them, and I've heard them less clearly than have some who are involved intimately with professional sports. But whites who have tuned in to the problem find many examples of sportscasters calling a good play an "athletic move" for a black and a "smart move" for a white. "There is a tradition in sports of saying that when the black guy succeeds, he's a great natural athlete," observed Richard Schaeffer. "When the white guy succeeds, it's due to hard work and perseverance and his own dedication to his sport." The implication is "that the black guy hasn't worked to get there, and that it's just a physical versus a mental thing."

Randall Cunningham, one of the few blacks who broke the barrier and played quarterback, got comments about his innate physical ability—"what an athlete," people said. "Whereas when you hear them talk about a white quarterback," Schaeffer noted, "it'll always be how heady he is and how much courage he has. For instance, you almost never hear people talk about a courageous black athlete. Courage is not something they'll attribute to blacks. It's what a miraculous physical phenomenon they are. But the white guys are cagey, heady, dedicated, hardworking, et cetera, et cetera." Schaeffer wondered if this amounted to "a feeling of white physical inferiority and your having to make up for it."

Cunningham's example provides a good yardstick for measuring attitudes. Cunningham was "the best black quarterback to ever play in the NFL, certainly one of the best," said John Feinstein three years before Cunningham's last season with the Philadelphia Eagles, in 1995–1996. "And yet when I go around the country, I always hear these whispers that Randall doesn't work as hard as Jim McMahon, his backup, that Randall's teammates don't think he makes good decisions. There is a local broadcaster on the all-sports station in this town [Washington, D.C.] who said repeatedly throughout the football season, 'The Eagles should be starting Jim McMahon because he's a better, smarter quarterback in the clutch.' Jim McMahon at this stage in his career can't carry Randall Cunningham's jock, to use a cliché. And yet in the white media—and most of us in the sports media today are white—you hear these whispers that put doubts in people's minds. Doug Williams for years was exposed to people saying he was not smart enough to quarterback a winning team in the NFL. But he did lead the Redskins to the Super Bowl and won the Super Bowl MVP."

Speaking on a radio talk show, Feinstein blamed sportscasters for spreading these images. " 'Athletic team' has become a code word for 'black team.' " he said. " 'Smart, gritty player' has become a code word for the slow white kid. . . . There was a player named Quin Snyder, who played at Duke a couple of years ago, who was always described as very 'heads-up.' Well, the fact is, Quin Snyder, relatively speaking as point guards went, was not a great thinker of the game but was a great athlete. But because he was white, that stereotype of nonathlete thinker was placed on him when in fact the person who had preceded him at point guard at Duke, a guy named Tommy Amaker, was not as athletic as

Quin but a much better thinker of the game. But that never came up, because Tommy Amaker was a black guy."

White and black coaches are treated with similar disparity, Feinstein remarked. A case in point was a 1992 game between Kentucky and Duke. "On the last play of the game, Rick Pitino, the Kentucky coach, made a stupid move: He didn't guard an inbounds passer. . . . If you interviewed a thousand coaches, nine hundred ninety-nine of them would say you guard the inbounds passer. I promise you, I promise you, if that had been John Thompson or another black coach, people would have gone around talking about how stupid he was. . . . Whereas with Rick Pitino, who is regarded as a great coach, when he did something stupid, there were all these reasons for the move that had nothing to do with the fact that at that moment in his life, he made a big mistake."

In racial thinking, it is assumed that the body reveals the mind.

CHAPTER FIVE

Mind

Through a Glass, Darkly

Comparing them by their faculties of memory,
reason, and imagination, it appears to me that in
memory they are equal to the whites; in reason much
inferior, as I think one could scarcely be found
capable of tracing and comprehending the investigations of Euclid; and that in imagination they are dull,
tasteless, and anomalous.

—*Thomas Jefferson*

White on Black

Roy and Diane Gordon, conscientious white parents, had three children
at once in the high school in Los Altos, California. When their two older
boys missed homework assignments and fell behind, teachers sent notes
home or got on the phone. But when their daughter had trouble, the
Gordons got no notes or calls. Neither teachers nor guidance counselors
seemed to expect or demand good schoolwork from the girl. The boys
were white; she was half black.

Rarely does the laboratory of human experience provide a test case as
clear as this for measuring the effect of race on assumptions about
mental ability. The boys were the Gordons' biological children; the girl
was adopted as an infant. Close together in age, all three were raised in
the same family, educated in the same schools, and exposed to the same
aspirations by parents with high standards. Yet the school system never
gave their daughter the same attention, despite her parents' pleas.

It could have been sexual discrimination, to which girls have been
subject in many classrooms. But to the Gordons, race seemed the
stronger variable, shaping their daughter's self-definition and the ways in
which others saw her. From first grade, she found her comfort zone
among black friends, and by high school she was traveling in a mostly

black group that "just did not have any expectations of themselves," her father said. They could not imagine excelling in school or going to college. They hovered at the margins of a high school community that drew from a broad area of cultural and economic backgrounds: white and black, Latino and Asian, wealthy and relatively poor. Many of the school's students were headed for good universities, but many of her friends would not go beyond a high school diploma, if they even graduated.

"All our experience said that the educational system failed those kids dreadfully," Roy Gordon observed. "The teachers totally had the expectation in their minds, and they reinforced it all the time: They did not expect the kids to do well, and the kids didn't do well, and so they didn't demand it of them. If they didn't do their homework, if they didn't turn up for classes, that's what they expected anyway, and they didn't do anything about it. . . . She was part of that group that they had basically written off. We're not passive people, and so we spent a lot of time in the school working with them. But it didn't help."

The teachers in question did not burn crosses or wear white sheets. They did not call black people "niggers" or stand defiantly in the schoolhouse door to fight integration. They stood instead in the center of mainstream America, where racist thoughts and images are quieter, subtler, insidious. Struggling to work professionally in classes too large, too unmotivated, too corroded by the ills of home and street, the teachers succumbed to assumptions and prejudices they probably did not know they had. In the end, the girl barely got her high school diploma, did not go to college, worked at a dry cleaner and other odd jobs, and then had a baby out of wedlock. She fulfilled her teachers' expectations.

Few white Americans will admit openly nowadays that they regard blacks as mentally inferior. But most harbor such beliefs, according to a survey conducted in 1990 by the National Opinion Research Center at the University of Chicago. The study had special significance because it used sophisticated methodology. Polls usually attempt to measure stereotypes by presenting bigoted statements to respondents, asking them to agree or disagree: "Black people are less intelligent than white people," for example. Or "Generally speaking, black people are lazy and don't like to work hard." The crude caricatures make many of those surveyed recoil; to agree is obviously racist, and not many Americans want to brand themselves that way, even in an anonymous poll.

So the National Opinion Research Center devised a questionnaire
with nuanced choices. Respondents were invited to consider the supposed characteristics of various groups—whites, Jews, blacks, Asian-
Americans, Hispanic-Americans, and southern whites—and rate them
on a scale from one to seven. Offering a continuum of gradations about
more than one group elicited prejudices that the blatant survey questions
would have missed, according to Tom W. Smith, an historian at the
center. "I must admit I didn't expect nearly as much stereotyping as we
found," he said.

The survey was given to a cross section of about 1,200 Americans,
150 of whom were black. It asked three questions relating to intelligence
and industriousness: "Do people in these groups tend to be unintelligent
or tend to be intelligent?," ". . . tend to be hard-working or tend to be
lazy?," and ". . . tend to prefer to be self-supporting or do they tend to
prefer to live off welfare?" In tabulating the results, characterizations of
whites were used as the reference point, with other groups placed higher
or lower along the scale of images.

In assumptions about intelligence, blacks and Hispanics were about
tied at the bottom; on the hard-working and self-supporting scales,
respondents put blacks at the lowest end; on all three questions, only
Jews scored higher than "whites."

Just 6.3 percent rated blacks as more intelligent than whites, while
53.2 percent rated them as less intelligent and 40.5 percent saw them as
equally intelligent. Smith pointed to a particularly significant result:
"Fifty-seven percent of nonblacks rated blacks as less intelligent than
whites," he said, "and a much smaller but still a not trivial thirty percent
of blacks rated blacks as less intelligent than whites." This was a glimpse
at the large minority of blacks—nearly one-third—who internalized the
anti-black stereotypes held by the white world.

Even more dramatically, 62.2 percent of the entire sample rated
blacks as lazier than whites, and only 5.9 percent thought of them as
more hard-working. A total of 77.7 percent thought blacks more likely
than whites to prefer living on welfare; just 1.9 percent believed they
would rather be self-supporting.

These are stunning statistics. They are measurements of a cruel wind
that whips across America. If more than three out of every four Americans believe that blacks are more inclined than whites to prefer welfare
over work, if nearly two out of three see blacks as lazier, if more than one
out of two regards them as relatively unintelligent, the consequence is a
corrosive chemistry of low expectations, closed opportunities, and ultimate defeat. The judgments that spring from the stereotypes become

self-fulfilling prophecies, creating a reality of failure that is then taken to justify the stereotypes themselves. And so the cycle is nourished with as much raw force as a hurricane accumulates over tropical water.

For the most part, white Americans nurse these images privately, entrusting them only to those who clearly share them—a bunch of bowling buddies, close family around a dinner table, fellow construction workers across a brown-bag lunch. Chris Johnson, a sturdily built white man with a crew cut, was watching the 1993 Super Bowl with friends in Millville, New Jersey, when Leon Lett, a black lineman for the Dallas Cowboys, picked up a fumble and lumbered toward the end zone. Just before he crossed the line, Lett started showing off and dancing and didn't notice a white player, Don Beebe of the Buffalo Bills, sprinting up behind him. Beebe slapped the ball out of Lett's hand and prevented the touchdown. "Stupid nigger!" shouted a couple of the guys in the room. The slur erupted naturally and comfortably, Johnson felt, and he kept his disagreement to himself. "Was he stupid? Yeah," Johnson told me later, "but not because he's black."

The assumptions of stupidity and laziness may be papered over in many quarters of America, but they come tumbling through the facade in many others. In Louisiana and elsewhere, some folks still use the term "nigger-rigged" as a substitute for "jury-rigged," meaning makeshift, put together or repaired sloppily and hastily and, hopefully, temporarily, as in "This will be nigger-rigged, but it will get you there." At a Goodyear tire plant in Alabama, where Robert Avery, who is very dark and bald, trucks green tires to the curing mold, "you hear a lot of racial slurs, a lot of racial statements, yeah," he says as casually as if he were saying, Yeah, it gets hot and humid down here. "I mean, you pick it," he goes on. "They use the word 'nigger' now and then to refer to you. They talk about being lazy: 'Black folk lazy, don't want to work.' They have a lot of references to welfare, just the normal everyday racial-type statements."

A kindly middle-aged black man is checking me in at the Budget car rental counter at O'Hare Airport in Chicago, but he is having trouble figuring the 6 percent tax on the calculator. He asks a white woman coworker for help. As she walks behind him, she shakes her head in disgust, almost imperceptibly, then says perfectly nicely, "You punch in point-oh-six." "Oh," he says and does it. Still standing slightly behind him, she rolls her eyes and purses her lips in disdain.

In Chatham, New Jersey, a middle-class suburb of New York, four white women sit in a Chinese restaurant talking about their children's school experiences. One dark-haired mother in her thirties recalls her own school elsewhere, and a sentence comes flashing across the room like a knife: "It was so black, there weren't very many of us who were smart."

The notion that blacks are not as smart, not as competent, not as energetic as whites is woven so tightly into American culture that it cannot be untangled from everyday thought, even as it is largely repressed in polite company. Sometimes it springs to the surface in trusting relationships like an eruption of hurtful truth telling. Such was the case one evening when Tony and Gina Wyatt were recounting their forbidden courtship as teenagers in Gadsden, Alabama. Tony, an African-American, was now an air force sergeant who trained armed forces personnel in the techniques of dealing with racial tensions; Gina, his wife of fourteen years, had the one characteristic that had made their relationship quite dicey in their hometown: She was white.

"I was attracted to him," Gina said. Other black guys approached her because they knew she liked soul music. "I always got out there dancing with them at school and stuff, but I was like, 'No, I'm just not attracted.' I guess maybe their personality had a lot to do with it. I got to know him at school before I actually met him that night. And I was, 'This guy's really different. He's really smart, really intelligent. I know he's gonna make something of himself.' "

Tony laughed. "You hear the word 'different'?" He laughed again. The previous day, he had talked with trainees about the backhanded compliments and veiled insults that blacks are often given by whites who call an individual with brains or talent "different," the "exception." Now he was hearing it from his own wife.

"Not colorwise," Gina protested. "You know what I mean."

"See what I mean?" Tony said to me.

"I mean, he was really smart," Gina insisted.

"Even with her. Even with her." Tony was laughing; Gina was not.

"I'm talking about personalitywise," she said. He was still chuckling.

In the realm of proper political discourse, where overt racial slurs can destroy a career, the expression of prejudice takes a more circuitous route. There, the lesser regard for blacks' intelligence and initiative is diluted into less obviously racist forms to please the current taste in acceptable debate. You can't speak of black people as indolent, but it's all right to urge that (black) welfare mothers be required to work. You're not allowed to characterize black people as incompetent, but you may preach the abolition of affirmative action because it promotes "unqualified" blacks over "qualified" whites. In American public life, where it is no longer admissible to assert the mental inferiority of black people, it is perfectly fine to argue policies that grow out of that assumption, so long as the core stereotype is left unstated.

I once got into an argument with an old friend over the racial redistricting instituted under the Voting Rights Act to give blacks majority legislative constituencies, resulting sometimes in oddly twisted, elongated regions whose only common characteristic was the race of most of their residents. The Supreme Court ruled 5–4 in 1996 that districts shaped predominantly by race were unconstitutional. But pro-black gerrymandering was designed to counter the decades of pro-white gerrymandering that had carefully blocked blacks from office. My friend was adamantly opposed, arguing that the criterion for elected representatives should be their competence, not their race. That sounded reasonable and fair-minded until the overtones of her theme began to emerge: She had an impulse to question the competence of blacks elected by blacks. She didn't raise a problem with Irish elected by Irish or Italians elected by Italians—or white Anglo-Saxon Protestants elected by white Anglo-Saxon Protestants, for that matter. But she gave every indication of feeling that blacks would be less capable than whites, especially blacks who were elected from mostly black districts. Black representatives of a truly mixed constituency would be acceptable and presumably qualified. I wondered if, at some buried level of attitude, she was saying that she trusted white more than black voters to make wise choices.

Something of that theme was struck by Jim Blacksher, a white civil rights lawyer in Birmingham, Alabama, speaking not for himself but for what he saw as the common denominator of white views in today's South. He described the popular thinking this way: "The question is whether or not the underlying structures of governance and political participation are fair. And we're convinced that they are, and the only problem that black people have is that they're not very good at playing the game, playing politics, and frankly—and this is the part we don't admit out loud—we're not surprised about that, because we've been raised to believe that blacks really aren't capable of managing affairs. . . . We have been taught, (a) to believe that this is our state, just like it's our country. It's a white man's country. We settled it, we built it, we made it what it is today. So it belongs to us as a matter of property. And secondly, now that we are beyond the civil rights revolution, we are willing to let blacks, previously held down by law, into the process, all the processes, private and public, and participate, sharing the benefits and all that. But we really don't believe that they're up to it.

"Our own experience teaches us that they're just not very smart,"

Blacksher continued in his portrayal of white attitudes, "that they're devious, and they're certainly not to be trusted—certainly not to be trusted with our money. But that's not racism. That is not racism, OK? If black people would just act right, they would be able to get the same things that we've got. If they would just work as hard as we work, if they would just take the time to build a community, the same way we and our ancestors before us worked to build this community, instead of going around tearing down, shooting, sniffing drugs, raping, and killing, they could expect to have the same things that we've got. But we'd be bloody fools to just turn it over to them now and say, 'Here, it's yours.' That's not justice. I mean, it's going to take a long time, because black folks really are, after all, just up from slavery."

You don't have to be a southerner to have these thoughts or even express them, of course. "Bob Edison," a New York architect who made sure people knew that he had gone to Choate and Harvard, mustered up a fine measure of gleeful indignation to tell of a black student who had failed to do the work in an architectural design class he had once taught. Edison had given him a failing grade and had then been raked over the coals for doing so; higher authorities had passed the student over Edison's objection, and Edison had been fired. The point of his story— his version of the story—was that many incompetent, lazy blacks were being coddled by white institutions. With some prompting, he admitted that he'd had several incompetent whites in the class as well; he had managed to scare them into dropping the course. Oddly, this did not lead him to sweeping generalizations about the stupidity of whites.

"I've had a situation where we've had an ad for a secretary, and black women showed up who were totally unqualified," he went on. "I had this woman that answered, couldn't type, couldn't spell, couldn't write, claimed she spoke French, didn't expect to run into somebody that actually spoke French—not that it was part of the job, but she wrote this thing down. She was an affirmative-action baby. She thought she could get the job because she was black. But it was just a one-girl office at the time. And it was very embarrassing. She came in for an interview. I tried her out. I dictated something, asked her to type it up, which is the only way to do it. And nothing happened. And she got mad."

Edison never expected to see a qualified black applicant for a job. "If a black guy came into my office wearing a Brooks Brothers suit, a button-down white shirt, his shoes were shined up, wearing a watch that had a brown leather band, and his hair was cut short, and he spoke regular English, he was saying to me, 'I want to get with the program,'

I'd have no problem with such a guy. I'd have one major problem—I wouldn't see a guy like that in a million years, wouldn't come into my office. A guy who figured that simple thing out would be working in the White House."

On the surface, this may look like an issue of attitude, appearance, and cultural assimilation—factors that do influence how an African-American is seen by whites. But in essence, Edison was taking account of deeper qualities that seemed to him less susceptible to revision. He explained them genetically and culturally. "I don't have any problem recognizing the fact that liberal European civilization is in very, very large measure the most refined and civilized civilization," Edison said. "When you look at the cultural achievements of the world of art, science, medicine, music, architecture, sentiment, it's European. . . . If I had to choose between the African tradition of medicine and the American–western European tradition of medicine, I think I'd choose our tradition. And the same is true in aviation, naval architecture, science, and so forth."

This man was saying what many whites think. His candor was unusual; his thoughts were not. At first, he was pleased to be heard and quoted; in the end, however, recognizing the social unacceptability of his statements, he decided not to permit his real name to be published unless he first had an opportunity to edit his own quotations. That spoke to the anxieties, the taboos, the inhibitions that white America now endures on the subject of race and intelligence.

In 1994, the issue flared into the open with the publication of *The Bell Curve: Intelligence and Class Structure in American Life* by the late Richard J. Herrnstein, a professor of psychology at Harvard, and Charles Murray, a Harvard graduate and research fellow at the American Enterprise Institute. Their work, one among several books on race and intelligence published during the same period, ignited a fleeting firestorm of debate, little of which took serious note of their findings. In large measure, it was a replay of the bursts of outrage that had greeted Arthur Jensen, an educational psychologist, when he wrote in 1969 that remedial programs did not help disadvantaged children because of their low IQs, and William Shockley, the Nobel laureate in physics who proposed paying those with low IQs to be sterilized. In 1971, Herrnstein also caused controversy by writing that IQ—and therefore economic success and social standing—was largely inherited. Blacks were not the only targets of the stigma. Earlier in the century, during an influx of eastern and southern European immigrants, the "I.Q. worshipers," as Brent Staples of *The New York Times* called them, aimed the arsenal of the intelligence test at Jews, Italians, Hungarians, and Russians in an attempt to portray them as "feebleminded" and keep them out of the country.

In *The Bell Curve*, Herrnstein and Murray examine numerous studies of IQ scores and conclude that the United States is being divided not merely into socioeconomic classes but into "cognitive classes," a hierarchy differentiated by widely diverse mental abilities. At the top, they see a "cognitive elite" that channels its children into advanced education and influential professions; at the bottom, an underclass of people ill equipped in reasoning ability to function well in modern society. Higher birthrates and younger childbearing by mothers with lower IQs threaten to pull the American population's general level of intelligence down a slippery slope of deterioration, they argue.

Recognizing Americans' obsession with race and surely anticipating charges of racism against themselves, Herrnstein and Murray take pains to build a careful framework for the discussion of IQ. Not until Chapter 14, 269 pages into the book, do they introduce ethnic differences. In the first half of the volume, they exclude blacks entirely from their observations. Among whites alone, they note, correlations exist between low IQ and many major social difficulties: poverty; unemployment; failure to complete high school; criminal behavior; out-of-wedlock births; and parenting deficiencies contributing to low birth weight, child abuse, and toddlers' poor motor and social development. Furthermore, in all those areas, IQ is a more powerful element than socioeconomic status. In other words, the authors conclude, your intelligence is more important than your parents' economic means in determining your life chances. "If you have to choose, is it better to be born smart or rich?" they ask. "The answer is unequivocally 'smart.' A white youth reared in a home in which the parent or parents were chronically unemployed, worked at only the most menial of jobs, and had not gotten past ninth grade, but of just average intelligence—an IQ of 100—has nearly a 90 percent chance of being out of poverty by his or her early 30s. Conversely, a white youth born to a solid middle-class family but with an IQ equivalently below average faces a much higher risk of poverty, despite his more fortunate background."

With this groundwork methodically laid, the book's relatively brief section on racial differences takes on severe import. On numerous tests, the authors say, black Americans come out with a mean IQ of about 85, compared with about 100 for whites. "This means that the average white person tests higher than about 84 percent of the population of blacks and that the average black person tests higher than about 16 percent of the population of whites," they write. They then assert that IQ is determined largely by genetics and less by environment, thereby sealing a doctrine of racial superiority into their research.

They also note that Ashkenazi Jews—those of European origin— score the highest of any ethnic group and that East Asians—specifically, Chinese and Japanese—test higher than American whites. But in the cross fire that followed publication, their discussion of Jews and Asians was practically ignored. It was the comparison of blacks and whites that caught the whirlwind of suspicions and fears raging through America.

In a tribute to the volatility of their subject, Herrnstein and Murray write defensively, lacing their analysis with caveats, qualifiers, and rebuttals designed to preempt attacks. Even as they emphasize blacks' lower test results, they caution that "the differences among individuals are far greater than the differences between groups." Even as they draw graphs to dramatize the black-white differences, they go out of their way to estimate that one hundred thousand blacks have IQs in the highest group, with scores of 125 and above. "One hundred thousand people is a lot of people," they say eagerly. "It should be no surprise to see (as one does every day) blacks functioning at high levels in every intellectually challenging field."

But none of their conciliatory noises or intellectual fortifications deflected the assaults. *The New Republic* published an entire issue of mostly critical essays on their book. *The New York Times Magazine* led with an unflattering profile of Murray, mentioning that, as a high school senior in Iowa, he had gone along with friends on a cross-burning spree, unaware (he now says) of its racist message. *Newsweek* put the controversy on its cover, and newspapers assailed the authors in editorials, even as the book reached the *New York Times* best-seller list. A few conservative scholars and right-wing Republicans praised the work, and it formed the silent subtext of many Republican proposals in Congress, from reducing (low-IQ) immigration to denying welfare benefits to teenage mothers (whose promiscuity, the book says, lowers the population's IQ level). But many other specialists denounced both the methodology and the infatuation with IQ as a measure of intelligence. Herrnstein and Murray were accused of relying on century-old science and omitting studies on human development, self-esteem, culture, and other environmental factors that are believed to shape intelligence. They ignore a dimension of capabilities that researchers call "emotional intelligence," which includes interpersonal skills and likability, which have been shown to be more influential than IQ in determining success.

Again and again, Herrnstein and Murray sloppily allow statistical correlations to slide into assertions of causality. If people suffering from unemployment are often found with a low IQ, for example, it does not necessarily mean that the low IQ causes the unemployment; both could be symptoms of educational, family, and experiential deprivation. Nor do the authors adequately discuss the dubious qualities of IQ as a yardstick, an issue that has produced long-standing controversy. Richard A. Gardner, clinical professor of child psychiatry at Columbia University, noted that IQ tests, originally developed by Alfred Binet in France to identify retarded children, are so closely linked to what is taught in schools that the scores are more indicative of educational performance than of intelligence. "If these tests were properly named," Gardner suggested, "they would be called Tests That Predict Success or Failure in the School System From Which the Questions Have Been Derived."

At its heart, then, *The Bell Curve* can be seen as a circular argument: Some people do poorly on IQ tests because they lack certain cognitive skills, and that lack leads them to do poorly on other tests—those that screen and filter for schooling, jobs, and the like. Consequently, a correlation between IQ and, say, educational achievement is about as significant as a correlation between a sore throat and a cough. IQ is merely an index of reasoning and other mental abilities, many of which can be acquired from family and school environments. When Herrnstein and Murray hold this index constant and show that blacks and whites who have the same IQ also have the same annual earnings, it should not be a major surprise. The only surprise is that a society is willing to tolerate the family, social, and educational conditions that breed failure in so many aspects of life.

If black-white differences in IQ scores are a measurement of those disparate conditions, then a discussion of the problem falls within familiar, comfortable parameters: Change the conditions and narrow the gap. Don't regard IQ as a fixed, God-given level of intelligence, immutable in all but extreme cases; see it, rather, as the confluence of all the forces exerted on a child by family, community, school, and the limits and opportunities that life seems to present to him. In such an interpretation, the gulf between black and white is theoretically possible to overcome eventually if one believes in the country's capacity for self-correction, albeit with such great difficulty that Herrnstein and Murray offer no real remedies. As part of the American inheritance, the gap reflects the society's tradition of racial wrongdoing. Harvard psychiatrist Alvin Poussaint put it bluntly during a debate with Murray: "Scientifically, if they wanted to compare so-called genetic differences between blacks and whites, then they would have to take a group of white people who have had similar experiences to black Americans. That is, they would have to find a group of white people that experienced 250 years of slavery, 100 years of Jim Crow segregation, and then let's compare our IQs."

If intelligence is biologically inherited, however, a different analysis applies, an assessment that invites both hopelessness and self-congratulation. When the authors of *The Bell Curve* make their central assertion that cognitive abilities are mostly genetic—a theory for which they provide only flimsy and unpersuasive evidence—they set up a proposition that is at once alluring and troubling. The scenario plays to a deep yearning for exculpation in portions of white America that embrace the notion that blacks' failure at present is the product of their own heritage and behavior, not of whites' malfeasance. Moreover, the authors argue, the society has become inherently just, for America has fulfilled its promise of enabling the brightest to rise to the top. As they see it, the severe problem that remains is the polarization between the smart and the stupid, a division that holds great dangers. But each group is about where it should be in the social hierarchy, they think. They reject the twentieth-century egalitarian ideal because "it fails to come to grips with human variation." Instead, in a vague and preachy conclusion mixing alarm and complacency, they urge the country to strive to make a "valued place" for every citizen and resign itself to "living with inequality."

Some people with experience in the real world will find this portrait of America amusingly infuriating. I've met enough senior corporate executives and members of Congress with mediocre minds and enough very bright farmers, lobstermen, and clam diggers—and quick-witted drug dealers as well—to appreciate the absurdity of *The Bell Curve*'s claim. This country has a long way to go in mining the talents of its citizens of modest stature. Nevertheless, it is hard to laugh off a book with such a racial message; it is safe to say that if Herrnstein and Murray had not tapped the pernicious well of semisecret beliefs about black people, their work might have been greeted by nothing more than derisive dismissal.

Instead, it became one of those books that many Americans discussed emotionally without undertaking the bothersome chore of actually reading. "The topic of genes, intelligence, and race in the late twentieth century is like the topic of sex in Victorian England," the authors observed. "Publicly, there seems to be nothing to talk about. Privately, people are fascinated by it. As the gulf widens between public discussion and private opinion, confusion and error flourish." And as *The Bell Curve* was distilled into a simplistic portrait of blacks as less intelligent than whites, it took its ominous place in the gulf between two competing beliefs: the private suspicion that blacks are mentally inferior and the public doctrine that every person in America, given opportunity and hard work, can reach success. That confrontation between private racism and public mythology touches the rawest nerve of the American experience.

A close reading of *The Bell Curve* gets to be a very personal and moral undertaking. Most of us have our views of intelligence—what it is, how it is acquired, who in our experience possesses more or less of it. Few of us have given much thought to how we come by these views, how we factor in gender, ethnicity, and class in making our assessments. We may be comfortable with the notion that an individual's intelligence is at least partly genetic; we all know smart parents with smart children, and we accept elementary schools' special programs for the "gifted and talented." Certain talent is a gift, to be sure. But we also want very much to believe that some spark of brilliance lies smoldering in every human mind, waiting only to be fanned into flame by the right mother or father or teacher. Otherwise, a person's level of intelligence becomes a life sentence rather than a life opportunity. Everyone might as well walk around with a name tag so we can all know how to relate to one another:

Hi! I'm
Joe
My IQ is
109

Despite all the cautionary caveats, the world constructed by *The Bell Curve* is even more severe, for it takes that fateful step from the individual to the collective. In it, everyone has a different sort of tag:

Hi! I'm
Black
The mean IQ of my group is
85

Satana Deberry was wearing the label, and her white second-grade teacher in North Carolina saw it clearly in the color of her skin. So Satana was placed in the middle reading group—not the lowest, but not the highest, either. "I kept telling my parents that I could read the book in the high reading group," she recalled, "and kept telling the teacher I could be in the high reading group, and she'd go, 'Oh, no, you can't. You can't be in the high reading group.' " Luckily for Satana, both her parents were teachers; her mother taught first grade in the same school and knew the second-grade teacher's prejudices. "They got me tested, and I actually tested out in a higher reading group," she said. And with that irrefutable evidence, her parents got her into the higher level, where she belonged. She ended up in the class of 1991 at Princeton.

This is a typical story for black children, except that most of them don't have mothers teaching down the hall and most of them don't end up at Princeton, even those who deserve to. Most of them don't have mothers who are brave enough to gird themselves against the rude school secretaries and imperious assistant principals. Most of them don't have mothers or fathers who know how to become their advocates or who even know that there is anything they can do about such a problem. School can be scary, and black parents, especially those in poverty, may have had bad experiences at their children's schools or during their own schooling. Often they don't feel listened to. They may not get positive feedback about their children. Or the logistics of getting to school for an appointment may be overwhelming: arranging for time off from work, finding care for a younger child, paying for transportation.

Barbara Wyche, now a sociologist, first realized that she lived in poverty when she was sent to a newly integrated, mostly white school in Hopewell, Virginia. Her family was crowded into a small place; her mother was separated from her teachers by an unbridgeable gulf. "One of the teachers said to me, and I told my mother, 'Mama, the teacher said if we're s'posed to really do well we have to have a desk with a light.' You know?" Wyche erupted into a deep, rolling laugh. "And nothing else can be on it. Like you can't eat on a table, you know, it had to be one function." Again the laughter roared out, shaking her body, stinging her eyes with tears, throwing her into a coughing fit until she got control over the delightful absurdity. "I went home and I told my mother, and my mother said, 'People live here.' " Wyche laughed again, long and hard. "At that point I made a decision: I never told my teachers what my mother said, and I never told my mother what my teachers said." Laughter once more.

Assumptions about black youngsters' inabilities taint the reactions of many white teachers—certainly not all, perhaps not even most, but enough to make an impact on the memories of black children and their parents. Sherlynn Reid, the black community relations director of Oak

Park, Illinois, recalls vividly the question her daughter Laurie's math teacher wrote on the bottom of an assignment at the beginning of an honors course: "Do you think you really belong in this class?"

Laurie's Spanish teacher never called on her, and when her mother asked why, the teacher explained, "I don't want to pick on her."

"Did you realize," Reid retorted, "that by not calling on her you *are* picking on her?"

And her swimming coach, after urging a white swimmer to "get us a first!," turned to Laurie and said, "Get us a second!"

"We called her over and said, 'Laurie, get us a first,' " her mother remembered with proud indignation. "She did. The coach said later he didn't want to put pressure on her."

But pressure is just what some black youngsters and their parents crave. "Michele" and "Frank," African-American high school students in Oak Park, actually wanted their teachers to sound the alarm to their parents, they explained as they sat in an empty classroom after school one day. Michele's father, a professor of physics, and Frank's, a professor of mathematics, had pushed them hard into honors courses, where they were struggling. But their teachers were not making sufficient demands on them, they felt. "My parents are very forceful as far as my teachers," Frank said. "They're here almost as much as I am, making sure that I'm getting a fair deal. That's really what's needed in order for African-American students to survive at this high school. If your parents are not involved, you won't do well."

Teachers' low expectations of black students sometimes produce an attitude of neglect, even undue tolerance of poor performance. During parent conferences, Michele was amazed as she heard white teachers sugarcoat her problems. "Since third grade, my mom started saying, 'You really need to work hard, 'cause the white teachers don't really care about you as much as they do about the white students,' " she explained. "I see it in my classes. I'm in honors classes; they definitely do treat black students a lot different. Last year I was doing pretty bad in math. I was in one of the higher math classes—this was in eighth grade—and I think I was the only black person in my class. And for all the other students they'd call the mom and say, 'You know, your child's having a problem.' "

But the teacher was too lenient with Michele. "She didn't really confront me about it," the girl said. "She really didn't pay attention to it. I think I really needed help, and I could have used a lot more motivation. She kind of gave up [on me] within the first week of school. . . . My parents go to the conferences: '[Michele's] such a great student, I wish I could have more students in the class like her.' They don't exactly say what the problem is. . . . I guess they're trying to make themselves look good so the parents will like the teacher. . . . 'She's so nice and she's so pretty and she has a lot of friends, blah, blah, blah.' And they never really talk about my grades." The anodyne approach to the black parents may reflect a mixture of prejudices and anxieties—low assumptions about Michele's abilities and nervousness that criticism could expose the teacher to the dreaded accusation of racism.

By taking honors courses, Michele and Frank were exceptions to a sad and destructive pattern. In much of American education, students are now placed on tracks from the elementary grades through high school, where honors or advanced-placement classes are obligatory for acceptance by the best colleges. Yet even in the best integrated high schools, only a small percentage of black students enroll in honors courses. In Oak Park, outside Chicago, where blacks make up 29 percent of the high school's student body, they constitute only 11 percent of the students in honors courses. Nearly 90 percent of the school's graduating seniors go on to college. Similarly, in Teaneck High School in New Jersey, the percentage of blacks taking various honors courses ranged from one-half to two-thirds that of whites in 1994. Eight percent of the white and 4 percent of the black students took eleventh-grade advanced-placement American history, for example, and 48 percent of the whites and 24 percent of the blacks took honors biology.

The fewer the blacks in honors, the fewer the blacks who want to be. At Teaneck one day, nine staff members—three of whom were black— sat around a conference table, discussed the problem, and quickly came to a consensus that black youngsters not only were tracked by the school system but also tracked themselves. "There is a lot of social pressure for kids to choose a class where they think they're going to fit," said Alice Twombly, a white English teacher with nineteen years of experience. "They don't want to be isolated." The black teachers nodded in agreement. So some of the brightest African-Americans, instead of selecting advanced placement, put themselves in less stimulating classes to be with other blacks. "In fact, they knock themselves down," she said.

Art Gardner, a black physical education teacher, supported her with a statement so blunt that no white could have made it. "The simple fact is," he said, "you have many minorities that just don't care if they don't make high scores. That is the reason why the test scores are so low. I have met a million and one black boys that do not care if [they do] well on the SATs. Couldn't care less. Some kids will go to sleep and say, 'I'm tired of this.' "

That kind of self-destruction grows out of a long legacy, in the view of Roger Wilkins, a civil rights activist who is now a history professor. "This society has done everything it could to disable black people," he said. "A society does that for three hundred years, it's going to have some successes."

Honors courses can be hostile environments where inadvertent, unconscious assumptions by white teachers often come through in thinly coded body language. Chris, a black student at Teaneck High School, described his white honors biology teacher this way: "Whenever she'd explain something, she'd look at me, sort of like asking me, 'Chris, do you understand?' " He interpreted this as racial prejudice.

A black girl had a typical story of being steered into lower-level courses. She was discouraged by her guidance counselor from taking biology her freshman year. "Meanwhile, I took physical science, and it was so easy, and I could have been finished with science last year. I could have been finished with history last year. I was totally misguided. I would have been able to take totally different courses. . . . I could have taken physics, which I haven't taken, which I need for the school I want to go to."

Some black youngsters channel their resentment at the low expectations into a kind of constructive anger, insisting on proving the opposite. Yoidette Myles, a black senior at Edward R. Murrow High School in Brooklyn, had heard from black friends that white guidance counselors had discouraged them from applying to competitive colleges. It had happened to her sister, so Yoidette was on her guard. "When I wanted to apply to Columbia, I was told, whoa, I should go for a safer school. My other choice was [State University of New York at] Stony Brook, and they said, 'You can probably try there, that's OK, that's more secure, but a lot of people want to go to Columbia, and it's hard to get into.' And I was sitting there, like, I can't believe this, because it was the same thing again. I applied to Stony Brook, Hofstra, Barnard—that was just in case I didn't get into Columbia."

But how malevolent was this, after all? Shouldn't a guidance counselor inject seniors with a dose of realism so they have a safe school on their list? Yoidette gave her grade point average as 91 and her class standing as fifty-eighth out of 693, well into the top 10 percent. But her SAT scores on the math and verbal tests combined totaled only 990. "It wasn't all that great," she admitted. Nevertheless, she added, "I took as many AP [advanced placement] classes as I could. I always tried to get into the best classes and challenge myself. I didn't see any reason why she should be telling me this." Yoidette was accepted by Columbia.

In many work situations, the assumption of lower ability has a silent, subliminal effect. It can corrode opportunity almost invisibly, without the conscious awareness of either perpetrator or victim. Take air force pilot training, for example. There are relatively few black pilots (1.8 percent), and in the air force, where pilots are the elite, that means relatively few black officers with the credentials to be assigned to senior commands and become generals. When I asked Lieutenant Colonel Edward Rice, an African-American B-52 pilot, why blacks were washed out of flight training in disproportionate numbers, he thought for a while and then gave an insightful answer.

The written tests are objective, he explained, but the flying exercises are subject to the constant judgments of the instructors who are in the cockpits with the students. If the student is black and the instructor is white, an image of black inferiority, even if deeply buried, gnaws away subtly at the instructor's sense of confidence, which is essential in such a risky enterprise. If a black student is at the controls, Rice asked, "how much does the instructor—how far does he let you go before he intervenes? If his perception is that you're dangerous and you can't fly and he doesn't really trust you, then he's not going to let you go as far as if his perception is [that] he does trust you and will let you go further. And you can't really learn unless you can kind of progress. And if he's always taking the airplane before you can get to a place where you're comfortable and can start to progress, then you're never going to make it."

In civilian offices on the ground, also, one often hears white supervisors of professed goodwill explain that they have covered for a black subordinate who cannot seem to do the job. They have saved him by doing his work for him; they have grabbed the controls of the plane before it crashed.

To counter the image of mental inferiority, some African-Americans project their intelligence like a huge snowplow, shoving away the stereotype before it takes on such bulk that it blocks their way. Veronica Valentine, a Boston child who went on to Bates College in Maine, learned this when she was bused to a mostly white suburban elementary school, where she was labeled a slow learner because she insisted on talking with a street accent, even though her speech had been constantly

corrected at home. "They said, 'Oh, my, this is a speech-impaired child.'
And they sent me to these special classes, and I hated it," she said. "I
called them the 'dummy classes,' and I felt like a dummy, and I knew I
wasn't a dummy, because I had all A's on my report card in second grade.
. . . She had us read a book that I remembered having read in kindergarten. I was reading all the words. I just didn't enunciate them the way
they wanted me to." From then on, she recalled, "that became a crusade
of mine: to always speak proper English in front of anybody who has any
influence over my grades and my education."

When Mellody Hobson got to Princeton, she said, "I wanted people
to know that I was smart, and I wanted them to know they couldn't
stereotype me—and this was both black and white people. And I think
that was a defense mechanism, and I hated myself for needing to do it.
But for some reason I had this desperate need to be like everyone else."
Perhaps, she explained, the need had been generated in grade school,
where she had been one of only a couple of blacks in a class. "My mom
always made sure that I had just the same things as everyone else. You
know, she would get mad at me if I wore a sock with a hole in it. She'd be
like, 'You're the first one that people are gonna look at!' And so that kind
of mentality became a part of me."

The sense of always being on display, and of performing a ritual of
proof in each encounter, chafes against the spirit of well-being. "It gets
wearing after a while," said a fine-boned black woman, a psychiatrist at a
Baltimore hospital. She was reminiscing with a thin, fluttering pain, the
kind that never overwhelms but never disappears.

Some years before, a white woman with psychological problems had
come with her husband to be admitted to the hospital. "I walked in the
room," the doctor remembered. "My name was Jones at that point. I
said, 'I'm Dr. Jones. I'll be admitting you to the hospital.' And she sat
there, and her husband was sitting there, and they looked at each other,
like, shocked." The doctor read with unfailing clarity the lucid language
of the body, which is more honest at the initial moment than the dissem-
bling words that tumble after. "She stayed in the hospital a couple of
days, and she left," the doctor said. "And I guess ideally I'd like to believe
she left because she didn't need to be here in the hospital, but I can't
quite fully accept that that was all there was to it. I think that one,
momentary look said so much, that she was very uncomfortable with me
being her doctor. And we talked about it. I was comfortable enough at
that point to talk about it with her. She said, 'Oh, no, no, no, no
problem, no problem.' But she left."

The doctor has developed "a whole range of reactions" inside herself when she gets that momentary look at a first meeting. Sometimes, when she is rested and in a good frame of mind, she throws it off as she would a virus—with her body's natural defenses. "If it's at the end of the day and it's been an irritating day, I might not take it so well," she explained. "Sometimes I feel, Here we go again. It's really their problem; it's not my problem. But it is irritating, and it adds an unnecessary element to the work. It can chip away at you if you let it. I try very hard not to let it do that. But it does happen. It's happened with patients. It's happened with families." It had happened several weeks before, when visitors had arrived to consult about launching a new program. "And they're coming down the hall and I go out to greet them. I think it was a group of four people, and they all looked at each other. Every single one of them looked at each other! And, I thought, Oh, great, this is going to be a short meeting. So they come in and we talk. . . . The more we got into it I could see them . . . relax and their posture was a little different, and I could see that they were hearing what I was saying, and start to ask more interesting questions. So they were valuing what I had to say. So it's an element of proving oneself, establishing one's credibility."

She smiled as she told the story, the same kind of aching, inward smile that dissidents in Moscow used to have when they talked of their imprisonment. When you know calmly that you are right and steady, and when you are the target of absurd hostility, it is hard not to smile, and it is hard not to feel hurt at the same time. The doctor overcomes. Again and again, every day, in virtually every conference she has with a patient and his family, she overcomes. "Part of the conference involves my interviewing the patient to get a sense of how they're doing, to establish the goals, and so on," she said. "Nine times out of ten, things change after the interview takes place, because I know that I do a good job. So I guess that's a way of establishing some credibility with this other person during the interview process. But, you know, it gets wearing after a while."

Some white people are profoundly unable to fit any African-American into their portrait of a highly skilled professional. So they instinctively withdraw the honorific title, probably without thinking. It just strikes them as nonsensical to call a black person "doctor." Dr. Jones occasionally has such patients, who call her "Ms. Jones." "And I say, 'No, it's Dr. Jones. I prefer Dr. Jones.' I've perfected it over the years. That's what I say now: 'I prefer Dr. Jones.' "

The problem arose even with a professional colleague who, with a single word, thoughtlessly punctured the young black woman's achievement of university, medical school, and psychiatric training. "When I was a resident," she recalled, "one of my supervisors referred to me as 'Miss Jones.' And this guy was an analyst, and he knew better. On many levels, he knew better. I felt very awkward. I was a first-year resident and this guy was calling me 'Miss Jones.' I said, 'You know, you've been calling me 'Miss Jones,' and I don't like that. Why are you calling me that?' He denied it and then went into this psychoanalytic thing about our relationship." His denial fell apart when he referred to her as "Miss Jones" at a meeting of all the supervisors. But he never repented and never called her "doctor." He continued sometimes to call her "Miss Jones." "Either that or nothing," she said, "and I preferred nothing."

The trouble is, prejudiced whites rarely appreciate blacks who advertise their brains or their energies; in violating the comfortable stereotype, they stir resentment. They're too smart, too eager, maybe even too rich—"uppity" is the old term, now translated into more coded adjectives. Two veteran military men, one black, one white, described the quandary for blacks who try to get ahead in the armed forces, which may be America's most successful institution in opening opportunities for minorities. Blacks have to push for good assignments, said Tony Wyatt, the black master sergeant in the air force. They have to ask where the openings are and go after what they want. "Otherwise, they're left behind," he said.

"And then," added David Baade, a white chief petty officer who serves on submarines, "the Catch-22 is that if they take the initiative themselves to seek and push the job, they may be viewed as pushy, overaggressive."

"Overaggressive," Wyatt agreed. "Think the system owes them something."

"Even to be labeled as far as 'militant,' " said Baade, "simply for trying to be equal."

To get along comfortably, many African-Americans adjust the level of intelligence they project to suit the circumstance; sometimes it seems wise to be smart, and sometimes it seems smarter to be dumb. Whites' reactions to those who seem too brilliant can be unpredictably hostile, and quite accommodating to those who seem a bit slow.

A black physicist in California vividly remembers driving across country with his mother when he was thirteen or fourteen. She was stopped by a cop in Texas for speeding and "played the dumb black," he said. "She played the dumb black and got off."

So did an army buddy of Robert H. Cooley III, the Richmond lawyer who traces his lineage back to Thomas Jefferson. The man had a flat tire, Cooley recalled, while driving in the snow from Washington to Macon, Georgia, in the sixties. He and a couple of friends were sitting in the car, needling each other about who was going to change the tire, when a state trooper sauntered up. "What's wrong with y'all, boys?" he asked. So the "boy" behind the wheel, articulate and college-educated, decided to play the acceptable role, Cooley said.

"We don't know what the problem is, Mr. Policeman," the driver whined in a thick accent straight out of *Amos 'n' Andy*.

"You've got a flat tire," said the trooper.

"What we gonna do now?"

"Well, don't you have a jack and a spare tire in the car?"

"I guess we do." Cooley imitated the driver shaking his head stupidly and putting a lost, confused look on his face.

The cop called them names, got the spare, and changed the tire himself while the blacks stood around trying to look dumb. "All right, well, go on," the cop finally snarled. And off they went, laughing all the way to Macon.

Another time, Cooley was working with a black man on a mail-sorting machine; you fed in piles of letters, the machine would tie them into a bundle, and you'd throw the bundle into the appropriate basket.

"Man, I'm tired," Cooley's partner complained. "I'm tired of working here."

"But you've got to keep on going," Cooley said.

The coworker didn't think so. "Where's the supervisor?" he asked, and then called to his boss, "Hey, man! Come here a minute, man!"

"What's your problem?" the supervisor asked.

"Man, I can't work. What's wrong with this machine?"

"Well, let me see."

"So," Cooley said, "he scooped up some mail—*whoom*—scoops up some more mail, got the machine working—this is the supervisor doing this."

"There's nothing wrong with the machine," the boss said.

"There must be something wrong with the machine," Cooley's coworker insisted.

"Look, I'll show you again," said the supervisor. He shoved another pile of mail into the machine, and another, until he had done it all. Then he called them "stupid."

"Well, I guess you're right," the worker admitted. "Maybe it was something I was doing." When the boss had walked off, the employee turned triumphantly to Cooley. "See, I told you I was tired of working."

The tactic of stepping into the stereotype and using it to outfox whites has been a standard weapon in the arsenal of survival. "Blacks have done that for years," Cooley said. "That was part of your defense." He appreciated the shrewdness of the prank but couldn't bring himself to participate in a demeaning victory. "I wouldn't want to be perceived as being a dumb jerk," he remarked.

If the twists about outsmarting whites were subtracted from these scenarios, they would have been considered hilarious television in the fifties, when blacks were caricatured as shuffling, scared, witless clowns and cheats. From Buckwheat's wide-eyed fright to Beulah's broad, jolly subservience, black characters were imprisoned in boxes of imagery that never allowed for intelligence or dignity. And their blackness was made integral to much of the comedy, which often turned on dialect, crooked-ness, laziness, gullibility, and other forms of incompetence thought to be particular attributes of black people. The humor of *Amos 'n' Andy*, which was canceled after two seasons on TV following complaints by the NAACP, relied heavily on the stereotypes.

"Why, you ain't got sense enough to come in out of the rain," Andy is told sternly.

An instant of confusion flashes across his dark, round face. "I is, too," he says. "I done it lots of times."

Kingfish, the miserly wheeler-dealer, defends a good-for-nothing friend against a woman's calumnies:

SHE: What, may I ask, has he ever accomplished?
KINGFISH: Well, he, uh—just yesterday he had a run of thir-teen balls in the side pocket without once leaning on the pool table.

Kingfish's famous gift of gab is considerably more facile than his brain. "See, Andy," he explains, "first, the atom splits into what they call the monocle. And the monocle breaks down into what they call neu-trons, potrons, Fig Newtons, and morons."

Whites were not the only fans of *Amos 'n' Andy*; the show had a black audience as well. "We thought the show was marvelous, the best thing on television," Colin Powell wrote in his memoir, *My American Journey*. "It was another age, and we did not know that we were not supposed to like *Amos 'n' Andy*." In recent years, certain black scholars have done some revisionist thinking about the show. True, it was full of stereotypes. But it was also a whole black culture, they point out, complete with black judges, black lawyers, black doctors—even a black doll, which Henry Louis Gates Jr., the author who heads Harvard's African-American studies program, remembers as the first he ever saw as a child. One recent Christmas, Gates pulled out tapes of the program as a nostalgia trip to show his daughters, ages twelve and fourteen. "I found myself laughing so hard at Kingfish's malapropisms and Andy's gullibility," he wrote, "that it took me a while to realize that I was laughing alone." His children denounced the show as "garbage," "stupid," and "fake."

James Baldwin once observed, "The country's image of the Negro, which hasn't very much to do with the Negro, has never failed to reflect, with a frightening accuracy, the state of mind of the country." And so the black images in that most cautiously commercial of media, television, have been closely attuned to the nation's attitudes of the time. The society bends and sways and shifts its standards and tastes on matters of race just as on the length of hemlines and the width of ties. The skirts and the ties of the fifties now look as awkward and unattractive as the black characters of the period's films; that they were all once acceptable now seems unimaginable. Surely the white producers, writers, and viewers—and the black actors—did not consider themselves racists when they created and appreciated Beulah, Buckwheat, Amos, and Kingfish. The shock comes only in retrospect. Infallibly, our eye adjusts to the present.

After the civil rights movement, television passed appropriately through an integrationist phase, with such black characters as Alexander Scott, the bright, multilingual Rhodes scholar played by Bill Cosby in *I Spy*, beginning in 1965, and, from 1968 to 1971, the character of "Julia," the slim, light-skinned black nurse who lived and worked in mostly white settings. Significantly, *Julia* was created by Hal Kanter, the white producer who had done *Amos 'n' Andy*. That show had been produced only with an eye toward entertainment, he explained in "Color Adjustment," a PBS documentary.

"I don't think that the sponsors or the network, and certainly not the writers, ever considered the questions of race relations, of stereotyping, et cetera," he said. "That was the farthest from our minds. What we were trying to do was present an amusing set of characters in as amusing a background as we possibly could, doing amusing things to entice the audience to come back next week." But in the next decade, his *Julia* was his response to a plea to Hollywood from Roy Wilkins, head of the NAACP. It was also his way of recognizing and correcting his misdeeds.

"I thought that I really owed to my black colleagues some sort of an apology for a lot of the things that we had done on *Amos 'n' Andy*," he explained.

In the waning years of the century, blacks have multiplied their identities and images to the point where they can be seen in practically every conceivable incarnation. In the sitcom *Night Court*, they were the only ones with any common sense, foils to the infantile white judge, the silly white defense lawyer, and the dogmatic white sergeant at arms. In police dramas, they often showed up as the steady, honest cops or the upright attorneys. On *The Cosby Show*, they finally became upper-middle-class professionals—a doctor and a lawyer—who personified solid family values. As Archie Bunker's wife once said on an episode of *All in the Family* when asked what she thought of black people, "You've sure got to hand it to them. I mean, two years ago they were nothing but servants and janitors. Now they're teachers and doctors and lawyers. They've come a long way on TV."

Add to the disjunction between image and reality the blacks who have increasingly been cast in commercials; the blacks featured in newscasts (often unfavorably, as criminals); and the black athletes who are scattered across the screen during football, basketball, and baseball games, and television looks like a cornucopia of racial diversity. (For many years, United Airlines has shown a safety video featuring a black man dressed as a pilot with a captain's four stripes on his sleeve. But in real life, passengers hardly ever see an African-American in a cockpit, since only 2.8 percent of United's pilots are black and fewer than one-fifth of the black pilots are captains.) The impression this picture has made is so powerful that when I asked a small class of whites at the University of Maine what percentage of the American population they thought was black, one woman said, "Fifty," another student agreed, and a couple of others estimated 40 percent and 30 percent. The actual figure is 13 percent. That most of the students came from Maine, whose population was only 0.4 percent black in the 1990 census, suggested that they were drawing conclusions not from their surroundings but from their television screens and perhaps from the tendency among many whites to magnify a few blacks into a horde.

In the early days of television, black Americans used to call one another in excited anticipation when a black actor or singer was scheduled for a broadcast, so rare was the event. Now, too, even in the midst of plenty, blacks gravitate to certain shows, and broadcasters play to a Balkanization of viewing habits. Not a single one of the top ten programs favored by blacks appears among the top ten for the country as a whole, according to a 1993 survey; the races are simply watching different shows. Advertisers and networks have discovered the African-American market. With the explosion of cable stations, a gradual realization that black audiences are sizable, and research data showing that blacks watch more hours of TV than nonblacks, African-American producers and writers are finally gaining a foothold.

But some of the black characters that are valued by African-Americans are not very bright. They convey old stereotypes dressed in different garb. There is the streetwise black youth, angry and violent. There is the sexually obsessive man (or woman), grabbing and joking suggestively. And there is the buffoon—yes, the stupid, silly, garish clown who says and does dumb, funny things, usually punctuated with jerky, goofy gestures or slaps alongside another actor's head. Such figures have appeared in the shows most popular among blacks, including *Martin*, *In Living Color*, and *Family Matters*.

The buffoonery also soothes white viewers by erasing any quality that whites might see as intimidating. As a result, black actors and writers in television contribute to an image of unintelligence that will surely be seen as offensive in some near future.

White on White, Black on Black

Not only do racial stereotypes shape one group's view of another, they also affect each group's view of itself. Whites who assume that blacks are mentally inferior automatically assume that whites are mentally superior; the two beliefs fit together as neatly as two pieces of a jigsaw puzzle.

This may seem obvious, but whites rarely put it so bluntly. Most white Americans are not aware of "whiteness" as a characteristic. Nor do they always display racial solidarity in judging people's intelligence: Some whites with college degrees look down on whites who haven't finished high school; some whites who work in offices think they are smarter than whites who work with their hands. Some whites named Smith are dubious about whites named Taglieri. Within the race, the contours of prejudice are marked by the crisscrossing lines of ethnicity and class.

But the line between black and white is the most severe, and whites seldom recognize what they gain from racial stereotyping. When they consider racism, they usually focus on what whites do to blacks, not on the benefits whites enjoy as a result. They may not consciously consider how their negative images of blacks naturally confer positive attributes on themselves or how they have gained privilege from long-standing patterns of prejudice and discrimination. They may not see what Peggy McIntosh, associate director of the Wellesley College Center for Research on Women, calls the "unearned advantage" of white skin, the "invisible knapsack" of assets they carry around.

McIntosh is a rare sort of white person, for she actually thinks about the prerogatives of whiteness. In 1988, comparing her circumstances with those of African-American women whom she knew, she devised a list of forty-six conditions that she, but not her black acquaintances, could count on enjoying. "I think whites are carefully taught not to recognize white privilege, as males are taught not to recognize male privilege," she wrote. "So I have begun in an untutored way to ask what it is like to have white privilege." Her resulting observations, while largely autobiographical, have struck a universal chord and are now routinely cited by scholars, diversity trainers, and others who write and teach on racial matters.

"In my class and place," she concluded, "I did not see myself as racist because I was taught to recognize racism only in individual acts of meanness by members of my group, never in invisible systems conferring unsought racial dominance on my group from birth." Her list of unseen privileges (unseen by most whites, vividly visible to most blacks) illuminates, layer upon layer, the acid coexistence of white benefit and black disadvantage. It includes the following:

• "I can do well in a challenging situation without being called a credit to my race."

• "I can be late to a meeting without having the lateness reflect on my race."

• "I can swear, or dress in secondhand clothes, or not answer letters, without having people attribute these choices to the bad morals, the poverty, or the illiteracy of my race."

• "When I am told about our national heritage or about 'civilization,' I am shown that people of my color made it what it is."

• "I can easily buy posters, postcards, picture books, greeting cards, dolls, toys, and children's magazines featuring people of my race."

• "If I should need to move, I can be pretty sure of renting or purchasing housing in an area which I can afford and in which I would want to live."

• "I can be pretty sure that if I ask to talk to 'the person in charge,' I will be facing a person of my race."

• "I can avoid spending time with people whom I was trained to mistrust and who have learned to mistrust my kind or me."

• "I can go home from most meetings of organizations I belong to feeling somewhat tied in, rather than isolated, out-of-place, out-numbered, unheard, held at a distance, or feared."

• "I can criticize our government and talk about how much I fear its policies and behavior without being seen as a cultural outsider."

• "I can worry about racism without being seen as self-interested or self-seeking."

Thus do white Americans, as a group, enjoy the comfort of basic assuredness. As black Americans look at themselves, however, no such confidence accrues to them. The stereotypes of mental inferiority infil-trate their self-assessments, forcing teachers and parents to struggle hard against the doubts that are imposed upon their children.

The father came looking for his son, who had not been in school and had not gone home the day before. The man was strong and lean, his face creased with worry. He wore a black baseball cap with a white X on the front, and he was carrying the radio from his car, which he had parked at a glass-strewn curb of South Central Los Angeles—on Crenshaw Street, to be precise, between Slawson and Vernon, in front of the small, dingy building where his son studied.

In the jargon of the struggling efforts against the urban tide of illit-eracy and decay, this was called an "alternative education worksite," where sixty youngsters unable to function in regular schools were embraced by a strict and caring structure of demands, expectations, and hopes. The forty-three-year-old leader of this enterprise, Chilton Alphonse, a former Black Panther and now executive director of the Community Youth, Sports, and Arts Foundation, sat in a large, stained couch that used to be beige. He was bald, with a full gray beard and lively eyes. This morning he wore a blue flowered shirt with the top two buttons open, and he stood up as the father was ushered in. He knew the case thoroughly, and asked simply, "The fact that he didn't come home?"

"Right," the father said.

The boy's name was Charles, and he had returned to class today, so Alphonse sent for him. His mother was a drug addict who had lost cus-tody, and the boy himself had been placed here by the probation depart-ment, one route by which teenagers were referred. Others were sent by juvenile courts, by surrounding schools, or by parents who had heard about the good things that happened inside these walls. "It's a very disci-plined, structured program that allows the kids to learn at their own pace, gives them an advantage," Alphonse had explained earlier. "Most of the time when the kids come to us, they read on a second-, third-grade level, so it's impossible for them to complete senior high school classes if they don't have the ability to read and comprehend." As a condition of enrollment, parents are required to attend parenting classes run by the school. "Many parents have just totally lost control of the children," he said wearily. His response is "tough love, as I like to call it," and an unusual belief never before encountered by most of these children—that each one of them has the brains to succeed.

As Charles walked in, he looked sulkily down at the floor, trying not to meet his father's eyes. He was a big boy, but in his gray pants and black sweatshirt, he almost melted away into the background—surely his fondest wish just then. "Why weren't you in school?" Alphonse asked sharply.

"I was mad."

"So you just want to call your own shots, do what you want to do. Do you buy any of your own food?"

"No."

"Do you buy any of your own clothes?"

"No."

"Do you buy any shoes?"

"No."

"You don't do shit. You want to get help?"

"Yes."

"You got to follow your father's rules. There are rules everywhere you go." Alphonse looked at the boy's transcript. "You can barely read."

Charles finally showed a flicker of defensive pride. "I can read. Mr. Williams said I did good on the test."

"You're reading on a seventh-grade level."

"I'm not reading on a seventh-grade level."

"You haven't been applying yourself, son. You haven't been doing your work."

"I've been doing some."

Alphonse spoke this boy's language, having been born and raised in the neighborhood and having grown up in a gang called the "Slawsons." It had been a more innocent time, when the weapons were merely sticks and "maybe knives every now and then," he said. But he understood the rough affection these youngsters needed; he saw how vulnerable they were beneath the surface of bravado. He looked at Charles's folder again. "You only completed one assignment. One assignment. One assignment since January sixth."

"Why not?" The father asked the boy.

"It's Math Two," said Alphonse. "You can do the work. You're no dummy." Charles mumbled that he did not understand the assignments or the contract that he and his teacher had drawn up. "It's not a crime not to know something," Alphonse declared. "But find out." Then came the threat. Charles liked the school and wanted to stay, Alphonse knew, so he took out his ultimate weapon. "Basically, I think we're wasting our time," Alphonse said, " 'cause he's not doing nothing. We can't do nothing about it. I don't have time to waste with you. I want to help those who want our help. If you'd been my son, I'da kicked your ass when I found you." He turned to the father. "I suggest you start documenting all this—date, what he does, get him categorized as 601A— incorrigible youth. He's assigned a probation officer, and if you break your father's rule, you go before a judge. Maybe you need to spend a night in Juvenile Hall. You're a big seventeen-year-old boy that wants attention. You're gonna be eighteen pretty soon and in that cold world. You got to get a job. . . . I'm raising kings and queens here." He was pausing after each word to heighten the punch. "Can't nobody make you do nothing. You got to take it in your own mind what you want to do. What are you gonna do, son?"

There was a long, long silence. Charles looked down at the floor and finally said softly, "I'm gonna try."

This was not enough for Alphonse, and he made an exasperated sound between his teeth. "Dad, do me a favor. I'm gonna get you a math book. Take him home. Bring him back Monday. He doesn't deserve to go on the field trip." This was true punishment, for the next day, the youngsters were going out on a whale-watching boat in the Pacific. "Come in Monday. If you want to stay here, you better have a stack of math work for me. You understand what I'm telling you? If you don't have it, I don't want to see you. Go on, then, and get a book." Charles sat there for a moment. "Now get up and go and get a book!" Alphonse shouted.

"Stop moving so slow!" his father scolded.

This was not the end of the session, for when Charles came back with the book, one of his teachers came too, a white woman who suggested that he be tested for dyslexia. She urged him firmly and gently to ask if he didn't understand. "Are you afraid of me, Charles? Are you afraid of me?"

"She's talking to you," Alphonse snapped. "Look at her, man. I'm about to write you off." Charles mumbled that he wasn't afraid. Therefore, his teacher told him, he shouldn't be afraid to ask for help.

Alphonse was bringing his rescue mission to a close for now, and so he deftly mixed more threats—"We'll take a little ride, let you meet my good friend Judge Randolph Moore, let him talk to you"—with that essential undercurrent of belief. At last he put an arm around the boy and squeezed his neck. "You're gonna bring the math book back, right?" Charles smiled for the first time. "You want attention, don't you?" The grin broadened. Father and son left together.

If you're black, you don't have to be a street kid in Los Angeles to doubt your abilities. You're immersed in the society's doubts from birth, and pretty soon you may believe them yourself. This can be true even if you get into Princeton. When Lisa Copland received her acceptance letter, it didn't occur to her at first that she might have enjoyed a preference because she was black. Her SAT scores were nearly 1200, and she was fourteenth in a class of 206 at her Catholic high school in Maryland. But in a couple of weeks, a little worm of a thought began to gnaw at her, a little question about how her blackness might have influenced Princeton's decision. She asked her father. He didn't know; he'd have to ask the admissions office. And so she willfully put it out of her mind, decided she had gotten in on her own merits, and resolved to "come here and do the best I could," she said. And she did.

"Then, like, during midterm week, I had so much to do, and it didn't seem like enough hours in the day, I was thinking, Maybe I'm not supposed to be here." The doubt stayed with her, and she learned that other black students shared it. "Someone brought this up last night," she said. "The work is so much, you're overwhelmed with things. Why am I here? Do I belong here with these people? Or am I only here because of the diversity thing? Am I here because they have the need to have a certain number? And I wonder if that's what people see when they look at me. If they say, 'Well, she might not be as smart as I am. Maybe her extra push in getting in was because she's black.' It makes you feel degraded, because you wonder if that's true."

This nagging question is not limited to African-Americans. Nell Painter, a black history professor at Princeton, heard it from wealthy whites at Harvard when she was a graduate student. "It was, 'I bet I'm here just because I'm wealthy,'" she said. "And from smart lower-class students it was, 'My God, they're going to find out I'm not as smart as I'm supposed to be.'"

For blacks, however, the uncertainty is even more corrosive, for the racial obsession can eat away at any trust of whites' judgments: Low appraisals are considered anti-black, while high appraisals seem self-consciously pro-black. Neither are credible. Flattery is sometimes taken as patronizing. If a white says that an African-American is articulate or creative, the black may hear a lilt of surprise in the statement. The compliment seems to bounce off the baseline of low expectations. When a white professor at Lake Forest College had good things to say about Michelle Pulce, an excellent student from Little Rock, Arkansas, she didn't believe him. "I've worked with him a lot," she said. "One summer I did my summer research with him. And he thinks I can go to Harvard and do these great things and whatever. But I know for a fact that I'm not Harvard material. Just looking at the scores I make in standardized tests, I don't meet those qualifications. But he pumps me up and all like this. It's good, I feel great and whatever, but I know that's not the real thing. . . . It gives you, like, a false sense of what your ability really is. . . . You have to have your own reality check for yourself." The difficulty is where to find the reality when it is shaped by such distorting lenses.

Although affirmative action is blamed as the catalyst for these attitudes, it is wise to remember that blacks were seen—and saw themselves—as mentally inferior long before the efforts to recruit them into colleges and workplaces. Indeed, that stereotype of stupidity and laziness formed the core of the bigotry that made affirmative action necessary. Three decades ago, if Lisa Copland had been rejected, she might legitimately have wondered whether that negative outcome was the result of her race. Being black, it seems, is never a neutral element in the equation.

Campuses and corporations are pervaded by a diffuse belief that African-Americans who get into coveted positions are being given special breaks that overlook their inadequacies. Black students routinely run up against this nasty assumption, and although many deflect the insult with a shell of hard antagonism, many others feel the hurt and nurse the doubts about themselves. Opponents of affirmative action cite this as a damaging feature of the policy, arguing that it is demeaning to blacks and erodes their self-esteem. There is a worse alternative, however: not getting in at all. In either case, the black is seen as less smart than her white peers. If asked to choose, a young, bright, ambitious African-American might prefer being at Princeton and being thought inferior over not being at Princeton and being thought inferior.

Every solution creates at least one new problem. But as affirmative action has created this one, among others, it has also exposed the durability of the old caricature of black people as inherently less capable than whites. Racism is agile enough to adapt itself to a different landscape, and it has done so deftly as anti-discrimination and pro-diversity ethics have gained ground. When African-Americans are excluded, it is because they are less capable. When they are accepted, they are still less capable, but their deficiencies have been unjustly ignored in favor of the color of their skin. The virus of bigotry mutates and survives.

"If you are a black person in this society, how in the hell do you maintain self-esteem?" wondered Richard Taub, a sociology professor at the University of Chicago. "So many blacks internalize the white standards about blacks . . . and it breaks your heart. I think about growing up as a Jew. My parents and all their friends thought that Jews were smarter than other people. . . . The Japanese in this country, they know they're smarter than other people. . . . All these groups really have deep cultural roots of self-esteem. Blacks have tried it with this black pride stuff, but that's fake. It's not really internalized. It's not real."

Haki Madhubuti, the African-American poet and book publisher, tries to inspire by turning the expectations upside down when he teaches literature to mostly black classes at Chicago State. "When I walk into the classroom the first day of class," he explained, "the first thing I'll tell the students is, 'One, all of you as far as I'm concerned—and I don't know you—are geniuses. Which means that you came out of your mother's womb at genius level. Unless there is something genetically or biologically wrong with you, you were a genius. Now, to nurture the genius, that means you have to be in a nurturing culture, a nurturing family. I don't know if you were in a nurturing family or not. I know that the culture, by and large, is not nurturing. I'm going to give you the benefit of the doubt, because I'm saying you're still a genius. Which means, essentially, you have to prove to me that you're not a genius. Which means if you're a genius, everybody starts off in this classroom with an A. You have an A; everybody has an A. What has to happen, you've got to lose the A. So in losing the A, that means you're proving to me that you're not a genius.' "

This is a nice idea but a bit of a hard sell, because it is not only white culture that has failed to nurture such confidence and commitment; it is black culture as well. One of the most painful vignettes of ghetto schools in recent years appeared on page one of the *Wall Street Journal*, which described how administrators at Frank W. Ballou Senior High in Washington, D.C., kept the true purpose of an academic awards assembly secret so students would not stay away. One winner, who had been tipped off, was so unwilling to endure his schoolmates' jeers and catcalls that he remained alone in a chemistry classroom when his name was announced. Another came forward only after a teacher ran to his seat and ordered him to walk up and receive his prize, as some taunted, "Nerd!"

You don't have to be black to smell the anti-intellectualism that wafts through hallways like acrid disinfectant. Making fun of "nerds" is a venerated tradition among schoolchildren generally, both white and black. But when the epithets become racial, when serious black students are branded "white" for taking honors courses and getting good grades, the condemnation takes on a bite and a magnitude that can be debilitating for all but the most tenacious young person. The charge of "acting white" and thereby abandoning your black identity is a severe curse.

Intricate divisions among black people result. Mickey, an African-American policewoman in Baltimore, worked very hard in school and endured cutting comments about her supposed brilliance, even to the point where she tried to convince friends that she wasn't as brainy as she seemed. "It's not that I was so smart," she insisted. "It's that I spent a lot of time studying because I wasn't smart." She also felt friction from black officers in the police department. "I find people looking to tell me, 'Oh, there's Mickey, she knows everything.' And one day, I just told them, 'You know something? I'm tired of apologizing for my knowledge, because I study, I read, I get involved in things, which is something anybody can do, and if I know something, I'm not going to try to sell myself short by acting as if I don't know it. . . . If you talk about things you know about, then you'll come across as a pretty smart person too.' "

The same conflict has developed between American and Caribbean blacks in such settings as Lincoln University, the black college in Pennsylvania; students from the Caribbean and Africa often go there on scholarships from their governments, and if they don't keep their grades up, they lose their funding. "When an African or West Indian student answers a question well in class," said a professor from Jamaica, "you can feel the tension." Some American blacks ridicule them as trying to act white; in turn, some Caribbean students stereotype the Americans as lazy and self-destructive. Some African students, so insistent on dissociating themselves from American blacks, angrily refuse to be called "blacks."

The image of smartness can intrude deeply into personal and family relationships. Barbara Wyche, the sociologist who felt neglected in her integrated schools in Virginia, nonetheless saw one benefit in leaving the all-black classroom. "I used to get beat up because I was very good," she said. "This was in the black school. I was relieved to go to the white school, because I didn't have to take the verbal abuse, nor the physical abuse, of being a smart child." Her black peers never accepted her. "I just was caught in that image, and even if I go home today," she said, "nobody would ask me to dance. You see what I'm saying? They wouldn't even think that I knew how to dance. I had an inferiority complex, because I really wanted people to like me, and I really loved people and I wanted to fit, and I couldn't fit."

Her father had three years of college and wanted his daughter to go on as well. He "wanted me to talk, like, very fine, like, 'Thank you.' " And here she put on an erudite, quasi-British accent. "My mother let me know that if I came back talking and acting like some of the people that were teaching, that I would not be her child," Wyche recalled. "That was again picking up those attitudes that we call 'white.' "

Thus did the racial imagery insinuate itself into the fiber of her family, setting up tensions over class, education, language, and identity that were played out against conflicts between her parents, whose marriage ended when she was ten. "I am a product of class warfare in my own family," Wyche said. "My mother went on a campaign and said I was never going to be like that man and his arrogant, his elitist-type attitude. And I love my daddy. All right? I love the ground he walks on, and I look just like him.

"I would come home from Johns Hopkins University," Wyche went on, "and you know, you pick up this way of talking to each other. I was good at it. . . . So I remember I went home one year, and I told my mother, I said, 'Mama,' I kept talking and talking and talking, and my mother said, 'I'm glad you learned how to talk at school' . . . and I was just talking, talking, talking, and my mama said, 'Speak English or don't talk at all.' I was using the GRE and SAT vocabulary. I had made the transition, so my mother didn't know what I was talking about."

Black on White

The exercise was simple. I asked the thirty students, all but one of them black, each to take a piece of paper and write down a list of stereotypes they thought white people held of blacks; then to make a list of stereotypes that black people held of whites. When they had finished, I asked them to read from their lists while I wrote their words on the board.

It was a sociology class at Lincoln University, whose students seemed as varied as they would be in a public school. Some were exceptionally bright and eager; others, considerably less so. But they reached a consensus on the images they saw projected across racial lines. Here were their lists, with the students' elaborations and reactions in brackets:

Whites Think Blacks Are:

Poor

Violent

Lazy

Athletic

Ignorant

Thieves

Inferior

Like to complain

Uneducated

Drug addicts, dope dealers

Not important

Fatherless

Radicals

Homeless

Alcoholics

Can dance

Entertainers

Perpetrators

Churchgoing

Blacks Think Whites Are:

Perpetrators ["They don't have nothing." "They pretty much want to tell somebody that they do have something even though they don't." "They, like, perpetrate a fraud."]

Bigots

Selfish

Critics

Financially secure

Devils [Murmurs.]

Supremacists

Funny ["Funny peculiar." "The various ways like
you see like mocking things or trying to copy
things—like for example with the lipstick, trying to
look like they have thicker lips."]

Scared

Confused

Ignorant

Good actors

Can't dance

No rhythm

They have complexes

Party animals

Alcoholics

Back-stabbers

Can't trust them. Untrustworthy

Conniving

Money-hungry ["Yeah."]

Later in the day, I did the same exercise with another sociology class,
which had only two whites.

Whites Think Blacks Are:

Hoodlums

Undereducated

Criminals

Lazy

Violent

Look alike [Laughter.]

Better athletes

Poor English speaking, broken English

On drugs and alcohol

Ignorant

Leech off society

Wanting sex [Lots of crosstalk and laughter.]

Can't handle stressful situations

Arrogant

Materialistic

Gaudy

Broken homes

Untrustworthy

Comedians [Meaning clowning around.]

Blacks Think Whites Are:

They all look alike

Funny

Powerful

Can't dance

Egotistical

Manipulative .

Dirty [Some people groaned, "Noooooo!"]

Rich

Opportunists

Superior race

Ignorant

Cold

Nerdy

Only one word turned up in all four lists, identified by both classes as the single characteristic that blacks and whites attribute to each other: "ignorant."

For many African-Americans thinking about white people, ignorance has a broad meaning, extending far beyond what standardized tests can measure. It encompasses a lack of street savvy, common sense, and instinct about human behavior. In the faintly amused assessment by many blacks, white people tend to be smart but stupid, intelligent but unwise. The 1990 poll by the National Opinion Research Center, surveying prejudices in a cross section of Americans, questioned only about 150 black people, not enough to be statistically significant in gauging blacks' attitudes. But the results hinted at one side of the conflicting views that seem to run through blacks' images of whites. Asked whether whites were intelligent or unintelligent, almost as high a proportion of blacks (56.5 percent) as whites (58.4 percent) put whites at the intelligent end of the scale. In all, 12.5 percent of the blacks, as opposed to 6.4 percent of the whites, labeled whites unintelligent. The rest were in the middle.

These figures suggest no particular anti-white prejudice among blacks, but conversations indicate otherwise. Many African-Americans say that when it comes to character, mental brightness leaves something out, and that whites often display blank spots in their understanding. "White people are somehow more intellectually oriented, square, concerned with the superficial, nonhuman kinds of issues than blacks are," said Laura Washington, the African-American editor in Chicago, when asked to describe the stereotypes. "Blacks are more interested in music, in things that are created by people, that people gravitate to."

Being more people-oriented, in this view, means that blacks have an empathy that whites do not, and the whites' gap is especially immense on racial issues; hence, the T-shirt logo: "It's a Black Thing. You Wouldn't Understand."

"Most of the time, I feel like it *is* a black thing, and you *wouldn't* understand, because you don't take the time to," said Shari Jones, the African-American college student from Memphis. "And you don't understand. I mean, you just don't understand." This came clear when she had a white teaching African-American history. "My mom's, like, fifty-eight years old, and she grew up in the South," Jones explained. "She'd tell me how she'd have to walk to school and white students would spit at her, you know, from the bus, and how during this time of season, this is cotton season, so they would have to stay out of school for a whole quarter, black students would, and pick cotton, instead of being in school and learning."

But that human trial never filtered into the history professor's antiseptic lessons. "He didn't understand. He just gave us facts about history. He didn't give us any perspectives. And that's why when I think about that T-shirt, I think about my mom and what she said and how things happened. . . . And then I think about this teacher who just gave us facts with no meaning. You know what I mean? Things that happened and no perspectives and no feelings, because he didn't understand. And I'm sure you can try, but you'd have to change your color to really understand. You understand?"

Yes, but how easily an experiential gulf translates into a racial caricature, imputing personal traits to all those of a certain color. Sometimes blacks laugh delightedly when whites seem to fulfill the expectations. Laura Washington remembered a bizarre accident in Chicago in which a drawbridge was raised as a cab crossed, suspending the taxi precariously before crushing it. "And there was a black girl and white girl, in their mid-twenties, in the cab," Washington recalled. "They'd been out to dinner together, and they were on their way home. . . . There was an opportunity for about thirty seconds for the two of them to jump from the cab onto the ground near the bridge. . . . The black girl, she told the story later that she jumped from the cab. . . . She told her girlfriend, 'Come on, jump! You're gonna get killed if you don't jump!' And the white girl couldn't jump, and she had to climb back up and get her and pull her down to safety. And so the chat in the black neighborhood was, 'Well, the white girl was too dumb to know to jump. She didn't even have the nerve to jump. This black girl had to go back and save her. We've got more nerve, and we've got more survival instincts.' "

And a lot more common sense, it seems, even when it comes to horror movies. A black woman at Spelman College once asked my daughter, Laura, "Why does the white woman always go into the house? That's so stupid!" Good question.

The pleasure that many African-Americans take in discovering, or inventing, whites' inadequacies is especially keen when the mirror can be held up to the traditional white stereotypes of blacks. When a white intern began work in the office of a black member of Congress, he was viewed with scorn by the all-black staff, according to a recent Princeton graduate who worked there. "They automatically assume he can't do certain things, that he won't be able to perform up to par as the other black staffers," the Princeton man said.

Sharon Walter, vice president of operations for the Urban League in Houston, remembers her mother's experience as a maid in a white household and lists among blacks' images of whites the belief that they can't cook. Miriam Edwards, a young black woman who went to college in Shreveport, Louisiana, reports that her sister, who cleans rooms in a hotel in Minnesota, has found that many of the whites working there can't read. The first inkling she had came when they were filling out some forms.

"Can you do this for me?" one white woman asked the sister.

"No, the answer's simple; it's just like this."

"I can't write," the white admitted.

The mirror images flicker back and forth across the line, but few people seem to see both reflections. One who did was a black man in one of those sociology classes at Lincoln. After looking over the two lists of stereotypes on the board, after listening to the discussion and exploration of their origins, he spoke up firmly and clearly. "I think it's the same for both of them, really," he declared. "White people are ignorant, black people are ignorant. It goes both ways. We got white drug dealers, we got black drug dealers. We got white people who are lazy, we got black people who are lazy. I figure it's just the way you're brought up."

CHAPTER SIX

Morality

Black Heat, White Cold

> We were so beautiful when we stood astride her ugli-
> ness. Her simplicity decorated us, her guilt sanctified
> us, her pain made us glow with health, her awkward-
> ness made us think we had a sense of humor. Her
> inarticulateness made us believe we were eloquent.
> Her poverty kept us generous.
>
> —Toni Morrison, *The Bluest Eye*

Honesty, Dishonesty

In practically every corner of the world where ethnic conflict grinds
away at the foundations of coexistence, the "others" are categorized as
morally inferior. "They" do not value human life as much as "we" do.
"They" do not love their children as deeply or care for family or practice
sexual propriety. "Their" religion lacks the essential values. "They" offer
false friendliness, then collude, deceive, and cheat. The glint of a smile
accompanies the flash of a knife in the back.

As a component of prejudice, moral judgment shapes itself to the specific contours of the local landscape, where it magnifies group differences into monumental contrasts of good and evil. This I saw soon after
arriving in South Vietnam in 1973. My Omega watch needed repair, and
a helpful Vietnamese man in my office warned me not to take it to any
Chinese jeweler. If I did, I would get back the Omega face and case, he
assured me, but the inner workings would be some cheap substitute. The
trick has surely been played by some jeweler somewhere. My colleague's
admonition applied not to that unscrupulous jeweler, however, but to all
jewelers of a particular ethnicity. He thus introduced me to the widespread belief among Vietnamese that ethnic Chinese in Saigon were wily
cheats, conspiratorial in their networks of dishonesty; they were cast in
images reminiscent of the anti-Semitic caricatures of Jews in Europe and
the United States.

When I got to Cambodia, I discovered that many Cambodians had precisely the same notions about the ethnic Vietnamese who lived in their midst. And in Laos, many saw Cambodians and Thais in a similar light. Indeed, Indian merchants in East Africa are often branded with these stereotypes, as are Georgians by Russians, Israeli Jews by Israeli Arabs, and Arabs by Israeli Jews. Over the decades, black Americans in poor neighborhoods have attached similar labels to whatever successive group has produced the proprietor of the local food shop, pawnshop, or liquor store: Italians, Jews, Arabs, Koreans.

In turn, African-Americans are targeted not as shopkeepers but as shoplifters; they have not gained enough of a foothold as retailers to be subject to the bigotry afflicting merchants, but they suffer other images of immorality that function silently and actively in debates about such public policy issues as crime and welfare. Taken together, beliefs about the morals of black people make up a bundle of stereotypes that can be seen in several parts: Blacks are dishonest and are prone to steal. They do not care enough about their children and have allowed their families to disintegrate. They are sexually aggressive and promiscuous. And they are violent. These are not new portraits; they date from the time of slavery. They find reinforcement today in social ills that seem to strike black Americans with special intensity, and they allow white people to slide easily into instant judgments about individuals who happen to have the physical characteristics that make them "black."

For his twelfth birthday, on May 18, 1990, Jason Deuchler's parents gave him a shiny black Dyno bike. As he went happily riding near his house on Carpenter Avenue in Oak Park, Illinois, a police car cruising the quiet suburban street pulled alongside.

Jason was an engaging, articulate boy whose skin was the color of cinnamon; his mother was black, his father was white, and they had lived in this integrated town since 1976. But to a white police officer, the sight was incongruous: a black-looking kid with a fancy new bike. Bicycles were being stolen in Oak Park, and the police assumed that the thieves were black youngsters from across Austin Boulevard in the slums of Chicago's West Side.

The cop asked where he had gotten the bike and did not believe Jason's answer, even when the boy pointed out that it was licensed and could be checked on the police computer. Only when Jason's friends came along and confirmed his ownership did the cop back off and invent a story about a report of a black bicycle stolen by a kid in similar clothes.

Jason felt "angry," he told me, "like I got ripped off or something." But he also had a child's capacity not to be consumed by rage. "There is still a lot of stuff going on that makes me angry," he wrote two years later in a *New York Times* op-ed piece, "but I really think most people are getting smarter. People don't really want to be ignorant."

He is probably right. People don't want to be ignorant. But they have a funny way of showing it. Consider the experience of Richard Orange when he flies first class, as he often does. Orange is a big, stocky man who does diversity training for corporations. His face is round, his hair and beard are short and salted with gray. He is usually warm and relaxed, but when he settles into a spacious seat in the first-class section of the plane, he waits tensely for the inevitable question. A flight attendant invariably stops beside him, smiles a plastic smile, and asks to see his ticket—his, not the white man's, not the white woman's, just his. Is it his race? "You see, that's very difficult to prove," Orange says. "So now I say, 'Ask him,' " and he points to the white man across the aisle. "On some days after I've worked a sixteen-hour day and I'm exhausted and I just want to get home: 'Ask him.' " He thereby fulfills the stereotype of the "arrogant, violent" black man, he realizes. "But, you see, after seven or eight times of asking me that, so that I'm almost looking for it, I can't just fall in my seat and relax."

The assumption that black people are dishonest is activated the moment an African-American walks into a store. It is probably the rare black citizen who has not been watched, followed, questioned, closely scrutinized, and repeatedly offered help while shopping.

The experience was carefully documented by two Lexington High School boys, one black, one white, who ran an experiment in clothing stores at the Burlington Mall outside Boston. The black came under immediate suspicion, although his teacher described him as soft and sweet-tempered, with velvet eyes and infallible courtesy, hardly presenting the threatening mien that storekeepers seemed to see. While he entered a store, the white stood outside watching how the clerks observed him wandering among the aisles, fingering garments. "He's followed with laserlike attention," the teacher reported, "and when he leaves the damned store, they're still looking at him outside the glass!" Then the boys switched. The black watched while the white handled merchandise ostentatiously and even pretended to put things inside his jacket. The clerks barely glanced at him. The boys then tried wearing suits and ties to make themselves look more respectable. The discrepancy in treatment remained: The black received enormous attention; the white was given free rein.

Janet Bowser, a black who grew up in rural North Carolina, watched in angry amazement one day as two black women tried to return a pair of pants in a store in Edenton. "The white lady said, 'I'm not going to let you return those pants, 'cause you wore them,'" Bowser said. "And the tags were still on the pants!

"And the [black] lady said, 'No, I didn't wear them. I tried them on, but I didn't wear them, and I want to return them.'

"And she said, 'You wore these pants, and you know you wore them. You wore them on the weekend, and you want to bring them back now and change them, and I'm not gonna let you change them.'

"And so her friend said, 'No, she didn't wear them, I was with her.'

"And that white lady looked at her and pointed her finger in her face and said, 'You shut up. You just shut right up. Don't you say anything.'

"And my mouth just fell open, and I just said, 'What? You're not supposed to tell her to shut up. You're not supposed to talk to her that way. She's in your store, purchasing things from your store, and you're telling her to shut up? She's securing your job by purchasing things.' So she threatened her if she didn't shut up she'll call the police."

Suspicions about blacks are often less direct and more difficult to decode. Shari Jones of Memphis thought she could smell the racism when she went to posh shops and department stores in Chicago. "People are, like, following you around, like, 'May I help you?' 'No, I'm just looking.' And ten minutes later, it's 'May I help you?' Five minutes later: 'Can I help you find anything? What do you want today?'"

Now, who can be sure that solicitous attention from a salesclerk is a racial insult? I've been in stores where I'd have been grateful for a little help—but then, I'm white. I've always assumed that a hovering salesman is just eager for his commission; it never crosses my mind that he might see me as a shoplifter. That is the privilege of being white in America: Almost never does your skin color make you an automatic suspect. You don't wrestle constantly with that little demon of a question mark that dances around every adverse experience.

Mellody Hobson, the Princeton student, puzzled over one incident and was unable to come to a clear conclusion. "I don't know if I can call this racist," she said. "I was with my sister, and we were shopping, and she was wearing a raincoat that she had bought at the store, and we were looking for one for my mom—the same raincoat—to give her for her birthday. So my sister took off her coat to try on the other one, just to make sure it was the same size and everything. She took it up to the counter and she put hers back on to go up to the counter and said, 'I'll take this.'"

As they continued looking around the store, they noticed a woman with shopping bags walking behind them everywhere they went. And as they tried to leave the store, they were blocked by several security men. "This was Bonwit Teller," Mellody said. "This man was messy. He looked horrible. He was like, 'Come with me.' " He took them to a dingy basement room, where he accused Mellody's sister of stealing the raincoat she was wearing. Fortunately, she happened to have the receipt for that coat as well as the one she had just bought, and they let her go. She was furious. "The next day she called the president of Bonwit's, and out of nowhere . . . she gets a check for $2,500 in the mail for her trouble," Mellody said. "See, I don't know if that was racism, or if it was a mix-up."

Compensation for such "trouble" is exceedingly rare. The most a black person usually gets is an apology, if that. Therefore, black parents warn their children. When Richard Orange was a boy, he made a deposit in his savings account, then ran out of the bank to catch a bus. "My father slapped me," he remembered. "He said, 'Never run out of a bank!' Today, at forty-two, I never run out of a bank, I never run out of a store."

In 1995, a black youth, Alonzo Jackson, was shopping at an Eddie Bauer store in a Maryland suburb of Washington, D.C., when he was accused by white personnel of stealing the shirt he was wearing, which he had bought on an earlier visit to the store. Despite his protests of innocence, he was forced to take off the shirt and return home bare-chested. Only when he brought the receipt the next day did he get his shirt back. And only an uproar from whites and blacks alike—with no small measure of bad publicity—provoked an expression of regret from Eddie Bauer, Inc.

The assumptions about black dishonesty were powerful enough in the little town of Union Point, Georgia, to stimulate some wicked inventiveness by the mayor, the City Council, the police, and many of the merchants. Shortly before Christmas 1994, they drew up a list of twenty-one residents who had been suspected of shoplifting and vandalism—but never convicted—and ordered them to stay away from more than two dozen stores, banks, laundromats, and video arcades. "You are not to enter said premises," the notice said. "If you do so, you will be charged with criminal trespass and/or disorderly conduct."

All twenty-one on the list were black. An outcry erupted. Sixteen of those targeted filed a lawsuit for $5 million, prompting the town fathers to retract the list in February 1995 and then settle the suit for $265,000 a year later.

The stereotype of black youths as shoplifters brought a knowing smile from the black manager of a B. Dalton bookstore in downtown Chicago, Nancy Deuchler. Trying to deal in realities rather than prejudices, she had learned that the best-dressed white could be a culprit. "A lot was ripped off by men in business suits on lunch hour," she said. "They'd just come and pocket the [paperback] that they were reading." While three or four black teenagers enter the store and galvanize white employees, she said, chuckling, "it's probably some lady in the back. While you're watching them, she's cleaning out a whole section."

"Danny," a white teenager in Brooklyn, made the prejudice work for him once, and he told the story to an appreciative audience in his high school course entitled "The Black Experience." He was the only white in the class and looked innocent enough with his short hair, blue-and-yellow-striped shirt, white shorts, and sneakers. But he was keenly aware of the stereotypes that "all Puerto Ricans and blacks are thieves," as he put it. "I'm gonna tell you something, but I'm not gonna mention the store. It's just a little supermarket around there, and I went in with a whole bunch of friends, white, black, whatever. And I walked over by myself, and the owner followed the black people around, and I tossed a couple of things in my bag, and he didn't even look twice at me." The black students, hearing this story for the first time, exploded into laughter. "He wanted to check them others walking out, and he had his eyes on them the whole time, and I put four cartons [of gum] in my bag. It was amazing." The black youngsters laughed and applauded delightedly. It seemed a kind of nice justice.

By that point in their lives, five of the eight black teenagers had been followed and hassled in stores, they said. They reacted variously.

"I just brush it off," one girl remarked. "It don't bother me. I don't let it get me down."

"It makes me mad," said a boy.

"I get upset," another girl declared. "That shouldn't go on. If he's not following that white person over there, why me? What makes me look like I'm gonna steal something?"

A third girl, Christie, described the little protests that some African-Americans have devised against such treatment. She was tall and wore her hair long, and her horn-rimmed glasses gave her a studious appearance. Nothing about her, except for her skin color and her age, should have triggered the unwanted attention she got when she went shopping in an upscale clothing store on Avenue U, in a predominantly white neighborhood of Brooklyn. "I was just looking around," she recalled, "but I was planning on buying something, and the man kept looking at me: 'Excuse me, can I help you? Do you need help?' And I was like, God, why is this man? Leave me alone already. So I decided I'm not buying anything, but I took the most expensive thing [a dress], and I went up to the counter, and I pulled out my money and everything. And I said, 'No, I think I changed my mind,' and I put it back and left." Christie never announced that she was protesting, however, so it's doubtful that the storekeeper got the message.

Other African-Americans are more explicit. They pick out an item, take out their credit card, let the clerk write up the sale, and then say, "I'm not going to buy this," and explain why. "I've come up with a creative idea," said Amir Abdussabour, a black Coast Guard lieutenant. "Now when I go walk in a store and someone thinks that we are a family of thieves, I go into my pocket and take out my wallet and take out a credit card and give it to them, and I say, 'Just in case my children fit the stereotype of the typical black thief and I'm not aware of that, hang on to the credit card—I'm sure you won't have any charges on that by the time I leave.' So now they have to process this: What have I done? Have I offended this customer? Am I going to lose sales? So I let them hold the credit card and intentionally find what we want, don't buy it there, and go somewhere else."

At a diversity workshop of some two hundred blacks, whites, Latinos, and Asians, the facilitator asked all those who never had to worry about a check or a credit card being refused because of their race or ethnicity to stand. Only we whites rose to our feet, and we were left standing for a long time looking at one another, and into the eyes of those still seated.

At many points along the color line, whites engage in the classic practice of prejudice: taking one black person's dishonesty and ascribing the trait to the entire race. One such point is politics. As African-Americans have clambered into elective office, a very few of them have been brought down by their own misdeeds of corruption, drug use, and other crimes. And in virtually every case, because of the volatile chemistry of race, the offender has been seen not merely as a man but as a black man.

A peculiar collusion by both blacks and whites turns him into a representative of his race. To many whites, he becomes a justification of their general distrust of blacks—or an acute disappointment to liberals who root for blacks' success; to many blacks, he becomes another persecuted victim of the racist white establishment, entrapped or framed by a criminal justice system determined to block blacks' progress. Almost never is his behavior divorced entirely from his race. Almost never is his lapse or his prosecution regarded purely as his own personal failing.

The difficulty of separating a black politician from his race was illustrated by *The New York Times* in a brief article from Richmond, Virginia, on September 18, 1995. In its editorial policy, the *Times* avoids identifying a criminal suspect's race unless it is deemed relevant. In this case, it reported on the arrest and resignation of Henry W. "Chuck" Richardson, "a black city councilman who was re-elected four times after being convicted of drug possession." He had been videotaped selling heroin to an undercover informer in a Richmond suburb.

Why black? Why not just a city councilman? Was his race germane? As the paper constructed the story, mentioning his race seemed unavoidable. He had come into office as a black, and African-Americans were now defending and denouncing him as a black. Elected initially in 1977 under a Justice Department mandate that had redrawn districts to yield blacks their first majority on the city council, Richardson "was a hero to many blacks despite almost annual brushes with the law," the paper said. "He lent money to constituents and elicited contributions from developers who nonetheless saw him as a disgrace." James B. Hughes, a chef who had voted repeatedly for Richardson, declared, "He stepped into the trap. He messed up for himself and for the whole black race."

The more significant trap was the one that black constituents stepped into, the one that inevitably caught the *Times* as it put the event into context. It was the snare of the double standard, in which a black wrongdoer is portrayed as a member of his race but a white wrongdoer is not. Senator Bob Packwood, for example, who was forced to resign his seat in 1995 for molesting women and other unethical conduct, was never identified as "a white senator" and was never denounced by whites for disgracing his race. William Aramony, the United Way president convicted in 1995 for embezzling $1.2 million of the charity's money, was never described as white, and whites didn't rally to his defense by claiming that he was the target of racial persecution. As the majority in power, whites don't think this way about each other; they enjoy the unconscious luxury of seeing individuals of their own race as individuals. Thus the trap of the double standard has a tight hold on white and black alike.

In 1990, when the Justice Department used a woman to lure Mayor Marion Barry of Washington, D.C., to a hotel room so he could be videotaped smoking crack, the racial lenses were immediately polished up and focused on the scene. Barry was suddenly cast in dual images—as sleazy black drug user and womanizer, as noble black fighter and victim, as a corrupting and arrogant role model for inner-city youth, as a hero of pride and accomplishment for young blacks. Reports had circulated for years about Barry's drug and alcohol problems. Many white residents of Washington were disgusted by his immorality. But in the poor neighborhoods of Southeast D.C., many outspoken blacks were more forgiving of Barry and angrier at what they saw as the excessive zeal of the U.S. Attorney's Office under the Republican administration of President George Bush. Such intricate and expensive efforts to entrap their mayor would never have been undertaken, they argued, if he had been white.

That is a thought-provoking charge, one often made and one that is usually unanswerable except with speculation. Would this or that have been done to a white man? It is a useful question, adaptable to many situations, although rarely susceptible to a clean yes or no. It could be asked more generally about the entire fate of Washington's municipal standing. If our capital were mostly white instead of mostly black, if most of its local officials were white instead of black, would Congress be less contemptuous of the city's striving for statehood, for self-determination, for liberation from the budgetary entanglements that are woven by the federal government? Even as congressional Republicans sought to transfer power from the federal level to the states, they reacted dismissively to Washington's pleas for similar autonomy. Could it have been that black people seemed morally less capable of self-government?

Barry was sentenced to six months in prison. When he got out, he returned to politics, campaigned on the theme of personal redemption, and was reelected mayor in 1994 with overwhelming support from blacks and hardly any from whites. In the Democratic primary, which has always been tantamount to election, Barry swamped the incumbent black mayor, Sharon Pratt Kelly. But in Ward 3, which is heavily white, he received only 601 votes to his opponents' 16,850. In the general election, the closest ever, his white opponent, Republican Carol Schwartz, won 42 percent in a city where only 8 percent of the voters were registered Republicans. Many whites were puzzled and troubled by the upsurge for Barry in black neighborhoods, and their comments were peppered with the epithet "corrupt" as they braced for a term of sloppy mismanagement and wasteful patronage. "When asked yesterday for her thoughts on the polling," Steve Twomey wrote in the *Washington Post*, "a Ward 3 woman, who declined further notoriety, opened her mouth and stuck her right index finger down her throat. . . . Several other white faces contorted in silent disgust in response to the same question."

A *Post* poll before the election recorded a deep racial divide. Three-quarters of the blacks surveyed thought Barry was a good role model for children; three-quarters of the whites thought he was not. Two-thirds of the blacks predicted that he would improve race relations; three-quarters of the whites thought he would not. Some 70 to 80 percent of blacks and fewer than 30 percent of whites thought Barry would do a good or excellent job of attacking crime and drugs, improving schools, attracting new business, dealing with the murder problem, eliminating waste, reducing corruption, improving the image of the city nationally, and relating to Congress. Most significantly, 83 percent of the blacks questioned agreed with the statement "I believe Marion Barry when he says he is a changed man." Only 31 percent of the whites agreed.

Barry hardly turned out to be a model mayor. His term was marred by abrasive conflicts as the city's problems deepened and he lost fiscal authority to a financial control board responsible to Congress. The schools continued to deteriorate, and his administration was rife with mismanagement. He did little to promote racial healing and occasionally contributed to tension—once by accusing a white member of the city council, Kathy Patterson, of trying to prevent blacks from getting a good education when she opposed a larger subsidy for the University of the District of Columbia. Even many black residents grew disenchanted.

Nevertheless, the concept of a man falling victim to drugs, paying the price, and then coming back home to declare himself reformed and ready to pick up life again "struck deep in the cultural recesses of Washington's heavily-churched black community," wrote Ron Walters, then chairman of Howard University's Political Science Department. "It especially resonated in the black community in 1994 because of the way the 'drug trade' has affected families and has corrupted and tested the old values. It was immediately accessible to mothers and fathers who have seen their sons, daughters, or other relatives and friends tormented by the tragedy of drug addiction." If Marion Barry could find salvation, so could others. He offered a way of hope.

Whites should have understood, Walters observed. "Whites seem to have an amazing capacity to put their own flawed white politicians in broader perspective," he noted. "Plenty of whites have ignored the racism of Jesse Helms, Ernest Hollings and others, reclaimed and revived a disgraced Richard Nixon, and accepted Oliver North. . . . The best explanation of this phenomenon comes from South Philadelphia, where Leland Beloff, a white former member of the City Council, was recently unanimously elected to be the chair of the area's Democratic Party just six months after he was released from prison after serving five years on a felony conviction. When asked why this happened, Beloff's opponent in the contest simply said, 'We stay loyal to our people.' "

Barry's drug arrest heightened black-white tensions elsewhere about the morality of African-American politicians. In 1991, Houston seemed poised to elect its first black mayor until the candidate, Sylvester Turner, got derailed by an ethics charge made by a television news program. As an attorney, he had written a will for a man who had then faked his own death to collect insurance that was payable to the man's father. The will had named a friend of Turner's as executor, and Turner had handled the estate for a year without knowing that the man was still alive, he said. The newscast's implication that Turner had profited by the fraud was immediately denied by a lawyer for the insurance company, the judge in the case, and Turner himself, who told me that he scarcely knew the client and had received just $500 for preparing the will.

But the charge, coming six days before the election, had a devastating effect on Turner's campaign. He was something of an outsider and had accumulated support with difficulty, even from the established black leadership. After the first round of voting, when he beat the incumbent white mayor, Kathy Whitmire, she endorsed him in a two-way runoff against another white candidate, Bob Lanier. Taking a strong anti-crime tack, Turner began to gain ground, and as the polls showed him pulling ahead, he got closer scrutiny from the press.

This is a natural process. "The job of the press is to be the equalizer," said Whitmire, "and whoever is on top, make it about as hard for him as you can possibly make it. When I was on top, they made it as hard for me as they could possibly make it. Going into the runoffs, Sylvester was going to win. He was the predicted winner. We were rallying behind him. He was going to make it. He was the leader, and it was their job to go after him." They did it unfairly, she added.

Turner and some of his black supporters saw the dynamics in more racial terms, as an attempt to cut down a black man who was about to gain power. After the ethical question mark was hung over his head, other frailties were publicized: He had once, in 1984, written a bad check to a grocery store for $24. He had been ticketed in 1983 for allowing an automobile inspection sticker to expire. He had been sued by Harvard Law School for falling behind on loan payments; he later paid off the loan. "When you go back and look, all of the negative crap did not materialize until after the polls had placed me ahead," he said. "I don't think you can eliminate race as a factor. I think I'd be naïve if I did. What that story did was, it conjured up all of their fears about another black mayor. And maybe it provided them with an excuse that they otherwise did not have. And so Lanier picked up on it and started running his own TV ad: 'What more do we not know?' "

"This is bullshit, to say this is racism," declared David Berg, a white lawyer who had done civil rights cases and worked for Lanier's campaign. "I'm in the middle of this. I know what's going on. I trust my instincts. . . . This isn't racism. This is reporting. And if a white man had been accused of these same things and had gotten beat, when it was over, he would say, 'Unfair reporting. Not fair.' " Berg agreed that the story about the insurance fraud was as unfair as it was decisive. "We couldn't have won without this happening," Berg said. "He was killing us. White liberals were flocking to Turner. And women. Our pollsters were telling us we're dead."

Still, the ethical question, especially the failure to pay the law school loan, activated uncertainties that seemed to carry racial overtones. "A lot of folks, white people who I know, were saying, 'God, you know, that's bothersome. I paid *my* loan,' " Berg observed. "Here you fulfilled this gestalt of black people as irresponsible."

Lanier beat Turner with 54 percent of the vote, mainly from whites and Hispanics. Turner got about 97 percent of the black, 30 percent of the Hispanic, and 22 percent of the white votes.

Honesty was not a quality that Joe Brown ever imagined seeing in African-Americans. A stocky white twenty-two-year-old, he had been raised on a constant diet of bigotry. Television news reports of black rapists and black shooters would provoke a running commentary of racism from his father. "I grew up always hearing black jokes, always hearing how bad black people were, never hearing any good," Joe said. "To this day, my grandmother will walk through the mall and still say, 'Hey, Joe, look at them niggers over there.' She does it out of complete ignorance. She doesn't do it because she's being prejudiced. That's the way she grew up and that's the way she's always lived. She still calls them, 'Hey, boy. Hey, boy, come here.' . . . So that's the way it was pounded into our head that blacks were just a total lower form of life."

Joe learned otherwise when he started dealing drugs in Stockton, California. At first he stuck with whites, mainly in the marijuana trade, but the product was cumbersome and the profits too slim for his taste. "For practical purposes, it just wasn't good business," he said. "It took this much marijuana to make a thousand, while it took only this much to make a thousand in coke. So I was thinking businesswise. And when I started realizing in the drug business that to get that money, to get higher power, I had to go with black people, I accepted it, I really did. I opened up to them real well, and a lot of them are really intelligent. It's kind of shocking."

Equally shocking to Brown was his discovery that white people could be untrustworthy. In fact, he ultimately flipped his stereotypes upside down, extolling blacks as intensely loyal and branding whites as the biggest cheats in the business. This, he said, he learned from rude experience as he moved ultimately into manufacturing and distributing methamphetamine, a stimulant known on the street as "crank."

"My first burn was a four-thousand-dollar deal with a white person, and he took my money away," Brown complained. "I've never seen it." It happened because a white supplier, suspecting that Brown might be an undercover cop, insisted on a precaution that he wrongly thought would guard against arrest: They would do the transaction in two parts. First, Brown would give the supplier the money, and then, at a second meeting, the supplier would give Brown the drugs. "In that way we're not exchanging money for drugs," Brown explained. "But I handed my money over and they ran."

Gradually, Brown moved away from dealing with whites and tiptoed into relations with blacks. "I've been burned—burned meaning ripped off and stabbed in the back—way more times by a white person than by a black person," he said. "My first deal with a black guy was a hundred dollars, 'cause I didn't trust him. I believed all my friends. And he made me, like, five hundred dollars profit. He read me pretty well that I didn't trust him. It took us several months, and before you know it he started introducing me to more of his friends and bigger friends, and I'd move out of his territory, and as I would go up and meet this higher person, another black guy that was even higher and bigger, he would accept me after a couple of weeks and a couple of big meetings with him. And then they'd trust you.

"See, I feel that black people are pretty open to white people," Brown continued. "They trusted me way more than I ever trusted them at the beginning. They looked at me as a potential, good business partner. I looked at him as a person who was probably gonna stab me in the back and steal my stuff. That was my image when I first met him and I shook hands with him—it was kind of a light shake, and I really didn't trust him. All my white friends who started me and got me going told me, 'Never do business with a black person. Don't trust them, 'cause they're just no good.' Hearing that, hearing my dad, it made a lot of sense to me."

But once Brown became established, he rid himself of most of his white contacts and set up an all-black team, including what he called "a six-pack" of black bodyguards whose deference and loyalty made him feel wonderful. "I call them my family," he said. "They acted just like my brothers. They protected me. They got me out of more jams than anybody could have." When Brown would visit his parents, he had to disguise both his involvement in drugs and his admiration for blacks. At Christmas, when his father would lace his conversation with the word "nigger," Brown would just change the subject. When his father told an anti-black joke, Brown would give a thin, brief "Hah" and leave it at that.

Brown entered that circle of intimacy where racial terms could be thrown around without offense. "You better haul your black ass out of here," Brown quoted himself as saying. "You're a punk nigger. You ain't nothing but trash." In turn, they would call him "honky." "I was one of them," Brown said. "They know I'm not putting them down as a nigger. But they accepted the name. Isn't it funny that blacks call each other 'nigger'?" Then he went into a black accent. " 'What are you talking about, nigger? You ain't gonna do that, nigger? Oh, bullshit, nigger.' They get into these 'nigger' contests—who can say 'nigger' more times in one sentence. . . . I don't think it's right. I never say it because of prejudice at all. They're all my friends. . . . I more or less became one of them. . . . I didn't see them as black, and they didn't see me as white. We were just friends, true friends. Like I said, I trusted my life with them. They're loyal, they really are, they're loyal people. Maybe not in all situations . . . in friendship they are. If they say that you're my friend, boy, you are their friend. Trust me."

Brown tested their honesty by setting traps around his house—money lying here and there, little tasks preparing drugs. Only the whites would steal the cash and adulterate drugs so they could pilfer the good stuff, he insisted. "I don't have any white friends left," he said. "They just turned on me, stabbed me in the back, took what they could. Right now I have probably fifty, sixty thousand dollars owed to me. I have about four hundred dollars from one black kid, strung out, and he ran on me. That was the only time I lost money to a black. It's really sad that all my white friends turned out to be trash. The black guys that were supposedly the trash were the good guys; they're the ones that will stick with you, businesswise, friendshipwise."

Of course, the power relationship was clear: Brown was in charge, and the blacks were his subordinates. He adopted a paternalistic role. First, he insisted that if they wanted to work for him, they stop taking drugs themselves. Then, with a certain noblesse oblige, he provided for them generously. "I took all my boys—I took very good care of them. They all have apartments. They all have cars. They had a lot. . . . It's really funny, if you took a picture? I'm the only white guy in the group. There's all these black guys and then there's me in the middle." He laughed and then added, "We never allowed pictures."

Family Values

In 1950, 16.8 percent of the births to black women in the United States occurred outside marriage. By 1960, the figure had risen to 21.6 percent. Through the following decades, as the phenomenon spread like an epidemic, the rate climbed to 37.6 percent in 1970, 56.4 percent in 1980, and 70.4 percent in 1994, when 448,315 black babies were born to single mothers and only 188,076 to married couples. Furthermore, nearly one-third of those single mothers were teenagers—children having children.

The African-American family has been disintegrating, or so it seems. White America shakes its collective head in disappointment and contempt and then comes to contradictory conclusions about the causes: Black families are battered by poverty, drugs, and other disabilities generated by the legacy of discrimination. Households are torn apart by welfare rules that penalize children whose fathers live at home. Black men, emasculated by unemployment, seek to prove their masculinity in irresponsible ways. Black women (and girls) fill the vacuum of loving relationships by having babies. Blacks wallow in victimhood, looking to everyone except themselves for salvation. Perhaps something in black culture, some absence of values, undermines family cohesion. And perhaps it is true, as many whites suspect, that *they* do not care about their children as much as *we* do.

The mixture of sociology and stereotype is intricate and compelling, fertilizing the ground in which a seed of truth grows into a tangled caricature. The devastating scope of what has happened to black families in reality is magnified by how the reality is seen, how it is fit into the context of what whites think they have always known about blacks. And such judgments are not unique to the black-white confrontation.

Family is often a touchstone of imagery in ethnic and national conflicts. Throughout the Arab-Israeli confrontation, each side has tended to regard the other as deficient in one or another form of family values, as did Russians and Americans during the Cold War. In 1985, as Soviet-American antipathy reached its final crescendo, a *New York Times* poll found a plurality of Americans (46 percent) believing that Americans cared more than Russians about their children. Russians often expressed the same sense of superiority about themselves; many were convinced that Americans could not match their own extravagant love of children.

White images of black America contain a similar indictment. They highlight the collapse of the black family without seeing the extended connections of caring support that do exist. Projected onto blacks generally are the most corrosive aspects of inner-city life, a portrait of stark decay without the shadings and nuances of human ambiguity. The perceptions are overwhelmed by the mothers on crack, the babies born addicted, the children shooting children. Crowded out of the picture are the quiet, heroic struggles by mothers and fathers to protect their children from the ravages of gangs, guns, and drugs. The statistics on out-of-wedlock births, for example, do not reveal the realignment of family ties that has taken place for many African-American children, the extended universe of "significant others" that includes grandmothers, grandfathers, aunts, uncles, siblings, and the web of caring that frequently—though not always—replaces the bonds of fatherhood. As grave as it is, the decline of the traditional, two-parent household does not in every case mean the decline of nurturing love.

Nor is it solely a black problem. While the percentage of out-of-wedlock births was increasing by four times among blacks, it was soaring by nearly fifteen times among whites, from 1.7 percent in 1950 to 25.4 percent of white births in 1994. The narrowing black-white gap was defined by Andrew Hacker using the multiples produced by dividing the black out-of-wedlock birthrates by the white. The black percentage of such births was 9.9 times the white rate in 1950, slid to 9.4 times in 1960, then dropped to 6.6 times in 1970, 6.1 times in 1980, 4.3 times in 1988, and 2.8 times in 1994. As some black people like to say, when white America catches cold, black America gets pneumonia. Putting it another way, severe social problems may first become visible in lower-income black communities, then grow to prominence among whites. The delayed discovery that births to unwed mothers are a white problem, not just a black problem, has finally hit the popular mind like a second wave of pain.

None of this diminishes the crisis of the black family. It is real, and it has loomed so large in the worries of whites and blacks alike that when a *Washington Post* survey presented a nationwide sample of Americans with a list of possible causes of African-Americans' social and economic problems, the breakup of the black family was picked as a "major reason" by 58 percent of the whites and 62 percent of the blacks. Indeed, the mantra of "family values" is now chanted across the political spectrum. On the right, the primary goal seems punitive: Cut off welfare to children of teenage mothers, cap payments after a certain number of births. Conservatives do not have to say "black welfare queens" for the white audience to recognize the coded references, despite the fact that two-thirds of those on welfare are white.

The concern takes a different form among African-Americans who counsel the rebuilding of community. At one level, they deplore the disintegration of the present; at another, they romanticize the closeness they remember from the past, a time when children respected their elders and their elders watched and comforted and disciplined them without fearing that the children would pull guns. "It takes a village to raise a child" has become a favorite saying of nostalgia and longing. And many blacks compare their village favorably to what they imagine to be the less cohesive and less supportive family structures among whites. "The one thing I think we had that European-Americans didn't have, familywise, was the extended family," said Richard Hawkins, who teaches communications technology at Southern University, a predominantly black college in Shreveport, Louisiana. "I understood, as a boy, that if my mother died I knew where I was going. There was no question. I knew where I was going. . . . See, I would never allow my grandmother, my aunt, my uncle to know that I got a whupping at that school. You know why, don't you? They'd give me another one. . . . We no longer have it. It's dying in our community."

No matter how much myth may be in the memory, the decay of community brings African-Americans an acute sense of losing something special, even in the ethics of the streets. "The gangs have changed," complained Sampson, a veteran gang leader in Los Angeles. "We should respect people's mothers and their kids and their women. You understand what I'm saying? You have a beef with somebody, it would just be with him. You would never go to their house; you would never shoot up their house. That was the law of the street." He had become so despairing of the collapse of honor that he was moving to suburban Orange County, he said, " 'cause I don't want nobody to shoot my daughter."

"We used to police our own neighborhood," said Snoop, a founder of the Crips gang. "Wasn't such a thing as breaking in the houses in our neighborhood or taking the women's county checks or whatnot. We didn't play that. Whereas now, I'd have to kill one of these youngsters to tell them about, 'Man, don't cuss in front of my mama.' We didn't cuss in front of each other's parents, whereas now these kids, you know, you see them on the bus, old folks are sitting up there scared to death, the youngsters in the back riding on the bus, cussing. We had more respect for ourselves."

Jim Galipeau, a white probation officer, told of a boy who shot a member of a rival gang. When gang members couldn't find him to retaliate, they shot and killed his mother instead. "I still can't believe that," said Snoop, shaking his head angrily. "I still can't believe that."

"We can bury our dead homeboys," said Galipeau, "but we can't bury our dead mothers. See, this is where it's gotten out of hand. There's no respect."

Mothers may command respect from these men, but some of the staccato banter in these neighborhoods is peppered with "bitches" and "hos" (for "whores") and hateful bragging about the power trips of sex. When misogynous sentiments find their way into "gangsta rap" lyrics that are disseminated by white-owned recording companies, white people glimpse a world of sexual tension that most blacks would rather not display for outside scrutiny.

Initially, in the late seventies and early eighties, the crude poetry of rap seemed like a radical chic exposure to gritty street life in the ghetto, an unvarnished reflection of the true mood at the bottom. And so it may have been. But gradually, as the lyrics got tougher and whites started buying the music, African-American writers, ministers, parents, and other adults began to worry about the impact on both their children and their images.

"The bitches look like hos," chants the rapper Ice Cube, pounding a message of raw rage into his tape *AmeriKKKa's Most Wanted*.

> *Then I looked down, she was fat in the front,*
> *I asked how long. Well, about seven months,*
> *Oh, how time flies when you're havin' fun,*
> *She said, yeah, but the damage is done.*
>   *. . .*
>
> *Then I thought deep about giving up the money,*
> *What I need to do is kick the bitch in the tummy,*
> *Naw, 'cause then I'll really get faded,*
>
> *That's murder one, 'cause it was premeditated.*

With a trace of satire, some rap becomes more biting than ugly. But that doesn't undo the damage. "It's like we have consumed the worst stereotypes white people have put on black people," the African-American writer bell hooks told *The New York Times*. Whites who buy rap music, she noted, may even find a certain appeal in black people acting out the caricatures.

"It's almost as if we have become the minstrels of the 1990s," agreed Kevin Powell, a music critic for *Vibe* magazine. "White people are sitting back and saying, 'Let's watch the niggas wave guns in videos . . . and grab their crotches and amuse us.' "

The timeworn picture of the black man as aggressively oversexed stirred a deep, defensive revulsion among many blacks when it was revived during the confirmation hearings of Supreme Court nominee Clarence Thomas. Testifying reluctantly before a televised session of the Senate Judiciary Committee, law professor Anita Hill described Thomas, her boss, as having made persistent, lewd suggestions that they have sexual relations and watch pornography together. He angrily denied the charge and called the hearing a "high-tech lynching," thus invoking the racial motive that he so often dismissed in his judicial opinions. While many blacks wanted Thomas rejected for the Court because of his rightist views, others were infuriated that a Senate committee of white men would give a black woman a national forum to tear a black man down, especially with sexual charges. A Lexington High School teacher reported that all eight black girls in his classes disbelieved Hill, thought she had been jilted, and had a gut feeling that she had fabricated the story as revenge. All the white girls believed Hill completely.

If the individual act could be divorced from the racial message, it could be seen more clearly. If Thomas were viewed as just a man rather than a black man, if rap were heard as just music instead of black music, the offenses would be judged outside the pernicious context of racial morality. Instead, the breach strikes a chord, the impropriety plays against the caricatures that have danced inside American minds for generations.

The racist stereotype has been given plenty of room to flourish by the large blanks, the vast silences, where competing images might have existed. Until very recently, popular culture never offered a portrait of a whole person who was black. For decades, viewers never saw a complete African-American family on television. Black maids and handymen existed in a kind of familial vacuum, without spouses or children or any personal lives outside the white homes where they served. "Julia," the light-skinned black nurse who came to the screen in 1968 as a token of integration, had no husband; she was a widow with only a young son. Not until the mid-1980s did *The Cosby Show* truly break the pattern with high visibility (though some blacks criticized the characters as too "white" and middle-class). And finally, by the mid-1990s, black families had gradually crept into some mainstream television advertising. Downy, Burger King, Advil, Doublemint Gum, Campbell's Soup, Children's Motrin, and insurance from New York Life were among the products being sold by blacks cast in family situations.

Another window for whites into the black world has been opened by African-American literature, increasingly so in recent years as high school and college courses have included black authors in the curricula. Like journalists, novelists write about problems. The African-American novelists who are most popular with whites include Alice Walker and Toni Morrison, whose biting chronicles of black family distress contain merciless portraits of black men; they rape their daughters, beat their wives, and turn their backs on their families. Against the onslaught, strong women struggle for harmony and dignity.

These works are powerful statements of feminism, written deeply and beautifully by women whose creative brilliance shatters the stereotype of mental dullness so often attributed to African-Americans. But the fictional pieces of truth offered by Toni Morrison in *The Bluest Eye*, for example, and Alice Walker in *The Color Purple* also affirm some of the most brutal images of black men. And so the reactions among blacks spatter the literature like competing whispers of conscience: image, truth; discretion, honesty; solidarity, imagination. Whites' perceptions are being reinforced; artists need to write what they need to write, free of political inhibition. Many African-Americans are simultaneously proud and troubled when they read their most famous living writers. Some tremble with humiliation when the book gets onto film, as did *The Color Purple*.

"I was very, very offended by *The Color Purple*," said Dorothy Redford, the black woman who traced her ancestry back to Somerset Place plantation in North Carolina. "There was no balance. [It] really fed into everybody's stereotype of what African-Americans were and what African-American men were."

Because the film was made by a white man, Steven Spielberg, some who had not read the book saw it as a white creation. That seemed the gist of a conversation one evening in a New Jersey suburb among several whites and a black man named Art.

ART: I just wish Steven Spielberg had balanced that movie and put in one black positive male. The whole movie—it was a great movie. The black women loved the movie, and I'm suspicious about this too: Black female and white male usually like the same damn thing.

WHITE MAN: He made a movie out of the book.

ART: Yeah, yeah, you're right. I'm just saying, from a technical standpoint, if he had just put a black male in there as positive, it would have meant a world of difference. The black guys sold their own children, they raped women—

WHITE WOMAN: But you've got to talk to Alice Walker, Art!

ART: You're absolutely right. She's a black female. Black female, white male, there's not a whole lot of difference.

WHITE MAN: There's a lot of difference. But she's a black female who doesn't like men.

WHITE WOMAN: Black men in particular.

ART: When she wrote the book, she reinforced the feeling of a whole lot of white males that we are animals. You know the one thing that black people remember in the movie *The Godfather*? Every black person who saw *The Godfather* remembers this: One scene, they're at the table talking, drugs were coming in; the Godfather says: No, I don't think we should bring it in. One of the younger ones says: You know, let it come in. We're gonna give it to the niggers cause they're animals anyway. Every black person who saw that remembers that. 'Cause that's the way we feel that white society feels about us—we're animals. We beat our women, we abuse our children, we have no values.

WHITE MAN: No self-restraint.

ART: And I am angry because, knowing so many people who've done so many things, knowing so many men who used to work in the forties and used to come home from work, twelve hours a day, and would tell his wife, 'Feed the children. I'll eat last.' The books never mention those people. . . . The books never mention that. Never mention that. They did such a job on us.

The current of belief flows in another direction, too. While many whites see only the collapse of the black family, many blacks regard whites as unemotional creatures devoid of the warmth and caring that supposedly characterize the noblest tradition of black culture. This gnawing image of white dispassion is a quieter, less virulent view than the white stereotype of black immorality. Yet it has been taught for generations. At Lincoln University, the African-American students who listed their impressions of whites included the following descriptions:

> Back-stabbers
>
> Can't trust them. Untrustworthy
>
> Conniving
>
> Cold

When white people are being discussed by blacks, "cold" is a word that occasionally flutters to the surface of the conversation. Some blacks feel a decided difference in temperature between the races, contrasting climates of family cohesiveness and emotional honesty. This stereotype underlies the dichotomy favored by some Afrocentrists that divides humans into the "sun people" of Africa and the "ice people" of Europe. The country's variegated white subcultures are generally invisible to those holding such extreme views; they tend not to distinguish among classes, and they do not see Italians, Jews, Irish, white Anglo-Saxon Protestants, or other groups as possessing family traits very different from one another.

This bundle of caricatures pictures whites as opportunistic and unable to express feelings, a "lack of warmth, you know, a kind of a cold-hearted, calculating view of the world," said Salim Muwakkil, a Chicago journalist and former managing editor of the Nation of Islam's newspaper, *Muhammad Speaks*. He was speaking not for himself but for what he saw in blacks' attitudes generally. And since he had broken with the Nation of Islam, he could candidly crystallize the opinions held by the movement's founder, Elijah Muhammad, who died in 1975. "Elijah Muhammad believed that, essentially, white people were genetically incapable of being benevolent, and they really hated black people from the depths of their being. So we should expect anything," Muwakkil explained.

"These things are real hard to articulate," added Laura Washington, the black editor, "but there's this whole thing about how white people are stiff and they're not as down-to-earth and easygoing as black people are, and they're more uptight, at least in the way they relate to one another. I don't think it's just the way they relate to us, but the way they relate to themselves. . . . And they're not as open, necessarily, or not as willing to speak their mind." She said that blacks often joked among themselves that they would never take the insults that whites often accept in silence. "If somebody did that to me I'd cuss him out or I'd tell him what I thought, whereas white people tend to be more reserved or unwilling to be more open about human relations." This seems a satisfying inversion of the abject deference forced on blacks for centuries; like most stereotypes, this one makes those who possess it feel better.

At a workshop on race and gender issues, Mary Wills, an African-American executive in Chicago, listened to black and white women comparing their approaches to men and concluded that white women were inclined to marry pragmatically rather than romantically, to "go to great lengths, even to the point of marrying somebody that they didn't really think was really compatible," she said. "And black women don't do that. Black women will tell you in a minute, 'If your act isn't together, don't waste my time.' On the other hand, the white women in the room are saying, 'Oh, he's a man and he's eligible, he's not married; you don't want to turn him off.' "

Such opportunism fit the white profile perceived by Floyd Donald, who used to be a bandleader in an integrated Alabama middle school. He is black, and he noticed that when his band won a tournament, white parents were a bit more cordial to him. "People like winners," he said. "If you're a winner, people can kind of overlook what color you are. . . . It makes it much easier for one of those daddies to come up and shake your hand. And his little daughter's a majorette, and you're a black man. But if you're a winner, if she's standing there with an eight-foot trophy, well, it makes it much easier."

On a cool, sparkling October day in 1995, hundreds of thousands of African-American men poured into Washington, D.C., for the Million Man March. Billed as a day of atonement, the gathering struck a deep chord across the breadth of black America, stirring the need to take some measure of control by turning inward to cure ills that no government seemed willing or able to address. "The purpose of the march is to improve the quality of life for black people—to get us, and black men in particular, to take greater responsibility for the care of our children, the care of our families, the care of our communities," Benjamin Chavis, one of the organizers, told CNN as crowds streamed onto the Mall. "This is a self-responsibility march," he continued. "So the measure of success of the march will be after this march, if black-on-black crime will go down, if drug addiction and alcohol abuse will go down, but if employment will go up, if education will go up, if black men taking care of their families will go up. That will measure the success of this march."

Beforehand, the concept of the gathering divided blacks deeply along several serious fissures. The anti-white, anti-Semitic ravings of its organizer, Louis Farrakhan, repelled many African-Americans and brought down a torrent of condemnation by whites. The exclusion of women caused distress, although a few did come, and support was also offered by many black women who yearned for strong, functioning black men to embrace fatherhood and avoid gangs and drugs and crime. This infuriated such black feminists as Kristal Brent Zook, who denounced "the march's dangerous nationalistic call for a romanticized black masculinity" whose "rhetoric of protection and atonement was just a seductive mask for old-fashioned sexism." Some blacks worried that the emphasis on self-help would comfort white conservatives who wanted to "blame the victims" and cut social programs. The march was boycotted by the NAACP, the Urban League, and many individual blacks. But many others looked past Farrakhan's bigotry and sexism to another core message; these included church groups from New York to California that were drawn by the promise of repentance and redemption.

"We seek your forgiveness," a gang member told the crowd, "for allowing your babics to lie in the street with that yellow tape draped around them. We seek your forgiveness, black woman, for not being present for those six-week checkups, for those PTA meetings, and for mistreating our most precious jewel—you, black woman. This day, we reconcile and atone before God."

With the gleaming dome of the Capitol behind them, speaker after speaker confessed, apologized, pledged, cajoled, preached, and promised. "What can a million men do?" asked Jesse Jackson in a growling shout full of desperate rage. "Take your child to school! Meet your child's teacher! Exchange home numbers! Turn off the TV three hours a night! Pick up a report card every nine weeks and sign your child's report card! We can send our children from jail to church to home! What can a million men do!"

Farrakhan, whose Nation of Islam movement advocates personal habits that would have delighted the Puritans, exhorted black entertainers to purge pornography and violence from their work, as the Senate's Republican majority leader, Robert Dole, had done just a few weeks before. "All we got to do is go back home and make our communities decent and safe places to live," Farrakhan told the assembled throng. "And if we start dotting the black community with businesses, opening up factories, challenging ourselves to be better than we are, white folk, instead of driving by and using the N-word, they'll say, 'Look, look at them. Oh, my God, they're marvelous. They're wonderful. We can't say they're inferior anymore.' But every time we drive-by shoot; every time we carjack; every time we use foul, filthy language; every time we produce culturally degenerate films and tapes—putting a string in our woman's backside and parading them before the world; every time we do things like this, we are feeding the degenerate mind of white supremacy. And I want us to stop feeding that mind and let that mind die a natural death. And so to all the artists that are present (you wonderful, gifted artists, remember that your gifts come from God) . . . demonstrate your gift, not your breast, demonstrate your gift, not what is between your legs. Clean up, black man, and the world will respect and honor you. But you have fallen down like the prodigal son, and you're husking corn and feeding swine. Filthy jokes. We can't bring our children to the television. We can't bring our families to the movies, because the American people have an appetite like a swine, and you are feeding the swine with the filth of degenerate culture. We got to stop it. We're not putting you down, brothers. We want to pick you up, so with your rap you can pick up the world, with your song you can pick up the world, with your dance, with your music, you can pick up the world."

Farrakhan threw out a lot of other concrete suggestions: about registering to vote (registration stations, scattered across the Mall, had stacks of forms arranged by state); about each man going home and contacting the local prison chaplain to establish a mentoring friendship with a black inmate; about adopting black children who were languishing in foster care. These were woven through a web of mystical numerology in which Farrakhan anointed himself as a prophet through whom God spoke. He avoided his customary anti-Semitic remarks, however. And at the end, in a moving conclusion to an uplifting day, he called on the masses of black men spread out before him to take a pledge. "I want you to shout your name out so that the ancestors can hear it," he told them. "Take this pledge with me."

And then, in the infallible rhythm of a preacher who has his congregation in a swaying cadence of compliance, Farrakhan recited and paused to hear the roar of repetition, recited and paused, recited and paused, and the Mall reverberated with the thunder of the words:

> I!
> *I!*
> Say your name!
> [*A multitude of names rolled up from the Mall.*]

Pledge!
Pledge!
That from this day forward!
That from this day forward!
I will strive!
I will strive!
To love my brother!
To love my brother!
As I love myself!
As I love myself!

I!
I!
Say your name!
[*A multitude of names.*]
Pledge!
Pledge!
That from this day forward!
That from this day forward!
I will strive!
I will strive!
To improve myself!
To improve myself!
Spiritually!
Spiritually!
Morally!
Morally!
Mentally!
Mentally!
Socially!
Socially!
Politically!
Politically!
And economically!
And economically!
For the betterment of myself!
For the betterment of myself!
My family!
My family!
And my people!
And my people!

And so the pledge proceeded, a gripping catechism of ills and hopes that rang out across the nation's capital like brittle poetry:

To build business
Build houses
Build hospitals
Build factories
And enter into international trade
For the good of myself
My family
And my people.

I will never raise my hand
With a knife or a gun
To beat
Cut
Or shoot
Any member of my family
Or any other human being
Except
In self-defense.

I will never
Abuse my wife
By striking her
Disrespecting her
For she
Is the mother of my children
And the producer of my future.

I will never engage
In the abuse of children
Little boys or little girls
For sexual gratification
But I
Will let them grow
In peace
To be strong men and women
The future of our people.

I will never again
Use the B-word

To describe any female
But particularly
My own black sisters.

I will not poison my body
With drugs
Or that which is destructive
To my health
And my well-being.

I will support black newspapers
Black radio
Black television
I will support black artists
Who clean up their acts
And show respect for themselves
And respect for their people,
And respect for the heirs of the human family.

I will do all of this
So help me God.

Trust, Distrust

Bruce King grew up on Chicago's South Side in the sixties and seventies, when it wasn't as rough and poor as it is now. He remembers it nostalgically as a tight-knit, hardworking neighborhood where people looked after one another. "We played in the streets," he said. "Everybody had to be in when the streetlights came on. You were respectful of your elders. . . . Everyone was 'ma'am' and 'sir,' and everyone would have the right, if you got out of line, to pop you and then go back and tell your parents. And then your parents would come home, and you'd get a whipping from your parents." He smiled fondly. "It was that kind of community. It was very close-knit. People worked very hard to maintain the little that they did have."

He was a burly man, open about his feelings. And as he sat in his office at Lake Forest College, north of Chicago, where he was director of minority affairs, he dredged up the memory of an old wound, a fleeting incident that left a long scar. He had made the journey from his black community to the whiteness of Iowa State University. "I was the only black person in our dorm floor of fifty-seven men," he said, "and I remember I had some friends over, some black friends over, like one afternoon." As they were leaving and stood talking at the entrance to the stairwell, two white students were horsing around, laughing. One ran from the other and dashed for the stairs, but the blacks were blocking the way and the other guy caught him. "So my friends left," King said, "and I'm walking back to my room, and those guys are still horsing around, and the guy says, 'I would have gotten away from you if those niggers weren't at the door.'" King stopped for a moment to let the words penetrate.

"There were a lot of people around," he continued. "I was just shocked, and sometimes it just hits you and it's so out of the blue that it's just—you don't feel like cursing—sometimes you do, sometimes you don't. You know, sometimes you just want to tell people that they're assholes. But you're standing there, and people are looking at you waiting for you to respond. What is his response going to be? And I just looked at them and shook my head and said, 'You guys are sick.'"

He needed to talk to somebody, so he went to a friend, a white student on his floor. "I thought we were very close friends," he said sadly. "I told him what happened: 'Can you believe it?' I was still kind of just shaken. 'I don't know if I responded well. If I didn't, what should I say?' And he says, 'Bruce, I don't know what the big deal is. They're just gonna do that. And it's no big deal at all.'" That comment "really just knocked me for a loop-the-loop," King recalled. "I couldn't believe that he said that. . . . It took me weeks to be able to go back to him and tell him how his reaction—not so much what they said—but it was his reaction. . . . I was just floored by that.

"He then tried to explain where he was coming from. He apologized that in some way he didn't give me the answer that I wanted. But his first answer was very honest. He didn't think it was a big deal, that it happens, you just should understand, and I was at fault for trying to make more out of it than there actually was. So subsequently we weren't friends after that."

Again and again, African-Americans tell the same story. White friends, white colleagues, white classmates who seem close and sympathetic suddenly veer off onto a different wavelength. "Stuff like that is very destructive," Bruce King said. "You venture out, you make friendships, you're conscious of who you are, but you think that you find a group that accepts you for who you are . . . and then you come to find out that that's not necessarily the case. You really have to question your-self then: Did I let my guard down too much? How did I let this happen? How did I think this guy was my friend? . . . And you start analyzing everything. Should I not have white friends? It has a lot of effects."

Distrust is a major obstacle to black-white friendships. It is the fault beneath the fragile common ground. It results from all that has gone before: the images of immorality, the hurtful expectations, and the pain of real experience, which undermine the belief that virtue can exist across the racial line.

If a thin filigree of trust adorns a black-white relationship, it is delicate and easily rent. In Birmingham, Alabama, in the early 1990s, Reverend Abraham Lincoln Woods of the St. Joseph Baptist Church thought he had built rapport with a white corporate president, part of a group called Leadership Birmingham that convened periodically to address racial problems. But when Woods had occasion to test that rela-tionship, he found it empty. A black employee with twenty years in the company had called in sick one day, saying that he had to go to the hos-pital. When his boss checked on him, it turned out that he had not gone to the hospital at all. He was fired. He appealed for help from Woods, who was one of Birmingham's senior civil rights leaders. "I called the president of the company," Woods said, "and I went and had a meeting with him, feeling now that we knew each other, having had that experi-ence together, feeling that there was some understanding on his part. I asked him to give him another chance, let me monitor it. But in spite of my appeal, he went along with his supervisors, and [the black employee] was fired. I felt very bad, I felt very bad." And this coldness seemed part of a pattern that held in other cases as well. "See," Woods said sadly, "those kinds of things make you lose confidence. That's per-sonal, you see."

A twisted trust is sometimes shown by whites who confide in black women and use them for emotional support. In offices and factories, and even in homes where they work as maids and housecleaners, black women complain that they serve as a convenience for whites who want to tell their troubles to someone safe—someone who is distant enough not to injure them with gossip and warm enough to listen sympatheti-cally. African-Americans tend to see this as an updated version of the "mammy syndrome," in which whites reenact old patterns of seeking maternal caregiving from subordinate black women.

One stocky black woman who had played that uncomfortable role found little emotional support from whites when she needed it, however. On a summer evening, at a workshop on racial issues for middle-level managers at AT&T and Du Pont, she sat listening to her African-American colleagues talk about racial slights in the office. Gradually, she grew pensive. She looked down at the floor. She began to cry quietly and dropped her head into her hands. Finally, prompted by the discussion leader, she spoke.

Like practically all Americans, she had watched the blurry images of white Los Angeles police officers surrounding and beating and kicking Rodney King, the black man who would have remained just another obscure victim had it not been for a bystander's video camera. The tape of the law enforcers enforcing their own law was televised over and over again like a flashback from an old national nightmare. She had followed the trial of the officers, and she had heard the unbelievable verdict of "not guilty"; it had been rendered by a mostly white jury in a mostly white Simi Valley community imbued with scary images of black hordes held back by the thin blue line of the police. Only later were two of the officers convicted and imprisoned on federal civil rights charges. Now their exoneration ignited rioting in South Central Los Angeles—and a riot of emotions inside many blacks and whites.

The next morning, the woman came to her office, where she had worked for many years. She was torn into shreds of outrage and agony. She looked for some comradeship among her colleagues, whom she knew well. But from the whites she encountered only silence. And silence was like an attack. She spoke to the workshop in fragments of grief. "Rodney King, blow after blow. You go to work. Nothing said. If anything's said, it's all among the blacks. And the whites are there, but they don't say anything. It's as if we can't share the pain. At work you can't share. You have to be quiet. You can't share. You can't share your pain."

Undoubtedly, there were whites who also felt pain—and shame—but they did not know what to do or how to behave or what to say to a black woman, even someone with whom they had worked for years. And their awkwardness compounded the hurtfulness and deepened the distrust.

"I understand what the woman was saying," Bruce King remarked, recalling his own feelings the day after the verdict. "I thought about not coming to work, because I did not want the liberal white person in my face telling me how wrong it was and how sorry they were. I didn't know what I wanted from white people. I think I wanted them to be as angry as I was but not be apologetic to me, because what happened to Rodney King in that whole case, it affects America, and so they need to be angry at themselves, and they need to be angry at our justice system. And I don't know how they could have articulated that to me. I don't know what a person could have done at that time. Most people did stay away. People were nervous. People didn't know what to say, and there was an awkwardness."

I pressed him. It sounded as if white people couldn't win, no matter how they behaved. Neither silence nor words would satisfy. What did he want from them? He wasn't sure. He didn't want the white guilt trip laid out on the table, he didn't want an argument, and he didn't want the subject ignored, either. One white friend, on the phone from California, did say just the right thing. "When I called him, he said, 'Man, it's just fucked up. That's all I have to say. It's just fucked up.' And that was good." King smiled, then laughed warmly. "You know, this was a white guy. 'It's just fucked up.' I said, 'I agree.' And that's all he had to say: that we were thinking the same things. . . . So that worked for me."

It seemed a matter of geometry, I thought. Ideally, he and I would be standing side by side, facing in the same direction with the same anger, rather than face-to-face with me trying to assure him of my outrage. Yes, King nodded. Yes. A difficult geometry to achieve.

And especially so given the long tradition among blacks of seeing whites as untrustworthy and deeply racist. "I was taught," said La Tanya Wright, a young woman who grew up in Washington, D.C., "that in general you just don't trust them. You can work with them, and they'll smile in your face, and you can smile back. But don't trust them, because they'll back-stab you. My mother told me that. My grandmother. My grandmother used to say, 'That white boss you have down at the Department of Agriculture, he don't care about you.' "

Like a walking time bomb, the racism inside white people would eventually explode. "Eventually, whites were going to slap you" was the way it was explained to Quentin Messer, a Princeton student from Jacksonville, Florida. "Every white has their day," he said. "I don't care how progressive they are. This was a saying I heard growing up: 'Every white has his day, and when that day comes, you're going to recognize that you're black and he's white or she's white.' . . . I don't believe that anymore," he added. "I think every human has his day. We resort back to what is comfortable, which is our own, and we lash out at anybody else that's different."

In Chicago, Laura Washington's mother tried to convey a dual message: Learn to deal with whites, but stay alert. "They don't have any good intentions as far as you're concerned," she quoted her mother as saying. "They're going to make you struggle to get everything you can get, because they are racists, and therefore you have to be watchful."

The words "evil" and "devil" come up in some blacks' conversation about whites, just as they did in Malcolm X's speeches. In a history course at Tougaloo, Jessica Prentice, who was the only white on campus, was driven from the classroom in tears by a black student who "started talking about how white people have perpetrated all the terrible things in the world, and how white people are the devil, and that's why she doesn't associate with white people, because if you associate with them, then they'll corrupt you, and they'll make you greedy, and white people are just pure greed, and black people love the earth and love everybody else."

African-Americans who come to a sense of tolerance sometimes find themselves in the presence of uncomfortable bigotry among fellow blacks, and they react variously. Trey Muldrow went to a mostly white private school in Baltimore, then to Princeton. When blacks would say, "They must be evil, they must be out to get you, they must talk behind your back, they must not be as hospitable or nice to you," he explained, "I have to say, 'No, they're not like that. You can't typecast people like that. You'd be very upset if they said that about you: "They must be drugged, they must be poor." You'd be very offended.' "

But it's often hard to muster the courage to speak up—as hard for blacks as for whites to reprimand friends who make racist remarks. One afternoon, Demetrius Childs was sitting with a group of other blacks in the cafeteria at Malcolm X University in Chicago when one of the few white students walked by. "Hey, devil!" said one of the blacks. The white continued walking. The black stood up at his table. "Hey, devil! Hey, devil!" The white pretended not to hear and kept on walking.

"Everybody at the table got a laugh out of it," said Childs. Did anyone raise an objection? "No, no, no. I didn't say anything. And I didn't say anything because it happens so often." Childs had challenged the black offender previously, asking him why he made such comments. "It's absurd at times, his response," Childs said. " 'I don't like white people. They're devils.' Or, 'God made a mistake.' " And what would have happened if Childs had spoken up then? "I would have been laughed at," he insisted. "I would have been laughed down. I think that there probably were some other people that were uncomfortable with what he said, questioned why he said it, but out of a nervous reaction laughed right along with him."

Reading racism and measuring trustworthiness is an uncertain business, and blacks often get it wrong, according to a white undercover narcotics cop in Washington, D.C. His professional responsibilities entail buying drugs so dealers can get caught. "There are a lot of contexts in my job where, if you were a fly on the wall, you'd think there was no hope for race relations," he said. "I've been in a room where I was the only white and I was sort of doing something and the blacks [policemen] in the room were talking among themselves . . . and to hear conversations in those settings, you would think that every black basically thinks every white is racist. 'You know how whites are. You know how they are. You hear where they got on the brother about this.' "

Similarly, when he and his white friends go camping, some of them slip into racist slang—"using the N-word," as he puts it delicately. But the reality is more complex than the language, this officer believes, and he cites the case of one white policeman in particular. "To hear his conversation, you'd think by day he's a cop, by night he's a rider for the Ku Klux Klan. And yet I've seen this same officer spend hours and hours and hours in an incident where it wasn't related to our job in the narcotics bureau. . . . He ran into someone [black] who had a problem with their car or they'd been robbed. And he spent far more time than somebody who was really a racist would have spent. My point is that if you heard his conversation, you'd think he was. But you reach a point where you start to go much more by people's actions. [He] married a black woman. Now how do you figure that out? It's bizarre.

"Another friend of mine uses the N-word, or there are a couple of others—'boofer,' just another slang word for it. But I've seen an officer who uses those words give mouth-to-mouth resuscitation to a black junkie who had OD'd—prior to the AIDS fear, but still, just a very unappealing thing to do—mouth-to-mouth resuscitation to a junkie lying on the curb. And the guy died. It didn't work.

"But I compare that with coming back from a run, when I lived down on the corner here, and seeing a pair of what we call 'biff and muffies,' a couple of Capitol Hill yuppies—middle-class whites—who are stopped by a black guy who's sort of sprawled across the sidewalk. And I stop to see what's going on, and the guy's drunk and just falling out. And I hear them saying, 'Where are the police? Why aren't they ever there when you need them?' The classic. So I stop. I don't identify myself as a cop. And I'm in my sweat outfit, so they don't know I'm a cop. And I squat down: 'Hey, buddy, what's the problem?' 'Wor, wor.' 'Where do you live, man?' He points. He was basically in front of his house. So I start to lift him up, and I tell biff, 'Hey, man, grab his other shoulder and we'll get him upstairs.' " The cop pauses and imitates the white yuppie's horrified face. "You know, this recoil. Complete unwillingness to go beyond the words. Now, his words are probably very proper. He probably never uses the N-word. He probably never called anybody a 'boofer.' Who is the racist?"

In the currency of race, the coin of distrust has its opposite side. There, in counterpoint to the usual patterns of suspicion, individuals manage to burnish the emblems of trust, loyalty, and regard, often in the midst of hardship. That flip side of the coin can be found in unexpected places, such as the grimy, prisonlike building in South Central Los Angeles where the probation department has offices. Voices echo in the large lobby. People sit on hard benches or stand talking on a pay phone, waiting, waiting, until their parole officer emerges through a locked door to escort them into a warren of cluttered cubicles.

Jim Galipeau's partitioned compartment is nearly swallowed by a desk strewn with papers. Looming behind the mess, a poster declares: "A Clean Desk Is a Sure Sign of a Sick Mind." But Galipeau doesn't spend much time in his office. His office is the street, his desk is his car, his file cabinet is a black briefcase containing a nine-millimeter with ten rounds of hollow-point in a quick-draw holster. He is white and big—a gruff, no-nonsense genie of six feet or so and more than 200 pounds, down from 260 since he went back to cigarettes and constant cups of coffee. He shaves his head and wears tinted glasses, a gold ring in his left ear, a gray and black beard and mustache trimmed short, and a gold medallion on a heavy gold chain around his neck. Today, he's got on a black-and-white-checked sweater with the sleeves pushed up to reveal thick forearms. This man sends a mean message: Don't mess with me. A lot of black gang members in the ghetto swear by him.

Some of them, especially O.G.'s—original gangsters, now in their middle and late thirties, who founded the Crips and the Bloods—have even taken Galipeau into the intimate fraternity of blacks who can call each other "nigger," that racist epithet that some blacks have turned into a term of rough affection.

"Snoop" and "Sampson," alias Fred Hill and Jimel Barnes, sit over a heavy lunch of ribs, pork chops, red beans, rice, and other soul food in a South Central restaurant, explaining their tough trust of Galipeau. Snoop wears a diamond earring. Sampson has a meaty handshake and is fueled by an obsession to fight Mike Tyson. To these men, battered by the brutal streets, the great divide is not between black and white. "It's

like this," says Sampson. "I believe in the world today, you got the real
people, and you got the phony people. The phony people have the most
control in the world and the most money."

Galipeau qualifies as real. "I first met him when I was about twelve or
thirteen," Snoop says. "He was gonna whup my ass back then. He always
been that kind of guy that come off joking with you. At the same time
with his joke, you can see the realness in him. And me and him do that
now. He makes the statement 'nigger' sometime, and I make the statement 'peckerwood' sometime. We'd laugh at it . . . because we see each
other as men first, see?" And are there things he can't understand
because he's white? "No," Snoop answers. "That ain't nothing but a
color. Deep inside, he's a black. He's black as me."

"We're both niggas," Galipeau says. "He's a black nigger, I'm—" and
then all three men announce in unison, "A white nigga!"

"That's it," Snoop says.

"That word describes the three of us," Galipeau declares. "We're
niggas."

"We all the same," Sampson explains.

"We understand from the bottom," says Galipeau.

"See," Snoop continues, "although he's got a professional job, he
gotta deal with the bottom to come out and be on top at his job. I mean,
he's got to ride through the ghettos."

"When we're down there, we're all the same," says Galipeau. "I go
to their neighborhoods at night with their permission. I could not be in
their neighborhoods at night, [even] if I had a tommy gun, without giving them respect. That's what it's all about. And what he's saying, it's
respect. When he calls somebody a nigger, it's not a slave word anymore.
What we're talking about when we're calling each other niggers is
respect."

For Snoop, the first glimpse of Galipeau's respect came at the funeral
of a homeboy; Galipeau had been his parole officer. Snoop was struck by
the mere fact that a burly white man was there. Then he was amazed by
the tears he saw in Galipeau's eyes. "He didn't see shit," Galipeau
insisted with a macho wave of his hand. "Well," he added gruffly,
"maybe I did have tears in my eyes."

For children from decaying, love-starved households, the gang becomes family, and—oddly—the parole officer sometimes becomes uncle,
older brother, pastor, teacher, coach. "He helped me get a durned good
job," Snoop says, "that I lost on account of me acting wild, not him, and
before I seed where I went wrong at. This last time I was on probation
for carrying a gun, I walked into Mr. Galipeau's office and I said, 'Mr.

Galipeau, this lady, they gonna put me on her caseload, and I don't want to be with her. I want to be with you, somebody I know's gonna be on my ass, 'cause I just got back to the city, and I know I'm gonna be doing things wrong.' He said, 'You serious?' He say, 'If you want to be on my caseload, and you serious, I'll help you.' "

Galipeau earned his credentials in his own turbulent youth, which he spent on the fringes of Hispanic gangs in Long Beach, smoking weed, experimenting with heroin, and stealing liquor and cars. Between the ages of thirteen and fifteen, he was arrested about ten times, and he remembers the last time vividly. The cops knew that he had been doing a lot of stuff that they couldn't quite pin on him, but this time they had him cold. "I'm a smart-ass," Galipeau recalls. "I'm talking back: 'Fuck you, do what you're gonna do. I ain't afraid of the probation officer. I ain't afraid to go to your camp. Send me to your camp, man, I'll kick ass'—all this type of thing. . . . My friends had gone to camp, and I wondered what it was like. . . . It was kind of a challenge to me. I wanted to get tougher, I wanted to learn more. But it's just like these guys out here; I deal with them. They know they're going to the penitentiary. Even at sixteen, seventeen, they know they're going to end up in the pen, and they're going to end up in county jail if they don't end up dead. . . . So I was very interested in finding out what the experience would be like. So I'm in there. They caught me dead to rights on something, maybe a stolen car or whatever, so they're calling me 'punk' and all this type of stuff, like I call these guys. And I was telling them to fuck off, I wasn't afraid of their camp, I'd go in and kick ass and be fine, that it wasn't scaring me, just go ahead and send me, don't talk about it. Here came my little five-foot-three father, walking into this police station."

Galipeau's mother was dying of multiple sclerosis; his father, working the night shift as a machinist in an aircraft factory, was barely holding things together. He wouldn't drive his 1950 Oldsmobile because he wanted to preserve it. So, Galipeau says, "he would walk about a mile to the bus stop, starting about two-thirty. . . . He would work from four to midnight, take a bus home, get home about one o'clock, at which time he'd have to totally change my mother's bed. She would defecate and urinate all over herself. He'd have to bathe her, totally change all the bedclothes, put her to bed. He'd probably get two or three hours of sleep, he'd be up at six o'clock in the morning to cook me breakfast—the only time we'd see each other on school days—make sure I was up, dressed right, and all of that. That was the only time we got to talk.

"At any rate, here's this man, killing himself like this—didn't drink, didn't smoke, didn't go out with women. His whole life was for my mother and I. And you know, I didn't see that. I just thought that's the way it is, that's the way it's always been. . . . He walked in and I looked at him—I'm in a repartee with the night probation officer and a cop—and he just looked broken. He was just hunched over. And I'd wrecked his car. He's trying to save the car, and I was sneaking out wrecking it. He came down, and they said, 'John'—I think one of them called him John. He said, 'We got to put him away this time. He's just into too much trouble. You can't take care of him. I know you're trying as hard as you can, I know your wife's sick, but you cannot control this boy, we cannot control this boy. This boy needs to be put somewhere where he can learn discipline.' 'Fuck you,' I said. 'Dad, don't worry, ain't no problem, I'll be back.' And all of a sudden, my father started crying."

Galipeau abandons his rapid talk and slows way down, pronouncing each word slowly, leaving a beat of silence after each one. "I had never seen this man cry in my life. And he didn't just cry. He broke out sobbing, begging these motherfuckers: 'Please don't do this. It'll kill his mother. Please don't take him away from us. I'll get another job. I'll have two jobs. I'll put him in a private school. Please don't do this, please don't do this to him.' And all of a sudden it hit me, like a kick in the head, you know, like a bolt of lightning. Looking back now that I'm a little more spiritually oriented, I think it was probably the Holy Spirit intervention, where I saw: I'm killing you. And all I ever prayed for was that he don't die. That's all I ever prayed for. I didn't pray for a Corvette. I prayed that he doesn't die, because I couldn't take care of my mother. I wouldn't know what to do with my mother if he died. So please, God, let him live to take care of my mother, till I'm old enough that I can do something. . . . I'd broken this guy. He was the strongest man I'd ever known, although I didn't realize it till I was older. And I'm the only thing that can hurt him like this, and I'm doing it, and I've been doing it. And I turned around to them and said, 'Give me a break.' And they said, 'Well, fuck you, you're nothing but a punk, you shouldn't treat your father like this.' And I said, 'I know. I never asked you guys for shit. I'm not afraid to go to your camp, you know that. Let me have a chance. This could kill him.' . . . And I start crying. And I didn't cry very often. And they were impressed, and they just laid it on me. They kept pushing and pushing, same technique I use a lot today, just to see if they could get me to kick back. No way. I said, 'You tell me anything. You want straight A's? I'll give you straight A's. You want perfect attendance? I won't miss a day of school. I won't get suspended. I won't smoke. But give me a chance. If I don't do it, put me in prison.' They said, 'OK, we don't like you, and you know that.' I said, 'I don't like you either, but I love him, and I want a chance to show you guys.' "

Galipeau did well enough in school to get into Berkeley, and after graduating in 1964, he went into the army and got sent to Vietnam. Crawling after Vietcong through the tunnels of Cu Chi and forging friendships in combat, he thought, made him focus on the essentials about people. When he came back to graduate school in psychology, everything seemed bland and false and unreal. And then, when he worked temporarily as a probation officer in Watts, he connected. "I found a vitality and a kind of a something in these people that I couldn't get out of the white middle-class people that I knew, because I was changed," he says. "Vietnam had changed me permanently. So in the brown and black people, I saw people who had values a lot like I did in terms of respecting word, honor, courage, physical prowess—you know, the kind of things that I'd been into."

High on the wall of Galipeau's cubicle is a poster of flowers and wine and the inscription "Friendship is the most constant, most enduring, most basic part of love." Nearby hangs an ink drawing of the faces of four children—white, black, Asian, Latino—and this declaration: "There is a destiny that makes us brothers. No one goes too far alone. All that we put into the life of others will someday come back into our own."

CHAPTER SEVEN

Violence

The Mirror of Harm

Everybody you kill in the line of duty becomes a slave
in the afterlife.

—*A white Los Angeles policeman,*
in a computer message

Fear

Apparently, Lauren Nile presented a terrifying sight. On a raw morning
in the early spring, she strode up Connecticut Avenue in Washington,
D.C., and turned left into the brick building where she worked. She
would be forty in August, but she was lithe and looked younger, a
diminutive African-American with the tight curls of her black hair
cropped close to her scalp. She had dressed casually in pants and a
hooded jacket that day because she had no important appointments on
her calendar.

Lauren Nile had been an assistant dean of admissions at Wesleyan
University, had done a year of graduate study in philosophy, had earned
a law degree, and was now counseling various institutions on overcoming friction between the sexes and races—in short, a typical mugger.
At least that's the impression she seemed to give a middle-aged white
woman walking several paces ahead of her up the street, through the
door, and into the elevator.

Lauren followed. The white woman may have been a resident; the
building, in a virtually all-white neighborhood, contained a mixture of
apartments and offices. When the woman saw the trim, jacketed black
person, her face twisted into such horror that Lauren could easily read
her thoughts: *Oh, my God, this woman has followed me into the building, into
the elevator!*

Lauren had a thought of her own, an urge to say something to com-
he woman and defend herself: *I'm a lawyer. I work in the building. It's*

all right. Instead, she just said, "Hi, how ya doin' today?" The woman gave no reaction. Then the elevator door opened, and the bitter little encounter was over. In her office a few minutes later, Lauren summed it up: "All she saw was black."

This treatment is usually reserved for black males, not females. White women clutch their purses, cross the street, choose another elevator. And not only whites stiffen with apprehension. "There is nothing more painful to me at this stage in my life," the Reverend Jesse Jackson told a conference in 1994, "than to walk down the street and hear footsteps and start thinking about robbery, then look around and see somebody white and feel relieved."

Nor are whites the only ones to advise taking precautions. One November evening, in a room at the village hall of Oak Park, Illinois, a black policeman gave some pointers to a dozen white residents from the southeast corner of town. Their neighborhood runs along Austin Boulevard, the frontier with the impoverished, mostly black West Side of Chicago. And although the policeman, Greg Hines, made no explicit references to race, the images in the whites' minds were clear enough. A white man described his anxiety as he waited at Madison and Austin for his wife to get off a bus from work every night around eight o'clock: "It gets pretty lonely out there." He did not have to say that the corner was populated mostly by blacks. A white woman added a reference to the intersection of Austin and North: "I've seen things there that I just couldn't believe. I saw a drug deal go on right in front of me. This kid, I thought he was waiting for the bus, his buyer came along, and it happened so fast. I thought, 'What if they start shooting?'"

Officer Hines was straightforward with them. "As you know," he said, "we are bordered by Chicago on two sides of the village. Chicago is a different place from Oak Park. . . . If you carry a purse, carry it under your arm. And if somebody comes and you have a gut feeling, there's nothing wrong with putting it on the other side and crossing the street. Run. You may embarrass that person and embarrass yourself, but there's nothing wrong with that. You've got to take care of yourself. You see those two thugs coming at you, walk the other way. You don't have to walk into that."

Young black men feel the pulse of pain when whites cannot see the decency behind the color of the skin. Tony Wyatt, the black air force sergeant, notices in a Florida Kmart where he shops that a white person often starts down an aisle, sees a black man there, turns, circles all the way around, comes into the aisle at the other end, takes the merchandise off the shelf, and travels the long way around again, just to avoid crossing paths with the black. "When you start to understand what's going on, it begins to make your stomach turn," Wyatt says.

For some blacks, a white's fear ignites a flash of insult and rage. When a black youth entered a subway train in Washington and stood next to a white woman, and she hugged her pocketbook close to her body, "I was so angry," he told a friend, "I wish I could have stolen her purse just to prove she was right. I don't want to steal anything from her, but she made me so mad."

Some African-Americans are amused by the dread they see in white faces, said Lorenzo Daniels, a seventeen-year-old with a shaved head. He and his friends in South Central Los Angeles like to "mess" with whites just to watch their expressions. "We might see some white people, and to tell you the truth, we might just be having fun, we might mess with them, call them a name or something, 'cause they dress funny and stuff like that," he remarked. "They might wear tight pants, you know. We'll just say something about them." When a white man with big sideburns came strolling down the street, "I said to my friend, like, 'Elvis ain't dead. There he go right there.' And then I start saying it really loud: 'Elvis is not dead! There he is right there!' And everybody started laughing. I could see by his face that he didn't like the way I said it. When I saw his face, I started saying more stuff. I was talking about his pants, 'cause his pants was tight." Lorenzo gave a merry laugh.

For a course at Dartmouth on social deviance, five African-American students—four women and a man—draped themselves with gold chains and rings, dressed in gang colors and baggy overalls, put baseball hats on backward, and talked loudly as they sat in a student lounge. "In your project you don't bother anybody," explained Zola Mashariki, a senior from Brooklyn. "You just stand there, and you kind of observe people's reactions to you. And people were really, really scared. . . . People felt that we were unapproachable. People would walk all the way around us."

The image of black violence spins through daily life like a dust devil across a plain. It filters so thoroughly into the American consciousness that nonblacks actually argue among themselves about whether or not they are justified in discriminating against all black males as a shortcut to security. A *Washington Post* columnist, Richard Cohen, wrote sympathetically of jewelers who refused to buzz black men through the locked glass doors of their downtown stores. A public-radio host in Washington allowed, without comment or objection, the assertion by Dinesh D'Souza, a right-wing writer originally from India, that taxi drivers should be legally permitted to refuse black men as passengers; this, he claimed, was "rational discrimination."

Some whites who think more reflectively find themselves at war with their instincts. "I remember waiting at Newark Airport, and we were on line, and there were youths walking around who were black, and they started towards the line, and I guess just to cut through," said Stephen Burka, a white in his twenties. His and his uncle's "first instinct," he remembered, was to move in front of his sisters and his aunt. "So we sort of covered them," he said. "I just did it, and then I noticed my reaction. I don't know, it hit me, Why did I do that?"

When a white man told me that he thought blacks' indignation at such treatment was misplaced, that they should be angry not at whites but at fellow blacks who commit so much crime and give one another the profile of violence, I took his argument to Lauren Nile. What was her feeling? "It's hurt," she answered. "It's a dagger to your heart. My response to that would be 'Listen, as an African-American I'm painfully aware that the vast majority of crime that's committed in cities is committed by African-Americans. The fact is that most of that crime is committed black on black. Only a small percentage of it is black on white. So there is a way in which the level of fear is irrational.' . . . So while I can see that white people might fear black urban crime, unless you are in one of those neighborhoods and happen to be caught in the crossfire or whatever, the chances are it won't touch you. It isn't rational. But it hurts because if a person were to see *me*, they would see I'm not a very threatening person because of stature. . . . But they don't see *me*. And that hurts. . . . And I'm a human being with feelings; my feelings don't have to make sense. When a person looks at me and clutches her purse and scurries out of the bathroom, that hurts."

Lauren added another thought: Whites may be afraid of blacks in the city, but blacks can be afraid of whites in the country. One night in rural West Virginia, a black consultant left his hotel to drive to the place where he had to be early the next morning, just to make sure he could find it easily and wouldn't be late. As he was leaving, he asked his colleague to call the police if he didn't return in an hour. Black college students from the East who attend Louisiana State University in Shreveport travel with strict instructions from parents to fill up on gas before driving through rural parts of Alabama and Mississippi so they don't have to stop. Lauren has the same fears when she's in some small midwestern town. She also had them as she looked for a homesite. "I want to build a round house with floor-to-ceiling glass," she said. "It has to be on an acre, a wooded lot. That means being out in the country. I've looked at a lot of lots, and I've thought, No, I don't want to be out here. It doesn't feel safe to be alone in this area—West Virginia, Virginia, Maryland."

The irony of whites' fears about African-Americans, Roger Wilkins observes, is that the bulk of the interracial violence has historically gone the other way, committed by whites against blacks. Slave owners who beat and maimed and killed were worried that they might be poisoned by their slaves, he noted wryly. The conspiracy of violence in the postwar South was constructed by law enforcers and vigilantes against black people. And blacks continue to face dangers from white policemen. "When white people think we're violent," Wilkins remarked, "there's a lot of projection going on."

The association of black people with violence produces a labyrinth of thoughts and deeds among white Americans, who wander the puzzling corridors along various routes. Some use the image as a vehicle of raw racism. Some react with nervous humor. Some incorporate the assumption into refined professional judgments. Some shrink from confrontation, even where it would be appropriate, as in a teacher-student interaction. However translated into behavior, the image is powerful and widespread. The National Opinion Research Center, surveying a multiracial sample of adults nationwide in 1990, found 56.1 percent believing that blacks were more violent than whites; no other ethnic group received such a negative evaluation.

To some whites at some level of consciousness, this seems a simple matter of biology. A Louisiana probation officer told a reporter for the *Shreveport Times* that black people carried a gene that fostered violence. For saying out loud to a newspaper what many of his colleagues probably believed, the officer was suspended.

The violent stereotype is close to the primitive, to the savage, to the caricatures that have long been used to brand blacks as subhuman. When I asked a focus group of whites at Drew University for some of their racist thoughts, Christina Fichera easily merged the primitive into the violent. "Spear chucker. Jungle bunny. Nigger. Chocolate bunny," she said, then immediately went to a stark recollection. "I remember when we were younger, before we'd go out, it would always be like a big joke: Do you have your nigger-be-good stick? Which is like just a stick, but it was used to beat up black people, so it was called a 'nigger-be-good stick.' "

"I remember," Stephen Burka said, "my mother always thought that African-Americans had something extra that made them crazy. They were wild. They just could not behave, act normal, could not settle, could not be civilized. . . . So today if I see the youths being crazy or black youths acting a little wild, that thought comes into my head almost immediately: 'Oh, boy, what's wrong with them?' "

He and the others were blinking in embarrassment at their own words; their eyes were stinging and watering as if noxious fumes had been let loose in the room.

"Violence and crime," said Christina. "Whenever the news shows the latest crime, it's always a black person who's committed it. . . . I try not to think of them as a culture that's violent, but you can't help but think that as a culture they're completely violent, when you look at TV and the videos on MTV—guns, violence. They're talking about guns and shooting their women and shooting white women. And that's a disgrace, and I think it's disgusting. When you're walking down the street and someone startles you or scares you, it's usually a black person. It's not a white person that you fear. It's the black person that makes you walk on the other side of the street or make you kind of start looking around to see who else is there. Whether it's true or not, this is what it is. Sometimes I think it is true, that black people do commit crimes more than white people. Or maybe you just hear about it more. I don't know which one it is, but it is truly frightening."

Apparently, one of Colgate's coaches was nervous, because he started making tasteless cracks as soon as a large number of black athletes began to arrive for a track meet at a mostly black college. Trevor Woollery, a tall runner from Jamaica, was working out early when the first remark came, and he tried to let it go by. "He said to me, 'Trevor, looks like we'll have to hang close to you, Julio, and Willie today for protection,' " Woollery recalled. "I just said, 'Ah, yeah, sure, whatever.' . . . I thought, Oh, it's just a random statement. I gave him the benefit of the doubt. But twenty to forty minutes later, the rest of the team came from the hotel, and I was told by the other two brothers that the coach came up to the van and said, 'Guys, you'll have to hang around Julio, Trevor, and Willie for protection today.' . . . We got very uncomfortable." Was he making a bad joke? "When he said it to me at first, he did not smile. But after the meet, we usually have a meeting just to go over the results and he praises us or whatever, and he opened by saying, 'First of all, we'd like to thank Trevor, Julio, and Willie for protecting us today.' . . . He just smiled. The rest of the team, the white guys, they laughed too, and that just pissed me off. I walked out of the room." Later, a couple of whites went to Trevor and made a statement of solidarity in a rough, macho way: Could you believe what the coach said? But Woollery never felt able to raise the issue with the coach himself. "I just avoided it," he said. "It just pissed me off so much."

More subtle, more polished, was the reaction of a committee of whites at a leading psychiatric hospital when a young black man was admitted suffering from manic depression. Only one black psychiatrist was in the room when his case was presented, and she was struck by how willingly these highly educated and experienced professionals believed the patient's fantastic tales of his own violence. The initial assessment was done by a student who was taken in by the young man's stories of murders he had committed and jail time he had done, and as the student reeled off the litany of supposed crimes, "I could just see the level of tension rising in the room," the psychiatrist recalled. "I said to myself, This is crazy here. It just seemed to me that what was being crystallized was a stereotype of the young black male being evil, being a criminal, as opposed to what was the truth about this fellow." Although he was not the first patient to arrive at the hospital with such stories, he was the first black to do so, and the staff was believing his fantasies. The doctors had been able to muster up some skepticism about the whites' accounts of their own dangerous exploits, but not about the black's.

Only when she recalled the earlier patients and called for the records—which showed no arrests—was she able to calm the mood. "This was the tool I used to deflate everybody's anxiety," she explained. "I said, 'Gee, Tom, remember that guy, Eric whatever-his-name-was? He had the thing about death, too. How did you handle it with him?' . . . I had to remind people of the history. I think they had forgotten that. It was striking that this guy was just a little bit more worrisome because of his color."

At some level of anxiety, mere difference is enough to activate the fear. "If you know that there's a rapist in the area," said Reverend Bill Lawson, a black pastor in Houston, "and you've seen a number of people walking around the area—some are black and some are white, some are wearing leather jackets and some are wearing suits and ties—you just kind of automatically look at the blacks with the leather jackets rather than the whites with the ties. It actually may be the white with the tie who is doing it, but there is still enough of a residual feeling that there is something ominous about people who are not like me. And we have the same feeling. If there's a white person in the black community, we may very well trust the black person who is going to rob us rather than the white person who is perfectly innocent, simply because we're more comfortable with a black person in our community."

Moreover, this pattern fulfills a need to keep violence at a distance.

Attaching the threat to people who are different from you makes your own group feel safer. When a white person hears of a brutal crime, assumes it has been committed by a black, and then learns that the offender is actually white, the revelation can be horrifying, for the sense of danger is heightened by a sense of proximity. The threat is too close, too intimate. If violence emanates primarily from blacks, it can be walled off.

Two days before the Million Man March, a white man at a dinner party turned to me to ask my advice. Knowing that I had been working on this book, he wanted my estimate of how dangerous it would be for him to attend a dinner in downtown Washington the night of the march. I asked what he was afraid of. The answer was so obvious that he paused for a beat, as if suddenly sensing—as whites often do—that he was not in company where he could candidly say what was really on his mind. He fumbled a bit as he tried to find a palatable way to put it. Given the kind of people who were demonstrating, there might be trouble. What kind of people? Young people. Maybe some group of whites would attack them. A white woman suggested that the young blacks might get "stirred up" by the speeches.

The specter of great masses of black men swarming into the capital to be addressed by the inflammatory Louis Farrakhan so frightened whites that thousands stayed home from work that Monday. The predicted traffic jams never materialized; it was easier than normal to drive into the city. The Metro system, which put subways on a rush-hour schedule all day, found most trains virtually empty. The downtown law firm where my son Jonathan worked was nearly vacant. When no violence erupted, most absentees insisted the next morning that they had just wanted to avoid the rush-hour crush; some conceded that they had been scared. The line between fear of traffic and fear of black men seemed difficult even for individual whites to define within themselves.

I had expected whites to take cover, at least as the marchers were gathering, but their absence from the streets around the Capitol was even more complete than I'd imagined. Usually on a weekday morning, the area is bustling with all shades of people going to and fro. But when my younger son, Michael, and I emerged from the Metro at Union Station and were carried along in a river of black men toward the Capitol, we were initially the only whites in view. Then, en route, an occasional white appeared, walking in businesslike fashion here or there. The same was true later as we walked past the White House, the Old Executive

Office Building, and the offices along K Street. The entire effect was more like a Sunday than a Monday.

Among the marchers, the mood was lighthearted, friendly, laid-back, "spiritual" in the words of some participants. Relaxed and almost jubilant, the men joked and laughed and greeted one another with hugs and slaps on shoulders. Michael and I saw none of the animosity that many whites had expected; we encountered no hostility, only courtesy, no hard looks, only an occasional gaze of curiosity. Unlike the 1963 March on Washington at which Martin Luther King Jr. delivered his powerful summons to the nation, "I Have a Dream," there was no room for me to participate in this gathering. It was not about me. The message was not about overcoming racial gaps or petitioning government, only about internal reform. And so I could only watch from the outside. Yet somehow the atmosphere reminded me of 1963, when strangers had spoken to one another, when all who had come were exceedingly polite. In 1995 as in 1963, a jostle or a bump brought a profusion of apologies and smiles unlike anything seen on a normal day. As some blacks said later, at the Million Man March they could finally look strangers in the eye without fearing that they would be seen as "dissing" them and risking attack.

As I was taking notes, a tall black man in a jean jacket walked up behind me, and as he passed, he said, "Black men are peaceful. Write that, right?" He didn't slow down for a reply. Indeed, black men were peaceful on the Mall that day, defying every white fear. Farrakhan saw this, looked over the crowd, and declared, "All of these black men that the world sees as savage, maniacal, and bestial, look at them: a sea of peace. A sea of tranquillity."

Afterward, however, the peacefulness of the occasion did not figure prominently in the commentaries. As a black friend of mine observed, the fact went unnoticed that in any gathering of such size, it is rare to have no violent acts; shootings have occurred on the Mall even during Fourth of July fireworks. In the news coverage and the myriad columns on the march, whatever mention was made of the event's nonviolence was often negated by the menacing portrait of Farrakhan. Whites' fears of black men, agile enough to find a niche in practically any setting, were focused on both ends of a spectrum—fear of the chaos of rampaging youths and fear of the rigid discipline of militants from the Nation of Islam. Many whites are haunted by the two images simultaneously—the primitive and the disciplined, combining, like two volatile chemicals, into a heightened threat. This is what made Malcolm X seem a fearsome figure, and it affected reactions to Farrakhan as well. My dinner companion's nervousness about the prospect of disorder was reinforced by a colder fear of order, triggered by Farrakhan's closely clipped, dark-suited bodyguards. Even as Frank Rich, a *New York Times* columnist, urged whites to drop their fixation on Farrakhan, he wrote, "His retinue of brownshirts injected the chilling trappings of fascism into an event otherwise resplendent in spirituality and peace." Who could stop fixating on Farrakhan after a description like that? Besides, if his guards are truly brownshirts and fascism is in the offing, wouldn't we be wise to remain quite deliberately fixated upon him?

Several months after the turbulent wake of emotions left by the march had subsided, a black cab driver in Chicago offered me a quick vignette of the fear on the other side. He and all his friends had carried their handguns, carefully concealed, to the Mall that day, he asserted: They had been determined to go down fighting if, as they believed likely, the white establishment had tried to gun them down as they assembled at the heart of power.

Sorting out responses to the images that are seen, and to the images that are carried inside minds, is the puzzle of the labyrinth that is so confusing to whites. When I taught at Princeton, white students didn't know quite what to feel about the rigid ritual that surrounded the pledge period for black fraternities. During several weeks in the spring, when they went "on line," as it was called, black pledges wore military clothing, spoke to no one except fraternity brothers and professors, and walked around campus as if they were marching in formation—turning square corners, keeping eyes ahead. Groups of men moved into each other's rooms, where the pledges were hit with paddles and subjected to other hazing. Black women were assigned as "sweethearts" to clean their rooms, do their laundry, bring them food, and perform other favors.

On one level, some whites tried to be tolerant of what blacks described as the process of asserting their blackness, finding solidarity, beating down in order to build up. On another level, however, many of the same white students found the spectacle frightening. On many campuses, largely white fraternities also practice hazing, of course, but this seemed to contain an aggressive, exclusionary overtone of anti-white, anti-female hostility. "So much for my thoughts that the black community was dedicated to liberal ideals," lamented a white whose African-American roommate brought three blacks into the suite for three and a half weeks as they pledged Kappa Alpha Psi. "I'm sure I'm far more liberal than they are," he continued. "The concept of these fraternities is militant, it's anti-individualistic, it's chauvinistic, and it's racist." The black students were noisy late into the night, were not allowed to wash for the entire time, refused to acknowledge him, and made him feel a stranger in his own room, he complained. Once, when several black women came in, he heard one say, "I don't know if I should be talking to white people." He was outraged: This is in my damned room! he thought. "I really feel like this whole thing is a disgusting throwback to slavery. They're sort of enslaving themselves. . . . It was just a really scary, scary situation to be in." So, at the end of the year, he decided not to room with any blacks again. "It wasn't the individuals," he explained. "It was the whole culture. It definitely made me less optimistic about racial harmony."

Joe Brown, the white drug dealer in California, used white fear to his advantage as he assembled an all-black squad of security guards around him. "White people are chicken on the street—seriously," he said. "They have this image of black guys as real hard people. I would never walk out my door with four of my white friends to fight anybody like my guards. I could go out with one black guy, and he would just come out of the door and the white people would go, 'Oooh, oooh, there's a black guy there, and he's probably pretty mean!' "

For Bill Page, the white diversity consultant who used to be a school superintendent in New Hampshire, the whiff of fear could be found intricately mingled with the exhilaration of urban street life. He came to feel this strange duality after a black colleague began taking him to Harlem. "There are a lot of people in the streets," he explained, "and there is a lot of energy, a lot of talk, a lot of movement, and I find that tremendously exciting. But I can flip over into fear of it real quick." He snapped his fingers. In his own culture, everything is done behind doors, he noted, so that life on city stoops and sidewalks strikes him viscerally as wrong, illicit, suspect. The same energy and movement and noise that excite him also startle him. "But," he added, "I end up coming out of the experience enormously refreshed."

In an acutely race-conscious society where racism is condemned, whites sometimes overcompensate for their image of blacks as violent. Debby, my wife, was looking for a store in Montgomery Mall, outside Washington, D.C., when she found herself at the end of a walkway. She began to walk down one side and saw a black man coming toward her. Suddenly she realized that it would be shorter to turn around and go on the other side. But mindful of how such a maneuver would be inter-preted by the African-American, she decided to keep going, pass him, and take the long way around to her shop. It was better to endure a little inconvenience, she felt, than to cause offense.

Whites take the long way around more often than most blacks realize. Michael J. Weithorn, the white writer who created the television sitcom *True Colors*, about an interracial marriage, bent over backward to write the black husband as gentle and innocuous. "I was guilty of what I think is a widespread phenomenon in the way television deals with black men," he explained, "and that is to really idealize them to the point of harmlessness. . . . I think the white audience in America is so much more predisposed to be threatened by the black character, particularly by a black male, that the shows go that much further to say, 'Don't worry. He's OK.'" Instinctively, unconsciously, he confessed, "I created a character who was such a basically good, nice, loving guy, who was so OK with everything, that he wasn't real. . . . I created a very nice, safe little world, like the interracial antagonisms within this family were never very serious. . . . So they [the Fox network] never resisted, to their credit. And they put it on at seven o'clock Sundays, which helped. . . . If I had it to do over, I would have approached it differently." However, Weithorn conceded, "all the things that I say that I might have done to it are probably things that would have kept it from getting on the air."

Here and there, compensating mechanisms have also been established in an effort to protect blacks from whites who stumble innocently into stereotyping. This was done in a massive old health clinic and community center at the edge of Cabrini Green, a notorious Chicago housing project. The building, which resembles a prisonlike school, is home to a tutoring program for children from the project. When the young white program director, Michelle Gauthier, found that many of the white lawyers and college students who were volunteering were also carrying assumptions about the black children's broken homes, academic failures, and violent lives, she instituted a four-hour training course for tutors to help them with the "unlearning process," as she called it. What had to be unlearned was a series of caricatures that made no room for complete families, youngsters who got good grades, and mothers who worked hard to get off welfare and keep their children from the lure of the gangs.

In some measure, Gauthier was going by her own experience. She had grown up in a white town in Michigan, in a "very Republican home," she remarked, "where your parents don't say they're prejudiced but they say, 'Well, why are black people so lazy?'" Working at Cabrini Green, she watched her stereotypes peel away. The reality she saw simply didn't fit the images she had been taught. "In my culture, the predominant ideas about this kind of community [were]: The people are lazy, they don't want to work, they want to have kids to get money, the welfare queen," she said. Sometimes the tutors would weave similar assumptions into the questions that they asked the children, questions that would sting: "How far behind are you in school? Do you know who your father is?" "We say to the tutors, 'Please, if you want to test a question, test it on us before you test it on the kids, so we can tell you, that's really not appropriate.' "

One afternoon, a white woman casually mentioned to her pupil, a high school girl, that she was going to Joliet to visit her brother. To anyone in Illinois, the name Joliet conjures up not just the city, where the tutor's brother resided, but the large prison that is located there. And when the black pupil replied that she also had a brother who lived in Joliet, the white tutor asked, "Oh, is he in the prison?"

"Unfortunately, he was," Gauthier explained. "So she couldn't even say, 'No, I can't believe you thought that, I can't believe you automatically assumed that.' " The girl had been labeled—and, even worse, labeled accurately. So, although she had been a serious student who had attended tutoring regularly, she stopped coming. The tutor was dismissed. "She felt bad," Gauthier observed of the white woman, "but she hadn't thought it through before she automatically said it." The girl resumed her lessons after being assigned a new tutor.

Although many blacks complain, rightly, that the image of violence leads authorities in various settings to crack down unduly on African-American males—that criminal charges, sentences, school suspensions, and the like are harsher for blacks—a curious countercurrent also runs through white behavior. More often than is commonly realized, whites bend the rules and shrink from confrontation, even where it would probably be good for all concerned.

That this goes unnoticed should not be surprising. Anger over blatant bias roils the waters and conceals the less dramatic depths. Larry Walker, an African-American who taught at Proviso East High School in a Chicago suburb, recalls a nasty dean in the late sixties dispensing summary punishment, mostly to blacks. After a fight between blacks and whites, Walker says, "he'd round them up, bring them into the auditorium or some large room, and start talking to them. Then he'd administer discipline to the black kids: 'You're suspended three days, you're suspended five days.' And he'd do all the blacks first. Then when he gets to the white kids he'd maybe suspend one for the day." Among the students at the time was Fred Hampton, who later became a Black Panther leader and was murdered by the Chicago police.

At Oak Park and River Forest High School, in the integrated suburb just west of Chicago, the apprehensions about black males create an odd contradiction. On the one hand, blacks are suspended at a relatively high rate; they account for 29 percent of the student body and 55 to 60 percent of the disciplinary cases. According to the principal, the main reasons are truancy, class cutting, and "insubordination," a vague charge that is subjective and easily abused. On the other hand, some members of the virtually all-white faculty say frankly that they are averse to confronting black males about misbehavior, especially in the halls. In a 1991 survey, thirty of the 182 teachers admitted that they handled African-American students differently in such situations. "African-American students seem louder," the report said. "There is a degree of apprehension that teachers feel when intervening in hallway situations because the students involved are anonymous and hostile."

There is reason to believe that intimidation is felt by more teachers than the survey revealed, for after attending workshops on racial diversity, some white staff members suddenly became aware of attitudes in themselves that they had never recognized before. "I did find out that I had a belief that African-American males are more aggressive," confessed Maryanne Kelly, head of the deans, or guidance counselors, "that I'm sometimes hesitant to confront African-American males, where I'm not with females." She realized this during an exercise in which teachers were shown pictures and asked to describe what they thought was portrayed. One, of a black male, looked to her like a gang member. "That was way off base," she said. "Not even close." He was a college student out to play basketball with friends.

The school's white teaching staff, especially women, occasionally called on an African-American history teacher, Mark Vance, to do the confronting. "A teacher came to me," he remembered, "and said, 'Mark, I asked this young man over here for his ID, and he wouldn't give it to me. I asked this young woman over here for her ID, and she wouldn't give it to me. Would you go over there and get it for me?'" He did, again and again, but the demands tired him and drained away much of his respect for the white teachers concerned.

Something of the same thing happens among white faculty at Teaneck High School in New Jersey. "In some situations they feel they don't want to discipline the kids, because they're afraid they're going to be insulted," observed Charlotte Scarbrough, who is white. Married to a black man who died some years ago, she worked as a reading specialist at the elementary, junior high, and high school levels. One day, she was entering Teaneck High through what is known as the "black door," the door facing the mostly black northeastern section of town, the door most convenient to most blacks walking to school, the door that has become a point of control and territoriality for black students. "I go through there to go up to my class every day," she said. "It's in the morning, so I walk into this stairwell, there are all these kids sitting on the stairs. If there are a lot of kids sitting on the stairs, what would you say?" she asked me.

" 'Excuse me,' " I replied.

"That's right. I said—" and she imitated her authoritative, no-nonsense teacher's voice in high volume, with the words drawn out: " 'EXCYOOOOOOZ MEEEEE!' They moved, and I went right on up the stairs to my class. I get to the top of the stairs, here come the two vice principals running. . . . Two of the teachers had called the vice principal and said that they went to the stairs, and the students wouldn't move." She paused to give a little chuckle. "Students wouldn't move, blocked them on the stairwell. They said, 'They do that to you?' I said, 'No, I went there and said "Excuse me." ' The teachers didn't say 'Excuse me' to the kids. And the kids were playing games: We're not going to move unless they say 'Excuse me,' and the teachers did not say 'Excuse me,' and they sat there."

Some teachers feel caught in the middle, damned whichever way they go. "If I come down too tough and too hard on my kids, then I'm being a mean SOB," complained a middle-aged white woman. "If I act too understanding, I'm 'enabling,' " meaning that she was enabling blacks to drift along on an undisciplined, unchallenged path that would never get them ahead. The label "enabler" had surfaced during a discussion among female faculty; she reported angrily that blacks had accused Jewish women in particular of having difficulty with black male students.

A similar pattern was described by the black Coast Guard officer Lieutenant Amir Abdussabour, whose white colleagues failed to discipline a black sailor despite repeated incidents of drunkenness and fighting. Abdussabour believed that the whites were thinking, "Black people, that's the way they act. They get drunk and they're rowdy, and that's the way they are, so you don't do anything to rehabilitate them." In the end, in the last bar of the night, a fight broke out and the black sailor was shot dead by a local man. Could his death have been prevented? Abdussabour thought so.

. . .

In the early days of September 1971, the leaves were still thick on the old trees that lined the streets of Attica, a town near Buffalo, New York. Decent, churchgoing white folks were enjoying the last mild weather before the autumn deepened. This was a good community—rock-ribbed, salt-of-the-earth, true-blue America. From its vantage point, a comfortable distance from the turmoil of the cities' decay and crime, life was wholesome and safe. And in their own way, the people of Attica felt, they performed a vital service for the country, doing their part to contain the wild streak that seemed to run angrily through some malevolent vein. Attica's major industry was the state prison, whose ugly walls disrupted the harmony of the tree-lined streets.

The vast majority of those locked inside the walls were black. All those who guarded them were white. The black inmates came from some sinister, malignant tumor of a world that had to be isolated from the healthy flesh of orderly society, townspeople thought. Conditions in the prison were cruel, and the prisoners seethed with rage. The guards beat them and called them "niggers." Finally, the prisoners rose up, took over part of the prison, captured guards and other employees, blindfolded them, and threatened to slash their throats with homemade knives.

On the last day of the rebellion, after fruitless negotiations, black inmates led eight white hostages onto a raised walkway in full view of the authorities and the cameras. With rags around their eyes like prisoners of war, the hostages were spaced some feet apart from one another, each with a black inmate as his guard. Each inmate held a blade to the throat of his hostage. The tableau was meant to bluff away the state police, who were massed for assault, but it merely played on the worst stereotypes of blacks as primitive, savage. Sharpshooters were positioned at high points, and angry "correction officers," who had watched their colleagues threatened and humiliated, broke out guns and waited for the word.

When the command was given, a helicopter dropped tear gas into the prison yard, hostages and inmates dropped to the ground, and the police opened fire, killing twenty-nine inmates. Nine hostages were also killed (a tenth died of his wounds several weeks later, and one guard had died earlier of a skull fracture), and word spread quickly outside the walls that their throats had been carved open by the inmates. Rumors circulated that one guard had been castrated, others disemboweled. In the whirlwind of the inmates' threats and posturing, in the deep tradition of seeing blacks as violent and uncivilized, the story seemed entirely credible.

When I arrived that afternoon, dispatched by *New York Times* editors to help with coverage, nobody was questioning the account—not families of the dead guards, not townspeople, not reporters. The story had been given an official imprimatur when it was disseminated by New York State authorities, and it was so believable, so obviously true, that none of us had any doubt. If further proof were needed, it came from four surviving hostages who had been cut in the throat, two superficially and two seriously. One of them required fifty-two stitches. Many news stories that day stated as indisputable fact, without attribution, that inmates had murdered hostages by slashing their throats.

The belief in the inmates' bestiality drove guards—who came from among the good, churchgoing people of Attica—to club and beat and scream "nigger" at prisoners who were forced to run naked through a tunnel into their cell block. Wounded inmates were struck on their stretchers, and a National Guardsman saw a guard ram a Phillips-head screwdriver into the "anal area" of an inmate who was too injured to follow the guard's orders to get to his feet.

The first crack in the story that the hostages had died from slashed throats came that afternoon, when a hospital told one family that it had been a bullet and not a knife that had caused their relative's death; the man's body showed that he had not even been touched except for a bullet wound in the side. The news was not immediately made public. The next day, September 14, I was sent to cover a news conference by Dr. John Edland, the Monroe County medical examiner, who had done autopsies on the remaining eight hostages. He looked exhausted, but he reported his findings with absolute clarity: Every one of the eight had been killed by bullets or buckshot, not knives. And since the police who had confiscated the rioters' weapons had found not even a single gun, the conclusion was inescapable: The black prisoners had not killed the hostages; the all-white assault force of police and guards had done so. Local reporters had been tipped off earlier that these would be the findings, so those of us in the small room had known what would be coming. Still, we sat for a moment, stunned by how swiftly a dreadful scenario that had seemed so certain could be turned upside down. I asked some questions and ran to call in the information to the reporter who was writing the story.

What happened then was enormously revealing: Many townspeople in Attica, whose brothers and husbands and fathers and sons had been prison guards through generations, angrily refused to believe that their friends and relatives had been shot by the police. They furiously continued to insist that the black inmates had slashed them to death in a brutal ritual of killing that only blacks could do. I spent the next few days deep in conversation with people in Attica, trying to thread my way through their hurt and conviction; I found very few who accepted the autopsy results. No other explanation was possible to them. They simply could not get their minds around the notion that the blacks had not fulfilled their worst images. They hated Dr. Edland, and they hated the press for reporting his findings. The retired guard from whom the *Times* had rented a house to set up a temporary bureau across from the prison turned less friendly, even cold. The folks in Attica were very glad to see all of us depart and leave them alone with their beliefs.

The young white couple, Carol and Charles Stuart, had begun childbirth classes at Brigham and Women's Hospital in Boston; their first baby was due in two months, around Christmas 1989. After the class on a Monday evening, they left the hospital, got into their Toyota Cressida, and headed home through Mission Hill, one of Boston's few racially diverse neighborhoods. Charles was behind the wheel. He stopped at a traffic light.

A 911 operator got the frantic call from the Toyota's car phone. He and his wife had both been shot by a black man in a jogging suit, Charles cried. The police located them, dispatched ambulances, and had them whisked to the hospital. Carol, gravely wounded in the head, died shortly after her baby boy was delivered prematurely. Charles, who told police he had ducked when the robber fired, lay in critical condition with a stomach wound, but not too critical to give the police considerable detail. The assailant had forced his way into their car, he said, ordered them to give up their jewels and cash, and then opened fire. Officers quickly pieced together a plausible explanation of why a robbery had turned into a shooting: When the robber had demanded his wallet, Charles had hesitated because he did not have his with him. The assailant had probably thought that Charles was a police officer and did not want to show a wallet containing a badge.

The crime tapped a deep well of frightened outrage in much of white America. The innocence of the white couple, cut down by a vicious black man at such a pristine moment of joyful anticipation, brought to a new height the savagery of the violence that had ravaged the country's cities. The *Boston Herald* published a grizzly picture of Carol Stuart's blood-covered body. There seemed no doubt about what had happened: Once again, a black man had ruthlessly murdered a white woman—and a pregnant white woman at that. Far beneath the surface of hysteria, the reverberations rumbled across decades of racial suspicion. The story seemed so thoroughly credible that journalists quickly suspended the profession's customary formulas of skepticism and attribution: Carol Stuart had not *allegedly* been murdered by a black man. She had, in fact, been murdered by a black man. The news accounts were written as if the reporters had been there to witness the event with their own eyes. The phrase "Charles Stuart said" or "Charles Stuart claimed" evaporated from the reports. All of America knew what had happened on that Boston street corner. Seventeen days later, the baby died.

The police, hastening to solve the crime, pressured a seventeen-year-old boy, Dereck Jackson, to state falsely that he had heard a confession from William Bennett, a black resident of Mission Hill. Stuart, in his hospital bed, was shown a photograph of Bennett and agreed that he resembled the murderer. Once discharged, Stuart identified Bennett in a lineup, and Bennett was arrested.

Then, as suddenly as the gunshots that October night, the entire story collapsed. Stuart's younger brother, Matthew, told the police that Charles had concocted the crime as an elaborate plan to collect a life insurance payment that would help him open a restaurant. Charles had shot his wife, then wounded himself, Matthew said, and had left the gun and the jewelry at the scene for Matthew to pick up. Sure enough, divers found the .38-caliber pistol at the bottom of the Pines River, where Matthew had dumped it. On January 4, 1990, Charles Stuart, now the prime suspect, committed suicide by jumping from a bridge into Boston Harbor. Matthew, who pleaded guilty two years later, was sentenced to a prison term of three to five years.

The same day Stuart took his own life, police in New Jersey learned that the Camden County prosecutor, Samuel Asbell, had faked an assassination attempt on himself several days earlier and had blamed two fictitious black men. They had shot into his car, he had claimed, and had then pursued him during an eighty-mile-an-hour chase. At a news conference, he had speculated that the assailants might have been drug dealers angry that he had increased drug convictions fourfold the previous year. He and his family were placed under police guard, and all the prosecutors in the state were warned to take precautions. As it turned out, however, his term had just expired, he was unlikely to be reappointed, and he had shot out the windows of his own car with a shotgun, the police reported. He was admitted to a psychiatric clinic.

Racial illusions seem impervious to experience. In October 1994, five years after the Stuart charade, Susan V. Smith, an appealing, bespectacled white mother, pleaded tearfully on national television for the safe return of her two little boys by the black carjacker who had abducted them. "I have prayed to the Lord every day," she said. "It's just so sad that someone could take such beautiful children. I have put all my trust and faith in the Lord that he will bring them home to us."

Her story was clear and credible: Stopped in her burgundy Mazda at a traffic light just outside Union, South Carolina, she had been approached by a stocky black man between twenty and thirty years of age, carrying a gun and wearing a lumber shirt and a wool cap. He had gotten into the car, ordered her to drive, and then forced her out after several miles. The two children, aged three and fourteen months, had still been buckled into the backseat as he had driven away, saying that he would take care of them. She had screamed after the car, "I love y'all!"

"I just feel hopeless," she said into the microphones. "I can't do enough. My children wanted me. They needed me. And now I can't help them. I just feel like such a failure." On NBC's *Today* show, she went on and on in a convincing display of maternal anguish. "I was thinking last night," she said, "as a mother, it's only a natural instinct to protect your children from any harm. And the hardest part of this whole ordeal is not knowing if your children are getting what they need to survive. And it hurts real bad to have that protection barrier broken between the parent and the child. . . . And, Michael and Alex, I love you, and we're going to have the biggest celebration when you get home."

Fifty investigators were put on the case. Hundreds of volunteers searched for the children. Smith helped police do a composite drawing of the suspect, and copies showing a black man in a dark wool cap were posted in store windows, broadcast on television, circulated throughout the state. Dozens of black men were rounded up and questioned. Once again, black villainy and white purity were placed in stark juxtaposition.

And then, once again, the entire fantasy came tumbling down. Smith failed two lie detector tests. Her story about the traffic light didn't make sense, because she insisted that no other cars had been there but the light was set to turn red only if a vehicle approached on the cross street. A few hours after her performance on the *Today* show, she broke down and told the police where to find the children's bodies: still in her car, which she had rolled down a boat ramp and into a lake. Apparently, she was distraught that a boyfriend had broken off their relationship because he did not want to marry a woman who already had children. Convicted of murder, she was sentenced to life in prison. She was twenty-three.

About the same time, in the small town of Dexter, Maine, three white girls reported to police that a seven-year-old friend had been sexually assaulted in a parking lot. The attacker, they said, was a black man in a red pickup truck. There are hardly any blacks in that part of Maine, but a wave of fear swept across the community for five days as police conducted an intensive search for the man and the truck. Finally, the girls admitted that they had fabricated the entire story. In a reflective editorial, the *Morning Sentinel* of Waterville took the measure of white America's credulity:

> "There was no black person," the district attorney, Christopher Almy said. "There was no one lurking in the bushes. There was no red pickup." Except, of course, in the minds of the people in the community, which is unfair and unfortunate. . . . It is unfortunate that some Americans, from rural South Carolina to rural Maine, believe the most plausible villain possible is an African American male. There is a vein of racism still running through our society. It is exposed at odd times, and in bizarre ways.

Something else was significant about the incident in Dexter. It was not reported nationally, only in the immediate region. Perhaps because no murder was involved—and no actual sexual assault, either—it did not reach the threshold of shock needed to propel it into the national news. So it raised a question about how frequently such fantasies and false reports were occurring at local levels. How common was the fictitious black criminal? Could real victims and witnesses sometimes color the assailant black out of a tangle of expectations?

The Color of Law

Data on crime have no pure objectivity. Measuring the incidence of rape or robbery or assault is not like measuring rainfall or temperature. Between the reality and the numbers is an array of lenses and filters that accentuate and distort and ultimately throw into question much of what we think we know when we look at the statistics.

The figures that show high crime rates, especially among African-Americans, bolster racial images that are subject to considerable exaggeration. By every available index, it is true that blacks are more heavily involved in violent street crime than whites. The question is what whites make of that truth. Many believe that the United States has endured unprecedented crime at the hands of blacks, that most blacks are prone to violence, and that whites are at particular risk from African-Americans. None of those deductions can be supported by the data.

The "fact" of rising crime since the 1970s has become a fixture of political campaigns and evening newscasts. Even as rates have dipped in recent years, the impression persists that violent crime has never been worse than in the 1990s. This belief has led to harsher sentences, a building boom in prisons, and sharper racial tensions. But it may be little more than a mirage shimmering up from dubious data compiled by the FBI's Uniform Crime Reporting Program. In a searching history of the Justice Department, *Above the Law*, David Burnham attributes the increasing numbers to several factors that have little to do with how much crime actually occurs and more to do with how numbers are generated. The figures have been driven upward partly by the introduction of new police procedures and technology, Burnham argues, including the following:

• In the 1950s and '60s, before the supposed crime wave of the last thirty years, many precinct commanders "concealed substantial numbers of crimes" to avoid creating a bad record for themselves, Burnham writes; only later did the police realize that higher crime rates would win them higher budgets.

• The gradual introduction of 911 lines across the country has permitted citizens to report crime more easily and has allowed central data collection, bypassing local precincts.

• Until the civil rights movement, during which blacks and other minorities protested a lack of police protection, many departments did not patrol black, Hispanic, Chinese, and other ethnic neighborhoods as actively as they do now. A greater police presence results in more crime reports.

• Police have begun to employ more aggressive techniques, such as decoys—officers who pose as bait for robbers.

• Crimes that previously went unrecorded, such as family disputes and child abuse, are now more likely to get into police statistics.

A great deal of crime still goes unreported to the police, so the actual rates are certainly higher than shown in the FBI's *Uniform Crime Reports*. But that does not necessarily mean that crime has grown more prevalent. Where the FBI shows a trend line upward into the early 1990s, another key source of data describes the rate of those victimized by the violent crimes of robbery, rape, and felonious assault as nearly flat, with a gradual downward slope. This is based on data compiled since 1973 by the National Crime Victimization Survey, in which the Census Bureau asks 50,000 Americans every six months whether they have been victims. The rates are considerably higher than the FBI's, since they include unreported crimes. But the conventional notion that violent crime has soared cannot be supported by the findings. Shifts in the homicide rate also look less alarming when the long view is taken. As compiled from coroners' reports to the National Center for Health Statistics, the murder rate dropped sharply from the 1940s into the mid-1960s, then rose again by the early 1990s to a level just below where it had been in the early 1930s. Since the early 1990s, it has been in a slow decline.

Take this uncertain equation, add the race of the alleged perpetrator, and the question marks multiply. Victims surveyed in 1994 pointed to blacks as responsible for 20.6 percent of the rapes, 51.1 percent of the robberies, and 23 percent of the assaults. Blacks make up 13 percent of the country's population, so these are disproportionately high rates. That same year, blacks accounted for 53.8 percent of the alleged murderers whose race was known to the police. The catch is that in 1989, the fictitious murderer of Carol Stuart would have been listed as one of them.

The figures on arrests, convictions, and prison sentences also paint blacks as overrepresented in violent crime. But there are additional caveats to insert. Arrests are discretionary, and their patterns reflect police policy more accurately than they indicate the distribution of crime. If more police are assigned to a narcotics squad, drug arrests may soar even if drug use remains unchanged. If a neighborhood gets more cops, arrests go up and the figures look like a crime wave. Furthermore, blacks seem to be arrested at rates higher than their rates of involvement, according to discrepancies between the Victimization Survey and the *Uniform Crime Reports*. For example, although 20.6 percent of the rape victims surveyed in 1994 reported blacks as the rapists, 41.7 percent of those arrested for rape in 1994 were black. In the same year, blacks committed 30.4 percent of the aggravated assaults, according to the victims, and accounted for 39.2 percent of those arrested for the crime. By 1994, 32.2 percent of all black males in their twenties were in prison, on parole, or otherwise entangled in the criminal justice system, compared with 6.7 percent of white men in the same age range. More black men were in prison than in college.

For these results to be perfectly fair, blacks would have to commit many more crimes, use much more crack and heroin, and be much more dangerous to society than whites. That is a hard case to make, and many African-Americans think otherwise. They see the old white fear of the black man's violence, that potent mixture of reality and fantasy, driving the laws, the police, the courts. The resulting biases are sometimes coded, sometimes subtle, sometimes difficult to discern. A flowchart of Maryland's juvenile justice system, for example, reveals how the percentage of black youngsters increases at each stage in the process leading to trial. At every juncture where a softer or harder decision is made, at every possible exit from the system where authorities choose either to release the youth to his parents or to send him on toward incarceration, the black child has less chance than the white for a softer disposition. The farther along in the process, the blacker the population. Why? Judges, prosecutors, lawyers, social workers, and criminologists at a conference on the subject offered a host of reasons, some of which may be stereotypes in themselves: More black youngsters may be accused of more serious crimes. They may not be able to afford good defense attorneys. Their families may not be cohesive enough to provide support. The factor of race is not easily isolated.

A similar pattern was noted by the Sentencing Project, a Washington-based advocacy group, which estimated that blacks represent 13 percent of the country's regular drug users, 35 percent of drug arrests, 55 percent of convictions, and 74 percent of those sentenced to prison. A white policeman working the undercover narcotics beat in black neighborhoods of Washington complained to me that his unit would gain credibility with black jurors if the department put as much effort into arresting whites in the clubs on Georgetown's M Street for the drug offenses that proliferate there.

Race and fear were mixed into crime legislation in 1986, when Congress set radically higher penalties for crack cocaine than for powdered cocaine. Crack is sold mostly by small-time black street dealers; the powdered form is smuggled and sold by large narcotics traffickers, most of whom are nonblack. As a result of the new statute, the sale of only 5 grams of crack (less than 18 percent of an ounce) brought a mandatory five-year sentence on the first offense. It took 500 grams of powder to trigger the same penalty. A mandatory ten-year sentence kicked in at 50 grams of crack and 5,000 grams of powder.

The hundred-to-one disparity was widely perceived in black communities as an unvarnished attempt to target young black men in inner cities while going more easily on nonblacks in the upper levels of the drug trade. That may not have been a conscious goal of the legislators, but the rhetorical mood of the time was infused by the specter of crack as an extremely dangerous narcotic in the hands of young blacks with guns. There is no denying the wave of violence that has surged over the crack business as shoot-outs have erupted, catching innocents in the cross fire and turning children into both victims and murderers. Homicide among black youths is the one area of violent crime that has, in fact, risen precipitously. From 1960 to 1993, the death rate by homicide among black males between the ages of fifteen and twenty-four nearly quadrupled, from 46 to 167 per 100,000, compared with a similar jump, but at much lower levels, from 4 to 17 for white males in the same age group. In 1994, that rate dropped to 158 for blacks and stayed about the same for whites. Among black males from twenty-five to thirty-four, the rate has been declining since 1970.

Crack is so easy to buy and so easy to use that youngsters are easily hooked. The crack subculture would be scary even without race; add race, and it seems more terrifying to many whites. In 1995, however, the U.S. Sentencing Commission found no scientific basis for the belief that crack was more dangerous than powder, and it recommended that the penalty differences be eliminated. "Injecting a solution of powder cocaine produces the most intense physiological and psychotropic effects," the commission wrote. "Smoking crack cocaine produces somewhat less intense effects, and snorting powder cocaine produces even less intense effects."

Because crack can be distributed simply and sold relatively cheaply in single doses for $5 to $20, it has become more popular in low-income neighborhoods than powder, which is sold by the gram at higher prices. Crack is peddled on street corners and in well-known crack houses, where the police can easily spot the low-level dealers, who tend to be younger than those selling powder.

Cocaine usage is not as widespread as commonly believed (involving 0.7 percent of the population aged twelve and over in 1995, down from 3 percent in 1985), and 83 percent of those who have used it at least once in their lives are white, according to federal studies. Only 1.1 percent of the blacks who were surveyed, 0.7 percent of the Hispanics, and 0.6 percent of the whites reported having used cocaine in any form. Among those who had ever used crack, 70 percent were white, 19 percent black, and 9 percent Hispanic.

It is traffickers, not just users, who are prosecuted under federal law, and here the disparity between crack and powder delineates a stark racial divide. In 1993, 89.5 percent of those convicted for crack were black, and 4.2 percent were white. Only 30.2 percent of those convicted for powder were black, while 35.3 percent were white. Furthermore, the Sentencing Commission found that "retail-level crack offenders are being sentenced like wholesale-level offenders and importers who traffic in other drugs," including powder cocaine, heroin, and methamphetamine.

The five-member Sentencing Commission, made up of three sitting federal judges and two former U.S. attorneys, usually sees its recommendations translated directly into policy. Only Congress can block them. But in this instance, both the Clinton administration's Justice Department and the Republican-controlled Congress reacted with all the sweet reason of a bull sitting down on a bee. The Justice Department conceded that the disparity in sentences "appears to have a racially disparate effect when applied neutrally by prosecutors and judges." But to eliminate the difference for racial reasons, the department argued in a snide memo to the commission, would be as sensible as equating the penalties for violent and nonviolent crime because blacks were more involved in the violent kind. In October 1995, both houses of Congress voted overwhelmingly to retain the more severe sentences for selling crack, and Clinton signed the measure. It was the first time that Congress and the president had ever intervened to thwart the commission's recommendations.

Bobby Rush is no longer a Black Panther. He is a congressman. Middle age has softened him. He wears glasses, a mustache, and a short beard and adopts a relaxed, reflective air more like a professor than a politician. He speaks in slow moderation about the concerns of his district, which is carved like a piece of a jigsaw puzzle, its fattest part in the virtually all-black South Side of Chicago and a thinner protrusion into the white suburb of Worth Township. In the interest of justice, he voted to eliminate the gap in sentencing between crack and powder. Yet his constituents of both races care very much about crime, and therefore it is very much on his mind.

Ten days after he was first elected in 1992, he addressed a celebratory gathering of his precinct captains and organizers at his headquarters, a storefront in a run-down shopping center just off Martin Luther King Jr. Boulevard. In a large room with picture windows sealed from the street by drawn venetian blinds, about fifty campaign workers, including a smattering of whites, sat on folding chairs and stood along the sides and the back. The crowd was full of friendliness and deep satisfaction, fed by its candidate's landslide, with 83 percent of the votes, over a black Republican.

"I'm not going to Congress with a chip on my shoulder, wearing a beret and sunglasses and a bandolier," Rush told them. "They're going to see the nicest—nice but firm, humble but direct. I'm gonna make friends and influence people. We've had enough of people with shrill voices. They hate everything white, including that white paper in front of them. But they ain't done nothing for black people."

Murmurs of approval floated up from the audience. Bobby Rush had made a long journey. In the late 1960s and early 1970s, a time of militant rhetoric and clashes with police, he had been "defense minister" and then head of the Black Panther Party's Illinois chapter. He had served a short prison sentence on a weapons charge. And in 1969, he happened to leave the apartment of Panther leader Fred Hampton just before fourteen Chicago policemen stormed the place, killed Hampton in his bed, killed another man, and wounded four. An investigation concluded that almost one hundred shots had been fired, all but one by the police.

Now Rush was telling campaign workers how tough he would be on crime. "We are not going to neglect the urban areas where we've lived all of our lives," he declared. "The urban agenda is on the front burner. We've got to talk seriously about crime. You don't want us to go there coddling criminals, right? You're the victims of crime, right? Nobody can tell us about crime in our communities. You don't want nobody to come and take our money, 'cause we've been working." The audience heard him warmly and agreed. They could have been white suburbanites, obsessed by crime, and he could have been a white Republican, responding to their fears.

Later, after he had reviewed his captains' accomplishments precinct by precinct, after he had bestowed thanks and congratulations on one after another, after a minister had closed with a prayer, Rush retreated to his small office in the back, where he settled down in a brown leather chair behind a wooden desk. I wanted him to elaborate on his remarks about crime, since crime among blacks had been a convenient vehicle for racist attitudes among whites.

He nodded. "I think that blacks are probably more in favor of strong law enforcement programs and policies than some whites are," he replied. "The way I see it, there's more probability of someone shooting me or one of my loved ones in my neighborhood. . . . I'm more prone to be a victim of crime, no matter what my lofty position might be, than 98 percent of whites. Now, intelligence should dictate that I'm for law enforcement. But on the other hand . . . I want to eliminate and resist the racial excuses that some law enforcement officials use in terms of misapplying or misdirecting their aggression. OK? Some of us, we're uniquely positioned to do that. We can stand up and we can talk about we want more police officers in our neighborhoods, we want better police patrols in our neighborhoods. . . . We want people who commit crimes to be punished. But on the other hand, we abhor the fact that there's more money being given to building prisons than there is for drug treatment centers or for providing job training programs."

His sense of being at greater risk than the vast majority of whites is supported by the data. White fears about black criminals contain a simple irony: Most victims of black criminals are black. To the extent that police believed that they knew the race of those who committed homicides in 1994, the vast majority of the murderers and their victims were of the same race. In general, most murders are committed by relatives or acquaintances of the victims; only about one-fifth are by strangers.

U.S. Homicides, 1994

Races Involved	Number
Black murderer, black victim	5,106
White murderer, white victim	4,445
Black murderer, white victim	790
White murderer, black victim	337

Similarly, most rapes do not cross racial lines. According to 1994 victims' reports, 78 percent of the rapes were white on white. Where blacks were identified as the rapists, 57 percent of their victims were black and 40 percent were white. The Victimization Survey found that only 2 percent of the rapes committed by whites had been against blacks; in 1992, no blacks reported being raped by whites.

Robberies with injury followed a similar pattern: 65 percent of the black perpetrators targeted blacks, and 35 percent targeted whites. Blacks were the victims of whites in only 4 percent of the cases. Assault was the only violent crime that went the other way: 58 percent of the black assailants attacked whites, and 40 percent made blacks their victims.

In all categories of violent crime, however, most of the attacks suffered by whites came from other whites, as shown in the following table.

Percentage of White Victims by Race of Offender, 1994

Type of Crime	Race of Alleged Offender		
	White	Black	Other or Unknown
Murder	83%	15%	2%
Rape	78	10	12
Assault	75	15	10
Robbery with injury	59	25	16

As the table shows, only a small fraction of the whites who are murdered, raped, assaulted, or injured during robberies are victims of African-Americans; most are attacked by whites. If fear were logical, whites would be more afraid of other whites than of blacks.

In all my travels and interviews across the United States, I rarely met a black male who had not been unjustly hassled by a white police officer. He might have been driving late at night through a white part of town, driving a fancy car, riding his new bike in front of his own house, or simply strolling back to his dorm at Princeton. The three-piece suit may be a defense, but not always. As a rule, the humiliation cuts across lines of profession and class. Among those who are routinely pulled over and questioned are off-duty black police officers themselves. Only when they flash a badge does the harassment quickly come to an end.

Sergeant Larry Jones, a nineteen-year veteran of the Baltimore police, was wearing a sweat suit and a baseball jacket on his day off and was driving his year-old Mazda MX6 through the wrong part of town—that is to say, the white part in western Baltimore. When he saw the lights in his mirror, he stopped. A white policeman approached cautiously, his gun drawn. "Place both of your hands on the dash!" he yelled.

"I am a police officer," Jones replied. The cop merely repeated his order once, twice: hands on the dash. Finally Jones realized that the cop was seeing but not hearing, seeing his fellow policeman as a casually dressed black man in a too-nice car, not hearing him as a police officer trying to identify himself. Before long, Jones was surrounded by ten white cops. The mood was nasty. They were about to search his car when "one officer finally recognized me," Jones said, "and asked me if I was Sergeant Jones from the Eastern District, and I said yes. And every last one of them disappeared, leaving that poor officer there that had initially stopped me." Jones asked why he had been pulled over. Because a helicopter patrol had reported his making a left turn through a red light, the officer explained. Jones denied it, but added a more pertinent question: "It took ten of you to stop me for a red light? Is this proper procedure, to stop a person with your gun drawn?"

"If you're a sergeant," the officer replied, "you should know this. This is the Western District."

Jones shook his head, drove off, and wrote a stinging article for the newsletter of the black police organization, the Vanguard Justice Society. "This humiliating, insensitive, and thoughtless practice has a name," he said. "It is called 'profiling.' Profiling is the act of categorizing, the targeting of a particular group or culture with a view towards labeling those individuals law enforcers believe are engaged in illegal activities. . . . Officers dedicated to servicing and protecting citizens cannot allow this 'profiling' disease to eat away at the fabric of reasoning, training, and rational thinking."

But they do allow it, as Lieutenant Barry Powell of the Baltimore police has discovered. Raised in East Baltimore, Powell wears the uniform well on his tall, thin frame. He is meticulously polished in his starched white shirt with its gold badge on the pocket and single silver bars on the collar. His black tie is perfect, his dark blue pants are sharply creased, and his black shoes are spit-shined. In civilian clothes, however, he has been stopped in the District of Columbia (by three white cops and a black who accused him of stealing his own car), in Baltimore ("We're just checking everybody out"), and in Prince George's County as an eighteen-year-old police cadet. That was in the early 1970s, but the memory is like a vivid videotape that plays again and again through his mind. It was late; he and three friends were lost. They stopped by a pay phone at a darkened shopping center to call for directions, and when they started to leave, a patrol car pulled them over. Powell tries to smile as he re-creates the dialogue:

"What you boys doing out here at the shopping center? Can't you see it's closed?"

"Can't you see that one person got out to use the phone?" Powell retorted.

"Oh, you getting smart, boy?"

"No, I'm trying to find my way to where I'm going. I'm lost."

"Well, let me see your registration."

"I'm not driving. My friend is." The cop looked at the friend's license, then asked Powell for some identification. Powell produced his police ID.

"Oh, you got a gun on you?" the cop asked.

"What are you, you ignorant or something?" Powell answered. "You see it says 'cadet.' Cadets in the state of Maryland don't carry guns."

"Oh, you're smart."

"No, I'm not smart. But you're trying to agitate me, and I haven't done nothing. Nor have my friends done anything. I think I have as much right to be here and make a phone call as you have to be on duty." So the cop returned his ID and told them to leave.

No black (and probably no white) who was not a policeman and was in his right mind would talk back to a cop that way on a dark, deserted street. Powell doesn't recommend it, either. "Don't give the police any reason to further abuse you," he advises. "Don't give them a reason to put handcuffs on you if you're not doing anything. Realize that some of them have certain attitudes and certain biases—and not that it's right, but that at that particular time, they've got the upper hand. So let us— the citizens—let us be the ones to be cool."

This kind of harassment does not happen to me, I explain. "You don't fit the profile," the lieutenant says with a smile. "You don't fit the profile that everybody puts out: Black is more likely to commit a crime, black is more likely to be involved in street-level narcotics. . . . So knowing that, and knowing that the police officer is supposedly there to protect the society, he feels or she feels that this is what they're supposed to do."

They certainly do it actively. Walterene Swanston worried every time her teenage son drove her old Mercedes from their home in suburban Virginia into Washington. "He'd get stopped. I mean, he'd just get stopped," she said. "He'd find himself in blocked alleys with police cars." Doug and Nancy Deuchler's son Tim, at age seventeen, was detained and delivered home by the Oak Park police for standing in a friend's yard at midnight, after curfew. "Had he been white, I don't think he would have been picked up," said his father. When Roy Gordon's bi-racial adopted daughter went out with black friends in the San Francisco area, "you could guarantee that their car would be stopped by a police-man," he said. "They just accept it; it's just part of life." A group of black Princeton students driving back to campus were pulled over by the town police and asked where they were going. A couple of black students, after dark, were made to produce their IDs for the campus police. Whites do not receive the same attention.

A computer conversation among Los Angeles policemen made the point graphically:

"U can c the color of the interior of the veh . . . . dig."
"Ya stop cars with blk interior."
"Bees they naugahyde."
"Negrohide."
"Self tanning no doubt."

Police brutality can also be white on white, black on black, black on Hispanic, or any other permutation. In Compton, California, a Latino teenager was videotaped being beaten by a black policeman. In Gadsden, Alabama, it took a black city councilman, Robert Avery, to make enough noise to stop white cops from abusing whites. "They just dog-beat white prisoners," Avery said. "I've got a situation where we had an individual who had already been arrested and was handcuffed and was in the process of being booked, and a police officer took him and slammed his head up against a brick wall. He got fourteen days off for it."

In South Central Los Angeles, a sixteen-year-old drug dealer named Denzil, a bright-eyed boy with an impish smile and curly shoulder-length hair, noticed that the presence of white cops could make black cops harder. "When you're driving in a car and there's three people or maybe four people in the car, you always up to something, in the police eyes," he said. "They're telling us, 'Too many black heads together. You-all are gonna do something.' . . . Sometimes black police try to show off for the white cops—you know, frisk you all hard, and you're like, 'Damn, brother, what's going on?' . . . When there's two blacks, they be cool. Sometimes, not all white police is like that, though. Some white police is just as cool as the next."

Some, perhaps most. But not the two white Detroit officers who beat a black steelworker to death with their metal flashlights in 1992; they were sentenced to prison terms of eight to twenty-five years. And not the four who were videotaped beating Rodney King. As the blurry images of King crouching, kneeling under the blows, were broadcast again and again, a line was drawn through the nation—not between those who thought the officers were justified and those who did not. It was hard to find whites who would defend the policemen, and when the mostly white jury in their state trial found them not guilty, a wave of disgust and outrage swept across white America.

The divide came along a different line: It separated those who were shocked by what they saw on that tape from those who were not surprised at all. In that way, it divided most whites from most blacks as decisively as a wedge splits a log. By and large, whites were stunned. African-Americans were infuriated but not amazed. This was not a new phenomenon to them. They had heard something like it described by close friends and relatives, had seen it with their own eyes, or had been through it themselves. The racial frontier, then, was a boundary between surprise and nonsurprise, and from each side blacks and whites saw very different pictures as they gazed at their country. As Jesse Jackson explained, one looks at a shiny red apple from above, while the other sees its rotten, worm-eaten bottom from below—same apple, two views.

Rodney King was an unlikely hero. He had been drinking and smoking marijuana before getting into his white Hyundai and tooling along Interstate 210 in Los Angeles. He was on probation, having been released three months before from a two-year prison sentence for armed robbery. Therefore, when a California Highway Patrol car tried to stop

him for speeding just after midnight on March 3, 1991, he was afraid
that his parole violation would send him back to jail. So he drove faster,
leading police on a chase at speeds variously put at 70, 80, 115 miles an
hour. Calls went out over police radios, and Los Angeles policemen
joined the pursuit; they ultimately became the offending officers. When
King finally pulled over, he put his hands on the steering wheel, then got
out, followed officers' instructions to lean on the car so they could frisk
him, took a few steps back, and lay facedown on the ground so he could
be handcuffed. He was eventually surrounded by twenty-one officers,
twelve of whom had come to the scene out of curiosity, even after radio
messages that no further help was needed.

King was unarmed. Whether he lunged at one of the cops or not,
whether he tried to run or not became a matter of dispute. The police
said that they believed he was dangerously high on the drug PCP,
although blood tests turned up only alcohol and a trace of marijuana. They shot him with a Taser stun gun, which delivered an electric
jolt; taunted him with shouts of either "What's up, killer?" or "What's
up, nigger?" (King was not quite sure which); then beat him and beat
him and beat him—fifty-six blows with clubs and six kicks during the
eighty-one seconds that George Holliday, who lived in a nearby apartment, happened to videotape. Afterward, nurses at Pacifica Hospital said
that the policemen who had brought King in for treatment "openly
joked and bragged about the number of times King had been hit."

Twenty minutes earlier, Officer Lawrence M. Powell, who landed
the most blows, had responded to a call about a dispute in a black family.
He had typed out a message on the portable computer in his squad car
describing the episode as "right out of 'Gorillas in the Mist,' " a film
devoted to the study of primates in Africa. The dispatcher responded by
mocking black dialect: "hahaha . . . let me guess who be the parties." The
exchange confirmed what black citizens of Los Angeles had long recognized in their police department. When Powell's raw racism came to
light, many whites were shocked once again.

The four officers were tried in suburban Simi Valley, where many
policemen reside, where the black population is minuscule, and where
every prospective black juror was honest enough to admit that it would
be impossible to be impartial. Consequently, no blacks got onto the
jury, which comprised ten whites, one Filipino, and one Hispanic. On
April 29, 1992, the jurors reported that they could not agree on one
charge against Powell, but on the rest they voted with resounding unanimity: Not guilty. Abiding fear had scored a victory over decency.

"These officers don't get paid to lose street fights," Powell's lawyer,

Michael Stone, had said in closing arguments. "They don't get paid to roll around in the dirt with the likes of Mr. King. If we as members of the community demand they do that, the thin blue line separating the law-abiding from the not-law-abiding disintegrates."

The thin blue line. The separation. The disintegration of the protective wall around the fortress of civilization. The apocalyptic vision was hammered home by Paul dePasquale, attorney for Timothy E. Wind, one of the officers. "This unpleasant incident is what we have police for. The circumstances here were consistent with the job the man was hired to do. He was part of the line between society and chaos." Society and chaos. Did these men truly not understand what chaos would be bred when those charged with upholding law and order abandoned law and became agents of disorder?

South Central Los Angeles erupted. Later, blacks who wishfully thought that power could be realigned called it "rebellion" and "uprising." But it was just a riot. It was a convulsion in a simmering fever of rage among people too abused by the police, too impoverished by the economy, too marginalized by the society to have much stake in the preservation of neighborhood or system. At its most dramatic level, it looked black and white. A white motorcycle rider on his way to help fix a black friend's car was beaten to death by blacks. A white truck driver, Reginald Denny, was beaten nearly to death by black youths, one of whom was captured on television doing a victory dance over the man's limp body. In many white minds, these scenes overlapped the image of Rodney King being broken by police batons and reinforced the durable notion of blacks as violent criminals. But other blacks rescued Denny, and Denny himself was generous in harboring no resentments. Furthermore, the fires that were set and the looting that was done relied on a multiethnic cast. Many targeted stores were owned by Koreans, but some Koreans who were good to neighborhood people were deliberately spared, and some blacks who cheated were burned out. Of those arrested, only 36 percent were black. Some fifty people were killed, and more than $1 billion in property damage was done.

In the midst of the riot, Rodney King appealed for calm, asking his simple, sad question to which Americans already knew the answer: "Can we all get along?"

After the acquittals, the Justice Department decided to prosecute under federal civil rights statutes, and one year later, a federal jury found that Powell, "while acting under color of law, willfully violated Rodney King's constitutionally protected right to be free from the use of unreasonable force during arrest." His superior, Sergeant Stacey C. Koon, "while acting under the color of law, willfully violated Rodney King's constitutionally protected right to be kept from harm while in custody." Both officers were sentenced to two and a half years in prison.

It is entirely likely that mixed into the bully mentality of such policemen is a measure of fear. They have spent enough years rubbing up against people who are not exactly model citizens, and they have seen enough of them pull guns, to be wary and scared. When the old prejudices about violent black men are added to the brew, spiced up by crude talk and true stories around the station house, the chemistry gets explosive.

Among the most vulnerable victims of the macho anxiety are black undercover cops. By virtue of their assignments, they must look like anything but policemen. They must dress down to their roles to blend in. And they carry guns, of course. As a result, white officers sometimes see only black, and black means bad, tough, dangerous. So it was with Reggie Miller, who was working undercover on a prostitution investigation in Nashville. When a white officer noticed that his police-issued, civilian-looking truck had an expired license, he ordered him over. He drove another few blocks so his cover wouldn't be blown in the neighborhood. Then he reached down to pull the emergency brake, and the officer thought he was reaching for a gun. Backup units were called, and five whites pulled Miller from the truck, gouged his eyes, and kicked him in the groin before his sergeant came to the rescue. Two of them were later fired.

In a New York subway, Desmond Robinson, a black transit policeman, was on pickpocket patrol when white officers, arresting two youths with guns, spotted him with his semiautomatic weapon drawn. Officer Peter Del-Debbio fired into Robinson's back and then kept firing after he was on the ground, hitting him four times and leaving him with nerve damage and constant pain. This followed another shooting in which white officers fired twenty-one times at a black transit cop, hitting him with three bullets. The incidents were just the tip of the iceberg, as Craig Wolff of *The New York Times* discovered when he interviewed a dozen black and Hispanic undercover officers. One black transit policeman, identified as "Michael K.," told Wolff that he had wrestled a suspect to the ground and was holding his pistol to the man's head when a white officer took aim. If Mike and the white cop had not worked together, if Mike had not known the cop's name was Joe and had not yelled, "Joe! Stop! It's me!," Mike would have been dead. In a smaller fraction of a second than it took to pull the trigger, Joe suddenly recognized his colleague, felt his knees go weak, and brought his gun down. Shaken, he stammered, "Oh my God, Mike. I didn't know. All I saw was a black guy with a gun."

Faceless black guys with guns seem to dance grotesquely through the nightmares of many white officers across the country, releasing racial stereotypes in bursts of ugliness. In Los Angeles, written police communications by computer left a rich record of racism for the commission that was convened after the Rodney King beating. In one exchange, officers bragged to each other about being ready to shoot people. "A full moon and a full gun makes for a night of fun," wrote one.

Another answered, "Everybody you kill in the line of duty becomes a slave in the afterlife."

"Then U will have a lot of slaves."

Making fun of black accents was a favorite theme. "Wees be reedy n about 5," an officer wrote. "Wees also bees hungry."

References to blacks were often surrounded by allusions to the primitive, or to animals, as in Powell's reference to *Gorillas in the Mist*. "I'm back over here in the projects, pissing off the natives," said one officer. "I would love to drive down Slauson with a flame thrower . . . we would have a barbeque," said another. "Sounds like monkey slapping time," wrote a third. In one exchange, as policemen told each other jovially that they were out "huntin' wabbits," one typed out, "Actually, muslim wabbits." In the exchanges about the King beating, the watch commander's desk at Foothill Sration responded to a gleeful report about the "big time use of force" with the remark, "Oh well . . . I'm sure the lizard didn't deserve it. . . . HAHA I'll let them know OK." The uninhibited nature of these slurs suggested officers' confidence that they would suffer no consequences, a reasonable belief given the views of the police chief, Daryl F. Gates. After three black prisoners died from choke holds in 1982, he commented that in blacks, "the veins or arteries do not open up as fast as they do in normal people."

In 1992, a one-page letter signed "For God, Race and Country" by Charles Lee, Grand Dragon, White Camelia Knights of the Ku Klux Klan, began landing on desks throughout the Harris County Sheriff's Department in Houston. In seven cunning paragraphs, the Klansman expressed sympathy with the frustration among white sheriff's deputies, called them victims of "anti-white unprofessional attitudes of some Black Officers," and said they had every right to take early retirement and work elsewhere "to get away from this White bashing that seems to be a constant burden on our Race." Noting that Houston had become mostly nonwhite and that "Harris County is not far behind," he played to the concerns about family and safety by writing, "One of the greatest dreams most of us have is to live in an area where our wives and children can live without fear, Houston and Harris County is [*sic*] not such a place." He asked them to "please read the enclosed literature," which "is not to persuade you to join the Klan but to give you a better understanding of our ideals and our beliefs."

The enclosed literature was emblazoned with a photograph of a hooded Klansman holding a flaming cross, and it contained the usual mélange of Bible, ethnocentric American history, vicious caricatures of blacks, and classic anti-Semitism, including the assertion that Jesus was not a Jew. The material was sent to ranking officers by name through the regular U.S. mail, according to Major Mark Kellar, an aide to the sheriff. Kellar received the packet himself. "We opened it, and I read it, and everybody on the staff read it," he said. "I know that several of the captains out in the districts received the same thing. Apparently it was a mail-out kind of thing. So what? They have a right to mail literature." The so-what feature of the episode came when the literature was then circulated through the internal mail system of the sheriff's department. Perry Wooten, chairman of the Afro-American Sheriff's Deputies League, learned of the internal distribution when a black secretary intercepted it, photocopied it, sent it on, and gave the copy to the league. Kellar professed to know nothing about the use of internal mail, but he insisted that if anybody in an administrative position, unprotected by the civil service, were a member of the Klan, "I would say they'd probably be terminated by the end of the day."

To Wooten, however, the likelihood that sheriff's deputies were sending Klan literature around the department fit the anti-black atmosphere that he and other officers had been struggling with for years. The former mayor of Houston, Kathy Whitmire, agreed. "I'd say he's right," she declared. "I'd say he is absolutely right, because in my view that's exactly what existed in the Houston Police Department back in the seventies." Her explanation was political: Harris County is mostly white, and "the elected officials are not in a position to be held accountable by the black community."

Around the time of the Klan letter, white deputies formed a Caucasian American Police Association with about two hundred members as a show of white solidarity. A United White College Fund was set up as an answer to the United Negro College Fund. A white deputy drew a semicircular configuration on the floor of an officers' dining room and asked a black deputy what it was. The correct answer: "That's when the Klan is throwing a nigger down a well," Wooten reported.

Wooten was a short, dark, muscular man with a thick neck and biceps that bulged like a prizefighter's. He draped his gun and gun belt on the brown vinyl couch in his league's sparse office and lit up a cigarette. As he spoke, he seemed to channel every ion of energy through an unwavering stare that locked the listener into intense attention. Nothing in his appearance showed the pain that could be heard in every word. On each sleeve of his blue uniform, he wore a blue, gold, and gray patch showing a blindfolded Lady Justice holding scales, and the words SHERIFF—PRIDE OF TEXAS.

"It is widespread," he said. "It is very blatant. It is hard-core, real blatant, abusive, and I would say even criminal, the type of things they do, the mentality. The mentality frightens the hell out of me, because you've got all these guys wearing guns. Put badges on them, and you legitimize the Klan."

Wooten listed several incidents: a white sergeant renowned for calling blacks "niggers"; a deputy on a jail's PA system announcing, "All right, we're having a nigger count. All niggers line up"; whites sketching plays for the Houston Oilers with the labels "NR," "NL," and "NC" and asking one of the blacks if he knows what that means: "Nigger right, nigger left, and nigger down the center." Several white deputies observed Martin Luther King Jr.'s birthday in 1992 by promoting the idea of a holiday for his confessed assassin, James Earl Ray. At the control center on one floor of a jail, black deputies coming to work at the start of a morning shift found a tape in a cassette player and turned it on. It was a patchwork of songs played on a banjo and sung by white deputies, Wooten said, "about niggers, jigaboos, coons, and everything of that nature, all kinds of filthy racial implications, slurs, about the nigger *Gemini*, taking all the blacks and putting them in a spaceship and the Klan launching it back up to the moon." One song recounted a ride through a neighborhood where "you'll see an old run-down shack and a Cadillac, and two niggers eating out of one can of beans," said Wooten. "It's a good-ol'-boy thing, and they're kickin' it up and having a good time."

Major Mark Kellar listened impassively to my recitation of Wooten's complaints. Then he spoke in a thick Texas accent that made him sound like Lyndon Johnson. Despite his rank, he was a civilian, called "Doctor" by everyone because of his degree in "interdisciplinary education." His thinning hair was combed back across his pale head, his metal glasses gleamed in the institutional lighting of his utilitarian office. He was in charge of the deputies who served as guards in jails and courtrooms.

Kellar acknowledged the "history of racism" in sheriff's departments, especially in the South, but insisted that "tremendous strides" had been made. "I wouldn't for a minute say that there are not individuals within this department who have racist attitudes and beliefs, but I don't think that's reflective of the administration, and I don't think it's reflective of the overwhelming majority of people within our organization. . . . I fail to see that we have problems as far as race relations are concerned." No friction, no remarks? "I do concede that there are remarks made sometimes. I think that those are probably few and far between. Now, again, do you have some people that are concerned about this? Yes, we do. We're all concerned about it. But I think if you take it into perspective, for every person who's hung up on this thing, I submit that we probably have ten or twenty who would feel that we have an excellent department."

The most impressive thing about Kellar was the aura of complacency that shone through his proper words, the bland vacuum where indignation might have boiled. He had a deft deflection for every charge. The PA announcement, for example, was not about a "nigger count" but about a "nana count," white deputies had told investigators. What did "nana" mean? "I don't know what it means," replied Kellar smoothly. How was it explained by the deputy who said it? "He didn't really say." Investigation closed. As for the tape, it was "filthy," Kellar admitted, "like some KKK thing out of the fifties." It had apparently been hanging around the control center for weeks, and lots of deputies had heard it. But everybody denied owning it, and an investigation could never find a specific individual responsible for bringing it into the jail. So no disciplinary action could be taken. Kellar gave no sign of recognizing that his real problem lay not in some single, elusive scapegoat but in a culture peopled by a whole crew of white deputies who enjoyed listening to that stuff. Was there nothing he had done? No retraining, education on racial issues, seminars, workshops? "Well, we do that normally as a part of our ongoing training," he explained calmly. "I'm not sure of the exact courses. . . . If I'm not mistaken, our jail school, under 'interpersonal relations,' includes some of that. I'm not really sure how many hours."

Wooten saw radical contrasts between the white deputies' treatment of black inmates and white inmates, black suspects and white suspects. "How cordial they are with whites," he said, "and how demeaning they are with blacks. You might tell a white to 'Step out of the car, can I see your driver's license, please? What's your name?' He might ask, can he have some water? 'Yeah, go get some water.' If you're black: 'Mothafucka, shut up. Son of a bitch this and this. I'll kick your ass,' et cetera, et cetera, et cetera. Whereas the white person, he could be the scumbag of the earth, the damn serial killer . . . and you treat the serial killer better."

Wooten was convinced that in exercising their discretion to arrest or not arrest, white officers targeted blacks most vigorously. "You can police the black community, but don't you police the white community," he said. "You can arrest all of the niggers down there that you want to, but just don't arrest white folks."

What particularly bothered Wooten was the ease with which the hateful language came tripping off the tongue. "They feel comfortable, and it's fashionable, to be a racist. They feel so easy saying 'nigger.' That bothers me. It feels so easy to tell nigger jokes. It comes too easy. . . . That's only letting me understand and reinforce in my mind that they have to allow *x* amount of blacks to work in law enforcement, but we're only two screwups from being in that jumpsuit behind those bars with the rest of those niggers."

The Simplicity of Conspiracy

"The police are the biggest gang of all."

The words were spoken to a *Washington Post* reporter by Janet Thomas, a thirty-five-year-old medical receptionist in the mostly black South Central section of Los Angeles. In a single sentence, she captured a sentiment that few white Americans could comprehend. Not until the former football star O. J. Simpson was acquitted in 1995 of murdering his ex-wife Nicole and her friend Ronald Goldman did whites get a clear look at the depth of black alienation from the criminal justice system. It was displayed in one of the most haunting visual experiences that Americans have ever shared as a nation—the contrasting faces of whites and blacks as they watched Simpson stand stiffly, turn toward the jury in the Los Angeles courtroom, and then hear the court clerk read "Not Guilty."

At the climax of the nine-month trial, at 10:00 a.m. Pacific Daylight Time on Tuesday, October 3, an estimated 107.7 million Americans, 57 percent of the country's adults, were gathered before television sets to await the verdict. Airline departures were delayed as passengers refused to leave the TV screens in the terminals and board their planes. Long-distance calls through AT&T dropped by 58 percent during the five minutes that it took to read the verdict and poll the jurors. Trading slowed on the New York Stock Exchange.

Cameras across the country recorded the reactions of dismay and jubilation, of shock and celebration, of anger and delight as the line was drawn not between women and men, as might have been expected, but

along that other basic divide: between whites and blacks. At the Juice
Club in Simpson's Brentwood neighborhood, whites who were poised in
tension suddenly dissolved into grimaces of horror and incredulity. A
young white woman's mouth dropped open in amazement; she stared for
a moment at the TV set, then turned away in disgust. In the First A.M.E.
Church in Los Angeles, however, African-Americans jumped to their
feet and cheered in an eruption of joy that reverberated across black
America. Outside the courthouse, blacks raised their hands and fists
and bounded up and down with abandon. Even at a shelter for battered women, black victims of domestic abuse hugged one another and
cheered the acquittal of the black man who had indisputably beaten
Nicole in the years before the murders. Their celebration said forcefully
that race still overpowered gender as a vehicle of identity, grief, and
struggle. At Howard University in Washington, D.C., black students
and faculty exploded in screams, hugs, and gleeful pandemonium. If you
stopped the tape, rewound it, and watched again, you could pick out one
or two black students still seated, looking glum. And in the background,
a white man joined the cheers. But otherwise, the images mapped an
unyielding chasm, a moment frozen by two photographs printed side by
side on the front page of *The New York Times*: on the left, several
whites—a woman holding her hand despairingly to her head, a man with
jaw slackened in gaping disbelief; on the right, several blacks—an ample
restaurateur with her arms outstretched, her mouth and eyes wide in
ecstasy, being wrapped in hugs by two other women. Never before in the
long and sorrowful history of racial conflict on this continent had the
American people watched themselves in such a stark mirror of difference. The reflections they saw were profoundly troubling but also
illuminating.

What had started as a titillating murder mystery of soap-opera significance had taken on the gravest dimensions of the nation's racial fault
line. The interracial marriage, the separation, the love that had soured
into jealous rage, the vicious slaughter itself gripped Americans at some
primal level of dread and fascination:

The black man rises to a pinnacle from childhood infirmity and
deprivation. He not only gazes and whistles at a white woman—
imaginary crimes for which blacks were once swiftly lynched—he mar-
ries her, fathers her two children. Then, according to white policemen,
the black man topples into primitive violence; he stabs, slashes, butchers
two whites. This struck many African-Americans as too close to the
familiar racial parable.

Simpson did not begin as a black hero but as a football hero who preferred the company of wealthy whites. In circles of Los Angeles blacks who tried to help the poor, Simpson was not particularly admired; he was placed disparagingly in the ranks of the many African-American athletes who had moved up and out without looking back. But as the trial progressed, he became more symbol than reality; he became every black man, every black man who dared to marry white, who dared to achieve, who risked being destroyed by the white structure that had elevated him. He became every black man who had been pulled over by a white cop, called "nigger," beaten to the ground, jailed without evidence, framed for a crime he didn't commit. Polls began to show that the prosecution's mountain of evidence—portrayed as more voluminous than in most homicide cases—did not convince most African-Americans. In general, two-thirds of whites thought Simpson was guilty, and two-thirds of blacks thought he was innocent. After the jury made its decision, a *Washington Post* poll found that 85 percent of blacks and 34 percent of whites agreed with the verdict; 8 percent of blacks and 55 percent of whites disagreed.

On the surface, the evidence had seemed persuasive: a bloody glove found behind Simpson's house matching one at Nicole's condominium, where she and Goldman had been killed; DNA tests from three labs matching Simpson's blood with blood found on Nicole's walkway, his Ford Bronco, and the glove; similar tests showing the victims' blood on the glove and in the Bronco; Simpson's lack of an alibi at the time of the murders, when a limousine driver sent to take him to the airport had gotten no response at his home.

However, Simpson's expensive team of defense attorneys and technical witnesses adroitly undermined the credibility of the evidence, in large measure by questioning the reliability of a police department long known for endemic racism. The jury, composed of ten women and two men, including nine African-Americans, two whites, and one Hispanic, seemed ripe for this approach; one could hardly live in Los Angeles and be oblivious to the police department's defects. The defense successfully raised reasonable doubt among the jurors by showing that the detective who had taken Simpson's blood sample had carried it around with him for hours, providing plenty of opportunity to plant it, before logging it in to the lab; that the Bronco had stood unsecured in a parking lot for weeks before the blood samples were collected; that the chain of custody of blood and other forensic evidence had been broken; that the glove was too small to fit Simpson; that the lead detective who had climbed over Simpson's fence without a search warrant and found the bloody glove had a history of virulent racism.

The name of that detective, Mark Fuhrman, quickly grew into short-hand for a piece of the national shame. Earlier, when he had testified calmly as a smooth-faced, clean-cut, and seemingly rational professional, he swore under oath that he had not used the "N-word" in the last decade. Months later, however, it was discovered that he had done taped interviews with a screenwriter over a nine-year period in which he had casually laced the word "nigger" into his conversation forty-one times. That discrepancy became the wedge with which the defense pried open the foul insides of Fuhrman's mind, and although the jury in the courtroom heard only a tiny fraction of his remarks on the tapes, the larger jury in America heard a good deal more. Fuhrman spoke in placid tones of ignoring the requirement for probable cause in making arrests ("Probable cause? You're God"); of officers falsifying evidence by squeezing a suspected drug addict's old scab to make it look like a recent injection ("That's not falsifying a report. That's putting a criminal in jail"); and of beating blacks ("Did you ever try to find a bruise on a nigger? It's pretty tough, huh?"). At one point, arguing against a new police station in South Central, Fuhrman declared, "Leave that old station. Man, it has the smell of niggers that have been beaten and killed in there for years."

Around the same time as these revelations, the country learned that a gang of five policemen had spent at least three years abusing and framing poor blacks in North Philadelphia. After the officers were indicted and pleaded guilty, more than 50 drug cases were overturned, and some 1,400 more, plus several murder convictions, were slated for review. One officer told investigators that his partner had planted narcotics in an upstairs bedroom as they searched the home of a fifty-four-year-old grandmother, Betty Patterson, in connection with suspicions that her three sons had been involved in a murder. Because of the phony evidence, she had gone to jail for three years. None of this was startling news to residents of North Philadelphia; they had long been talking about the bad cops, but nobody outside the neighborhood had been listening. Lynne Abraham, Philadelphia's district attorney, managed a pithy observation: "When the police are indistinguishable from the bad guys, then society has a serious problem."

A serious problem is the deteriorating credibility of the police with jurors, especially black jurors. So distrusted are the police that federal prosecutors said they made a calculated decision in 1997 not to rely heavily on New York City Police Department evidence in the civil rights trial of a black man, Lemrick Nelson Jr., who had been found not guilty by a state jury for the murder of Hasidic scholar Yankel Rosenbaum during 1991 riots in the Crown Heights section of Brooklyn. The tactic worked. After hearing testimony from civilian witnesses, the federal jury convicted him and a second man, Charles Price. An undercover narcotics policeman in Washington, D.C., recalled that after Mayor Marion Barry's drug conviction, it had become more difficult for him, as a white cop, to get black jurors to believe his testimony against black drug dealers. His job was to pose as an ordinary buyer—many whites buy crack cocaine in the ghettos—and then to arrest the seller. But sometimes he would notice that as soon as he raised his hand to take the oath, several black jurors would look away from him, stare at the clock on the opposite wall, or sit skeptically with arms folded. That was enough to tell him that his case was in trouble. Talking about this among colleagues back at the station house, however, he was careful never to mention the race of the jurors in question; he didn't have to, because everybody knew.

The several Simpson jurors who explained their verdict insisted indignantly that race had not been an issue, that their decision had been governed purely by their doubts about the evidence. Brenda Moran believed that the glove had been planted and that blood samples had been handled in a questionable manner. Lionel Cryer pointed to the opportunities for contamination. "It was garbage in, garbage out," he declared. Whether or not racial solidarity with the defendant was a factor, whether or not the jury had been swayed by the advice of Simpson's lead defense attorney, Johnnie Cochran, to "police the police by your verdict," race probably had a diffuse impact. Being black in America tends to heighten one's skepticism of the police. Given the separate worlds in which blacks and whites generally reside, given their disparate encounters with the criminal justice system, at least some of the black jurors undoubtedly required, perhaps unconsciously, that a higher burden of proof be met by the prosecution. A lifetime of racial experience can permeate perceptions and decisions as invisibly as the air we take into our lungs.

Many outraged whites saw only race, and some fell back on timeworn caricatures of blacks to explain the verdict: that the jurors had been emotional, not rational, and that they were too stupid to understand the complex genetic matching of the blood. A New York talk-show host agreed with a caller who said that the average IQ of the jurors must have been about seventy-five. And Gil Garcetti, the Los Angeles district attorney, contended, "Apparently their decision was based on emotion that overcame the reason." To be fair, district attorneys who lose cases routinely make this slur against jurors of whatever race, and Garcetti may not have been thinking in racial terms. But the assessment was shared by 49 percent of the whites versus 14 percent of the blacks who were asked by the *Washington Post* to agree or disagree with the statement "The jury ignored the evidence and decided the case on their feelings and emotions." The notion of the jurors as stupid found less support; only 26 percent of the white respondents thought that the jury "wasn't smart enough to understand the evidence."

Beyond their appraisal of the jury's motives, many whites were astonished and bewildered by the pictures they saw of blacks rejoicing in virtual unanimity. Some whites who knew that I was working on this book asked me to explain. Eventually, I decided to make a suggestion. If you attend school or work with African-Americans, sit down one day with a black person, preferably a male, and ask a simple question: Have you ever been hassled by the police? I guarantee that when you listen to the answer, you'll get an education. You'll learn something about the sense of powerlessness and marginalization that has been imposed on Americans who are black.

The racial disparity in opinions about Simpson's guilt or innocence persisted virtually unchanged through the civil trial in 1997, when a mostly white jury (nine whites, one Asian, one Hispanic, and one black Asian) unanimously found Simpson responsible for wrongful deaths and awarded the victims' families $33.5 million. The public reaction, muted this time, echoed the earlier verdict, with 74 percent of whites and only 23 percent of blacks agreeing that he was guilty, according to an ABC News poll.

In keeping with Alexis de Tocqueville's observation that Americans talk about everything and converse about nothing, most blacks and whites found discussion of the Simpson case impossible, except among themselves. After the verdict in the criminal trial, white and black staff at the Good Eats restaurant in Jackson, Mississippi, clustered separately until a white waiter walked up to Tiffany Francis, a black waitress, and asked, "Can you believe this shit?"

"Yeah!" she said. And that was the end of the dialogue. She had regrets later but could not bring herself to open a conversation. "We didn't talk about anything else," she said. "I guess after seeing my reaction, after seeing his reaction, we didn't talk about it. And I was really wanting to talk to somebody who felt different from me."

Perhaps the rush of joy after the Simpson verdict came from a burst of empowerment, a sudden feeling that black people could finally penetrate the high walls of the system to make something right. That may also have been a source of much of the white distress—the notion of blacks having power, of blacks wielding their authority as unjustly as whites have wielded theirs. Black violence and black power seem part of the same continuum.

Powerlessness contributes to conspiracy theories, and black America is full of conspiracy theories that attribute immense capability and nefarious cunning to such institutions as the Los Angeles Police Department. The force of such beliefs comes partly from the impossibility of proving or disproving them; they lie beyond the reach of evidence. I heard an example as I drove through South Central with the retired gang members, Snoop and Sampson, and the probation officer, Jim Galipeau. Snoop described how the police, in several instances he knew of, had taken care of drug dealers or gang members on whom they didn't have enough evidence. "The guy got, say, a nice blue Cadillac," Snoop said. "They arrests the guy on a trump charge and take him to the police station. Impounds his car. He's in the station waiting to bail out. During the time he's in the station, two officers, all black, put on a black beanie, some local gloves, and get their weapons and drive through his rival gang area, drop the windows out of his car, shoot somebody down, take it back to the lot, put it back. In the morning the youngster bails out of jail, gets in his car, and soon he drives in that area and stops at a gas station, he gets killed." Galipeau said nothing in contradiction.

One of the most popular theories, believed by 60 percent of black New Yorkers polled in 1990, holds that the government deliberately makes drugs easily available in poor black neighborhoods. A 1994 survey found that 80 percent of black men under forty without a college degree subscribed to the belief. The notion gained credibility in 1996 after the *San Jose Mercury News*, in a report that other papers denounced as flawed, asserted that the Central Intelligence Agency had enabled the Nicaraguan Contra rebels to raise money in the 1980s by introducing crack into Los Angeles. Amid a flurry of denials of any CIA involvement, Eden Pastora, a Contra leader, testified before a Senate committee that the Contras had received funds from a man they had not known was a Nicaraguan cocaine dealer in southern California.

Support for the theory of government complicity in the narcotics trade comes from surprising quarters, including some policemen and drug dealers. Denzil, the teenage dealer in South Central, gave a unique response to the standard question of what he wanted to be when he grew up. "I want to be a politician, 'cause they have all the power and all the say-so. If I was a politician, I know I could change this world to help minorities," he said, "because politicians get the drugs in this world, you know? They give us the drugs, and then after we sell it to them, they take us to jail for it. I feel if they didn't want drugs in this country, they wouldn't be here."

The key word is *feel*. The feeling, the hunch, the surmise seemed to govern the views of Richard Wright, a linguistics professor at Howard University. "It's because of the respect that I have for what the white scientific, military, technological, industrial mind has accomplished," he said. "I can't imagine that we are as incompetent as we appear to be in terms of stopping drugs from crossing borders and entering urban centers in the USA."

Perry Wooten, the sheriff's deputy in Houston, had the same feeling, although he conceded that he could not document it with any professional experience as a law enforcement officer. "Just like the Tuskegee thing where they had that experiment," he said, a reference to the federal government's having withheld treatment for 399 poor black men with syphilis from 1932 to 1972. "Sometimes I look at it, and I really think this is what drugs is all about sometimes in our community. I really think they're practicing whole-scale genocide. If it's not a conspiracy, it's something that they feel is acceptable." Otherwise, he insisted, the police could clean it up in no time. "I'll put it this way. I'm aware of police officers on the street allowing it to happen and not busting them if it's in the black community, 'cause it's 'just another bad nigger.' . . . That's the reason why it's flourished. They don't give a damn." (This contradicted his earlier assertion that blacks were vigorously targeted for arrest.)

"Too many big people got too much money tied up in it," said Robert Robinson, president of the NAACP chapter in Bergen County, New Jersey. "Who is making the money off it? It's not African-Americans. We don't have any ships. We don't have any yachts. We don't have any small planes to bring drugs in, and that's how it comes in. So why can't we stop? Why won't we stop? It's become a major industry. Put a kid in jail for drugs, you've got to feed him, so that creates an amount of jobs. You've got a lawyer that's got to get a job. You've got a guard that got to get a job, you know? It costs $35,000 to keep a kid in jail, $20,000 to send him to college.

Surveys have shown that a large minority of blacks—29 percent to 34 percent—believe that the AIDS virus "was deliberately created in a laboratory in order to infect black people," as the question was worded for a *New York Times*/CBS News Poll. The African-American poet Haki Madhubuti agreed. "AIDS came out of a laboratory in the United States and has been dropped around the world," he declared. "It became very clear AIDS is another germ, biological warfare, that whites have created in order to essentially try to maintain their sense of control of the world." The belief has been echoed by John Singleton, the young film director who did *Boyz N the Hood,* and by Abdul Alim Muhammad, the chief doctor of Louis Farrakhan's Nation of Islam. In 1992, Muhammad blamed President George Bush for playing "a leading role in developing a policy of genocide against nonwhite people all over this earth, and we believe that the AIDS virus is a direct consequence of that plotting and planning in secret."

Accepting this scenario requires thorough distrust not only of government but of private medicine, individual research laboratories, the mainstream press, scholarly journals, professors, medical schools, and other institutions ostensibly established to convey information and render aid. To believe in the conspiracy, people must ascribe enormous powers of coordination and control to the white-dominated machinery of society. It is as if people lived so far outside a household that they imagine a grand design whenever a dish is dropped, a phone call is missed, a drain is clogged, or a conversation is misunderstood. It is as if the concepts of inadvertence, accident, coincidence, and incompetence did not apply to the white power structure.

The implicit violence that runs through these conspiracy theories suggests that many African-Americans are as imprisoned in their images of white brutality as whites are shackled to their caricature of the violent black. As in the folklore about "night doctors" seizing blacks for their blood, these notions go back a long way. A mutiny by slaves on the Spanish ship *Amistad,* en route from Havana to Puerto Principe, Cuba, was provoked by a mulatto cook's warning that the white crew planned to slit the slaves' throats, boil their flesh, then salt and dry the meat for later consumption. The Africans believed that the white men were cannibals, and when the mutineers were captured, press reports indicated that the whites believed that the Africans were cannibals. It seems necessary to add that neither was true.

True or fictitious violations of the body, particularly with sexual connotations, have run through much of the black-white relationship, just as in conflicts elsewhere. During the Cambodian war in the early 1970s, troops of the Cambodian government and of the Khmer Rouge guerrillas used to cut off the genitals of each other's dead and stuff them into their mouths. During massacres in Bosnia in the summer of 1995, Muslim prisoners were forced to bite off a fellow prisoner's testicles, a *New York Times* investigation found. Lynchings in the South were frequently accompanied by castration, as if to drive home whites' anxieties about the specter of the sexually aggressive black male. "Many accounts speak of a black man whose attackers presented him with the chilling alternative of either being strung up or 'just' castrated as punishment for having sex with a willing white female neighbor," Patricia Turner writes in her study of rumors and conspiracy theories, *I Heard It Through the Grapevine*. Maya Angelou recalled a lynched man whose body had been thrown into a pond near her grandmother's home. "The man's thing had been cut off and put in his pocket." Lawrence Guyot, a voter registration worker arrested in 1963, was not only beaten, his penis was burned.

These real experiences have created a set of expectations that are easily triggered by rumor. When Norplant was introduced as a long-lasting contraceptive that could be implanted in a woman's arm, the *Philadelphia Inquirer* ran an editorial suggesting innocently, if tastelessly, that welfare mothers be given a financial incentive to use the device. In an uproar of outrage, black leaders accused the paper of devising a scheme akin to forced sterilization, and the *Inquirer* felt compelled to print a retraction. The specter of sterilization also turned up in Turner's research on a host of conspiracy theories directed against manufacturers of consumer items from soft drinks to fried chicken and cigarettes. Coors Beer, Church's Fried Chicken, Kentucky Fried Chicken, Kool and Marlboro cigarettes, and a fruit-flavored soft drink called Tropical Fantasy were all rumored to contain chemicals aimed at the sterilization of blacks. Manufacturers of athletic wear, including Adidas, Converse, Nike, Puma, and Reebok, were said to be linked to the apartheid regime in South Africa or to the Ku Klux Klan. Turner found absolutely no merit in any of these claims, but even some black youngsters who didn't believe the stories avoided the clothing for fear of being assaulted. And many who were skeptical that food companies were trying to sterilize blacks decided nonetheless that they could do without certain brands of cigarettes, fried chicken, and soft drinks, just in case.

Perhaps if Judge Michael T. McSpadden had been tuned in to this long history of real and imagined racial violence, he would not have stepped so unwittingly into the parable. But he had been fascinated for a while with an idea for treating sex offenders that had been tried with some success in Denmark, Norway, Sweden, and Germany: castration to reduce the production of testosterone. According to scholarly studies that he had collected, underlined, and annotated in his office on the seventh floor of Houston's criminal court building, the procedure had reduced recidivism rates dramatically, from as high as 84 percent to as low as 2.3 percent. The judge had written a newspaper article advocating that the method be used, especially since only 200 of the 8,000 imprisoned sex offenders in Texas were receiving psychological help, which didn't seem to work anyway.

One of McSpadden's readers was a twenty-eight-year-old black man named Steven Allen Butler, who had been arrested for raping the thirteen-year-old daughter of a neighbor and longtime family friend. Butler did not want to go through a trial with the risk of an extended prison term, so he offered to plead guilty if he could be castrated instead of jailed. McSpadden approved. He ordered Butler to undergo four psychiatric examinations to be sure that he was of sound mind, that he understood the consequences of castration, and that he was making this decision on his own, without encouragement or coercion. Then all hell broke loose.

In Houston, where McSpadden was known as a "hang 'em high judge" with a "country club mentality," black leaders were incensed. They smelled the stench of raw racism, and they mobilized all the rhetoric, publicity, and countervailing expertise at their disposal to throw a spotlight on the impending outrage. The story got national coverage, bringing Jesse Jackson for a visit with the prisoner. "The judge ought to know that this is a remedy that's beneath the dignity and character of American justice," Jackson declared.

Less diplomatic comments came from Reverend Jew Don Boney, chairman of the Houston chapter of the Black United Front. "Frankly, I think the judge is titillated by the idea of cutting the balls off a black man," he said. The NAACP demanded McSpadden's resignation, calling his decision "an effort to set a precedent and open doors of opportunity to castrate thousands of black males legally." In the end, no doctor would perform the surgery, Butler's family pressed him to withdraw his request, and he did so. McSpadden recused himself from the case.

Three weeks later, when I walked into McSpadden's office, he was still smarting from the charge of racism. He attempted an air of confidence about the correctness of his decision; he even produced a letter from a white prisoner in Dallas requesting castration as the only way to curb the aggressive sex drive that had landed him in jail. Subsequently, in 1997, the Texas legislature legalized voluntary castration for sex offenders. But now McSpadden could not conceal the hurt, which burned with startling clarity in his blue eyes. "I've worked hard at getting a reputation around here," he said wistfully. "If he had been a white, it

would be over by now." Would he do it for a white? "Sure." Never had
he thought of himself as a racist—quite the contrary. And since this was
a Friday, he was going to prove it by taking me along on his weekly
Friday routine: a visit to one of the city's black elementary schools.

McSpadden's office was crammed with memorabilia. Bookcases
running from floor to ceiling were full of thick law books. Walls were
covered with pictures, certificates, honors, his college diploma, and his
law degree from the University of Oklahoma. A five-foot-tall cigar-
store Indian, peace pipes, and other Native American paraphernalia
completed the decor. "I'm one-eighth Cherokee," he said. "My great-
grandfather led the Cherokees along the Trail of Tears." But McSpadden had grown up in discomfort as the only fair member of his family.
Tall and slim, he had longish gray hair with traces of blond that swept
back over the tops of his ears. His blue eyes were set off by a slight tan,
which gave him an outdoor, patrician look. Between his wide black sus-
penders hung a flamboyant green tie with American flags and fireworks;
"Persian War tie," he explained.

After lunch from the seafood buffet at the Courthouse Club, open to
judges, lawyers, and others associated with the courts (a nearly all-white
clientele served by black waiters), we got into his bright red Porsche and
set out for the J. C. Sanderson Elementary School on Houston's North
Side. Every Friday afternoon he visited a different inner-city school to
lecture youngsters on the law, the courts, the penalties for crime, the
virtue of honesty. He then brought classes to his courtroom, let them
watch trials, and showed them what he hoped they would remember
vividly: the holding cells.

The school was a handsome, neat, two-story brick building, and as
we walked in, an unspoken question buzzed around inside my thoughts:
How would he be received? How would the black staff greet this preppy
white Republican who drove up in his flashy sports car and looked more
suited to a golf course than a city school? How would they react to his
vilification as an unalloyed racist?

The answer was unambiguous. When he entered the principal's
office, three black women blossomed into smiles and large welcomes.
Frenda Lightfoot, a teacher, wrapped him in a huge hug. Iris Ashley, the
principal, radiated warmth. When I called her later to check that her
effusive friendliness had not been just for show, she was adamant in her
admiration. "How noble I think what he's doing is, because he's making
such an impact on our students," she said. As for the castration issue, "I
was glad I knew him before it happened," she explained. "I knew he
made the best decision, because I knew him. He just kind of became our

hero. When he comes to the school, the ladies argue about who's going to greet him. He's so genuine." And what about the charges the black leaders have lodged? "Some of them are making names for themselves," she declared. McSpadden's sentiments exactly.

Upstairs, in a fourth-grade class, the judge looked out over the eighteen children, all black, and began by explaining that this morning he had been picking a jury in a capital murder case and that he would take the youngsters on a tour of the courthouse and let them talk to inmates. "What is the first thing that inmates tell kids?"

" 'You should have finished school,' " a girl answered.

"Right. They're gonna tell you to finish high school at all costs. That's what I'm gonna tell you today. What are most of the inmates in for?"

"Doing drugs," said another youngster.

"Right. Doing drugs. Who knows who a drug dealer is in your neighborhood?" Eight children raised their hands, then a ninth, hesitantly. Others seemed on the verge.

"We don't have to tell you who, do we?" asked a boy.

"No. Next time you see them, tell them Judge McSpadden says hello and looks forward to seeing them real soon." The kids giggled and laughed. He warned them that if they were with someone possessing drugs, they could be charged with possession too. Let's say you're in a car, the driver runs a light, the police pull him over, and somebody throws a little bag of cocaine under the seat or out the window. The policeman asks whose it is, and nobody says a word. "Who in that car gets arrested?"

"Everybody," said a girl in the back row.

"Everybody, right. And the penalty is two to twenty years. You'll have a record the rest of your life. If you've ever been arrested for a felony and you're applying for something, you have to put down 'Yes' on the application. . . . You wouldn't be able to get into that college you want to go to, you wouldn't be able to be a policeman or a fireman or a teacher. You might want to be a doctor or a lawyer, and one mistake— being around somebody with cocaine—can ruin your life." And then he asked them what they wanted to be: There were three or four lawyers, lots of teachers, a doctor. He went into a lecture about how much athletes were paid and how little teachers were and how "this society should honor its teachers more." Miss Taylor, the teacher, was beaming and nodding. The children asked him lots of not-so-hypothetical questions about how the law works when somebody tries to kill you and you kill him, when somebody beats up a policeman and the policeman shoots him in the foot, when a woman being chased around an apartment shoots the other person, whether a policeman who stops a car at night will shoot if the driver opens the door and runs away.

"My uncle Charles stole dope from someone and was shot," said a boy in the front row.

"Did he die?" the judge asked.

"Yeah. The guy is in jail for murder." Another boy in the front told a similar story.

"There's another uncle that died," McSpadden said. "The toughest ones I see are the ones where a child is killed," he told them. "Sometimes after the trial, I'll invite the jury in and we'll close the door and we'll all cry." A girl in a white blouse told about her uncle's girlfriend, who called the police to report that he had drugs. The policeman called him racist names, threw him on the ground, and knocked out his teeth. "They shouldn't do that," McSpadden said. "If anybody does that, call somebody a black this or a nigger this or that, you should call the police chief. At the same time, don't use it as an excuse." And then he launched into a little sermon on how they shouldn't ever use race as a reason not to do their very best. Miss Taylor, who was black, was nodding approvingly.

As McSpadden left, a boy asked, "Were you the judge for Mike Tyson?"

"No, I was not the judge for Mike Tyson. If I had been the judge for Mike Tyson, Mike Tyson would have gotten fifty years and not six years." The boy was left looking nonplussed.

All this proved that reality was more complicated than theory, whether conspiracy or otherwise. But the most riveting moment of the visit came somewhere in the middle, when Judge McSpadden asked the little, neatly dressed fourth-graders sitting in their sunny schoolroom, "How many in this class hear gunshots at night?"

Every child's hand went up.

CHAPTER EIGHT

Power

The Natural Order

We are a very tribal people. We take care of our
friends, and I don't have any problem with that. But
black folks ought to be able to have the same empowerment.

—Jim Blacksher,
a white lawyer

The Assumption

The smells of lunchtime meat loaf and coffee smoothed the listlessness
of the large café on Forrest Avenue, just a block from the courthouse in
Gadsden, Alabama. A portly white waitress slid with surprising ease
among the tables, delivering tall glasses of "sweet tea," gravy-covered
plates, and sly remarks of camaraderie. The room undoubtedly contained a multitude of silent grievances, as would any town's main-street
gathering place. But one complaint among them, nursed for twenty
years, was bursting to be heard now, long after it might reasonably have
aged into mellow memory.

Lawrence "Coach" Presley settled onto a hard-backed chair across
from me, just the two of us at a table for four. He was a stocky man, very
dark, in a gleaming white short-sleeved shirt; his gray hair and metal
glasses made him look all of his sixty-seven years. Everybody in town
called him "Coach," from the two decades or more when he had coached
football, basketball, and everything else at the black high school named
after George Washington Carver. With integration, he had moved to
Gadsden High School to be assistant principal and then, for a year, principal. By retiring, he quipped, "I made a whole lot of folks happy."

He was the object of the grudge, and the white waitress the holder of
it. She brought it with the menus, tossing it teasingly into her banter, her
honey voice sliced by a whine. Long ago, it seemed, when she was a student and he assistant principal, she had played hooky one day, and he
had suspended her for two weeks. "My mother, she's settin' right over

there," the waitress complained with a sugary lilt. "She ain't forgiven you in twenty years."

From a nearby booth, a pallid woman turned around. "I'da rather her been in school," she told Coach Presley. And then she turned away from us again. Coach explained gently to the mother's back: Well, those were the rules—cut a day, get suspended. He was not a harsh man, and when the waitress returned with our iced tea, he smiled at her and said, "You put your finger in it? It'll make it sweet."

An anthropologist would have had a field day decoding the saccharine bitterness of this exchange, unraveling the ritual to reveal the doctrine. Perhaps any schoolgirl would remember a suspension, but something else was needed for the memory to burn with such fiery obsession for twenty years. That something was a reversal of power. No upheaval in the normal order of life could quite compare with the disturbing novelty of a black exercising power over a white, especially in Alabama in the early 1970s. How galling for a white mother and daughter to feel helpless before a black man in authority. How vividly the echoes of resentment reverberate into the present.

When the waitress had left us, Coach considered my racial explanation for a moment, agreed that it was possible, but wasn't completely sure. It took a white southerner to be sure. Steve Suitts, the native Alabaman who runs an old-line civil rights organization in Atlanta, listened to the story and instantly recognized the message. His whole face crinkled into a smiling look of understanding, and then he laughed. "That's right," he said. "And that's when you really do get insight into what these little tags mean when they say, 'Hell, no, we won't forget.' "

More than forty years after school segregation was declared unconstitutional, more than thirty years after the Jim Crow laws were erased, more than twenty years after affirmative action began to place blacks in supervisory positions, you would think that whites would be entirely used to blacks in power. Here and there, African-Americans run city governments, police departments, high schools, military units, university programs, corporate divisions, newspaper staffs, and manufacturing teams on factory floors. Probably more white people in America take orders from black people than ever before. Undoubtedly, more whites than ever accept with equanimity the notion of blacks in authority. The sheer force of everyday personal experience can eventually realign the most stubborn of attitudes. Even network television, which holds its finger to the winds of acceptability, has created black authority figures in the roles of police commanders in such weekly shows as *Homicide* and *NYPD Blue*.

Nevertheless, a strain of discomfort remains. White anxiety over black authority runs like a hidden stream that courses underground, erodes the earth, and reemerges now and then. Power in black hands can still surprise, concern, annoy, and frighten. Individual blacks who manage or govern may still defy expectations, violate assumptions, and disrupt some idea about the natural order of things. Moreover, the uneasy sensations are strengthened when African-Americans are taken as a group; white America has been most alarmed not by the injustice of black powerlessness but by the rhetorical assertion of black power. Indeed, African-Americans are often seen by whites as more numerous and more powerful than they are in reality.

Polling shows that most whites imagine blacks as having much better access to the tools and rewards of economic influence than whites themselves do. In a 1995 study, 58 percent of the white adults surveyed said they thought that the average African-American was better off than the average white in terms of jobs. The facts speak otherwise, of course. As of 1994, the percentage of whites in professional or managerial positions outran that of blacks 29 to 19, and the percentage of blacks in low-skilled service jobs outran that of whites 23 to 13.

Similar disparities between beliefs and facts marked other areas. Whites finish college at more than twice the rate of blacks, yet 56 percent of the whites thought that blacks were better off than whites in education. Nearly twice the percentage of whites as blacks are homeowners, and the average value of white-owned homes is considerably higher, but 45 percent of the whites thought blacks had the advantage in housing. And 41 percent said that blacks had higher incomes, although average earnings for black families are less than two-thirds those of whites.

At the heart of this immensely exaggerated view of blacks' position in society is a growing sense of white disadvantage, a broadening tendency by whites to see themselves as victims, to transfer onto themselves the handicaps long attached to minority status. Some whites even imagine themselves as a minority in America, picturing their country being overwhelmed by a burgeoning black population (and inflating the percentages of Hispanics and Asians also). Just as a couple of students at the University of Maine estimated blacks at 50 percent of the American population, white respondents more generally hold the conviction (which blacks share) that the United States is at least one-quarter to one-third black and less than half white. A white woman in Florida who estimated African-Americans at more than half the population refused to believe the actual census figures of 13 percent black and 74 percent white. "That can't possibly be," she said. "The census must not have been done correctly. . . . It's only common sense. They have very, very large families, and there are getting to be more and more of them all the time." Studies have discerned a correlation between the higher estimates and racial prejudice; whites who imagine a greater number of blacks perceive more threat from black influence.

Imagination, not reality, has driven attitudes about power. The real quagmires of blacks' impotence—their tightly circumscribed political influence and their hollow economic stature—have hardly mobilized the country into a consensus of outrage. More emotion is directed against the remedies than against the problems. White anxiety and anger boil up over redistricting, affirmative action, and other government efforts intended to redress the imbalance of power. As a result, integration has failed to keep its promise. True integration means power sharing and has worked only where blacks and whites have both had access to power, as in the armed forces. Integration has not succeeded in institutions where power has been reserved to whites, as in most private corporations, or has been shifted completely to blacks, as in some school systems. Now as ever, power stands like a sentry at the color line.

The initial signal that a white person thinks in racial hierarchies is sent by the first impression, the opening remark, as when a white customer approaches Nancy Deuchler, the black manager of a B. Dalton bookstore in Chicago. "People would come in and ask me for the manager," she said without rancor, as if describing the law of gravity. "You could see they were kind of taken aback. 'Oh.' But then they would just get over that and deal with me." She refused to be bothered by this assumption that a black woman could not run a store. "I have no problems," she said lightly. "I've never had problems."

Still, she mentioned it. She had mentioned it to her husband, too. And other African-Americans mention it as well, sometimes with a shrug, sometimes with indignation, usually with at least a touch of pain. Janet Bowser heard about it from her cousin, a black teacher in North Carolina whose white assistant always seemed to be the one to whom parents went for consultations about their children. Black parents often did the same, sharing the assumption that the white must be the teacher and the black must be the aide. The cousin was frankly annoyed, especially because the white did nothing to correct the parents' misimpression.

As a black basketball coach in New Jersey, Mel Henderson got more loyalty from his assistant. Henderson would run into the assumption the moment he boarded the bus with his white deputy behind him. The white driver "would invariably say to my assistant coach, 'Where are we going, Coach?' Not to me. My assistant was a fantastic guy. He'd say, 'I don't know. You'll have to ask the boss here.'" Henderson ended the slights by switching to a bus company with black drivers. Still, when his team arrived at an opposing school, the welcoming athletic director would look through him as if he weren't there and address the white assistant: "Come with me. I'll show you where you can dress." "This is an everyday occurrence," lamented Henderson, who later became a high school principal in Englewood. "Every day of my life I've got to first demonstrate that I'm where I'm supposed to be and that I'm who I am supposed to be and I'm the one in charge."

Whites sometimes bridle when they encounter a black with more authority—or with the power that is brought by expertise. That might have been happening when a middle-aged white woman asked for help from Mary Bowman, a black librarian at the University of Louisiana in Shreveport. "She approached me with such a superior attitude, I thought she knew what she was talking about," Bowman recalled. "And then when I suggested some avenues to her, to try the *Reader's Guide*, and then move from there to the psychological abstracts, and then I would look at the education index, and she was looking at me, like, as if I was speaking some foreign language. And I realized that she just did not know what I was talking about. So I took her by the hand, just like I would any person, and I explained step by step what she needed to do. Well, she still did not understand. And she went all over the library asking white librarians to help her. And I saw this taking place, and I just kind of sat back and looked." Eventually, Bowman realized that the woman was being cantankerous with everyone, regardless of race, creed, color, or national origin. "At one point, one of my fellow librarians was trying to help her, and she just threw up her hands, and said, 'Mary, will you come and help this person?' I said, 'I cannot help that woman. That's all there is to it. I have tried and cannot help her.'" The woman then demanded Bowman's name so she could make a complaint.

The significance of the event lay in its ambiguity. As a rule, racial attitudes are heavily masked and not easily isolated from the host of factors governing behavior. It takes careful watching and a certain intuition to discern the ingredient of race within the mixture. A lifetime of observing white-black interaction told Bowman that this woman did not fit into the pattern. "I'm in a service position here, and I don't think that most white folks have problems with black people in service positions," she said. "But when black people are in more of a position of authority, that's where the problem occurs. You see, I'm not giving any grades. When a person comes to me, he's coming seeking something I can give to him." Yes, but the something is superior knowledge, familiarity with reference books and other resources of intellectual power, and that can reverse the comfortable relationship. "White people," Bowman added, "are the nicest people in the world when they're trying to get something. They will kiss my butt." She laughed at her own language. "They will be as kind to you as they can be and give you the greatest respect ever, until they have in hand what it is they're seeking, and then they may walk out and say, 'Yeah, that nigger got it for me.' But I have been 'Ms. Bow-man'ed, and 'Yes, ma'am'ed to death, and it's kind of fun. It's all a game; you know what's happening."

When authority is the issue, however, whites sometimes play by uglier rules. Moreover, aspects of the game retain an unhappy continuity across demarcation lines that ought to separate one era thoroughly from another. In 1962, as the South was emerging turbulently from the age of segregation, Charles Hines was a young army lieutenant, eventually to become a major general. Maneuvers with the code name "Operation Swiftstrike" carried him and his self-propelled anti-tank platoon from Fort Bragg, North Carolina, into South Carolina. The countryside seemed to be littered with the letters "KKK," and when the troops stopped for lunch and white officers went to the restaurant, Hines had to eat in the truck. At a traffic circle in Aiken, South Carolina, Hines stood in the road and made the usual pumping motion with his fist as a signal to his vehicles to tighten up their convoy. "The next thing I felt when I turned around was something very hard against my temple," Hines remembered. "And it was a police officer who had taken his weapon out and had placed it against my head, and he said, 'Nigger, I'll blow your brains out if you give me the finger.' . . . And I remember, my company commander came over and said, 'What's wrong?' And he wasn't going to aggravate this guy, 'cause he didn't know. . . . He explained to him, 'He wasn't telling you, up your whatever—he was motioning his unit to close up.'"

In the late 1980s, as a brigadier general, Hines was visiting Alabama on a study for the army. He and his escort officer went to a restaurant for dinner. "We sat there, we sat there, we sat there," Hines said. "No one came. So he got up and went over to find out—he was white—to find out why no one had come to take our order." He didn't get an answer, so he suggested that the two of them walk over to a waitress and place their order. When the white officer asked General Hines, "Sir, what would you like?" the waitress broke out laughing. "Just broke out in hysterical laughter when he called me 'Sir,' " Hines recalled. "And he said, 'Well, what's funny?' I said, 'Carl, I think we better leave.' And he was mortified. He said, 'But I don't understand.' I said, 'I do.' So we just left."

In 1989, after Hines became the first black to command a military installation in the South (Fort McClellan, Alabama), he was welcomed by the nearby community of Anniston in a formal gathering. He cut an impressive figure—his skin very dark, his head bald, his eyes piercing, his voice remarkably gentle for a general's. He wore his uniform with meticulous polish. Even in battle fatigues, which were starched and pressed, Hines gleamed with precision; in dress uniform, his chest was adorned with ribbons. As he stood in the receiving line with his deputy, who was white, he felt a proud exhilaration. Local citizens filed by, giving him their greetings.

Then several people refused to shake his hand. They simply shook hands with his white deputy and the deputy's wife and passed Hines by. He was stunned and saddened, but he refused to be consumed. "I could dwell on that," he declared. "I could say, 'See, I knew I shouldn't come to Alabama.' But I said, 'But look, there were two hundred people in the line, and a hundred and ninety-seven of them shook my hand.' So I feel sorry for the other three for being so stupid, rather than being furious and angry and rebellious. I just feel sorry for the three idiots who didn't feel that they could shake my hand. I feel sorry for those people, I really do. But by and large I love this community."

Compared to the army, the rest of America seems as if it's caught in a time machine, and when military people step on and off base, they seem to travel back and forth between epochs. Not that the armed forces have solved all their racial problems—not at all—but to find patterns in the army as blatant as Hines encountered in the restaurant and receiving line, you usually have to go back twenty or thirty years. In those days, whites who didn't want to take orders from blacks were rewarded with transfers, recalled Sergeant Major Edgar Adams Jr., the black commander of the drill sergeant school at Fort McClellan. A sturdily built soldier with a ready grin, Adams seemed tough and compassionate at the same time. In the late 1960s, he said, "if you was a black drill sergeant trying to make a [white] soldier do what they were supposed to do, they would holler, 'He's prejudiced! He's prejudiced!' " Few company commanders were black back then. "If one of them privates would holler, 'He's prejudiced!' the commander automatically plucked him up and put him in a white drill sergeant's platoon, 'cause they didn't want to deal with the issue. . . . It's not like today. If one of the noncommissioned officers in the drill sergeant school or MP school says 'Adams is prejudiced,' 'OK, come in, let's talk about why Adams is prejudiced. Lay me down some facts. I'm going to look into it, but lay me some facts out.' We stop everything, we do an investigation. They wouldn't do no investigation. They didn't want to hear it. They'd take him and put him over here. That's how we used to deal with it."

By 1973, Adams had developed a more effective tactic. His platoon was lined up one day for the battalion commander's inspection on a base in Missouri. Adams gave his men a quick smoke break, then told them to put out their cigarettes as the commander approached. That was one order too many from a black man to suit a white soldier from Arkansas. "Where I come from," the soldier cracked, "we tell boys like you what to do." Adams kept his cool, told him to douse his cigarette, and added that they'd discuss the comment later.

"After the inspection," Adams said with a smile, "I took him in the little platoon office there, and I made him stand at parade rest, and I said, 'Just tell me exactly what you mean by the remark you made outside.' And I guess, because we were one on one, his whole upmake and his expression changed altogether." It turned out that he came from a rice farm where he had never seen blacks except as field hands, Adams said. "He broke down and began to cry, and it was during that time that I realized that he had never been exposed to blacks, he had never had a black over him. . . . I talked to him. I didn't use any profanity toward him. I talked to him. I was more than nice to him, I think. Since both of us were young, I was more than nice." Adams let out a deep laugh. "I said, 'You know, we live very close together. Can you imagine what would happen if you go around and say "boy"? Now, what you're gonna do when we leave here, I'm gonna get the platoon together, we're gonna go out in the field here'—it was on a Saturday morning—'and I'm gonna let you apologize.' " So the soldier made his apology and got put on a punishment detail for a week. "You do it through education," Adams explained. "But you have to be very patient—very, very patient when you're dealing with soldiers, because they do come from all geographical locations. Very patient and understanding."

Nowadays in the army, whites who have trouble with blacks in authority usually find more indirect means of expression. White subordinates sometimes used passive resistance with Lieutenant General

Andrew Chambers, failing to act vigorously on his commands, going behind his back to pass information and undermine his goals. He couldn't prove that his race was the cause, but knowing the individuals' records, he suspected as much. And he was tuned in to the issue after serving as the army's director of equal opportunity in the mid-1970s, a critical period when basic racial policy was being revised; he retired in the early 1990s.

"If you divide the army into classes," he said, "there are four classes: white males, white women, black males, black women. Sometimes, black men might be even with white women—might. The black women are definitely rated down. . . . My assessment is that it's easy for a white person to accept a black woman if she's in a typical woman's position, like secretary, clerk, or a supply person. But when she is the leader, in charge, it's very difficult."

In civilian life as well, African-American women often encounter double resistance when they attempt to project authority. Mental images confine them by both their race and their sex, and they are twice condemned as they step out of subservient roles. Mary, the black director of diversity planning for a major corporation, was told openly by a white manager that he thought women should stay home and that "people of color" (her term) should go only so high in the organization, "that I was higher than most and I should be thankful for that," she said. "He didn't want me to work for him. I was clearly too articulate, too assertive— which was not viewed as assertive but aggressive."

The terminology betrays the image. From white to black, as from male to female, the adjectives switch as quickly as a blackjack dealer turns a card. An assertive white is an aggressive black. A resolute white is a pushy black. A confident white is an uppity black. And white discomfort with a black who is proud of her blackness, forthright about her views on race, and ambitious in her career is often disguised in reservations that sound nonracial: She has a prickly personality, she has trouble getting along with people, she doesn't work well with the team. Whites themselves may be unaware of how race-based these assessments can be, how their reactions may be distorted by the way in which a person's character traits violate the preferred model of black subordination, acquiescence, assimilation. But there is no doubt that many blacks' careers have been derailed in this netherworld of subjective intolerance. "It is about power," said Mary. "Things start happening, like people get appraisals that are not fair, or that the word is spread that this person is too big a risk and they're radical, that you don't want this person in your organization. So when the person comes up for consideration for promotion or [as a] high-potential candidate, it's amazing that these people don't show up on lists."

Perry Wooten, the sheriff's deputy in Harris County, Texas, identified the same reflexes in his fight to expose racism in the department. "If I drive the old Ford, it's OK," he explained. "If I walk around in a suit like some Billy Bob, I'm OK. But if I dress out in anything over fifty dollars that don't come from the Salvation Army, I'm in trouble: 'That boy's getting too uppity.' So it's the same old thing that come through history: As long as you stay within your place and your confinement, you be subservient, nonaggressive, be seen and not heard, you can make it in law enforcement. As long as you go along with the gang and keep the code of silence, you'll be OK." It is a long-standing tradition for bigoted whites to complain about blacks in fancy suits or fancy cars.

The dynamic operates more subtly against black men and women in corporations, in government hierarchies, and in universities, whose faculty departments search for new professors who will be personally and professionally compatible. White employers often see assertive, independent-minded blacks through a lens that projects them as brash and abrasive. Another favorite word is "arrogant." When a black dean—an open and caring man—had to reject a white mother's appeal of her son's suspension for cheating, she told me repeatedly that she found the dean "arrogant," which he is not at all. That single term carried a heavy and complex burden of insidious expectations and resentments stored up over a lifetime, now released in socially acceptable fashion. Perhaps any stranger with such power over the fate of a child seems to arrogate unwarranted authority to himself. But for the stranger to be black and possess such power is deeply infuriating to some whites. Arrogance implies an exaggeration of one's importance: No matter how courteous the dean's manner, his blackness was supposed to render him unimportant and compliant, and when his power and his adverse ruling clashed with his racial role, he appeared truly arrogant in the mother's eyes.

Unconsciously, perhaps, some whites try to enforce the black's subordinate standing by using his first name or denying him the honorific title he deserves. Some northern blacks who visit their parents in the small-town South are bombarded by the grating sound of whites calling black mothers and fathers by their first names and of their parents calling whites "Mr. This" and "Mrs. That." John Charles Thomas, the first black justice on the Virginia Supreme Court, now back in private practice, was stung by whites' repeatedly calling him "John" instead of "Judge" or "Justice." He would enter a room full of high government officials and hear each judge introduce himself and each official respond with "How do you do, Judge?" Then, at his turn, he would say, "I'm John Thomas," and the officials would reply, "Hi, John." It took him a while to notice, and chances are that the whites involved were not even aware of how reflexively they were diminishing the man. But even close black friends and relatives called him "Justice," he explained. "They surely don't have to do it," he said. "They're proud of it, and they love me, and they want to do it. And so it's an odd thing. It's almost like the people who are closest to you want to give you that title, because they know how hard it is to come by. And then you got people who try to pretend they're close to you—this is when I was a judge—and they would do the first-name thing, making a horrible mistake when it comes to black-white relations."

Like many other slights to which whites are deaf and blacks are keenly attuned, this one comes from slavery, when blacks were given only first names, symbolizing their status as mere property. Today, then, some African-Americans erect defenses against the practice. "I stopped saying 'John Thomas,' and I started introducing myself as 'Judge Thomas' so nobody would do that anymore," the judge explained. "This is an ancient thing. I know black women in the South who will only introduce themselves as 'Mrs. John Doe' because they know if they say 'Mary Doe,' a store clerk will say, well, 'Mary' this and 'Mary' that. And to stop that they'll say, 'I'm Mrs. John Smith,' and then the clerk has to say 'Mrs. Smith.' "

For whites, the use of a first name is often meant as a sign of intimacy, not disrespect; the line they are crossing is one of familiarity, not authority. Whites can therefore be confused by blacks' intimacy with one another, as when African-Americans refer to Jesse Jackson as "Jesse" and Clarence Thomas as "Clarence." Whites then pick up the style, not realizing the insult it carries when it comes from their lips. In an essay on the nomination of Clarence Thomas to the Supreme Court, Michael Thelwell, a black novelist who teaches at the University of Massachusetts, repeatedly uses the judge's first name alone and then chides the White House for doing so. "For these White House aides it had been 'Judge Ginsburg will' or 'Judge Bork won't,' but in this case, at least in the beginning, it was 'Clarence will,' 'Clarence thinks,' etc. Black people, being cursed with oversensitivity, notice such things, as someone else must have, for it abruptly ceased."

The justifiable "oversensitivity" also brought protests in 1991 when the U.S. Postal Service issued sheets of stamps honoring a black inventor, Jan Ernst Matzeliger. "Jan invented and patented a shoe-lasting machine," the marginal notes explained. When complaints were made about the use of the first name alone, the post office dismissed it as "an editorial slip" that did not justify reprinting 150 million stamps. But some prominent African-Americans saw deeper themes of condescension, whether intended or not. "By using 'Mr.' or 'Mrs.' the speaker acknowledges that the black is an adult," said Ethelbert Miller of Howard University, "and the use of first names is a sign of a certain power relationship, that the black is kept subservient."

"That happened with Harold Washington when he was mayor," said Laura Washington, the Chicago editor, who had been on his staff and was no relation. "Sitting around the pressroom, the white reporters would refer to him as 'Harold,' whereas they would always refer to Jane Byrne as 'Byrne,' and they'd always refer to [Richard] Daley as 'Daley.' " Black reporters also used Washington's first name, she said. "People would refer to him that way in quotes. He resented it and would speak out about it, and the reaction that whites who used the reference had was 'Oh, black people refer to him as Harold.' . . . And blacks resented that. They felt that was a sign of disrespect."

The Danger of Politics

Coach Presley was still bantering with the white waitress he had suspended twenty years before. He had to send back his pear salad because the dollop of mayonnaise on top was sour. When she brought the second, it was sour, too, and he joked with her about how hard it was to kill him off. She got a touch defensive, blamed it on the kitchen, and cleared our dishes away with a clatter. And we got back to our discussion, which was about the Supreme Court case he had just lost.

On January 26, 1992, Coach Presley had learned the bad news in a most awkward place, where everyone could watch his reaction. He was in his seat at the right-hand end of the curved dais that crowns the Etowah County Commission's hearing room, a modest chamber whose plaster walls are covered shoulder-high with wooden paneling that furnishes a facade of dignity. Presley was the only black among the six commissioners, and almost all of the white men to his right looked like Central Casting's idea of southern sheriffs: ample beer bellies and a little meanness in their faces. Billy Ray "Bulldog" Williams had a full head of gray hair and fleshy pink jowls. Thomas "Bull" Smith had a nasty squint in his eye and a paunch that hung over his belt; he chewed constantly on a toothpick. Like most of the others, Billy Ray McKee was a burly man, and he walked stiffly with a cane. Robert "Booley" Hitt, the chairman, presided.

Suddenly a red-bearded reporter from the *Gadsden Times*, Andy Powell, walked into the room with the news. Hearings were casual enough that Powell often acted as a virtual commissioner, intervening in the middle of testimony to question witnesses, clarify issues, and get a story. So he told them straight out: The Supreme Court had just ruled, six to three, against Coach's suit charging that the county commission had violated the federal Voting Rights Act by denying him the same budgetary authority that white commissioners had long enjoyed. "The county won," Presley remembered Powell announcing. All but one of the whites jumped up, yelled, "Bravo! Yay! I knew we were right!" and then failed to extend a hand of condolence to Presley, who sat in stunned silence. "I was kind of hurt by that. I was hurt by the fact that that would have been the reaction," he said. And he couldn't believe that Clarence Thomas had joined the majority against him. Like many blacks who saw Thurgood Marshall's seat as a "black seat" on the Court, who were moved more by a racial loyalty than by a careful reading of Thomas's conservatism, Presley had supported Thomas's nomination to succeed Marshall. "I thought that was the one vote I would have had," he said sadly. "I felt let down. I felt hurt. I felt that he didn't even look at the case. He didn't even look at what was happening. Had he known what was taking place, I believe he would have reacted differently."

On the surface, it was a classic case of a white power structure's changing the rules in the middle of the game just as a black gets into scoring position. The county commission's then five seats had always been filled by whites chosen in countywide, at-large elections by an over-whelmingly white constituency. In response to a challenge under the Voting Rights Act, the county signed a consent decree in 1986 designed to give black voters the chance to elect a black commissioner. At-large voting was phased out, and six districts were drawn, deliberately pro-ducing one that was 65 percent black, mostly in the small city of Gadsden. Those black voters elected Presley; an adjacent, mostly white area elected a white banker, Billy Ray Williams. The two newcomers were added to four white incumbents.

The members were essentially highway commissioners with the task of maintaining county roads and bridges; in the past, each man had been allocated a sum of money, mostly from state gasoline taxes, to hire his own crew, buy his own equipment, and set his own priorities of repair and construction in a given district. The practice had produced a comfortable archipelago of little principalities, providing each prince with opportunities for patronage, nepotism, and other forms of gain. At first, the four white incumbents acted as if nothing had changed; they retained control over the highway money and excluded the newcomers. Then, faced with the likelihood of a lawsuit, a dilution of money and power, and the obligation to share with Presley and Williams, they abruptly revised the system. Instead of each commissioner's having autonomy over his own funds, the entire commission would have to approve a countywide budget from a "common fund."

The principle wasn't bad; it could make spending policy more transparent and guard against individual abuses. The execution, however, shortchanged the new black and the new white. No "common fund" was set up, and the four white incumbents (three of whom were related to one another by marriage) worked things so that they controlled the bulk of the funds and deigned to distribute crumbs to Presley and Williams. One white commissioner made patronizing offers to send his crews into Presley's district now and then. In racial terms, it was an arrangement quite satisfying to some white sense of where blacks should be; in political terms, it was a convenient way of controlling turf, and Williams, the new white, was equally a victim.

Presley and his civil rights lawyers, teaming up with black commissioners who were facing a similar subterfuge in Russell County, argued that the commissioners had violated the Voting Rights Act's requirement that, before altering any "practice or procedure with respect to voting," they obtain approval from the Justice Department or a federal court. The Bush administration agreed, arguing that otherwise a locality could "negate the election of a candidate favored by minority voters simply by reallocating the successful candidate's authority to other elected or appointed officials." However, the Supreme Court ruled that altering a budgetary process did not alter voting practice and that no "preclearance" was needed.

Civil rights advocates were shaken by the decision, and a liberal-conservative debate erupted on editorial pages condemning or praising what seemed a narrowing of the act's application. If localities could be put through contortions to ensure the election of blacks, only to strip the blacks of power once they reached office, the federal guarantees of universal suffrage would be rendered meaningless. And that was a reasonable interpretation of what had happened to Presley; in effect, his black constituents had ended up with little impact on county spending. On the other hand, if every procedural change in governance needed prior federal approval, courts would be flooded and home rule denied. So went the arguments.

But the case was more complicated. As in many such conflicts, it was about race, but not only race. It became an instructive study in the overlapping forces of racial politics, old-boy power networks, and governmental accountability. On one level, white county commissioners were adroitly maneuvering to deny power to a new black official. On another, they were protecting their traditional fiefdoms against all newcomers, without regard to race. Indeed, Williams was as frustrated as Presley; he was no flaming liberal, but he was the one white in the commission chamber who pointedly abstained from celebrating the Court's ruling. "I think that I have been raped and Coach Presley has been raped to a certain degree," Williams declared angrily as he played with a stainless-steel letter opener at his desk. "I expect to be treated the same as the rest of them. Although I'm white, I think I've been discriminated against."

At a deeper level, in trying to deny blacks and other newcomers access to a spoils system, the old guard was poised to dismantle the system itself by lurching unwillingly toward an arrangement called the "unit system" that would have pleased any liberal-minded promoter of good government. That envisioned a unitary, countywide approach to budget decisions and road maintenance. So some liberals had mixed feelings, as one confided to Presley's attorney, Jim Blacksher. "I have a good friend who's a voting rights lawyer of national prominence, who's told me to my face that he understands my arguments about the technical aspects of the Voting Rights Act," Blacksher said. "But he hopes that I don't upset the unit system, because that's good government and he's for it." Blacksher took another tack. "I don't have any problem with being tribal," he remarked, "if that's what the democratic process produces and that's what we want—and that's sure as hell what we want in Alabama. We are a very tribal people. We take care of our friends, and I don't have any problem with that. But black folks ought to be able to have the same empowerment. They ought to be able to participate in that system. They ought to be able to take care of their friends, as well as think about all the larger good-government issues that technocrats are supposed to think about."

Therefore, Presley and Williams argued that each should receive one-sixth of the county's highway funds. But they were placed on weak ground by one telling fact, a detail that didn't make it into news reports on the Supreme Court ruling. While the other four districts contained 150 to 260 miles of county road each, Williams's had only 35 miles and

Presley's just 2.6 miles, or 0.3 percent of the county's total. Almost all of Presley's roads were inside the Gadsden city limits, where most of the blacks resided—and the city, not the county, maintained those streets. So what would Presley have done with the money, even if he had received it? "In-kind work for schools," he said. Although state gas tax funds are supposed to be used only for roads, "if a commissioner could go on school grounds and build access roads and build up playground areas and drainage and stuff like that, I felt I ought to have the same kind of privilege," Presley declared. Furthermore, Blacksher explained, he could do some horse trading with other commissioners to get funds that were free to be used for nonroad projects. "We always made clear that the remedy we were talking about did not have to rigidly track the former system that they were using before these additional seats were added to the commission," Blacksher said. "The problem here is that in these county commissions the road and bridge budget is the entire discretionary playing field for the politicians. It's the only area where they get to make any real decisions that affect their constituents."

Presley had already been embarrassed by his inability to fulfill a campaign promise to pave Owls Hollow Road, which began inside Gadsden (where the city had blacktopped it), then, after a half mile, turned into dirt as it crossed the city line into wooded countryside, along and above a rusty, unused railroad track and past an occasional cottage and some shacks and run-down trailers with junked cars and other trash in front. One house had little yard statues of two black children, the kind of ornaments you don't see anymore in most of the country. "This was the only thing I had going for me," Presley said. "Another commissioner did go in and he fixed a portion of the road and paved in front of [one] house, you know, killed the dust and what have you in that dry season and everything, and mud when it got mud season. But that did not eliminate the total problem for people who live there, especially people who can least afford."

W. A. Lutes, a white steelworker turned commissioner, took a beneficent posture toward Coach Presley. Out of the goodness of his heart and his obligation to serve all the people, Lutes would dispatch his crew and equipment to Owls Hollow Road. "I agree that it needs to be paved, just as the miles that I have need to be paved, and as far as I'm concerned it will be paved," he offered magnanimously. Sharing control over the pot of money was out of the question, of course. "I could not bring myself to agree to give them one-sixth of the money when they didn't have the road mileage. But as far as voting is concerned, their voting rights have never been violated"—here his voice rose to a squeak of joy and he gave a sly grin—" 'cause they have voted every time. It just happens that they was outvoted!"

Lutes had a revealing prescription for how a newcomer should have behaved, how he himself had acted when first elected. "I didn't come here on bended knees," he observed, "but I came here humble. 'Now, fellers, I need your help. What can y'all do for me? I'll take anything you can do.' . . . I came to them and said, 'Hey, man, I'm at your mercy now. I need help.' " If he had been stricken by candor, he might have added that the humble act is especially satisfactory when performed by a black man.

Lutes pointed out with some delight that Presley had been given a very important job by the commission: "He was put in charge of the courthouse. And he was in charge of the whole maintenance of the courthouse and the crew. He had more people working for him than I did. . . . He was here with a nice budget, more people than I had, and he was serving all the people of Etowah County. He was seeing to their comfort here in this building. He was put in charge of the upkeep and taking care of this whole building."

"A glorified custodian," Presley sniffed.

Walking around town with Coach Presley, having lunch with him, sitting in his office, or gathering random comments from white folks, you would never have thought that he was at odds with anybody. People seemed to like him, and some said outright that they were ashamed at the way he had been treated by the commission. At the café, where I was having tea alone in the morning, a young white fire inspector sat down when he heard I was talking to the commissioners and said, "Don't hold it against us—we're not all like that." In the hallway outside the hearing room, while the commission was in closed session, a stout blond woman who ran programs for the aging condemned the commissioners for treating Presley unfairly and offered a concise summation of the Supreme Court's opinion: "It was a crock." Presley himself was in constant banter with whites who inquired after his health, compared notes on kidney problems, and joshed him sympathetically about having no work to do.

We were sitting in his tiny office when a white cleaning woman in a gray apron stuck her head in. "What drug you in today, Coach?"

"This young man here," Coach said.

"I knew it was something—wasn't your job." She laughed and shuffled off. Presley smiled, but I'm not sure he found it funny.

Finally, in City Hall, after he and the city's white finance director kidded each other all the way up in the elevator about whether the city or the county had more money, I decided to ask him about this informal friendliness I was seeing, this liquid easiness that white southerners often hold up as an example of the accommodating race relations they have achieved. We sat down with Robert Avery, one of two blacks on the seven-member Gadsden City Council, and I put it to them. Avery was the first to reply: "They'll pat you on the back with one hand and try to stab you with the other at the same time," he said.

"I have to agree," said Presley.

"They've always done that," Avery continued. "There were always certain particular people in the black community in certain positions that whites dealt with and felt comfortable in dealing with and still feel comfortable dealing with: schoolteachers, like he was; professional people; ministers; people like that. And believe it or not, even prior to the civil rights movement, the Civil Rights Act, those blacks had a little bit more freedom."

"They had a little more freedom," Presley added, "but they had to have a different attitude." He scolded himself for naïveté. "We should have known," he said. "We've lived here long enough to know that they weren't gonna break their hearts down and give us anything, but we just assumed that they would, and we hoped that they would."

Avery had wisely assumed no such thing when he was elected to the city council in 1986, also under a court order that eliminated at-large voting. He was thirty-seven years old then, a man as dark as ebony who worked in a tire plant and didn't mince words. From the first day the council met, he was treated to a virtuoso display of maneuvers aimed at curtailing powers that individual councilmen had traditionally possessed when all were white. The mayor wanted the members to sign a list of restrictive procedures, including no contact with department heads or other city employees without the mayor's approval. Avery objected, and he could feel the members stiffen with the thought, Uh-oh, this guy's going to be a troublemaker. But at his insistence, a few provisions were removed as the members were waiting to go into their initial session, and Avery signed with reservations. "The paper didn't stay in effect for long," he observed with a laugh. "When the white boys found out it applied to them too, then they kind of pushed it away."

Avery's next task was to get the chairmanship of an influential committee. Traditionally, each member picked his own post. The members "assumed that I was gonna take the chairmanship of the Community Development Committee," Avery recalled with a chuckle. "But when I said 'Finance Committee,' you should have seen the look on their faces, 'cause they didn't think I had sense enough to realize the importance of the Finance Committee chairman." From that position he "made some of the local businesspeople stand up and start acting right when it came to dealing with minorities." When whites tried to get him out of the job in his second term, he threatened to stage a run for council president— for which he had three of the four votes needed—and then agreed to back off if he could keep Finance. The deal was done.

With his hardball politics, Avery also protected the kind of backward procedure on the city council that Presley was unable to retain on the county commission. By long-standing practice, each council member had the right to name one school board member, and the council would simply ratify the choice—an undemocratic approach but one in which newly elected blacks wished to share. When it came Avery's turn, how-ever, "all of a sudden they wanted to devise a new system," he said. "They wanted to have an interview process, and then they wanted to solicit a couple of names, as opposed to just one. And of course I objected to that and reminded them that we didn't do that when other council members made their selection. I think they finally realized the fight they had, so they gave in."

Sweet reason did not always prevail. After a white councilman's wife was given a speeding ticket on Eighth Street, which runs down a hill past a virtually all-black Catholic school, the councilman mustered a narrow 4–3 vote to increase the speed limit to thirty-five miles an hour from twenty-five. Avery spoke out vociferously against the change, and the issue prompted some violent protests in which a black youngster threw a brick at a white woman's car. "I was accused by this council member of inciting a riot," Avery said. "He just flat told me one day that if anything ever happened to his wife coming down off of that mountain, then I better find myself a deep, dark hole. . . . I said, 'Are you threatening me?' So he pushed himself away from the table and said, 'You can take it the way you want to.' . . . I said, 'Well, I appreciate your telling me.' And I laughed it off 'cause I didn't have any gun. But I knew he had his gun on. Of course, the next time I came to City Hall I had mine."

These experiences in the back rooms of Gadsden's government merely confirmed what Avery had learned long before. "What people got to realize is that racism has always been a power thing," he explained. "It hasn't been race per se. It's always been the fact that you could have power over another. It just so happens in this case that whites want power over blacks." And then he added a grim assertion in a single sen-tence, which Coach Presley completed:

"No white man, no matter who he is, doesn't matter whether he's a northern liberal, a southern liberal, northern conservative, or southern conservative, he's not gonna do any more—"

"—than the law requires."

Coach Presley died in 1993. Alabama's Republican governor appointed a black Republican, David Williams, to serve out Presley's term. And in 1994, Williams was defeated by Presley's widow, Alice, who moved into his small office in the county courthouse. According to Presley's attorney, Jim Blacksher, evidence in a follow-up hearing before a federal district judge showed that the commission "had misrepresented the facts to the Supreme Court." Contrary to what the Court had been told, money had never been placed in a common fund and a unit system had never been installed; the four incumbent white commissioners were still splitting up the money as before. The judge therefore ruled that the 1986 consent decree had been violated and ordered the commission to do what it had told the Court it had already done: take a series of complicated steps toward the unit system, in which a county engineer would supervise road repairs and the commissioners would act as a body, not as autonomous individuals. Alice Presley declared herself satisfied as the transition progressed. She had even been able to pave Owls Hollow Road.

One day around election time, a white woman who headed a city department in Birmingham, Alabama, confided to the black mayor, Richard Arrington Jr., that her neighbors were asking a pointed question: "What is it like to have a black man for your boss?" Her answer, she assured him, gave him full credit as a good mayor and a good administrator. And then she described to Arrington the question behind the question, the disoriented curiosity that comes from seeing that unnatural oddity, a black above whites.

"She said, 'I just hope you'll understand and not get discouraged,' " Arrington recalled, " 'because as whites growing up here, we were always taught that you should never have a black for your boss. In fact, our parents would always say, "If you don't get your lessons done and you don't do this, you'll end up with a nigger for your boss one day." ' She said, 'For us, that was the worst thing that could happen.' "

Of course, that was in another era. But a childhood curse does not easily evaporate. It was still "ingrained in a lot of us," Arrington remembered her admitting. And after that, he paid a little more attention and heard other white staffers tell him similar stories of similar questions and similar old impulses deeply rooted. "I had another young lady on my staff," Arrington remarked, "and she came one day and she said, 'I want to tell you, I have this dear old lady, white lady, who lives next door. She must be eighty-some years old, and I'm out in the yard working. She comes out and she talks, and what does she finally say? "I want to ask you something. What is it like to have a black man for a boss?" ' It's something that's difficult for people to accept."

Arrington is a courtly gentleman who retains the soft-spoken, distinguished calm of the biology professor he once was. He walked around in front of his bare, wooden desk, which is shaped like an oval with the ends cut off, and visits with a guest by sitting in an easy chair, relaxed. He is soothing in a brown suit, rimless bifocals, gold cuff links, and a sandy gray mustache. Whether by nature or by careful cultivation, the steely core of principle that his associates sense within is padded with a reassuring charm. This he used effectively to defuse the white business community's initial jitters over a black running City Hall. "He's not a confrontational individual," observed Ted Kennedy, a leading figure in town and the white chairman of a large construction company. "He's not out to challenge you because you're white or challenge you because you disagree with him. His style is much more subdued than that, and I think a lot of his successes have been because of that."

And that is the nonthreatening posture a black in power must carefully adopt to ease white worries. In 1979, when Arrington was elected the first black mayor of a city that had been shaped by segregation and riven by racial strife, two themes of concern rippled through the white commercial hierarchy. "Their own personal lack of experience with blacks as peers," said Ed LaMonte, Arrington's white executive secretary during his first two terms, "and secondly, probably a skepticism that any black mayor could be competent." LaMonte set out to promote personal contacts and let Arrington's personality be the balm. "I would always say to business leaders, if they had a true concern, that rather than assuming it would be an unpleasant experience dealing with the mayor, they ought to simply call the mayor and deal with him. And after that initial experience, many developed a very effective working relationship."

In this regard, black officeholders must prove themselves in an extra dimension of moderation. To allay suspicions, the most successful blacks in political, corporate, academic, and military life are usually those who attain a certain racelessness by not emphasizing their blackness, playing down the racial tensions in their surroundings, and avoiding any agenda with a hint of pro-black militance. Shelby Steele, a black conservative, calls this "striking a bargain for racial innocence"—an unspoken agreement with whites to confirm their racial innocence in exchange for acceptance. "No black candidate will have a serious chance at his party's nomination, much less the presidency, unless he can convince white Americans that he can be trusted to preserve their sense of racial innocence," Steele writes. "Such a candidate will have to use his power of absolution; he will have to flatly forgive and forget."

In most places, white voters have been slow to embrace black candidates, and black mayors have been the products largely of demographics—white flight to the suburbs and the rise of African-American majorities in such cities as Detroit, Atlanta, Baltimore, Washington, Newark, Birmingham, Atlantic City, Memphis, New Orleans, and Richmond. Still, some black candidates have attracted sufficient white votes to win major elections where blacks are in the minority. L. Douglas Wilder, the grandson of slaves, turned history on its head in 1989, when he was narrowly elected to preside from the former capital of the Confederacy as governor of Virginia. In 1992, Carol Moseley-Braun became a senator from Illinois. Since 1967, when Carl B. Stokes of Cleveland became the nation's first black mayor of a major city, four of the country's five largest cities—all with black minorities—have elected African-Americans as mayors: New York, Los Angeles, Chicago, and Philadelphia. (Houston is the exception.) Their victories proved transitory, however, since whites ultimately returned to office in all of them, and almost always in racially charged campaigns.

Smaller cities with black minorities that have elected black mayors include New Haven, Connecticut (36.1 percent black); Seattle (10.1 percent black); Denver (13 percent black); Kansas City, Missouri (30 percent black); Cincinnati (38 percent black); Dayton (40.4 percent black); Hartford, Connecticut (38.9 percent black); Roanoke, Virginia (24.3 percent black); Cambridge, Massachusetts (13 percent black); Rockford, Illinois (15 percent black); and Charlotte, North Carolina (31.8 percent black). But racial crossovers at the ballot box have been most pronounced when the black candidate has been careful to soothe and reassure whites by avoiding any emphasis on race or pride in his blackness. Thomas B. Edsall, a *Washington Post* reporter who has written on race and politics, finds that many black mayors garner support from whites by opposing busing and taking a tough stand on crime, positions that black voters increasingly endorse as well.

Indeed, Colin Powell rose to become the first black chairman of the Joint Chiefs of Staff not by flaunting his black identity but by submerging it in a corporate mentality of cautious harmony. He kept his head down, blended in, and displayed no rough edges—or so it seemed to an American public that indicated in polls its overwhelming affinity for the man as a potential presidential candidate in 1996. When he decided not to run, he cut short a process of discovery about where his race—plus his emerging policy positions and personal qualities—would fit into the equation of electability. But in his noncampaign (his book tour), he sent signals that clearly counteracted the images associated with being black: He was a Republican, albeit a centrist who cared something about social problems. He was a military man who had demonstrated his patriotism—a quality believed to be less prevalent in blacks than whites, according to 50.6 percent of a national sample of Americans. In accent, dress, and public conversation, he kept his race in the distant background, enabling white people to feel good and open-minded about liking a black man. Moreover, he was not a politician, and every refreshing sentence reminded his audiences of that endearing fact.

Some blacks have to go to great lengths to make their newly acquired power nonthreatening. Steve Suitts tells of a locally famous black minister, Tom Gilmore, who was elected sheriff of Green County, Alabama, by black votes but then, with white acquiescence, stayed alive and in office by refusing to wear a gun. "Most of what sheriffs do is deal with domestic disputes, white and black," Suitts said, "and here's this sheriff going out to deal with this domestic dispute out in this white part of town where somebody's got a gun, shooting at somebody, threatening to kill their wife—and he ain't got a gun. Well, it took courage. And Tom did it. And ultimately, two elections later, in this profoundly plantation culture . . . Tom was getting half the white votes."

On the other hand, David Dinkins lost his reelection bid as New York's mayor in 1993 partly because he failed to bend over far enough to maintain that essential impression of racial neutrality. Three incidents were particularly damaging: a black-led boycott of Korean grocers in Brooklyn after a Korean store owner got into a scuffle with a black woman in 1990; attacks by blacks on Lubavitcher Jews in the Crown Heights section of Brooklyn in 1991; and the mayor's condolence call on the family of a drug dealer who had been killed by a white policeman, in 1992, in what a grand jury later termed self-defense. In the first two cases, Dinkins was widely viewed as biased and unwilling to stand firmly against militant blacks who were indulging in racism of their own. In the third, he triggered deep-seated fears that are generated by most black politicians who try to combat police brutality—the fear of crime and violence breaking through the emasculated front lines of law enforcement. Police officers demonstrated angrily, some carrying placards calling Dinkins a "washroom attendant" and denouncing his "true color" as "yellow-bellied." In all three incidents, Ian Fisher of *The New York Times* reported, white residents of Brooklyn's Canarsie neighborhood saw the nonblack victims—Koreans, Jews, and police—suffering "injustice that the Mayor failed to correct." Whites told Fisher that Dinkins "favors his own kind," "put his own people first," and ran a "racist" administration. "I think they have proven themselves to be a hostile race," one voter said of blacks generally.

The police brutality issue got Richard Arrington into office, kept him there, worried whites, and may also have contributed to a long-running, failed plot by the Justice Department to induce him into taking bribes so that he could be arrested. Official documents, including a stack obtained by Arrington under the Freedom of Information Act, showed him as one among half a dozen leading blacks in Alabama targeted for phony prosecutions by the Republican administrations of Ronald Reagan and George Bush.

Like virtually all black males in America, Arrington had his share of unpleasant experience with white police officers. Growing up in the rigidly segregated South, he and his brother were worried over by their anxious parents, who feared that a random encounter with racist cops would get them beaten or arrested. Arrington suffered nothing physical, but his memories were vivid nonetheless.

As a seventh-grader, he delivered the *Birmingham Post-Herald*; one day, copies of the paper were late in arriving at the distribution point in the suburb of Fairfield, leaving more than twenty delivery boys of both races with nothing to do. "We decided to play football, blacks and whites," Arrington recalled. "We were having a great time." At another place, in another era, a neighbor looking out her window might have found the scene heartwarming, but not then, not there. The embryonic experiment in integration so alarmed a resident of the white neighborhood that the police were called. "These two officers came—of course, all officers were white at that time," Arrington noted. "While they said nothing to us—those of us who were black—they just cursed the white kids out for playing with the 'niggers,' I mean, said all kinds of things about us. . . . It was a very embarrassing situation."

But it wasn't the last of its kind. He and his cousin, also a paper carrier, made the mistake another day of pausing by a baseball field and putting down their papers to watch the game for a while. "Officers threatened to put us in jail," he said. "They never spoke to you in a respectful fashion. It was always in a threatening fashion."

Arrington's journey out of intimidation was long and arduous; as opportunity developed, he felt a chafing doubt about his adequacy. His father, a sharecropper, moved his family to Birmingham so he could work in the steel mills, and Arrington did not leave Alabama until graduate school. He studied at Miles College, a black school in Birmingham, and never socialized with white people until he went to the University of Detroit for his Ph.D. in biology. There, he mixed uneasily with his white peers. He carried "a deep suspicion of all whites," he confessed. "What I knew at that time of whites was that whites felt and expressed openly here a sense of superiority, or more importantly, a sense that blacks were always inferior. As a black, you were always in a position of having to prove yourself." Furthermore, those white views made an impact. "I even had some fears about inferiority," Arrington said. "In the classes, even if I were called upon I was so sensitive about the whole racial matter, I always felt as if I had to know everything: If I didn't know it, I'd let my whole race down. That was the kind of crippling effect it had on me." At first he reacted awkwardly to the familiarity, the intimacy of the white students who included him in their wrestling and horseplay. It was so strange to be on a par with whites. Ultimately, however, it gave him a sense of identity and self-confidence and made him look back more clearly on Alabama, where "blacks were always frightened," he said. "Police brutality was so pervasive here in this area. It was still a time when there was a place for black folk, and you were supposed to stay in your place. I didn't know at the time how bad it was, to tell you the truth. And I just began to sense it as I got away from here and got a different perspective."

Birmingham presented a fearsome spectacle as the dominion of Eugene "Bull" Connor, the police chief who enforced segregation by setting dogs on peaceful civil rights demonstrators. And when Arrington returned to teach at Miles, he reawakened his instincts of wariness. If he was pulled over at night, he said, "I was very uneasy, even when I had done nothing wrong. I glanced in my rearview mirror, because there were all kinds of stories, and they were basically true stories, about the treatment of blacks by police officers." So in 1971, when he became the second black member of the city council, he explained, "I decided right away that the only way we could deal with the issue, especially one that sensitive, was to try to focus a spotlight on it. So I began doing that by bringing the victims of police brutality to city council meetings. Nobody could deny it. See them firsthand while they're still beaten. I began to record every complaint over a period of time, with a report on it. I would take pictures of the victims. I began slowly to put in place little policy decisions that, though small, had impact." They included a requirement that whenever an officer used force, he had to take the defendant to the hospital. "And I began demanding of our internal affairs division that we get a report on every complaint of every allegation of mistreatment of a citizen, [which] had to be investigated. And I would air those reports, and it just kept the attention on it and really built up pressure so that eventually police brutality diminished." As a result, he acknowledged, he became the darling of the black community and thus built his political career.

While Arrington was monitoring police brutality, the Federal Bureau of Investigation was monitoring Arrington. When he obtained his heavily censored FBI file, Arrington discovered that he had been under surveillance as a national security risk. "Don't ask me why," he said with a laugh. "I'm a quiet, laid-back guy. When my friends heard that, it was humorous to them." The file named him as a member of something called "the Alabama Black Liberation Front, which they said was a branch of the Black Panthers," he noted. "I really never was, except I was outspoken on police brutality and I very well may have spoken up for some of them. I spoke up for everyone." He was listed as a target of COINTELPRO, the "Counter-Intelligence Program" developed by the FBI's director, J. Edgar Hoover, to undermine American Communists and, later, outspoken black leaders as well as the KKK and white student radicals. The program used anonymous letters, false news leaks, and other "dirty tricks" that sowed the seeds of mistrust within their organizations and families. Precisely what clandestine activities, if any, were directed against Arrington were not specified, according to David Burnham, who sifted through the voluminous documents for his 1996 book on the Justice Department.

Arrington was elected mayor in 1979 after a white policeman shot and killed a young black woman near the scene of a robbery; she was merely driving by but was mistaken for an accomplice. Rioting ensued. The white mayor, David Vann, transferred the officer but refused to fire him, and an enraged black leadership drafted Arrington to run. He entered office in a swirl of telephoned threats and real dangers. The FBI now became his protector, making sure he had adequate security around his home, he recalled, and passing on information about several plans to kill him. In one plot, he was informed, a suburban Klansman had been hired to do the job; in another, a racist from Colorado was camped in the woods waiting for his chance.

After a year or so, as the threats tapered off, the FBI switched roles again, emerging as the instrument of what Burnham calls "an ugly guerrilla war" devised by the Justice Department in an effort to bring Arrington down by his own hand. From 1984 to 1992, the U.S. attorney for the Northern District of Alabama conducted eleven investigations of the mayor in a campaign the FBI code-named "Bowtye," spelled just that way in the memoranda and other documents. A team of agents, including some who posed as businessmen, tried to tempt Arrington with offers of bribes, and the U.S. attorney's office waged a scurrilous campaign of leaks about grand jury proceedings, which often seemed to surface during election seasons. Just prior to the election of October 8, 1991, the Justice Department named Arrington as an "unindicted co-conspirator" in a corruption scheme for which, obviously, the U.S. attorney had no evidence, not even enough to bring a charge. Such actions cut into Arrington's white support, but not sufficiently to defeat him; in 1995, he was elected to his fifth straight term.

Two episodes in particular revealed the unsavory nature of the Justice Department's campaign. In the late 1980s, Burnham reports, the FBI and the IRS offered immunity from prosecution in a criminal tax case to a real estate developer, Robert Moussallem, if he could get Arrington to take a bribe. Moussallem, who had known the mayor for some years, made several tries and then told him of his undercover role. He "also provided the mayor with revealing tapes of some of his conversations with his FBI handlers," Burnham writes. In retaliation, the federal government indicted, tried, and convicted Moussallem on the tax charges, which prompted *Newsweek* to run an article on the case in July 1989 raising the possibility that federal authorities were going after black political figures. In September, as Moussallem was awaiting sentencing, he was murdered by a shotgun blast to his face. A copy of the *Newsweek* article was found at the scene.

In the second incident, another informant swore shortly before the 1991 election that he had paid Arrington $5,000 in two installments in the mid-1980s to secure contractual work from the city. But it proved to be an amateurish fabrication, for it happened that on the two dates that the man asserted that he had handed Arrington envelopes of cash in his City Hall office, Arrington was, first, in Washington attending a luncheon of the Alabama congressional delegation, and then in Israel on a fifteen-day visit. "So we immediately pointed that out," Arrington said wearily. "That, I guess, made them angry, and it's just gone on and on."

After he won reelection, the Justice Department subpoenaed his appointment books. But by now Arrington had good reason to suspect that if he turned his calendars over, the authorities would use them to concoct another episode, being sure to pick a day when he was in his office. He refused to comply with the subpoena, and when he was cited for contempt of court in January 1992 and sentenced to a night in jail, he made his surrender a demonstration, marching to jail in the symbolic chains of slavery and imprisonment.

"They're motivated by pure, raw, unadulterated racism," Arrington said of the U.S. attorneys who conjured up the nightmare. "That's what I think it is. I really do." In November 1992, ten days after Bill Clinton defeated George Bush, the U.S. attorney's office notified Arrington that the investigation was over and there would be no prosecution.

From the Bottom

Powerlessness is a vantage point, a perspective, a revealing angle on life. It generates convictions about those on top and questions about the self at the bottom. It can invigorate or alienate, motivate or defeat.

Black people appraise white people through the lens of the long American legacy. Consequently, just as whites tend to envision blacks as subordinate, many blacks assume that whites hunger for power. White people are conditioned to sit in the front of the bus, a Spelman professor told a class. "Powerful," "rich," "financially secure," "supremacists," and "perpetrators" were among the characterizations of whites listed by black students at Lincoln University. They imagined that whites saw blacks as "inferior," "uneducated," and "not important." To Denzil, the teenage drug dealer in Los Angeles, vivid terms came to mind when he thought of whites: "Punk rock. Surfers. People that talk funny. Nerds. Rich man. Powerful man. Man that puts you in jail. Try to always keep the black man down."

David Murphy carried the image and the grudge until he went into the army. He had grown up in a black neighborhood of Chicago where he had had no egalitarian contact with whites. "I thought that to a large degree a lot of problems that were caused in our country was caused by white people and their drive for power and control," he said. "They would do anything for money or dominance, you know, control and power." But in the army he was suddenly thrown in with whites who did not fit the description. "What they do is they mix you up," he explained. "The black people are not in groups. They make a conscious effort to put black people where there are a lot of white people and then give you a white bunkmate, normally. They force you to become integrated. And you have to start depending on your fellow soldier by doing certain things with him. That person becomes your buddy. You guys march together, you guys eat together, you guys live together, you do everything together, and so you break down all those stereotypes." And one of the stereotypes was whites' alleged lust for power. "A lot of my friends, they were not like that," Murphy said. "They did not care about power or controlling people or dominating. They just wanted to live and have a good life."

But for many other blacks, the image holds. It is reinforced by history and experience. It is generated by the flow of power and privilege in America, which—translated into the measurements of money and class—invites many African-Americans to carry assumptions not only about whites but about themselves.

Subordination works its way into the fiber of self-appraisal. It encourages the sense of incapacity. It weaves defenselessness into helplessness, acquiescence into doubt, producing a tapestry of internal limits, of circumscribed ambition. Generations spent looking up from the bottom, gazing in from outside, cannot easily be torn away, even by new-found opportunity. In this region of powerlessness, subservience and rage coexist, along with a disability that Shelby Steele terms "hesitation."

Steele remembers admiring a fellow black graduate student until a shattering moment when the student summed up his postdoctoral aspirations in a devastating sentence: "Man, I just want to hold on, get a job that doesn't work me too hard, and do a lot of fishing." Steele decries what he calls the "victimization mentality" in black America. He concludes that the man was afraid—afraid of rejection, afraid of ambition—and that "as a group, we have hesitated on the brink of new opportunities that we made enormous sacrifices to win for ourselves."

Whatever psychological process is at work, the white-black power relationship has surely damaged the way many African-Americans see themselves and one another. As in the areas of imagery that surround body, mind, morality, and violence, whites' attitudes toward blacks regarding power and class have contaminated blacks' attitudes toward themselves.

One result is contempt among some upwardly mobile African-Americans for those left behind in poverty, squalor, and crime. Class-consciousness, like color-consciousness, creates a divide; some blacks who have moved up feel threatened by those who have not, as if the tentative hold of the upwardly mobile on rank, authority, and economic well-being will be weakened by the supposed sins of the poor. A white woman, an anthropologist, discovered the phenomenon when she married a black man, also a professor, and was thrown into circles of black professionals. At conferences, she noticed black academics making fiery presentations about those caught in the ghettos. But later, at the bar, "when they get drunk, when the panels are over," she said, "they'll talk about the 'Negroes' they study. They say 'Negroes.' "

Her husband, laughing sourly, added, "When they talk to me, it's worse. They say, 'the niggers.' "

Some middle-class African-Americans feel that they have more in common with whites than with poor blacks. "When I went to the inner city, it was a whole new culture, a new way of looking at things, and it wasn't one that I was very comfortable with and was accepting of me," said Russell Ballew, an African-American who moved to a black section of Milwaukee for his last two years of high school. He had spent ages nine to twelve in a small white Wisconsin town and then three years in Liberia. "So there was a lot of inner turmoil in myself in trying to adapt," he said. "There were really some crude ideas of what was important, like money, the way you dressed, clothes, the way you talked, whether you were cool. It was repulsive, you know what I'm saying?"

Despite the fact that two-thirds of those below the poverty line are white, the close identification of blacks with poverty is an indelible racial label, accepted by many blacks themselves. Richard Taub, the white sociologist at the University of Chicago, has found in researching city neighborhoods that blacks, as well as whites, associate racial change with deterioration. It is no news that whites who see their neighborhood changing racially are pessimistic about its future. But Taub discovered something more. "If you look at minority neighborhoods, we have the same phenomenon, but it's by class," he explained. "You ask black people, 'Is your neighborhood changing racially?' " Middle-class blacks in an all-black neighborhood who answer "yes" also complain that "it's going down the tubes," he observed. What they mean by "racial" change is that lower-class blacks are displacing middle-class blacks. "For these people, it's almost as if the definition of black is being poor, and if you're not poor, somehow you escape the definition."

At the bottom, the reactions to white power run from acquiescence to withdrawal to rage. In studying economic development, Taub found that many African-Americans had difficulty handling white authority because of what he called "the black conception of honor," in which "lots of things that look like just an order or a command you would give some-body just feel like a personal offense." He admitted that he would "get thrown out of the liberals' club" for the thought, but he declared, nonetheless, "Young black men have a real problem with close super-vision in that they really see it as insulting and degrading. . . . That is why I think if I were making policy, I would be doing a lot more to encourage blacks into those occupational worlds where close supervision isn't the issue, and that is the trades and over-the-road trucking and things that also have a certain inherent honor in them."

The history of exclusion has also heightened a sense of alienation from the "system," whatever system it happens to be. A white administrator in a government agency observed that when something goes wrong, black employees, more than white, seem inclined to throw up their hands, blame the institution, and resign themselves to the problem. Where change looks essential, he maintained, whites seem more willing to work through the system, employing whatever self-correcting mechanisms the agency provides. In his view, blacks often confront the problem either by individual recalcitrance or by group protest, rarely trusting the built-in institutional pathways to reform. A white police sergeant in Washington saw the same thing: Blacks do not feel they can make a difference, so they stop coming up with ideas, he said.

But when fellow blacks turn the oppression inward, Perry Wooten, the sheriff's deputy in Houston, feels the fury rise. "After you get browbeaten, you get brutalized, your self-esteem has been brought down so low—your integrity, your pride, you've been stripped of those things, and it continues day in and day out, degraded, and you've been brainwashed to the point where you don't care, it's OK for you to be called a 'nigger,' and that's what scares me," he declared in a torrent. "Because it's said so regularly that blacks are accepting it, and that makes me angry as hell, because to me, you've got a generation of people here that, depending on what frame of mind they're in and how secure they are in themselves, is going to determine how their offspring are. So if you . . . take away their self-esteem, pride, and self-respect, then they're going to be losing something when they're relating to their kids. . . . How do you lay down at night? How do you talk to your kids? How do you correct them? What kind of person are you? Well, we as a black community have become so passive-aggressive. We have become complacent. We have become so dependent to a certain extent. We want people to give us something. We lost that fire. We lost that spiritual awakening that we had over the years. We've lost that. We are able to tolerate anything in order to go along to get along. And it's a sad state of affairs."

A certain generational divide runs through blacks' reactions to subordination. Angered by the alleged subservience of their elders who were caught in a rigid social and economic hierarchy, some younger African-Americans recall with pain and shame the deference of their parents to white people. One woman gets edgy when she visits her mother in the South and hears her cooing to whites and calling them "Mr." and "Mrs.," "sir" and "ma'am." Bruce King, who grew up on Chicago's South Side in the 1960s, was introduced to whites through the shift in his mother's inflection when she spoke with those whose houses she cleaned. "You always knew when a white person was on the phone, because my mother's voice would change," he said. "She'd be very pleasant, and she'd chuckle and laugh . . . and as I recall now, that's how we were taught to respond to them—to be very friendly, to be very nice. We respected them because they were white. You stood up straight, and they would come by the house and you would always put on your best. They were special company."

In some eyes, that brand of imposed respect looks like submissiveness. It angers and humiliates many young African-Americans so intensively that they cannot bring themselves to gaze into the face of America's racial past, even when a work of fiction carries an anti-racist theme. For them, an act of memory and portrayal somehow seems tantamount to endorsement. Therefore, when white playwright Alfred Uhry created the gentle companionship of a wealthy white woman and a black chauffeur in his play and film *Driving Miss Daisy*, he did not receive unanimous praise from African-Americans. Uhry won a Pulitzer Prize for the play and an Academy Award for his screenplay; the film won three other Oscars in 1990, including best film and, for Jessica Tandy, best actress. But it was excoriated bitterly by some blacks who could not see beyond the mistress-servant divide.

The story is drawn from Uhry's own childhood in Atlanta. Like Daisy, his grandmother stubbornly drove her automobile long after aging had overtaken her. Like Daisy, "she really did put a car over a hill and knock down a garage," Uhry said merrily. "That really happened. And they hired this man to drive her. And it all went on in my house." With a good ear for the cadence of the language in his home, he writes spare, affecting dialogue to sketch the developing tenderness between the two. As Daisy resists and then reluctantly yields piece after piece of her proud independence, her black chauffeur, Hoke, navigates with nobility and grace across the line of race and class and power into a close regard. By the end, in frailty, when they declare and acknowledge their friendship, *Driving Miss Daisy* has risen beyond race and power into the realm of fine theater.

Because the play's characters were real to Uhry and he was not doing a treatise, he never expected the firestorm of attack. "I was writing not so much about the black man in America as two lonely old people in

Georgia in the 1940s, '50s, and '60s," he explained. "I just wanted to re-create these two people who sort of found a way to bridge a gap across a big, big, big patch of loneliness toward each other." So he simply wrote the truth. "The Miss Daisy character is really pretty much a composite of my grandmother, her sisters," he said. "The scenes with the son—she didn't have a son, so I was writing about me and my mother. But that black man is pretty much Will Coleman, who is the man that was in my house for my whole childhood, died when I was about forty. He was the only grandfather I ever had, and I loved him dearly." And as played by Morgan Freeman, the character of Hoke brought Uhry the most rewarding reactions he received from African-Americans. They recog-nized in the chauffeur models of their youth. "Several black people said, 'That was my grandfather. That was my father,' " Uhry reported. "I got that a lot. 'How did you remember the way they talked?' That's what I usually got. Arthur Ashe is one that I treasure. I met him at a party once, and you could just see his eyes light up, said, 'You got it right. . . . It was people like your character and my grandfather that put all the rest of us where we are now. They made the money, they put us through school, and they lived their lives. And they were good, decent, solid people.' The fact that there were only certain professions open to them is not the point. The point is, they did the best they could."

But numerous black college students and young adults resented the very concept of *Driving Miss Daisy* so thoroughly that they denounced it without having seen it. "I once spoke at Brown," Uhry recalled, "and some kid stood up and started talking about it and I asked him if he'd seen it. He said no. So there was nothing to talk about. What's to talk about?" Indeed, the refusal to see the film often occupied a central place in the statements of condemnation. "I purposely didn't want to see it," declared a young professor in Louisiana. "I didn't go see it," announced a professor in California. "I am not ready to see a black male chauf-feuring somebody around." Most students in an all-black sociology class at Lincoln University had not watched the film or the play, but they were repelled by the mere idea of a black man playing servant to a white woman. And even some who had seen the movie could not get beyond the uncomfortable symbolism of the white-black power relationship; these students, so wounded by the past, found themselves unable to see that any human caring could be contained in that past. They could not admire the tender, evolving friendship between Daisy and Hoke. They did not notice how much control Hoke gained over the relationship. They could not appreciate the agony of lonely aging, so universal that it could transcend even race in that place and time. Their racial experiences had stolen their capacity to appreciate this piece of literature at the multiple levels where art resides.

"If I was a black man," a woman in class declared, emphasizing gender as well as race, "I don't think I would have played in that role in which he was playing, which was a stereotype, back to being the shuffling Negro who did anything this white woman told him. I just didn't appreciate the whole thing, especially since you're supposed to be projecting positive black male role models for the black youth. The role in which he played just made me think, 'Boy, you're stupid, why would you want to play in anything like that?'" She went on: "I just hate the way he talked—'Yes, Miss Daisy.' 'No, Miss Daisy.'" She imitated the lilt and slur of the black southern dialect.

"I don't believe that I wrote a stereotype," Uhry countered, "because I knew that the man that I wrote about was a real man in my life. I just kind of played a tape recorder in my head about the way he talked, which I think was a rich, rare, and beautiful locution. I wish there was still more of it."

Albert Johnson, a black film critic who taught at Berkeley, got impatient with his black students who dismissed the film; he concluded that they didn't understand the context, the South before the civil rights movement, "a time when blacks and whites recognized the parameters of their social behavior and worked within that, and blacks had to be very subtle and clever in manipulating the white racism," he explained. "I said, 'Listen, we'll go back and look at it again. Pay attention, because Morgan Freeman is born in Mississippi; he knows that character; he's seen that character growing up, and I think he's playing it very well.' But I think a certain cynicism and hardness of heart has crept into our society so that any intimation of sentiment is immediately rebuffed and looked upon skeptically."

As for Uhry, the criticism has made him a bit gun-shy about his future work. "I don't want to write any black servants," he declared. "If I want to write about the South of my childhood, I just don't want to deal with writing black servants. . . . I just have to avoid it. . . . I just don't want to hear all that. I don't want people on me about that stuff, and I'll find ways to get around it."

The ambiguity of the mistress-servant relationship, which often combines exploitation with genuine friendship, became apparent to my daughter, Laura, as she interviewed black women and white employers for her sociology thesis on the subject. Whites who say a maid is like a member of the family "can be self-absorbed—blinded by their place of luxury," she remarked. Yet some blacks say the same thing: that they feel part of the white family. "Domestic workers relay one anecdote filled with resentment," Laura reported, "and, in the next moment, their eyes soften as they remember a particular employer or a past conversation over the kitchen table." In many cases, she found, "white women struggling to make a connection and black women struggling to maintain dignity" managed to shift the dynamics of control. "When you wend your way into such a relationship," she observed, "even who holds the power is not so clear-cut anymore."

Nevertheless, some white people damage themselves with African-Americans by speaking fondly of black drivers, black gardeners, black maids. Even the most admiring remarks can trigger the worst assumptions about patronizing white condescension in unequal relationships of power. This happened unknowingly to a white woman who applied for a fellowship from a prestigious foundation. A black man and a black woman were among the six panelists who made the selections, and they reacted sharply to the applicant's personal essay, recalled Barbara Green, a white member of the committee.

She was "a lovely young Jewish woman in her late twenties, very impassioned, very committed to social justice," Green said. She wrote of the black woman who had cared for her as a child, the "person she was closest to in the world for the first five years of her life. She went everywhere with this person. She went to her home, and she went to church with her, and she went shopping."

The black woman's attitudes about herself had helped to shape the young woman's worldview, by her account. "Much of what this woman does and thinks and feels is in response to this [black] woman," Green explained. "Well, you know, it could be a wonderful story. [But] they saw it like some southerner saying, 'Of course I love Negroes. My mammy, Jemima, was very dear to me. She was a member of my family.' " Consequently, when the applicant came in for an interview, everything she said was filtered through that unhappy prism. "They were going to turn her down flat," said Green. "I asked that we reconsider her at the end of the week, and we did. . . . But this story, which she invoked in all good faith, absolutely did her in. And they saw it, and I didn't see it. . . . They were operating on different wavelengths."

PART THREE

Choices

CHAPTER NINE

Decoding Racism

We're just as prone to see everything as racism as whites are to see nothing as racism.

—*David Greene,*
an African-American employee
of the Defense Department

Listening

Americans make choices constantly as they try to navigate through the racial landscape. They hear, or they do not hear. They speak, or they remain silent. They keep a racist thought to themselves, or they translate it into behavior—overtly or covertly. They select one or another mechanism by which to control the prejudices inside them. They confront or evade, question or teach, learn or regard themselves as above learning. They are not helpless in all of this, not mere prisoners of the past or pawns of the present. They are shaped by their surroundings, to be sure, but they also have free will. They act. They choose. And their first choice is how they listen.

Blacks and whites do not listen well to one another. They infer, assume, deduce, imagine, and otherwise miscommunicate. They give each other little grace and allow small room for benefit of the doubt. Dialogue is exceedingly difficult. Nor do blacks and whites listen well to themselves as they stigmatize, derogate, slur, slight, and otherwise offend. Quite innocently, whites make comments that trigger old stereotypes and then get defensive when blacks take umbrage. Blacks sometimes think their persecuted status cloaks them in permanent absolution for the sin of racial bigotry. And so they commit the sin without acknowledging it, infuriating whites and forestalling conversation.

It takes practice to learn to listen, and whites don't get much because most of them rarely think about race. If you are black in America, however, the chances are that you think about race every single day. When this simple fact was mentioned by Richard Orange, the black consultant, to a workshop for Meridian Bancorp in Pennsylvania, the bank's chairman, Samuel A. McCullough, found it such a stunning revelation that he was still talking about it months later. It had opened a window onto a hidden universe. As a white man, he went through most days without race ever coming to mind.

That is the smooth luxury of the majority. Immersed in the harmony of sameness, bathed in familiar chords of culture, white people don't usually notice their whiteness, any more than someone speaking his native language notices his own accent. The senses are so soothed that they are dulled. This means that whites can be comfortably deaf to the racial overtones that blacks hear so vividly. And from across the line, blacks can imagine racial dissonance where none is intended. So it happens that blacks and whites tune in to different melodies.

If you are black in America, you stand somewhere along a spectrum of assumptions about what is really happening behind the code of white behavior. At one end are those African-Americans who tend to see racism in every adverse encounter with a white. At the other end are those who try mightily not to see it at all. Those extremes are the easiest positions; little thinking is required to apply ready formulas. But in the middle of the spectrum, where most blacks seem to be, deciphering whites' comments and actions is an exhausting effort. Was it because of your blackness that you were denied the promotion, excluded from the meeting, treated rudely by the salesclerk, ignored by the professor? Was the unpleasant remark, glance, or laughter an encrypted expression of racial prejudice?

Many African-Americans, reluctant to jump to automatic conclusions, find themselves expending enormous emotion trying to figure white people out. "It's very difficult," says Sharon Walter of the Houston Urban League. "I have had instances where I'm in a room with white people and there will be discussions going on, and I feel left out. . . . In waiting rooms or lobbies, you feel like you want to talk, 'cause you're sitting and waiting—the weather or sports or politics, whatever. And I've tried to initiate a conversation, and I could tell that they don't want to talk." But when a white person walks in, conversation begins. "I don't want to think it's racism," she says. "The better part of me wants to think otherwise."

"We all walk around with a little radar system," says Bruce King. "Often it's confusing, because you're in conversations with people and things happen and you don't know. You have to think about it, analyze it. . . . Those people who are oppressed have to put so much energy into rethinking, into going back over situations over and over and over and over again, always hoping that a comment maybe wasn't meant the way it sounded. Did they really mean that? What did they mean? Why am I angry right now if they didn't mean it?"

The label "racism" is such a fierce and categorical condemnation that its features are commonly disguised and submerged to create a benign mask of subtleties. Almost nobody wants to consider himself a racist. "My experience is that when many white people think of prejudice, they think of the institutions: Jim Crow, slavery; they think of the extremists, the hate groups," says Lauren Nile, the diversity consultant. Racism is not considered racism unless it wears a hood and burns a cross and explicitly keeps blacks down, agrees Jim Blacksher, the white civil rights lawyer in Alabama. But to "people of color," Nile believes, racism means something less dramatic: "the daily indignities, the look [of fear] on that woman's face when I was standing at the elevator, the fact that I can go downstairs to this pharmacy, and if I take too long looking at what I want, the pharmacist will start looking at me as if I'm going to shoplift something."

Racial aversion often takes the form of personal aversion, and someone who dislikes another individual personally rarely notices when the root of that distaste lies in racial stereotypes. Such failure of introspection can afflict both whites and blacks.

This can lead to stark black-white differences of interpretation, a Rorschach test in which contradictory perception becomes divergent reality. The late Mitchell Goodman, a white anti-war protester from Vietnam days, once said that he thought black Americans possessed X-ray vision about this society, an ability to see through the platitudes and self-deceptions into the essentials. There is a valid point here, for whites could learn a great deal about themselves and their country if they would only listen to what blacks have to say. They might see how events are compiled into patterns. They might tune in to the racial vibrations in their own remarks. They might come to understand how insidiously their behavior is shaped by the shapeless caricatures that lurk in the unlit corners of the mind. Instead, whites usually just get indignant when they think blacks are imagining racism that isn't there. And those blacks who do fantasize about racism are often disgusted by whites' denials.

Some also manage a laugh at themselves, though. Wilbert Tatum, publisher of the *Amsterdam News* in Harlem, tells of a party on the yacht of the late media mogul Robert Maxwell. All the guests were asked to remove their shoes as they boarded. Tatum noticed that, unlike many of the white luminaries, he was not given any slippers to wear over his socks. He shambled around, looking at people's feet, and determined that none of the blacks had slippers. Feeling insulted, he confronted the attendant, who explained simply that slippers were being given to people who had holes in their socks.

An ambiguous episode occurred on a fine spring day when Trevor Woollery, a sophomore on Colgate's track team, came happily down to the track to stretch and warm up. "The weather is propitious for a good workout," he announced with delight.

A white teammate guffawed. "Did you say 'propitious'?"

"Yeah, why?"

"Oh, I didn't know you knew such words!"

As an African-American stereotyped as mentally inferior, Woollery had no doubt about the meaning of the remark. He knew the white student, so he could fill in the character behind the comment. But wasn't it conceivable that the student would have teased a fellow white for using such a fancy word in such a mundane setting? "It is conceivable, yes. But they use the words all the time," Woollery said. And was he certain that it was because he was black? "Well, from my standpoint, yes."

Rarely is it possible to pass beyond speculation in such a matter. To know whether the white student was teasing innocuously or insulting racially would require a formidable capacity to read his mind. Only occasionally can the question be tested, and Senator John Danforth unwittingly provided such a case. In the lobby of a Senate office building, Danforth was approached by Roger Wilkins, the insightful black attorney, professor, and Pulitzer Prize–winning journalist. The two had never met. Wilkins stretched out his hand. "Hello, Senator. I'm Roger Wilkins."

Danforth shook hands. "Hello, Roger." And in that too-intimate use of a black man's first name alone, Wilkins heard the reverberating echo of white condescension across a long legacy. He told me the story to illustrate how thoroughly the practice was ingrained. But wait, I said, Washington is a town full of phony familiarity where even young secretaries give their elders the first-name treatment. Ah, Wilkins replied, but Danforth is different: well-bred, proper, an Episcopal priest. He knows better. But he's a politician, I countered. Wouldn't he have done it to a white man as well? Not a chance, Wilkins insisted. I wondered skeptically about this for a year or so, until I happened to attend a luncheon where Danforth spoke. Now I could check it out, for I had never met him either. I walked up to the senator, put out my hand, and told him my full name. "Hello, David," he said.

When I returned to Wilkins with the result of my experiment, he acknowledged that politicians use first names to diminish distance. Still, given the racial legacy, he argued, Danforth should have known better. "If you're a black person my age and were born in segregation, as I was, you are just steeped in the lore of segregation," Wilkins explained. "You had to understand it to negotiate it. One thing we all knew was that white people had to use first names with black people to establish the superior-inferior relationships. Black people started giving their kids names that required white people to address them with respect; they'd name their kids Major, General. You would expect that a man like Danforth would know that racial etiquette. On the other hand, Danforth thought he was doing a good racial thing by promoting Clarence Thomas for the Supreme Court, showing that he was tone-deaf on race."

Breaking the code is difficult because the motive is masked, the wellspring of the comment is concealed. Even a man with a good ear, with intuition finely honed, can be mistaken. Salim Muwakkil may be wrong, or he may be correct, in thinking that racism got him transferred out of Germany when he served in the air force. He dated an attractive German woman who picked him up almost daily in a nice Mercedes; he would see the faces of white officers peering enviously from the windows of their quarters as he rode away. Mark Vance, the high school history teacher in Oak Park, Illinois, may be right or wrong that racial prejudice induced a white mother to demand the transfer of her child out of his honors course in world history. The whites involved would surely deny—perhaps even to themselves—that bigotry played a role.

The accusation of racism flabbergasted Susan Jacox, a white official in a state university's development department. She fell into a misunderstanding that could have been choreographed in a comedy routine, except that nobody was laughing. Sitting in her office with her door open, she was concluding a meeting with three or four people who had been brainstorming over a problem. The session had gone well, and Susan was summarizing as she happened to notice the black assistant to the vice president for development walking by in the corridor. "I said hello to her, and she turned and nodded to me," Susan recalled, "and in the same breath I turned to the people in my office and said, 'I always believe in calling a spade a spade.' "

The daughter of a diplomat, Susan had grown up overseas, unexposed to most of the racist slang that young people learn in America. She had no idea that "spade" was a derogatory term for a black person; the black assistant evidently had no idea that "calling a spade a spade" meant telling a plain truth in plain language. "She came to me later that afternoon and was furious with me for that insult to her," Susan said, "and I asked her what insult she was talking about, and she said, 'I'm not going to say it. Don't ask me to say what your insult was.' " For a time, they groped toward each other through obscurity until enough clues were given that "it dawned on me," Susan said, "that in the realm of card playing, spades are black." But that's not what she had in mind at all, she told the assistant. That's what the phrase means, the assistant said. "I didn't know that," Susan pleaded. "How could you not know that?" countered the assistant. "Well, I didn't. And I'm terribly sorry, and I will never, ever say that again."

Susan was stricken at the offense that she had caused. "So I called her that night from home, and I said, 'I am appalled at what I said and appalled that I used a phrase that has this connotation, and I apologize to you and I thank you for telling me discreetly, privately about it. And I will never, ever say that again, I promise you.' " The assistant thanked her, said she accepted the apology, and came to Susan the next day to say that she appreciated the call.

Several weeks later, Susan once again stepped into that battle zone of miscommunication that rages along the racial frontier. She had occasion to telephone the assistant one evening on some work-related matter and decided to compliment her. "She was a very beautifully tailored black person, a very elegant woman," Susan explained. "She was a refreshing, stunning-looking individual in the office. I complimented her frequently on what she was wearing. . . . As part of thanking her, and saying how super she was and how special her sparkle was to me, I said, 'You remind me of a sapphire.' And I was thinking on the phone about a magnificent blue and white silk pants-suit outfit she had worn, and she truly was as elegant as a star sapphire."

The comment brought a long silence. Then the assistant asked, "Do you remember *Amos 'n' Andy*?" Susan vaguely recalled seeing some of the shows when she was a young child, but she didn't get the connection. "Well," the assistant explained, "Sapphire was the woman on the show."

"So?" Susan asked.

"So! You've just called me 'Sapphire.' " And then came a torrent of invective about the program, about Susan as the worst racial bigot the assistant had ever known.

None of Susan's pleas of ignorance, her explanations about living overseas, were received as credible. "The next day, she studiously avoided looking at me," Susan said. "The tension was just horrible." As working hours ended, the assistant walked into Susan's office. "She said, 'I just don't know where to begin.' She would not look at me, she would not sit down. She was ramrod straight, absolutely furious, shaking with anger. . . . 'What crap do you hand me that you don't know those phrases? You claim to be so innocent of them, then you turn around and use the worst kind of slur possible. I detest you. . . . I will not accept this apology. You don't deserve to be treated civilly.' And she stormed out of my office, and I broke down. I was absolutely overwhelmed."

Susan pressed the university's vice president to institute diversity workshops, and the vice president hemmed and hawed, arguing that to do so would be to admit to a problem that did not exist. When the assistant heard that, she spoke privately to the vice president, and workshops were begun. Susan thanked the assistant for her intervention. In turn, the assistant circled around Susan, apparently looking for ways to have a conversation. One day, "she sat down next to my desk and sat forward and was really very eager, and didn't know what to say. I said, 'You don't have to say anything . . . this is a long process.' " Again she praised the assistant for standing up at the right time to get the diversity training started. "She said, 'Good,' and then left."

Two months later, Susan's husband was transferred out of state, and she left the job. The assistant did not attend her farewell reception.

At the other end of the spectrum, where blacks don't want to see racism, they can seem oblivious to what is obvious. It may have been just politics, but Clark Kent Ervin, an unsuccessful black Republican candidate for Congress, sat in his echoing storefront campaign office in Houston and proclaimed in sincere tones that George Bush's infamous Willie Horton ad contained not an ounce of racist appeal. Horton was a black murderer who raped a woman and assaulted her fiancé after escaping from a furlough program during the administration of Massachusetts Governor Michael Dukakis, Bush's opponent. By using Horton's African-American face to sinister advantage, the commercial pushed some powerful buttons of fear. But Ervin insisted that the ad was "about crime; it wasn't about a black person committing a crime. It would have been politically more correct, obviously, to have had a whole bunch of criminals of different races and religions and sexual orientations, and then we wouldn't have had that charge leveled against us. But it's essentially about crime."

African-Americans sometimes feel they have to educate one another. Renea Henry, a black Princeton student, took on the task with a fellow black Princetonian who had grown up affluent in a white community. He was driving with a white friend in a white neighborhood when a white cop pulled him over—and he had no idea why. "You think it's because you're black?" she asked rhetorically.

"Oh, no. It probably wasn't that."

When it happened again, and then again for no good reason, he began to accept her racial interpretation. Finally, he "got it" and had his white friend do the driving through white neighborhoods.

Sometimes whites are the ones who have to point out the racist dimension of an incident. Sitting around a table at Birmingham Southern University in Alabama, four white students and a black were telling of a black student recently charged—unjustly, they felt—with peering at a white woman in a shower. She had noticed a black man looking at her, she had screamed, he had run, and she had seen that he was wearing a yellow T-shirt. Campus police quickly found a black student doing his laundry in a nearby dorm and accused him, although his shirt was not yellow and he had checked in at the campus gate only two minutes before the incident—hardly time to park his car, go to the shower, then put in a load of laundry.

A couple of the whites believed that the authorities had been ready to grab the first black man who was handy. "I definitely saw it as racist," said Leigh Haynie, a white senior from Hartselle, Alabama.

But Carlton Chamblin, a black junior from Birmingham, thought otherwise. "More than an issue of race, it was an issue of justice," he said. "It wasn't like someone stole something and you don't know who stole it. I mean, she saw a black person. We can accept what she said. . . . That's why I don't make it an issue of race, because it was a black person," even though, he conceded, the wrong black person may have been accused.

It was an odd moment, with whites charging racism and a black dismissing the charge. Wesley Edwards, a white from Columbus, Georgia, tried to explain to Chamblin. "You know, if it had been a white person, they wouldn't have grabbed up the first white person on campus who happened to be near the place near the time, so easily. It made it very easy on the college to dispense with the problem." Chamblin thought for a moment, then nodded.

For some blacks, avoiding the racist interpretation is a protective doctrine that allows them to avoid a state of constant anger and to function with composure in a white environment. "I'm quite sure it's out there, and I've probably run into some situations where the intent was to let me know that they didn't like me because I was black," said Major

Craig Adams, an air force navigator on C-130 cargo planes. "But I would say, generally speaking, I have never perceived things that way—or even if I thought it was, what I try to do is, I try to look at other alternatives. I say, 'Well, I think he's trying to tell me he doesn't like me because I'm black. What other reasons could there be for that?' I try to explore those before I look at it as a black-white issue."

Another black air force officer, Lieutenant Colonel Edward Rice, had something of a bizarre experience in this regard. He was sitting in the cockpit of a B-52, preparing for a flight evaluation, which is done periodically to keep pilots in top shape. The evaluator was white, and Rice's grave manner during the preflight checkoff seemed to be making the man nervous. "I'm normally very serious," Rice explained. "I don't joke around a lot during a flight." Finally, the evaluator couldn't take it anymore and said, "Come on, Rice, lighten up."

"I took no offense," Rice said. "I didn't think he meant anything other than relax a little bit. But the next day, he came up to me and said, 'Hey, I hope you didn't take offense to that remark. I didn't mean anything by it. I was just trying to say "lighten up," but I started to think about it.' " And the white evaluator went on to explain awkwardly that he was afraid that Rice might have interpreted it as a racial comment. That cracked Rice's seriousness, and he laughed deeply. "It obviously dawned on him that it could have been interpreted that way, even though it was clear to me in the circumstance that that's not what he meant."

In their interactions with blacks, white Americans fall along a broad spectrum themselves, from the self-questioning extreme of the flight evaluator to the dense, don't-get-it (or don't-care) mode of the majority. Unlike the black spectrum, which probably forms something of a bell curve with the bulk of blacks in the middle, the white spectrum seems to be skewed toward the less perceptive end, with a substantial tail that extends through the continuum into regions where whites get uptight, tiptoe around, walk on eggshells, choose their words, calibrate their statements, and otherwise display acute discomfort in dealing with blacks. As Wesley Edwards put it, "In any kind of interpersonal relationship between blacks and whites there's always that little impediment there of not being willing to be completely honest and open with each other. . . . It's always with us to some degree or another, whether we recognize it or not."

To avoid being accused of racism, these whites may use extreme restraint and careful calculation, which enforce the distance. That often seems the safest course, but it avoids intimacy—no teasing about a big word, no first names on first meetings. Hypersensitivity also brings paralysis, as it did to two white women at Princeton who felt so inhibited in a course on race relations, taught by a white woman and dominated by minority students, that they said practically nothing in class the entire semester. "Being white people, we don't feel qualified to speak," Anastasia explained simply. "I listen," added Loren. "I love hearing other people's stories, but I don't know what narrative I can tell to contribute." At the end of the course, some minority students expressed bitterness that the whites had said so little. But the two women had been intimidated by their whiteness and by their lack of suffering, which they thought deprived them of anything interesting to tell about themselves. Furthermore, they had accepted the admonition that as whites, they could never understand the black experience. This was all the more poignant for Loren, who was doing a concentration in Afro-American studies courses in which she routinely took a backseat. "I'm always second-guessing myself in those classes," she said. "I never felt the authority, and it's really hard for me. I don't know why I chose to concentrate on something that I'll never feel the authority in."

Other sensitive whites at this end of the spectrum have healthier reflexes. They listen to themselves and to the way their language comes across to blacks, and they deepen their understanding. Steve Suitts got an education when he reacted angrily to an anonymous memo that had been circulated about someone in his civil rights organization. "I think I referred to it as a pusillanimous and woolly-headed approach," he said. "I thought 'pusillanimous' might have been a little strong, but really what some of my black colleagues took offense to was my referring to it as 'woolly-headed.' Where I grew up in Winston County [Alabama], if somebody would bump into a door, we'd say, oh, he's just woolly-headed." In fact, the term "woolly-headed" may have racist origins, judging by its two definitions in The American Heritage Dictionary: "1. Having hair that looks or feels like wool. 2. Vague or muddled." The experience was a lesson to Suitts about how language naturally emerges from a warren of images and attitudes. "Sometimes you check yourself, sometimes you don't," he said, "and sometimes even with the best of intentions, what you say and what you do express a sentiment that others have heard as something quite different from what you heard it as."

But vocabulary is not always reliable as a guide to attitudes. "The operating theory in the civil rights movement was: If some southerner said 'Negro,' he was a liberal; if he said 'nigra,' he was a moderate; and if he said 'nigger,' he was a conservative," Suitts recalled. "I will always remember hearing a debate in Alabama by two old codgers who were sitting by a cedar tree on some red clay in a courthouse yard. I was interviewing them years ago. . . . And I'll never forget this fellow talking about the Negroes, and how the Negroes were taking over and how the Negroes were the closest thing to the ape that society had, and this other old white codger stopping him right in the middle and saying, 'Now, wait a minute. Niggers are people too.' "

Some whites who tune in to themselves discover their own prejudices, thereby taking a step toward controlling them. Jessica Prentice was unaware of her attitudes before she spent a year as the only white student at Tougaloo, the black college in Mississippi. She counted herself as liberal and open-minded but found herself seeing people's shortcomings through a racial prism. Some of her racist thoughts grew out of "a certain snobbishness in general that I acquired over the years," she confessed. "In a racially charged situation, that can often play itself out in a racist kind of way. [At Tougaloo] I had a certain frustration, sometimes, finding intellectual peers." Instead of looking around and seeing specific individuals who didn't measure up, she added, "I would understand it racially, instinctively. And even though by the time I left, I had found those people, it took a lot longer." She was jolted into self-examination when a black friend told her that no matter how nice and liberal a white person may be, "if you push them far enough the n-i-g-g-e-r word will come out of their mouths," as she remembered the comment. "That hit home, because in a certain sense I spent my whole time there dealing with my own racism. That was just a constant—my own prejudices," she confessed. "Some little thing would come up, and I'd just react in a way that five minutes later I'd be able to see was racist. I wouldn't react overtly, but just in my mind I would interpret it."

At another, less introspective part of the white spectrum, a dozen or so white middle-class parents are sitting in a church basement while their sons hold a Boy Scout meeting upstairs. We are there for an unhappy purpose, but you would never know it from the faces. We are discussing a flash of racism in the troop and the complicated fallout, which included the resignation of the black youngster who was the target. But no emotion is registering on the white faces, no pain, no hurt, no guilt, no concern, just bland complacency, as if this episode were nothing more than a shooting star that had skipped off the distant reaches of the atmosphere and never had a chance to penetrate the defensive layers of ignorance that surround the soul of morality.

The story is simple. Three boys—my son Michael, a white friend, and a black friend we'll call "Tommy"—had just joined the troop together from their Cub Scout pack and were wisely placed together in the same patrol. On one of their first camping trips, their white patrol leader, an older boy, ridiculed Tommy by calling him "blackie" and "black boy." Michael and the other white complained to the senior patrol leader, who notified the white scoutmaster. The scouts' version of a court-martial was convened, and the patrol leader was demoted. No counseling was done for him, and no support for Tommy was given by either the older scouts or the scoutmaster. Michael and his two friends, who were close pals, were worried that their patrol might be disbanded and they might be split up. Their parents—concerned that their alertness to racism would in effect result in punishment—asked the scoutmaster to be sure that didn't happen. The scoutmaster rudely ignored the appeal—at one point, he hung up on Tommy's father—and without warning, the boys were scattered into different patrols. Angry and upset, they discourteously demanded a meeting with the scoutmaster, who adopted an imperious air and made insulting declarations about the other white boy's mother. Michael and Tommy then resigned in protest; the other boy remained temporarily, later switched troops, and went on to become an Eagle Scout.

So, this evening, the white parents involved have decided to bring the matter before the other parents. We are sitting in a tight circle, all facing one another. I am expecting compassion, indignation, a resolve to make amends with Tommy, to deal firmly with the scoutmaster. After all, a racist incident, plus the scoutmaster's abusive behavior, has led a black scout to conclude that he cannot be comfortable in this virtually all-white troop. That should be a matter of grave concern.

Instead, the chairman of the parents' committee, an older white man, dismisses the entire episode, accepting the scoutmaster's denial that he insulted the mother or was nasty to the youngsters. We point out that two boys have resigned, that the racism has been handled mechanically, not sympathetically, that nobody has even called Tommy or his parents to apologize or inform them of the action taken. I mention that this may have been Tommy's first contact with racism, one that he will never forget. I look around the room. A chill has descended. The shields are up. The other parents are deflecting the discussion away from race; their faces are frozen, expressionless, almost lifeless. *They don't care*, I realize. *They don't care.*

Finally, we persuade them at least to talk to the boys. Two white fathers are appointed to the task. Weeks later, they write a report that, predictably, exonerates the scoutmaster. It makes no mention of the racial slurs or of the fact of Tommy's resignation. It is as bland and uncaring as the white faces in the church basement.

Most white people probably do not feel guilty about race relations, and they certainly do not feel the guilt that black people think they should. They never owned slaves, they never discriminated. Many of their ancestors came to America after the Civil War and scrambled up the hard way. In fact, they are the new victims. If they are males, they are vilified, blamed, and pushed aside. Richard Orange finds that in corporations, most hostility comes from white men in their twenties and thirties who are trying to climb upward in an era of "downsizing" and affirmative action; they see undue, unfair competition from women, blacks, and other minorities.

Unsolicited comments by whites about race usually come to me in three forms. One is a category of complaints about blacks who get preference in hiring and then display either incompetence or dishonesty. Another is a lament about violence and disorder in the schools and neighborhoods of the inner city. The third is one story or another that casts the white as the target of black racism. Being the victim seems to have become the most fashionable American pastime.

To Larry and Rufus, twenty-one-year-old whites in Louisiana, the underdogs were white. "Blacks are killing whites, and it never hits the papers," said Rufus. "But one black gets killed and the whole place riots."

"It's so unequal," Larry added. "The cops will not pursue blacks for fear of being called racists. . . . A black can walk down my street, but a white can't walk into their neighborhood. If I went down there, I'd get stopped by a cop. They'd think I was down there buying drugs. . . . A black police officer let a black leave after he ran into my friend from the rear. My friend got a citation: failure to maintain control or something. My mother was in a wreck with a black person who was drunk with no license, no insurance. We had to pay for our car. . . . The blacks have an innate prejudism born inside against whites." And so on.

But white interpretations of black bigotry are subject to some of the same ambiguities that apply to black perceptions of white prejudice. That is to say, they are sometimes wrong. Laura, my daughter, laughed at herself for being so paranoid, when she arrived for a semester at Spelman, that when she went out walking to the supermarket with a few black women, she thought she heard one of them say, "Who's that white fool?" She was stunned, but only for an instant, because somebody asked, "What?" and the woman repeated her question: "Who's gonna buy the food?"

John Graham, the descendant of plantation owners, once went through something of the struggle that blacks experience in trying to delineate the racism within the coded behavior. "I worked as a waiter at one point down in New Orleans," he said, "and it was at a nice restaurant, and my captain for the room was black. I hadn't even said a word, and he immediately came down on me and was very negative the entire time we worked together. And there was nothing that I could do in terms of doing a good job or kind of being responsive to what he needed that ever made a difference. Now, it may very well have been that he just didn't like me—not because I was white, but that he just didn't like me." But Graham leaned toward the racial explanation. I asked how the captain had dealt with black waiters. Graham paused in thought for a long time. "That's actually a very good point," he said finally. "There were some that he seemed not to be down on regularly, but there were also some that he was also a pain in the ass for." Graham hadn't thought about that before, and it seemed to diminish the weight of race.

Many blacks define racism as prejudice plus power, thereby labeling the practice so that it lies beyond the reach of powerless people like themselves. According to the formulation, if you're not in a position to translate your prejudices into discriminatory action, if you don't have the authority to make your attitudes felt in people's schooling, housing, jobs, and lives, then you cannot be racist.

Such a narrow rendering of the term will not be found in the dictionaries. But the issue is more than a semantic one. Many blacks have used it to confer a kind of immunity on themselves, a permission to be racist without admitting to it. As Gus Savage declared in defending an anti-Semitic campaign speech when he was a congressman from Chicago, "Racism is white. There ain't no black racism."

Suffering

From behind that protective screen of powerlessness, many blacks listen to themselves just as poorly as many whites do. These African-Americans do not hear themselves parroting age-old slanders against Jews and others. They do not hear themselves echoing the pernicious logic, under which they themselves have suffered, that projects one individual's faults onto an entire group.

Negative imagery travels in many directions across America's ethnic lines; no group has a monopoly on malice. Unkind caricatures of African-Americans flourish among Latinos, Asians, and Jews just as they do among the majority Christian white population. And in return, such visible blacks as Louis Farrakhan, Al Sharpton, and Leonard Jeffries find license to express their prejudices acerbically, souring the atmosphere of debate and making black America appear more bigoted than it is.

Blacks who work with members of other minorities to overcome ethnic tension do so almost invisibly, in hidden pockets of goodwill, with little attention from newspapers and television broadcasts. Their struggles face huge obstacles of culture and history, and even small gestures come hard. That lesson was learned by a compassionate man named James Smith in Nickerson Gardens, a shabby public housing project in Watts.

On a January Sunday, a family from Guatemala was driving to church from among the pale blue, two-story buildings where they lived. Although the houses were built of cinder block, they looked from a distance like temporary plasterboard that could be swept away in a stiff breeze, as fragile as life. A twenty-year-old black man knocked on the driver's window, broke the glass, waved a gun at the father from Guatemala and demanded money, then shot the man, shot his daughter, shot his nephew. The father and nephew died. The mother was left with eight or nine children.

James Smith, the black director of the project's community service center, knew the family well; they were active in the center. He appealed to the all-black tenant board to show the widow and the children their concern by attending the funeral, by sending at least a representative. Nobody came. "Where was everybody at the funeral?" he asked, his voice tight with shame. Where were his fellow African-Americans saying, " 'Hey, we're with you,' " he demanded in anguish, " 'we're gonna stick with you till you get a place to live again, since you're not coming back into Nickerson'? 'We're gonna stick with your kids to make sure that they make it through school, through college.' They're brilliant kids, but they're impacted, impaired kids right now." James Smith felt very much alone.

One might think that divergent peoples who suffer together would form bonds of mutual caring and support. But the boundaries dividing them by race and ethnicity have proven stronger than the common ground of deprivation. Many blacks remark bitterly on what they see as the negligible participation by Latinos in the fight against discrimination, for example. "They won't join in. They won't stand up," complained Perry Wooten, who tried to enlist Houston's Latino sheriff's deputies in his efforts to reform the department. "It's the same thing that happened during the civil rights movement, when we got out there and got the water hose turned on us, got the dogs sicked on us, locked in jail and got beat with the billy club. . . . They didn't struggle for it. They didn't pay no dues, no price, no nothing. They don't try to fight for their rights, even when we call upon them. They have fewer numbers than we do and less representation, but they're too busy trying to play like they're white." The charge is not entirely fair, since Latino organizations have existed for decades to press for rights, and they mounted a large march on Washington in October 1996. But they have rarely combined forces with blacks.

Nor are Koreans and blacks united by their mutual hardships. In the inner city, both peoples exist at the society's lower edge, scrambling for survival. The Korean immigrants who open small stores in the ghettos may look rich and exploitative to many blacks, but most cling desperately to slim livelihoods, having bought their businesses with funds scraped together from networks of friends and relatives. Many Koreans, who have learned stereotypes by watching American television shows back in South Korea, arrive seeing virtually all blacks as violent and dishonest. To many blacks, Korean shopkeepers seem rude and greedy.

"Mama-san is selling spoiled milk and won't take it back," sneered a young black woman from Washington, D.C. "I bought some milk for my grandmother when I was home last summer, and it was all spoiled, and I took it back and he knows my face, he knows I'm from here. 'No, you can't bring it back. You didn't buy it from here.' I mean, they have just as many stereotypes against us as we have against them. When you walk into the store, when you go up to the counter, there is a bulletproof glass around. They are stuck inside this cage. Before that, when it was owned by the black folks, there was just a counter there, just a little counter with a register. For some reason, it was more of a community then than it is now."

The sense of alienation runs very deep, and while many Koreans fear and detest blacks, innocent cultural differences are also interpreted as racial insults. Jim Galipeau, the white Los Angeles probation officer who identifies closely with blacks in the ghetto, put it bluntly: "You see," he said, "the Koreans' problem is not that they're Koreans, it's that they treat people like shit. See, if you treat people like shit, they're gonna treat you like shit back, particularly down here. And they try to call it 'cultural,' " he snorted. And what outrages do Koreans commit? "Oh, they're rude. They don't smile."

"In our culture," countered Marcia Choo, a Korean-American, "if you smile too much, you're a fool because you're just going around smiling for no reason. It's considered not very mature, and you have an addled brain or something."

When African-Americans complain that Koreans don't look them in the eye or that they refuse to put change directly into their hands, Choo explained, the blacks are misreading a cultural custom as a racist practice. Eye contact is easy to misinterpret. A gaze may be more or less direct, lingering or fleeting. It may be deemed appropriate to one situation but not to another. Whites may be accustomed to more eye contact than blacks, and blacks to more than Asians. "You expect me to look at you when we're talking," Choo noted. "But in the Asian culture, that's not a sign of respect. In fact, it's very rude. You're looking someone in the eye, and therefore you're challenging their authority. So when I cast my eyes downward, or away, I'm actually lowering my status and elevating yours. That's my sign of respect to you." Touching has similar implications, she said. "It's not correct or proper for, particularly, women to touch strangers' hands and those of strange men. . . . So when they give you your change, instead of putting it in your hand, they may put it on the counter. And so that's a cultural thing. But the African-American customer will often interpret it as: 'They won't touch me because they don't want my blackness to rub off, or they think that I'm dirty.' And that's how it gets interpreted."

Language problems among Korean shopkeepers have also led to misunderstandings, Choo observed. "English becomes very choppy, and it's not a pleasant, 'Hello, how are you, and how are your children?' " Instead, it becomes: " 'That's five dollars. Yes. No. OK.' And so then it takes an appearance of rudeness."

These are among the issues that Choo confronted as she helped run a dispute resolution program in Los Angeles. With mediation, conflicts that looked racial—a black security guard fired by an Asian-American employer, for example—were defused before they turned violent or ended up in court. But she also believed that cultural clashes were merely corollaries to the main proposition of economic oppression, which had put the blacks and the new immigrants at each other's throats. That was her main explanation for the explosion of attacks on Korean-owned stores by rioters in April 1992.

"I get very angry when people say it's a black-Korean conflict," she declared. "It absolves too many people of their responsibilities. . . . These are disenfranchised communities who have been shut out of opportunities. They're literally at the bottom, fighting over the crumbs. . . . A lot of the perception of the African-American community has been 'I have not, so if you are doing better than me, it has to be because you're taking something away from me.'

"Don't look to Koreans as having realized the American dream, because our parents didn't come to the United States with the dreams and hopes of owning a liquor store in South Los Angeles," she continued. "You have professional people with high education pumping your gas and selling produce and opening up these little mom-and-pop shops. The Koreans didn't come in to be in the next class of oppressors. But that's how they're perceived. . . . I think that sentiment has been aimed at a lot of other immigrant groups."

Blacks' attitudes about Jews have followed similar patterns of stereotyping. Polls sponsored by the Anti-Defamation League of B'nai B'rith show a higher level of anti-Semitic views among blacks than among Americans as a whole. About 20 percent of all Americans surveyed, and 41 percent of blacks, agreed with six or more of the following eleven stereotypes:
- Jews stick together more than other Americans.
- Jews always like to be at the head of things.
- Jews are more loyal to Israel than America.
- Jews have too much power in the U.S. today.
- Jews have too much control and influence on Wall Street.
- Jews have too much power in the business world.
- Jews have a lot of irritating faults.
- Jews are more willing than others to use shady practices to get what they want.
- Jewish businessmen are so shrewd that other people don't have a fair chance at competition.
- Jews don't care what happens to anyone but their own kind.
- Jews are not as honest as other businessmen.

Moreover, only 7 percent of blacks rejected all of the stereotypes and another 9 percent accepted just one, responses that describe a very narrow ground of true tolerance.

Verbal assaults on Jews have proven more likely than most other expressions of bigotry to get African-Americans into the news. Louis

Farrakhan has received more media attention for his vile anti-Semitism than for preaching black separatism. Black student audiences have gained their colleges fleeting prominence by cheering approval as Farrakhan's aide, Khalid Abdul Muhammad, has denounced Jews as "bloodsuckers" who owned 75 percent of the slaves. And Leonard Jeffries propelled himself out of obscurity as a professor at the City University of New York by accusing Jews of financing the slave trade and taking a lead in stereotyping blacks in Hollywood films. His slurs against whites in general and non-Jewish white ethnic groups such as Italians have generated less uproar than his anti-Semitism.

The concoction that Jews were prominent in the slave trade gained such ground among so many African-Americans that in 1995 the American Historical Association felt compelled to issue a statement denouncing the notion as a distortion of history and "part of a long anti-Semitic tradition." Jews played only "a marginal role in a vast system," the historians said.

The synthetic scholarship of Jeffries and other Afrocentrists further contaminated a relationship that already contained considerable poison. For many blacks in New York and certain other cities, Jews became the handiest whites to hate. They were vilified as exploitative shopkeepers and ruthless slumlords, representatives of a racist power structure. Many who had worked closely with blacks to end segregation were eventually edged out of the civil rights movement by the drive for black pride, black power, and black self-determination, which strove for an end to dependence on even the most liberal whites. And since that time, New York has become the capital of black-Jewish animosity.

In 1968, tensions between blacks and Jews flared over an experiment in school decentralization when a local board of black residents in the Ocean Hill–Brownsville section of Brooklyn summarily dismissed a number of white teachers and principals, many of whom were Jewish. In 1991, an innocent traffic accident exploded into black-Jewish violence in the Crown Heights section of Brooklyn, where a seven-year-old black boy, Gavin Cato, was killed by an automobile in the motorcade of Rabbi Menachem Schneerson, the leader of the Lubavitcher movement; crowds of blacks then attacked Hasidic Jews and stabbed one of them, Yankel Rosenbaum, to death. Days of rioting ensued. As Arthur Hertzberg wrote in *The New York Times*, both sides were haunted by their distant histories. "When Gavin Cato was killed accidentally . . . blacks saw the ghosts of slavemasters riding into their quarters and not caring whom their horses might trample. The Hasidim saw ghosts of their own when the police tarried during a riot that followed the accident and when a jury later acquitted Lemrick Nelson of the murder of Yankel Rosenbaum. For many centuries, mobs carried out pogroms against Jews while the authorities stood by."

In 1995, a Jewish-owned clothing store in Harlem, Freddie's Fashion Mart on 125th Street, became the target of angry black demonstrators who staged prolonged protests against the store's plans to expand by evicting its neighbor and subtenant, a popular black-owned record shop. At times, police said, anti-Semitic epithets were shouted, including a threat to "burn and loot the Jews." In the end, a black man carrying a pistol and a container of flammable liquid burst into Freddie's on a Friday morning, ordered the black customers out, then shot and wounded four people and set the place on fire. Eight died in the blaze, including the assailant.

Nevertheless, Jews and blacks devote more effort toward accommodation than do most other ethnic groups in America. In many parts of the country, Jewish and black children and adults conduct workshops, dialogues, athletic programs, and other searches for understanding across the difficult lines. Black and Jewish teenagers travel to Israel and Senegal together. The Anti-Defamation League's curriculum on tolerance, "A World of Difference," is used in many schools to combat stereotyping of blacks and other groups as well as of Jews. The league has run seminars for student editors aimed at diminishing the anti-Semitic content—and the anti-black content—of high school and college newspapers. Substantial accord also exists on public policy issues. Although the Anti-Defamation League and certain other Jewish organizations oppose the most aggressive forms of affirmative action, such as government set-asides for minority contractors, the American Jewish Committee, for example, has joined with the NAACP Legal Defense and Educational Fund in court cases on voting rights, minority broadcast licenses, school segregation, and other matters. In Congress, black and Jewish Democrats usually find themselves on the same side of social legislation.

After the riots in Crown Heights, the New York Times Company Foundation organized a "tolerance committee" of prominent blacks and Jews to discuss ideas for bridging the gap. One approach, which the foundation helped fund, was the creation of museum exhibits and community focus groups in Brooklyn to foster dialogue on the neighborhood's history and the traditions and perceptions of its three main groups—Lubavitcher Jews, Caribbean blacks, and African-Americans. Oral histories, puppet shows, and various displays were aimed at educating each people about the other's religious and cultural practices. Grassroots efforts were also launched by Crown Heights residents to bring blacks and Hasidim together to play music, play basketball, clean up vacant lots, hold joint celebrations of Kwanzaa and Hanukkah, and talk through their mutual images. At the same time, a black drama professor from Stanford, Anna Deavere Smith, was roaming the neighborhood with a tape recorder to catch the angry, pompous, pained, self-righteous, bewildered language of twenty-six characters whom she then portrayed in a one-woman show, *Fires in the Mirror*, which drew thoroughly mixed audiences in many parts of the country. At the Arena Stage in Washington, it was even presented as a fund-raiser for the Hebrew Academy in suburban Maryland.

As with all such efforts that intuitively seem good and helpful, a question arises about their impact. The exhibit on Crown Heights at the Brooklyn Historical Society, for example, drew few Lubavitchers and no Hasidic school groups, according to the curator; practically all the schoolchildren who were shepherded through by their teachers were black, and there was no research on whether the experience changed their attitudes. The joint black-Jewish neighborhood programs, as vibrant and well attended as they were, may have struck only a glancing blow at the underlying enmity. *The New York Times* gave that impression in a front-page article that Crown Heights activists found cynical and something less than thorough, since it failed to mention most of the programs, including those funded by the Times Foundation. News organizations rarely report on quiet, undramatic attempts to reduce stereotyping, especially when the efforts are aimed less at achieving immediate results than at starting a process.

Black-Jewish dialogue groups have run into trouble in many instances, partly because each side views itself as a victim. As an Israeli once said about Israeli-Palestinian interaction, when you put two victims together, it's like mixing fire and kerosene. The same is often true of Jews and blacks, whose discussion frequently degenerates into a contest of sorts over who can claim the prize for suffering. If blacks seem to diminish the relevance of the Holocaust to America, Jews are deeply offended. If Jews maximize it as unique in human history, blacks are hurt at having to compete for uniqueness in their victimhood. As a debating point, some blacks may present slavery as their Holocaust, triggering a fear among Jews that blacks do not quite understand Jews' special sense of vulnerability. The discord derives from blacks' tendency to see Jews not as a beleaguered minority but as part of the nation's privileged white majority, a disconnection that was illustrated in a brief exchange between a Jewish and a black teacher at Teaneck High School in New Jersey. "To be very honest with you," the Jewish woman declared, "I don't identify with the white Christian community. All right? So here I am as a white Jew caught in no-man's-land."

The black man countered dismissively, "But you're more accepted as a white Jew than I am as a black person because of race. There's the biggest difference."

And the Jewish woman tried to explain as her eyes filled with tears. Her maiden name was ambiguous, she said; her husband's, clearly Jewish. Her aunt had scolded her for marrying into a Jewish name, warning, " 'You are announcing who you are now. Before, you could pass.' So you have your skin color, I have my name," the teacher told her black colleague, "I have a mark of Cain on my forehead here. . . . When people look at me they see it, just the way you feel that when people look at you they see you're black. My father was raised in a ghetto, and I have a mark here, and anybody looking at me knows what I am. I cannot hide it."

If the black man heard her, he gave no sign.

The dynamics of such conversation can worsen the pain. As Jews try to educate blacks about their feelings of marginalization and their history of persecution, blacks reply by citing the success of Jews in finance, law, real estate, the press, and other endeavors, arguments that can easily slip into classic stereotypes about Jews' power and control. To make matters worse, many blacks resist as Jews implore them to denounce the anti-Semitism of Jeffries, Farrakhan, and company. Blacks often insist that their choice of leaders will not be dictated by others; for most Jews, however, the refusal to reject such bigotry becomes a litmus test of a person's attitudes.

It can be argued that pain is a necessary part of the process and that worsening the pain does not mean failure. But many dialogue groups get hung up on these points of disagreement without progressing into overlapping areas of interest, and blacks are the first to lose enthusiasm. "We are always like supplicants," a Jewish woman from Manhattan observed. As blacks began to drop out of her group, "I was always trying to call and ask them to stay in there," she said. "It became clearer and clearer, and they even said this to us: 'For you it's more important than to us.' "

Frequently, Jews want conversation, while blacks want action. "Learning about African-Americans seems forever interesting to Jews," notes Fern Amper, a Jewish resident of Teaneck who has hosted a group for years. "Learning about Jews seems interesting for African-Americans for about six months, and then they want to move on into coalition building. Jews at times agree and at times do not support the particular form of action proposed, like supporting an all-black municipal slate."

It is a Monday evening in December. Fern and her husband, Eli Schaap, have arranged a comfortable circle of upholstered and straight-back chairs in their living room; five Jews, three blacks, and a black Jewish man have settled in, the core of a group that has been gathering every month or so for two years. Despite the Jews' concerns over black anti-Semitism, the interplay of interesting personalities has kept the dialogue alive and has created some close friendships. When two blacks, weary of being badgered to denounce Jeffries, stopped coming, "we changed our format," Fern explains. "We now choose one topic of mutual interest each session, like raising children, assimilation versus group identity, education, our own childhoods, et cetera."

Michele March, a black woman who dropped out, has returned this evening, and perhaps it is her presence that draws the conversation back into its old ruts. Jeffries, a Teaneck resident whom she knows, is not anathema to her. She accepts his "information," as she calls it, perhaps because of a personal quest. In researching her roots, she discovered that her maiden name of Felder, which she assumes was Jewish, appeared on antebellum census rolls in the South Carolina county of Clarendon, where her ancestors lived in bondage. She rejects being labeled anti-Semitic for accepting the "fact" of Jewish involvement in slavery. "I grew up in a Bronx neighborhood," she tells the group. "God, I didn't even know what anti-Semitism was. Jews were my friends. I was in the hospital, working, all the doctors Jewish, the nurses were black. I mean, the encouragement and the nurturing that I got where people were saying, 'You can be a doctor, you can be, you can be'—I have to be honest—came from Jewish people. So that was my experience. . . . On the flip side of that, my landlords were Jewish. When they came for rent money and my mother didn't have it, you know, there was some resentment there, because, you know, your mom would say, 'He should understand. They own everything. Just understand. Can they miss a dollar today? Come back next week?' "

The anti-Semitism of some outspoken blacks remains a sore point in this group. "One of the primary differences we have not been able to come to grips with is the Jewish concept that we must renounce certain things, i.e., our leaders or our spokespersons," explains Ray Kelly, who is black. "One of the key individuals was Dr. Jeffries. Another one was Reverend Jackson, and another one was Reverend Sharpton. It was their opinion . . . that if we didn't renounce these so-called leaders or spokespersons of ours, then we didn't have anything to talk about. And I personally felt that that was their problem and not our problem, OK? Because even though we may not look upon these individuals as leaders, they are spokespersons who deserve some recognition and attention, whether you agree or disagree. . . . If we're gonna dialogue, then we're gonna dialogue amongst ourselves, and don't tell me about who I should renounce before we can talk."

The Jews get mixed messages from the blacks about the power of words. On the one hand, the blacks have educated the Jews in the trigger terms that make many blacks bristle—the adjective "qualified" that always seems to precede the noun "blacks" when hiring is discussed, for example, implying that a qualified black is an exception to the rule. "It was really very annoying to you," Eli Schaap tells his black friends. "I had not thought about it. It was very important to me to hear that."

On the other hand, Art Gardner, a black high school teacher, and Mel Henderson, formerly a black high school principal and town councilman, have tried to persuade the Jews that words, and even symbolic actions such as cross burnings, are ephemeral and ought not be exaggerated. "It was an eye-opener," Fern explains. "When we were responding to the Jeffries thing, we were just responding to words. . . . And Art and Mel were both saying, 'We live with this all the time, we live with this constantly, and there's no reason to react. We know where we stand with certain people, these are just words, you have to move on.' And our orientation is so different, because the lessons that we feel from history are that you need to respond when things are at the level of words. If you don't respond very strongly at that level, then things begin to be action."

As the evening wears on, the conversation spins back into the old issue as a floating leaf is drawn into a whirlpool. The Jews try, as they have for two years, to convince the blacks that Jews are at risk in America. And the blacks simply cannot fathom the Jews' anxieties.

"They appear to have all the comforts of America," says Ray Kelly, "and here they're feeling insecure. . . . It's a surprising statement." He has heard them explain about Germany, about their lives collapsing suddenly into Holocaust. "So I can understand their feelings," he says. "But again, my feeling is that it's really not realistic for them to feel that way."

"Do you think if some social conflagration were about to occur that it would hit African-Americans first before it would hit us?" asks Manny Landau, a school psychologist.

"Yeah," says Kelly. Marilyn Taffet, who is Jewish, agrees that the Jews would be next, after the blacks.

"Jews do not necessarily perceive themselves as being terribly powerful," says Chaim Frazer, a black man who has converted to Orthodox Judaism.

"Why? Why?" Kelly asks. "Look at all of the money that's available to the Jews, as far as assets and as far as institutions. Now how can you not relate that as being powerful?"

"An excellent question," Frazer replies, and then instructs his listeners in the basics of history: On the whole, Jews from Europe, and especially from Poland, have been extremely poor, he argues to murmurs of dissent. Their success in the United States has been partly due to "the fact that Jews were not the victims of choice," he says. Blacks were. Therefore, "Jews have also benefited from blacks in ways that are not terribly obvious."

"We all know that," Kelly retorts. "You didn't answer my question. How can Jews not recognize their power?" Frazer starts lecturing on Weimar Germany, igniting a flurry of crosstalk about the relevance of history. Declarations surface in fragments. "Everyone hates us," says Fern. "The Muslims, the Hindus, everybody hates the Jews," says Frazer. "And we're very few in number—" Fern declares.

"You're very few in number," counters Kelly, "but you're very large in power as far as economic dollars."

"It can all be confiscated," Frazer says.

"Can it?"

"It has all been confiscated."

"It has? In America?"

"Not in America, no," Michele March intervenes. "You've got to live with what's happening now." Jews are protected by their influence in the press and other industries, she insists. No, Eli Schaap counters: Jews are practically excluded from the top ranks of many major corporations. His wife, Fern, tries to draw a distinction between wealth and power, one the blacks find hard to accept.

"I can see the look of disbelief on your face," she says, but "power that is based on the acquisition of a certain amount of wealth can be taken away by taking away that wealth. . . . What you said is that it's surprising to you that we feel as insecure as we do, because first of all there's an amount of material assets, and that we're white."

"Most of us, not all of us," remarks Frazer, the black Jew, with a little laugh.

"OK," Fern continues. "In this country most are white. . . . We don't feel white. We don't identify with white. . . . People who feel themselves superior by nature of their skin being white do not consider Jews part of that group." People who regard their white skin as a badge of supremacy provide no privilege or comfort or security to Jews.

"Fern, let me ask you something," Art Gardner says in a voice as quiet and deep as a river. He is a brawny physical education teacher who has made close friends here. Later in the evening, he explains that whites often put him down, but not these folks. "This is the only white group I've ever spoken to that people didn't say to me, 'You are an angry young man.' " Now he is slowing down the discussion to a reflective tempo. "I understand how you feel, and I think we all are aware of that," he tells Fern. "As a matter of fact, you said that months ago, how you don't view yourself as being white. The American white society as a whole, who do you think they would accept if they had a choice—Jewish people or black people?"

"I think if they had a choice they would like to be rid of both of us," she replies. "But if they had to pick, it's obvious that, as Chaim says, we are number two. We're not number one and the most hated. Around the world I think we're very hated. But I think in this country because you're here, we're number two in terms of being hated. Being number two is not a very happy place either. It's nicer than being number one, but it's not really nice. And so, because of that, it feels very insecure. . . . I would venture to say that there's no Jew sitting in here—and I've never spoken to you about this—who does not have an up-to-date passport for yourself and your kids in your desk drawer. Tell me if that's true."

"It's true," one says. "Absolutely," says another. "Absolutely," say all.

"Why? Why?" asks Kelly incredulously. "Are you really serious with this paranoia?" A moment of silence, a couple of voices say, "Yes," and the conversation whirls away as Kelly challenges, questions, tries to understand, and gets no answers concrete enough to persuade or satisfy.

Finally, Art Gardner and Ray Kelly have something to say about fleeing. "I am prepared to leave this world before I would let my children be brought up the way I was brought up in the South," Gardner declares. "No way. I would take some people out, and they will take me out, but I would not let my children be raised the way I was raised. No. I am definitely prepared to leave. Definitely."

"The point that Art just made," Kelly adds: "You're going to carry us out of here. We're not going to take a passport and leave here. We have no intentions of nobody sending us back to Africa or back to anywhere. Where you all are saying, 'Hey, my passport's up to date, and so are my kids' '? Your thing is, hey, I got to escape. Israel. We're saying we're not going anywhere. . . . Hey, this is where we are. And this is where we're going out. OK?"

Conversing

Talking about race is one of the most difficult endeavors in America. Shouting is easy. Muttering and whining and posturing are done with facility. But conversing—black with white, white with black—is a rare and heavy accomplishment. The color line is a curtain of silence.

When Kathleen Sherrell, who is white, was seriously dating Bob Sherrell, the black man who became her husband, her brother and sister-in-law paid her an urgent visit with a vitriolic appeal. "They came in the door, and both of them started attacking me," Kathleen recalls more than two decades later. "Just a vicious attack: That I was trying to kill my father. I would kill my father. That I was rebelling, that that's all I was trying to do, was hurt my parents. On and on. 'You know those people are different. How are you going to handle your children?' The whole thing. And I kicked them out of my apartment. I called them names and told them to go back to church and pray. . . . I didn't have much more to do with them until after we got married. . . . My brother since then has come to me and said, 'That's one of the most shameful times of my life.' He has really talked about it as being something he's very ashamed of."

"But interestingly," Bob says, "he's never told *me* that." Bob is sitting beside Kathleen, and a wince of pain crosses his face. "I—I—I frequently—I think I've forgiven him. I think I have forgiven. I feel that I've forgiven. But I also feel that a piece of me really wants that out on the table. That needs to happen in order to have the closeness, because it is so phony to me to be received and to be hugged and welcomed when I know how they initially reacted to me in 1971. And it just still gnaws in a way."

And has Bob raised it with the brother? His eyes flicker with surprise at the idea, and he shakes his head: no.

If a black and a white in the same family who agree on the shamefulness of a racial episode cannot bring the subject into their conversation for more than twenty years, then a black and a white in a workplace who disagree cannot even think about talking the next day, the next week. In a newsroom, a white reporter wrote a summary of the story he was about to do on the civil war in Somalia. He commented on the country's "tribal politics," and a black reporter who saw the summary bristled. The black went to a white editor and objected to the word "tribal" as a racial allusion to primitive blacks. The white editor went to the white reporter and suggested it be changed. The white reporter, infuriated, defended the word. It had nothing to do with race, he said; Arabs and Jews in Israel, Muslims and Serbs in Bosnia, ethnic groups in confrontation around the world were properly described as "tribes"—a perfectly appropriate anthropological term. The white editor insisted, so the white reporter reluctantly changed it to "Byzantine politics." This so confused a second editor, who knew nothing of the black reporter's objections, that he called the white reporter and suggested that "Byzantine" be changed to "tribal." The white reporter had to be honest and mention the dispute. So, in the end, it came out in the paper as "murky."

The white reporter was still angry the following day, when he told me the story. He was mad not only that he had been misunderstood but that the black reporter had not gone to him directly and that the white editor had shown such cowardice. In that event, I suggested, why didn't he sit down with the black reporter and talk it over? Perhaps they could learn something from each other. He thought for a moment. He hadn't considered such an approach, he said, but he might. Two weeks later, I checked. No, he had decided against a discussion; he was afraid that he would simply lose his temper. And so the incident will remain frozen in the memories of the two reporters just as they initially perceived it—as a piece of subtle racism, on the one side; as a case of false accusation and "politically correct" censorship, on the other.

It is always difficult to begin such a conversation. Anyone who has been present when a racist joke or racist slur is made knows how hard it is to be the first to speak up in protest, for much moral energy is required to overcome the inertia of silence. Usually, a vacuum of acquiescence prevails. If a black person is in the room, she notices what "good" whites fail to say. A doctor, the only African-American in a staff meeting at her hospital, was the only person to object when a white doctor complained about having too little help during a conference. "All I had to count on was this big, fat black woman who was sitting in the chair," he remarked.

"I said, 'Excuse me? What's the relevance of that last statement to the issue?' " she recalled. "He blushed and tried to clean it up, but I never forgot it. Never forgot it." No whites seconded her disapproval. "They just kind of got real uncomfortable and shifted around in their chairs."

Blacks can be so hurt by white silence that the memory of the moment lasts for decades. In 1973, Craig Adams was the only black in his high school in Havre, Montana, where his father was stationed at an air force radar site. Adams was a senior, destined for the Air Force

Academy and ultimately a seat as a navigator on a C-130 cargo plane. In Havre, he was a high school football star, an academic star, and the subject of a good deal of attention in the local paper.

Perhaps a bit of jealousy was aimed in his direction, but the whites on the team were good to him. They introduced him to blue jeans, which he had never worn before. They took him out for his first keg, got him drunk, brought him home. They were his pals, all in it together, wanting to win.

He was running around the track one day when a white man zoomed by on a motorcycle and shouted, "Hey, nigger!" The words came to him unclearly, and Adams was not quite sure of them. Or maybe he was trying to believe that he had not heard what he thought he had. But when he saw how his white teammates reacted, he knew what he had heard. When he glanced toward them, they just looked down or away.

Racist remarks paralyze most whites. They don't know what to do. They also don't know how to apologize. "We were sitting in the lounge one day," said Mary Bowman, the black librarian at Louisiana State University in Shreveport, "and one of the staff members got overenthusiastic trying to tell us her favorite mechanical shop, and we were having a hard time figuring out the exact location that she was talking about, and she said, 'Oh! You know where it is? It's right up there beside that nigger bar.' And of course she kept on talking, and I listened to her, and I said, 'Now what was the name of that bar, again?' Well, only then did she realize what she'd said. And needless to say, my colleagues were flushed red." But nobody said a word of apology. "I was not offended by the remark," Bowman insisted. "I know that these remarks are made. I had no personal feelings against the person who made them: she would have made them anywhere. It was a natural thing, it was natural to describe blacks in that manner, and it was not a personal attack."

But left unresolved, such incidents can fester and infect a relationship fatally. A white friend was lost this way to Russell Ballew, the African-American who became Student Senate president at St. Olaf College in Northfield, Minnesota. He lived for a time in the little white town of Oconomowoc, Wisconsin, where "a very, very close friend" said one day as they were playing in his basement, "Whites are better than blacks."

"That's not true," Ballew remembers himself replying. "We're all equal." But in a long look back, he now wishes that he had felt comfortable enough to do more than argue, had felt enough self-assurance to steer conversation and not merely react, to adopt clear lenses with which to choose his friends, and to demand their loyalty. "It was something that was never resolved," he says of that argument in the basement. "And if it's never resolved, it comes back and acts as a specter to haunt the relationship."

Many whites never learn how blacks feel, because many blacks avoid confrontation. This often seems the safest, least unpleasant course, but it lets whites off the hook. Carlton Chamblin, a black college student from Birmingham, Alabama, dodged and weaved his way around a racist white woman during a job at BellSouth one summer. Older black women working there had warned him that she would interfere with his tasks, would foil his efforts, and "won't be good for you," he said. So he approached her as warily as he would a scorpion. When he needed information from her, "she would not always respond." When he needed it by a certain deadline, "she would not be on time." He took to going over her head and evading her.

Chamblin also abstained from an encounter when he realized that it would have been uncomfortable for his white friends, as well as for him. Spring break was coming up, and Clint Peinhardt, a clean-cut white student from the Alabama town of Cullman, invited Chamblin and some whites up to his parents' house on a lake. They planned to go horseback riding on his grandparents' nearby farm. Something clicked in Chamblin's memory of a remark that Peinhardt had once made about his grandparents being very racist, so Chamblin asked whether there would be any problems in his going.

"What I was thinking," Peinhardt recalled, "was that we would actually have to get my grandmother out of the house and off the farm while we went to ride horses. Or somehow allow us to sneak in there and ride horses without her knowing what was going on." If Chamblin had simply arrived at the door, Peinhardt surmised, "she really would not have confronted the issue, I don't think. But it would have made her very uncomfortable, and it would have made me very uncomfortable."

"Clint said, 'If there is gonna be a problem, then none of us go horseback riding,'" Chamblin remembered. "I said, 'Wait a minute. I'm not gonna be the reason why everyone else is not going to enjoy spring break by not going horseback riding. If anything, I will not attend any of the events at all that week, because I'm not going to stand for it.'" His white friends properly insisted that he be included. But in the end, Chamblin managed to stay behind in Birmingham for most of the vacation to finish some work, "so I never got to Cullman in time for horseback riding."

"It sort of fizzled out," said Peinhardt.

"Had he encouraged me," Chamblin added, "I think I would have enjoyed myself, and I would have been just as congenial and just as nice to his grandmother, knowing probably what she was sensing, and I would have taken full advantage of it." He smiled impishly. "Oh, gosh, I would have asked her for iced tea and everything. I would have been all in her face. That's probably what I would have done, just to see how she would react." But he did not.

It's hard to blame anyone for sneaking around to avoid experiencing racism, or even to avoid talking about it. But that kind of self-protection tends to leave the status quo intact. It fails to provoke any change of interaction or any exploration of self. And while both blacks and whites are prone to the aversion, professionals who instruct and facilitate in this area tend to see whites as considerably more inhibited. "You'll see a black person or a minority open up about these issues, because nine times out of ten they can speak from experience," said Horace Little-john, a black lieutenant colonel in the air force who supervised diversity trainers at a Pentagon institute in Florida. "And whites, 'Oh, no, here we go again. And then the finger's going to be pointed at me, like it's my fault.'" From behind one-way observation mirrors, Littlejohn watched this pattern unfold in many groups. "I do believe that whites have a tougher time dealing with issues of race discrimination," he said. And that can become a problem, for the institute is where the army, air force, navy, marines, and Coast Guard send carefully selected career people to be schooled in the art of managing racial and gender conflict in the ser-vices. "If they can't get in touch and deal and talk about this business, if they can't get in touch with where they are themselves with this and open up and let it come out at this time, we're very hesitant about sending them back out in the field . . . to work and advise that com-mander." The taciturn student is tutored, counseled, told "that you need to talk about these issues, overcome these fears, these blockages," Little-john explained. But if he cannot open up, he is "disenrolled" from the school.

The all-black Russian language class at Lincoln University was on edge, ready to pounce. Islanda Goode, Paul Robeson's niece, was fresh from Moscow, and she had just begun teaching here. She looked white, although she was biracial. She wrote on the board the Russian words for various colors: *byely* ("white"), *chyorny* ("black"), *krasny* ("red"), and *sinyi* ("blue"). From among the students, a woman's voice rang out: "Why did you put 'white' first? That's racist." Goode stopped short. She screwed up her face into deep thought and pretended to ponder the accusation. "Yes," she said finally, "it is deeply racist. So perhaps we should put 'yellow' first. But that would mean Asian, so non-Asians would find it racist. We could begin with 'blue,' except that's what we call gay people, so that would seem to favor them. How about beginning with 'green'?" By then, the class had started to laugh, and the complaining student had as well.

A little humor is a good antidote in a moment of racial tension, but it probably takes someone in Goode's unique position as an outsider-insider to defuse such a charge by laughing at it. Few white Americans would be bold enough to try, and it's a technique that can easily go wrong. Indeed, many techniques go wrong. Talking is not a panacea, and even when whites and blacks make an attempt, they often fumble around awkwardly with each other.

As a black man in a mostly white setting, and as a person who believed in clear communication, Bruce King traveled this terrain extensively. "When people say things that puzzle me and I don't understand it, I've learned to just ask them," he explained. " 'I don't understand what you're saying. Can you help me better understand it?' " That was enough to stimulate some useful discussion. But he also found that discussion could become burdensome, especially as a black alone at an all-white dinner table, peppered with questions.

At the time, King was the director of minority affairs at Lake Forest College, north of Chicago. He and his wife, Marcine, were the only blacks at a dinner meeting where I gave a speech about race and made the point that we don't talk to one another very well, don't listen to one another, and don't hear ourselves. Then we sat down to eat. Unfortunately for King and his wife, my remarks prompted a barrage of inquiries from genuinely interested and concerned white people who had probably never had such an easy opening to vent their curiosity on African-Americans.

How does it feel to be black? What is it like to be black in Lake Forest? Why aren't you angry? "I was asked that question," King told me the next morning. " 'With all that's going on, how come you're not more angry? Shouldn't you be angry?' " He thought talking was healthy. "It gives people an opportunity to be honest and ask questions," he said. "But seldom are you in an atmosphere where they just come at you and they're constant. At our table, they were just constant. Before I could sit down, one of the women at the table said, 'I'm sorry he didn't talk more about solutions.' And she saw me coming to the table, and she says, 'Well, here's a guy who's going to give us the solutions to these problems.' At first, I thought she was joking, 'cause surely—even if you listen to your presentation last night, it's clear that there really are no clear-cut solutions. But I mean, every five minutes, it was like, 'So what is the solution? What is the solution to what happened in L.A.? What is the solution to black-on-black crime?' She wanted to know." He seemed bemused and weary. "It would have been nice to have a few more black people at the event, because I really seriously got tired of answering the questions," he said. "I mean, you would finish one, and somebody was coming with another one. And these were not just yes or no, and people wanted articulate answers."

Being on stage, even at casual parties, became so exhausting that King and his wife decided to avoid the subject of race if possible. "It's no longer fun to be someplace when you are speaking and having to think and articulate at a party," he complained. At a dinner the previous summer, he and his wife had been grabbed by a white woman on the staff who wanted to check his view on something a black student had told her: that she couldn't imagine how hard being black was in this environment. Was that true? King tried a short answer, explaining that most black students, including those who have gone to mostly white high schools, have never lived immersed in a predominantly white environment with no black family to go home to for support. Another white woman disagreed that the campus was such a hostile place. King replied by citing some of his unpleasant personal experiences. Soon he and his wife were encircled by a group of whites listening to the debate. "Then I was told that I was too sensitive," he said in annoyance, "that she didn't believe me or tried to write it off as me being sensitive. Then I was angry, I became frustrated, and we were ready to go home."

Coping

"Being a black person in a racist society is like being the moon going through meteor showers," Nell Painter, the history professor at Princeton, remarked laughingly. She admired undergraduates who expended enormous effort combating racism. But she had come to a different stage in life. "I am so hardened that it's almost impossible for me to see or feel things unless they're really gross," she said. "You could learn that there are some things that you just can't deal with and let them go, or you could spend all your time responding and being torn." She recalled a graduate student in his mid-thirties who was perpetually infuriated by the racism he saw around him. "My thought was, You're just going to have to let some of this go, because there are other things you have to do with your energy, and what's the use of getting an ulcer? I mean, you can get an ulcer and you can have an ulcer, or you can do your work and pick your fights."

Every African-American adjusts her level of sensitivity and outrage, either by instinct or by force of will. Daphne LeCesne's coping method involved intellectualizing the bigotry. A black school psychologist in Illinois, she occasionally had white parents of troubled children erupt in racist vehemence. "I've sat at tables with people who said, 'You black people don't know how to handle my kids, and the reason we don't live near you and we don't let you live near us is we knew you would do this to our kids, and you bused my kid in here, and nigger this and nigger that,'" she reported. She learned to take this not as a personal attack but as a symptom of a problem. She showed parents how the racial issue was being used by the child to mask or excuse deeper troubles. "Even if your kid says he hates all the black kids in the class," she would explain, "even if your kid says he hates all the black staff, there's a reason for that. And I will propose to you that the reason is, it serves something here. You wouldn't hear it, and he wouldn't also be failing, and he wouldn't also be encountering behavioral difficulties if that's all there was to it." She added, "I learned, I guess, to take racism along with everything else and try to interpret what it accomplished for the child and what it accomplished for the parents."

Putting a psychological label on racism is one way of impersonalizing it, detoxifying it, sealing it off. Every person defends herself in one or another manner, but the method selected does not always improve the chemistry across the racial line.

A black policewoman in Baltimore adopted an intentional pose of cockiness to keep the bigots away. They said she had an attitude and called her a bitch, but she thought it was worth it. "To me it was more or less a defense mechanism," she said.

A male colleague, also black, took the opposite tack. He recognized that white cops who told racist jokes in his presence were testing him "to see what I'd do and what I would say and if I was militant or if I was going to let anything just go on by." He chose silence. "I just wouldn't say anything. I would try to lead them around to where they didn't know where I was coming from. I more or less just kind of eased on away." But the soft approach had an unintended effect, he admitted: "They'd take my kindness for weakness, and they'd just run with it."

A black air force officer, Captain Will Gunn, searched for a safe harbor of people he could talk to, sympathetic peers or mentors. "There has to be a cone of silence or some kind of sanctuary," he said. "It helps if it's somebody in that environment who knows exactly what you are talking about."

For racially mixed couples in many parts of the country, avoidance of conflict is a principle that permeates everyday life, from big decisions to small. Valda Smith Jungblut moved with her white husband to Teaneck, New Jersey, because it is a multiracial town. "I wouldn't live in some of the other towns around here," she said. "Not at all." The family picks every vacation spot cautiously, checking it out to make sure "it's a place that's very tolerant," as she put it. Doug and Nancy Deuchler, who are white and black, respectively, carefully chose Oak Park, Illinois, as their home because it has been self-consciously integrated. When they drive in the Chicago area, they shun single-ethnic enclaves, such as all-white Cicero or all-black sections of the West Side.

Gina and Tony Wyatt have set a pattern of secrecy throughout their entire relationship. "Our first date was March 5, 1976," she remembered, not long after their high school in Gadsden, Alabama, had been integrated. She was a white senior with thick brown hair, drawn to this slim young man with a complexion like mocha. "We went out to a dark spot, close to the vocational school," she said. "I drove up in my car, turned my lights out. He jumped the fence over the vocational school, got in the car, and we set there talking, trying to get to know each other."

This represented the deepest rebellion Gina could have conducted against her upbringing. "I remember in Sears when I was young, they had two water fountains," she noted. "And over one, it said: 'For Whites Only.' And every time we'd go in there I'd say, 'Mom, what's the other one for?' And she'd say, 'That's for colored people.' And I'd say, 'Well, why are there separate water fountains?' And she'd say, 'Well, colored people are dirty, and you don't want to drink from the same water fountain that they do.' So I remember as a child, wondering: I don't understand. I don't see why you say that they're dirty. And every time, I would go over and drink out of the colored water fountain, and she'd always get on me, 'Don't do that!' . . . When I came into high school, I always tried to be friends with the black girls: 'Oh, hi, how ya doin'?' "

"We used to sneak off to Birmingham," said Tony. That was a place where nobody knew them and he and Gina could be together openly. When his family found out, they mostly feared for the couple's safety. Her mother had a different reaction. Tony had enlisted and was stationed in California. He had been writing Gina letters, full of poetry and love, which she had been hiding in her car. Her mother found them.

"What's the big secret about these letters?" her mother asked. "This sounds like a really nice guy, you know, and sounds like he really loves you. Why are you hiding this guy?"

"Because he's black," Gina answered. Her mother fell down crying and forbade her daughter to see him again. So Gina ran away, flew to California, married Tony, and so far has lived happily—but warily. Both of them are gun-shy about disclosing their mixed marriage to people with power over them until they know it is safe to do so.

Near Patrick Air Force Base in Florida, where Tony served as a diversity trainer for the military, Gina got a job as a dentist's receptionist, and during her two-week trial, she was careful not to mention that her husband was black. She scrutinized the reactions of the staff to a black patient who came in. "Everyone was really nice," she said. "It didn't matter to them, and I thought, Well, I'm gonna like it here." After her trial period had passed, "I showed them pictures of the kids," she said. "I didn't say anything, I didn't say anything about Tony being black or anything. And they said, 'Oh, what beautiful kids.' Well, about a week or so later we just happened to be talking, and I jokingly said to one of the other girls I worked with, 'Well, you know my husband is black.' She said, 'Yeah, I saw when you started showing pictures of your kids, I sort of had that feeling, but I told the doctor, "Did you know that Gina's husband is black?" And he said, "No, but what does it matter? It doesn't have anything to do with her job." . . . I don't care.' I said, 'That's good, 'cause if you guys had had a problem with it, then I couldn't work here.' "

When Tony arrives at a new assignment, he also lets a period of time pass before he introduces Gina to his colleagues. While he regards the military as a refuge for mixed couples, he has felt a sudden coldness descend over some whites and blacks once they discover that his wife is white. In the civilian world, he habitually goes alone to discuss such matters as automobile loans. "I'm not sure how in tune she is to how I do this, because I've never voiced it," he said with Gina sitting beside him. "She'll never be with me when I go to get a loan, because I believe it has a direct impact on my dealing with a loan officer."

Had she known? She shook her head. And if he had told her, how would she have felt? "Well, I would have agreed with him," she said softly. "I would have, you know, thought if I went with him that whoever the loan officer was probably would not have pushed it through."

Techniques of survival are passed from generation to generation, both by example and by conscious decision, and no two parents are quite alike in teaching children how to cope with bigotry. In mixed marriages, the black partner tends to take the lead in setting the style and giving the advice, for the white mother or father rarely has a sense of what skills are needed by a youngster who is considered black.

Gina Wyatt was inclined to try to protect her three children, especially her two daughters. But Tony wanted all of them to learn to deal on their own, and he resisted the temptation to rush into school whenever a racial incident occurred. His thirteen-year-old son, Justin, began running into problems after he revealed in class that he was not merely white, as he appeared, but biracial. The teacher started grading him down, and other youngsters gave him trouble. A white boy told him that blacks shouldn't be allowed onto the golf course because they would tear it up and trash it. Justin exploded in anger and walked out of class.

He was coached through the crisis by both parents, primarily by Tony, who counseled firmness, hard work, and nonviolence. "I grew up violent," Tony said, "and I know that violence does not solve anything. . . . What I told him to do was to go back and just continue doing what he was doing and address the issue directly, because I want him to be able to confront these issues. . . . We really don't want to go out and rescue them every time. We do want to protect them, don't get me wrong. But they need to develop the skills to do it themselves."

The obligation to give a black child the tools he needs to function and survive amid racial bias adds a layer of duty to African-Americans' parenting that whites simply do not confront. So trying is the task that entire books of advice have been written to help point the way. In *Different and Wonderful: Raising Black Children in a Race-Conscious Society*, a married couple, Darlene Powell Hopson and Derek S. Hopson, who are black psychologists, lay out a series of steps designed to encourage open discussion and maintain a youngster's self-esteem amid pejorative portrayals of blacks. "Children should be taught about race at the earliest possible time," they state. "It is a parent's obligation to learn a child's innermost thoughts about race." If a child is afraid of white people, parents are advised, she should be helped to associate with whites "with whom you yourself feel comfortable."

Nancy Boyd-Franklin, a noted black psychologist, urges parents to assist children in developing a sense of "Blackness" and to give them "enough information about the realities of the world so that they are prepared without becoming immobilized or so bitter that they are unable to function." This is a tricky balance to achieve, for children must be taught to believe in themselves and to embrace a "philosophy of hope" even where "an older child succumbs to drugs, truancy, and/or other destructive activities," she writes.

Racial problems can be masked by their symptoms, and parents who don't talk openly with their children risk missing the core issues. Boyd-Franklin cites the case of Melanie, a black girl who developed serious academic problems after moving from a public to a private school in New York City. During counseling, the mother was asked by the therapist to talk to her daughter about her experience in the new school. "Melanie burst into tears. She told her mother that she had never felt so alone. She was used to having lots of friends at her other school. Here she was the only black child in her class. None of the other kids ever invited her to do things with them." One child informed her that she was too black to be her friend.

The mother "was shocked," Boyd-Franklin writes. "She asked Melanie why she had not told her before. Melanie stated that she had tried but her mother was so angry at her for not doing well that she was afraid." The therapist then took several steps. First, she "normalized Melanie's struggle" by assuring her that the sense of aloneness was quite common for black youngsters in mostly white private schools. Second, she encouraged the mother to talk with her children about how she felt as one of the few blacks on her job, pointed out that Melanie and her mother shared the common trait of being "different," and asked the mother to explain how she handled it. Finally, the mother was urged to contact the teacher, call parents of schoolmates to arrange get-togethers, and help Melanie maintain contact with her old friends in the neighborhood.

In large measure, parenting is autobiographical. Most of us raise our children approximately the way we were raised. And therefore, as African-American parents discuss race or avoid it, they often echo their own upbringing and reflect their own intimate sensations of comfort or awkwardness. For many blacks, race can be as difficult a subject of conversation as sex is to most parents. A riot of conflicting emotions storms through such dialogues. In an effort to help, Hopson and Hopson have drawn up a self-test for parents, who indicate the extent to which they feel exhausted, nervous, frustrated, irritated, disappointed, regretful, depressed, angry, embarrassed, guilty, desperate, calm, confident, patient, helpful, enthusiastic, friendly, happy, or concerned when they talk about race with their children. The authors note that many of those who have never had an open conversation on the subject "usually express regret. When racism surfaces the child is often devastated. ('Why didn't you tell me?' is a sad and frequent refrain.)"

Racial sensibilities are swaddled in ambiguity. That is something of the lesson that Sharon Walter of the Houston Urban League tries to impart to her children: Be tough-minded, but give some grace and don't automatically condemn others as racists. "I try to teach my children that racism is real, 'cause it is," she says. "But you can't let that stop you. I teach my children that you've got to be the best, not because you're black but just because you are. . . . If they come home and they tell me that something happened and they perceive it to be racist, I try to present two views. . . . One, so that they'll be able to recognize it, if it was, the next time it happens. Or the other side, so they'll be able to take a look and say, 'Well, maybe that wasn't racism. Maybe I did something. . . . Was I really up to par? Was I really all I should have been?' "

It is a great burden to place on children.

Bob Sherrell's family never gave him the tools. His father was a very light-skinned automobile mechanic with a seventh- or eighth-grade education who "was able to get along by going along," Sherrell said. "If someone called him a 'nigger,' my dad would say, 'Oh, I'm sorry you feel that way.' And then when he and I were together—'cause I'd work with him in the summer months—then he would grouse and say, 'Son of a bitch,' or 'What the fuck is he thinking?' But then we'd get back in that larger gathering; my dad would be just as accommodating, just as friendly. . . . That's how I learned. I learned how to live with that. And I suspect that I have my own source of anger about what I saw happen to my father and how he accommodated."

Sherrell's wife, Kathleen, was a psychologist, but as a white person, she knew no more than he did about teaching a black child to handle racism. When their son, Matt, would bring white friends home, Sherrell said, "they would bullshit and jive and all that, and I would listen to them, and I would try to—again—accommodate, because I know how important it is for Matt to have friends. But most of those guys, Matt would tell me about some of the statements they would make: 'Look at that big-ass nigger on the television,' you know. That would slip out." And Sherrell would be accommodating by saying nothing.

Then, one Memorial Day, everything blew up. Matt was fifteen, and he came home crying. He was tired of his friends calling him 'nigger,' he said. His father exploded, marched down their street in Oak Park, Illinois, and yelled and scolded and shouted at the boys, "No nigger-calling on this block!" Stunned, his pals deserted Matt like drunkards scurrying from the Salvation Army. Friendships that had been formed in eighth grade suddenly evaporated. Matt was miserable and angry at his father—and at himself for having fudged the facts a bit.

They had not called him "nigger"—not that day, at least, although they had done so in the past. "I made a mistake," Matt confessed. "I wouldn't really call it a lie, but I guess my father mistook it for something else, 'cause I said I was sick of them calling me a 'nigger.' " What happened that day had nothing obviously to do with race. "I was having a really bad week, and I've always been the guy who got picked on, because I was the smallest of them all. . . . They tied me up in a hose and turned the sprinkler on. I had Rollerblades on, so it was hard for me to stand up. Every time I stood up, they pulled the hose so I'd fall back down again. Then I just like got up and blew up on them and just went home."

It had been a long time in coming. Like his father and his father's father, Matt had made his accommodations with the swirl of ethnic slurs that his friends enjoyed. "Like this kid Seth, he's Jewish, so they called him 'kike,' " Matt said. "And these kids Anthony and Nick, called them 'dago,' 'wop.' This kid Dave down the street, they used to call him 'mick.' . . . Usually I wouldn't start it. Usually they would start it. I would just listen and chuckle at some of it. I wouldn't really say anything, because I would know how they felt if I had said anything."

He objected when they called him "nigger," Matt said, but ineffectually. "I told them a lot of times before that I didn't appreciate it. It was, like, persistent. They wouldn't stop even if I told them that that was wrong."

What got to his father was the boy's sense of powerlessness. "Matt said, 'Dad, the terrible thing is, how can I come back? I can't come back. You never heard any good comeback that says something about a white guy being white.' The joke was 'How do you get five black guys off raping a white girl? You throw a basketball at them.' OK, so Matt says, 'I don't have any comebacks. . . . I can't hurt them as much as they can hurt me.' "

The day after Bob Sherrell assailed Matt's friends, he had to go pick his son up from school, the atmosphere had turned so nasty, said his mother, Kathleen. "They're jeering him for bringing his dad in," she remembered. "So Matt said to me, 'Why did Dad have to do that?' He was really upset with him that he had interfered. It has never mended. That rift has never mended, and he's had to accumulate all new friends since that happened." She turned to her husband. "If we replayed that," she said, "I think that I would have stopped you from going down there and gotten Matt more involved in deciding what was the best thing at that moment, even though I understood how you felt and how angry you were. I think maybe if I were going to replay that again, I think it probably would have been better to have Matt fight back than to have Bob do it."

"See, I think that's the difference, again, between our perspectives and culture," Bob shot back. "While I agree with you very rationally and very logically, the thing to do would be to sit down and problem-solve . . . I feel at that time the only thing I could do—and I feel strong-ly about it—was to show those white kids that there was a line being drawn. . . . So maybe for the rest of his life, Matt will hate me for having done that, maybe his friends will hate me and hate him, but I think the tension . . . gets focused when I think about what happened on that par-ticular day, that Memorial Day in the most tolerant of communities, allegedly, in the most idyllic of settings, this block here. My kid comes home and says that he's just had to deal with that. So I can't be like Kath-leen and say I can deal with this kind of thing—emotionless and do problem solving. Hell, no."

Eventually, Matt moved into a new group of friends, both black and white, who did not use ethnic slurs.

Conventional wisdom has long held that every baby is born pristine, pure, completely free of prejudice. Bigotry must then be learned. Intol-erance must be taught and taught until it builds up in layers of tarnish on the silvery mind of the child.

This is undoubtedly so, but there is another perspective. In American society, a child has only to breathe and listen and watch to accumulate the prejudices that govern ordinary thought. Even without willful inten-tion, with no active effort, a youngster absorbs the images and carica-tures surrounding race. Nobody growing up in America can escape the assumptions and expectations that attach themselves to one group or another. Intolerance is naturally learned. What must be consciously taught is tolerance.

Steve Suitts teaches tolerance. He does it in his civil rights work, and he does it at home. So when he heard his six-year-old son try to choose between two toys by saying, "Eenie, meenie, miney, moe—" Suitts inter-rupted him right there, with a harsh shout of "Stop! Don't say that!" The boy was so startled that he finished the rhyme by reflex: "—Catch a tiger by the toe." And Suitts was cooled by a rush of relief, for when he was a boy, the rhyme he had learned ended "Catch a nigger by the toe."

"We stopped, and he was sort of speechless," Suitts said, "and he was just confused as to what I'd done." Where had his son heard the "tiger" version? Suitts asked. From his black kindergarten teacher. "I told him his daddy had grown up in a place where that rhyme was said differently and it hurt people," Suitts said, "and I didn't explain to him what the difference was, but I said it was a lot different. 'But the way your teacher taught it to you was fine, and that just remember that if you say things that hurt other people, then you have to expect to have people say things that will hurt you.' " Then Suitts mused, "I had sort of let the old ghosts take over."

CHAPTER TEN

Acting Affirmatively

I believe that segregation was planned, and if you're going to have racial diversity, you better plan it.

—*Sherlynn Reid,*
community relations director of Oak Park, Illinois

Controlling Racism

Prejudice is merely a thought. It can be as fleeting as the darting shadow of a squall or as constant as the grip of a deep winter. It can dance invisibly at the edge of consciousness or grotesquely at the center of imagination.

But it needn't be expressed in action. Contained inside the mind, a belief may remain a belief and never be transformed into behavior. So it is with many thoughts: perverse sexual thoughts, violent thoughts. Fortunately, most people never act on them. And to that end, to curtail and manage the acting out of racist thoughts, American society has erected a superstructure of manners, ethics, laws, regulations, institutional customs, and training programs. Americans invoke the power of government, employers, and peers against the demons within.

As the country's experience with race has become more sophisticated, the machinery of control has grown complex. Lessons have been learned about how cunning bigotry can be, how slyly thought may corrupt action, and what subtlety the means of correction must possess. There are many ways of discriminating racially; they lie along a broad continuum from the overt to the unconscious. The corresponding ways of preventing or dampening discrimination cover as wide a range, from the punitive to the intuitive.

The crudest and most blatant forms of anti-black behavior are the most familiar and the most easily recognized. When blacks are excluded from jobs and labor unions, rarely promoted, kept out of fraternities and country clubs, denied apartments, turned down by colleges, and refused service in restaurants, few people have trouble identifying racism as the cause and legal sanction as the appropriate reaction. Public values, revised in the long aftermath of the civil rights movement, no longer allow race to be the sole basis for rejection. Against that shifting morality, racist incidents stand out like stark aberrations; many whites see them as pesky weeds that poke up through the lush countryside of American goodwill.

Where the discrimination is subtle, however, or expresses itself in reasonable, nonracial terms, it is cloaked in the camouflage of legitimacy. It blends into the background of propriety, where it is difficult to discern, to analyze, to correct. If a black employee is regarded by white supervisors as lacking leadership ability—a flaw that can curb a career—it may be true, or it may come from that silent assumption that blacks don't quite belong in positions of power. If a black army officer is repeatedly marked down for "lack of sociability" and poor communication skills, the judgment may derive from that diffuse sense of blacks as different, other, apart. Indeed the perception of difference can magnify other negative traits: A black worker will "go it alone" or won't be "a member of the team." A black professor's unusual ideas put him "out of the mainstream" or reveal his "political agenda," which means that he doesn't get hired or doesn't get tenure. In the case of the pilot trainee, a black's supposed inferior competence prompts the white flight instructor to intervene again and again, seizing the controls and never allowing the student to progress.

Whites who discriminate subtly may not even be aware of what they are doing; almost all would vehemently deny being racists. They can fool themselves into honestly thinking that what they are seeing is one characteristic (lack of leadership ability) when their perception is actually triggered by another (blackness). Suitably disguised, prejudice can operate without being noticed, unseen even by those who hold the biases. Bigotry is an adaptable shape-shifter, mutating to survive in a hostile climate by translating itself into accepted behavior and fastening onto the handiest rationale.

Tools have been developed to fight that insidious bias, and good people across America labor with them to carve out myriad zones of sincerity, small regions of earnest effort that go largely uncounted by the press and the public. But most individuals do not pick up the tools, and most institutions do not make them available. They prefer to think that race has no role in their actions.

The denial is understandable in a society that excoriates racism so that little room is left for any admission of even the mildest guilt. Racism is seen as an absolute—either you're infected, or you're not—rather than what it truly is: one ingredient of behavior that is either more or less pronounced. White people are told, first, that racism is a severe sin and, second, that they must acknowledge and purge the racism within themselves—but without any promise of a secular form of salvation. This is asking a lot of human nature; it leaves no space for serious self-examination except, perhaps, in carefully controlled workshops.

Consequently, many white Americans are quite generous in giving themselves the benefit of the doubt. They tend to define racism narrowly enough that it does not tarnish them, and they approve only the most tightly focused methods of prevention—which they themselves, of course, do not need. Along the continuum, as the blatant prejudice becomes subtle, as the obvious discrimination becomes indirect, as the control mechanisms grow more complex, the consensus about what is happening and what must be done falls away. Fewer and fewer whites agree that racism is involved, and fewer and fewer endorse the measures designed to counteract its effects. As a result, the broadest support goes to the crudest instruments, such as the most basic anti-discrimination laws; the most refined mechanisms, such as affirmative action and sensitivity training, are often seen as neither necessary nor legitimate.

So most blacks and whites work and study in settings where disguised racial discrimination could probably be curbed, at least to a degree. But it is left fairly free to operate by police chiefs, university presidents, government leaders, and chief executive officers of corporations who refuse to face up to the pervasive qualities of racial bias. It takes only a modicum of education for people to recognize that if a black candidate for a job or a promotion is judged to be a poor team player, it may be another way of saying, "You're different, and I have less tolerance of your difference than I would of a white's; I am more comfortable with people like me, and you and I have no common ground to outweigh our dissonance." Similarly, the white flight instructor who has been taught about the classic patterns of anti-black stereotyping might examine his own assumptions about blacks' incompetence as he moves to take control. This is the ideal: to search your attitudes, identify your stereotypes, and correct for them as you go about your daily duties. In the end, managing prejudice becomes a very personal task. Yet it can be facilitated by institutional mechanisms.

On a late summer day in the early 1990s, the dean, who was white, rose to welcome the black and Hispanic students entering one of the country's leading law schools. They had been invited a week early for special orientation, and he had a delicate message for them. His remarks were born of anguish, for he knew something that they did not: They had been admitted with lower average scores than their white classmates had earned on the Law School Aptitude Test.

He wanted to warn them but not defeat them. He could not tell them of the disparities in test scores, because his school, like virtually all others, tried to keep such information secret. So he took an oblique approach. He himself had come from a small town, not an intellectual background, he told the new students. To overcome that deprivation, he had been forced to apply enormous effort, and so would they. "If you work extremely hard," he remembered himself saying, "you can make up for differences in past credentials."

His talk was as welcome as an earthquake. "I was deeply criticized by a number of faculty who felt I had hurt these people on their first day at the institution," he said. "I felt terrible."

The issue confronted him more directly when a group of Hispanic students approached him for reassurance. They were being tormented by white classmates who insisted that Hispanics had scored lower than whites on the LSAT and did not deserve to be there. They wanted the smear refuted. "I tried to be very candid with them," the dean recalled. It was true, he told them: Their scores had been somewhat lower, but with hard work they could erase the deficiencies of their pasts.

An awful silence descended. "I just looked into their eyes as I was talking," the dean remembered, "and I thought, 'I can't bear this; it's too painful.' Their hopes and expectations about what would be said were defeated. There was just a feeling of betrayal."

So goes the conversation about one of the most critical methods used to pry open doors long locked against Hispanics, blacks, and other minorities. The truth cannot be told on any campus without stigmatizing those being aided, without giving a weapon to conservative opponents of such efforts. This law school cannot be identified, the dean cannot be named. He cannot be quoted, except anonymously, as he reveals that if only scores and not race were taken into account, only five or six blacks would be admitted each year instead of forty or fifty. A full and honest discussion of how colleges and graduate schools increase the numbers of African-Americans in their ranks cannot be had.

But why not? How shameful can it be, after generations of imprisonment in inferior educational systems, to score lower on a standardized test? How unfair can it be, after three hundred years of white advantage, to spend thirty years redressing the imbalance? And how unwise can it be, after failing to tap the vast resources of black America, to search affirmatively past the sterile test scores into a rich human potential not easily measured?

Instead of wearing this practice as a badge of honor, most universities fudge the facts. They are devoted to a racially diverse student body as being essential to their educational mission: to provide for members of groups that have been deprived of opportunity, to educate the future leaders of all groups in the country, and to create a campus community with a variety that will enrich everyone's experience. You can't prepare young people to live in the United States of the twenty-first century by confining them for four years in a homogeneous setting. So the best colleges trip over one another competing for the small pool of black students with high grades and test scores. Recruiters visit inner-city high schools, generous financial aid is offered, and the best black candidates are flown to campus for free weekends.

But the differences in scores on the Scholastic Assessment Test are shrouded in silence. The Consortium on Financing Higher Education, which collects member colleges' statistics on the racial breakdown of their students' scores, guards the figures jealously; it complained to the publisher of *The Bell Curve* about printing "confidential data" without permission—namely, a bar graph showing twenty-six top schools where black students' SAT scores had ranged from 95 to 228 points below the white mean. The reason the scores are kept secret is that "they tend to be taken in isolation," explained the consortium's director of research, Larry Litten. "When used in the admissions process, they're taken with other data to give a big picture. The SAT scores alone do violence to this big picture. All the other subtle, less quantifiable, issues get lost. They don't give people access to the other parts of the picture that admissions officers have."

What would happen if admissions officers made their case openly and fully, putting the lower scores into that broader context? In an unfriendly racial climate, conservative whites would use the numbers in bruising condemnation of black classmates, and blacks would surely feel inadequate. "Of course we're all concerned that releasing those figures would be damaging to the self-esteem of minority students," said Mary Childers, director of equal opportunity and affirmative action at Dartmouth. "But I think the hidden secret is doing a lot of damage also. So if we released the figures and talked about what they meant, we might be able to handle the situation better."

The hidden secret is more like an open one. Many students think they already know the score differentials; the confidentiality just makes the whole enterprise of minority recruitment seem vaguely illicit, and that feeds majority resentment as much as if the disparities were announced. When the numbers leak out, as they did at Georgetown Law School several years ago, they cause an outcry of pain and anger. And when sued, an institution is often forced to reveal the data, as the University of Texas Law School did for its entering class in 1992: The mean LSAT score of all 500 new students was 162 (on a scale of 120 to 180), putting them at the 89th percentile; the mean for blacks was 158, at the 78th percentile. It was a small difference, but if only grades and test scores had been considered, the school stated, only nine blacks instead of forty-one would have been admitted, and only eighteen Mexican-Americans instead of fifty-five. Indeed, after a federal court struck down the law school's affirmative action program, only five blacks and eighteen Mexican-Americans were admitted for the fall of 1997.

While individual colleges avoid publicizing the SAT scores of their own students by race, the College Board provides a breakdown for all high school students who take the test. Here, too, blacks' average scores have trailed whites' (434 to 526 on the verbal test in 1996, 422 to 523 on the math), but the gap has been closing. Furthermore, scores have a socio-economic component: the higher the parents' income and educational background, the better the scores in both racial groups. Among blacks and whites with the same income, however, the blacks' scores remain behind the whites'. The 1996 mean scores for whites with family income of $20,000 to $30,000 were 505 on the verbal test and 499 on the math; for blacks in the same income bracket, the scores were 431 and 417. Over $100,000, the whites scored 582 and 567; the blacks, 509 and 488.

Since a person cannot be reduced to a test score, the most skilled admissions officers use the SATs only to a point. In weighing an applicant's test performance, many say, they try to correct for background. If a black student from the South Bronx gets a 650 and a white from Scarsdale gets a 700, one admissions director explained, "the 650 probably represents a greater achievement, given the circumstances, than the 700." The circumstances include a host of environmental factors, he noted. "A lot of it is family-based, going back into primary education, reading. And then instruction in schools, going back into primary schools. That doesn't deal with an unresolved question on whether tests are culturally biased."

This joins the old argument about whether reaching out to minority applicants results in lower standards, a central issue that would have to be discussed openly if the racial breakdown of the scores were released. "We should talk about the presumed and the actual relationships among

SATs, achievement in college (and I would define achievement broadly), and the contributions people go on to make to society," Mary Childers declared. "We know you can have a C average and become a vice president. We know that students who have a C or B average go on and do remarkable work in a variety of communities."

Although SAT scores are reliable predictors of freshman grades, they forecast later achievement less accurately. Harvard studied alumni in its classes of '57, '67, and '77 and found that graduates with low SAT scores and blue-collar backgrounds displayed a high rate of "success"—defined by income, community involvement, and professional satisfaction. Here is where race and socioeconomic background mix; some admissions officers believe that if affirmative action were aimed particularly at lower-class students, it would generate less opposition. But it would also yield fewer blacks, since two-thirds of eighteen-year-olds below the poverty line are white. Furthermore, giving preference to students who need financial aid would cost more in scholarships than most colleges have. Consequently, some universities seek upper-middle-class blacks, who can bring diversity and also afford the tuition. However, other elite schools, such as Dartmouth, Harvard, and the Massachusetts Institute of Technology, do give a nod to lower-class applicants. "We have particular interest in students from a modest background," said Marlyn McGrath Lewis, director of admissions for Harvard and Radcliffe. "Coupled with high achievement and a high ambition level and energy, a background that's modest can really be a help. We know that's the best investment we can make: a kid who's hungry."

The two words "affirmative action" were first put together during the inauguration of President John F. Kennedy in 1961, when Vice President Lyndon Johnson, standing in a receiving line, buttonholed a young black attorney named Hobart Taylor Jr. and asked him to help advisers Arthur Goldberg and Abe Fortas write Executive Order 10925 barring federal contractors from racial discrimination in hiring. "I was searching for something that would give a sense of positiveness to performance under that executive order, and I was torn between the words 'positive action' and the words 'affirmative action,' " Taylor recalled in an interview for the Lyndon Baines Johnson Library. "And I took 'affirmative action' because it was alliterative."

From that poetic genesis has come an array of requirements and programs that stir resentment in most of white America. An elastic concept

with many definitions, affirmative action is broadly seen as unnatural and
unfair, yet it has begun to work its way into the standard practices of so
many universities, corporations, and government agencies that it seems
sustained as much now by habit and ethic as by law. Even as the courts
whittle away at affirmative action's constitutional rationales, more and
more institutions are following the military's lead in justifying racial
diversity as pragmatic, not merely altruistic. They strive to avoid not
only legal punishment but the punishment of a marketplace that is pro-
ducing fewer and fewer white males as a percentage of workers and customers. As the Pentagon realized after the draft ended in 1973, if the
armed services were to compete for good people and tap the entire reservoir of potential recruits, those who were not white men would have to
be convinced that unfettered opportunities existed in the ranks. Some
corporations have experienced a similar epiphany of self-interest, and at
many universities, an admissions officer observed, "success in minority
recruitment has become a kind of coin of the realm to indicate institutional success."

It may be a comment on corporate values that opening opportunity
for blacks is justified less as a moral enterprise than as a practical method
of enhancing the bottom line. But that rationale has made affirmative
action easier to swallow among middle managers. AT&T's global operations stepped up the push for minority personnel in response to simple
demographics in its marketplace. "I'm not driven by any I-want-to-
make-things-right-for-what-happened-by-my-forefathers [argument] or
anything like that," one executive declared. "I think of it in very
businesslike terms. . . . I think there will be economic benefits to us for
having that happen."

A company vice president justified both minority recruitment and
diversity training in terms similar to those used by military officers who
argue that racial tension undermines a unit's combat readiness. "If
decent numbers of people on a team feel uncomfortable, they're not welcome, et cetera, then that team is not going to be as effective as it would
be otherwise," the executive observed. "And AT&T and every other corporation recognizes the brutality of competition in the world we live in.
. . . You die if you're not at, or at least very close to, the best."

At Simon & Schuster, the publishing house, special attention to hiring and training a diverse staff has been given in the large unit that pub-
lishes textbooks for middle and high schools, according to Michael
Carroll, vice president for human resources. To appeal to the diverse
clientele who will buy and use the texts, he said, the company "makes

sure books are reviewed by a wide variety of reviewers, that products reflect a multicultural experience, that they try to hire from a multicultural point of view."

The military approaches the task with intense seriousness, training a good number of senior sergeants and middle-ranking officers in the dynamics of race. One afternoon, in a compound of squat buildings at Patrick Air Force Base in Florida, a group of trainees got a graphic demonstration of what affirmative action was all about. Their instructor, a black navy lieutenant named Lance Harris, asked for two volunteers from the class, which comprised Defense Department civilians and uniformed men and women from the army, marines, navy, air force, and Coast Guard. A middle-aged white civilian, "Al," and a slim black air force major, "Delores," went to the front of the room.

The lecture hall was about forty feet wide. On the left-hand side stood a lectern, onto which Harris placed a dollar bill. He put his two volunteers shoulder to shoulder on the right-hand side and told them that the first to reach the dollar bill could keep it. But there were some rules. Delores could walk normally; Al had to take a step, then turn around, touch his toes, and take another step. "Begin," Harris said. As Delores strode directly toward the bill perched on the lectern, Al turned, bent, grunted, straightened, and was quickly left behind.

"Stop!" Harris commanded. They froze in place, Delores with a clear lead. Now they could both walk normally, he said. "Go!" They set off again, but Al was hopelessly in the rear. "Stop!" said Harris. "What do we call this? Equal opportunity. If this person performs just as well," he pointed to Al, "he will still not win." Then Harris took Al by the elbow and moved him forward until he stood beside Delores. "What is this called? Affirmative action. Have I given this person anything extra? No." Then Harris put Al ahead of Delores. "What is this? Reverse discrimination or preferential treatment."

In practice, the distinction between bringing a black person evenly alongside a white and putting him slightly ahead is not as clearly defined as in the exercise. It's like trying to straighten a piece of bent metal: You bend it the other way, farther than you want it to go, so that, hopefully, it will spring back into a straight line. If the process works in racial matters, it neutralizes the aversion to hiring blacks and levels the playing field. Thus, institutions often raise the stakes as they scramble for the best black candidates. When top universities compete for the small pool of black faculty members, they frequently get into bidding wars, throwing in extras they might not offer whites: a higher salary, a job for the professor's spouse, research money, and the like. To motivate such recruitment, colleges may entice the faculty search committee by creating an added position in a department if a black is hired. Corporations may give managers better evaluations and bonuses if they hire and promote minorities and women: The Xerox Corporation's chairman, Paul Allaire, has told his managers that they will be held accountable for such performance; Harvard Pilgrim, which delivers managed health care in the Boston area, uses the advancement of minorities and women as one factor in calculating executives' bonuses.

A cynical side effect can develop. Some big universities increase their black enrollment by recruiting star athletes and relaxing the academic pressure on them, giving them an education in name only. Some faculty departments turn the incentive system around and use it as a bargaining chip: They will hire a black *only* if an extra position is created. Occasionally, the enticements may do more than neutralize the aversions; they may give an advantage to certain highly skilled blacks with an elite education. That putative black advantage is perceived by white employees, who sense reverse discrimination.

Therefore, the problem created by the solution of affirmative action is this: It allows whites to imagine themselves as victims. Polls find about two-thirds of Americans believing that a white has a smaller chance of getting a job or a promotion than an equally or less qualified black does. When asked why they think this, however, only 21 percent can say that they have seen it at work, 15 percent that it has happened to a friend or relative, and just 7 percent that they have experienced it personally. "With blacks, who are such a small fraction of the population," says Barbara Bergmann, an economist at American University, "the lost opportunities to white men are really minuscule."

Furthermore, some of the personal experience is suspect. Affirmative action transports long-standing biases against blacks into the realm of reasonable discussion: It gives whites permission to affirm the stereotype of blacks as less competent by saying, or thinking, that this or that African-American was not good enough to have been admitted, hired, or promoted without a racial preference. Unscrupulous white supervisors contribute to the slander either by hiring less qualified blacks, just to get their numbers up and avoid discrimination suits, or by disingenuously telling whites, "Gee, I'd love to promote you, but I have to take a black or a woman." Affirmative action thus becomes, in the first case, an excuse for sloppy recruiting and, in the second, a handy pretext to spare a manager the discomfort of telling a white colleague why he doesn't deserve to be promoted.

These are perversions of affirmative action's purpose, and they undermine its viability. In its many forms, from intensive recruiting to hiring goals to set-aside contracts for minority-owned businesses, the effort is designed to remedy unjustified exclusion by seeking out qualified people from the excluded groups and accepting the best of them. It recognizes that passive color blindness is not enough, that people do not deal with one another purely as individuals, and that even if overt discrimination is eliminated, the handicaps of poor schooling and impoverished family life, of subtle prejudice and institutional intolerance, remain severe obstacles to advancement by African-Americans.

More fundamentally, affirmative action arouses objection because it acknowledges the mythical quality of the American dream. It clashes with the nation's most treasured creed by vitiating the belief that the country's bounty is open to anyone who has brains and works hard. It sees people's fates determined not merely by their individual merit but also by their membership in groups. It does not matter that this is a realistic appraisal of the way society operates; it is one that defies the way most Americans would like society to be. The principle of group preference has been rejected when it favors whites, many argue, so why should the discredited concept be sustained to favor blacks?

As pollster Daniel Yankelovich has found in discussing affirmative action with focus groups, whites and blacks want exactly the same results, but they have different appraisals of what is required to get them. Both want fairness. Whites fear that *with* affirmative action, less qualified *blacks* will be hired and promoted over more qualified whites. Blacks fear that *without* affirmative action, less qualified *whites* will be hired or promoted over more qualified blacks.

Affirmative action has surely smoothed the path of upwardly mobile blacks into the middle class. It has made institutional leaders think about the complexion of their workforce and managerial ranks. But it has also left behind a massive, impoverished class of African-Americans trapped in urban neighborhoods of crime and decay. The destitute have been largely untouched by the anti-discrimination laws, the hiring goals, the contract set-asides, the recruitment drives, the incentives. In other words, some things have been done for some blacks but not much for others. Yet the publicity and political argument surrounding affirmative action have given many whites the impression that they are doing a great deal—too much, in fact.

Some whites know precisely how to aim their resentment. When a white college student was turned down for a summer job on a newspaper in Louisiana, the editor said he would like to hire him but had to take a black. The student's mother was angry, not at the metaphorical or mythical black but at the editor for not having hired a black person twenty years ago.

Few white people are as discerning, and some wait in ambush for a frail black recruit to come along as a symbol of the whole. This played out during a staff meeting at a major corporation. The only African-American in the room was "Barbara," the department's human resources manager. She listened in astonishment as a white woman commented on the efforts to bring in diverse people. "Well," the white woman remarked, "I went and I got this guy from Harvard, an M.B.A. from Harvard, and he worked for the company six months, and he just didn't work out. And that was just a waste of the company's money, and I just don't know how hard we need to be working on this."

"I was just floored," Barbara recalled. "I thought that was the most— not even racist—that was stupid. . . . How many people have been put in jobs where they didn't do well in the first six months and we didn't say, 'We don't want to go out and hire any more of that kind of person'?" Barbara kept this thought to herself; something in the atmosphere of the meeting prevented her from saying it. She wondered how anyone, especially a woman, could make such a leap from an individual to an entire group, given how effectively women had been locked out. "And if they had stopped giving women a chance," Barbara thought in silence, "you wouldn't be here today."

Less harshly, but pointedly, the white vice president chairing the meeting turned the spotlight on the manager herself as the possible cause of the problem. "You have to understand," he told her, "you were looking at him through white eyes." The woman didn't seem to get it. "The mannerisms, the way people relate," he explained. "You were expecting something different." No, the woman didn't think that was it. She had recruited a black person from the best school to ensure that he was good, and she had been disappointed.

Emboldened by the vice president's opening, Barbara spoke up, though awkwardly, she realized later. If such a highly educated black person was dismissed after six months, she suggested, perhaps the company was doing something wrong, failing to communicate or to develop people well. But then she stopped talking. "I could feel the pressure mounting," she said, "and I didn't know how to do it in an intelligent way." The manager was unmoved; she merely repeated her conclusion: "I don't know how far we should go to make this thing happen."

It is very hard to address that kind of aversion by counseling managers individually, so institutions usually take another tack: They force up the overall numbers of blacks, thereby going straight for the results and sidestepping their supervisors' personal qualms. This is a shortcut that can stop short of providing full opportunity.

"I get to work with these white officers," said Richard Orange, the corporate consultant, "and some of them just inherently do not believe that blacks, Hispanics, people of color, and [women] can bring added value to the company. They try not to hire them. They try to hire them at a lower level in the organization, but they will never move. They will never move."

You wouldn't be able to tell that by blacks' evaluations, though. "A black woman was just taken on as a kind of administrative assistant in an area where I'm consulting," Orange said, "and she used to work at Bell Labs, and for eight consecutive years she was rated 'far exceeds.' That's the highest rating you can get. And she hasn't had a promotion. You see a lot of that, an extraordinary amount—people just buried, just buried in the organization. They don't know what to do. They become dispirited. They don't know what to do." He pointed to another black woman who had been rated as having little leadership potential. He laughed. "And what she did, she became president of the black professional group at AT&T. When she took over as president, they had seven hundred and something dues-paying members. Four years later, they had seven thousand. . . . See what I mean? That's a huge disconnect."

Nevertheless, rummaging around in companies across the country turns up a significant number of white executives who anguish and struggle to right the racial wrongs. And they would rather do it out of their own sense of justice than out of a fear of government retribution. "I don't want to be told about what is legal," said Ted Kennedy, the chairman and chief executive officer of B, E & K Construction Company in Birmingham, Alabama. "I want us to do what is right, and I think, in almost every case, that will also mean you're doing what is legal."

Kennedy is a case study in how the values of affirmative action have passed by osmosis into the bloodstream of certain influential whites. Dissatisfied with the pace of black hiring and promotion by his company, he compromised one principle—his opposition to quotas—in behalf of a higher principle: opportunity for African-Americans.

Kennedy was relaxed, informal. His whole face crinkled into a slight smile as he spoke reflectively, gesturing with a letter opener carved of dark wood. But his sense of calm was cut by ambivalence. "I'm not very fond of the idea of quotas, on the one hand," he said, leaning back behind his sweeping wooden desk inlaid with tooled leather. "On the other hand, I end up finding that I'm setting them myself." He gazed through his large office windows, which opened onto a forested industrial park south of the city where so much shame and promise had been gathered together.

"So I'm on both sides," he continued. "I've gone to my personnel group, my HR people, our recruiters, and I've said, 'OK, you can't come to me with white engineers until you can also show me that you have tried on females and blacks. And you have to show me those first, and then I'll let you come in and bring a white, no matter how talented.' In fact, I've put them on a quota system. I say I don't like quotas and don't believe in them, but internally I'm doing exactly that. I don't believe just letting the natural course of things happen that we can get there. Some kind of affirmative action is necessary. I've almost come to the point where I believe in quotas personally, but I don't want the government to tell me to do it."

Kennedy's company does engineering and construction for smoke-stack industries such as pulp and paper, steel, chemicals, and fertilizers, and has also built churches, office buildings, and shopping malls throughout the South. To attract the best people, he decided to establish an elite corps of full-time, year-round workers. "The construction industry is a volatile, seasonal business," he explained. "A construction worker, most times, doesn't really get a full year." So he created an annual salary that would be paid to some employees even when there was no ongoing project—on the condition that they would travel anywhere the company had work. To determine those eligible, he and his managers came up with a set of criteria: years of experience, high skills, a good safety record, and continuing education to enhance performance. He wanted this "to be something that people strive to get into," he declared. "We're saying we're going to have the best people in the industry, we're going to keep them busy."

When the criteria were applied to the company's list of employees, however, those who made the cut included "a very low percentage female and a very low percentage black," Kennedy said. "It was strictly done by the computer. There wasn't anybody saying, 'Well, I think that's a good person.'" So he told his subordinates, "'We've got a problem. I'm not willing to start the program.' At that moment, the people who were doing it said, 'Now, wait a minute. You told us that you were creating this really top-notch crew. Now you're telling us that we have to bring in so many blacks and so many females.' And one of the managers said, 'You said you don't like quotas, and now you're establishing them.' " Kennedy replied that he wanted to broaden the standards. "I'm not going to keep anybody out," he said. "Therefore, it's not a quota system." He smiled at himself.

One reason the computer selected few blacks and women was their lack of longevity; Kennedy wanted people who had worked on at least four or five jobs. The echoes of past hiring inequities were being felt. "We didn't know how to recruit blacks," Kennedy admitted. When he asked the advice of the NAACP in Mississippi, he found that his advertising had been misplaced. "We were in the wrong newspapers. We were on the wrong stations when we were on the radio." So he cut the requirement to three jobs.

He then discovered that few African-Americans had enrolled in training programs. "That's as much our problem as theirs," he observed. "Most of these projects are in rural areas, poor school systems. Many of the blacks are dropouts from the school system. No matter how you try to make [the training] hands-on, you end up with a certain amount of mathematics, a certain amount of reading skills. I think they get discouraged." So he changed the criterion to demand not that they already have the training but that they enroll and remain in training. Remedial reading, basic computer skills, and other fundamentals were added to the courses. "I almost could say that it's not so much a black issue as it is a poor issue, a rural issue," Kennedy commented.

At higher skill levels, the company confronted different obstacles. "Among engineers, to get blacks and women, I don't find that I have to bend the qualifications," Kennedy said. "I just find that there aren't that many out there. You have to really hustle . . . and I'm competing. Take a black engineer, and I say, 'I'd like you to come to work for us.'

" 'What am I going to do?'

" 'Well, I'm going to send you into the construction business.'

" 'Where will I be located?'

" 'Well, I'm gonna send you to Crossett, Arkansas, or Pine Bluff, Alabama.'

"In the meantime, IBM is saying, 'Yeah, but I am going to send you into a nice shiny steel building with glass and air-conditioning, and if you do well you can be in Paris.' Now, I come out second on that. Maybe fifth." So the problem is not quality but quantity.

And how did a man who grew up in a racist family, who attended segregated schools all over the South as his father moved from one construction job to another, come to such conviction about opening doors for blacks?

Kennedy laughed. "I have no idea," he said. "But I'll tell you one thing. If I didn't have this position, I couldn't live with my wife. She'd kick me out. It's more a sense of right and wrong. I'm not sure it's race-related; it's just whatever is right is right."

On the eleventh floor of the massive headquarters building in Chicago, at the end of a maze of white marble walls and narrow hallways, an African-American woman with the title "director of diversity planning" was poring over printouts of spreadsheets when she noticed something awry. Of one hundred or so promotions in a key division over the previous few years, all but ten had gone to white males.

What happened next tells a significant story of painful racial change in the heart of American business. This was one of the largest corporations in the United States, sprawling and powerful. Yet racial problems and their remedies were so controversial that neither the company nor its executives were willing to be identified in print, even when they had something to brag about.

The woman in Chicago, writing up the division's quarterly "report card" on diversity, noted the problem of the promotions and mentioned some negative "feedback" from nonwhite employees about the racial situation. Then she sent the report off to "Bernard," the vice president in charge of the division.

Bernard was a white man with thirty-three years in the company. He had been "on a journey," as he put it, "to try to get the organization to a place where everybody feels comfortable and that they are in a position where they are allowed to and encouraged to and rewarded for doing their best." So the figures on promotions came like a thunderbolt. He had not been paying attention. His department had been squeezed into "terrible layoffs," he said, and had had no time to monitor the racial situation. "Last year I started to see light at the end of the tunnel and started to pay a lot more attention to how people were feeling and what was right and what we should be doing. In fact, the words we used were 'thriving and not just surviving.' And so we started to think about diversity."

He summoned his subordinate managers, all whites. He pointed out to them, and then noted in a videotape shown to the entire division, that the higher up you looked, the whiter and more male the organization became. More intensive efforts were needed to find minority candidates whenever promotion opportunities materialized, he told them.

"People went crazy," Bernard said. "White people in the organization went crazy. Not all of them. But people started saying, 'Well, I guess there's no opportunity for me here anymore.' " So he had to make another tape. "I said, 'Let's be reasonable about this thing. Ninety percent of the promotions went to white people. Let's say we doubled the percentage of minority promotions, so we'd be down to eighty percent, right? Because we'd be going from ten to twenty [nonwhites]. Now, if you're going to argue that eighty percent is no opportunity, first of all I'd say that's a twisting of the language that's hard to accept. If you want to argue that you'd rather have it ninety than eighty, then what I've got to tell you is that the only thing you're asking for is to continue an unfair advantage. And I can't deal with that. So what is your issue?" One white man went as far as to argue that he felt underrepresented as a midwesterner. Bernard retorted wryly by asking for his help in addressing differences that created real problems for people.

One of the vice president's white subordinates, "Carl," took on the mission with alacrity. When he arrived on the job, all fifteen members of his department were white. As business improved and he expanded to fifty employees, he imposed a quota of sorts. "I've taken the position that I want one out of every two," he said. "So if we hired one white male last time, we don't fill the next job until we find a talented person who fits our other needs," meaning the need for racial diversity. "I have a fellow who works for me in Denver, and he's starting our training business—a real start-up, entrepreneurial kind of thing—and he's having trouble getting diversity candidates. . . . He had two jobs to fill. . . . A white male, living in Washington, D.C., exactly fit the requirements of one of the jobs. The second job, he had a candidate that really fit the job, but it wasn't a diverse candidate, so we put that on hold." The manager in Denver was told to find a minority person for the second position.

This pressure created fierce competition inside the corporation, with departments raiding one another for outstanding blacks, Asians, and Hispanics who came to be known through the grapevine as excellent. "You don't get candidates," Carl complained, "because somebody who has somebody isn't gonna let him go. They will let him go for promotion . . . but they won't go out of their way to make a good diversity candidate available. You're often faced with, do I take somebody that almost fits, or do I let the job stand empty?"

Carl was in his forties and, on a "dress-down day" when suits and ties were not required, he sat at a round table in his windowless office, looking sporty and relaxed in a yellow shirt and bright plaid sweater. He had grown up in a segregated town in the middle of Kansas, and he had lost jobs early in his career because he was white and a black was needed.

"That has happened to me, yes," he said. It might have made him bitter. "Well, for some reason it didn't. You can tell from where I am, I have a good job right now. It didn't set me back for long." And he became a true believer. "I think there's a lot of learning going on across the organizations," he said. "We've focused a lot on education the last couple of years, so people understand the value of diversity, and the learning that I've seen has been as good for the people of diverse backgrounds as it has for the majority."

Characteristically, he noted, jobs had been filled through the old-boy network by people the managers happened to know, and those people happened to be a lot like the managers—white and male. "To improve the penetration of minorities and improve the diversity profiles, you've got to break ranks," Carl observed. "You've got to be willing to say, 'I'm going to take somebody for this job based on what the paper says about them, based on the way they come across in the interview, and I'm willing to take a risk, 'cause I don't know them.' "

Managing Diversity

Once blacks get through the door, their difficulties don't evaporate. In fact, both Carl and Bernard discovered that it was at least as hard to manage diversity as to create it. Part of the problem was the sense of alienation that many blacks felt in mostly white settings.

An African-American woman, promoted from the sales force to middle-level management, had a college degree and a professional quality to her work that had earned her the respect of her boss and her colleagues, all of whom were white. "I have seen this lady do spectacular work," said Carl. "I am very pleased. She is really coming in and learning this business, and I couldn't be happier—with the exception of two times: She had to provide a readout on her project beyond me, to my boss and then to his boss, who happens to be the lady who's the president of our business. And I saw a complete change. . . . What I saw was the inability to articulate, crisply respond to questions. . . . She got out of the comfort zone that she sees with me and her boss, who she knows are really committed to her success, and got into the next level. And instead of being extremely effective, I would say she was barely adequate. The material she knew extremely well, but she began rambling and not having cohesive, clear thinking. And we're trying to figure out how to deal with that. . . . It was an absolute shock to us."

Carl also puzzled over a black man who looked good on paper but was slated to be laid off from another department. He asked why. The answer came back: "He's the best hardworking guy you'll ever have. He's smart. But he can't interview. He can't interview." As a rule, Carl would devote only a few minutes of small talk to such a candidate. But this time he took the trouble to spend two hours with the man, who did not present himself well. "Based on the interview, I would not have hired him," Carl said flatly. "He didn't come across any way as good as he looked on paper. Yet one of our staff members had shared an office with him for the last two years [and said], 'This is one of the best people you can get in the business.' " And so, after a long conversation that Carl kept deliberately low-key, he hired him. "I believe that this guy is worth taking a chance on," he said. "We're going to work together to make him successful. We probably won't put him in some of the stand-up presentations that he wouldn't be successful in."

Whether it is a real risk or just an imaginary gamble, taking a chance is probably essential to advancing many African-Americans who have not had the opportunity to prove themselves. But bending efforts to promote employees because they are black can sometimes be damaging, for if they are advanced too early and are thrown in with more experienced people, they may look less competent and simply reinforce whites' stereotypes. Carl was also responsible for such a case in the 1980s, he admitted, and it gnaws at him to this day. A good staff manager who was black was about to leave for a smaller company that had been spun off from the parent. "We decided it's the wrong thing to do, to have a high-performing Afro-American leave our business," Carl recalled. "We happened to have a job opening. He wasn't, at that point in time, considered at the very top of the promotable list. We took a risk and sat down and talked to him and said, 'We would like you to stay, and we'd like to put you in this job. But you have to understand that there will be some people who will think you went around them. There's gonna be a lot of pressure on you to perform, and all we're doing is creating an opportunity for you—you have to take advantage of it.'

"And he failed miserably," Carl declared. "I began doing too much of this guy's work. . . . The harder he tried, the more perplexed he got. . . . Some of my senior managers would ask very probing, very hard, very direct questions, which I think they had every right to do. He never created himself as the expert on top of his particular job." Although he was well liked personally by his staff, he shared the sense of aloneness that many blacks feel in predominantly white workplaces. He was never embraced closely enough to feel entirely safe; he never felt free to unburden himself to his colleagues about the problems he was having. "We gave him a couple of years, we went through another downsizing, and in that new population he was right at the bottom of the population," Carl said. "He had a very positive attitude, his [boss] liked him. I was as supportive of him as I could be. And yet he came out at the bottom of the population, below the cut line.

"So we took a guy who was doing an outstanding job, we tried to create an opportunity in order to keep him from leaving the business, so as a result he went . . . back to the lower level." Carl looked pained. "He thanked us for the opportunity, and he fully realized that he hadn't been able to keep his part of the bargain. The tragedy in my mind wasn't that we tried something and failed. It was that he changed his outlook on life: 'Well, maybe I can't do it.' I would say that at the lower level, when he was perceived as a high-performance, upper-tier kind of guy, he had a dream. He had a lottery ticket, and as long as he had that lottery ticket, he could win. When we helped him fulfill a piece of the dream, he lost the lottery ticket."

Anyone who works anywhere could point to examples of whites as well who are promoted beyond their abilities; after all, the Peter Principle holds that an employee will advance until he reaches the level of his incompetence. In this event, however, Carl said that he would not have selected this man if he had been white. And so the fickle component of race creates an obstacle one moment, then an advantage that turns out to be a mirage. What was the lesson learned? "I would probably be less willing to take the risk with another person, because I saw what it did to this guy as an individual," Carl remarked. "The person I cared about was hurt. And so I would probably make sure the next person was even more ready than that person was."

Favoring African-Americans by doing some of their work, as Carl did, or by hesitating to give them poor evaluations that they deserve, is called "dysfunctional rescuing" by Thomas Kochman, the specialist on black-white cultural differences. In his seminars, when he asks how many people feel that they have to be extra careful when evaluating blacks and women, most of the white men raise their hands. A white professor at a Florida university was stuck for years with his dean's choice of a black secretary who was cordial, charming, and well liked by people who never had to depend on her to get anything done. She procrastinated, forgot, and refused to take dictation even from a tape, so he had to write his letters in longhand for her to type. And she couldn't, or wouldn't, learn to use a computer, so she worked on an electric typewriter. If she hadn't been black, he declared bitterly, he would have fired her.

Although affirmative action brings people into the same room, it does not teach them how to deal with one another once they are there. Every workplace is a warren of unseen walls and barriers.

Blacks are often left out of meetings, committees, and brainstorming sessions, not to mention luncheons and golf outings where connections are made and policy is forged. A young black sales representative worked at an IBM office in New Orleans for a full three years before he was invited to a happy hour that he hadn't even known was taking place every evening. "They were making decisions, making business deals, handing out territorial assignments—no females there," he said. "Eventually, I left IBM because it was just too tough to break into it."

In Carl and Bernard's division, a black woman who monitors racial issues heard constantly from black employees that they felt invisible. "They don't know most of the time what's going on around them," she said. "They're not in the loop, they don't understand the rules of the game, so they don't know what to do. Just Friday a young man was telling me that his organization has formed this task force to look at market intelligence. They get all this research information and they spoon it out to the rest of the business. And he does that. He sets up all the stuff. They formed a task force to find out why people weren't using it, and they didn't put him on the task force."

Bernard, the vice president, had a clear explanation: "I know I'm guilty of this myself. You tend to trust and therefore give important assignments [to] and strategize with and share important information with those people that you feel the most comfortable with, and those usually turn out to be the people who are most like you." And what were the definitions of comfort, what people were most like him? "I don't know," he began. "I don't know the answer to that one. I don't think skin color, at least for me and what I have noticed, is a primary variable. More primary variables are cultural things." Such as what? He paused for a long time. "I'm not sure I can describe it. This isn't right, but it's close. I think—I hate this, 'cause you're forcing me to generalize, and I really don't want to do that; I really like to treat people as individuals. But there are two stereotypical black people: There are inner-city black people, so there you have a culture that is different from the white majority. And there's a southern black culture, and that's also different. . . . Then there are different kinds of white cultures too. You almost have to think of these in pairs rather than white versus black. I'm an inner-city person. I'm a technically trained person, and relatively speaking an intellectual person . . . and I come from a lower- to lower-middle-class background. And I deal every day with white people who come from a middle-class to upper-middle-class and suburban midwest majority background. And those are very different. I don't feel real comfortable with them; they don't feel real comfortable with me either. So there are a set of white cultures and a set of black cultures, and the various pairings don't match up."

The impact on blacks of cultural clashes can be crude or subtle, vivid or barely visible. Thomas Kochman sees the disharmony reflected in the decorum of the office. In a discussion, blacks will often employ dynamic argument and emotion to convey sincerity, he says, while whites "regard the black argumentative mode as dysfunctional because of their view that reason and emotion work against each other." Blacks may distrust as disingenuous "the dispassionate and detached mode that whites use to engage in debate." The whites seem to be hiding something.

"African-American is a high-offense, high-defense culture, compared to Anglo culture," Kochman told a workshop in Washington, D.C. He was using "Anglo" to represent the common denominator of corporate culture and to distinguish it from such white subcultures as Hispanic, Italian, and Jewish. "Anglo culture compared to some Asian cultures is a high-offense, high-defense culture. It depends on who you compare yourself to. In African-American culture, the valued person is the one who can churn up, arouse emotion—the rapper, the preacher, the signifier. The person on the receiving end is taught to accommodate the asserter."

These generalizations might have triggered an objection from someone who could have cited that eternal exception to every rule. But the several blacks in the group around the table—managers from the World Bank, Kaiser Permanente, the U.S. Postal Service, the Bureau of Engraving and Printing, and elsewhere—were smiling and nodding in agreement.

Kochman illustrated his point with an example: A white official in the Justice Department was accused by a black minister of processing discrimination cases too slowly. The official was patient and polite and, he thought, quietly reassuring. The minister wasn't buying any of it, and he escalated and escalated until finally the white official exploded in rage, throwing down the files and swearing and yelling that he was just as eager to prosecute these cases as the minister was to have them prosecuted. The official thought he'd blown it. But the minister, finally recognizing the man's commitment, then shifted ground to a more productive discussion of what the Justice Department was doing. "Our lack of passion looks like insincerity," Kochman concluded. "One could construe the pursuit of peace and the anti-emotion as being anti-truthseeking," he said. "Keep it calm, keep it peaceful, don't make waves."

"One of our survival strategies," a black woman chimed in, "is that we go off. You can't use it every day, but it's part of our bag of tricks. When I use it, especially with Anglos, it has a very powerful effect on them." As a doctoral candidate, she said, she once took her shoe off, à la Nikita Khrushchev, and pounded it on the desk of a recalcitrant professor. "It got things done." She wished that her office had an atmosphere conducive to expressing emotion. "I'd like to be able to talk and bring passion," she said. "I would like to bring spirituality—I don't necessarily mean prayer. It would open us up and help our organizations go forth."

But African-Americans in small numbers, even those who exhibit the cultural characteristics that Kochman describes (and not all do), cannot reframe the mores of a workplace. While some diversity trainers try to persuade institutions to open themselves to diverse cultural styles, successful "diversity" usually goes the other way: Blacks adapt to the dominant mode. "You have to peel off that visible blackness about yourself, that cultural blackness," said a black human relations officer in one company. If you do not, there can be unhappy consequences.

Kochman pointed to a few, and he did so in the name of educating people to recognize differences, thus to accept them. "One constant pet peeve whites have of blacks is tardiness," he said. Some blacks jokingly call this "c.p.t."—colored people's time—and Kochman tried to put a virtuous face on it. "Anglo culture expands the future. African-American and Hispanic culture expands the present. Anglo culture tries to get as much done as possible. The locus of control is external—it's the clock. . . . The Anglo orientation is one foot into the activity you're in, the next in the next thing. We bring the future into the present. We're not wholly into what we're doing now." When white and black churches have joint meetings, he said, the whites ask when it is going to be over, and the blacks are saying that it's over when it's over. "When is it over?" he asked the group.

"When everyone has had their say," a black woman replied.

"Right, and when everything that has been aroused is processed. Rude behavior by black standards is 'I can't talk to you now.' Because in black culture, people count first."

A case in point was offered by Kenneth Addison, a black trainer who worked with Kochman. His daughter's performance, in a job with a company that marketed an automated payroll system, was measured by the number of calls she made. She had come under criticism for making too few, and she was about to be shown the door, when the results of her too-few calls started coming in. "She's a great phone person," Addison said. "She made more sales even than her supervisor, and she got letters saying how pleased people were. The supervisor had the sense to say, 'Hmmm, maybe we have to change the criteria.' "

The trouble is, if a black shows up late for work or meetings, he violates the dominant cultural norm in the United States, and a meaning will be attached to his tardiness. In a highly complex society and economy, promptness is pragmatic; its absence damages efficiency. Furthermore, being on time is associated with hard work, interest in the job, and professional courtesy: chronic lateness, especially in a black person, activates the traditional stereotypes of laziness and incompetence. And white supervisors will react not merely to the act of tardiness but to the meaning they have given it.

Authority is another area of conflict. Anglo and African-American styles contrast and clash as vividly as classical music differs from jazz, Kochman explained. "Anglos come from a text orientation," he said. "You've got the text, and you've got the plan. The composer is never subordinate to the performer. The performer reveals the hidden qualities of the text. A performer couldn't change a Bach piece from B to B-flat. You couldn't do that. We're talking about a degree of freedom here and at what point it should be criticized. In the African-American tradition, the performers are often the composers. Where in Anglo culture the context is shaped to fit the text, the African-American concept is to shape the text to fit the context.

"Where blacks get into trouble in the workplace," he continued, "is precisely where they have made changes to get the job done where it has not been authorized by their managers." In Kochman's view, a black might assume that if he is delegated to do the job, he is authorized to revise the plan. "If it succeeds, Anglos will say, 'OK, you got lucky. It worked.' It's too unpredictable. Also, it takes the play out of the manager's hands. By black standards, you would be at risk if you carried out the plan and it failed." The answer seemed to lie on some middle ground. "A good composer tries to give some spontaneity to his form,"

Kochman said, "and a good performer tries to give some form to his spontaneity."

Then he closed with a kicker that had the African-Americans in the room laughing and nodding in glee. "If I've lost my parking ticket at O'Hare Airport, I want a black woman clerk. She'd feel she had the authority to make a decision:

" 'Why'd you do that, honey?'

" 'I guess I'm not perfect.'

" 'OK.' "

Like a company or a college, an entire town can manage racial diversity, or it can neglectfully allow conflict to take root. It has the choice of attentiveness or heedlessness, which leads to comity or strife. Doing nothing is an act in itself, for when a garden is not well cultivated, it quickly goes to seed.

Few towns in America spend much energy managing diversity. One that does is Oak Park, the enclave of integration adjoining the predominantly black slum of Chicago's West Side. For a quarter of a century, Oak Park has worked assiduously to maintain its racial mixture, to defuse internal tensions, and to guard against the segregation and decay that have festered next door. To cross Austin Boulevard, Oak Park's border with Chicago, is to move between what America might have been and what America has become.

Roberta "Bobbie" Raymond drove across Austin, leaving behind the trim shops and stately homes and plunging into a universe of boarded-up buildings and tacky storefronts offering liquor, check cashing, money orders, meats, and Salvation Army bargains in used clothes. "Look in both directions as we cross this intersection," Raymond suggested. "On one side it's totally slum, and on the other it's yuppie. The Chicago side is totally sleaze." She cruised along Madison. "You're gonna see burglar gates on the doors. That is, what, two minutes from my house? Now you see a lot of gang graffiti." On the porches of two-story frame houses, black men lounged idly; rusting hulks of old cars sat in the front yards. "This was a very beautiful neighborhood until the sixties. It was all white."

It had changed quickly, block by block. Driven by panicky whites and panic-sowing real estate agents, some eighteen blocks on Chicago's West Side went from all white to virtually all black in five years. "By about 1971, all of the experts in the Chicago area were predicting that Oak Park would resegregate," Raymond said, meaning that it, too, would change from all white to all black, "based on the fact that the West Side ghetto had expanded to our doorstep."

But she and a few other Oak Park whites had other plans: not to flee, and not to hold some futile, immoral line against black Americans coming to live with them. Their idea, which took hold in pockets of decency throughout the country in the early sixties, was to create a truly integrated community by enacting an anti-discrimination law and appealing to the long-term interests of the real estate industry. And it came to pass, producing a dramatic frontier at the eastern edge of town. There may be no boundary in the United States quite as flagrant as Austin Boulevard.

The line stirs anxieties in Oak Park about the encroachment of crime, fear, poverty, and bigotry, and a resulting collapse of property values. Yet housing prices in the town, which ranges from working-class to upper-class, have soared by five or six times in the last two decades and now range from $110,000 to $1,100,000. The schools have remained among the country's best, and the town has largely resisted the siege mentality that afflicts some of its all-white suburban neighbors. Oak Park's population of 54,000 is about 18 percent black and 7 percent Asian and Hispanic, a level that could trigger white flight if the town did nothing to alleviate concerns.

The tools employed in this endeavor are not esoteric; they are available to most communities. In 1968, after four years of work, Bobbie Raymond and her associates got the board of trustees of the village, equivalent to a town council, to pass a fair housing law that prohibited racial discrimination. In 1972, she led a group in establishing a housing center to use what she called "intervention strategies" that would "manipulate the market" to create and maintain an integrated town. That meant showing prospective black and white residents housing on blocks they might not naturally consider, with the goal of dispersing the races around town to avoid segregating neighborhoods. The center also held seminars for apartment owners and real estate agents to puncture burgeoning myths about the decline of the community; they were taken to schools, for example, to see for themselves that the quality remained high; most became convinced that if they wanted to remain in business, and not just scare white people and then get out, they would need to support integration.

The trustees also took a series of steps to codify the village's commitment. They banned for-sale and for-rent signs from all housing to obviate the panic that might erupt if two or three appeared on a block. They set up a town office of community relations to monitor and address racial tensions and fears. They enacted a program to insure 80 percent of a home owner's equity, guaranteeing payment if a house couldn't be sold in five years. In 1973, the trustees passed a policy statement in support of racial diversity; renewed every several years, it constitutes a little sermon extolling the virtue of Oak Park's "stimulating mixture of racial, religious, and ethnic groups" and warning that "efforts to achieve diversity are nullified by the resegregation of neighborhoods from all white to all black." The policy declares, "We must not succumb to Big-City-style residential patterns. A free and open community—equal and diverse— can only be achieved through dispersal, a mixture of racial and ethnic groups throughout the Village."

Printed on little cards, the statement is handed to every prospective renter who walks into the housing center and to most buyers who approach real estate offices. "We very specifically did not want a situation where blacks all lived in one section of Oak Park," Bobbie Raymond explained. "If you don't do something special to keep up white demand, white demand isn't going to continue. And if you don't do something special to be sure that blacks are not steered to one section of the village, [they] end up getting the short end of the real estate market. . . . History told us that, left alone, the real estate community, the apartment building owners and managers, the banks and other lending institutions, business, et cetera—all the basic institutional forces—would work against us."

White demand was the key, Raymond believed. "We didn't have to advertise for blacks," she said. "The longer you're integrated, the more blacks who live in a metropolitan area like this want to live in the community. So we had a constant flow of terrific blacks wanting to move into Oak Park. It was the white thing that we had to work on. We were aiming for intellectual, liberal whites who would move in."

The housing center took out magazine advertisements and printed a full-color brochure headlined "Oak Park, the People Place." Its photographs subtly convey a reassuring image of whites predominating in a milieu with just a smattering of nonwhites. Artfully composed, the images place nonwhites in slightly less obvious positions. A posed picture on the cover shows eight young adults gathered in a living room where only whites sit in the foreground; the two blacks and an Asian are relegated to the background, along with two white men. Inside the pamphlet, on a page labeled "Fine Schools," three students are pictured in a chemistry lab: The centerpiece is a white boy who is the only one actually doing anything; he is observed by a black boy, half hidden in the farthest background, and a white girl in the foreground. A street scene shows only whites, no blacks. A group of four children in a greenhouse contains no blacks, only a small Asian girl and an olive-skinned little boy dwarfed by two taller, older, white youngsters. The brochure also emphasizes Oak Park's more upscale houses, some of which were designed by Frank Lloyd Wright.

Renters who approach the housing center are encouraged to avoid the path of least resistance. "What we do is expose people to everything," Raymond said. "So if you're white and you come in here, we're probably going to make sure that you see apartments in buildings that are on Austin Boulevard or fairly close to Austin or elsewhere in the community where we need white demand. It could be a building in Oak Park that's 80 percent black or whatever, where we need to get some whites in. . . . We're definitely going to get you to consider things not otherwise considered. If you're black . . . we're going to give you listings in Oak Park that are less integrated. We're going to try to get you something that's going to be a positive move in terms of integration."

The technique has been criticized as racial steering in reverse; instead of nudging blacks out of white blocks, the housing center is nudging them in. "We're into expanding people's options rather than limiting people's options," Raymond countered. "I think it's quite different from steering, because we tell everyone right up front what we are doing. 'Steering' to me implies that something's being done to me without my knowledge of it."

These efforts may not have changed the thoughts that occur inside people's minds, but they have changed behavior, in the view of Sherlynn Reid, the black director of the town's Community Relations Division. Today, she notes, if a real estate agent encounters a white who wants to be shown houses where no blacks live, the broker no longer winks and says, "I know what you mean." He says instead, "You need to talk to somebody in Community Relations." And Reid gives it to them straight: "If you're white and you want to live in an all-white community, you must go someplace else. If you're black and you want to live in an all-black community, you must go someplace else, 'cause this community has said it intends to be racially diverse."

Frequently, the fears are unfounded, and simple facts erase the hesitation. If white buyers are scared by friends into believing that the house they are considering is on an all-black block, the broker may call Reid and ask her to come meet with them. "So I get my books, brochures, and I drop into that office," Reid said. "See, I believe that segregation was planned. And if you're going to have racial diversity, you better plan it." She laughed at the common sense of this. "First of all, I tell them what the racial makeup of the block is—actually is. Then, you know, talk to them about what we're trying to do in terms of our policy statement . . . and then I'll give them the names of at least two [white] people who live on that block who are willing to talk to them about the block." If the prospective buyers are black and worry about being in a mostly white neighborhood, Reid sets them up with black residents. The objective is to get people to make "nontraditional choices" to live where they're least expected to live. "The final choice is always theirs, but our experience says that if people don't have the information, they tend to follow the same patterns."

This brand of troubleshooting occupies Reid and her staff in a whirl of constant vigilance over racial tension in Oak Park. Whites often imagine that services are declining because blacks have moved onto their street. A white family was sure that the presence of black neighbors was responsible for garbage not being picked up. Reid's office discovered that the trash collectors had simply made a mistake; they had stopped for a lunch break, had forgotten where they left off, and had missed the white family's house when they resumed. Another white called Reid and told her that the Public Works Department had started construction on an alley behind the houses on her block and hadn't notified residents because "niggers" were living there. It had been just an oversight, Reid discovered. "So I got the Public Works Department to send a letter to everybody on the block apologizing. She came in to thank me, and when she saw me, I thought she was going to faint. She probably thought there was nobody black working in the village office."

Casting a wary eye toward the West Side, some Oak Park residents fret about their modern West Suburban Medical Center, which draws blacks from Chicago and treats its share of Saturday-night shootings. Some whites won't take the El into Chicago because it makes stops in the ghetto. And the mostly white Oak Park police force earned a reputation long ago for hassling black youths with accusatory questions—even youngsters who live in the town.

"Everybody is concerned about safety," Sherlynn Reid declared. "The blacks' concern about safety is: 'Is somebody going to bomb my house? Is somebody going to put a cross up in front of my house? Am I going to be called names?' The white [concern about] safety is: 'Am I going to be robbed? Is somebody going to rape my wife? Am I going to be hit over the head?' " When prospective residents ask about "safety," she always asks them to define the term. "Yes, we have crime in this community. Tell me where the community is where there isn't any, and I'll beat you there."

Black residents complained about the police so persistently that in 1989 the village trustees appointed a citizens' committee to investigate the department. Its 138-page report documented inadequate hiring and promotion of blacks and little training in racial awareness and other necessary skills. As a result, recruiting of blacks was stepped up, a black deputy chief was hired, diversity workshops were instituted, and officers were punished for using racial epithets. One white policeman, talking on the phone from headquarters, was suspended for a day without pay after a black employee heard him say, "Well, you know how those niggers are." As minor as a one-day suspension may seem, the deputy chief, Edward Buckney, insisted that it had sent a shock wave through a department that was unaccustomed to such discipline.

"There were allegations that this department was discriminating against black officers, and it had the reputation of being ass-kickers, especially against blacks," said Buckney, who came to Oak Park after retiring from a thirty-four-year career with the Chicago police. Some in the Oak Park force "would always be bigots," he said flatly. "I have to be honest about it: I am not comfortable here. We've come a long way. We've done a lot of hard work with the administrative end. We've developed new rules and regulations. We have a lot of general orders, special orders, training bulletins, and a number of things to try to guide our people. But one of the things that I learned in Chicago was that people certainly mirror the community."

And much of the community is afraid of blacks. One day, a white woman who telephoned 911 with a complaint about black youngsters hanging around an alley referred to them as "these colored people" and declared, "They're like roaches." The police dispatcher happened to be a black woman. She told the caller that she was black and was offended— and then threatened not to accept any more of her calls, which drew her a reprimand from the department. That was going too far, Buckney said. But the episode illustrated the context in which white police officers were operating.

The white chief, Joseph Mendrick, took a tough, pragmatic line. "As far as changing other people's values and attitudes, I don't even try to do that," he said. "Alls we try to do is change your behavior here. They know the rules, they know what's expected of them, they know how they're supposed to behave. It's reinforced with discipline and rewards, up to and including discharge from the department. The officers understand that we recruit minorities. They're not opposed to it. If they are, they don't say anything about it. That's just the way it is."

Clarified rules were issued on many matters. For starters, all graphic opportunities for the display of racist or sexist materials were erased by a new policy banning drawings, pictures, and most reading matter from headquarters, which occupies the basement of the town hall. "You can go through our station, you will see no cartoons, nothing other than work-related things on the bulletin board," said Mendrick. "We don't allow any of that. You're not allowed any reading material other than . . . a newspaper for their personal use to read on the lunch break or something. But you're not allowed to have any *Playboy* magazines. None of that's allowed in this building. That's the starting point. That sets the tone. There's no writing on the walls of the washrooms, in the stalls. We fired an officer for doing that. . . . He was writing racially derogatory comments."

In addition, Mendrick believed that behavior had been influenced by the creation of a citizens' oversight board to review allegations of police misconduct. It had no power to discipline, which displeased some town residents, but its very existence served notice on officers, he insisted. In addition, citizens who had dealt with individual cops were now surveyed for the periodic evaluations that went into their files. And rules were set down to curb the kind of harassment that led to complaints from blacks.

With about 125 officers on the force, there used to be about 125 policies on stopping black people randomly on the street, Mendrick conceded. There was no guidance from the top; each patrolman had his own method. "Today in policing, for our officers, they've been trained not to look at an African-American as a potential prime offender," he said. "We don't stop people for no reason. We have an order that it must be based on reasonable suspicion or probable cause."

When Mendrick's words were quoted to several black teenagers in Oak Park, they laughed sardonically. The policy sounded fine, but down on the street, it was unrecognizable. The clearest explanation came from Buckney; as an African-American, he could be more candid on the subject. While Mendrick estimated that "over fifty percent" of the crimes in Oak Park were committed by blacks, Buckney put it at more than 90 percent. He noted that most 911 calls described the perpetrator as a black male. "If you have ninety percent or better of your crime committed in this village by blacks," he said frankly, "then it doesn't make sense to me that a crime is committed, and you go looking for a white offender."

Still, the department responded to complaints by instituting a beat system known as "community policing," an elastic term with many definitions in many towns and cities. In Oak Park, officers had been given no geographical assignments; they could drive anywhere in the town's 4.5

square miles. Now they were given beats and schedules to put them on patrol in the same blocks during the same hours of every day. They were encouraged to get out of their cars and do some of what they called "walk and talk" to get to know the residents and storekeepers in their zones. One purpose was to hone the officers' sensibilities to the neighborhood and diminish their tendency to stop and question and harass the people they were supposed to protect.

By contrast, when a racial crisis erupted in Teaneck, New Jersey, the police department adopted a sulky, defensive posture, and the town government descended into testy paralysis. It was left to the clergy and other townspeople to rally themselves into constructive efforts to address the divisions.

Before April 10, 1990, Teaneck was a place of smug complacency about its ethnic diversity. Situated a few miles west of the George Washington Bridge, it basked in its progressive aura, proudly advertised itself as the first town in the country to have voluntarily integrated its schools, and enjoyed being a haven where interracial couples rarely got hard stares or unwelcome comments.

Then, in an instant, a white policeman named Gary Spath shattered the illusion. Summoned by an anxious neighbor who reported seeing black youths with a gun, Spath chased and shot sixteen-year-old Phillip Pannell in the back, killing him. A .22 starter's pistol, converted to fire real ammunition, was found in the boy's pocket. Pannell's friends insisted that he had put his hands up, an assertion supported by forensic evidence. But Spath, who contended that Pannell was reaching for the gun, was ultimately found not guilty of reckless manslaughter.

The shooting immediately revealed racial rifts long masked by the town's middle-class contentment. The next day, near Teaneck High School, several white students were targeted by blacks hurling fists and epithets. That evening, following a protest meeting outside police headquarters, a small crowd of black teenagers and young adults overturned a police car, damaged other vehicles, broke store windows, and threw stones at whites. Many of the white policemen on Teaneck's force, unaccustomed to handling much more than burglaries and traffic violations, called the disorders "riots," which brought derision from one of their white officers, Captain Gary Fiedler, a former marine who had fought in Vietnam. "This is magnified by people that had never done anything otherwise exciting," he scoffed. "To me this was nothing."

The town quickly became polarized, not only between black and white but also between liberal and conservative, clergy and police, healer and zealot. Suddenly exposed were the simmering suspicions among many blacks, their sense of exclusion from Teaneck's power structure, their deep alienation from the police. And when these long-standing, unarticulated emotions exploded in rage, when some white leaders joined the clamor for Spath to be suspended and prosecuted, most of the ninety police officers on the force were sincerely shocked and truly hurt. "We didn't expect when this happened that they'd turn on us before any of the facts were in," lamented Donald Giannone, a veteran of twenty-six years in the department who became chief seventeen months later. "That they would do that and didn't have confidence in us!" His voice rose to a high tone of pained surprise. "Knock you back. What the heck can you do? You're not racist. You never saw anybody make a decision based upon race. I can honestly say that."

Neither Giannone nor his predecessor stopped to ask themselves why the feelings were there or whether their department might now do something to alleviate them. From the front desk of headquarters, policemen sold T-shirts emblazoned with the declaration "Never a Doubt," a reference to the contention that if Spath had not shot Pannell, Pannell would have shot Spath. Officers from surrounding areas responded to blacks' protests by joining Teaneck cops in a countermarch through town. Furthermore, the police force received no sensible guidance from the township manager (who left thereafter) or from most members of the township council, who were crippled by internal bickering and a sense of siege. "The council couldn't even talk to each other because we were so divided on the issue," said a councilman, Peter Bower.

Facing a vacuum of leadership from the town government, citizens organized dialogues and advocacy groups to reach across the gulfs and press for reforms. The high school set aside two days for conversation, permitting students to gravitate as they wished to teachers and other adults who made themselves ready to facilitate discussions in classrooms and offices; some white teachers were hurt that black students with whom they thought they had close relations chose instead to confide in black faculty.

The Teaneck Clergy Council, a loose assortment of religious leaders, opened houses of worship to any residents who wanted to gather and talk. The first day or two, several dozen police officers participated. But as time wore on and abrasive activists grabbed the public spotlight, policemen grew disenchanted and defensive in their belief that community organizers were merely out to bash the police. Officers reported that their union had ordered them not to attend any more sessions. And in the end, Captain Fiedler was left practically alone representing the department at the community dialogues until he was instructed by the township manager, Jack Hadge, to stop going.

Hadge also told Reverend Bruce Davidson, leader of the Clergy Council, that "it was none of our business, he was going to handle things, and our concerns were not things anybody should do anything about," Davidson recalled. "We had to stop listening to the wrong people. We should shut our mouths. This was just an incident, just a bunch of troublemaking kids, no racial problems, nothing wrong with the police force. A lot of the town leadership adopted that stance. On the town council, the attitude was that anyone who thought there was a problem was the enemy."

Giannone, Fiedler, Bower, and others saw police officers retaliate for the criticism by enforcing laws less vigorously, writing fewer tickets, taking less initiative. "The enthusiasm for the job dropped off," Fiedler said. "You also heard attitudes from some of the guys: 'Fuck this place, it's only a paycheck. I don't give a shit.' "

Some of the recommended remedies, including affirmative action and sensitivity training, drew derision from Chief Giannone, who cautioned that white cops who didn't get promoted or hired would go to the bar and gripe about affirmative action. "And now he tells twenty or thirty or whatever it happens to be, plus his own family," Giannone said. "Now they're anti-black or anti-minority because their Johnny dear didn't get the position, and the reason why is this. Nobody has taken that part of the equation into account."

As for diversity training or sensitivity workshops, Giannone was simply impatient. "From our perception, we were not the problem," he declared. "Whatever societal ills are there, we're not the problem, don't even cause it. If we go to a scene and somebody says that they screwed with my mother and she's the best piece of ass they ever got and stuff, or I'm a dirty m.f. or whatever it happened to be, and I haven't used any derogatory terms, if their answer to that is to send *me* to sensitivity training, well, so be it. That's the political answer."

Still, some sensitivity training was instituted for the department. And Giannone professed a desire for more black officers, at least to diminish blacks' ability to throw the racial motive at the cops. "It helps to be a composite of what the community is," he said. And the department did move very slowly in that direction following the shooting. In 1990, Teaneck had 38,000 residents, of whom about 33 percent were black (other minorities included 30 percent Jewish, 6 percent Hispanic, and a growing number of Muslims of Indian and Pakistani background). By 1992, only seven of the ninety police officers were black (8.8 percent), and blacks were still underrepresented in other areas, accounting for just one of the top thirteen police officers (7.6 percent); one of the township council's seven members (14.2 percent); two of the nine members of the board of education (22 percent); and about thirty of the 160 staff positions in the high school (18.75 percent), where 40 percent of the students were black. The principal, the superintendent of schools, the president of the board of education, the police chief, and the township manager were all white (although the manager's deputy was black).

By 1995, thanks to a recruitment drive organized by Gary Fiedler, who was elected to the township council and then left the department, the police force expanded to ninety-seven members, and the number of blacks doubled, to fourteen. Community policing was introduced, which some black residents thought had eased tensions. But black youths still complained of being stopped randomly.

Sherlynn Reid of Oak Park was invited to Teaneck in 1996 by a citizens' group that had set up a foundation to encourage interracial dialogue. She met with four council members, visited schools, and explained to everyone who would listen how Oak Park went about the business of managing integration. She found the high school impressive and the community discussions encouraging but the government "kind of hush-hush about the subject," she remarked. "We tend to be out there," she said of Oak Park, "so we tend to get into more conflicts, open discussion, where it's clear that people don't agree. But at least we get it out and move on."

CHAPTER ELEVEN

Breaking the Silence

I cheated myself, because I didn't speak up.

—A white military man

Officers of the Law

When John was a rookie cop in Baltimore, fresh out of the academy in the early 1980s, he was the only black on a squad of experienced whites, and none of them would speak to him. "None of them. Nobody. They wouldn't even say 'Good evening,' " he remembered acidly. That was the code: You didn't talk to a rookie, white or black. A white might escape the rule by having a cousin or a classmate or a friend on the force, and that connection would open a way out of the cell of silence. In those years, a black had no one. And so he would be imprisoned in muteness until he proved himself.

When John would say, "How ya doin'?" others would not reply. When he would get called to a robbery in progress, the others would come and back him up, doing their duty. "Then, if you wanted to say something, they'd just get in the car and fly off," he recalled. For six weeks he was isolated in this way, less time than most. It could go on for as much as a year.

"But then I got a call one time in the projects for Signal Thirteen—officer needs help," John said. "And it was one of the older officers. This guy was, like, the oldest guy in the squad; amid all the other officers he was well respected. . . . Guess who the first officer on the scene was. Me. I go to the door. It was shut. I can hear him battling in there. I kicked the door open. There he was, tussling with this big guy. . . . They were fighting over his gun, and his gun got loose. When I got there, the guy was on top of him, getting the best of him, and I grabbed him and began to kick his butt all over that house. . . . Then I got the cuffs on."

When it was all over and other cops from the station had arrived, John asked the older officer, Jack, if he was all right. Jack was covered with blood, but he had the stamina to make a crucial gesture. "He came to me, right in front of all the guys in the house," John remembered, his eyes twinkling, "and puts his hands on my shoulder. This was the first time he speaks to me. This guy wouldn't say, 'Hi,' or 'Good evening,' or 'Good morning.' . . . He says, 'Good work, man. I really appreciate what you did for me.' I said, 'No problem, Jack.' And that made me feel good inside, that he at least appreciated it. And then, bam, everybody in the squad starts talking to me."

The streets, like the trenches, are sacred ground where race disappears as cops and soldiers battle shoulder to shoulder. No quiver of doubt entered John's mind that a white officer would have done the same for him. He felt not the slightest wisp of a question about that. The racial lines are drawn only when the moment of crisis has passed. "If you had a shooting," he explained, "and you were going looking for someone that was armed with a gun, you didn't find any prejudice there," he said. But if he was the first to arrive at a murder scene and therefore became the officer in charge, his white colleagues would provide only perfunctory assistance in holding back a crowd while waiting for the lab technicians and the homicide detectives. Then "they'd just kind of ease their way away without trying to be a help. I can't knock all white officers, but there were many, and they made it blatant."

When a black woman gets trouble from white men, she cannot easily distinguish the anti-black from the anti-female attitudes. Sometimes they get thoroughly mixed together into a potent brew. That's the way it looked to "Helen," a black Baltimore policewoman, when she entered the police academy in 1979. In the self-defense course, Helen was paired with a strapping, sneering white man who told racist jokes. She is not a big woman. She is sinewy and slender with dark olive skin; her straight black hair is pulled back tightly and tied with a black ribbon.

"When I was paired up with him, I says, 'Oh, God, I know I'm gonna quit now, I know this is it.' He would look at me and smile, you know, one of those numbers. . . . This guy was just throwing me all over the place, and I was scared, so I was afraid to defend myself, and I says, 'This stuff doesn't work.' " The trainer, a sergeant, told her every day that if she was going to be out on the street, she would have to have confidence and learn the moves. But she had no confidence, only fear.

One day she wasn't feeling well, and her patience was at an end. She said to herself that she simply wasn't in the mood to deal with this immense "hilly billy," as she called him. "So when it was our turn to get on the mat with our defense tactics, I just somehow picked him up and body-slammed him," she said. "And I stood there and I was shocked. I says, 'My goodness, did I do that?' He turned around and he looked at me and he says, 'You're gonna get it.' And when he said that, I said, 'No, I am not,' and that day I made up my mind that I was gonna fight back, and that's what I did, and I was just throwing him all over the place."

He had a friend, though, another white trainee. And on a later day, as she was driving out to the pistol range, his pal was tailing her so closely that he was practically on her bumper. When they pulled into the parking lot and got out, he made some insulting remarks about her car and her driving, and "we both pulled our guns on each other," she said. "We were gonna shoot each other, and the officers had to wrestle him down and take his gun and take my gun." Nevertheless, she and both white men were then graduated from the academy and became career police officers.

The hostility has grown more difficult to sustain as more African-Americans have entered the department under affirmative action requirements. One witness to the changing climate has been Lieutenant Barry Powell, who joined the force in 1971 and has served as president of the Vanguard Justice Society, the black police association. "Back during that time, words were used such as 'nigger,' " he said, "not only outside in the car but at roll call at times." That meant that when the sergeant briefed the oncoming shift, he would read out the incidents of the last twenty-four hours by reporting that a "nigger" committed this crime or that. "All I can say is that when the consciousness became more open about not doing these kinds of things, and as there was a changeover of personnel," Powell observed, "these kinds of things stopped, as far as it being out in the open. What people think is something different."

And what they think finds more circuitous routes of expression. In New York City, African-American policewomen who pull over a car that seems suspicious and call for a backup using the code "10-85" have sometimes found that as they're talking, the radio goes "ep, hep, ep, ep," blocking their transmission. In some departments, this is known as "clicking," an untraceable form of harassment accomplished from another car when an officer simply presses the transmit key of his radio while the black is trying to get her message through. This looked purely racial, not sexist, to James Hargrove, a black assistant police commissioner in the early 1990s, because white policewomen often got the opposite treatment, he noted: Other officers flocked to their aid, albeit in patronizing fashion.

The discrimination that John encountered as a Baltimore cop came in a score of subtle ways. Supervisors approved days off for white officers more frequently than for blacks. Whites knew how to manipulate the scheduling book and never told black officers the techniques. "They would switch days around for one another so that a certain officer could get off," he said, "where they would end up closing you in so you couldn't get a day off close to a holiday—Thanksgiving, Fourth of July, or Christmas."

White officers would receive higher evaluations, less criticism, and assignments on easier beats than blacks, he observed. When a supervisor was off and an ordinary patrolman had to fill in as officer in charge, the privilege would invariably be awarded to a white. "The white officers would always be in supervision, ordering blacks," he said. "We wouldn't be given the opportunity to learn."

That was then. "I think it has changed a lot," John continued. "I see more black supervisors coming in. . . . I got a black sergeant, and he knew my potential. He knew I showed the same potential as the white officers who were in the squad, and he immediately put me in place [as an officer in charge], not because I was black but because I showed the skill to do the job. And he was knocked by many white sergeants, but he believed in standing on right." With more black officers hired, whites' attitudes seemed to shift. "I mean, you spend more time with guys in your squad than you spend with your wife," he observed. "You kind of come to respect one another, and then racism goes out the window, because it's what's being seen every day. I come to know you and you come to know me."

That was Hargrove's formula as well. "I found that the greatest training and understanding—the hell with all the police academies and the human relations and everything else—is blacks and whites working together and riding together for eight hours in a radio car, and finding out that your family problems and my family problems are very similar, and that your grandmother's attitudes toward certain things are like my grandmother's attitudes toward certain things." The trouble is, people usually get the partners they ask for, and they ask for people like themselves, he said. "I think the police department accommodates that too much."

Furthermore, many white officers, coming from virtually all-white communities, see black partners as mere exceptions to a pattern that assaults them daily. They see the worst of all people in every racial group. "They never get an opportunity to go to the woman's house that's immaculate, whose family sits down at the table together for dinner," Hargrove observed. "They don't get the calls for those houses.

So to them, who have no interaction with those community people, that doesn't exist. Every house in that area is rat- and roach-infested, you know: kids eating cereal for dinner."

In police business, cross-cultural sensitivity is not just a touchy-feely creed of compassion; it has a practical effect on black-white interactions, and on the street its absence can be deadly. "If you have a white officer that was born and raised pretty much in a middle-class family in Hartford County somewhere," said Helen, the black policewoman in Baltimore, "and he comes down here to the inner city to work in a black neighborhood, you know, he's not used to dealing with black people, he's not used to seeing the poverty, neither do he understand why this is happening. What happens is that he begins to formulate his own opinions as to what the problem is or whatever, and he begins to act out the solution; he's gonna be the solution. 'I'm gonna make them stop hanging on the corners, I'm gonna make the men take care of their children, I'm gonna make them act right, I'm gonna do this and I'm gonna do that.' So he starts to take it on as a personal thing, and this is where a lot of the problems are created: simply not being able to conceive of people living a certain way, of people doing certain things, because, you know, it's foreign to you. You've never seen it. It takes some adapting and getting used to."

Such cultural biases have kept many blacks off the New York police force, according to Hargrove. The filter comes in the form of psychological testing. "One of the questions asked of all the candidates is to describe the most traumatizing experience they had," Hargrove said. "Now you talk about a kid that comes out of Bedford-Stuyvesant, where I came from, that can describe a homicide scene, shootings nightly, and, 'Well, how does that affect you?' 'Hey, I deal with it.' 'What happened that day when you found the body?' 'I went to school.' 'You went to school?' Now, some psychologists, based on their background, might not be anxious to give that kid a gun and hire him as a cop. Whereas the kid from Okadonk, Long Island, if that happened to them, they would need therapy for a year. However, that psychologist feels comfortable giving that person a gun. And that person from Okadonk is gonna police in Bed-Stuyvesant. Personally, I'd rather give a gun to the kid in Bed-Stuy, 'cause he can deal with that situation." In other words, there is a difference between being callous and being street-smart.

Police departments generally let their members deal with race on an ad hoc basis, and that doesn't always work very well. It is such a sensitive matter in a unit of the mostly black Washington, D.C., force that black and white officers tiptoe around the subject with acute wariness. "There is an incredible amount of joking directed at every other aspect of a person's makeup," said a white officer. "We have one black officer who's rather portly. Every time he walks in the room, everybody starts oinking, black and white. We have another guy who's white, who's portly. Everybody calls him 'Fats' and 'Doughnut' and all this sort of stuff. It's brutal. I mean, we are basically pretty cruel with each other." But never do they dare to be racial in their joking. "We don't talk about race a lot, which I think is healthy," he said. "I think it's a no-win situation, basically. This isn't *Hill Street Blues* and shows like that where people walk around with their hearts on their sleeves. This is a working police unit that has to keep doing its job on the street. If you got all twisted in second-guessing yourself, what other people did because of the racial permutations and combinations, you'd be paralyzed. So we don't talk a lot about it."

Addressing even racially motivated brutality can be a ticklish business for a good cop. John has tried to find acceptable formulas to curb police violence without quite breaking the cops' code of solidarity. "I feel that there are many officers, white officers, that are prejudiced, who treat blacks wrong—many," he said. "I know police, white officers, that should not be police. I've seen them do things where I've had to step in . . . and say, 'You're not gonna do any more, you're not gonna hit him anymore, you're not gonna kick him anymore.' Or 'The cuffs are on, man.' They are so prejudiced that they think that all blacks are dirty, or because they're poor they're good for nothing. There are some who feel that their rights can be violated just because they may not be as knowledgeable with the law as we are. . . . For example, just walking up to somebody and searching them on the street, or stopping a car and saying, 'Get out, stand here!' and go rifling through their car and find something and then lock them up—with no probable cause. Or just calling, saying, 'You're nothing but a no-good nigger anyway. You was born a nigger, you'll die a nigger, all of you niggers are the same.' Just verbally abuse them." Sometimes when a black officer arrives, the abuse slacks off, but even when he is there, John has seen it explode in the heat of anger. "There's such rage that they can't control themselves," he said. "They're not even thinking about you. Their true feelings, their true nature comes out. And then you see it."

Later, with a bunch of officers sitting around in conversation, he can sometimes approach the issue indirectly. "While you're talking, you can work in how you feel," he explained, "and every one of them would know exactly what you're talking about." If Joe, who's sitting there, "kicked the mess out of somebody five times" a few weeks ago, John might say, without looking at Joe, "Man, I don't think that's really necessary, kicking somebody five times." The message gets across.

If policemen find it awkward to combat racism when it's so crude, they are even less inclined to fight it when it's undercover. In principle, the New York City Police Department has something of the same philosophy as the army, which Hargrove described this way: "I cannot control what you think, but I can control your behavior—that you come to work, you hang it up in the locker room, you go out on the street, and you do your job." But only the most egregious violations are considered subject to control, and many of those go unpunished, he admitted. "We still get the ethnic slurs, we still get the violence by police officers that's accompanied by an ethnic slur, which translates into our own definition as a bias incident. So it's not to say that it does not occur. It does." The more insidious behavior escapes attention. "I think the racism in the New York City Police Department is very subtle," he said.

Subtle or explicit, its cost to the fulfillment of the police function became clear after the Los Angeles department's record of racism helped to lose the prosecution's murder case against O. J. Simpson. If there had been no detective Mark Fuhrman spouting "nigger" on tape and boasting about beating blacks and fabricating evidence, if the police force had not been stained by a history of brutality and bias, the evidence might have seemed credible. But the Simpson case was just the loudest alarm bell. In little-noticed trials across the country, skepticism about police testimony has been introducing "reasonable doubt" into jurors' minds for years. The doubts reached the bench as well when a federal judge in New York, Harold Baer Jr., threw out drug evidence because the arresting officers, seeing the occupants of a car flee, believed that gave them "probable cause" to search the vehicle. Baer ruled that in light of minorities' abuse by law enforcement officers, it was no surprise, and no indication of guilt, that people ran when they saw the police. Under a storm of pressure from the Clinton White House and the Republican Congress, the judge reversed himself.

The bottom line of a business is profits. The bottom line of a police department should be convictions, even though most departments measure their performance by arrests. If convictions are undermined by endemic racism—and they are—a prudent police department would reasonably be expected to launch a major campaign to educate its members, screen those entering, and rid its ranks of those who act on their bigotry. The tools are available; they are simply not used.

For example, the New York City Police Department does not scrutinize its applicants thoroughly for racism, Hargrove said; the eight-hour battery of psychological tests provides no such information. Nor are sergeants, precinct commanders, or other supervisors held responsible for the performance of their subordinates around racial matters. "I always criticize police departments, and I guess New York City included, for the fact that we do not give the same attention to issues of discrimination and brutality that we give to corruption," he declared. "I don't know of a department where rules and regulations and practices and policies that deal with combating corruption are duplicated for racism and brutality." If an officer at the lowest level is instructed to report the passing of so much as a $5 bribe, Hargrove insisted, that same officer should be trained to report "those racist statements that are made in locker rooms, that are made in radio cars, the beating of a handcuffed prisoner." He added, "I know of no police department that does that."

Only a few departments have used existing technology to monitor patrolmen's behavior. Only some have equipped their cars with video cameras to tape automatically as soon as the siren goes on. Almost all— except for the police in San Diego County and Irvine, California—have ignored a device that could be installed in each patrol car to record its location at all times: a receiver that is fed constantly by signals from the Pentagon's array of navigational satellites, the Global Positioning System; it is used widely by private boat owners and airplane pilots. Getting it into police cars has been the brainchild of Sam Knott of San Diego, who believes it would make policemen less cavalier about stopping blacks, pulling over Hispanics, and harassing young women. In particular, he believes that his twenty-year-old daughter, Cara, would still be alive. She was murdered in 1985 by a California highway patrolman who pulled her over to harass her sexually, as he and other cops had done to other women. She was white, and so was he. But Knott thinks the potential for racial abuse would also be reduced if officers knew that they could not deny that they had been at a particular place at a particular time.

Police departments are way behind the military services in assigning equal opportunity officers to deal with racial problems in commands and in educating personnel in racial matters. Some of that is done, but not extensively. When it comes to controlling racism in the ranks, police departments are among the country's least effective institutions, and the armed forces are among the best. With few exceptions, police departments tolerate remarks and actions by officers that would derail careers in the military. Black cops who encounter racial slurs and discrimination have considerably less recourse than black soldiers and sailors do. And police culture, while changed from thirty years ago, remains inhospitable to the intensive training, constant monitoring, and candid self-evaluation that the military employs to hold racial tensions to a minimum.

Soldier Citizens

The armed services have their problems, of course—some subtle, some overt. In December 1995, a white supremacist army private, accompanied by two buddies, gunned down a black couple in North Carolina, prompting the army to comb its ranks for extremists. In 1997, amid reports of widespread sexual abuse, five white women said they had been pressured by army investigators to charge their black drill sergeants with rape. But such incidents are rare. In general, the armed services have learned to manage race relations well enough that they have lessons to teach civilian organizations and a few tools that are adaptable to nonmilitary settings. "Private industry ought to be as good as we are," said Major General Charles Hines, the first black commander of Fort McClellan in Alabama.

When President Harry Truman ordered the integration of the armed forces in July 1948 (largely to draw black support in the upcoming election, his staff papers show), he set in motion a great wheel that turned with ponderous reluctance. Misgivings were expressed on both sides of the color line, and eighteen months after his order, the air force still contained some all-black units, despite cajoling memoranda from the top. Ultimately, the doubts and the segregation disappeared, but even as the races mixed together into barracks and mess halls, the more complex task of managing the mixture was neglected. In 1961, there were fewer black master sergeants in percentage terms than in 1948, and not until the Civil Rights Act of 1964 did the military address off-base discrimination in surrounding communities, which had created hardships for blacks in uniform.

General Hines started as an enlisted man in 1954, when the army gave no slack to a black. He was left as the lone African-American in an artillery battalion in Panama after the only other black soldier was discharged for "some minor infraction on guard duty," as he recalled. So when Hines had guard duty, he spent the whole time walking around or doing jumping jacks so nobody could accuse him of falling asleep. Assigned once to run a movie projector, he plugged it in and burned it up—and was promptly charged with destroying government property. Just before his court-martial, a white investigating officer discovered that the outlet had no label showing it as carrying 220 volts, and that saved him.

As a junior officer, Hines had contradictory experiences with white superiors. Some he remembered as "princes of people," he said, "and they treated me extremely well. And there were others who wrote in my efficiency report, 'the best colored officer I've ever seen.' " He snorted a sour laugh. "You could not get away today with saying 'the best colored officer I've ever seen.' But that was in my record."

The slow awakening in the armed forces was hastened by the decay of military cohesion in the early 1970s, toward the end of the Vietnam War, when race riots broke out on bases and aboard aircraft carriers. Newly dependent on voluntary enlistment, the military leadership was galvanized into establishing what is now called the Defense Equal Opportunity Management Institute (DEOMI) at Patrick Air Force Base in Florida to address racial problems. It has developed into one of the country's foremost training institutions on issues of diversity. In addition, nondiscrimination policies were reinforced with promotion goals, not quotas, aimed at advancing at least the same percentage of minorities and females as that of all officers under consideration. This objective has not always been met, but it is probably safe to say that in the army, more whites take orders from more blacks than anywhere else in America.

Moreover, those inside and outside the services who have studied the issue believe that within the last ten or fifteen years, the climate has gone through a sea change: Career officers and noncommissioned officers have come to understand the professional consequences of racism. "The worst thing that can happen to an army officer or a leader," said General Hines, "the worst thing that can happen—other than robbing a bank downtown—is to be found guilty of depriving a member of the organization of equal opportunity. Or of being insensitive—grossly insensitive. Now, when I say insensitive, I'm talking about overtly insensitive. But there's still covertly insensitive kinds of things that happen."

These can take many forms, for even if institutional discrimination is eliminated, personal prejudices remain; one army diversity trainer worried that he was doing no more than teaching people how to discriminate covertly rather than overtly. "The one thing about the army— good, bad, or indifferent—they follow orders," Hines said, "and if the chief of staff of the army says there will be equal opportunity in the army, I'm just gonna tell you, you can take it to the bank: There will be. If the secretary of the army says this will happen in the army, it will happen. There will be no debate. But it takes time for the insidious

things. The overarching things and concepts and policies that are cen-
tralized and managed from above, they will be majestic. But down in the
pits, down in the human dimension where people are degraded and
demeaned, their dignity is excised, it takes time. It takes time for people
to change their ways."

Off duty, military people cluster pretty much as civilians do. "If you
go to a service gym, you'll have blacks on one side, whites on the other,
playing half-court basketball, or black teams and white teams," said Alan
Gropman, a former air force historian. "If you go to the mess hall, you'll
have blacks at one table, whites at another. If they're at the same table,
they'll be at opposite ends of the table. That's where the breakdown
occurs. Worse yet is in the off-post activities in camp towns like Fort
Benning, Bragg, Campbell, where there are bars that are exclusively
black and bars that are exclusively white. This is true in Germany. There
will be bars that are all black and bars that are all white, and you really
don't want to go to one or the other. You want to be very careful about
that. If you do go, you have to be sure that you're accompanied by somebody. Alcohol is a dangerous fuel.

"The army has a main officers' club where everybody is welcome, but
the Fifth Battalion will have one, and the Sixth Battalion will have one,
the Seventh Battalion will have one . . . and one of those will be black.
And the enlisted will have several NCO clubs, and one of those will be
black. Nobody will be hurt for going in there. It's just de facto. That's an
ugly little secret that the services would like to hide."

One of the most insidious devices of racial discrimination is the
evaluation form, the performance report, the "ticket," as it is often called
in army slang. The upper end of the scale measuring promotion potential is stacked with superlatives, which can mask the nuances of bias.
"Always exceeded requirements" is the top grade, and "Usually exceeded
requirements" is the next; a black who gets merely "usually" (and doesn't
know that an equal white gets "always") is hardly in a position to complain. The form's other scale, for "professionalism," has number grades
that are nearly as subtle: Both "1" and "2" are used to indicate a "high
degree" of achievement in various areas.

Until shortly before retiring in 1989, Lieutenant General Andrew
Chambers never questioned his evaluations or imagined that he might
be the target of a refined put-down. "Anybody who's retired as a three-
star general shouldn't have any complaints," he remarked. But then he
became senior enough to sit on promotion boards with access to the
evaluations that his white colleagues had received over the years. Around
the table, perusing the files, he was stunned to see how much better they

had been rated than he. "I cried a number of times," he confessed. "The time that hurt the most was when I was battalion commander." The battalion was in disastrous condition; Chambers put it on its feet and established a warm friendship with his superior, the white brigade commander. "I loved the guy. I had the highest respect for him. And I was his man. I mean, he leaned on me big time. We had been to Vietnam together, and I know he liked me and respected me and still does."

But years later, Chambers picked up the file of a white officer who had been under that brigade commander, an officer who had also commanded a battalion but was "not even in the same class," Chambers insisted, "and the brigade commander said so, and he didn't even like that guy, couldn't stand him. But you know he gave him a hell of a lot better ticket than he gave me?" Chambers took a breath. "I stopped. I had to go out of the room."

While Chambers did not suffer professionally, other African-Americans' careers can be misshapen by the slights. The process has been closely observed by Sergeant Christopher Condon, a veteran equal opportunity adviser who is white. "If I'm a commander of a unit," he explained, "I have a certain control over what is done in that command, and I can use my own prejudices to lower the type of award an individual gets because I don't like a certain race of people. I can sit there and instead of giving them the highest award, I can just knock it down a couple of times. It doesn't look so bad—you know, I'm still giving people awards. . . . Commanders are allowed to give a soldier two hundred promotion points when they go up in front of a board, and just because I don't like a certain race of people, I can sit there and say, well instead of two hundred points, I'm gonna give you a hundred and forty. I'm still recommending you for promotion, but I'm cutting back on what I give you. It's very subtle." Correcting for such hidden bias is one reason the military uses percentage goals for promoting minorities, one form of affirmative action.

Duty assignments have proved more difficult to equalize, however. The job you get in the military is largely a function of how you score on the ASVAB (the Armed Services Vocational Aptitude Battery), plus your preferences and the service's needs. As a group, African-American enlisted personnel score lower than whites or other minorities; consequently, they tend to be concentrated in the military occupations requiring lower skills. In the army, blacks are underrepresented in the military police, aircraft maintenance, electronic warfare, special forces, public affairs, and electronic maintenance; they are overrepresented in petroleum and water supply, data processing, and other unsophisticated

fields. In all the services combined, only 6 percent of the blacks are electronic technicians, while 8 percent of the Hispanics and 11 percent of
the whites fill those positions. Conversely, 12 percent of the blacks are
service and supply handlers, compared with 8 percent of the whites. The
racial distribution of infantrymen, gunners, and seamen has been kept
about equal, however, with 16 percent of the blacks and 17 percent of
the whites in those tough and dangerous assignments. During the 1991
war in the Persian Gulf, blacks made up 17 percent of the combat and
noncombat casualties.

Remarkably, the gulf deployment saw no racial incidents serious
enough to be reported to the military police, in part because incipient
crises were defused by the equal opportunity advisers assigned to various
units. One of them, a white sergeant who was furnished with a jeep and a
broad mandate to roam among the troops, happened upon a sit-down
strike more appropriate to a factory than an army base. A white commanding officer had ordered a squad of black soldiers to load a truck by a
certain time. The blacks had taken offense at the officer's manner and
were sitting on the ground, refusing to work. Deftly, the sergeant got the
blacks together with the officer, helped them talk it through, and the soldiers ended up apologizing to their commander, who may have learned
something about the unintended messages his style conveyed.

"The big thing there is being proactive," Sergeant Condon explained. "If you're sitting back in your office waiting for a complaint,
you're being *re*active." You're not doing your job unless "you go out and
try and educate and try and stop it before it happens," he said. It is a
standard not always observed by the army and met even less often by
police departments, high schools, colleges, and companies, which tend
to wait complacently until a racial crisis explodes under their feet.

Racial tension cannot be defused unless the top executive is attuned
to the overtones of racial discourse. In the armed forces, the best officers
have learned how to step into that rough territory, once avoided like a
minefield. At a base in Germany, for example, a tasteless joke confronted
a white brigadier general, Tom Jones, who later became the army's
deputy chief of staff for manpower. His white deputy, a colonel, walked
by a room full of soldiers who were fooling around and said through the
open door, "OK, you slaves, get to work."

All were African-Americans, and two days later the unit's equal
opportunity adviser went to Jones. "Sir, we've got a problem," Jones
remembers him saying. "I've got a complaint that the deputy is racist.
He called a bunch of black soldiers 'slaves.'" So Jones called in his

deputy, took him to lunch, and told him of the allegation. At first the colonel had no recollection of any such thing. Then he remembered his wisecrack but insisted that he had paid no attention to who was in the room, whether black or white.

"So I got the soldiers that were in the room," Jones recalled, "and I brought them in and sat them down in my office and said, 'OK, you guys have indicated that you feel that the deputy's a racist. Put this in context. Let's talk about it. What happened?' And so they all explained it to me. It was kind of an interesting dynamic. . . . One of them said, 'Well, I didn't really think it was racist, but then we talked about it, and as we talked about what he'd said and we looked around and we were all black, then somebody said, "You know, he's a racist because he saw all of us blacks and he called us slaves." '

"So then I brought him in," Jones continued, "and we all sat down together, and we talked about the context. We ended up agreeing that that was not a very wise thing for the colonel to have said, but that in the context in which he said it, it certainly wasn't a manifestation of racism. It was simply a comment that he made without paying any particular attention to who was there. He apologized for the fact that his comment had been misinterpreted by them, and they accepted the fact that it was not a manifestation of racism. But I will guarantee you that he isn't gonna call anybody 'slaves' again!"

That kind of face-to-face resolution, brokered by the boss, is exceedingly rare in civilian life, where police commanders, high school principals, college presidents, and chief executive officers don't usually care to get involved. Without visible commitment from the leadership, a tone of concern is never set throughout an institution. Without mechanisms of monitoring as well developed as the military's, the wounds are left to fester. And where education in the form of diversity training is done sporadically, poorly, or not at all, people may remain insensitive to the signals they are sending, to the complicated messages that travel back and forth across the color line.

Diversity instruction has burgeoned into a business. Government agencies, corporations, and universities across the country are hiring growing numbers of trainers and facilitators to conduct programs whose titles include "sensitivity," "multicultural," and other warm terms of tolerance. Many trainers are freelance consultants, others are in-house employees; some are excellent, others are uninspired. Their sessions may stimulate true learning or angry resistance, introspection or polarization. Rarely do institutions spend the funds required to research the impact of such workshops, however, so the results cannot be measured precisely.

Intuitively, it seems reasonable to believe that the more employees know about the dynamics of prejudice and the subtle clashes of culture in a workplace, the more considerately they will relate to others. Few people get pleasure from hurting their colleagues, after all. But it takes more than half a day in class to understand the nuances of cross-cultural friction, and managers are usually unwilling to give the days or even weeks that may be necessary. Many funnel employees through a quick diversity session as if it were an inoculation against office strife. Some wait until after an incident, then call consultants to parachute in and try to pick up the pieces. Others use the training as a preemptive strike against accusations of racism or sexism that might arise. In short, some executives think they can write a check to a consultant and purchase values.

A diversity workshop's effectiveness probably depends largely on the institutional environment in which the training is delivered. Without a surrounding atmosphere conducive to racial tolerance, without clear support from the top for nondiscriminatory hiring and promotion, even the most brilliant diversity instruction can hardly stand on its own. If it is offered merely as a response to a crisis or as an antidote to a poisonous climate, the managers, workers, students, or faculty members who are requested or required to attend may react defensively, taking it as an insult, an accusation of guilt.

It need not be framed as such. No intelligent professor would assert that he has nothing left to learn about Shakespeare or physics or European history, for example. Nor would he consider a free lecture or workshop on those subjects an affront. Why, then, is he offended at the suggestion that he might have something to learn about the highly complex subject of racial interaction? Because it touches the nerve of personal decency; all of us are supposed to be experts on race in America, pristine in our thoughts, immaculate in our deeds. We are supposed to have no gaps in our knowledge, especially about our own behavior. If we admit otherwise, we admit to being part of the problem.

In many organizations, the price for improvement after diversity training is anger among white men who insist that the workshops have created friction where none existed before. But typically, the white males who dominate a workforce fail to feel friction that is obvious to minorities and women. And trainers note that exposing the friction is not the same as creating it, that discomfort in discovering the tension is a key to resolving it.

Another assault on diversity training comes from conservatives who denounce the messages of the seminars as "political correctness," a form of political indoctrination. But "political" seems an odd choice of terms. There is nothing political in teaching tolerance, unless you believe that only liberals or Democrats or those who support trade with China can be free of prejudice. There is nothing political about combating racism unless you think that racial bigotry occupies a legitimate place on the American political spectrum. The subject of diversity training is not political but moral. Perhaps "moral correctness" would be a more accurate label.

Since few mature adults are any more enthusiastic about being taught morality than politics, institutions often try to disconnect diversity training from any notion that the trainees might achieve personal betterment or improved moral values. Instead, the workshops are billed as purely pragmatic means to pragmatic and impersonal ends: In the military, the goal is unified fighting ability; in business, it is profits.

Simon & Schuster had its diverse clientele in mind when it developed multicultural workshops. "Diversity is good business," says the mission statement of its textbook-publishing group, which comprises Prentice Hall and Globe Fearon. "Part of my criteria up front was that diversity training had to be market- and customer-focused," explained Michael Carroll, vice president for human resources. As for "sitting people down and trying to unearth their racial inclinations," he said, "I don't think it's healthy, and I made sure the consultant who came in here understood that."

No matter how the training is pitched, however, the result may be heightened self-awareness. The calculating, bottom-line rationale for summoning employees to a diversity class may unintentionally open the door into their attitudes. As Carroll himself acknowledged, the training can create a workplace culture that values diversity, which affects behavior, which in turn may influence private thinking. "We would like people, if they do harbor certain racist tendencies, to be introspective about them and behave in a dignified fashion," he declared. "We would like you to behave in a way that reflects well on this company. And the best judge is the customer. . . . We have white male sales reps who have been here twenty years, good people, make us money. As they were able to get engaged in a positive way, I have no doubt that they increasingly began to look at their own behavior, look at their own attitudes, and adjust their behavior. . . . One of the things we're trying to motivate is candor. We shouldn't be ashamed of mistakes. We're all trying to learn to communicate. Part of diversity is having a dialogue about our differences and how we make mistakes."

Some instructors confront attitudes head-on, creating confrontational workshops that force people through a catharsis; the facilitator may cajole and badger until participants confess their prejudices and are thereby purged. It is not a popular approach.

"Chase the honky around the room" is what people in the army called the technique when the military started using it in the early 1970s. Colonels rarely enjoyed having sergeants tell them they were bigots. So the Pentagon switched styles. By the late 1970s, the method had mellowed into pragmatism. The military "does not do the equal opportunity and fair treatment business because it's the nice thing to do," said Eli A. Homza Jr., a white army colonel and director of training for DEOMI. "We do it because we have learned that if we don't do it, we will not have cohesive and battle-ready units."

The current philosophy is simple: You can think anything you want; that's your affair. What you do, however, is our concern. "The reality is that in the military context, I may not be able to change your attitudes, but I can sure change your behavior," said Brigadier General Tom Jones. "You may never change your attitude. I hope that through our education process, and I hope that through your own experiences, your attitudes change. But if they don't, that isn't of much concern to me as long as your behavior changes."

That nonthreatening, educational approach is favored not only by the military but probably by most civilian facilitators as well. Lauren Nile, who works primarily in corporations and government agencies, tries to construct what she calls "as safe a learning environment as possible." It wouldn't be necessary if participants arrived in a mood of emotional neutrality, as they would at a session on, say, sales techniques. "But when I do sexual harassment and diversity training," Nile observes, "I find people come with all kinds of feelings: 'I don't know why I have to be here. Once again we have to cave in and give all this time to minority concerns. . . . I don't want people to think I'm a racist.' Anger on the part of many people of color: 'Once again I've got to sit here and be a bug under a microscope and tell white folks what it's like to be black.' "

So she establishes "norms" with her group by asking them what they need to make this somewhat safe. Usually they weave a web of wishes: that they be listened to, that they be respected, that what they reveal will be held in confidence. "And I say, 'If at any point during the day, if you're feeling the need to revisit those norms, let me know,' " she explains. " 'We will make our mistakes, and we will use our mistakes as learning opportunities. If somebody uses a term that you're not comfortable with or a term you'd rather they not use, we will use that as an opportunity to learn.' . . . By then I've really set the tone that this is not a white-bashing session, this is not a male-bashing session. This is a session in which we are here to learn what's appropriate and inappropriate, hurtful or helpful behavior in a work environment."

Nile and many other trainers alleviate guilt by telling participants that they all possess mental tapes, recorded from childhood by parents and teachers and the rest of society, and that the key is to recognize the tapes as they play and notice their impact. "Those mental tapes affected our behavior and our attitudes and indeed our emotions, filled us with fear, anxiety, mistrust," she says. "Most of us, by the time we were ten, eleven years old, we were on automatic. We had automatic responses, emotional and behavioral responses to people who were different from ourselves. . . . The good news is that we can get off of automatic, and rather than have our tapes be in control of us, we can be in control of our tapes."

DEOMI is located just inside the main gate of Patrick Air Force Base, a missile test center on a narrow barrier island south of Cape Canaveral. On the eastern shore, the flat land tapers down to a narrow beach of fine sand smoothed by long Atlantic rollers.

The visitors' office on the base, where passes are issued, is staffed by retired military people, including an aging ex-colonel known as "a character." One morning, when he noticed that a young white sergeant worked at DEOMI, the colonel cracked a scraggly grin and quipped, "Oh, you're from Watermelon U." It is a local "joke" that makes DEOMI people shrug wearily and confirms them in their mission.

The institute occupies a complex of two-story, cream-colored stucco buildings trimmed in brown and constructed in neat, utilitarian military style. A mélange of uniforms moves among the structures: air force blue, navy white, marine khaki, army green, and a smattering of casual slacks and sport shirts indicating the civilians who are sent by the Defense Department and sometimes police departments. For a fee, civilian institutions are welcome to enroll employees at DEOMI. Too few use the opportunity.

The school offers several tiers of instruction. The most extensive is a fifteen-week course for officers and enlisted men about to begin full-time assignments advising commanders on racial and gender matters. Called "equal opportunity advisers" by the army (and given other titles by other services), they immediately stand out from most of their civilian counterparts in the "human relations" field. Where corporations tend to fill such posts with blacks and women who may be relatively new to the firm, the military prefers seasoned officers or, more frequently, senior sergeants and navy chiefs with chests full of battle ribbons. Their military credentials, vividly established, arm them with unassailable credibility. Nobody can ever call them novices or outsiders or say that they try to graft alien ideas onto a military culture that they do not understand. They are the essence of the service, the core and the heart.

In addition, the Pentagon cleverly structures the lines of authority so that the equal opportunity adviser is charged not with judging but with enhancing the unit commander's skill and sensitivity in dealing with race and gender. This is to be accomplished by making the adviser not a watchdog or a gadfly who can bypass the chain of command, but rather an assistant and ally to the commanding officer, a trusted aide who is well schooled and devoted to the commander's success in managing the diversity of his troops. It is in the commander's own interest to listen to the advice and respond to the suggestions of his aide.

In DEOMI's austere classrooms, the concept is drilled into the trainees repeatedly. "Never forget that the equal opportunity program is the commander's program," a group was told by a black instructor, Sergeant Major Claude June of the army. "It's the commander's responsibility. Everything you do, everything you try to accomplish, go back to the commander, talk to the NCOs [noncommissioned officers]. Get the commander's approval. Your job is to tell the commander what's going on in the unit. Tell the good things as well as the bad. The worst unit's got something good going on. The worst thing an equal opportunity adviser can do is report only negative things to the commander."

Gradually, over the weeks, this utilitarian message quenched a smolder of rage that had been consuming a tall black Coast Guard lieutenant in the class. He learned the difference between zealotry and advocacy, he said. Before the course, he confessed, he had been drifting over the line into fanaticism. He had hung his picture figuratively next to that of Malcolm X; now, he explained, he would take it down and put it next to his commander's. "I used to tell people to do things because it was the right thing to do and the moral thing to do," he explained. After training, "I'm focused more on mission effectiveness: 'We're not performing as an effective team.' " That approach, he said, "doesn't isolate any group, doesn't make any group feel they're being held accountable for two hundred years of oppression."

However, the advising system succeeds only if the commanding officer buys into the goals, only if he cares to know what is going on in the trenches and the engine rooms, only if the surrounding military culture promotes racial fairness. That is a good model for civilian institutions as well, and it is why the atmosphere varies from one branch of the service to another, from one company and ship to another. It is why Defense Secretary William Perry, beginning in 1994, ordered all newly promoted generals and admirals to attend two-day workshops in diversity training.

. Budget cuts have been forcing trims in DEOMI's program. The fifteen-week course used to run for sixteen weeks, and a further reduction is planned. Since the belt-tightening, the Pentagon has assigned full-time equal opportunity advisers no lower than the brigade level— 3,000 to 5,000 troops. Below that, battalions, companies, and most ships are given "equal opportunity representatives" who deal with racial matters part-time, as a collateral duty. They are trained in abbreviated courses conducted in the field and in turn hold sessions twice a year for their units. Some doubt their effectiveness. "They're useless," said a senior chief petty officer named Eugene Earhart, a white navy veteran who was well into the course at DEOMI. He gave his navy low grades. "They wait until something happens," he complained, "and then they have this massive reaction and everybody gets retrained with some quick, one-day thing."

In an effort to avoid problems that fester unseen, DEOMI has developed a diagnostic tool for commanders who want to keep in touch with the mood in their units. Called MEOCS, the Military Equal Opportunity Climate Survey, it can easily be adapted for use by private companies, universities, police departments, and other institutions. In fact, however, few civilian organizations take the temperature of their workforce; if they did, most would probably find powerful undercurrents of resentment and would hurry to establish preventive programs.

The survey is done in the least threatening manner that the military can devise. The top brass does not require the poll; a commander may request it, and only he—not his superiors—sees the results, tabulated and analyzed by DEOMI. Thus he takes no risk that poor results will go into his record. As word of the MEOCS has spread, it has grown so popular that DEOMI can barely keep up with the demand.

The questionnaire, given to all members of a unit, offers vignettes of positive and negative incidents and asks the respondent whether they might have occurred. "You need not have personally seen or experienced the actions," the survey explains. "We only want your opinion on the chances that the actions might have occurred at your location in the past 30 days." Each answer is recorded along a scale running from high through reasonably high, moderate, and small to almost no chance that the episode took place.

The first item in the army's version reads, "Unit special events (athletic programs, picnics, etc.) were attended by both majority and minority personnel." The fifth says, "Majority and minority officers were seen socializing together at off-duty locations." Other scenarios describe both discrimination and reverse discrimination: "A minority person was reprimanded by a commanding officer for dating a same ranked White person of the opposite sex (who is not in their chain-of-command)." "A minority enlisted person was assigned less desirable living quarters than a White." "The commanding officer changed the duty roster when he or she discovered that two Blacks were assigned to guard duty on the same shift." "A minority enlisted man was selected for a prestigious assignment over a White enlisted man who was equally, if not slightly better, qualified."

The answers add up to a sense of the "climate" in the unit, "a collection of everyone's perceptions about what's going on in an organization," said Lieutenant Colonel Philip A. Irish III, the air force psychologist and DEOMI's research director. "It may or may not represent what happens in actuality, but it represents people's perceptions about what's going on, and consequently, it's held that perceptions constitute reality."

That picture of reality shocks most commanding officers, especially those who are white males; they are rarely aware that subordinates, especially minorities and women, perceive such tension and injustice. "People in power at the top of organizations tend to feel very ego-involved, very ownership-oriented toward the organization, committed to it," said Irish, who used to design cockpits and instrument displays before getting into the business of race and gender. "And of course most organizations homogenize people as they mature and grow" and rise through the ranks. "So we do find people at the top feeling more positive about things than people at the bottom."

The surveys also reveal an intriguing symmetry of majority and minority beliefs. The more minorities perceive discrimination in a unit, he said, the more white males perceive reverse discrimination. "A polarization is taking place," he observed, "like two parts of a magnet." After

finding such underground tensions, the responsible commander—
and police chief, corporation executive, or college president—would do
something about them.

Despite the military's policy of focusing on action instead of thought,
behavior and feelings are not easily separated in the DEOMI classrooms. As Colonel Irish noted, many of his fellow psychologists believe
that behavior drives attitudes, "that if you continually behave in the
appropriate way, that sooner or later your attitudes will come into con-
sistency or in parallel with how you behave. It's a chicken-and-egg
issue." Furthermore, instructors are interested in getting trainees' attitudes out on the table now, so they don't interfere on the job later.

In the fifteen-week course, everyone comes together for factual lectures and videos about racism, sexism, the dynamics of prejudice, communications and listening skills, and the like. They play games such as
"Star Power," a team exercise in which participants accumulate chips
representing status and influence, just as classes and races gain wealth
and power in real life. As in literature, fiction seems to clarify reality.
They play "Bafa Bafa," an exercise widely used in diversity training to
sensitize students to the difficulty of interaction across cultural boundaries. DEOMI usually runs it for an entire day, dividing the class into two
artificial cultures, each with a language, a value system, a set of beliefs,
and customs of which the other is ignorant. One culture might be laid-
back, the other pressure-driven. One might denigrate females; the other
might elevate them. One might be hierarchical, the other democratic. In
one, a failure to make obvious gestures of deference to the chief brands
you as rude and uncivilized; interaction with those at lower levels is not
permitted. So if those from the democratic culture dismiss the chief as a
figurehead and try to communicate with the ordinary population, they
inadvertently insult. They quickly learn that what is acceptable in their
own culture can be taboo in another—an important revelation for many
participants.

Once or twice on most days, the students break into groups of twelve
to fifteen, to which they are assigned for the entire course. The groups
are carefully created as diverse collections: male and female, white and
black, Hispanic and Asian, officer and enlisted, army and navy and air
force and marines. And into these complex mixtures are thrown the hard
questions of attitude.

A session usually begins with a discussion of a film, a lecture, or a
game just experienced. "We have to process that information, we have
to talk about how we feel about this, that, and the other thing," said
Chief Earhart. "There's a person there who facilitates or guides us,

asking the proper questions to try to bring information out of every person in the group. Their key role is, if they find someone who appears to be hiding something, they try to bring that out so it can be discussed in the group. We've gotten to the point where the group can look at that person and tell whether or not they're hiding something, and we'll try to bring it out."

Hiding what? A chorus of answers came from four trainees: "Attitudes. Feelings. Prejudices."

"Body language," said Jennifer McNeill, a black army sergeant from Fort Benning, Georgia. "You can tell that they're very uncomfortable with the subject that's being discussed."

"And would prefer not to expose themselves," added Amir Abdussabour, the black Coast Guard lieutenant.

"But the idea is for them to bring it out here," Earhart explained, "so that later on they don't bring it out in the wrong place." On the job, for example.

"A part of that also is getting the individual to understand what their feelings actually are," said Abdussabour. "Many times the individual may have suppressed something for so long that they don't know how they will react when confronted."

"Or they're just learning about their feelings right now," Earhart said.

In any event, it seems deliciously incongruous for an instructor, a beefy white sergeant, to ask his charges in a heavy drawl, "Now, how do y'all *feel*?"

After six of their sixteen weeks at DEOMI, a group of trainees felt ready to go into the field and do some good. They were eager and confident that they could be surefooted on rocky terrain.

"I'm looking forward."

"It's a new challenge."

"It's going to be very interesting, exciting."

"I can't wait."

"It makes me nervous and happy. I love challenges."

But they had no idea what was about to happen to them, how the next day would shake their certainty.

The morning after they had made their dauntless pronouncements, they gathered at 7:30 in the auditorium of Building 558 to hear a guest speaker. A light green handout identified him as John Gray, a former personnel manager with an M.B.A. from Harvard, "an authority on minority and gender issues." DEOMI's director of training, Colonel Homza, stood onstage before a colorful array of flags and began his introduction:

"We have a speaker this morning who will use a psychodrama approach to focus on the dissonance, both personal and organizational, that can arise when working with members of different racial, ethnic, gender, and cultural backgrounds. Mr. Gray, a former personnel manager . . ."

Approximately sixty-five trainees sat in the auditorium, about half of them black, one-third of them women, half in combat fatigues, the rest in tropical uniforms. They applauded politely as Gray walked in. He was the picture of a distinguished, urbane, white executive—over six feet tall in a dark blue double-breasted business suit, glasses, a white shirt, and a conservative tie. His facial features were angular and prominent; his hair was straight and gray. He began in a smiling, pleasant fashion, saying that he had not come with a prepared speech.

"I'm going to start first of all by saying to you that if you're gonna be silent with me this morning, I'm going to be making what I call three basic assumptions about your silence," he explained. "The first assumption I'll be making about your silence is that all of you will be understanding everything that I'll be saying to you. Secondly, you're going to be agreeing with everything that I'll be saying to you. And thirdly, you're going to be supporting everything that I'll be saying to you. Those are the three basic assumptions I'll be making about your silence if you're going to be silent with me. And the only way I'm going to know differently is if you break that silence. Because silence for me is a very critical issue—a very critical issue, because your inaction becomes action. Your inaction becomes action." He paused, and the audience was silent. "So you just sent me a message: you understood, you agreed, and you certainly supported me in your silence."

There was light laughter. Inadvertently, the class had just entered into a crucial contract.

"I usually use what I call three basic instructional concepts," Gray continued. Unbeknown to them, he was about to hand them a map to guide them through the day; it would not register, however, and they would kick themselves later. The first technique was the lecture, which Gray called the "tell-me approach." The second, which he told them he always employed, was the "show-me approach." He flipped on an overhead projector and showed a slide of a man riding a bicycle while a boy watched. "Now, can I teach you how to ride that bicycle through a show-me? I think it would be very difficult to do that." In the next slide, a boy rode a bike while a man helped. "So I always tie in what I call a third piece, the 'involve-me.' See, once you involve me, that's when I really begin to understand."

Gray proceeded into an engaging lecture, mixing slides on the screen with questions to the class. He asked the trainees for definitions of prejudice, got good answers, and praised them. "I'm an active anti-prejudice person at this point in my life," he asserted. He asked if they had cleansed themselves of prejudice. "Is there anyone in the room that's not prejudiced? OK, I'll assume through your silence, then, that all of you admitted to being prejudiced. Isn't that the first step in beginning to deal with it—to recognize you are?

"I'll give an example of some prejudices I have. For example, I have a bias toward apple pie. I'm crazy about apple pie. And guess what my prejudice is on apple pie. All apple pie is sweet. That's why I like apple pie. Now, I have a bias against cherry pie. I don't care for cherry pie, and my prejudice on cherry pie is that all cherry pie is sour. Now, I have a right to think that, right? You have no right to tell me to think like you in order to be a good person. So prejudice is a thought. Now, when I carry out that thought and institutionalize a policy in the military that says from now on, everybody's gonna eat apple pie, there will be no more cherry pie eaten in this organization, then we get into a thing known as pie-ism. That's when we begin to get into conflict, and that's when we've got to break the silence."

After nearly an hour of lecturing, Gray suddenly declared, "I'm gonna stop this" and turned off the overhead projector. He had been "shocked" by the invitation to DEOMI, he said, "because people do consider me to be somewhat controversial." He had insisted that he be given freedom of speech. "So I'm going to share a point of view with you that's my point of view, and I'm not here to force my point of view on you." Then he eased into a criticism of affirmative action as "nothing but a quota system."

"And I know you're gonna differ with me on that because of who you are and what this school is about," Gray told the trainees. "When they came out with this affirmative-action order, I had to hire a certain number of minorities and women to work in my organization, and I resented that. The reason I resented that: I didn't like being forced into anything. And I spoke out about that. So I found myself being a former personnel director as a result of that. . . . I said to myself, 'Hey, are my children going to have to come out with an ID card that says they're minority or female before they're going to be considered for a job? Because if so, I've got to fight back, I've got to break my silence.' "

The class was silent.

"So I felt that what I've got to do is to start reaching young people in our schools, because they're our future. . . . I want to encourage them to speak out."

Still the military men and women, the blacks and whites, Hispanics and Asians, sat silently.

"I personally think that schools like this might have been appropriate at one time," Gray continued. "But knowing what I know about the military, you've made a heck of a lot of progress—a heck of a lot of progress. And I think when you have schools that emphasize differences rather than similarities among us, it creates more conflict than solves conflict."

The first faint stirring rustled through the audience.

"Now, when you didn't see color before, people are forcing you to see color and see gender. I don't think I could function in the military today, because of what's happening. . . . It's human nature when you mix males and females together, things are going to happen. . . . It would make me less effective in a combat situation. Because as a man, if I went into combat, and I had women next to me in combat, I would unconsciously try to protect that particular female in those kinds of situations. It would make me less effective. And that's why I stand behind the military in keeping women out of combat, because in my thinking we all have certain superiorities and inferiorities as human beings, and I'm saying let's build upon those superiorities that we have. And maybe then we can start to work better together. I'm not saying there's not a role for women in the military. There is, because you have made progress in solving a lot of the problems of color."

Gray delivered his patter with a disarmingly calm inflection, a tone of voice designed to soften the growing harshness of his words. "That's why I think that schools like this are outdated, or you could better use those dollars maybe in giving you pay raises for what the school spends to educate all of you. You see, I think schools like this are set up to give minorities and women something to do, in a sense. Because I'm looking at the makeup of this audience, and it looks like the majority of you almost look like you're minorities in here. And, you know, it's an assumption that I have. I may be incorrect. But I know I get tired of being the whipping post for all the problems in the United States as they relate to racism and feminism."

Finally, the silence was broken by a Hispanic man who began a question. Gray talked over him, raising his voice to a higher pitch. "You have some self-interest in keeping on perpetrating that there's a lot of prob-lems. . . . I think there's less today than there was in the past, and that we've made a lot of progress."

A black sergeant in the front row started to raise a polite objection. "Sir, I don't know where you've been, but—"

"The problems exist because of what goes on in Los Angeles, where your people commit violence." Gray's voice grew more emphatic. "That's where the problem begins." Derisive laughter rippled up from the class. "No, now look, you've got to learn to resolve issues without using a lot of physical violence." The audience broke into lots of crosstalk, then settled back into sudden silence. "That's when you're making progress."

The black sergeant in front exclaimed, "This is an exercise!"

Gray didn't miss a beat. "But you see," he said, "when you're con-fronted with the truth, you want to start to get into whether this is an exercise. I'm just here to share a point of view with you, as I said earlier. I'm not here to force my point of view on you. OK? All right. There are plenty of people here in the room who probably do support me but can't speak out as openly as I can." This brought a few murmurs, interspersed with laughter. "No, because you'd be out of the school tomorrow if you spoke the way I'm speaking today."

From an aisle seat halfway back in the audience, another black sergeant, a chunky man named Thomas, spoke up. "You know, the refer-ence that you made about the violence in Los Angeles, OK, I agree that the violence was nonsense and it was wrong. But when the system is designed and run by only one side of established society to oppress other people—"

"Let me ask you," Gray interrupted. "No, it wasn't set up to oppress people. Do we not have the strongest political and economic structure in the world today?"

"I don't think so," Thomas replied.

"It may be that we're having some problems, but don't we have the strongest political and economic structure in the world today?" The sergeant tried to speak; Gray drowned him out. "And it was built by us. That's not to say that you people didn't contribute. I'm not saying that at all. OK? I'm not saying that at all. That's what you have to look at. Look at your history."

That triggered a flurry of laughs and inchoate comments. "Who's 'you people'? Man! Who's 'us'?"

"See, this is what gets you in trouble," Gray continued smoothly.

"I would say 'you people' to any group. I don't necessarily mean anything negative. It's just like you jumped on Perot because he said 'you people.' . . . If you have a problem with 'you people,' that's your problem. See, you used to run me around the room with all that stuff at one time, 'cause I'd start apologizing. But I am who I am. The way I'm talking now, I'm not doing anything wrong. I'm not trying to put you in an unkind light. I'm not trying to do that."

Off at the far right-hand side, a black air force sergeant rose to ask a question in a lilting foreign accent. "Do you understand 'you people' to be what people?"

"Sir, where are you from?" Gray shot back.

"I'm from Africa."

"Yeah. Let me suggest something to you. You're in the military. When you learn how to speak like a good American, then I can look at you as a good American that can understand what I'm trying to say. Why don't you solve your problems that you've got going on in Africa instead of getting upset with me?"

Colonel Homza stood. "Mr. Gray, I did promise you academic freedom, and we have that here. I would ask you, however, please try not to make your comments personal, if you don't mind. And I would ask the students, please, one at a time. If you want to talk to Mr. Gray, you don't have to wait for the Q and A, that's fine. But one at a time."

"Well, I think they're showing me disrespect through their laughter," Gray replied. "I feel like I'm entertainment up here, and I'm not here to entertain you. And by the way, I do appreciate the support that I have from my white brothers and sisters here, and I do appreciate that."

"Oooh, oooh." The groans writhed through the class. He had them. Thus far, not a single white person had spoken up.

Thomas, the black sergeant, snapped. He stood up angrily and walked toward the back exit. "Where are you going?" asked a major at the door.

"I've just got to get out."

"Take a seat," the major ordered. Thomas did so, in the back. If he had not walked away from Gray, the sergeant said later, he was afraid that he would have walked toward him.

"You see, that's the problem," Gray insisted. "That's the problem with you folks, because when you get into combat, you do the same thing. You do the same thing. You see, that's why we don't hire you for certain jobs."

"How much combat have you seen?" asked a black soldier.

"I've been in combat before," Gray replied evenly. "I was in Korea."

Finally, a white man had something to say. "You were in Korea?" he asked. "Were there black soldiers?"

"Yeah, and they're good fighters. They're good in that area. I don't have any problems with that. But I think you're bringing that statement and asking that question because you're trying to show how liberal you are in front of the minorities that are here, so I know where you're coming from." Again, derisive laughter.

A black lieutenant asked what jobs Gray thought blacks were suited for.

Gray began by citing the lower IQ scores of blacks. "That's not to say that you're not intelligent, and I'm not saying that at all. But it's been validated that you people cannot pass tests."

"You didn't answer my question," said the lieutenant.

"But I'm going back to answering your question by saying this to you: You have excelled in other areas. You have excelled—and I don't think it's anything to be ashamed of—you've excelled in the area of sports, and that's a great-paying field." The audience rumbled. "Now, in acting, in acting. You're doing a great job in the area of acting. And I think even in the military, looking at the leadership of General Powell. You're making progress, that's what I'm trying to show. But if you continue to raise these issues of racism, sexism, or whatever it is, you're gonna create more problems."

Black trainees were now peppering him with objections. One protested his notion that blacks were good for only entertainment and sports. "What's wrong with that?" Gray asked. Another disagreed that DEOMI was wasting tax dollars. "I think it is," Gray countered, "because you've just demonstrated—I get a sense that there's more hatred in you than there ever was in me, toward people like myself, and that's what I hate."

"I think you're ignorant," said a black sergeant.

"Huh, uh, you're just as ignorant, OK? As far as I'm concerned. You know, you could learn a lot from the women in here. At least they know their place. They know how to sit here and listen, and you could learn something." The class exploded in an uproar of laughter and crosstalk.

"I don't know why you're laughing. I'm not here to entertain you. I resent your laughter." And then he called on the first woman of the morning to raise her hand. "Yes, ma'am."

She was a white air force sergeant. "Yes, sir, I just wanted to say something: Earlier you said that you wanted to thank—the support of all your white brothers and sisters. I would just like to say, personally, I don't feel like I fall into that category. I do not support—"

"Well, there is a category that you might fall into, ma'am, because there was a recent study done at Fort Gordon, Georgia, on women in the military. They found that 13.7 percent of the women in the military were working as prostitutes. They found that 6.6 percent of the women in the military are lesbians. And the balance of those women are in the military simply to catch a man. Now, I don't know what category you fit into, but what I'm saying is that right now you're making that statement, again, like this other person to show how liberal you are in front of the minorities that are here. So I know where you're coming from."

The indignant laughter, the whoops of amazed outrage, the incoherent sentence fragments now boiled up from the class in rising volume.

"You know, maybe I'm wasting my time with you as a group," Gray said. "I really resent the way that I've been treated. I don't know if you planted people in the audience, but I resent the way that you treated me, from your laughter through putting me down because I have a view that differs from yours. I've got better things to do with my time. . . . I feel insulted by you as a group. That's why you're gonna be ineffective out in the field no matter how much time you spend at this school. And I have better things to do with my time. I really resent the way I've been treated."

He picked up his slides and walked out to a burst of applause—that he was leaving.

After John Gray stormed out of his presentation, Colonel Homza told the military trainees that the lecture was apparently over and they should adjourn to their small groups. So they walked to an adjacent building and settled into their meeting rooms, knowing that their discussions would be monitored through one-way mirrors and closed-circuit television cameras.

In the darkened "fishbowl," a control hub where TV screens flickered and a large window opened onto Group One's seminar table, DEOMI instructors sat quietly, ready to watch and listen through earphones as their students "processed" what they had just endured. The instructors were soon joined by John Gray himself, who entered the fishbowl and took a seat.

Each group had a facilitator at its table. And each facilitator nudged the trainees to answer the question "How do youse feel?" as one hard-bitten sergeant framed it. For most, the feelings came down to shame, frustration, regret that they had not handled Gray with some skill. And in spitting out their emotions, they did not converse with one another; each seemed to be having a disjointed conversation with himself:

> WHITE MAN: I feel a little embarrassed because I didn't speak up, and he probably thinks we agreed with him.
>
> BLACK WOMAN: We're gonna have to deal with this in the military atmosphere.
>
> THOMAS (who had tried to walk out): One on one I could have sat and listened to him all day long. But when you can't be in a conversation, I got to a point where I took it personal, and I got up, and that was wrong.
>
> BLACK WOMAN: I didn't get nothing out of it, because I've been dealing with what he was saying my whole military career.
>
> WHITE MAN: I resented it when he said, "And I appreciate the support from my white brothers and sisters."
>
> BLACK MAN: I'm from the South, so it didn't bother me. I've heard worse than that all my life. I wonder if he's a minority.
>
> WHITE WOMAN: I got pissed off. All I heard was my father's voice. All I saw was my father's face. I've been hearing that all my life.
>
> WHITE MAN: I still feel as a class we did not handle it properly.
>
> WHITE MAN: A year or two ago, I would have agreed with him. But now I just laughed at him.

"But how is that laughter interpreted, kid?" The question came inside the control room, from a black army instructor, Sergeant Dorothy Maney, so the young man in the group couldn't hear it.

The facilitator at his table rattled off each trainee's failure: "You walked out," he said. "You laughed. You confronted him unemotionally."

"I think I'm ineffective as an EOA [equal opportunity adviser]," a white man confessed. "I thought I was doing pretty well here. I made a prejudgment. I wasn't an effective listener. I didn't listen to what he had to say, try to get his views and figure out how to change his views. I laughed, which is wrong. That was wrong."

A black woman tried to explain that she did not speak up "because of the way that he attacked."

"So we don't object to those that are forceful," Maney said sardonically behind the mirror.

"Why was it that 99.9 percent of the people who responded were minorities? Why?" asked a white man.

Another white man answered, "I didn't speak because I knew he'd call me 'liberal.' "

And in other groups, whites who had been silent in the confrontation spoke in a mixture of voices. One white man denounced the "white bashing" that he thought had been going on in the course. Another resented being associated with Gray's bigotry. A third declared simply, "I cheated myself, because I didn't speak up."

John Gray, sitting in the dim light of the fishbowl, watched the facilitators lead their trainees into a listing of strategies that might have defused his attacks. From time to time, he whispered a thought to an instructor. And as the sessions ended, Gray remarked that he had deliberately tried to "push all the buttons" by insulting many different groups so that the tensions did not create only black-white divisions. He gestured toward television images of the students as they left their rooms. "They're doing the teaching now."

Back in the auditorium, with the entire class, Sergeant Maney stood to lead the discussion. "Anybody think we were wrong to bring John Gray here?" she asked. Not a single hand went up. But a black man wearing sunglasses had something to say.

"I was personally afraid," he admitted. "I never have encountered personally an overt person who distilled racism and sexism overtly. It just shocks you. I don't know how to handle it, and I hope I can learn that at DEOMI. I was afraid, because I know there may be some real individuals out there that I'll have to deal with—may come into my office or be the male or female I may work for."

What did others feel? "Anger, shock, distrust, embarrassment," said a spokesman for Group Four, "especially when he said he'd like to thank all his white brothers and sisters for not saying anything. Shame, powerlessness, frustration, and disbelief."

"Shame?" Maney asked.

"I was starting to internalize what he was saying," a white man confessed. "When he made the comments about white brothers and sisters, it shocked me, because he wasn't speaking for me."

Suitably humbled, the trainees were eager to hear one another's solutions, so each group reported on its list of strategies: Confront the issue, not the speaker. Be prepared; know your facts. Use your resources; use your chain of command. Be open-minded; listen to what the individual has to say. Speak up and don't tolerate it. Expose it; put the individual on the spot. Take charge. Don't be emotional. Don't take it personally.

They broke for lunch and, soon afterward, gathered outside to watch a launch of the space shuttle *Columbia*, which soared from the Kennedy Manned Space Center in a spectacular plume of fire and smoke. It was a clean display of human accomplishment amid the confused frustrations down below.

When the discussion continued in the auditorium, a white man declared in a southern accent, "The first thing that bothered me is that he said we'd solved the racist problem. I sat there and laughed about it 'cause I couldn't believe it was happening. That's when I should have got up and broke that contract that we had. But I didn't."

John Gray walked silently in from a door at the left front of the hall. Murmurs skidded across the class: "He's back."

Smiling, he addressed them in a friendly way. He reminded them of some clues in the morning's introduction: that the program would be a psychodrama, that he would use three instructional techniques—tell me, show me, and involve me. "Did I do that?"

"Yes, yes," the students acknowledged. Slowly, disorientation gave way to realization that it had been a performance.

"I want you to know it's very difficult for me to do what I did here, presenting that psychodrama," Gray said. "Those stereotypes are mine. I heard them in my growing-up process, and I still hear them today. . . . I tried to be as equitable as I could in my discrimination. I apologize to anyone that I left out. I only had so much time. I know I didn't get into Hispanic, Asian. I didn't get into if you were Polish, Irish. . . . Are you angry at me, or are you angry at self? Because you had an opportunity to visit with self today, and sometimes when we visit with self we don't like what we see."

What they would see tomorrow, he told them, were videotapes of themselves compared with other audiences. "I hate to disappoint all of you, but your reaction to me is no different from any other group," he said. "Compare yourselves with young students in a high school. See how effective they are, see if they're any different. . . . The first coping behavior is usually laughter. I always get a lot of strong laughter. I ask, 'Why were you laughing?' I remember one person standing up, facing me, and saying, 'Buddy, the only reason I'm laughing is I'm trying to prevent myself from coming up there and carrying you out that door, and you better hope I keep on laughing.' "

Besides laughter, he asked, "how did most of you cope with me?"

"Silence," the students answered in a chorus.

"Silence. And that happens with every audience. The majority of people are silent. And I've asked people, why were you silent? 'Well, I thought you were so sick I'd just be wasting my time. I was silent because I didn't know whether I could really handle you, cutting me down the way you were cutting other people down. Oh, I was trying to think of what to say, that's why I was silent.' There's a variety of reasons for the silence. You know, one of the ways that Hitler got into power was by people sitting there quietly and not saying anything."

If a white student in a school yells "nigger" in a hallway, Gray went on, "that minority student does not hear one white person saying 'nigger.' [He] hears the whole school saying it, hears the teacher saying it, the principal saying it, the cafeteria workers saying it, the custodian saying it, see. Because of the silence. So one of the most effective strategies you can use, to begin with, is to—" and here he paused for emphasis after each word: "break—your—silence. So what we have to focus on is developing skills as to how to break that silence."

He had a few suggestions. "When you're in a group situation like this," he advised, "stand up, take your eye contact off of me. Take it off of me, and let it float around the group. 'That statement that John Gray made on intelligence, there is no known measurement for intelligence that I'm aware of today. Thank you.' And then sit back down. Now, be careful, because I might come back and ask you, 'Are you Jewish?' You see, you may want to keep silent, because you stated your point. We don't only want to state our point of view, we want the person to accept it. . . . You might be able to come out with another study to contradict me. And also, I won't be able to go on about the study at Fort Gordon, Georgia, because there is no such study. Something I created at the moment."

Gray couldn't help smiling as he remembered two dramatic rebuttals that he had encountered. "In Heidelberg, Germany, I was doing a session for staff officers there, and I was into the psychodrama. All of a sudden a colonel stood up and said, 'Let's pray.' I said, 'Wait a minute, Colonel, are you a Catholic?' He said, 'No.' I said, 'Well, if I wanted a prayer service I'd go to church for it. Take a seat.' And he started to sit down, but he caught himself. And then he walked toward me. Now, when you walk toward me, I stop talking. Then he stood over me and put his hand over my head, and said, 'God, give your blessings to this man, and, my God, touch him so that he may see the light.' He did a prayer service. And by praying, he did defuse the group. He took that group away from me—excellent strategy.

"I remember a session in Italy," Gray continued. "And all of a sudden a woman in the audience jumped out of her seat, 'cause I'd told her she had more male hormones than female hormones in her body. . . . She walked toward me, and I stopped talking again, and turned her back to me. She ripped her jacket open and said, 'Does this look like I have more male hormones than female hormones?' She took the audience from me. She defused the situation. An excellent, excellent strategy." The class laughed, but it was a different, genuine laughter.

Despite all the clues and hints, John Gray had fooled them into thinking that he was an authentic bigot. Now, the seeds of doubt sown, a black air force sergeant had anther suspicion. Gray had said that he was from Cleveland. "I'll be interested to know which side of Cleveland he's from," the sergeant said during a break.

When the class reconvened, Gray ended the day by opening the discussion to personal questions. A white man asked, "Where did you grow up in Cleveland?"

"The East Side," Gray said, "and I'll talk about that tomorrow." The black sergeant clapped and laughed in the jubilation of discovery.

The following morning, John Gray shed his double-breasted business suit and appeared before the uniformed students in a casual, light blue sweatsuit. The neutral outfit allowed the eye to concentrate on his face. The skin had an indeterminate ashen hue; the cheekbones, nose, and eyebrows added up to a craggy sum that suggested a touch of Greek, perhaps, or American Indian.

"You're going to have another experience in cognitive dissonance today," he said.

After a few slides and a discussion of how he helped remedy institutional intolerance, he showed two videotapes. The first, an edited version of the confrontational session with the DEOMI students the day before, included his comments and their reactions on the Los Angeles riots, the African, taking a lesson from women, the support from his white brothers and sisters, Thomas's walkout, blacks' unfitness for combat, the fictitious study on prostitution and lesbianism, Gray's indignant departure, and the students' applause. They sat in mute embarrassment.

The screen went blank for a moment. Gray was out of the auditorium now. Then the second video came on, a television news feature on Gray and his techniques. Various audiences, completely untrained and less sophisticated, reacted precisely as the DEOMI students had.

Finally, interviewed on tape, Gray moved smoothly into what he called "the disclosure." For decades, he explained, "I have been using my physical appearance as an educational tool, because under that myth of race, I'm classified as black. I'm black, both my parents are black, and both sets of my grandparents are black."

The auditorium was frozen in absolute silence, broken only by a single gesture. A black Coast Guard lieutenant, sitting in front of the black air force sergeant, turned around and put his hand over his shoulder so the sergeant could slap it in a high-five that said, "We guessed it!" Everyone else seemed stunned.

The tape rolled on. Gray said he knew of no whites among his ancestors, that culturally he felt African-American, that he had taken the pseudonym "John Gray" because of threats, and that he had chosen the name because "you can think of gray as a mixture of color," adding, "When I was growing up, 'the grays' was more or less another term for whites."

The DEOMI trainees spent the rest of the day working all of this through, first in their small groups, then back in the auditorium with John Gray answering a barrage of questions. He would not do this exercise anywhere, he said, without extensive follow-up to help his audiences think and talk about what they had experienced. He had been doing it at DEOMI since the school's inception.

Close to the end of his visit, he left the military men and women with a parting message: "Break the silence."

CHAPTER 12

A Country of Strangers

White privilege is like an invisible weightless knapsack of special provisions, assurances, tools, maps,
guides, codebooks, passports, visas, clothes, compass,
emergency gear, and blank checks.

—*Peggy McIntosh*

At the end of my journey, I suddenly came upon a new chasm. It marked
a divide that I had not encountered in all my wandering and listening
across the country, because, as a white person who had grown up in
privilege, I had not thought to ask the question.

The question was posed by the leader of a workshop in Washington, D.C. He had begun an exercise by having us circulate among one
another in the room until we found someone fundamentally different
from us and paired up. A young black woman and I chose each other.
We were instructed to sit down together and look in silence at different
parts of our faces: the eyes, the nose, the lips, the hair. Then we were led
by the facilitator through a structure of conversation until we had built
some rapport. And then he asked us questions:

How many of us found that we had to leave our culture at the door
when we went to work? To answer yes, we were told to stand. The
blacks and Latinos and Asians stood, leaving us whites in our seats. How
many of us had been stopped by the police because of our color? Virtually all the black men, and a few black women, rose to their feet. How
many of us could be sure that the next president of the United States
would be of our race or ethnic group? Only we whites got up from our
chairs. As troubling as it was to see these differences in stark personal
terms, nothing in the gaps was new to me—until he asked the question
that I had never asked:

How many of us had considered not having children because of
racism?

I caught movement out of the corner of my eye and turned and saw
the young African-American woman, my partner, push her chair back

and rise as gracefully as if she were at a funeral. I looked up into her sorrowful eyes, and she looked down into mine, through the immense distance that had been revealed between us. A dozen or so others, most of them black and Latina women, had also stood. The facilitator left us there for a long, long time, staring at each other across the chasm.

She was married, she told me later, and her husband wanted children. But she was frightened of the burden that her country, my country, would bring to them and to her. As she spoke, she wept. She had asked her African-American friends and coworkers, she said, both those with and without children, and they had agreed with her. At the end of this century and the beginning of the next, the trials of raising a black child in America would be too severe.

Since my children are my fondest joy, I cannot imagine sadness more profound than this. It is one thing to choose freely not to have children, as many people do; it is quite another to have the decision imposed by despair. I had often heard from my wife's parents about their conviction, as Nazism and fascism arose in Europe in the 1930s, that even in the safety of the United States, they could not bring children into a world so scarred by tyranny. Fortunately, their resolution proved transitory, but it reflected the traumatic future they foresaw.

When I spoke of the workshop to a white woman who had grown up on welfare and had gone on to a Ph.D. in English, she nodded with understanding. She too had decided not to have children, she explained, because the other white women in her world who did were never able to free themselves from poverty. She had been forced to make a calculation to save herself.

Poverty and racism have not led to a massive renunciation of childbearing by either whites or blacks, of course. Birthrates have declined among upwardly mobile African-American women, but they have remained high among unwed black teenagers. The human instinct to create new life, to nurture and love and be loved, cannot be overcome except by formidable hopelessness. It was into the face of that hopelessness that I stared as the young black woman answered the question by rising gracefully to her feet.

This divide is no more clearly defined than others separating black and white. It is about race, but not only race; it is about class, but not only class; it is about gender, but not only gender. It is a line woven of many differences.

This and all the lines that separate us also entangle us. Even as we look upon each other like strangers from afar, we are trapped in each other's imaginations. We cannot escape from our intimate histories, our unacknowledged racial mixtures, our awkward and unsatisfying efforts at integration. We have not completely purged the prejudices from our inner thoughts: We do not discount the body's appearance, the voice's sound, the suspicions of the mind's inadequacy. We do not refrain from moral judgments; at the very least, we make them secretly inside our heads. We fear violence from the other, and no reasoned understanding entirely extinguishes our apprehension. We do not share power easily—not whites, who have almost all of it, and not blacks, when they get a piece.

Since we do not know each other very well, we do not know what the other thinks of us. This failing is truer of whites than of blacks; as in many other multiethnic societies, the minority understands more about the majority than vice versa. Few white Americans have much grasp of how they are seen by African-Americans because few whites ask the question—and if they did, most blacks would probably be more polite than honest. We do not converse across the racial line.

Inevitably, that means that whites rarely know how their behavior is perceived, how their comments are taken, how their actions may be subtly shaped by latent biases. Not that African-Americans have a monopoly on truth, not that they always read correctly what lies behind white behavior. But in many instances they can teach white Americans how to examine themselves, how to interpret their own attitudes, how to gain self-knowledge. There is much that is deeply buried, and unless we work at digging it up for inspection, we remain strangers to ourselves as well as to each other.

Whites probably cannot do this effectively without blacks' help. Understandably, many African-Americans feel unduly burdened by the demand that they cajole, instruct, and lead white people by the hand toward open-mindedness. Irritated blacks sometimes delight in mocking the whining tone of whites who plead, "Tell me what I did wrong. Tell me what I can do." Without aid from blacks, however, few whites seem likely to reach the level of sophisticated sensitivity needed to foster racial harmony. By and large, white America has not tuned in to the subtleties of race that black America understands very well.

Consider Cindy, the white receptionist at an insurance office in Jackson, Mississippi. She made friends with Kimberley Brown, a young African-American who wore her hair in intricate, tiny braids. Born in Shreveport, Louisiana, Kimberley had been raised in Los Angeles, where her considerable experience across racial lines had taught her the patience and forgiveness that are often required in relationships with whites like Cindy.

"We were really good friends," Kimberley began, her voice bubbling with laughter just beneath the surface. "One day, she was talking about *Gone With the Wind* and how she loved the movie, how much she wished she could have been back there during that time. And she looked at me and she said, 'Wouldn't you have loved to be there?' " Kimberley's laugh broke free and tumbled out in a torrent.

"And I looked at her, and it did not dawn on her," Kimberley went on, "and I said, 'Cindy, I would have been a slave.' "

"And then it was, like, this look came over her face, and she goes, 'Ohhhh, my gosh, I didn't even think about that. . . . Oh, I'm so sorry.' "

"I'm like, 'It's OK, but, I mean, next time you should really think about that 'cause you might make somebody very mad.' " The innocence of Cindy's ignorance prompted Kimberley to spell it out simply for her. A different black person, she explained, might have taken the comment to mean "You could have been my servant." Cindy was mortified. She had intended nothing more malicious than an admiration for a bygone era of genteel southern belles and wanted to share her nostalgia with her friend. "For her it was beautiful, and it meant something totally different than it would for me," Kimberley said through giggles. "She never considered that *Gone With the Wind* was not the most fantastic movie of all time for me."

Why did Kimberley find this funny rather than insulting? "Because I thought about it in the sense of her not knowing, of her not even understanding," Kimberley said. "Funny in the way of, gosh, people really are out of touch."

Sometimes the soft response from blacks is not helpful. It can be misinterpreted as indicative that no offense was taken. Whites often need to hear blacks' anger—and not be so consumed by guilt that they cannot receive the lesson. Gentle explanation works where friendship is strong enough, as Kimberley understood.

If as much grace were given at every point along the color line, if each side were allowed room to make small mistakes without instant condemnation, we might feel safe enough to have the dialogues we need to have. In such dialogues, we could tune in to the nuances of bias, which must be discerned if we are to move toward racial justice. Prejudice shows no sign of disappearing from human thought, and its manifestation in behavior can be controlled and contained only if it is recognized. That task of recognition looms as a major obstacle in American society, where bigotry has become so unfashionable that it is heavily encrypted. It was easier to identify when it was blatant.

Failing to recognize the sophisticated symptoms of racial bias is the largest pitfall Americans face as they try to cure the affliction. If the disease is diagnosed, honest men and women can have honest disagreements about what treatment to apply. But the American debate increasingly separates those who see racism from those who do not. Much of the conservative argument against affirmative action and race-conscious electoral districts, for example, is based on a belief that racial discrimination by whites has dwindled to negligible proportions. Those who make that assessment do not define as racism a good deal of the ambiguous, camouflaged behavior that emanates from racial biases. As bigoted action has become less visible, then, it has eroded the common ground on which many white Americans stood together immediately after the civil rights movement.

"The people, white and black, who are pressing for more racial justice, for freer interchange, for more accurate understanding of America have not been able to describe what the country is like in terms that people understand or that people find persuasive," says Roger Wilkins, the historian and civil rights activist. "We haven't found a way to engage the emotions or the intellect of the American public."

The United States is no longer dominated by an ideology of racial separation or exclusion, notwithstanding the pockets of hatred tucked away among extremist groups. Political leaders do not preach segregation, even as the vast majority of Americans live segregated lives. Most business leaders do not deride blacks as unqualified to be executives, even as few blacks are admitted to the upper ranks. Civic leaders do not urge that black children receive inferior education, even as most predominantly black schools provide precisely that. Some might call this hypocrisy; it is more complicated.

Racial issues confront the country on three levels—public policy, institutional, and individual—and at each one, the response is now a curious coexistence of intensive effort and cold neglect. In public policy, three decades of government initiatives growing out of the civil rights movement are being whittled away by court rulings and legislative retreats. While some officials and agencies work feverishly to enforce anti-discrimination laws, promote affirmative action, advance minority voting rights, and preserve what they can of the safety net for the poor, the tide runs inexorably the other way. The prevalent notion that white racism has ebbed is used to rationalize a proposition that government should do less. The corollary holds that blacks can fend for themselves.

This trend infuses many blacks with a sense of urgency. "We suffer with such great dignity," says Richard Orange, the African-American diversity trainer. "Black folks are so reasonable. We're unreasonably reasonable. I'm trying to get us to be less reasonable. . . . I'd like for us to suffer with less dignity. The window's closing. The window's closing. We need to go for it."

Sadly, race is such a flammable issue that most politicians either exploit it or run from it, forfeiting the chance to lead intelligent discussion. One exception was President Bill Clinton's call for a national conversation on race, but it came only after he was safe in his second term. In his first term, he withdrew his nomination of Lani Guinier to head the Justice Department's Civil Rights Division because of her ideas on guaranteeing minority voting rights. His unwillingness even to allow her to testify before the Senate Judiciary Committee deprived the country of what might have been a healthy consideration of how best to ensure that black citizens are not denied power in this democracy—a vital matter that is ripe for serious analysis.

In his 1996 presidential campaign, Clinton threw away a chance to educate the public and lead a national dialogue on affirmative action, which he endorsed perfunctorily but failed to explain convincingly. Had he used his multitude of appearances in California to spell out the need for such programs, he might have influenced the outcome of Proposition 209, the anti–affirmative action measure that California voters approved. Nor did either Clinton or his opponent, Bob Dole, make the plight of America's inner cities a subject for discussion. They practically banned the issue from their campaigns. The silence of neglect seems likely to prevail until the next riot.

At the institutional level, contradiction abounds. Even while the ethic of racial diversity has taken hold in many companies, universities, and government agencies, where whites struggle sincerely to open opportunities for blacks, endemic racism continues to work its will. African-American customers are routinely quoted higher prices by automobile dealers and harsher terms by mortgage lenders, studies have found. Loan applications from African-American farmers are "discouraged, delayed, or rejected" by U.S. Department of Agriculture officials, ostensibly for sound financial reasons, driving thousands of the farmers out of business.

At Texaco, the fourteenth largest corporation in the country, the glossy brochures featured the requisite photographs of racially diverse teams of employees and carried stirring statements on tolerance. "The company believes that a work environment that reflects a diverse workforce, values diversity, and is free of all forms of discrimination, intimidation, and harassment is essential for a productive and efficient workforce," one booklet proudly declared. But as *The New York Times* discovered in perusing court papers and government documents, Texaco permitted the development of an atmosphere that condoned racist slurs against black employees, sometimes from supervisors, and a culture of hostility that frightened many blacks into keeping silent even while they were confined to the company's lower ranks. Sheryl Joseph, a black secretary in Louisiana who was pregnant, was deeply offended when her white boss gave her a birthday cake decorated with a drawing of a pregnant black woman and the words "Happy Birthday Sheryl. It must have been those watermelon seeds." She said nothing because she needed her job, the *Times* reported.

When the *Times* also revealed that senior Texaco executives had been taped making contemptuous remarks about African-Americans and plotting to destroy documents in a discrimination lawsuit, a public fury suddenly embroiled the company. The reaction illustrated a defect in the way American society confronts racial bigotry: The most flagrant incidents often divert attention from less obvious, insidious conditions. Civil rights organizations called for a boycott of Texaco, the company's share price dropped 3 percent in a single day, and the chairman, Peter I. Bijur, tripped over himself to apologize, pledge company reform, and quickly approve a record $176 million settlement in the two-year-old discrimination suit. But many corporations damage black employees subtly and silently, without Texaco's obnoxious style and without their executives' racist remarks being tape-recorded and printed on the front page of *The New York Times*. Boycotts would be equally justified in such cases. The threshold of outrage is too high.

On the individual level, white Americans have a lot of learning to do about the "invisible weightless knapsack" of privilege that they carry effortlessly. Most whites do not think of "whiteness" as an identity, and doing so carries risks. Skinheads and other extremists use whiteness as a weapon of supremacy or a symbol of victimization, juxtaposing themselves against blacks, Jews, and others. For most white Americans, however, the concept of whiteness seems too broad to fit a majority people, especially one so divided along intraracial lines of ethnicity, religion, and class. Nor can many whites who are struggling in poverty or minimum-wage jobs easily think of themselves as privileged.

Still, being conscious of the unearned benefits of whiteness tends to help whites clarify their thinking about race and relate more openly to black people. Since blacks know very well what advantages white skin brings, whites who acknowledge the reality put themselves on the same wavelength.

Attaining such awareness can be a difficult task, as a group of middle managers from AT&T and Du Pont learned during a five-day retreat held in a Virginia suburb of Washington. Among the forty-six participants, who came from throughout the country, twenty-nine were white, and they were encouraged by facilitators, both white and black, to probe the meaning of their whiteness—the privileges they enjoyed and the prejudices they held. This they did in an all-white session; then they met with their black colleagues to discuss what they had discovered.

As the workshop demonstrated, whites have trouble talking about race not only with blacks but also among themselves. They tune their antennas to one another's vibrations of intolerance to measure how much latitude exists for jokes, epithets, and derisive remarks. One gathering may encourage slurs, another may send signals of inhibition; many whites are adept at adjusting for the tone of present company. But few explore deeply, even with close friends, the cysts of bigotry that may be buried, that may need to be talked through in order to be excised. That was what the white facilitator Bill Page was hoping could happen in that circle of whites, all anxiously leaning forward in their chairs.

Again and again, when a man or a woman would reveal a pulse of anguish, a racist thought, or a piece of hurt or anger, the rest of the group would veer away from the uncomfortable, changing the subject and running for safer ground. At times it seemed as if each person were having a monologue with himself, listening only to himself, never daring to interact with what had been "put into the room," as Page characterized it. He had the skillful timing of a musician, waiting for just the right number of beats before entering the discussion to remind them of what one had revealed or another had confessed, asking them to work with that, put it onto the table, examine it. But they did so with trepidation.

"I'm proud of my heritage," remarked "Cheryl," who was in her forties, "but I'm ashamed to be white. Sometimes I'm angry to be white." Nobody picked up on that. The conversation spun away into others' disjointed remarks.

Cheryl came from a family steeped in such vitriolic racism that now, when she went home, she had trouble sitting through a meal. She told of a training session at Du Pont that had used a short television film in which hidden cameras followed a white and then a black into an apartment rental office, a car dealership, and elsewhere to document the disparity in treatment. It was a searing lesson that had left her deeply troubled. And immediately afterward, shopping with her daughter, Cheryl was overcome by the realization of how different her life would be if she were black. Now, in recollection, her voice trembled as she told the group: "It slammed into me that I never had to sit my daughter down and tell her she will not be able to do certain things because she's black, that some people will not talk to her because she's black." Cheryl had to leave the store, she said, and sit in the car and cry and cry. "I tried to explain to my daughter." And now, again, she was on the edge of tears.

She told the story after her all-white session had rejoined the blacks. But most of the other whites who spoke to the mixed group got nowhere near a nerve. One man admitted that race did not concern him because it didn't touch him. Another confessed that he had never cared about the drug problem until his daughter got involved with drugs. Others tried to assess the issues analytically, intellectually.

Some blacks found this frustrating. "I have a problem when I listen to whites talk," a black man said. "They always talk about being unemotional, and everything is intellectualized. I think whites do that as a means of self-denial. The real problems are there, and until you understand, we're going to sit around and intellectualize to death."

"Most of the time, in order for white people to listen to black people, you have to get dramatic," said an African-American woman; she had announced at the outset that she would not be crying here, because she had done all her crying by the age of twenty. "They let us talk, but they don't listen to what we're saying," she continued. "White people have a way of saying, 'If I don't deal with it, it'll go away.' "

"It's unfortunate," added a younger woman, "that you have to get emotionally involved to do something about it. That really pisses me off to hear white people say they are not personally involved so they don't care about black people. Fuck that—excuse my language. You know what's right and wrong."

Only after two or three days did most of the whites seem able to reflect on their prejudices and privileges. That opened pathways to closeness with the African-Americans; whites and blacks stayed up half the night talking and talking.

Bill Page told them a story. He had taken a trip to Dakar, Senegal; to the island of Gori in the harbor; to the old stone slave house there, where Africans had been warehoused before being loaded onto ships; to the Door of No Return—now a stark rectangular cut in the stone wall—through which the slaves passed and only the endless sea can be seen. "How did we do it?" Bill asked. "If we learn, we won't need people of color to remind us. I need someone to help me. It is a long journey. It is a lifetime journey."

The journey does not have to be a guilt trip; it is just an encounter with the facts of life.

Two of my children, Laura and Michael, were introduced to some of these facts of life when they participated in City at Peace, a program that gathers teenagers from throughout metropolitan Washington white and black suburban kids, black and Latino inner-city kids—to talk to one another, to confide in one another, and finally to help write and perform a musical on themes of pain and hope.

When Laura was involved, the virtue lay in "the hanging-out times," she remembered, the "flashes of insight" that came from going to each other's homes, walking along each other's streets. "It's not that hard to give kids a chance to come together across these lines," she said. "It's just rare."

By the time Michael participated several years later, a structure of dialogues had been created as a preface to the play. For weeks before they began composing and rehearsing, the teenagers sat in circles and told their own stories—often tales of shootings, drugs, and family strife that opened Michael to worlds he had witnessed only on television. Race was put squarely out on the table, inspiring candor and making a safe place for honesty. Both Laura and Michael gained insight into what it is like to be black in America and, therefore, what it is like to be white.

As the teenagers spent months working together, they found themselves embraced in growing affection for one another, and their hugs and quiet words and silent understandings testified to the caring that developed among them. For the most part, the friendships did not last; blacks and whites, city kids and suburbanites withdrew afterward into their own spheres. But City at Peace lasted in their memories as a magic moment.

Michael's lesson was powerful in its simplicity. "It taught me that to talk to people is the best way to connect with them," he said four years after the experience. "I know it is possible to connect with kids who have never had friends of other races. . . . Regardless of all the cynicism of all of the people who tell me that it's not possible, I know that it is. And I carry that ideal with me in all my relations."

For the shows, the youngsters put their compelling issues into brief skits, which were held together by affecting songs by Rickey Payton, a black composer who later wrote a number performed at Clinton's second inauguration. Between Laura's and Michael's years, the production moved from picturing a Utopian "city of peace" in its finale to vignettes with a sharper edge. Only a few of these had race as their subject; more often, the teenagers gravitated to concerns that crossed racial boundaries: conflict with parents in families that did not communicate, the lure of drugs, teenage suicide, gang cultures that substituted for loving homes. Onstage, a son sang of his father's hypocrisy, a girl accused a boy of date rape, a boy shot himself in the head while his stepsister watched, a gang leader killed a defector, black-white tension erupted over interracial dating and polarizing insults. And rising above all of this was a call for healing.

Parents and others in the audience could feel the bonds the children had forged with one another, and the children could feel our feeling. There was a sad joy in seeing tenuous strands of caring across the line that runs through the heart of America.

"You are my brother, you are my sister," our children sang. "We are the voices for peace, wish that all the world could see the light. . . ." In gospel style, they sang a song of yearning that built gradually to a demand and a challenge as more and more voices joined in:

> *Change the world,*
> *Change the world,*
> *I believe together,*
> *We can find a way.*

Notes

Introduction: The Color Line

PAGE 7 "CHANGE HAS BEEN MADE": In 1967, the U.S. Supreme Court, in *Loving v. Virginia*, ruled unconstitutional a Virginia law prohibiting interracial marriage.

13 RODNEY KING CASE: In the end, two of the four officers were found guilty of violating King's civil rights and given prison terms, and there were no disorders.

13–14 DATA ON HATE GROUPS: Bill Moyers, *Hate on Trial*, PBS, February 5, 1992. Current Klan figures from the Anti-Defamation League of B'nai B'rith.

16 PERCENTAGE OF ELECTED OFFICIALS: *Black Elected Officials: A National Roster*, 21st ed. (Washington, D.C.: Joint Center for Political and Economic Studies, 1993), pp. xxii–xxiii, xxvii, xxxiii–xxxiv, xxxviii.

17% OF WHITES: U.S. Bureau of the Census, *Statistical Abstract of the United States 1995* (Washington, D.C.: U.S. Government Printing Office, 1995), p. 159.

DATA ON BLACK PROFESSORS: *Journal of Blacks in Higher Education*, Spring 1996, pp. 32–33.

BLACKS EARNING PH.D.'S: U.S. Department of Education figures, reported in *Chronicle of Higher Education*, June 28, 1996, p. A30.

16–17 BLACKS DIVERSIFYING THEIR PROFESSIONS: Thomas Byrne Edsall with Mary D. Edsall, *Atlantic Monthly*, May 1991.

17 BLACKS' EARNINGS PER $1,000 OF WHITES': Data from U.S. Bureau of the Census, *Current Population Survey* (Washington, D.C.: U.S. Government Printing Office, March 1996), Table PINC-06.

PERCENTAGES BELOW THE POVERTY LINE: Ibid., Table 2, "Historic Poverty Tables—Persons." The black-white gap may appear less than it is in reality, because 800,000 blacks in prison are not counted and recent Hispanic immigrants with low incomes are counted as whites.

EARNINGS BY FEMALE-HEADED HOUSEHOLDS: Ibid., Table F-4a, "Historical Income Tables—Families."

17–18 NET WORTH DATA: Melvin L. Oliver and Thomas M. Shapiro, *Black Wealth/White Wealth: A New Perspective on Racial Inequality* (New York: Routledge, 1995), pp. 86, 94.

18 QUOTATION FROM ANNA DEAVERE SMITH: *New York Times*, "Week in Review," July 5, 1992.

One · Integration: Together and Separate

39 "BANG-YOUR-HEAD-AGAINST-THE-WALL": Isabel Wilkerson, *New York Times*, May 4, 1991.

41 "KNOW YOU'RE SCARED": James Percelay, Monteria Ivey, and Stephan Dweck, *Snaps* (New York: William Morrow, 1994). Foreword by Quincy Jones.

62 DATA ON SCHOOL INTEGRATION: Report of the National School Boards Association, *Status of School Desegregation, 1968–1986; New York Times,* January 19, 1992; *Harvard Educational Letter,* January–February 1994; Gary Orfield, Mark D. Bachmeyer, David R. James, and Tamela Eitle, *Deepening Segregation in American Public Schools* (Cambridge, Mass.: Harvard Program on School Desegregation, 1997). The states with the highest percentages of blacks attending schools with more than 90% minorities in 1995 were Illinois (61.9%), Michigan (59.6%), New York (57.1%), New Jersey (53.7%), and Pennsylvania (47%). In the South, previous gains are being reversed. In 1967, only 14% of black children attended mostly white schools. That rose to 36% in 1972 and reached a peak of 44% in 1988, then fell to 39% in 1991 and 36% in 1994.

64 "TIPPING POINT": Andrew Hacker, *Two Nations: Black and White, Separate, Hostile, Unequal* (New York: Charles Scribner's Sons, 1992), p. 36.

POLLS ON SCHOOL INTEGRATION: Computer printouts provided by Tom W. Smith, National Opinion Research Center, University of Chicago.

73 "BLACK NARCISSUS": Gerald W. Barrax, *Another Kind of Rain* (Pittsburgh: University of Pittsburgh Press, 1970). Reprinted in Arnold Adoff, ed., *The Poetry of Black America: Anthology of the 20th Century* (New York: Harper-Collins, 1973), p. 223.

76 LINGUISTIC SOCIETY AND OAKLAND SCHOOL BOARD: Rene Sanchez and Rick Weiss, *Washington Post*, January 6, 1997; text of Resolution No. 9697-0063, Oakland Board of Education, January 16, 1997.

79 "STRIP MINING": As told to Thomas Kochman and mentioned to the author in an interview.

89 DEATH THREAT ON HER LOCKER: Associated Press, *New York Times*, November 25, 1993.

99 BOOKS BY VIVIAN GUSSIN PALEY: *White Teacher* (Cambridge, Mass.: Harvard University Press, 1979) and *Kwanzaa and Me* (Cambridge, Mass.: Harvard University Press, 1995). This section is drawn in part from the author's review of *Kwanzaa and Me* for the *New York Times Book Review*, February 19, 1995.

103 "WE AIN'T NO BETTER": As quoted by Steve Suitts to the author.

107 "OBSESSED WITH IT": Interview of Lewis Nordan by David Molpus of National Public Radio, December 23, 1993, about Nordan's novel *Wolf Whistle* (Chapel Hill, N.C.: Algonquin Books, 1993).

Two · Mixing: The Stranger Within

112 MALCOLM X'S WHITE GRANDPARENTS: Bruce Perry, *Malcolm: The Life of a Man Who Changed Black America* (Barrytown, N.Y.: Station Hill Press, 1991), pp. 2–5.

113 WHITES OPPOSING INTERMARRIAGE: Computer printouts provided by Tom W. Smith, National Opinion Research Center, University of Chicago, from a 1994 survey of 1,606 whites. In a nationwide sample of whites polled in 1990, 66.2% opposed intermarriage with blacks, 46.3% with Asians, 44.2% with Hispanics, and 15.6% with Jews.

117 BLACK-WHITE MARRIED COUPLES: Black men married to white women totaled 196,000; white men married to black women, 100,000. U.S. Bureau of the Census, *Current Population Reports*, P20-483, "Household and Family Characteristics" (Washington, D.C.: U.S. Government Printing Office, March 1994), Table 13.

"UNRELENTINGLY NEGATIVE ARTICLE": Lydia Long, letter to the editor dated December 3, 1991, reacting to article by Isabel Wilkerson, *New York Times*, December 2, 1991.

120 "ABOUT MY CHILDREN!": Walt Harrington, *Crossings: A White Man's Journey into Black America* (New York: HarperCollins, 1992), p. 1.

Three · Memory: The Echoes of History

150 "IN THE FIELDS DOING OUR WORK": Mary Ann French, *Washington Post*, January 18, 1996.

153 "BY THEIR FIRST NAMES": Dorothy Spruill Redford, *Somerset Homecoming: Recovering a Lost Heritage* (New York: Doubleday, 1988), pp. 6, 21–22.

161 RECONSTRUCTION AT SOMERSET: By 1996, an archaeological dig had uncovered artifacts and remains from the field kitchen, chapel, cistern, and hospital. Among the discoveries were ivory-handled knives, pieces of pottery, beads, shot, and medicine bottles used by slaves.

169–70 ON JEFFERSON AND HEMINGS: Fawn M. Brodie, *Thomas Jefferson: An Intimate History* (New York: Norton, 1974).

175 QUOTATIONS FROM CHARLES MILLER: Charles A. Miller, "Jefferson's African-American Dilemmas and Ours," unpublished paper, November 16, 1992. Additional comment in letter to the author, November 17, 1992.

175 "ONE FATAL STAIN": Edwin Morris Betts and James Adam Bear Jr., eds., *The Family Letters of Thomas Jefferson* (Columbia: University of Missouri Press, 1966).

175–76 "THIS EXECRABLE COMMERCE": Quoted in Douglas L. Wilson, "Thomas Jefferson and the Character Issue," *Atlantic*, November 1992, p. 72.

176 FOSSETT AND OTHER JEFFERSON SLAVES: Lucia Stanton, "Those Who Labor for My Happiness: Thomas Jefferson and His Slaves," research paper published in Peter Onus, *Jeffersonian Legacies* (Charlottesville: University Press of Virginia, 1993), pp. 147–180.

177 "OVER THOSE OF HIS OWN SPECIES": Thomas Jefferson, *Notes on the State of Virginia* (New York: Harper & Row, 1964). All excerpts from pp. 133–139, 156.

177–78 "AN UNPREDICTABLE FUTURE": Stanton, "Those Who Labor."

179–80 "ABANDONING CHILDREN": Jefferson to Edward Bancroft, January 26, 1789, in Julian Boyd, ed., *Papers of Thomas Jefferson*, vol. 14 (Princeton, N.J.: Princeton University Press, 1950), p. 492.

181 *GEORGETOWN WEEKLY LEDGER* REPORT: Lerone Bennett Jr., *Before the Mayflower: A History of Black America* (New York: Penguin, 1984), p. 75.

BANNEKER'S LETTER TO JEFFERSON: Ibid., p. 76.

184 WILLIAMSBURG'S SLAVE AUCTION: Tamara Jones, *Washington Post*, October 11, 1994, p. 1.

186 "REVISED, RETHOUGHT, AND RENAMED": *New York Times*, February 12, 1993, p. A14.

191 FROM THOMAS JEFFERSON TO JAMES MADISON: According to Lucia Stanton, research director at Monticello, the man was an indentured servant who worked in the president's dining room and had about four years left before freedom.

192–93 GARRETT MORGAN AND OTHER BLACK INVENTORS: Most details of inventors and other prominent blacks in this section are drawn from Rayford W. Logan and Michael R. Winston, eds., *Dictionary of American Negro Biography* (New York: W. W. Norton, 1982).

193 STAMP OF BILL PICKETT: Unfortunately, the Postal Service's artist used a photograph of Bill Pickett's brother, Ben, according to historians and Pickett descendants.

QUOTATION FROM WILLIAM KATZ: Letter to the editor, *New York Times*, June 2, 1993.

194 TRANS-CONTINENTAL FLIGHT: The first flight across the United States was made in 1911 by Calbraith P. Rodgers, who was white, from Sheepshead Bay, New York, to Long Beach, California, in eighty-four days.

197 A DEFINITIVE BIOGRAPHY: Silvio A. Bedini, *The Life of Benjamin Banneker* (Scribners, 1971). Bedini was an historian at the Smithsonian.

199 BIOGRAPHY OF DREW: Spencie Love, *One Blood: The Death and Resurrection of Charles R. Drew* (Chapel Hill, N.C.: University of North Carolina Press, 1996).

200 AFRICAN-AMERICAN FOLK TALES: Gladys-Marie Fry, *Night Riders in Black Folk History* (Knoxville: University of Tennessee Press, 1975), p. 175.

201 QUOTATION FROM ANTEBELLUM PHYSICIAN: Love, *One Blood*, p. 191.

202–3 "INGATHERING OF THE PEOPLE": Maulana Karenga, *The African American Holiday of Kwanzaa* (Los Angeles: University of Sankore Press, 1988).

204 "METAPHYSICAL SYSTEMS": Cheikh Anta Diop, *The Cultural Unity of Black Africa* (Chicago: Third World Press, 1978), p. 195.

206 JONES SIBLING NAMES: The linguistic origins of these names are unclear. *Meta* in Swahili means "shining" or "twinkling," not "falcon black beauty."

208 "TO DESPISE THE AFRICAN": Carter Godwin Woodson, *The Mis-Education of the Negro* (Trenton, N.J.: Africa World Press, 1990). (First published in 1933.)

209–10 OLDEST HUMANS: The most recent discovery, subsequent to the publication of the *Baseline Essays*, was reported in *New York Times*, September 22, 1994.

211 "SCIENCE OR INTELLECT": "Exhibit A," Boogie Down Production.

213 *BLACK ATHENA*: Bernal is not black, but just as African-Americans often follow autobiographical urges in their research, so did Bernal. He began by exploring his Jewish roots. Formerly a Fellow of King's College, Cambridge, and then a government professor at Cornell University, he was educated in Chinese studies and after twenty years became fascinated by ancient Jewish history. As he began to study Hebrew, he found similarities with Greek, which piqued his interest in searching for contacts between ancient Greece and Semitic cultures. That drew him also to Egypt, and it is there that his work intersects with the Afrocentrists'.

"COLONIZING AFRICANS AND SEMITES": Martin Bernal, *Black Athena: The Afroasiatic Roots of Classical Civilization*, vol. 1 (New Brunswick, N.J.: Rutgers University Press, 1987), pp. xv, 2.

214 "MUSEUMS WITH EGYPTIAN COLLECTIONS": Diane Ravitch, "Diversity and Democracy: Multicultural Education in America," *American Educator*, Spring 1990, pp. 16–20, 46–48.

216 "STRONGLY NUBIAN FEATURES": Frank J. Yurco, "Were the Ancient Egyptians Black or White?" *Biblical Archeological Review*, September–October 1989, pp. 24–29, 58.

219 "THE HEALTHINESS OF AFRICAN CUSTOMS": Diop, *The Cultural Unity of Black Africa*, p. 93. See also his *The African Origin of Civilization* (New York: Lawrence Hill, 1974) and *Civilization or Barbarism* (New York: Lawrence Hill, 1991).

221 "THEIR RESEARCH WITHSTOOD CRITICISM": Erich Martel, "And How Not To: A Critique of the Portland Baseline Essays," *American Federation of Teachers*, Spring 1994, pp. 33–35.

223 NOT MERELY A QUESTION OF HISTORICAL ACCURACY: Molefi Kete Asante, "Multiculturalism: An Exchange," *American Scholar*, Spring 1991, pp. 267–276.

"ESCAPISM AND ROMANTICISM": Henry Louis Gates Jr., quoted in *New York Times*, June 3, 1992.

225 QUOTATIONS FROM DIANE RAVITCH: Opening quotes from interview with the author, remainder from Ravitch, "Diversity and Democracy."

Four · Body: Dark Against the Sky

232–33 "A FAMILIAR THEME": Harold R. Isaacs, *Idols of the Tribe* (New York: Harper & Row, 1975), pp. 55–59.

233 "SKEIN OF OUR CULTURE": Harold R. Isaacs, *The New World of Negro Americans* (New York: John Day, 1963), pp. 74–75.

234 "ICE AND SUN": Leonard Jeffries Jr., address to the Empire State Black Arts and Cultural Festival, July 20, 1991.

236 "SWEETWHITE BLOOD": Toni Morrison, *Beloved* (New York: Alfred A. Knopf, 1987), p. 198.

"THEIR OWN SKINS": Andrew Hacker, *Two Nations: Black and White, Separate, Hostile, Unequal* (New York: Charles Scribner's Sons, 1992), p. 32.

"A DARK BLACK": Quoted in Isaacs, *The New World of Negro Americans*, p. 79, from the 1920 edition of *The Story of Doctor Dolittle* by Hugh Lofting. Lofting died in California in 1947, and his family revised the chapter in the 1988 edition by Delacorte Press to delete all references to Bumpo's blackness; the prince is merely hypnotized into releasing the doctor and his animal friends. In an afterword, Christopher Lofting writes that some episodes, "in light of today's sensitivities, were considered by some to be disrespectful to ethnic minorities and, therefore, perhaps inappropriate for today's young reader. . . . Hugh Lofting would have been appalled at the suggestion that any part of his work could give offense and would have been the first to have made the changes himself."

240–41 STUDY OF REACTIONS TO SKIN COLOR: Nayda Terkildsen, *American Journal of Political Science*, 37 (4) (November 1993), pp. 1032–1053.

242 "THE LIGHTER THE SENTENCE": Kathy Russell, Midge Wilson, and Ronald Hall, *The Color Complex: The Politics of Skin Color Among African Americans* (New York: Harcourt Brace Jovanovich, 1992), pp. 36–38.

MORRISON QUOTING DANFORTH ON THOMAS'S LAUGH: Toni Morrison, ed., *Race-ing Justice, En-gendering Power: Essays on Anita Hill, Clarence Thomas, and the Construction of Social Reality* (New York: Pantheon, 1992), pp. xii–xiii.

242–43 STUDY OF BLACKS IN ADVERTISING: City of New York, Department of Consumer Affairs, *Invisible People: The Depiction of Minorities in Magazine Ads and Catalogs*, July 1991.

245 "SKIN COLOR COUNTS": Richard G. Carter, *New York Times*, April 6, 1991.

248 "PALLIATIVE OF A DARK COMPLEXION": Charles W. Chesnutt, *The House Behind the Cedars* (London: Collier-Macmillan, 1969), pp. 180, 188.

"LIGHTEN UP DE RACE": Zora Neale Hurston, *Their Eyes Were Watching God* (New York: Harper & Row, 1990), pp. 128, 134. (First published in 1937.)

249 "BLACK FOR THE FIRST TIME": Alice Walker, *The Color Purple* (New York: Harcourt Brace Jovanovich, 1982), pp. 86, 202, 147.

"MADE HIM VERY SAD": Alice Walker, *The Temple of My Familiar* (New York: Harcourt Brace Jovanovich, 1989), pp. 113, 171–172.

253 "ENTRY WAS DENIED": Russell et al., *The Color Complex*, p. 27.

257 "EVEN SHE DIDN'T KNOW": Morrison, *Beloved*, p. 247.

258 "THEY DO HAVE AN ODOR": Lynne Duke, *Washington Post*, December 24, 1991, p. A4, reporting on focus groups conducted by People for the American Way, a liberal lobbying group.

262 MONKEY PICTURES ON A SUPERMARKET BULLETIN BOARD: A Giant investigation, in response to a lawsuit, also found that racist jokes had been told and black employees had been threatened with nooses hung in a warehouse. David Segal, *Washington Post*, September 5, 1996.

GOODWIN'S SPEECH: *New York Times*, February 22, 1992.

271–72 DATA ON BLACKS IN PROFESSIONAL SPORTS: Unpublished statistics compiled by the Rainbow Coalition, 1996.

272 ROYKO'S COLUMN: *Bangor Daily News*, July 23, 1993.

273 "HE'LL BECOME A DEFENSIVE PLAYER": *The Diane Rehm Show*, WAMU-FM, Washington, D.C., February 12, 1993.

"FINESSE, TECHNIQUE, AND CONTROL": Jomills Henry Braddock II, *Institutional Discrimination: A Study of Managerial Recruitment in Professional Football* (Baltimore: Center for Social Organization of Schools, Johns Hopkins University, September 1980).

274–75 QUOTATIONS FROM FEINSTEIN: *The Diane Rehm Show*, WAMU-FM, Washington, D.C., February 12, 1993.

Five · Mind: Through a Glass, Darkly

278 DATA ON IMAGES OF BLACKS: The figures in the text are relative: They record the differences between the images held of blacks and of whites by all respondents. The absolute percentages of white respondents who made negative, neutral, or positive judgments about blacks are contained in the following table:

	Negative	*Neutral*	*Positive*
Lazy/hard-working	46.6%	35.7%	17.6%
Violent/nonviolent	53.7	30.1	16.2
Unintelligent/intelligent	30.6	48	21.3
Welfare/self-supporting	58.9	27.8	13.3

283 WORKS ON RACE AND INTELLIGENCE: Richard J. Herrnstein and Charles Murray, *The Bell Curve: Intelligence and Class Structure in American Life* (New York: Free Press, 1994); J. Philippe Rushton, *Race, Evolution, and Behavior: A Life History Perspective* (New Brunswick, N.J.: Transaction Publishers, 1994); Seymour W. Itzkoff, *The Decline of Intelligence in America: A Strategy for National Renewal* (Westport, Conn.: Praeger, 1994).

284 "HIS MORE FORTUNATE BACKGROUND": Herrnstein and Murray, *The Bell Curve*, p. 127.

284–85 "16 PERCENT OF THE POPULATION OF WHITES": Ibid., p. 269.

285 "DIFFERENCES BETWEEN GROUPS": Ibid., pp. 270–271.

"EVERY INTELLECTUALLY CHALLENGING FIELD": Ibid., p. 278.

PROFILE OF MURRAY: Jason DeParle, *New York Times Magazine*, October 9, 1994.

EMOTIONAL INTELLIGENCE: *New York Times*, "Week in Review," September 10, 1995, p. 6. See also Daniel Goleman, *Emotional Intelligence* (New York: Bantam, 1995).

286 QUOTATION FROM GARDNER: Richard A. Gardner, letter to the editor, *New York Times*, November 12, 1994.

286–87 QUOTATION FROM POUSSAINT: *Carleton Voice*, Summer 1995, p. 23.

287 "WITH HUMAN VARIATION": Herrnstein and Murray, *The Bell Curve*, p. 532.

293 BLACK PILOTS IN THE AIR FORCE: As of August 31, 1996, only 263 of the 14,842 pilots (1.8%) were black, whereas 5.7% of all air force officers were black.

295 "I PREFER DR. JONES": In her actual quotation, she used her married name, by which she goes professionally but which she preferred not to have published.

298 QUOTATIONS FROM *AMOS 'N' ANDY*: Excerpts here and below from "Color Adjustment," a public television documentary produced, written, and directed by Marlon Riggs.

299 QUOTATIONS FROM GATES'S CHILDREN: Henry Louis Gates Jr., "An 'Amos 'n' Andy' Christmas," op-ed page, *New York Times*, December 23, 1994.

301 DATA ON TV WATCHING: According to studies reported in the *Washington Post* of November 29, 1994, blacks watch an average of about seventy-five hours of television a week, and nonblacks watch about fifty hours.

302–3 QUOTATIONS FROM MCINTOSH: Peggy McIntosh, *White Privilege and Male Privilege: A Personal Account of Coming to See Correspondences Through Work in Women's Studies*, 1988 Working Paper 189, Wellesley College Center for Research on Women, Wellesley, Mass., pp. 1–2, 5–9, 17–18.

308–9 ACADEMIC AWARDS ASSEMBLY: Ron Suskind, *Wall Street Journal*, May 26, 1994.

Six · Morality: Black Heat, White Cold

319 "DON'T REALLY WANT TO BE IGNORANT": Jason C. Deuchler, *New York Times*, May 6, 1992.

321 LAWSUIT AGAINST UNION POINT, GEORGIA: Each plaintiff received $10,000, the five who did not join the suit got $1,000 apiece, and each of the two lawyers representing the plaintiffs received $44,000 plus expenses. Ronald Smothers, *New York Times*, February 5, 1995, and February 20, 1996.

325 QUOTATION FROM TWOMEY: Steve Twomey, *Washington Post*, September 15, 1994.

325–26 POLL ON BARRY: *Washington Post*, October 2, 1994.

326 QUOTATIONS FROM WALTERS: Ron Walters, *Washington Post*, September 18, 1994.

331 DATA ON OUT-OF-WEDLOCK BIRTHS: National Center for Health Statistics, telephone communication.

331–32 POLL ON AMERICANS' IMAGES OF RUSSIANS: Only 10% said that Russians cared more than Americans about their children, and 34% thought them equal. *New York Times Magazine*, November 10, 1985.

332 DATA ON BLACK-WHITE GAP IN OUT-OF-WEDLOCK BIRTHS: Andrew Hacker, *Two Nations: Black and White, Separate, Hostile, Unequal* (New York: Charles Scribner's Sons, 1992), p. 80. Figures after 1988 from the National Center for Health Statistics, telephone communication.

POLL ON BLACKS' PROBLEMS: *Washington Post*, October 8, 1995.

334 "IT WAS PREMEDITATED": Ice Cube, "You Can't Fade Me," from *AmeriKKKa's Most Wanted*, Priority Records, Inc., 1990.

335 QUOTATION FROM BELL HOOKS: Michel Marriott, *New York Times*, August 15, 1993.

QUOTATION FROM POWELL: Calvin Sims, *New York Times*, November 28, 1993.

340 QUOTATION FROM ZOOK: Kristal Brent Zook, "A Manifesto of Sorts for a Black Feminist Movement," *New York Times Magazine*, November 12, 1995.

346 MAMMY SYNDROME: Laura Shipler, "Reliving History: The Relationship Between Black Domestic Workers and Their White Employers" (senior thesis, Haverford College, 1994).

Seven · Violence: The Mirror of Harm

357 QUOTATION FROM JACKSON: *Washington Post*, January 8, 1994.

371 ATTICA PRISON RIOT: For a detailed account of the riot and its aftermath, see Tom Wicker, *A Time to Die* (New York: Quadrangle/The New York Times Book Company, 1975).

372 RAMMING A SCREWDRIVER: Ibid., p. 291, quoting *The Official Report of the New York State Special Commission on Attica*, Dean Robert B. McKay of the New York University Law School, chairman.

376 *MORNING SENTINEL* EDITORIAL: "Racism Arises in Bizarre Ways," *Waterville (Maine) Morning Sentinel*, November 5 and 6, 1994.

377 BURNHAM'S CRIME ANALYSIS: David Burnham, *Above the Law: Secret Deals, Political Fixes, and Other Misadventures of the U.S. Department of Justice* (New York: Scribners, 1996), pp. 105–130.

DEFINITION OF "ROBBERY": Robbery, as distinguished from burglary, is theft by the use or threat of force against a person. Burglary is defined as theft of property from, say, an apartment when no one is home.

378 DATA ON BLACKS' PARTICIPATION IN CRIME: Only homicides with one victim and one perpetrator are counted. Cases of multiple victims and multiple murderers are not tabulated by race. Bureau of Justice Statistics, U.S. Department of Justice, telephone communication.

ARREST RATES: U.S. Department of Justice, *Crime in the United States 1994, Uniform Crime Reports* (Washington, D.C.: U.S. Government Printing Office), Table 43.

378–79 BLACK CHILDREN MORE SUSCEPTIBLE TO PROSECUTION: From "Children of Color and the Juvenile Justice System," conference held by the Juvenile Justice Advisory Council, State of Maryland, at the University of Maryland, November 30, 1994.

379–80 DEATH RATES FROM HOMICIDE: Centers for Disease Control and Prevention, National Center for Health Statistics, *Vital Statistics of the United States,* vol. 2, *Mortality,* part A (Washington, D.C.: Public Health Service, 1996), pp. 150–151. The following data from coroners' reports are provided:

Deaths by Homicide per 100,000 Population

Age and Race	1960	1970	1993	1994
Males				
15–24:				
Black	46.4	102.5	167.0	157.6
White	4.4	7.9	17.1	17.4
25–34:				
Black	92.0	158.5	116.5	112.1
White	6.2	13.0	14.4	14.3
Females				
15–24:				
Black	11.9	17.7	22.0	18.7
White	1.5	2.7	4.2	3.9
25–34 (25–44 in 1994):				
Black	24.9	25.6	25.2	19.5
White	2.0	3.4	4.7	3.7

380 CRACK COMPARED WITH POWDER: Powdered cocaine is produced in a reaction of hydrochloric acid with coca paste, made from coca leaves. It can be injected, snorted, or eaten. Crack, which is made by cooking the powder with baking soda and water, can only be smoked. In both forms, the drug heightens alertness, energy, sexuality, and extreme pleasure. Although it is not addictive physiologically, it creates a psychological craving that is more potent when injected than when smoked.

DATA ON COCAINE USAGE: Advance Report No. 18, *Preliminary Estimates from the 1995 National Household Survey on Drug Abuse, Substance Abuse and Mental Health Services Administration* (Washington, D.C.: U.S. Government Printing Office, August 1996).

383 TABLE OF HOMICIDES: U.S. Department of Justice, Bureau of Justice Statistics, telephone communication. The tabulations, covering murders of a single victim by a single perpetrator, both of whose races are known, account for about half of the 1994 homicide victims.

TABLE OF WHITE VICTIMS BY RACE OF OFFENDER: All categories except assault are single-offender victimizations; Table 42, U.S. Department of Justice, *Personal Crimes of Violence,* Bureau of Justice Statistics, printout from computer database. Assault figures include multiple-offender cases in which all offenders were perceived to be black, from Table 48.

386 "SELF TANNING NO DOUBT": *Report of the Independent Commission on the Los Angeles Police Department*, Warren Christopher, chairman, 1991, p. 76.

388 KING SURROUNDED BY TWENTY-ONE OFFICERS: Ibid., p. 5.

"OPENLY JOKED AND BRAGGED": Ibid., p. 15.

BLACK JURORS EXCLUDED BECAUSE OF PARTIALITY: Jim Newton, *Los Angeles Times*, February 6, 1993.

390 NASHVILLE OFFICERS FIRED: *Los Angeles Times*, December 19, 1992.

OFFICERS ROBINSON AND DEL-DEBBIO: The shooting shattered both men's lives. Robinson was physically unable to continue as a policeman; Del-Debbio was dismissed from the force and found work doing street construction. He was convicted of second-degree assault but was sentenced only to probation and community service after Robinson appealed to the judge not to send his assailant to prison. Adam Nossiter, *New York Times*, June 22, 1996.

390–91 "A BLACK GUY WITH A GUN": *New York Times*, November 22, 1992.

391 "THE LIZARD DIDN'T DESERVE IT": Christopher Commission, op. cit., pp. 14, 52, 72.

QUOTATION FROM DARYL GATES: Ibid., p. 203.

393 JAMES EARL RAY'S CONFESSION: Ray withdrew his confession and was joined by the King family in 1997 in asking for a full trial and a new investigation.

395 "THE BIGGEST GANG OF ALL": Jessica Crosby, *Washington Post*, March 12, 1993.

TV AUDIENCE FOR SIMPSON VERDICT: Rating survey by Nielsen Media Research, reported in *New York Times*, October 5, 1995.

AIRLINE DEPARTURES, LONG-DISTANCE CALLS, AND STOCK TRADING: N. R. Kleinfeld, *New York Times*, October 4, 1995.

397 POLL ON SIMPSON VERDICT: The telephone survey was conducted among 684 randomly selected adults, including 315 whites and 312 blacks. The margin of sampling error was plus or minus four percentage points. *Washington Post*, October 8, 1995.

398 QUOTATIONS FROM FUHRMAN: William Claiborne, *Washington Post*, August 30, 1995. In 1996, Fuhrman pleaded guilty to perjury and was sentenced to probation.

BAD COPS IN PHILADELPHIA: Don Terry, *New York Times*, August 23, 1995.

399–400 POLL ON SIMPSON JURY: *Washington Post*, October 8, 1995.

401 POLLS ON DRUG CONSPIRACY: In the *New York Times*/CBS News Poll, 25% of blacks thought it was true, and another 35% thought it was "possibly true." The figures among whites were 4% true, 12% possibly true. *New York Times*,

August 11, 1991. The 80% figure comes from a survey of 812 black adults done for the Anti-Defamation League of B'nai B'rith by Marttila & Kiley, Inc., of Boston: *Highlights from the National Survey of Attitudes Among Black Americans,* January 26, 1995.

PASTORA'S TESTIMONY: *New York Times,* November 27, 1996.

402 QUOTATION FROM WRIGHT: Interview with Daniel Zwerdling, *Weekend All Things Considered,* National Public Radio, October 8, 1995.

SURVEY ON AIDS CONSPIRACY: In the 1990 *New York Times*/CBS News Poll, 10% of black New Yorkers said they thought the statement on AIDS was true, and 19% more said they thought it "might possibly be true." A separate survey of nearly 1,000 black members of churches in five cities was done in 1990 by the School of Public Health at the University of North Carolina in Chapel Hill.

402–3 QUOTATION FROM MADHUBUTI: Interview in *The Black Collegian,* September–October 1990.

403 FEAR OF CANNIBALISM ON THE *AMISTAD*: Patricia A. Turner, *I Heard It Through the Grapevine: Rumor in African-American Culture* (Berkeley: University of California Press, 1993), pp. 14–15.

404 QUOTATION FROM ANGELOU; CASE OF GUYOT: Ibid., p. 62.

EDITORIAL ON NORPLANT: *Philadelphia Inquirer,* December 12, 1990.

405 QUOTATION FROM JACKSON: Roberto Suro, *New York Times,* March 17, 1992.

QUOTATION FROM BONEY: Lawrence Wright, "The Case for Castration," *Texas Monthly,* May 1992, p. 160.

Eight · Power: The Natural Order

411 SURVEY ON BLACKS' ACHIEVEMENTS: *Washington Post,* October 8, 1995. The poll, conducted by the *Post,* the Henry J. Kaiser Family Foundation, and Harvard University, surveyed a random sample of 1,970 adults, 802 of whom were white. The margin of error was plus or minus three percentage points overall and four points for the white subsample.

412 "MORE OF THEM ALL THE TIME": *Washington Post,* October 8, 1995. Also, a Gallup Poll in March 1990, reported in *American Demographics* magazine, found whites guessing 32% for the black population.

419 THELWELL ESSAY: Michael Thelwell, "False, Fleeting, Perjured Clarence: Yale's Brightest and Blackest Go to Washington," in Toni Morrison, ed., *Race-ing Justice, En-gendering Power: Essays on Anita Hill, Clarence Thomas, and the Construction of Social Reality* (New York: Pantheon, 1992), p. 108.

420 QUOTATION FROM MILLER: Barth Healey, *New York Times,* August 4, 1991.

429–30 QUOTATION FROM STEELE: Shelby Steele, *The Content of Our Character* (New York: St. Martin's Press, 1990), p. 13. Steele is a conservative black English professor who opposes affirmative action.

430 BLACK MAYORS: The first black mayor of a town is believed to have been Monroe Baker, who became mayor of St. Martin, Louisiana, a century earlier, in 1867; Lerone Bennett Jr., *Before the Mayflower: A History of Black America* (New York: Penguin, 1984), p. 479.

431 SURVEY ON PATRIOTISM: Asians and Hispanics were judged to be less patriotic than whites by 55.2% and 60.4% of the respondents, respectively. National Opinion Research Center, *GSS Topical Report No. 19* (Chicago: University of Chicago Press, December 1990), p. 9.

432 CANARSIE VOTERS: Ian Fisher, *New York Times,* October 17, 1993.

435 MOUSSALLEM'S CONVICTION AND DEATH: David Burnham, *Above the Law: Secret Deals, Political Fixes, and Other Misadventures of the U.S. Department of Justice* (New York: Scribners, 1996), p. 252.

437 QUOTATIONS FROM STEELE: Steele, *The Content of Our Character,* pp. 38–39.

442–43 "WHO HOLDS THE POWER": Laura Shipler's written comments on the author's manuscript. Also, Laura Shipler, "Reliving History: The Relationship Between Black Domestic Workers and Their White Employers" (senior thesis, Haverford College, 1994).

Nine · Decoding Racism

460 QUOTATION FROM SAVAGE: *Washington Post,* March 30, 1990.

464 SURVEY ON ANTI-SEMITISM: Marttila & Kiley, Inc., *Highlights from the National Survey of Attitudes Among Black Americans,* January 26, 1995, pp. 9, 13. As with most stereotypes, some are regarded as "good" by bigoted people. "Jews stick together more than other Americans" was labeled as positive by 83% of all black respondents and by 85% of those who endorsed most of the other caricatures and were therefore considered most anti-Semitic. "Jews always like to be at the head of things" was labeled "good" by 47% of all respondents and by 53% of the most anti-Semitic.

465 ATTACK BY JEFFRIES: In a rambling speech in 1991, Jeffries went after both Jews and Italian-Americans. "For years I grew up as a youngster just like you did, going to movies where the African peoples were completely denigrated," he declared. "That was a conspiracy planned and plotted and programmed out of Hollywood by people called Greenberg and Weisberg and Trigliani and whatnot. It's not being anti-Semitic to mention who developed Hollywood. Their names are there. MGM—Metro Golden [*sic*] Mayer. Adolph Zukov. Fox. Russian Jewry had a particular control over the movies, and their financial partners, the Mafia, put together a system of destruction of black people." In the same address, reacting to white scholars who emphasized the role of Africans in selling other Africans into slavery, Jeffries repeated his assertion of Jewish financing but then spread the guilt around. "Let's talk

about who financed, planned, operated, maintained the slave system," he said. "Let's talk about every slave ship being blessed by a Protestant minister or a Catholic priest. Let's talk about the Catholic Church initiating slavery in Africa. Let's talk about the Danes, the Dutch, the Portuguese, the French, the Scots, the Swedes, the Brandenburg Germans that were involved in enslaving Africans for hundreds of years—Jews and Gentiles, Arabs and Christians. Let's deal with the whole ball of wax. Let's not just say Africans sold Africans into slavery." "An African-Centered Education," videotape of address, July 20, 1991.

465 STATEMENT BY THE AMERICAN HISTORICAL ASSOCIATION: Compiled by two experts on the history of slavery, David Brion Davis of Yale University and Seymour Drescher of the University of Pittsburgh, the statement read:

> During the past few years there have been a number of egregious assaults on the historical record [which] implicate Jews as a dominant group in the Atlantic slave trade and the enslavement of Africans in the New World. The claims so misrepresent the historical record, however, that we believe them only to be part of a long anti-Semitic tradition that presents Jews as negative central actors in human history. In such scenarios, Jews are the secret force behind every major social development from capitalism to democracy, every major cataclysm from the Medieval Pandemic of the plague through the French and Russian Revolutions to the collapse of Communism, and now, incredibly, appear for the first time, as the secret force behind slavery. Unfortunately, the media have given the latest charges wide currency, while failing to dismiss them as spurious. As professional historians who have closely examined and assessed the empirical evidence, we cannot remain silent while the historical record is so grossly violated.
>
> Atlantic slavery was an intercontinental enterprise extending over nearly four centuries. Ethnically, the participants included Arabs, Berbers, scores of African ethnic groups, Italians, Portuguese, Spaniards, Dutch, Jews, Germans, Swedes, French, English, Danes, white Americans, Native Americans, and even thousands of New World people of African descent who became slaveholding farmers or planters themselves. Since Portugal and Spain barred Jews from their empires, and since, by the 16th century, most of the Jews who weren't either killed or converted in Western Europe had fled eastward, it was impossible for Jews to play more than a marginal role in a vast system that attracted tens of thousands of pagans, Muslims, Catholics, and Protestants. Even in Holland and the Dutch colonies, where Jews were allowed to make their main "contribution" to New World slavery as merchants and planters, they always formed a minority. Similarly, Jews played only a nominal role in the slave system in the American South. Never more than a tiny fraction of the white population, they never formed more than a minuscule proportion of slaveholders.

465–66 QUOTATION FROM HERTZBERG: Arthur Hertzberg, *New York Times*, December 23, 1992.

467 ARTICLE ON CROWN HEIGHTS: Joe Sexton, *New York Times*, January 27, 1994.

483 HOPSON AND HOPSON: Darlene Powell Hopson and Derek S. Hopson, *Different and Wonderful: Raising Black Children in a Race-Conscious Society* (New York: Fireside, 1990), pp. 5–13.

483–84 QUOTATIONS FROM BOYD-FRANKLIN: Nancy Boyd-Franklin, *Black Families in Therapy: A Multi-systems Approach* (New York: Guilford Press, 1989), pp. 26, 29.

484 "A SAD AND FREQUENT REFRAIN": Hopson and Hopson, *Different and Wonderful*, pp. 14–19.

Ten · Acting Affirmatively

493 RACIAL GAP IN SAT SCORES: Richard J. Herrnstein and Charles Murray, *The Bell Curve: Intelligence and Class Structure in American Life* (New York: Free Press, 1994), p. 452. At the twenty-six colleges, Asians' SAT scores ranged from 57 points below to 70 points above the whites'.

494 TEXAS LAW SCHOOL CASE: The statistics proved effective in persuading Federal District Court Judge Sam Sparks that without affirmative action, the small representation of minorities would amount to unacceptable tokenism. But while upholding the overall strategy of including "nonobjective factors" beyond grades and test scores in selecting students, he threw out the school's particular mechanism of having dual admissions committees evaluate whites and minorities in two separate pools. A federal court of appeals went further, deciding that "no compelling justification" had been presented "to elevate some races over others." When the Supreme Court refused to hear the case in 1996, it let stand a ruling that effectively barred public universities from considering race in admissions—a departure from judicial precedent. This left the issue in ambiguity, for the Fifth Circuit's order applied only in Texas, Louisiana, and Mississippi. It severely cut minority admissions throughout the Texas state university system.

495 QUOTATION FROM TAYLOR: Cited in Nicholas Lemann, "Taking Affirmative Action Apart," *New York Times Magazine*, June 11, 1995, p. 40.

498 XEROX AND HARVARD PILGRIM: The Xerox and Harvard Pilgrim examples are from Claudia H. Deutsch, "Corporate Diversity, in Practice," *New York Times*, November 20, 1996.

SURVEYS ON AFFIRMATIVE ACTION: National Opinion Research Center, University of Chicago, surveys of representative samples of adults from 1988 to 1991.

510 "REASON AND EMOTION WORK AGAINST EACH OTHER": Thomas Kochman, *Black and White: Styles in Conflict* (Chicago: University of Chicago Press, 1981), pp. 19–20.

520 PANNELL SHOOTING: For a detailed account of the shooting and its after-math, see Mike Kelly, *Color Lines: The Troubled Dreams of Racial Harmony in an American Town* (New York: William Morrow, 1995).

Eleven · Breaking the Silence

532 TRUMAN'S STAFF PAPERS: Alan L. Gropman, *The Air Force Integrates* (Washington, D.C.: Office of Air Force History, 1978), p. iv.

OFF-BASE DISCRIMINATION: Ibid., pp. iv, 117–124.

533 RACE RIOTS: Racial disorders occurred at Travis Air Force Base in California; on army installations at Chu Lai, Danang, and Camp Baxter near the demilitarized zone in Vietnam; in Germany and Korea; at Fort Bragg and Camp Lejeune in North Carolina and Fort Dix in New Jersey; on the aircraft carriers *Kitty Hawk*, *Constellation*, and *Franklin D. Roosevelt*; and at other installations. Department of Defense, *Black Americans in Defense of Our Nation* (Washington, D.C.: U.S. Government Printing Office, 1990), p. 85; Gropman, *The Air Force Integrates*, p. 215.

536 GULF WAR CASUALTIES: Blacks made up 30% of the army's deployment in the gulf area, 19% of the navy's, 18% of the marines', and 13% of the air force's.

Twelve · A Country of Strangers

560 QUOTATION FROM MCINTOSH: Peggy McIntosh, *White Privilege and Male Privilege: A Personal Account of Coming to See Correspondences Through Work in Women's Studies*, 1988 Working Paper 189, Wellesley College Center for Research on Women, Wellesley, Mass., pp. 1–2.

WORKSHOP IN WASHINGTON: The workshop was led by Lee Mun Wah at a conference organized by the National Multicultural Institute.

565 LENDING BIAS IN AGRICULTURE DEPARTMENT: In response to lawsuits and complaints by hundreds of black farmers, the Agriculture Department conducted an internal investigation that found blacks underrepresented on local committees that decide on loans; black farmers had to wait longer and suffered a higher rejection rate than whites, partly because their anticipated crop yields—against which they were seeking to borrow—were calculated less favorably than whites'. Michael A. Fletcher, *Washington Post*, December 11, 1996.

566 RACISM AT TEXACO: Kurt Eichenwald, *New York Times*, November 10, 1996.

TEXACO EXECUTIVES' TAPED REMARKS: Kurt Eichenwald, *New York Times*, November 4, 1996.

Index

A NOTE ABOUT THE AUTHOR

David K. Shipler grew up in Chatham, New Jersey, was graduated from Dartmouth in 1964, and spent two years in the navy as an officer on a destroyer before joining *The New York Times* in 1966. He reported on housing, poverty, and urban affairs in New York City, then served as a correspondent in Saigon, as bureau chief in Moscow and Jerusalem, and as chief diplomatic correspondent in Washington, D.C., before leaving the *Times* in 1988. He is the author of two previous books, *Russia: Broken Idols, Solemn Dreams* and *Arab and Jew: Wounded Spirits in a Promised Land*, which won a Pulitzer Prize. He has been a guest scholar at the Brookings Institution, a senior associate at the Carnegie Endowment for International Peace, and a visiting professor at Princeton University and American University.

A NOTE ON THE TYPE

This book was set in Janson, a typeface long thought to have been made by the Dutchman Anton Janson, who was a practicing typefounder in Leipzig during the years 1668 to 1687. However, it has been conclusively demonstrated that these types are actually the work of Nicholas Kis (1650–1702), a Hungarian, who most probably learned his trade from the master Dutch typefounder Dirk Voskens. The type is an excellent example of the influential and sturdy Dutch types that prevailed in England up to the time William Caslon (1692–1766) developed his own incomparable designs from them.

Composed by Creative Graphics,
Allentown, Pennsylvania
Printed and bound by Quebecor Printing,
Fairfield, Pennsylvania
Designed by Virginia Tan